LITERARY HISTORY OF CANADA
VOLUME I
Canadian Literature in English

LITERARY HISTORY
OF CANADA

Canadian Literature in English

Second Edition

VOLUME I

General Editor

CARL F. KLINCK

Editors

ALFRED G. BAILEY, CLAUDE BISSELL,
ROY DANIELLS, NORTHROP FRYE,
DESMOND PACEY

UNIVERSITY OF TORONTO PRESS

TORONTO AND BUFFALO

First Edition 1965
©University of Toronto Press 1965
Toronto and Buffalo
Reprinted with corrections 1966, 1967, 1970, 1973

Second Edition 1976
©University of Toronto Press 1976
Toronto and Buffalo
Printed in Canada
Reprinted with corrections 1977

ISBN 0-8020-2211-1 (cloth)
ISBN 0-8020-6276-8 (paper)
ISBN 0-8020-6265-2 (boxed paper set)
LC 76-12353

This edition of the *Literary History of Canada* has been published with the assistance of a grant from the Ontario Arts Council.

Contents

Introduction

to Volumes I and II

THE *Literary History of Canada (Canadian Literature in English)* is a co-operative project which began in 1957. Its Editors have had two principal aims: to publish a comprehensive reference book on the (English) literary history of this country, and to encourage established and younger scholars to engage in a critical study of that history both before and after the appearance of the book.

The programme for basic research into the literature in English which led to the *History* in a massive single volume in 1965 required six years and the work of many hands. From the beginning, the task of survey and assessment was seen to be beyond the scope of any one man; it was accomplished by the Editors and twenty-nine other scholars, almost all of whom are named in the list of contributors at the end of Volume II.

With deep regret we record the loss through death of three of these original contributors, the Very Rev. James S. Thomson, Professor John A. Irving, and Professor Desmond Pacey, and of one of our most vigorous supporters, Professor Roy M. Wiles.

Now, in 1975, the 1965 book is being revised and republished as two volumes, parts I to III as Volume I of the new set, and part IV as Volume II. There is also a new Volume III, devoted to the years 1960–1973. The preservation of continuity throughout the series has involved chiefly minor revisions, but also the rewriting of certain chapters. We extend our welcome and our thanks to three new contributors, professors Sheila A. Egoff, Thomas A. Goudge, and John Webster Grant, while we remain sincerely grateful to all who wrote in 1965, no less to those who were prevented by various circumstances from revision or further writing for the series.

Although the purposes of the *Literary History* have remained the same, the climate for studies in Canadian literature has improved remarkably since work on the project began in 1957. The difficulties facing the original contributors are now part of Canada's literary history, for they had not the advantages, however limited, prevailing in contemporary scholarship in American literature or in general Canadian history; Canadian literary history and criticism (in

English) had been provided with a much narrower base of authenticated information. The amount of primary research needed to establish a foundation for this work, especially with reference to all periods before 1920, was unusually large for a subject of such national significance.

There cannot now be any doubts about the existence of literature in Canada, yet the terms in the subtitle "Canadian ... in English" may require definition. Although "Canadian" has a clear reference in external matters, it often has to be qualified when the reference is an internal one and the context is historical, sociological, or cultural. "English-Canadian" and "French-Canadian" are commonly used to emphasize a "bicultural," certainly a bilingual, situation in a land settled by people of many different origins. We employed "Canadian literature in English" here, rather than "English-Canadian literature," because the former term puts the name of this country first and suggests unity rather than division. We still hope for "Canadian literature in French" to be given treatment paralleling our work in an "Histoire de la littérature canadienne-française." We were so fortunate as to have our *History* translated into French by Professor Maurice Lebel, an honour conferred by this most distinguished scholar of the Université Laval. It would be of immense value to have a similar French-Canadian *Histoire* and a translation of it into English. The time will come, one may hope, when it will be possible to facilitate a comparative study of both literatures.

Now the term "Canadian." Referring to our thought, culture, and especially the art of writing, Northrop Frye has said that Canada is "an environment, the place where something has happened." It has been our task to discover what kind of "place" Canada was and is, and what has happened here in the realm of literature and of closely associated writings. "Canadian" has been broadly used for whoever or whatever is native, or has been naturalized, or has a distinct bearing upon the native—that is on people or events which had their focus here, although one could insist in some other context upon employing the label of the author's home country, as one might in referring to the New World novels of John Galt, known as a novelist of Scotland.

Historically, Canada was a number of "places." After the power of France in the northern part of North America fell before General Wolfe in 1759, the noun "Quebec" and the adjective "Canadian" were used to designate the old French colony and (from 1774 to 1791) also the "Old North West." After 1791 there were two Canadas, Lower (the old province) and Upper (now called Ontario); but between 1841 and 1867 there was once more a single Canada, with East (Quebec) and West (Ontario) sections. The British Atlantic provinces of Nova Scotia and New Brunswick did not bear the name of Canada before 1867, the date of Confederation with Quebec and Ontario by the British North America Act. Other colonies in the East joined later: Prince Edward Island in 1873 and Newfoundland not until 1949. In the farther Canadian West new provinces were formed as settlement progressed: Manitoba in 1870, British Columbia in 1871, Saskatchewan and Alberta in 1905. The Yukon and other Territories extend beyond the provinces. Canada is now the name for the whole northern half of the continent, except Alaska; it refers to the units and their common area and identity. Historically, the name often groups them all together in spite of what they were called in their own right in the period before federation.

The Editors and contributors have not joined in a chauvinistic hunt for "the great Canadian novel" or even for "Canadianism." They wish to demonstrate, not to argue about, what and how much has grown up in Canada. Their attitude resembles that of the painter Homer Watson, expressed on September 30, 1930, in a letter to Mr. Arthur Lismer: "Myself being so much Canadian, why should I think of trying to be Canadian? . . . Things form naturally, not by forcing. . . . I was born amid the hardwood trees and noted the beech, oak and elm, as native as the jack pine. And the trees mentioned are not as those of England. There is a difference which I hope anyone with a [discerning] mind will see."

Our writers have recognized no embargo upon foreign subject-matter, no restriction upon intellectual trade. "Canadian" culture has concerned itself, for example, with the classics, Freud, and international affairs as well as with Huron Indians or Montreal's social problems. The report given here has tried to show how the best writing in this country has reflected local, national, and universal matters which have engaged our serious thought. If we do not launch out from a studied knowledge of ourselves and of our own ways, no one else will.

That writing of intellectual and artistic quality has a history in Canada cannot be doubted; but readers may still have some misgivings about the title, "literary history." If a study with any foundation was to be made, "literary" had to be employed in a generic sense. Authors and books of slight importance could not be set aside without investigation; these volumes may give some names their first and last mention in a discussion of Canadian literature. Descriptive reference, however, without the addition of a specific claim for artistic value, must not be construed as anything more than an illustration of what was in the "environment." Whenever values are being critically assessed, "literary" is used, of course, in its restricted meaning.

These volumes treat, not only works generically classified as "literature," but also, chiefly in separate chapters, other works which have influenced literature or have been significantly related to literature in expressing the cultural life of the country. Canadian achievements in writing on philosophy, general history, the social sciences, religion and theology, and the natural sciences have been outlined. It would be too much to claim that we have here the intellectual history of Canada, even with restriction to the humanities, but these volumes do deal with much that would have to be taken into account in such a desirable production.

"Literary history" has been chosen as a main title instead of "history of literature" because the latter carries too limited a suggestion of a review of books. Each term indicates that temporal sequence is not to be neglected; but the latter would not have conveyed fully the purpose of noting whatever germinates, grows, continues, recurs, or becomes distinctive, perhaps unique. These volumes represent a positive attempt to give a history of Canada in terms of writings which deserve more or less attention because of significant thought, form, and use of language. They also aim to contribute to criticism by offering reasons for singling out those works regarded as the best.

The divisions and periods of this history have not been arbitrarily imposed, but have rather been discovered in the light of the evidence. Literary history need not match exactly the main lines of political events, and uneven progress in different genres can upset any pre-established system of dates for groups of chapters. No formula was laid down for the approach to, and the internal organization of, these chapters. It was suspected that some ready-made categories and descriptive headings hitherto solemnly accepted in Canadian literary history might prove to be part of the folklore, and thus hamper basic research. It seemed better to allow the systematic process of finding, sifting, and interpreting facts to dictate the approaches, methods of classification, critical concepts, and descriptive styles most appropriate to the truth as the respective authors saw it. The styles in the various chapters differ, of course, for other reasons: the contributors are experienced writers, proficient in their own idioms; they were free of cumbersome regulations, and *con amore* responsive to the spirit and shape of their discoveries. Differences in interpretation and opinion expressed by various contributors have been respected, for each bears the authority of dedication and research.

Flexibility, freshness, and authenticity were placed in the balance against strict orderliness, but an order emerged. Four major parts were recognized (as they are set forth in the Table of Contents). Part I was necessary to supply the framework, to show how the Old World grew in knowledge of the New Found Lands through the accounts of voyages and explorations. Part II, from the beginning of settlement to the decade after the British North America Act of 1867, had to record a period of "literary activity" rather than of production of memorable imaginative works; it called for more historical description than critical assessment. Part III, from the early years of Confederation to the end of the First World War, a period in which literary products accumulated, required much pioneer work of sifting. Part IV, from 1920 to 1960 [now constituting Volume II], covers a period in which critical evaluation of the best-known authors had to be made; it demanded at times extended treatment of their work.

These four parts mark the shape and suggest the pattern of volumes possessed of unity although there are many chapters and dozens of contributors. Introductory chapters (4, 12, and 26) for Parts II, III, and IV effect further consolidation. Each of these historical essays was written by an editor after the evidence of all the component chapters was at hand, the tone had been established, and the threads to be drawn together were visible. In addition, a critical conclusion was written by Northrop Frye after the manuscript for the rest of the book was complete.

For the sake of convenience, long discussions on a major topic, for example "Fiction (1880–1920)," were cut into two or three chapters; short discussions on limited topics were joined with other short ones. The aims of this project could not have been realized, and the volume would have gone beyond all bounds, if it had been necessary to include biographical data and a large bibliographical appendix. For details about the lives of Canadian men and women the reader may consult Dr. W. S. Wallace's *The Macmillan Dictionary of Canadian Biography* (1963) and successive volumes of the comprehensive *Dictionary of Canadian Biography*. Wherever it was possible, dates of authors' lives were inserted in the text of this *Literary History*, especially for writers no longer alive.

The "Bibliographical Notes" which follow the text are brief and highly selective; they were appended only if the author of a chapter felt that they were essential. The entire omission of notes for certain other chapters means only that these contributors rely upon the reader to seek out the numerous sources recorded in bibliographies of Canadian literature, especially in Reginald Eyre Watters' *A Checklist of Canadian Literature and Background Materials, 1628–1950* (Toronto, 1959; rev. 1972), which is virtually a companion volume. It is a record of books. Professor Watters and Dr. Inglis F. Bell have published *On Canadian Literature, 1906–1960*, "A Check List of Articles, Books and Theses on English-Canadian Literature, Its Authors and Language." The "Index" of this *Literary History* will be useful for reference and cross-reference, but also uniquely for tracing authorship of books known to the searcher only by titles. Some items in the Index and in the text of chapters will inevitably require correction. Assistance in this regard provided by readers, researchers, and critics will be welcome and will be acknowledged if communications are addressed to the General Editor in care of the University of Toronto Press.

It was possible to wait a reasonable number of years for thorough research and preparation of most of the manuscripts, but certain contributors, whom we were fortunate in enlisting during the last year, rendered full service under the shadow of the deadline. Among these were professors Henry B. Mayo, and Allison H. Johnson. Since Professor John Irving could not complete his chapters on Philosophical Writings because of illness, Professor Johnson quickly adapted and revised, with Professor Irving's permission, two of the latter's earlier articles on this subject and added a section on recent books of philosophy. Time was also a factor in decisions about a terminal date (roughly 1960) for books to be included in the discussion in various chapters. A few contributors attempted to review publications which appeared as late as 1964.

The Editors and contributors were assisted by other persons named in the notes and a host of helpers insufficiently acknowledged and described as a group of colleagues, students, academic officials, librarians, representatives of foundations, publishers, wives, and secretaries. All of these were singularly possessed of patience and all are remembered with admiration and gratitude. No editor or other writer received any payment for his labours or fees for his manuscript, but each one has the satisfaction of knowing that the six years of preparation of the *Literary History of Canada* saw a remarkable growth of interest in, and many scholarly recruits for, the critical study of Canadian literature. Almost all who wrote chapters have other books and articles now in progress on topics which emerged during the course of their research.

The loyal service of the writers and the support provided by the Humanities Research Council of Canada and the Canada Council can never be suitably acknowledged. During every year of preparation the Humanities Research Council provided funds for occasional meetings and other ordinary expenses. The encouragement given by that Council was also invaluable. The Canada Council made twenty-two separate short-term grants in aid of research to individuals who were working for the *Literary History*; not one application was refused. It was a heart-warming experience of scholarly co-operation and of national recognition of our literature—for which all concerned deserve our personal thanks.

Such support was carried over into publication. The Editors gratefully acknowledge a substantial grant-in-aid for the first edition from the Humanities Research Council of Canada, using funds provided by the Canada Council. The Publications Fund of the University of Toronto Press similarly receives our thanks for a large grant-in-aid, and the Press itself for friendly assistance since 1957. Mr. Marsh Jeanneret, Director of the Press, and the late Dr. George Brown gave encouragement and help from the day on which the project was initiated. The editorial competence, dedication, and firmness of Miss Francess Halpenny, then Editor of the Press, made this almost her own book; she deserves thanks and praise, but no blame for errors perpetrated by others. Many other publishers named in the "Acknowledgments" at the end of Volume II made a generous contribution by allowing free use of copyright material.

The Editors wish to express their thanks for financial support for the second edition to the Canada Council and the Humanities and Social Sciences Research Councils; and for courtesy and the amenities of publication to the University of Toronto Press, especially to Miss Jean Jamieson (Editor, Humanities), to Miss Jean Wilson (who coped with the manuscript and saw three volumes through the press), and to Mrs. Sally Wismer (who prepared the indices). We are also especially indebted to Mrs. Pauline Campbell for secretarial assistance.

None of the editors or contributors received any payment for his or her labour in research and writing, or fees for manuscripts. To those who contributed so graciously and generously, the editors offer this most sincere expression of their gratitude.

For the Editors

CARL F. KLINCK

October 10, 1964

May 24, 1975

PART I

New Found Lands

1. The Voyagers

DAVID GALLOWAY

I. THE PRELUDE

THE NEW WORLD was not discovered; it just grew. Plato's *Lost Atlantis* in the western ocean beyond the Pillars of Hercules, St. Brandan's Isle, the Earthly Paradise, the Fortunate Islands, and the Islands of the Blest, are all part of man's longing to find a Never-Never Land in the reality of dreams. Throughout the Middle Ages these legendary islands floated dimly beyond the fringes of the known world across the Western Seas. Human aspirations are etched in the early fourteenth-century poem, "The Land of Cockayne," "Fur in see bi west Spaygne," where there is a kind of satirical, anti-clerical, pre-Rabelaisian Big Rock Candy Mountain in which the rivers are of oil, milk, honey, and wine, and water is used for washing only. In some medieval maps and manuscripts the Earthly Paradise appears in Asia or Africa, but after Christopher Columbus it is often identified with the west, and Columbus thought that he was near it when he reached the mouth of the Orinoco.

Accounts of early travellers to the New World tell tales of mountains whose sands sparkle with gold, and of natives who "seeme to lyue in that goulden worlde of the whiche owlde wryters speake so much: wherin men lyued simplye and innocentlye without inforcement of lawes, without quarrellinge Iudges and libelles. . . ."[1]* Such ideal pictures live in the work of many sixteenth- and seventeenth-century writers. For Robert Greene, Cuba is ". . . a Region so inricht / With Savours sparkling from the smiling heavens." For Edmund Waller, writing of Bermuda about forty years later, "Heaven sure has kept this spot of Earth uncursed / To show how all things were created first."[2] Donne, as we might expect, in "Love's Progress" places the Fortunate Islands in his mistress's lips, and places "my America! my new-found-land" even nearer to paradise. The realities, of course, were not always so delectable, and early travellers also tell spine-tingling tales of "People called *Cannibales* or *Anthropophagi*, which are accustomed to eate mans fleshe." If the Earthly Paradise, El Dorado, the Seven Cities of Cibola, and King Solomon's Ophir were never actually discovered, lands where "neyther the coldnesse of

*The references required for this chapter are incorporated with the Bibliographical Notes.

wynter is sharpe . . . nor the heate of sommer intollerable" seemed to contain riches beyond the dreams of avarice.

In the minds of men who saw their fondest dreams beyond the setting sun, what is now Canada was, in the sixteenth century, a mere footnote to the countries of perpetual spring farther south. If Canada resembles any of the legendary lands of the Middle Ages, it probably resembles *Ultima Thule*. In a general sense, *Ultima Thule* was simply the "farthest land," and more often than not the Ancients had placed it in the land of the Midnight Sun. For various writers it later became Ireland, the North Pole, the Orkneys, the Shetlands, Norway, or the Faroes. For Sir Francis Bacon, Seneca's prediction in *Medea*, "The time will come . . . When men no more shall unknown courses measure, / For round the world no 'farthest land' shall be," led to America. Although there was no widespread identification of Thule with the New World, it was generally recognized to be a cold northern land, and often it was placed somewhere near the routes which men were later to follow in search of the Northwest Passage.

Historians, writing of the New World in the sixteenth century, often give the impression that the Elizabethans, fired by the voyagers' reports, dreamed of golden opportunities in America. True, the New World represented aspects of men's dreams, but men would still have dreamed even if it had not gradually taken physical shape in the sixteenth century. The New World is important to us because we live in it, but the vast majority of Elizabethans took no interest in America as an object of colonization, trade, or missionary endeavour; in the creative imagination of the age, as judged by its literature, America is comparatively unimportant. In the web of Elizabethan life the strands of the New World are few, and such interest as there was, was expressed by a tiny minority of dedicated men such as Richard Hakluyt, John Dee, Sir Francis Walsingham, and some of the voyagers themselves. Historians, who have often been the victims of that "gigantic optical illusion" of which Professor Butterfield writes in *The Whig Interpretation of History*, have organized past history "by reference to the present" and have made inferences "from a particular series of abstractions from the past—abstractions which by the very principle of their origin beg the very questions that the historian is pretending to answer" (p. 30). That arch-Whig of historians, G. M. Trevelyan, for example, sees Richard Hakluyt as one of the two most influential writers in the age of Shakespeare, and writes that "Hakluyt, in narrating the deeds of our explorers and seamen, directed across the ocean the thoughts of adventurous youth, of scholars, statesmen and merchants and of all who had money to invest. Even up-country squires and farmers began to dream of boundless expanses of virgin soil, waiting since the dawn of time to be broken by the English plough." (*Illustrated English Social History*, II, 52.)

The absolute importance of Richard Hakluyt has blinded historians to his relative importance in the age in which he lived. His *Principal Navigations, Voyages, Traffiques and Discoveries of the English Nation* (1598–1600) is so important to subsequent generations because much of his material is unique; most of it was unknown to the reading public until he printed it. However, the number of his readers has probably been over-estimated.[3]

There are, of course, many incidental references to the New World in the literature of the sixteenth century, and tags such as the "wealth of the Indies" are quite common. But in assessing the importance of the New World to the creative imagination, historians have often quoted a few well-known passages *ad nauseam* as though they were typical. J. Holland Rose, and R. B. Nye and J. E. Morpurgo, for example, quote Maria's description of Malvolio— "He does smile his face into more lines than is in the new map with the augmentation of the Indies"—as an indication of the groundlings' interest in the New World.[4] In fact there is no record of a public performance of *Twelfth Night* at all, although the play was performed at Court and in the Hall of the Middle Temple. So what has been taken to be an indication of widespread knowledge of a map in the *Principal Navigations*, based on Molineux's globe which stood in the Hall of the Middle Temple, could well be an allusion directed specifically at the Court or the Inns of Court.[5]

It is, of course, impossible to assess popular interest in events by counting allusions to them; the tavern talk of the day is silent, and the ordinary seamen are mute and inglorious. But if we are trying to assess popular interest in a subject, the broadside ballad might provide us with a key. There are, apparently, more ballads about the Revolt of the Northern Earls in 1569 alone than there are about the entire New World in the sixteenth and seventeenth centuries.[6] The popular imagination as expressed in the ballad seems to have been fired more by a single spectacular event at home than by the birth of a whole new world overseas.

If the impact of the New World as a whole on the creative imagination of the Elizabethan age was less significant than is commonly supposed, the impact of what is now Canada was definitely insignificant. In contrast to the first voyage of Christopher Columbus, who found, in Espaniola, a land of perpetual spring, the Cabots, on their first voyage, found a sterner, harder land. Prominent in accounts of subsequent voyages to Canada, in fact, are descriptions of struggles against the elements. The time available for the completion of a northern voyage is limited. The little ships leave Dartmouth and St. Malo, Harwich and Honfleur, in April or May; they must be back by October, and over them hang the urgent shadows of the coming winter. In the voyages to Virginia and the Indies there is no such sense of urgency, and whatever the dangers of sailing to the south, there is no danger of having to experience the frozen horrors which Cartier endured in the St. Lawrence winter of 1535–36.

From its very beginnings, the "literature" of Canada was stamped by a struggle against the climate and against the land itself. For Northrop Frye, reviewing A. J. M. Smith's *Book of Canadian Poetry* in the *Canadian Forum* four centuries later, "the outstanding achievement of Canadian poetry is in the evocation of stark terror. Not a coward's terror, of course; but a controlled vision of the causes of cowardice. The immediate source of this is obviously the frightening loneliness of a huge and thinly settled country."

Scant as references to Canada are, the country seems to have made its appearance in English literature earlier than did the warmer and wealthier lands to the south. The voyages of the Norsemen, unknown to Europe as a whole, may have been known to the seamen of Bristol, who were making regular visits to Iceland by the end of the fifteenth century. The voyages of the Cabots, of the Company Adventurers of the New Found Lands, of John Rut, and—no doubt—of others of whom no trace remains, seemed to herald a dawn of colonial expansion in the northern part of North America. The dawn was a false one and nothing was done for another half a century, but some of these voyages do seem to find dim reflection in Tudor literature. The interlude *Hickscorner* (written *c.* 1510) contains a reference to the 'new founde Ilande,' and a comparatively extended treatment appears in John Rastell's *A New Interlude and a mery of the nature of the iiij elements* (1519?).[7] In 1517, John Rastell, brother-in-law of Sir Thomas More, had set out for North America, but his "mariners, / False of promise and dissemblers," had put him ashore in Ireland. Rastell's "interlude" "may be accepted as the first work in modern geography of English authorship." In the hundred lines or so in which he deals with the "new lands," we have a glimpse of "Canadians" as they appeared to an intelligent man of the court of Henry VIII:

> And what a great meritorious deed
> It were to have the people instructed,
> To live more virtuously,
> And to learn to know of men the manner,
> And also to know God their Maker,
> Which as yet live all beastly.

In these lines appears a strain which was later to be developed in the promotion literature of colonization. Moreover, in the copper that the natives have, in the "Great abundance of woods," and in the "Fish they have so great plenty," can be dimly seen the ingredients of Canada's economic future.

When we contrast the amount of material that was published in Spain about the Spanish colonies, however, with the meagre scraps that were published in England about North America, Canada remains very much the poor relation of the American dream. Throughout the sixteenth century many of the northern voyagers, in fact, regarded Canada as a nuisance—an obstacle which lay across the path which led to the golden gates of Cathay.

The accounts of the voyagers themselves, the most direct expression of the New World, are, of course, the base upon which Canadian literary history in the sixteenth and seventeenth centuries must rest. Hakluyt's *Principal Navigations* (1598–1600) have been called, in Froude's well-worn phrase, "the Prose Epic of the modern English nation." Epic in scope and action they undoubtedly are, taken as a whole; as literature, they vary a great deal, although about one third have "significant literary merit."[8]

Some of the narratives of the voyagers to Canada, such as Christopher Hall's account of Frobisher's first voyage to the Northwest (1576; Hakluyt, Everyman ed., V, 131–37), Silvester Wyet's account of a voyage to "the Bay of Saint Laurence" (1594; Hakluyt VI, 98–100), and Charles Leigh's account of his voyage with "divers other to Cape Briton and the Isle of Ramea" (1597; Hakluyt VI, 100–14) are of the practical, log-book, journal-jotting variety. Dangers and excitements seldom ruffle the matter-of-fact surface of the style, although some of the details about the Indians, the vegetation, and the wild life are interesting enough in themselves. In contrast, George Best's "discourse" of Frobisher's voyages (1576, 1577, 1578; Hakluyt V, 170–276), and Edward Haye's account of Gilbert's last voyage (1583; Hakluyt VI, 1–42), are among the most lively in Hakluyt.

Like most of the accounts, Best's contains much unexciting detail, but it also contains what is, perhaps, the earliest effective description of a battle with the Canadian elements:

There arose a sudden terrible tempest at the Southeast, which blowing from the maine sea, directly upon the place of the Streites, brought together all the yce a sea-boorde of us upon our backes. . . . And again some where so fast shut up and compassed in amongst an infinite number of great countreys and Islands of yce, that they were faine to submit themselves and their ships to the mercy of the unmerci-full yce, . . . for plankes of timber of more than three inches thicke, and other things of greater force and bignesse, by the surging of the sea and billowe, with yce were shivered and cut in sunder, . . . that our ships, even those of greatest burdens, with the meeting of contrary waves of the sea, were heaved up betweene Islands of yce, a foote welneere out the sea above their watermark, having their knees and timbers within boord both bowed and broken therewith. . . . And albeit, by reason of the fleeting yce, which were dispersed here almost the whole sea over, they were brought many times to the extreamest point of perill, moun-taines of yce tenne thousand times scaping them scarce one ynch, which to have striken had bene their present destruction. . . . (Hakluyt, V, 238–39)

Best's account shows a humour and a humanity lacking in most of the others. He clearly admires Frobisher, but he does not suppress the fact that one of the "salvages" "hurt the Generall in the buttocke with an arrow, who the rather speedily fled backe. . . ." The savages are treated as human beings—if somewhat recalcitrant and "subtill" ones—and Best's description of the touching devotion between a captive man and a captive woman, "so that (I thinke) the one would hardly have lived without the comfort of the other," strikes the tender notes of an incipient idyll of love. In an age when the hardships of the ordinary seaman went largely unrecorded, we learn that "we lost in all the voyage only one man, besides one that dyed at sea, which was sicke before he came aboord, and was so desirous to follow this enterprise, that he rather chose to dye theerin, then not to be one to attempt so notable a voyage."

Unlike Best, Haye introduces a moralizing, religious tone into his treatment of Gilbert's last voyage, but the account has, on the whole, a restrained simplicity with few rhetorical devices. The disasters of the voyage are the work of God, and over the expedition hang hints of a tragically inevitable conclusion. One passage almost hints at a preview of the scene in Shakespeare's *Antony and Cleopatra* (IV.iv), when Antony's soldiers hear "hautboys . . . under the stage" and fear that ". . . the god Hercules, whom Antony lov'd, / Now leaves him."

The evening was faire and pleasant, yet not without token of storme to ensue, and most part of this Wednesday night, like the Swanne that singeth before her death, they in the Admiral, or Delight, continued in sounding of Trumpets, with Drummes, and Fifes: also winding the Cornets, Haughtboyes: and in the end of their jolitie, left with the battell and ringing of dolefull knels. (Hakluyt, VI, 28)

Haye's account has a dying fall and music at the close, and Gilbert passes through his travail, before finally meeting his Maker, "sitting abaft with a booke in his hand," and crying "out unto us in the Hind (so oft as we did approch within hearing) We are as neere to heaven by sea as by land."

The voyagers' accounts, plain, concrete, and incisive as they usually are, are relatively free from the rhetoric and conceit which are so characteristic of Elizabethan prose as a whole. Many of the accounts were, of course, written by seamen and merchants with no pretensions to literary skill, but "this plainness of style" extends to "the writings of university-trained men" who "were aware of the literary fashions of their age, but did not give way to them in their narratives." The accounts "are the unstudied and natural outpourings of men's expressions of what they saw and did. Men told these tales for what was in them rather than to achieve any special effect."[9] Descriptions of landscapes are especially bare and unadorned, and part of the reason is that there were simply no techniques available to writers at that time which they could use to describe natural scenery. "When the feeling for landscape was still in its simplest stages, so that the eye of painter and engraver, fascinated by space and sky, simple forms and elementary masses, was not yet trained to render the specific, the unusual, and the scientifically exact, small wonder that the writers of voyage literature were equally unskilled to describe in words what perhaps had vividly impressed them."[10]

If none of the accounts of sixteenth-century voyages to Canada can compare, as literature, with Sir Walter Raleigh's account of Guiana, some of them do rank high as voyage literature. They show the first attempts, in the English language, to come to grips with the vast loneliness of Canada, and with the vaster loneliness of the seas around her coasts.

Ballad writers were sometimes inspired by the exploits of the Elizabethan seamen, but the New World, when it appears, is usually incidental to the struggle with Spain. The few ballads about the Northwest have a pathetic minor key quality, compared to the more full-blooded expressions of Drake's adventures in the Caribbean. The second half of a ballad (c. 1584) about Drake's return from his voyage around the world refers to the loss of Sir Humphrey Gilbert on his way back from the "New-found-land" in 1583.

> Gallants all of British blood,
> Why do ye not saile on th'ocean flood?
> I protest ye are not worth a philberd,
> Compared with Sir Humphry Gilberd?
>
> For he walkt forth in a rainy day,
> To the New-found-land he took his way,
> With many a gallant fresh and green;
> Ne never came home again. God bless the Queen.[11]

The quality of the verse as a whole does not suggest that the last line is ironical.

On May 20, 1577, there was entered in the Stationers' *Register*, a ballad (now lost) called "Ffullers ffarewell to master Ffourbousier and the other gentlemen adventurers whoe labour to discouer the right passage to Catay," while a "thing" on Frobisher was entered six weeks later, on July 1. A poem called "Thomas Ellis in praise of Frobisher,"[12] which seems to refer to Frobisher's expedition of 1577, makes a few oblique references to such things as "countrise strange" and "men of savage kind," and compares Frobisher to Jason; but the golden fleece, of course, turned out to be mere dross after all.

II. THE SETTLEMENTS

When Queen Elizabeth died, on March 24, 1603, most of the hopes represented by the voyages of men like Sir Humphrey Gilbert and John Davis, and by the laborious compilations of Richard Hakluyt, Preacher, were still the stuff of dreams.

> . . . . Sir Humfrey Gilbert sure,
> and all his troupe is gone.
> But whether, no man knowes. . . .

Ever since—and perhaps before—John Cabot had come back from his voyage of 1497 and found the seas full of fish, fishermen from France, Spain, Portugal, and England had cast their nets on the Grand Bank and in the Bay of St. Lawrence. Some of them had even wintered on the shores, but the sixteenth century passed without permanent settlement.

With the formation of the Royal Council for Virginia in 1606, and the first permanent settlement at Jamestown in the following year, there seems to follow a period of popular interest in colonization. Several ballads, sermons, and pamphlets in praise of "the noble enterprise" came from the London printing presses. "The persons interested in Virginia increase daily," wrote Zuñiga, the Spanish Ambassador, to his King in a letter dated March 28, 1608. "R. Rich, Gent., one of the voyage," gives us in *Newes from Virginia* (1610) what is perhaps the first real affirmation of faith in the future of colonization in ballad literature.

> Let England know our willingnesse,
> For that our worke is good,
> We hope to plant a nation,
> Where none before hath stood.

The Virginia voyages were undoubtedly talked about a great deal in the years immediately before and after the founding of Jamestown, but it is easy to over-estimate the enthusiasm which they aroused. Their "literature" is propaganda, rather than the spontaneous expression of interest in a subject which had caught the popular imagination. Much of it represents an effort to combat scepticism and hostility. R. Rich's confidence is tempered by the "scandall" and "false report" which have attended his voyage, and by the discomfort and discontent of the colonists. A sermon of Daniel Price, preached on Sunday, May 28, 1609, includes a "reproofe of those that traduce the Honourable Plantation of Virginia."[13] Even Michael Drayton's "Ode to the Virginian Voyage," which is quoted so frequently, as though it were typical of poetic enthusiasm, is, in fact, the only known poem of real literary merit on the Virginian expedition by a major poet.

In spite of their many hardships, the colonists in Virginia clung on, to be joined on the American coast by the Pilgrim Fathers in 1620. In what is now Canada, in the meantime, three permanent settlements had been founded before the independent, God-fearing, Puritans had landed on Plymouth Rock. The French had already settled at Port Royal (1605) and Quebec (1608), and the English at Cupar's Cove in Newfoundland (1610).

The cultural—and even the political—history of English Canada in the seventeenth century is sparse, desultory, and shadowy compared to that of French Canada and the New England colonies. There is nothing in the English language which can compare in detail and in literary quality with the accounts of the early French settlements given by Lescarbot[14] and Champlain,[15] and nothing later in the century which can compare with the vast bulk and minute fascination of the *Jesuit Relations*.[16] Short histories of Canada, when dealing with the seventeenth century, often devote about ninety per cent of their pages to the French. Lescarbot may have been the first European to write verse in North America, and he probably staged the first dramatic production there. His fastidious regard for detail does not allow him to overlook the humming-bird, which supplants the wren as the smallest bird in poetry:

> *Niridau* oiselet délicat de nature,
> Qui de l'abeille prend la tendre nourriture
> Pillant de nos jardins les odorantes fleurs,
> Et des rives des bois les plus rares douceurs.

Lescarbot's pageant, *Théâtre de Neptune,* written especially for the Sieur de Poutrincourt's return to Port Royal, was presented "sur les flots du Port Royal" on the 14th day of November, 1606. Ten months later, on September 5 and 30, 1607, "*Hamlet* and *Richard*" were acted on Captain William Keeling's ship, the *Dragon,* off Sierra Leone. The very fact that Lescarbot could write and organize his entertainment in the wilderness and that Shakespeare could be acted on a cramped ship off the Guinea coast should warn us against being too dogmatic about "first performances." Long before *Hamlet* and *Théâtre de Neptune* were written, amateur actors may have fretted their hours on improvised stages in North America and signified nothing to posterity.

It is unlikely, nevertheless, that much literature was written, or that plays were performed, in Acadia by the French settlers who followed Lescarbot and de Poutrincourt. Although the ritual of the Church may have helped to satisfy incipient dramatic instincts, the churches and priests, like the settlers, were scattered, and even by the end of the century the two thousand Acadians of the Port Royal, Chignecto, and Minas areas were still concerned mainly with simple physical needs. Even in the more populous and concentrated society of the fortress of Quebec itself, attempts to produce Corneille, Racine, and Molière were short-lived. "The theatre was not a vigorous form of artistic expression in Quebec until recent years, because of the Jansenist element in French-Canadian Catholicism, which also gave a puritanical tone to society in other respects."[17]

Narrow as the culture of New France may have been during the second half of the seventeenth century, "the colony showed some signs of breaking through the narrow intellectual limits which had been imposed by frontier toil, and ignorance and clerical control."[18] In Quebec there were at least some of the trappings of a cultural life—a Jesuit college with a faculty of theology, private libraries of three and four thousand volumes, a fairly good assortment of recent and contemporary literature, church choirs, an organ, and a developing tradition of folk song. "Of the seven to ten thousand songs collected in the Province of Quebec in recent years nine tenths are derived from songs brought to Quebec before 1673."[19]

Narrowly theological and utilitarian as the taste of New England also often seems, it produced, by the end of the seventeenth century, a culture which New France could not rival. Religious opposition to plays persisted in New England as it did in New France, but, farther south, in Charleston, the first professional actors to perform in the colonies offered a play in 1703. By the year 1701, there were universities at Cambridge (1636), Williamsburg (1693), and New Haven (1701). Three years after the founding of Harvard a printing press was set up in Cambridge (1639), to be followed by presses in Philadelphia (1685) and New York (1693); whereas the first result of a printing press in Canada was the *Halifax Gazette* of 1752, and there is no conclusive evidence of printing in New France until 1764. The first newspaper in the American colonies, however, appeared in Boston in 1690, and by 1735 there were five newspapers in the town. By the early eighteenth century, Edward Taylor (*c*. 1645–1729) had written—even if he had not published— the best poetry in New England before the nineteenth century.

In the sparse, primitive English settlements in Newfoundland, Nova Scotia, and Isle St. Jean (Prince Edward Island), however, the taste for learning hardly existed. During the seventeenth century there were no printing presses, no bookstores, no colleges, no centres of population, and, apparently, no Edward Taylors. There was no Cotton Mather who, in his *Magnalia Christi Americana* (1702), produced at great length and in great detail "the Ecclesiastical History of New England, from its First Planting in the year 1620, unto the Year of our Lord, 1692."

Meagre as English literary achievements in, and about, Canada were, English literature was written in Canada as soon—or nearly as soon—as it was in the American colonies to the south. In it there are no elaborate prospects of El Dorados, but there are modest hints of promised lands. Those men who had favoured colonization in the days of Elizabeth had naturally been concerned not to give the impression that life was one long battle against the elements. Anthony Parkhurst, in a letter to Richard Hakluyt (1578; Hakluyt V, 343–49), had said that "Newfoundland is in a temperate climate and not so cold as foolish mariners doe say. . . ." Sir George Peckham, in "A true Reporte of the late Discoveries . . ." (Hakluyt VI, 42–78), had stressed "manifold benefits, commodities and pleasures heretofore unknowen" and had talked of the "wholesome air and fertile soil." Frobisher commended Peckham's "report" in, for him, the unusual medium of verse: "A pleasaunt ayre, a sweete and firtell soile, / A certaine gaine, a never dying praise."[20] John Guy, the founder of the Cupar's Cove settlement and its first governor, writing home from the Cove in a letter dated May 16, 1611, speaks in a quiet, modestly optimistic manner of a temperate winter in which "not onely men may safely inhabit here without any neede of Stove, but Navigation may be made to and fro from England to these parts at any time of the yeare."[21]

In spite of the hardships of the early days of the colony, the twenty years following Guy's settlement were to produce bursts of minor poetic activity on the parts of some of the leading colonists. Among the "divers honourable persons and others who have undertaken to helpe advance his Majesties Plantation in the New-found-land," was "the Worshipfull William Vaughan of Tarracod, in the Countie of Carmarthen, Doctor of Civill Law." Vaughan (c. 1575–1641) had already published *The Golden Grove* (1600), a general guide to morals, politics, and literature, in which he had shown himself to have at least one admirable quality for a colonist by denouncing plays as folly and wickedness. In 1622 the fantastic Welshman may have visited Newfoundland, although it is unlikely that he did so, where he had bought a grant of land in 1616, "and hath in two severall yeers sent thither divers men and women." In 1626, in England, he published *The Golden Fleece*, partly in verse, partly in prose, to encourage emigration.

Prefixed to the book were commendatory verses by Guy, and by Captain John Mason (1586–1635). Guy, in a burst of poetic optimism, foresaw "A trade more rich than Jason brought to Greece / From Colchos land," and Mason wrote of ". . . how my heart doth leap with joy to hear / Our New-found Isle by Britons prized dear!" Mason, classical scholar, governor of the colony from 1615 to 1621, and later founder of New Hampshire (1629), had already published his *Briefe Discourse of the New-found-land* (1620) to encourage settlement. He too tried to counter the rumour that the winters were unbearable, although he admitted that the mosquitoes were a nuisance in summer. Sir Richard Whitbourne (fl. 1579–1626) also, in *A Discourse and Discovery of Newfoundland*, published in the same year (1620; reprinted in part in Purchas XIX), had described the colony and assured prospective settlers that "even in Winter, it is as pleasant and helthfull as England is." For him, too, the mosquitoes were troublesome, but mainly to "loytering people . . . when they find any such lying lazily or sleeping in the Woods. . . ." The old sea dog, author, judge, and colonial governor, had made his first trip to Newfoundland in 1580, had seen Gilbert "take possession of that Countrie in the Harbour of St. Johns" (1583), had commanded a ship of his own against the Spanish Armada, and, after many more voyages, had been to Newfoundland again in 1618. Safe in port at Exmouth, writing his *Discourse*, he can be forgiven if he remembers "a strange Creature . . . in the Harbour of Saint Johns, which very swiftly came swimming towards me, . . . whether it were a Marmaide or no, I leave it for others to judge." Whitbourne's *Discourse*—conceited, humorous, tongue-in-cheek—is one of the most charming records of early Newfoundland.

How much of *The Golden Fleece* Sir William Vaughan—or Orpheus Junior as he called himself—might have written in Newfoundland, we do not know, but we are virtually certain that Robert Hayman (1575–1629), who succeeded Captain John Mason as governor, did indeed write his contribution to Canadian literature there, because all of his "Epigrams and other small parcels, both Morall and Divine" were "Composed and done at Harbor-Grace in Britaniola, anciently called Newfound-land." Hayman's *Quodlibets, Lately Come Over from New Britaniola, Old Newfound-land* (1628), is probably the first book of original English verse written on the North American continent.[22]

Hayman dedicates his "few bad unripe Rimes" to Charles I. Several of his friends, including Vaughan and George Wither, wrote poetic forewords. Wither cries: "Behold, e'en from these uncouth shores, among / Unpeopled woods, and hills these straines were sung." Over the 350 "epigrams and other small parcels" hangs an air of rustic urbanity—a moralizing on the ways of men in the Old World, recollected in the tranquillity of the New. There are epigrams in rhymed iambics on God, religion, papists, fools, drunkards, liars, doctors, merchants, tobacco, universities, mayors, and usurers; there are epigrams on John Donne, Ben Jonson, and Michael Drayton "whose unwearied old muse still produceth new dainties"; there are epigrams on our old friends, Mason, Vaughan, and Whitbourne, and on others who have laboured in the cause of Newfoundland. There is a charming nostalgic memory of Sir Francis Drake whom Hayman remembers from his boyhood in Totnes. Over a span of forty years or so, he recalls Drake's "walking up Totnes long Street," giving him "*a faire red Orange*," kissing him, and saying "*God blesse my boy*: / Which I record with comfort to this day." Drake had no children.

Hayman's sentiments about Newfoundland, in verse, are often similar to those of Mason, Guy, and Whitbourne, in prose. The four elements are "wholesome," "sweet," and "rich." The winter is ". . . short, wholesome, constant clear, / Not thicke, unwholesome, shuffling, as 'tis here," and although Newfoundland cannot compare with England for "cloaths, company, buildings faire," a man may find peace of mind:

> Always enough, most times some what to spare,
> With little paines, lesse toyle, and lesser care,
> Exempt from taxings, ill newes, Lawing, feare,
> If cleane, and warme, no matter what you weare,
> Healthy, and wealthy, if men carefull are. . . .

In spite of such delights Hayman is conscious of the eternal problem of getting English women to live in Canada:

> Sweet creatures, did you truely understand
> The pleasant life you'd live in *Newfound-land*,
> You would with *teares* desire to be brought thither. . . .

The tiny renaissance—or naissance—of literature in English in Newfoundland was short-lived. Modest as it was in quantity and quality, however, we have to wait until after the coming of the Loyalists towards the end of the eighteenth century before anything better developed in Canada.

In 1621, the year Robert Hayman probably became governor of Newfoundland, King James I made an enormous grant of land between the Gaspé Peninsula and what is now Maine to his fellow Scotsman, Sir William Alexander (1567?–1640), later Earl of Stirling. Alexander almost immediately made a sub-grant to Sir Robert Gordon of Lochinvar (1580–1656) in Cape Breton or New Galloway. There were several vigorous attempts at settlement, complicated by rivalries among the settlers themselves and by war with France. The dispute about Nova Scotia–Acadia, in fact, was only the symptomatic beginning of the long and bitter struggle for Canada as a whole.

Hayman had been optimistic about Alexander's projects, when, in *Quodlibets*, he had written: "Old *Scotland* you made happy by your birth, / *New-Scotland* you will make a happy earth." But the Scots of Nova Scotia inspired even less of literary merit than the English and Welsh of Newfoundland. Lochinvar's *Encouragements for such as shall have intention to be undertakers of the New Plantation of Cape Breton . . .* (1625) is precise, clear, and practical, but undistinguished; Alexander's *An Encouragement to Colonies* (1624) is scholarly and pedantic and lacks the inspiration of direct experience. Alexander was, of course, a poet, but most of his poetry was written before James's grant of 1621 and shows no debt to the New World, although his *Encouragement* does seem, at times, to be fired by his poetic imagination. In 1613 he had written an addition to Sir Philip Sidney's prose romance, *Arcadia*, and "the curious reader can detect some traces of the influence of the *Arcadia* in the brocaded prose of Alexander's *Encouragement to Colonies*."[23]

While the settlers of Newfoundland and Nova Scotia were trying to lay foundations, others were still building castles in the air of the Northwest. Hard as life in pioneer settlements is, the good settler has an essentially domestic mind which leads him to clear woods, build houses, and till the soil. But the New World was also built by those who moved through unpathed waters and unmapped forests. The strains run through American life and through human nature itself.

The dream of a northwestern passage to Cathay persisted. "The desire of Riches in some, of Knowledge in others, hath long wheted mens industries, to finde out a more compendious way to the East Indies . . ." (Purchas, XIV, 297). For Henry Briggs, the mathematician, in his *Treatise on the North-West Passage to the South Sea*, . . . (1622), the way lay through the ever-beckoning Strait of Anian "where are seated (as they fable) the large king-domes of Cebola and Quivira, having great and populous Cities of civill people; whose houses are said to bee five stories high . . ." (Purchas, XIV, 424).

The dream ended for a long time in the frozen reality of the northern seas. After a winter of smouldering hatreds and personal feuds, Henry Hudson's men baulked at the terrors of bleak rocks shrouded in frost and mist, and set their captain adrift in an open boat. Button, Hall, Baffin, Bylot, Hawkridge, Luke Foxe, and Thomas James were all to follow Hudson to the Northwest. But with the return of Foxe and James, who had sailed independently and met one another, in August 1631, near Cape Henrietta Maria, at the western entrance to James Bay, the voyages were over for more than a century until Captain Christopher Middleton set out, once more, in 1742.

If the voyagers to the Northwest did not gain their ultimate objective, at least they left many of their names on the map of Canada. If they are not great literature themselves, the voyagers' accounts at least helped to inspire great literature later on, "and as we read [Coleridge's "The Ancient Mariner"] we catch again the very savour of countless phrases in Hakluyt, Purchas and James." "That stubborn and pious old Bristol seaman, Captain Thomas James had provided in his *Strange and Dangerous Voyage*, with a certain grim satisfaction in his hardships, the raw material for a new *Inferno*, all ice; and Coleridge could no more have escaped in Bristol the shade of his ancient fellow-townsman than the Wedding-Guest could have given the ancient mariner the slip."[24]

It is natural that with the English settlements established—however precariously—in Newfoundland and Nova Scotia, and with the establishment of "The Governor and Company of Adventurers of England trading into Hudson's Bay," after 1670, information about Canada in England should increase. But the information takes the form largely of petitions from the colonists to the government at home, acts to encourage trade, treaties with, and accounts of war against, France. The "literature" on Canada, in fact, becomes more "official" and moves away from such charm as is found in Whitbourne, where facts and sound practical advice mingle with fancies and quaint conceits.

As the seventeenth century goes on the New World finds more factual and informed expression in England. Sir Francis Bacon was one of the first writers to put the voyagers' accounts to critical tests, and he significantly acknowledges having taken one piece of information from "an intelligent merchant who had carried out a colony to Newfoundland." References to

Canada in literature proper are still meagre, although the ones that there are tend to become more specific. Thomas Heywood in *Londons Peaceable Estate* (1639) refers to "Harber-grace in Newfoundland," and William Drummond of Hawthornden, poet-friend of Sir William Alexander, in an *Entertainment of King Charles* (1633), speaks of one of the characters as having "attyre . . . of divers coloured feathers, which shew her to bee an American, and to represent new Scotland."[25]

In the ballad literature of the seventeenth century Canada is mentioned only once. While there are half-a-dozen ballads on Cromwell's war with Spain in the West Indies, only one—on David Kirke's capture of Quebec—touches on England's struggles with France in Canada.[26]

It is natural, perhaps, that interest in the New World as a subject for literature should still concentrate on the Indies, the long-standing rivalry between England and Spain, and the cruelty of the Spaniards to the natives. Spanish cruelty had dramatic possibilities and was a convenient vehicle in which to express the idea of "the noble savage." It is easier to visualize innocent, primitive man in the sun-lit lands of the south, than to picture him squatting squalidly through a long Canadian winter. In the work of several English writers the Spanish conqueror became a symbol of the corrupt civilization which degraded natural man, hitherto happy in his long, golden days of nature. On the whole, the "noble savage" reached greater theoretical and philosophical expression in France than he did in England, in the writings of such men as Montaigne, Montesquieu, and Rousseau. In that gay, charming, anti-clerical, half-charlatan Baron Lahontan, in fact, France produced both a voyager and "un 'philosophe,' qui dépasse en hardiesse bien des 'philosophes.' "[27]

In England, however, the noble savage appears on the stage in Sir William D'Avenant's *The Cruelty of the Spaniards in Peru* (1658), which shows us the happy state of the natives before the Spaniards arrive, and even shows us —in dumb show—one Spaniard "basting an Indian Prince which is roasted at an artificial fire." In Sir Robert Howard's *The Indian Queen* (written in 1662) and in John Dryden's sequel, *The Indian Emperor* (first acted in 1665), the selfless innocence of Indian life is once more contrasted with the rapacity of the "civilized" Spaniards.

The seventeenth century seems to have produced no literary work with Canada as its main subject, and even the plays of John Crowne (1640?–1703?), who spent seven or eight years in Nova Scotia and New England, show no trace of Canadian influence.

At last, however, John Dennis (1657–1734) moves the noble savage to Canada in his play *Liberty Asserted* (1704), "a Satyr upon Arbitrary Power, a Satyr upon the Government of the French." The play deals with the struggle, in Canada, between the French and Hurons on one side and the English and

Iroquois on the other. There is no local colour, however, and Canada is merely described, in Dennis's preface, as "a vast Tract Land in Northern America, on the Back of New England and New York." Ulamor, the General of the Five Nations, is a very noble savage indeed, and a fast friend of the gallant English General Beaufort. Both Ulamor and Beaufort love Irene, the daughter of chief Zephario of the Angians, but Beaufort nobly renounces his sweetheart in favour of his friend and, as Zephario says:

> The English always were a gallant nation,
> And foes to Force and friends to Liberty.

After a peace, the French under Frontenac perfidiously break their word, but when Frontenac discovers that Ulamor is really his son by the Huron Princess, Sakia, even that hardened old warrior relents, repudiates the tyranny of his government, and accepts Ulamor's offer—"I'll make thee King of all Canadian France."

The play, which seems to have been quite popular, has a promising dramatic situation, a tightly knit plot, and moving moments often shattered by lines of appalling banality. Canada, in name if not in spirit, had made its début on the London stage.

Six years after the first performance of *Liberty Asserted*, the London public had a chance to satisfy its curiosity about the noble savage at first hand when four Iroquois "Kings of Canada" visited England. (Indians had, of course, been brought back to England occasionally from the time of the Cabots, and frequently from about the beginning of the seventeenth century.) The four kings had an audience with Queen Anne, dined with the Duke of Ormonde, were "mightily pleased with their reception at Whitehall," saw a literally riotous performance of *Macbeth* at the Haymarket Theatre, and did not "refuse a Glass of Brandy or strong Liquor from any hands that offer it." In short, they received the kind of hospitality that an Englishman expects to find in America today. Ballads, pamphlets, poems, dramatic epilogues, engravings of the kings themselves, poured from the press. Addison, Steele, Swift, and Defoe wrote about them. A group of young bloods even called themselves "mohocks" and acted in a natural manner which terrified the citizens and brought the young bloods into conflict with the authorities.[28]

Canada had now made a definite literary and physical impact on the old world of England. But, for English literature in the eighteenth century, Canada was merely a minor vehicle, and the elemental force of the country lay tamed under literary forms and conventions. The early voyagers—plain and crude as their accounts usually were—are the real forefathers of later poets such as Earle Birney, for it is they who held in their "morning's hand / the welling and wildness of Canada, the fling of a nation."

2. Explorers by Land

to 1867

VICTOR G. HOPWOOD

I. EUROPEAN AND FRENCH-CANADIAN BACKGROUND

UNLIKE EUROPEAN CONSCIOUSNESS, which goes back directly to ritual and myth, Canadian consciousness, especially that of English-speaking Canada, was born literate into history. European culture has immediate roots in the rituals, myths, legends, folktales, and folk songs of feudalism, classical antiquity, mid-eastern agricultural mystery kingships including the Judaeo-Christian, and prehistoric tribalism. This tradition belongs to Canada, but only as altered and diluted by transplantation and assimilation to North American capitalism, although our uprooted traditions sometimes gain hybrid vigour by cross-fertilization with non-British, non-French forms from other developed cultures. Thus, if the growth of European literature can be seen as statement and restatement of myth within a fundamentally continuous community, English-speaking Canadian consciousness, in contrast, faces from the start the problem of creating literature from direct experience, memory, and written records according to the sense of history which begins to mature within societies dominated by commodity production. Some regions of Canada, for example Newfoundland, are partial exceptions to the above statement. However, in general, the problem for our writers is difficult, particularly in dealing with those elements of consciousness which correspond to the foundation myths of primitive society which later found literary expression in epic and drama. The proto-form of our still largely unwritten foundation literature is of necessity the record of our explorers, fur traders, and pioneers. The transformation of such material has already begun. A significant recent example is Margaret Laurence's novel, *The Diviners* (1974), which draws on Scots, Métis, and Indian traditions to bring the past into the present.

Our explorers and fur traders left much fair to excellent writing, although the bulk of what they produced is simply historical source material. Few people were actually engaged in exploration and the fur trade, but of these a large proportion were literate since both activities require records, the ubiquitous log or journal from which more subtle forms of writing can evolve. Further, there was an interest in the homelands in discoveries, and a guaranteed market for accounts of them.

Canadian culture is marked by the parallel growth of two Canadian literatures, one in English and one in French. Each began within a parent European literature, slowly developed its own characteristics, and took its departure from its mother culture in the European metropolis. In the case of English Canadian literature at least, the new literature was modified by the influence of the more quickly maturing extension of British culture to the south.

Even before Canada was actually settled by Europeans the story of French exploration in North America appeared in English literature. Florio's translation (1580) of Jacques Cartier's account of the first two of his three voyages to Canada in the early sixteenth century reappears in the second edition of Hakluyt's *Principal Navigations* (1598–1600) along with such English voyages as those of John Cabot and Humphrey Gilbert. Hakluyt added a translation of the third voyage.

Today, every Canadian school child hears the story, either in English or in French, of how Jacques Cartier first found the great gulf he named for St. Lawrence, and a country called Canada. On his second voyage he sailed up the St. Lawrence, and wrote in his chronicle, "On both shores of it we began to see as goodly a countrey as possibly can with eye be seene," and thus started the historical process of creating an image of the new land. From Cartier's account of his voyages numerous events have become part of Canadian consciousness—Cartier raising the fleur-de-lis and cross, Cartier seizing two friendly Indians to take home as exhibits, Cartier's party nearly dying of scurvy during the winter until the Indians showed them how to make medicine from the "anneda" tree, possibly the white cedar or *arbor vitae*. And along with such stories, occasional phrases echo from Cartier's chronicle, such as the later translation of his description of the Labrador shore, "the land that God gave Cain."

The second great English collection of voyages, *Purchas His Pilgrimes* (1625), contains a translation of Champlain's account of his first voyage to North America in 1603, *Des Sauvages*. In the same collection also appears the tragic story of Henry Hudson.

Samuel de Champlain (1570?–1635) is certainly the central figure and writer of the French exploration of Canada inland from the sea. He was responsible, personally and through his agents, for the basic exploration of the St. Lawrence and its tributaries. From that valley, French explorers spread out to the Mississippi and the Gulf of Mexico, to Hudson Bay, to the prairies and the foot of the Rockies. After the British conquest, French-Canadian voyageurs pressed on with the explorers of the North West Company to the Arctic and the Pacific. The St. Lawrence became the portal of half a continent, the symbol of a nation's founding, expansion, and unity, a recurring theme in the poetry and romance of the new country.

After Purchas published Champlain's account of his first visit to the St. Lawrence, no more of his writings were translated into English until the nineteenth century. Nevertheless, the story of Champlain entered English-Canadian consciousness through various interpreters and popularizers. In the translations are found memorable images of the founding of Canada, all expressed in grave and unassuming narrative: the raising of buildings at Quebec, the fateful campaign against the Iroquois, the winter with the Hurons. From these and other incidents of the struggle of Champlain to establish New France emerges our picture of Champlain himself, the prototype in Canadian consciousness of the French administrator, pioneer, soldier, and explorer. Companion figures to Champlain in this tradition are the later explorers, La Salle and La Vérendrye.

The missionary explorer is a second major type, originating in the *Jesuit Relations*, a series of narratives, set down mainly between 1632 and 1679 by various members of the Jesuit order, telling of the progress of their missions. Written by men trained to observe and record, the *Relations* are basic documents of Canadian literature, history, ethnology, and geography. The character and quality of the writings are as varied as the men who wrote them: often crude, but frequently vivid in description and expressive of powerful feeling; sometimes wearisome in detail, but often dramatic in conflict and story. At their best, the *Relations* are well described by the man who first Englished them in full at the end of the nineteenth century, Reuben Gold Thwaites:

[The narrator's] meaning is seldom obscure. We gain from his pages a vivid picture of life in the primeval forest, as he lived it; we seem to see him upon his long canoe journeys, squatted amidst his dusky fellows, working his passage at the paddles, and carrying cargoes upon the portage trail; we see him the butt and scorn of the savage camp, sometimes deserted in the heart of the wilderness, and obliged to wait for another flotilla or to make his way alone as best he can. Arrived at last, at his journey's end, we often find him vainly seeking for shelter in the squalid huts of the natives, with every man's hand against him, but his own heart open to them all. We find him, even when at last domiciled in some far-away village, working against hope to save the unbaptized from eternal damnation; we seem to see the rising storm of opposition, invoked by native medicine men,—who to his seventeenth century imagination seem devils indeed,—and at last the bursting climax of superstitious frenzy which sweeps him and his before it.

Thwaites's description touches on the dramatic heart of the *Relations*, the conflict between the Jesuits' evangelical zeal and the beliefs of primitive nomads, between feudal theology and Stone Age superstition. From this matrix emerge the various figures of the drama—Lalemant, the gentle martyr; Brébeuf, the lion of the faith; Marquette, the proselytizing pathfinder of the wilderness. Behind the devotion and the strength we can see the more problematical qualities which helped produce the many martyrdoms, such as the over-zealousness of Father Jogues and the *donné* Goupil in teaching Iroquois children to make the sign of the cross against the wishes of their parents.

The most famous parts of the Jesuit chronicles are the tragic stories of the victims of the French-Dutch struggle, the Huron Indians and Jesuit missionaries killed or tortured by the Iroquois. Short English versions of the already legendized events were available even before the general translation of the *Relations*. The French wars against the Iroquois occupy a large place in literature based on Canadian history, although the possible mobilization of Six Nations' braves was only about two thousand. These stories have been the inspiration for literary works in English as well as French, including the poems "Père Lalemant" by Marjorie Pickthall and *Brébeuf and His Brethren* by E. J. Pratt. Leonard Cohen's novel, *Beautiful Losers*, makes perverse and exploitive use of the strangely hypnotic effect on the Canadian mythos of French attempts to suppress Indian beliefs. Pauline Johnson's poems about the Iroquois-Huron conflict are free from the condescension of white interpreters. Part Mohawk herself, she expresses clearly the courage and social solidarity of the women and men of the Iroquois Confederacy.

Francis Parkman's ability to grasp the conflicts in the life of New France made this American historian the outstanding interpreter of early French-Canadian society to readers of English. His work has been pre-eminent because of his wide acquaintance with the original sources, his direct experience of the Indian reaction to Europeans, and his gift for vigorous description, in addition to his strong sense of character and drama. Modern historians tend to be sceptical of imaginative attempts like Parkman's to make the past live, but the fact is that it is Parkman's Champlain, Frontenac, Father Jogues, La Salle, and Pontiac which have become fixed in the minds of English-speaking Canadians.

Unlike the political and religious explorers, the majority of French fur traders left indifferent narratives or none at all. The *coureurs de bois*, often illiterate, and frequently operating illegally, had seldom the ability or the desire to record their wanderings and transactions. Among them were many important explorers and historical figures, but we are concerned with two only, Radisson and Groseilliers, for their adventures are contained in a manuscript which may well be the first primary account in English of Canadian land exploration.

II. FROM THE BAY

Pierre Esprit Radisson's *Voyages* were written in England in 1668–69 to impress Charles II and various courtiers and merchants. The manuscript of the *Voyages* that has survived is either an original in Radisson's English or a translation from a lost manuscript in French. In the latter case, the founders of the Hudson's Bay Company paid for a translation of almost dazzling illiteracy. English syntax and diction have seldom been murdered as wildly as in Radisson's *Voyages*, a fact which seems to give them a life all their own. They describe an uncertain number of fur-trading journeys taking place at uncertain dates early in the second half of the seventeenth century.

The *Voyages* express a great new insight into the geography of the continent in the form of a traveller's narrative as admirable for its qualities as fiction as for its real adventures and its ideas. Radisson in his third voyage makes a doubtful claim to have been with Médard Chouart des Groseilliers on his trip to Lake Michigan and beyond. In the fourth voyage he makes a dubious assertion that Groseilliers and he reached the Northern Sea from Lake Superior. In spite of the mixed truth and fancy, Radisson's story contains a new and brilliant concept—that the centre of North American fur production was more accessible by Hudson Bay than by the St. Lawrence. The idea was not acceptable in New France, and the two *coureurs de bois* went to England for support. The outcome was the founding of the Hudson's Bay Company.

The psychology of the *coureur de bois* is well expressed by Radisson, for example in the contempt he shows for some faint-hearted Frenchmen who turned back to civilization when confronted with the Iroquois. He describes these men as "Gaillards" who only desire to do well, and then proceeds to contrast their idle boasting with the deeds of real woodsmen. Elsewhere, in a few words, he conveys the individualism of the trader, the eager welcome of the Indians to the bringer of invaluable European goods, and the power the goods gave the trader over the Indian:

We weare Cesars, being nobody to contradict us. We went away free from any burden, whilst those poore miserable thought themselves happy to carry our Equipage, for the hope that they had that we should give them a brasse ring, or an awle, or an needle.

Radisson also expresses the vision of what America was to mean to the multitudes of Europe, though it is hard to guess how much is fancy in his description of the country south of the Great Lakes.

The Europeans fight for a rock in the sea against one another. . . . Contrarywise those kingdoms are so delicious & under so temperat a climat, plentifull of all things, the earth bringing foorth its fruit twice a yeare, the people live long & lusty & wise in their way. What conquest would that bee att litle or no cost; what laborinth of pleasure should millions of people have, instead that millions complaine of misery & poverty!

Radisson's first two voyages deal with his adventures as a youth in the wilds of North America. Although they are not as important historically as the third and fourth voyages, as dramatic adventure stories they are scarcely to be surpassed. The first voyage constitutes a superb example of the story of escape by adoption, from death, of which the Pocahontas and John Smith tale is the American prototype. The stories of John Gyles, Alexander Henry, John Tanner, and John Jewitt are later Canadian versions. After adoption, escape, recapture, and re-acceptance by the Mohawks, Radisson went with some young braves on a hunting and war party to the west of the Appalachians. Few if any white men had yet penetrated that wilderness, and, more important, Radisson saw his adventures on this journey practically from the point of view of an Indian. Radisson's final escape from the Mohawks, and his later return in his second voyage to Iroquois territory, this time with the Jesuits, is as wild an adventure as the rest of his career.

Radisson's English manuscripts also had their share of adventures. They came into the hands of Samuel Pepys, the diarist, and were in a part of his collection which was being used for waste paper by a London shopkeeper when they were saved by Richard Rawlinson in 1750. Eventually Rawlinson's collection became the property of the Bodleian Library at Oxford, where the Radisson manuscripts lay unnoticed until nearly 1885, when they were published.

The charter of the company formed to exploit the inspiration of Groseilliers and Radisson is not in itself a literary document, but its words are quotable and have attained some literary fame. Even the name, "Company of Adventurers trading into Hudson's Bay," has helped to cast a glamour over a basically commercial enterprise. The terms of the charter (1670) have a certain legal grandiloquence in their bestowal of almost kingly powers. The Latin motto, *Pro pelle cutem*, has had the power to provoke speculation on its origin and meaning, ranging from variations on Juvenal (*pro cute pellum*) and the Vulgate book of Job (*pellum pro pelle*) through the idea of barter (skin for skin), to the facetious "Either way we skin you." E. E. Rich suggests that it refers to the process of making felt for beaver hats and means the skin for the fur.

After the Radisson papers and the charter, the early literature on the Hudson's Bay Company is disappointingly dull. In the 1740's, Arthur Dobbs, Henry Ellis, and others published attacks on the Company for its monopoly and alleged its failure to fulfil the obligation in its charter to carry out exploration. The Company's attempt to vindicate itself brought a counter-attack from Joseph Robson, an English mason who had worked at Fort Churchill. Robson's *An Account of Six Years Residence in Hudson's Bay* (1752) is memorable for a certain eloquence in its animus against the Company which had "for eighty years slept at the edge of a frozen sea." The same volume also contains several contributions to the mythology of Henry Kelsey (d. 1729), including the statement that the Indians called him "Little Giant" for shooting a grizzly bear.

The most complete known journal of Kelsey came to light in the papers of Arthur Dobbs in 1926 and was published by the Public Archives of Canada in 1929. It can barely be classified as literature, although much romance attaches to the adventures it tells. In 1690 "the boy Henry Kelsey" joined a band of Indians and travelled with them to the prairies, staying inland two winters. He was probably the first white man to see the Canadian prairies, to kill a grizzly bear, and to see an Indian buffalo hunt.

Kelsey is unique among explorers in providing a verse introduction to his journal, perhaps the first English verse written in mainland Canada. Poetry will never be Kelsey's chief title to fame, but occasional doggerel couplets are vigorous, such as these on the grizzly:

> His skin to gett I have used al ye ways I can
> He is mans food & he makes food of man
> His hide they would not me it preserve
> But said it was a god & they should Starve

Kelsey's journal, the introduction in verse, and an appendix on the beliefs of the Indians he met, are the earliest descriptions we have of the Plains Indians. There are not only sharp observations but also occasional touches of reserved humour, for example, with the medicine men who "by their singing will pretend to know w^t ye firmament of heaven is made of," some claiming to "have been there & seen it."

Antony Henday journeyed in 1754 to the prairies between what is now Calgary and Edmonton, nearly within sight of the Rockies. Henday's superiors were sceptical of his account, partly because he described the Plains Indians as having horses. His journal was published in 1907, by the Royal Society of Canada, from a copy in the Public Archives. It is clearly written and extremely matter of fact. Here is an entry describing a meeting with a band of the later dreaded Blackfeet:

16 [May, 1755] Friday. Paddled 30 Miles N.b.E. when we came to 30 tents of Archithinue Natives: I talked with them as I did with the others; but all to no purpose. Our Indians traded a great many Furs from them. They have the finest Horses I have yet seen here, and are very kind people.

This is a typical entry in the journal of an explorer or fur trader. Its form is like, and probably based on, the ship's log; it states daily, as relevant, the course travelled, weather, surrounding country, and incidents of discovery or trade. A useful record, it is usually tedious, all bare facts, all equal. Exploration tends to be repetitive, and the fourth or fifth adventure with a bear, boring, at least in the telling. If journals are to become interesting to the ordinary reader, they need suppression of repetitive detail, expansion with incident and description, and development of direction and purpose. The account may then be called a "narrative." Perhaps some of the more sober quality of English-Canadian fiction as compared to French-Canadian can be ascribed to the different emphasis in the early years of the two cultures on the journal and the narrative.

The model, and one of the best narratives of Canadian land exploration, is Hearne's *Journey from Prince of Wales's Fort in Hudson's Bay to the Northern Ocean*, published in 1795. It begins a series of major narratives, notably by Mackenzie, Henry, Harmon, Thompson, and Ross, all conforming more or less to a pattern. They are written in the first person, are factual, and derive their interest from the novelty of their material, their story of endurance, adventure, and discovery, and the incidental insight given into the character of the author.

In his dedication, Hearne (1745–92) rightly describes his style as "plain and unadorned." Its other virtues include clarity, definiteness of statement, sure choice of appropriate detail, combined with quick and unfaltering transitions and a firm but not obtrusive prose rhythm.

Hearne's book describes his two failures and final success (1769, 1770, 1771–72) in walking across the Canadian Barrens to the mouth of the Coppermine River on the shore of the Arctic Ocean. From each of his two failures, Hearne drew the appropriate lesson. Indeed, one of Hearne's outstanding characteristics was his ability to learn both from his own experience and from the people he travelled with and among. This capacity, combined with expressive power, becomes a literary quality in an explorer's narrative, since, almost by definition, exploration literature expresses the experience of seeking and finding the geographical unknown. Here in Hearne's words is how a Chipewyan leader analysed Hearne's difficulties after his second failure:

He attributed all our misfortunes to the misconduct of my guides, and the very plan we pursued, by the desire of the Governor, in not taking any women with us on this journey, was, he said, the principal thing that occasioned all our wants: "for," said he, "when all the men are heavy laden, they can neither hunt nor travel to any considerable distance; and in case they meet with success in hunting, who is to carry the produce of their labour?"

In effect, Hearne adopted the Indian method of travelling to reach the unknown coppermines. He placed himself under the protection of an Indian of some standing, and lived the Indian life, following the nomadic wanderings of the band for fish and animals, while it worked its way generally towards his goal.

Between the lines of Hearne's book can be read the near certainty that he was adopted into the tribe of his adviser, Motanabee, and, according to the custom of the Chipewyans had at least one wife to make his exploration possible. Traders seldom understood that they were being accepted into Indian society when a woman offered herself or was offered, even though European folk and fairy tales include many examples of a traveller being given the hand of a beautiful subject or daughter, a surviving echo among civilized peoples of parallel early customs. Much of the drama between whites and Indians developed because whites did not recognize or live up to the obligations of kinship, being concerned only with gaining trade.

Hearne's *Journey* is interesting not only as adventure but also as keen and accurate observation of nature. Hearne was alert both to the facts and to many ridiculous travellers' tales which had been accepted as true. His description of the beaver and his debunking of the surrounding mythology are noteworthy. He analyses the beaver's anatomy, for example, and points out that:

It would be as impossible for a beaver to use its tail as a trowel, except on the surface of the ground on which it walks, as it would have been for Sir James Thornhill to have painted the dome of St. Paul's cathedral without the assistance of scaffolding.

The historian Brebner has called Hearne's account of his journey "one of the classics of the literature of exploration," partly because of the author's "odd, judicious literary artistry," but also because it "conveys unconsciously a portrait 'in the round' of a very likeable and inquisitive, if somewhat timorous man." R. Glover in a recent edition of Hearne's work supports Brebner's opinion, except for the inappropriate word, "timorous." Nevertheless, the word points to something essential in Hearne's character, although grossly misrepresenting it. Hearne was willing to achieve his purpose by surrendering his command to the purposes of others. Possessed of the courage, persistence, and understanding to reach his goal, he still had an aversion to any struggle to bend others to his will. There was also a touch of the sceptic in his outlook, an attitude reinforced by eighteenth-century French rationalism or Humean scepticism. Hearne approached his difficulties with "philosophy" and found something corresponding to his own view in the attitude of the Indians. The result of his undogmatic attitude, almost at times complaisance, is a realistic yet sympathetic and discerning account of Indian life.

The *Journey* is one of the most sophisticated early journals and narratives, perhaps as the result of a bent more speculative and literary than was common among fur traders. Hearne is frequently moved to compare European and Indian ways, to comment on the effects of environment and custom on the outlook of people, and to raise such questions as whether Indians really benefit from European trade. There is also, one suspects, a touch of Dickens' fat boy in Hearne; he seems to like taking advantage of his cosmopolitan outlook to make his readers' flesh creep with accounts of outlandish foods and customs. He takes apparent relish, for example, in comparing the dish the Indians made of the contents of a caribou's stomach to a Scotch haggis. Even before publication the literary and scientific importance of Hearne's journals was recognized by the French geographer La Pérouse, who was in command of the French ships to whom Hearne surrendered Prince of Wales's Fort (Fort Churchill) in 1782. La Pérouse returned the captured manuscript to Hearne, stipulating that he publish it as soon as he returned to England.

A few other eighteenth-century documents on Hudson Bay deserve notice. Matthew Cocking's journal of a trip to the prairies in 1772, published in 1908, is similar to Henday's. Isham and Graham, stay-at-home factors on the Bay, wrote accounts of the region's natural history, Indians, and fur trade. James Isham's *Observations on Hudson's Bay*, published by the Hudson's Bay Record Society in 1949, contains much information and the occasional piece of lively writing, such as the speech of an interior Indian on coming to trade:

we Livd. hard Last winter and in want. the powder being short measure and bad, I say!—tell your Servants to fill the measure and not to put their finger's within the Brim, take pity of us, take pity of us, I say!

Andrew Graham's account of the Bay was published in 1969 with the same title as Isham's book, parts of which it repeats, although the natural history sections are more extensive. Both Graham and Isham indicate continuing connections of a few of the Hudson's Bay Company employees with scientific organizations such as the Royal Society and the Edinburgh Society.

In general, however, towards the end of the eighteenth century, a few years after the conquest of New France, the initiative in the exploration of the interior of Canada passed from Hudson Bay to the new British traders in Montreal. At the same time, the exploration of the northwest coast of America was beginning.

III. FROM MONTREAL

The merchants of Montreal who came to control trade up the St. Lawrence after the British conquest were from both Britain and the American colonies. Alexander Henry the elder (1739–1824), a New Englander fired by French-Canadian accounts of the fur trade, was one of the first white men to venture to the western Great Lakes after 1759. His *Travels and Adventures in Canada and the Indian Territories between the Years 1760 and 1776* (1809) is probably the most skilfully written fur-trader's narrative. Henry had a story to tell and made the most of it; as a result his book not only achieved immortality in its own right, but parts of its most exciting sections were incorporated almost word for word into Parkman's history of the Pontiac war.

At Michilimackinac in 1763 Henry saw the massacre of the English garrison which followed the famous game of baggataway or lacrosse. He himself avoided immediate death but was later captured, only to be spared again, this time by the intercession of an Indian friend who claimed him as a brother and then helped him to escape. The later parts of Henry's *Travels and Adventures*, while not so bloodcurdling, are still well written and interesting. When he describes being lost in the woods or crossing the prairies without food, he uses events, scenery, and thoughts to build up a strong feeling of anxiety and urgency. He reports the customs and legends of the Indians with sympathy and keen observation. Among the early writers he carried one of the lightest baggages of civilized preconceptions. To use social workers' jargon, he was not "judgmental"; he was, rather, almost pure adventurer. He reports what he sees objectively, with a certain amount of amusement, but nevertheless appreciatively:

The bear being dead, all my assistants approached, and all, but more particularly my old mother (as I was wont to call her), took her [the bear's] head in their hands, stroking and kissing it several times; begging a thousand pardons for taking away her life: calling her their relation and grandmother; and requesting her not to lay the fault upon them, since it was truly an Englishman that had put her to death.

Alexander Mackenzie's *Voyages from Montreal through the Continent of North America to the Frozen and Pacific Oceans in 1789 and 1793*, which was published earlier (London, 1801) than Henry's book, quickly went through three editions and aroused great interest. For example, Marshal Bernadotte claimed that the *Voyages* were smuggled into France and translated for him at Napoleon's command to provide information essential to a planned attack on Canada via Louisiana. Among the books Napoleon had on St. Helena were the three volumes of the French edition.

The "from Montreal" in Mackenzie's title was like a gauntlet thrown down by the Montreal traders in reply to the "from Prince of Wales's Fort" of Hearne's *Journey* published in 1795. It reflects the crescendo of opposition to the Hudson's Bay Company from the "peddlers from Quebec" who in 1787 sank their differences to form the North West Company. The voyages of Mackenzie were in a sense the first fruit of that amalgamation.

Mackenzie's *Voyages* opens with a history of the fur trade, probably written by the explorer's cousin Roderick, valuable to the historian but colourless. Yet even this matter-of-fact document grows lyrical over the beauties of the historic Methy Portage. The second and the third parts of Mackenzie's book are in journal form. The third, the most interesting, describes the crossing of the Rocky Mountains to the Pacific Ocean, where Mackenzie painted on a rock near Bella Coola the famous words, "Alexander Mackenzie, from

Canada by land the twenty-second of July, one thousand seven hundred and ninety-three." Here Mackenzie unknowingly missed meeting Vancouver by only six weeks.

The *Edinburgh Review* of October 1802 touches shrewdly upon the attraction of Mackenzie's *Voyages*. It brings out, indeed, a thread of Canadian literature which runs from its very beginning right through to the present.

There is something in the idea of traversing a vast and unknown continent, that gives an agreeable expansion to our conceptions; and the imagination is insensibly engaged and inflamed by the spirit of adventure, and the perils and the novelties that are implied in a voyage of discovery. . . . His narrative, if sometimes minute and fatiguing, is uniformly distinct and consistent; his observations, though not numerous, are sagacious and unassuming; and the whole work bears an impression of correctness and veracity, that leaves no unpleasant feeling of doubt or suspicion in the mind of the reader.

Mackenzie himself had a fair idea of the literary quality of his own book. In his preface, he carefully put aside any claim to "the charms of embellished narrative, or animated description." What he did claim was "the approbation due to simplicity and to truth." It is a claim which readers have found every reason to allow, although recent research adds an ironic footnote on the matter of simplicity. A preserved copy of parts of his original journal shows that the version published by Mackenzie contained a number of "improvements." These were made by William Combe, the creator of Dr. Syntax, who had previously edited Meares's voyages. An example is the description of a portage as "very commodious" which Mackenzie had called "good." W. Kaye Lamb's 1970 edition of the voyages deals definitively with Mackenzie's texts and includes his letters. Roy Daniells' *Alexander Mackenzie and the North West* (1969) discusses Mackenzie's journeys as proto-epic.

The power of Mackenzie's journal resides mainly in its story and the force of character of the man who wrote it. Prosaic and repetitive, it is nevertheless an account which enlarges the horizons of human knowledge and reveals the man, the very type of pushing Scot who has contributed much to Canadian development. Mackenzie overcame human and natural opposition by sheer drive. He had imagination, but it was not sensitivity; it was rather a compelling vision of what single-minded ambition could achieve.

Simon Fraser's journals describing the exploration of the Fraser River in 1808 possess to a superlative degree the best qualities of Mackenzie's journal. The brief account by Fraser (1776–1862) of his thousand-mile journey to the sea and back was included with some other English and French journals in a much-edited form in L. F. R. Masson's *Les Bourgeois de la Compagnie du Nord-Ouest* (1889). In 1960 Lamb's text of all the known *Journals and Letters* was published. Some of Fraser's descriptive passages have been frequently quoted as catching the force of the river or the immensity of its chasm. The power of his description comes, not so much from diction or imagery, as from the sense of appropriate activity on the part of Fraser and his men—activity which in its turn is the key to our sense of Fraser's character. Anyone who has seen the Fraser River in its canyons must find it hard to believe that any human being had the hardihood deliberately to descend it in a birchbark canoe or the power to command twenty-three other men to accompany him.

It being absolutely impossible to carry the canoes by land, yet sooner than to abandon them, all hands without hesitation embarked, as it were *à corps perdu* upon the mercy of the Stygian tide. Once engaged the die was cast, and the great difficulty consisted in keeping the canoes in the medium, or *fil d'eau*, that is to say, clear of the precipice on one side, and of the gulphs formed by the waves on the other. However, thus skimming along like lightning, the crews cool and determined, followed each other in awful silence. And [when] we arrived at the end we stood gazing on our narrow escape from perdition. After breathing a little, we continued our course to a point where the Indians were encamped.

Fraser's writing, as shown above, is blunt in statement, despite its clichés. The French expressions are in no sense an affectation. French was probably then the main language of the fur trade in *le pays d'en haut*, a sparsely settled Babel of half a continent, where English and some Gaelic were spoken by the masters, French by the bulk of the employees, and a score of languages and dialects by the native Indians.

Daniel Williams Harmon (1778–1845) was, like Alexander Henry, a Yankee adventurer in the Canadian fur trade, but far less colourful. His *Journal of Voyages and Travels in the Interior of North America* (1820), reporting his years, 1800–1819, in the Northwest, is generally marked by neither literary skill nor heroic endeavour. It is notable, however, for containing in its routine pages an intimate record of an inner struggle against the common practice of the traders of abandoning their Indian wives on returning to civilization, although more white men might have taken their wilderness wives out with them had Indian women been generally willing to leave their female kin.

My intention now is, to keep her as long as I remain in this uncivilized part of the world; and when I return to my native land, I shall endeavour to place her under the protection of some honest man, with whom she can pass the remainder of her days in this country, much more agreeably, than it would be possible for her to do, were she to be taken down into the civilized world, to the manners, customs and language of which, she would be an entire stranger.

Harmon's complaisance was eventually shaken by the death of a son and by his Puritan conscience. The outcome was a religious conversion and a rejection of his earlier intention.

We have wept together over the early departure of several children, and especially, over the death of a beloved son. We have children still living, who are equally dear to us both. How could I spend my days in the civilized world, and leave my beloved children in the wilderness? The thought has in it the bitterness of death. How could I tear them from a mother's love, and leave her to mourn over their absence, to the day of her death?

Alexander Henry the younger (d. 1814), the nephew of the author of *Travels and Adventures*, like Harmon kept a journal in detail for the whole length of time, 1799–1814, that he spent in the western fur trade. A transcript has survived, which was edited by Elliott Coues and published in 1897 as *New Light on the Early History of the Greater North West*. The frankness of the author on all matters is sometimes the result of prurience rather than objectivity. Like the majority of traders, he was unable to realize that the offer of women was hospitality, and that the offer of a wife was part of tribal initiation. Henry saw instead prostitution, pimping, and lasciviousness. In the same way he saw the Indian eagerness for gifts, especially alcohol, as savage greed and laziness, when in fact the Indians were expecting the generosity appropriate from a wealthy brother. In a remarkably short period of time the net effect of the emphasis on making every transaction an exchange of goods was to make both prostitution and drunkenness essential features of the fur trade. However, in spite of his limitations and a tendency to prolixity, Henry's book has many interesting anecdotes and much information.

The Journal of Duncan M'Gillivray of the North West Company at Fort George on the Saskatchewan, 1794-5, edited by A. S. Morton and published in 1929, is about a tenth the length of Henry the Younger's. In the events and descriptions it is as vivid as it is short.

They were hurled down with surprizing velocity thro' three successive cascades, nothing but the particular dirrection of Providence could have saved them in such imminent danger—for the Canoe was several times overwhelmed with water, & threatened every moment with being dashed to pieces in the windings of the Rocks, and after arriving in the dreadfull whirlpool below, it remained a considerable time under water.—At length however the Current drove it towards shore, with the men still hanging after it, and tho' they at first seemed insensible yet after a little assistance they recovered their strength, & before night renewed their labours, with as much alacrity as if nothing had happened them, a convincing proof of the force of their constitutions. About 3 O'clock P.M. a Roll of Tobacco fell into the water & F Lussier dived to the bottom to recover it.

The writing of Duncan McGillivray (17??–1808) is also exciting for the very lucidity of its bias and calloused understanding, for example when he discusses the independent attitude of the Indians of the plains.

It is then our luxuries that attract them to the Fort and make us so necessary to their happiness. The love of Rum is their first inducement to industry; they undergo every hardship and fatigue to procure a Skinfull of this delicious beverage, and when a

Nation becomes addicted to drinking, it affords a strong presumption that they will soon become excellent hunters. Tobacco is another article of as great demand as it is unnecessary.—Custom has however made it of consequence to them as it constitutes a principal part of their feasts & Superstitious ceremonies, and in these treaties of peace and councils of War, a few whifs out of the medicine pipe confirms the articles that have been mutually agreed upon.—As for amunition it is rendered valuable by the great advantage it gives them over their enemies in their expeditions to the Rocky Mountains against the defenceless Slave Indians who are destitute of this destructive improvement of War. It is also required to Kill Beaver, but if the Fur Trade had not allured adventurers to this Country there would be no necessity for hunting this animal. The rest of our commodities are indeed usefull to the Natives, when they can afford to purchase them, but if they had hitherto lived unacquainted with European productions it would not I beleive diminish their felicity.

Such a passage should make it clear that Duncan McGillivray was above all the Nor'Wester who possessed powers of commercial vision, morally uninhibited expression, and personal ambition and drive parallel to those of the Hudson's Bay Company's George Simpson. It is interesting to speculate that had this McGillivray survived, he might well have ruled the inevitable union of the rival fur monopolies in a manner even surpassing that of Sir George.

As a transition to the work of David Thompson, whose resolute opposition to the use of alcohol as a trade good is too well known to need illustration, a word on the vulnerability of the natives of North America to alcohol is in order. The evidence is shaky that either heredity or unfamiliarity is the deciding factor. Probably Indians wanted spirits to induce *ekstasis* (a state of being out of place or out of one's mind), ecstasy being highly valued by Indians and Eskimos in communal rituals and in attaining personal visions for establishing individual identities and names. This outlook gives some substance to the title of George Ryga's play, *The Ecstasy of Rita Joe*. Indian drinking was far removed from the individual alcoholism of European victims. Indeed, early Indians coming to the Bay would carry home untouched spirits which they had been commissioned to purchase. The deliberate exploitation of alcohol by the traders for the reasons given by McGillivray produced the problem. In the fur trade dead Indians produced no furs, so the only good Indian could not be a dead one. However, an Indian addicted to alcohol might well be more valuable than a sober one.

The pre-eminence of David Thompson's narrative of his twenty-eight years in the West among travel literature is emerging belatedly but unmistakeably, as has his genius as a mapmaker and explorer. Thompson never completed the narrative of his *Travels*, in spite of his constant rewriting of the work between 1846 and 1851. For some parts there are three revisions of the narrative in addition to the original journals in one or more versions and some reports to the North West Company on particular journeys. Through the various versions, it is possible to see his struggle to subordinate the great mass of his information to the narrative form, a process never finished but still carried to the point where his writing is the major primary work in English on the exploration of Canada. It first became available in the limited edition, splendidly annotated and introduced by J. B. Tyrrell, published by the Champlain Society in 1916 under the title *Narrative of his Explorations in Western America 1784–1812*. This book was reissued in 1962 with an inaccurate and vituperative introduction by Richard Glover, including in the text a grossly careless transcription of a hitherto missing chapter of the book identified in the Ontario Archives by Victor G. Hopwood in 1956. In 1972, the latter brought out a modernized edition of Thompson's travels, shortening part of the earlier editions, correcting textual misreadings, and adding unpublished accounts by Thompson of some of his journeys. The title of the new edition is *Travels in Western North America, 1784–1812*, since Thompson himself always called his book his "Travels."

One of the colleagues of Thompson (1770–1857), Dr. J. J. Bigsby, in *The Shoe and Canoe* (1850) describes him as a conversationalist, and indeed it is almost possible to hear the voice of the story-teller himself as we read the *Narrative*. Says Bigsby:

No living person possesses a tithe of his information respecting the Hudson's Bay countries. . . . Never mind his Bunyan-like face and cropped hair; he has a very powerful mind, and a singular faculty of picture-making. He can create a wilderness and people it with warring savages, or climb the Rocky Mountains with you in a snowstorm, so clearly and palpably, that only shut your eyes and you hear the crack of the rifle, or feel the snow-flakes melt on your cheeks as he talks.

Such an example of Thompson's image-making power can be found in his description of how, as a boy, he was introduced to the young Piegan war chief, Kootenae Appee, by the old chief Saukamappee. The meeting can almost be seen, and the words of the old man take on a mythic quality.

the war chief . . . gave me his left hand, and I gave him my right hand, upon which he looked at me, and smiled as much as to say a contest would not be equal; at his going away the same took place. . . . The old man now remarked to me that as we proceed [ed] on, we should see a great many Indians who had never seen a white man, as very few of them went to the trading houses. If one of our people offers you his left give him your left hand, for the right hand is no mark of friendship. This hand wields the spear, draws the Bow and the trigger of the gun; it is the hand of death. The left hand is next to the heart, and speaks truth and friendship, it holds the shield of protection, and is the hand of life.

Thompson's descriptions of people, events, and scenes are direct and rich in detail. He uses figures of speech only occasionally, although probably more often than the other explorers. Where he does use them, they are apt and forceful. More often than not they are in the mouths of one of the many characters who fill his pages, as in the above example.

The lesser units of Thompson's narration are brief descriptions or anecdotes, such as might be found in the author's speech. There are scores of interesting tales in his pages, each like a good nut, full of meat. Many a brief page or two contains what could be the kernel of a whole novel in its graphic description of events and shrewd revelation of character. Some of the anecdotes have a condensed epic quality which contributes to the character of the work as a whole. The following passage is an example of such quality, and also of Thompson's humour and his ability to catch the flavour of dialogue.

They soon broke silence, and Cartier [a Salish Indian chief] mildly said, You know our law is, that a man that seduces a woman must be killed; I said I have no objection to your law, to what purpose do you tell me this; the Orator then spoke, my daughter with her mother has always sat quietly in my Tent, until these few days past, when one of your men has been every day, while we are hunting, to my tent with beads and rings to seduce my daughter. Looking round on my men, he said he is not here, (on their entering my servant had gone into my room, I knew it must be him; the men and myself were every day too much fatigued to think of women.) But wherever he is, we hope you will give him to us that he may die by our law. I told them I had no inclination to screen the Man, but as they were much in want of guns and ammunition for hunting and to protect themselves from their enemies, if they wished me to return with those articles, and various others, they must give me a Man to take his place, otherwise I could not return; they looked at each other, and said we cannot find a man capable, besides his going among strange people where he may be killed; very well, then if you kill my man I cannot return to you, but shall stay with the Peeagans, your enemies; then what is to be done, exclaimed the Orator. I replied, let him live this time, and as you are noted for being a good gelder of Horses; if this Man ever again enters your Tent, geld him, but let him live; at this proposition they laughed, and said, well let him live, but so sure as he comes to seduce our women, we shall geld him; after smoking, they retired in good humour. But my men, all young and in the prime of life, did not at all relish the punishment.

The larger units of the book are the dozen or more major journeys and explorations which Thompson made, with visits to or life among new groups of people. These journeys give a picture of the life and customs of the Cree, Chipewyan, Assiniboine, Blackfeet, Mandan, Chippewa, Kootenae, and Interior and Coast Salish. Some sections record Indian myths, folklore, and beliefs; others describe animals and plants and their place in Indian life. Thompson's account of these matters must be considered to be especially authoritative, as he spent half a lifetime among the Indians, was the first white man to see some of them, and got most of his information directly in the language of several of the tribes.

All of Thompson's journeys and explorations fit into a panorama of tremendous scope, greater than that of any comparable North American work, stretching over twenty-eight years, including service in both the Hudson's Bay Company and the North West Company, and ranging from London to

Hudson Bay, Reindeer Lake, the sources of the Mississippi, and the mouth of the Columbia. The unity of the whole work is both that of an epoch and that of the story of a fourteen-year-old charity-school boy who made himself into a great scientific geographer, able to say on the completion of his exploration of the Columbia:

Thus I have fully completed the survey of this part of North America from sea to sea, and by almost innumerable astronomical Observations have determined the positions of the Mountains, Lakes and Rivers, and other remarkable places on the northern part of this Continent; the Maps of all of which have been drawn and laid down in geographical position, being now the work of twenty-seven years.

A contemporary poem, "The Pride" of John Newlove, draws extensively on travellers' writings and anthropological material, including Thompson's *Travels*. (In the same manner Newlove in "Wintertime" also made use of Hearne's *Journey*.) An interesting attempt to join fur trade background to modern experience can be found in Wayland Drew's novel, *The Wabeno Feast* (1973). The resulting book is unfortunately a bit schizophrenic, partly because of Drew's inability to distinguish between Indian communal values and primitive superstitions, an error Thompson does not make, and which, moreover, he shows some of the Indians capable of recognizing:

In the night the Gale had thrown down the Pole to which the Tambour and Medicine Bag was tied; and the Dogs had wetted them; he was indignant, and took the gun to shoot the Dogs, but his good sense prevented him; and looking at his Tambour and Medicine Bag with contempt, exclaimed "If you, the Wahbino had any power, the Dogs would not have treated you as they have done."

The story of Jacob Astor's Pacific Fur Company establishment, Astoria, is best known as told by the American, Washington Irving. In his *Astoria* (1836) he refers, rather condescendingly, to "literary" and "scribbling" clerks although he drew rather heavily on their memoirs with only a perfunctory acknowledgment. Two such clerks were Gabriel Franchère (1786–1863) and Ross Cox (1793–1853).

Franchère's *Relation d'un voyage à la côte du Nord-Ouest de l'Amerique Septentrionale* (1820), covering the years 1810–14, was translated into English in 1854. With the exception of a few purple passages, introduced by his editor, its easy direct style is most appropriate to the simple almost archetypal story which it tells: a voyage from New York around the Horn to the mouth of the Columbia, adventures while trading for furs, and a journey by canoe across the continent to Montreal. In 1969 an unembellished transcription and English translation by Wessie Tipping Lamb of Franchère's original manuscript was published. The restoration should bring increased respect for Franchère as an author.

Cox's *Adventures on the Columbia River* (1832), referring to his service first with the Pacific Fur Company and then the North West Company, was written in later life after the author had returned to Ireland. There his work included journalism, an occupation reflected in the style of the book, which is not improved by the fashionable loading with allusions and quotations. As an historical source, Cox is unreliable, for he wrote largely from memory and hearsay. As a story of adventure, however, his book is quickly and easily told, and contains some humour.

Alexander Ross (1783–1856) is unusual among the fur traders in having written a series of books. Like Franchère and Cox, he was a clerk among the Astorians, and his *Adventures of the First Settlers on the Oregon or Columbia River* (1848) tells much the same story. It is a rambling and racy book, written with a keen eye for character. Ross had a satirical gift, and he did not spare either Astor's direction from New York of the affairs of the settlement or the officers of his fur company who carried them out. But it was not until Ross was describing Astoria after it had become Fort George, in *The Fur Hunters of the Far West* (1855), that his satire really flowered. Ross lost his seniority twice: once when the North West Company absorbed Astoria during the War of 1812, and again when the Nor'Westers joined the Hudson's Bay Company in 1821. To him in each case the villain was the bureaucracy of the North West Company; both the decadence and the romance of its last years appear in his pages:

The Bourgeois is therefore carried on board his canoe upon the back of some sturdy fellow generally appointed for this purpose. He seats himself on a convenient feather bed, somewhat low in the centre of his canoe, his gun by his side, his little cherubs fondling around him, and his faithful spanial lying at his feet.

No sooner is he at his ease than his pipe is presented by his attendant. He then puffs the Indian leaf in curling clouds. His silken banner undulates over the stern of his painted vessel. Then the bending paddles are plied, and the fragile craft speeds through the currents with a degree of fleetness not to be surpassed. Yell upon yell from the hearty crew proclaims the prowess and adroitness.

The books of Ross, Franchère, Cox, and the later *Traits of American Indian Life* (1853) and *Snake Country Journals* (1950) of Peter Skene Ogden (1794–1854) have a new subject-matter in the expeditions of armed parties of company trappers into Indian territory, according to the American system of obtaining furs. The change of atmosphere from Thompson to these men is instructive. Henry, Harmon, and Thompson seem at home among the Indians. The new men, brave as they were, seemed to walk with their fingers to the trigger, expecting and nerved for armed conflict. There is danger and adventure enough in these expeditions, but the sense of enlarging the known world that is found in Hearne, Mackenzie, and Thompson is gone.

Ross's last book, *The Red River Settlement* (1856), tells of the hardships of the settlers who were brought to the prairies after 1811 by Lord Selkirk, and who became the pawns of the Hudson's Bay Company in the last ten years of near civil war between the two great fur companies. Ross writes as if the Hudson's Bay Company charter was not only royal but divine. However, one-sidedness allowed for, the book is a moving account of the settlers and their difficulties, both natural and man-made, before and after the joining of the companies.

Although established within the fur trade, both the Métis and Scots communities on the Red River implied the eventual development of agriculture and self-government in the West. After Ross's books, the literary value of fur trade writing declines except where new motives replace the original informing interest in unknown lands and peoples. Samuel Black's *Rocky Mountain Journal* (1955) of his explorations into the Finlay and Stikine River country is an example: prolix and hard to read, it still contains some clear descriptions, especially of geological formations.

Perhaps the most interesting reflection of the period of Hudson's Bay Company hegemony are the journals and letters of George Simpson, Sir George after 1841, "the little emperor." His official narrative of a semi-diplomatic tour for the Company, *An Overland Journey Round the World during the Years 1841 and 1842* (1847) is pompous and dull, but his journals and reports as published from 1931 on are more revealing of the man and the tensions of his rule. Here, as in his letters, largely concerned with the management of a trade stretching from Labrador to the Pacific, can be observed the shrewdness and skill with which Simpson manipulated his less tenacious or amoral subordinates and the Company's directors in London. Simpson's unfailing eye for the individual vulnerability and commercial value of each employee found expression as a secret art in his private notebook "Servants' Characters and Their Histories." This book of acerbic vignettes, often quoted by historians, should be published by the Hudson's Bay Record Society by the time this chapter appears in print. Here is Simpson's description of Dr. John McLoughlin, often considered to be the father of the American state of Oregon:

About 48 years of age. A very bustling active man who can go through a great deal of business but is wanting in system and regularity, and has not the talent of managing the few associates & clerks under his authority; has a good deal of influence with Indians and speaks Sioulteaux tolerably well. Very zealous in the discharge of his public duties and a man of strict honour and integrity but a great stickler for rights and priviledges and sets himself up for a righter of Wrongs. Very anxious to obtain a lead among his Colleagues with whom he has not much influence owing to his ungovernable Violent temper and turbulent disposition, and would be troublesome man to the Company if he had sufficient influence to form and tact to manage a party; in short would be a Radical in every country under any Government and under any circumstances; and if he had not pacific people to deal with would be eternally embroiled in "affairs of honour" on the merest trifles arising I conceive from the irritability of his temper more than a quarrelsome disposition. Altogether a disagreeable man to do business with as it is impossible to go with him in all things and a difference of opinion almost amounts to a declaration of hostilities, yet a good hearted man and a pleasant companion.

Aphoristic and penetrating as the characterization may be, it is still the response of a mean person to a great-hearted one. In contrast, McLoughlin's letters, also largely business correspondence, reveal the vision and warmth which inevitably produced the drama of his conflict with Simpson.

In some ways, what other people say about Simpson is more interesting than his own writing. John McLean's *Twenty-Five Years' Service in the Hudson's Bay Territory* (1849) gives a vigorous and uncomplimentary picture of the great man's rule by an aggrieved employee. It also gives an unadorned exposition of the methods of the fur trade, particularly in areas where there was competition, such as north of the Ottawa and St. Lawrence rivers. McLean's narrative not only covers twenty-five years, but stretches across the continent from New Caledonia to Labrador, where he discovered and described the Great Falls. His descriptions of the Labrador trade, its Eskimos, and the Moravian missionaries to them, form part of the background for Harold Horwood's recent novel, *White Eskimo*. McLean also gives an account of the work among the Cree at Norway House of his missionary father-in-law, James Evans. In spite of the obstacles placed in his way by Simpson and the Hudson's Bay Company, Evans printed the first book in the Canadian West, *A Cree Syllabic Hymn Book* (1841), on an improvised press with the type cast in lead from old bullets and the lining of tea chests. The printed characters were a special syllabic alphabet developed by Evans.

While there has been much discussion about the real value of missionaries to the native peoples of Canada, there can be little doubt that the shortage of missionary accounts of the early Canadian West results from commercial hostility to missionaries by the fur companies. An additional reason for their absence is the suppression in 1773 of the Jesuits by Pope Pius XIV, thus breaking the earlier tradition of French Catholic missionary explorers. The first missionaries in the West were not to the Indians but to the settlers of Red River. The earliest missionary journals, such as those of John West (1775?–1845) and Pierre-Jean de Smet (1801–1873), indicate the weakening of monopoly control of the Hudson's Bay Company territories. The American Jesuit of Belgian descent, de Smet, tells mostly about American Indians in his *Life, Letters, and Travels* (1905), but he also gives many interesting stories and accounts of the Kootenays. Later, the discovery of gold on the Fraser brought a few clerics into British Columbia, among them Robert Christopher Lundon Brown. He was one of several writers who wrote small books giving general information on the colony. He also wrote books on theology and several missionary reports, one of which played a part in causing shiploads of brides for miners to be sent to Victoria in 1862 and 1863. A couple of Brown's missionary articles indicate the problems the miners produced for the Indians. *Klatsassan*, published in 1873, includes a valuable contemporary account of the Chilcotin rising led by a chief called Klattsasine against the encroachment of miners and roadbuilders on tribal lands.

The great period in British natural history which reached a climax in the theories of Charles Darwin brought a number of naturalists to the territories of the Hudson's Bay Company, among them three ex-students of William Hooker: John Scouler, David Douglas, and William Fraser Tolmie. All wrote informative accounts of their work, but none of them showed in their writing much of the intellectual breadth and excitement which marked Darwin's observations during the voyage of the *Beagle*. John Scouler's journal, covering roughly the year 1825, was published in the *Oregon Historical Quarterly* in 1905, and contains material of interest on the northern Indians of the Pacific coast. Douglas stayed on in North America into 1827. His *Journal* (1914) where he told of his botanizing is written in fluent and eloquent but florid prose. In it he described the great fir, actually not a fir, which bears his name and is almost synonomous with the idea of British Columbia.

Tolmie, who came out as a doctor for the HBC, did his best to combine the collecting and classifying of specimens with trading. His discontinuous *Journals of William Fraser Tolmie* (1963) for the years 1830–1845 present a young man who took his work as physician, naturalist, and agriculturalist very seriously indeed. His rather solemn writing is saved by an introspective and self-analytical streak which allows us to understand his gradual change from a very orthodox youth to the later British Columbia MLA who sponsored such causes as free education, women's suffrage, and aboriginal rights. Tolmie's association with John McLoughlin and the take-over of the Hudson's Bay Company in 1858 by the International Financial Society were among the influences bringing about the change. His unpublished papers of later life are at times lively and even amusing.

John Keast Lord came to British Columbia with the international boundary commission to survey and mark the 49th parallel. He wrote two books, knowledgeable and informal, *The Naturalist in Vancouver Island and British Columbia* (1866) and *At Home in the Wilderness* (1867). The latter presents in an entertaining manner a great deal of early woodcraft lore which should come to be of increasing value to the growing number of people interested in finding themselves at home away from cities and roads.

While the BC boundary was being established, important surveys were also going on between the Great Lakes and the Rockies. The British or Palliser expedition of 1857–1860 produced numerous reports, well worth reading although only available in libraries. These introduced a number of concepts which have become familiar, such as the three prairie levels or steppes, the fertile belt, and the Palliser triangle. During 1857–1858, the Canadian exploring expeditions operated in parties led by Simon J. Dawson, Henry Youle Hind, and W. H. Napier. Hind published in 1860 a two-volume *Narrative* of the explorations. These are very readable, but lose to a degree the immediacy of the reports to the legislative assembly in 1858 and 1859. Here is Dawson's description of the plains west of Red River for June 12, 1858:

Such a country as we have passed through to-day I have never before seen in a state of nature. . . . It required no great effort to the imagination in weary travellers to see civilization advancing in a region so admirably prepared by nature for its development, to picture herds of domestic cattle roaming over plains still deeply furrowed with the tracks of the buffalo, which with the hunters who pursued them had disappeared forever; or to plant cottages among groves which seemed but to want them, with the stir of existence, to give the whole the appearance of a highly cultivated country.

Later social changes may have led many Canadians, especially in central towns, to see the wilderness as inimical to civilized humanity, but the explorers from Radisson to Hind saw it generally as welcoming, as did most of the immigrant settlers.

The last years of Hudson's Bay Company rule produced several books of interest. Letitia Hargrave's *Letters* (1947) are lively and discerning, largely concerned with domestic matters at York Factory where she lived from 1840 to 1851. R. M. Ballantyne's *Hudson's Bay* (1848) is a romanticized and rather adolescent account of six years he spent in the fur trade. This experience is important for such vitality as his later fiction for juveniles contained. His eye for immediate detail was good, but he was unable to see through the stereotypes which he transmitted of British imperialism.

In 1846–1848, the painter Paul Kane (1810–1871) travelled west, consciously seeking to record the images of an epoch before it faded forever. His *Wanderings of an Artist* (1859) is a lively and unpretentious portrait of the artist as a preserver of history, and, at the same time, it is the swan song of the "Old Northwest." Only a few years later, when Viscount Milton and Dr. Cheadle, an irrepressible tourist team, wrote their jaunty travelogue, *The North-west Passage by Land* (1865), the centre of interest had already changed from furs and exploration to settlement, mining, roads, and railways. Dr. Walter Butler Cheadle's *Journal* of the 1862–1863 crossing was eventually published in 1931 as volume one of the Canada Series edited by Frederick Philip Grove. It is clear that this was the main original of the 1865 volume, and further, that Milton (William Wentworth-Fitzwilliam) would hardly have survived the journey had it not been for the care of his more robust and enterprising companion. For authenticity, frankness, and ease of style, Cheadle's journal deserves in every way to be regarded as the primary and superior source.

Cheadle and Milton arrived in British Columbia towards the end of the decade of the Cariboo Gold Rush. The first substantial find of gold was on the bars of the lower Fraser, beginning about 1857. Later the centre shifted upstream to the bench diggings of the Cariboo. Books on this period tend to be more common than on the earlier periods, but most of them are factual surveys. One exception is Francis Poole's *Queen Charlotte Islands* (1872), the work of a lesser Munchausen in charge of an attempt to mine copper in the Queen Charlotte Islands. His observations of the Haida were unperceptive, but he claimed superhuman optical vision and steadiness of aim, "I killed a fine crow . . . with my Enfield rifle, as he was perched on the top of a tall pine tree, at a distance of 750 yards." John Emmerson's book, *British Columbia and Vancouver Island* (1865), tells a story both harrowing and amusing of his party's labours up the Lillooet trail to the Cariboo. As the overweight Emmerson and his companions packed from the coastal rain forest to the semi-desert interior, hunger and toil left his trousers hanging ever slacker about his waist.

The great story of the gold rush is that of the Overlanders, about 200 men, nearly all Protestants from Canada West or East. Setting out from Canada in small parties, they made their various ways in 1862 to Fort Garry via the United States. At or soon after leaving Fort Garry, they united into three main contingents, the largest of which elected Thomas McMicking as leader. He wrote the main account of the crossing, published in 1862–1863 as a series of letters in the New Westminster paper, the *British Columbian*. These letters deserve to be gathered together and republished as a book. In a thesis in preparation, Joanne Sawadsky says, "McMicking's style is distinguished by its clarity and smoothness, and by his ability to pack many details into a short space without producing a cluttered effect." Although his tone, like that of most of the Overlanders, is sober, McMicking had a dry sense of humour. He sums up the experience of his group and of most gold seekers after giving an itemized account of the Overlanders' expenses: "Our mining tools were the only articles in the above list that were found to be unnecessary."

One of the numerous Overlander journals was published in 1973 by the Alcuin Society, with a narrative excerpted from letters written back to Ontario, the whole called *The Diary and Narrative of Richard Henry Alexander in a Journey across the Rocky Mountains*. The memoirs of another Overlander, A. L. Fortune, deserve to be rescued from obscurity in local periodicals and republished. He wrote fluently and eloquently and has a special chapter of the adventure to tell. Fortune chose to go with the group which came down the Thompson. He thus became the chronicler of the only woman to accompany the Overlanders, Mrs. Augustus Shubert, who gave birth to the first white child born in the interior of British Columbia, the day after their party arrived at Fort Kamloops. Margaret McNaughton wrote a memoir of her husband, Archibald, which she called *Overland to Cariboo*. Unfortunately, much of it was plagiarized, probably naïvely, from Thomas McMicking. The only general history of the trek, *The Overlanders of '62* (1931), an admirable piece of research and writing by Mark Sweeten Wade, is regrettably a rare book. It quotes liberally and judiciously from nearly all the original sources.

For Canadian literary history, perhaps the most significant part of the gold rush was the formation of what was probably the first literary and theatrical group in Canada west of the Great Lakes. In the long winter evenings at Barkerville, a group met in a public reading room to produce concerts, recitations, skits, and even plays. The plays and many of the songs came from Great Britain, but some of the poems and skits were written locally. The leading spirit was James Anderson (1838?–1923), who sang, recited, and acted. In 1865 the *Cariboo Sentinel* was established and included in its columns poems by Anderson and his friends. In 1868 the paper printed two selections of Anderson's poems. In 1869 it brought out a collection incorporating the two previous leaflets and additional poems by Anderson along with selections from other local poets. The small volume, *Sawney's Letters and Cariboo Rhymes*, may be considered an anthology of gold rush verse with Anderson given the place of honour. A slightly larger collection with the same title was printed in Toronto in 1895. Anderson was undoubtedly the best of the Barkerville group. He wrote directly and humorously in a well-established form, Scots radical verse. He was much concerned with the working conditions of the miners, who needed considerable capital for the most part to reach the goldfields and to remain independent. Many were frequently reduced to working for wages on the roads or on other miners' claims. Anderson's verse has been frequently quoted to liven the pages of historical and economic writing, which it does very well. His work deserves some attention for its quality as direct and forceful writing:

> Weel, here at last I'm workin' oot
> A lab'rer by the day,
> 'Mang face-boards, water, slum an' mud,
> To keep the wolf away!

The gold that was to be easily found and extracted was soon exhausted, and most of the miners and their dependents left the country. As in the Yukon at the end of the century, the temporary and uncertain prosperity of the miners plus the long winters of enforced idleness favoured the production of popular literature. Also like the Yukon, the stimulus was brief and the movement quickly died, leaving only an inheritance of a few poems worthy of later recovery, along with a legend.

At the time Confederation came to the East (1867), human life in the West was at its lowest ebb in centuries, both in quantity and quality. The fur trade was all but dead as early as 1833, "knocked up" to use John McLoughlin's phrase of that year. The Indians had been reduced to a fraction of their original number and were unable to return to their previous mode of life. The white population, too, was at an ebb. The cluster near Red River amounted to perhaps twenty thousand. British Columbia, which had over forty thousand whites in the gold rush, was down to no more than ten thousand, almost entirely in the southwest. A gap of half a century of stagnation lay between the collapse of the fur trade and the coming of railways and settlement towards the end of the nineteenth century. Literature in the West would have to wait on the basics of the new farming for the world market and the acquisition of literacy by the new population.

IV. THE NORTHWEST PASSAGE

In 1818, the search for the Northwest Passage was renewed with the voyage of John Ross (1777–1856); the Canadian Arctic became, as Jeanette Mirsky suggests in *To the Arctic!*, the stage for a drama which entered its climax thirty years later with the loss of the Franklin expedition and the beginning of ten years of search for it, after which the stage lights were dimmed for generations. The simile of a drama is apt, not only because many of the central characters appear and reappear throughout the four decades between curtains, but also because character and event lock in a chain leading to the Franklin catastrophe. Because of this unity, almost that of a plot, the voluminous literature of the nineteenth-century search for the Northwest Passage has a power over the imagination which in most cases is not intrinsic in the individual works.

John Ross's *Voyage of Discovery* (1819) set the pattern for the opening chapters of the voyages to follow. He rediscovered Baffin Bay, thus refurbishing the tarnished name of its original discoverer and restoring it to the map; he described the cliffs of crimson snow on the Greenland shore; he met and observed the famous group of West Greenland Eskimos whom he called "Arctic Highlanders." Unfortunately he imagined seeing a range of mountains closing off Lancaster Sound and his passage to the west. William Parry (1790–1855), in command of the second ship, did not make the same mistake; he was sent out again the following year.

The liveliest part of Parry's *Journal of a Voyage for the Discovery of a Northwest Passage . . . 1819–20* (1821) describes sailing right over what Ross called "Crocker's Mountains" and westward through thirty degrees, almost halfway to Cook's nearest point of exploration east from Bering Strait. After the hopes, the noise, and the excitement, the ships were stopped by winter and had first to find and then cut an entrance into a harbour till spring: "The seamen, who are always fond of doing things in their own way, took advantage of a fresh northerly breeze, by setting some boats' sails upon the pieces of ice, a contrivance which saved both time and labour."

Some dramatic and publishing history arises out of Parry's winter in the ice, since the officers produced a number of London plays, including Garrick's *Miss in her Teens*. For Christmas they produced their own operetta, *Northwest Passage*, with F. W. Beechey as stage manager. Edward Sabine edited a weekly paper, the *North Georgia Gazette and Winter Chronicle*, certainly the first literary magazine in the Canadian Arctic, but there is little to glean from its combination of youthful facetiousness and pious reflections. Beechey (1796–1856) and Sabine (1788–1883) wrote books on their various Arctic experiences.

Parry and Ross both made further voyages into the Arctic, less significant than Parry's first as exploration, but more interesting for first descriptions of Innuit or Eskimos north of Hudson Bay. Ross and Parry were verbose sermonizers, whose books are saved by the intrinsic interest of their material and their sincerity.

Parallel to Parry's and Ross's voyages were a number of land journeys from the interior of Canada to and along the Arctic coast. The most famous of these is the first by John Franklin (1786–1847), in 1819–22, reported in his *Journey to the Polar Sea* (1823). His *Narrative of a Second Expedition* (1828), is of lesser interest.

Like many of the best narratives of exploration, Franklin's are organized around a geographical hypothesis—in this case the existence and continuity of a North American Arctic coastline. Subordination to such a purpose is broken in the first book by an unnecessary introduction giving largely second-hand information about the travel to the point where actual exploration began. This slowness in getting to the intellectually significant and therefore exciting events is typical of the Arctic narratives of the time. The concluding third of Franklin's *Journey* becomes absorbing because of the speed and intensity of the events which he describes. The struggle to live, involving both starvation and cannibalism, is one of the most intense ever recorded. Franklin, with part of his expedition, survived—in spite of almost complete ignorance of life in the region—to set down an indelible image of the hostility to man of the Arctic.

Powerful as Franklin's description is when taken at its face value, it becomes even more dramatic when read with irony as well as sympathy, for we see in his *Journey* the seeds of his final disaster. A certain stiffness in the verbal quality in Franklin's writing, combined with a constant exhibition of fortitude and will power, raises the question whether the extreme horror of the events was not partly brought about by the character of the leader plus the rigidity of naval discipline. Such critical reading does not remove Franklin's major work from its place among the best told and most thrilling narratives of exploration. It does, however, point to the difference between a British naval officer's image of the Arctic and the developing Canadian one. The exploration of Canada's Arctic, like her Pacific coast, was in its beginning mainly a British enterprise which only gradually took on a Canadian character. And it was only as the experience of the Canadian frontier was transferred to the Arctic, and the knowledge of the Eskimos was incorporated into that experience, that our Arctic began to become "friendly" to civilized man. Even now, the image of the Arctic as a home for man has only won a beachhead in Canadian consciousness in contrast to Franklin's *Erebus* and *Terror*.

Franklin's journeys were in part written by his subordinates: Hood, Back (1796–1878), and John Richardson (1787–1865). The latter two afterwards conducted their own expeditions of which they wrote accounts, which did much to reinforce Franklin's image of the north although Richardson, by travelling with John Rae, came to understand better the ways of Arctic life. George Back's *Narrative of the Arctic Land Expedition to the Mouth of the Great Fish River* (1836), describing an attempt in 1833–35 to find Ross, lost on his second expedition, is among the more readable of the travel books of the period, in spite of Victorian diction and roundabout sentence structure. One reason is Back's sense of scenery. He was a landscape artist of considerable ability who had the gift of putting what he saw into words. Also, he was a much easier character than Franklin, enjoyed whatever company he was in, relished conversation and anecdote, and had some facility in catching them in words. His writing is cumulative in effect rather than strikingly apt in individual phrase and therefore hard to illustrate by quotation. What follows indicates the man and his prose at its relatively unimpeded best.

I took upon me the part of amusing the Esquimaux, by sketching their likenesses and writing down their names. This gratified them exceedingly; but their merriment knew no bounds when I attempted, what was really no easy task, to pronounce what I had written.

The works of two fur-trader explorers, Thomas Simpson and John Rae, introduce a more indigenous image of the Arctic. That their writing is little known is testimony to the dominance, even to this day, of the Franklin view.

Thomas Simpson (1808–1840), nephew of George, demonstrated how explorers could live off the country in the Arctic. His *Narrative of the Discoveries on the North Coast of America, 1836–39* (1843) published posthumously, tells of his four years of exploration in the Arctic, in which he not only traced hundreds of miles of unknown coast, but showed conclusively that Arctic explorers could live almost completely on the resources of the country. His *Narrative* is competently written but strangely muted for so strident, egotistical, and persistent a personality. Part of the lack of drama is the result of his very capability as a wilderness traveller, a competence which prevented crises of the Franklin type. It is noticeable, however, that the writing, always clear and usually without affectation, becomes more expressive in the later parts. Simpson's character finds full expression in his letters, which are outstanding for colour, forcefulness, and aphoristic derogatory characterization of his associates. Thomas, save that his mania was for fame as an explorer, was very much the nephew of Sir George.

John Rae (1813–1893), as modest as Simpson was egotistic, is now becoming recognized as one of the greatest of Arctic explorers. His *Narrative of an Expedition to the Shores of the Arctic Sea in 1846 and 1847* (1850) describes the first successful wintering off the land north of the tree line by white men. Rae's writing is very plain, but it improves with each reading because of its economy, intellectual clarity, and sympathy with nature and men.

When Franklin set sail on his last expedition in 1845, all but a few miles of the Northwest Passage were known. Franklin's men felt confident that the explorer's prize of the centuries would fall to them and the splendidly equipped *Erebus* and *Terror*. They sailed into Lancaster Sound, never to be seen alive again by civilized men. Fourteen years later, and after the failure of nearly forty search expeditions, Leopold M'Clintock found the first of their corpses.

British naval officers commanded most of the rescue expeditions, and usually published official accounts, in addition to which their subordinates often prepared unofficial versions. For the most part these volumes are hard to tell one from another. With a few notable exceptions they are written in turgid prose expressing high moral purpose and a determinaton to conquer the Arctic; they are boy scoutish without a boy scout's understanding of how to cope with the wilderness.

The main discovery of the Franklin search was the Northwest Passage, although it was not actually navigated. In an expedition of 1850–54, Robert McClure sailed the *Investigator* from Bering Strait to within twenty-five miles of Parry's farthest exploration from the east, only to be forced to abandon his ship in the ice. He and his crew completed the passage—on foot. Their route, between Banks Island and Victoria Island, is the only passage of sufficient depth for commercial traffic across the Canadian Arctic, and is the channel the American oil tanker *Manhattan* was forced to take in 1969 after being defeated like all other ships by the icepack of McClure Strait. McClure's story was edited into a panegyric by J. Sherard Osborn in his *Discovery of the North-West Passage* (1856). Alexander Armstrong, the ship's surgeon, gave a hostile version in *A Personal Narrative of the Discovery of the Northwest Passage* (1857). Johann A. Miertsching (1817–1875), a Moravian missionary who had learned Innuit in Labrador, wrote an informative and more objective record of the voyage. His book was published in German, *Reise-Tagebuch* (1855), translated into French, *Journal de M. Miertsching* (1857), but translated into English only recently by L. H. Neatby, *Frozen Ships* (1967).

Joseph René Bellot, a French volunteer, accompanied one of the expeditions sent out personally by Lady Franklin. Bellot's *Journal d'un voyage aux mers polaires* (1851), translated into English as *Memoirs* (1855), is one of the few flashes of gaiety in the final Franklin gloom. Although his work has little interest as history and science, it does present, as Leslie H. Neatby says, "a lively picture of a gay and intelligent Frenchman amid a shipload of Scottish Calvinists."

Two of the outstanding books on the search, *The Grinnell Expedition* (1854) and *Arctic Explorations: The Second Grinnell Expedition* (1857), are those by Elisha Kent Kane, the medical officer for the first and the commander of the second American expedition. Kane's prose is balanced and cadenced according to mid-nineteenth-century ideas of rhetoric, slightly verbose, but made tense by sudden colloquial statements—Kane's personality bursting through the Philadelphia norms.

Having begun to apply the approach of the American frontiersman to the Arctic search in the first expedition, Kane went on in the second to become a master of Eskimo technique. The Pennsylvania gentleman took to the life of the Greenland "Etahs" as though born to it, describing his contact with it frankly, vividly, and sometimes amusingly:

The kotluk of each matron was glowing with a flame sixteen inches long. A flipper-quarter of walrus, which lay frozen on the floor of the netek, was cut into steaks; and the kolupsuts began to smoke with a burden of ten or fifteen pounds apiece. . . . I broke my fast on a handful of frozen liver-nuts that Bill brought me, and, bursting out into a profuse perspiration, I stripped like the rest, threw my well-tired carcass across Mrs. Eider-duck's extremities, put her left-hand baby under my armpit, pillowed my head on Myouk's somewhat warm stomach, and thus, an honored guest and in the place of honor, fell asleep.

Kane's reporting is lively, but his intellectual comprehension of his savage environment is even more outstanding. Had there been a Kane among Franklin's officers, their story might have been different. As it is, Kane's hopes for the lost expedition twist in the heart like knives:

My mind never realizes the complete catastrophe, the destruction of all Franklin's crews. I picture them to myself broken into detachments, and my mind fixes itself on one little group of some thirty, who have found the open spot of some tidal eddy, and, under the teachings of an Esquimaux, or perhaps one of their own Greenland whalers, have set bravely to work, and trapped the fox, speared the bear, and killed the seal and walrus and whale. I think of them ever with hope.

How different the real story! The first definite information was brought back by the John Rae mentioned earlier. Here is what the Eskimos told him, according to his report in the British Parliamentary papers of 1855:

In the spring . . . a party of "white men," amounting to about forty, were seen travelling southward over the ice, and dragging a boat with them. . . . by signs the natives were made to understand that their ship, or ships, had been crushed by ice, and that they were now going to where they expected to find deer to shoot. . . . At a later date the same season . . . the bodies of some thirty persons were discovered on the continent, and five on an island near it. . . .

From the mutilated state of many of the corpses, and the contents of the kettles, it is evident that our wretched countrymen had been driven to the last resource,—cannibalism,—as a means of prolonging existence.

Rae's report roused horror when it was made public, and Rae was forced to defend his conclusions and his own integrity in a set of magazine articles which could be taken as models of closely reasoned argument. One set of such articles appeared in Dickens's *Household Words*.

The final solution of the Franklin mystery—a vindication of Rae's conclusions in all essentials—is told in Leopold M'Clintock's *The Voyage of the 'Fox' in the Arctic Seas* (1859). The story it tells is at once a summing-up of the Franklin expedition and search, and the most thrilling and the best-written of all the nineteenth-century books concerned with the Northwest Passage. Here is M'Clintock's arrival at the scene of the disaster:

The skeleton—now perfectly bleached—was lying upon its face, the limbs and smaller bones either dissevered or knawed away by small animals. . . . This poor man seems to have selected the bare ridge top, as affording the least tiresome walking, and to have fallen upon his face in the position in which we found him.

It was a melancholy truth that the old woman spoke when she said, "They fell down and died as they walked along."

M'Clintock's outstanding characteristic, which enabled him both to solve the Franklin mystery and to write a good book, was straightforward intelligence interested in everything. Nothing seems to escape his attention—men, dogs, wild life, the weather, the ice, the ship—all are set down in unencumbered quick marching prose. His description of the escape of the *Fox* from pack ice shows his observation, his style, and his affection for his ship—a feeling one would expect to find expressed frequently in sailor's narratives, but which turns out to be surprisingly rare.

Our bow is very strongly fortified, well plated externally with iron, and so very sharp that the ice-masses, repeatedly hurled against the ship by the swell as she rose to meet it, were thus deprived of their destructive force; they struck us obliquely, yet caused the vessel to shake violently, the bells to ring, and almost knocked us off our legs. On many occasions the engines were stopped dead by ice choking the screw; once it was some minutes before it could be got to revolve again. Anxious minutes those!

. . . What a release ours has been, not only from eight months' imprisonment, but from the perils of that one day! Had our little vessel been destroyed after the ice broke up, there remained no hope for us. . . . Should I ever have to pass through such an ice-covered, heaving ocean again, let me secure a passage in the 'Fox.'

M'Clintock's investigations made it clear that, after Franklin's death, some of his men on their death march had come within miles of the crucial waterway of the southern possibility for the Northwest Passage, Rae Strait, a route navigable only by small vessels, such as the later *Gjoa* or *St. Roche*. Although the basic questions about Franklin and the passage were settled, to this day expeditions set out in search of relics of the great disappearance. A few later explorers produced memorable books.

The Narrative of the Second Arctic Expedition made by Charles F. Hall (1879) tells of an American navy captain's private search between 1864 and 1869 in the hope of finding some remaining survivors. Travelling with another white and two Innuit, he found no one still alive but heard some Eskimo accounts of Captain Crozier (Franklin's second-in-command) and two or three other men having lasted a year or so beyond the general disaster. He also gathered traditions of how the two ships were destroyed. Hall's narrative conveys the intensity of his hopes and disappointments.

In the belief that the records of the expedition might still survive, another small expedition, led by the American, Lieutenant Frederick Schwatka, visited the disaster area. The second-in-command, William H. Gilder, wrote the report, *Schwatka's Search: Sledging in the Arctic* (1881). He learned that some Eskimos had found and opened a tin box of books near a ship's boat containing human bones, including limbs which had been sawed off, which "led the Inuits to the opinion that the white men had been eating each other." Some of the books were left to the elements; some were given to children as playthings and lost.

The Northwest Passage was finally navigated by Roald Amundsen's expedition of 1903–1907 to the North Magnetic Pole in the *Gjoa*. The Norwegian explorer tells of some Innuit traditions about Franklin's disappearance in *The North West Passage* (1908).

Hall's research had a part in leading a St. Lawrence River sea dog, Captain Joseph E. Bernier (1852–1934), to become the grand old man of Arctic navigation. When only nineteen years old and already a captain, Bernier saw Hall's new ship, the *Polaris*, prior to its leaving on Hall's third and last expedition; Bernier accurately predicted that the shape of the hull would lead to its being crushed in the ice. His memoirs, *Master Mariner and Arctic Explorer* (1931), give an immediate and sometimes startling view of seafaring life when Quebec was a major builder of wooden vessels. Bernier intended to drift in a ship frozen in the ice across the Arctic Ocean as Fridtjof Nansen later did. He was diverted by being appointed by the Canadian government to assert his country's rule in the polar islands by patrolling them in his ship, the *Arctic*. The high point of his career was the formal proclamation at Parry's Winter Harbour on July 1, 1909 of Canada's sovereignty over its sector of the Arctic, to the pole. Bernier's work and memoirs are the basis of a story for young people, *The True North* (1957) by Thomas C. Fairley and Charles Israel. Fairley subsequently prepared *Sverdrup's Arctic Adventures* (1959), a reworking of Otto Sverdrup's *New Land* (1904) on his discoveries in the Canadian high Arctic. Sverdrup's advice on polar exploration is "Eat well or nothing will come of it."

Vilhjalmur Stefansson (1879–1962) in his 1908–1912 expedition came near enough from the west to the region of the last Franklin ships to gather some related Innuit traditions. These are included in his classic of wilderness travel and anthropology, *My Life with the Eskimo* (1913), one of his more than twenty-five books, in which he shows himself a master of clear prose, whether of narration or scientific exposition. *The Friendly Arctic* (1921) reports on his Canadian Exploring Expedition (1913–1918), which made the last major discoveries in the exploration of Canada. On this long journey Stefansson also recognized that the practical Northwest Passage was through Melville Sound. In the introduction to Stefansson's *Unsolved Mysteries of the Arctic* (1938), Stephen Leacock expresses pride in having "a personal share in the initiation" of the volume. Speaking of the analysis of what happened to the balloon expedition of S.A. Andrée, Leacock says, "I felt towards Stefansson that despairing admiration in which Dr. Watson lived towards Sherlock Holmes." One of the explorer's best discussions of an Arctic mystery is a critique of the loss and search for the Franklin expedition. As lucid iconoclastic exposition it is superb; it also provides an invaluable synopsis of the literature of the search. Another work with similar qualities is Stefansson's readable philosophical study of the relation between scientific method and commonplace fallacies, *Adventures in Error* (1936). *Discovery: The Autobiography of Vilhjalmur Stefansson* was published posthumously in 1964.

Three-quarters of a century after the disappearance of the Franklin ships, the part Innuit Danish anthropologist Knud Rasmussen travelled from Greenland to Siberia, making a comparative study of the various tribes of the Arctic coast. He enquired into, among other things, the part played in the native economies by the wreckage of ships searching for the Northwest Passage. To follow his progress westward is to have the story of the search retold from the Eskimo point of view. The eloquent Innuit traditions as told to him are probably to be trusted, partly because they check with the records, and partly because Rasmussen understood the language and the people. Here, from *Across Arctic America* (1927), is what an old Innuit told him of the end of the crews of the *Erebus* and *Terror*:

My father, Mangak, was out with Terqatsaq and Qavdlut hunting seal on the west coast of King William's Land, when they heard shouts, and perceived three white men standing on the shore and beckoning to them. This was in the spring, there was already open water along the shore, and they could not get in to where the others stood until low water. The white men were very thin, with sunken cheeks, and looked ill; they wore the clothes of white men, and had no dogs, but pulled their sledges themselves. They bought some seal meat and blubber, and gave a knife in payment. There was much rejoicing on both sides over the trade; the white men at once boiled the meat with some of the blubber and ate it. Then they came home to my father's tent and stayed the night, returning next day to their own tent, which was small and not made of skins, but of something white as the snow. There were already caribou about at that season, but the strangers seemed to hunt only birds. The eider duck and ptarmigan were plentiful, but the earth was not yet come to life, and the swans had not arrived. My father and those with him would gladly have helped the white men, but could not understand their speech; they tried to explain by signs, and in this way much was learned. It seemed that they had formerly been many, but were now only few, and their ship was left out on the ice. They pointed towards the south, and it was understood that they proposed to return to their own place overland. Afterwards, no more was seen of them, and it was not known what had become of them.

To leave Rasmussen without paying tribute to him as a recorder and translator of Innuit oral literature would be unthinkable. His transcriptions and translations of songs and folktales can be found in a number of sources, especially the reports of the Fifth Thule Expedition. Other writers have mined his works for several volumes of songs. Here is Rasmussen's Bathurst Inlet version of a folktale which can be recognized as circumpolar:

A fox and a wolf met one day out on a frozen lake.

"I see you catch salmon, Fox," said the wolf. "I wish you would tell me how you manage it."

"I will show you," said the fox. And leading the wolf towards a crack in the ice, it said:

"Just put your tail right down under the water, and wait till you feel a fish biting; then pull it up with a jerk."

And the wolf put its tail down through the ice, while the fox ran off and hid among some bushes on the shore, from where it could see what happened. The wolf stayed there, with its tail in the water, until it froze. Then too late it realized that the fox had been deceiving it; there was no getting the tail free, and at last it had to snap off the tail in order to free itself. Then following on the track of the fox, it came up, eager for revenge. But the fox had seen the wolf coming, and tore a leaf from the bushes and held it in front of its eyes, blinking and winking all the time against the light.

Said the wolf: "Have you seen the fox that made me lose my tail?"

Said the fox: "No, I have had a touch of snow-blindness lately, and can hardly see at all." And it held up the leaf and blinked and winked again.

And the wolf believed it, and went off on the track of another fox.

The epilogue is too good not to be included:

This seemed an odd sort of ending, and I said as much. "What is it supposed to mean exactly?" I asked.

"H'm, well," answered Netsit, "we don't really trouble ourselves so much about the meaning of a story, as long as it is amusing. It is only the white men who must always have reasons and meanings in everything. And that is why our elders always say we should treat white men as children who always want their own way. If they don't get it, they make no end of a fuss."

Even the composer of folk songs must measure the shortness of life against the difficulties of the art. Rasmussen was a modest man who accomplished a prodigious task. The spirit of his art as a transcriber and of the original artists can be found in one of the many songs he preserved for us. Tom Lowenstein translates:

> I, aya, am arranging
> I am trying to put together song this one,
> taking it apart, I aya
> why I wonder is it always on the tip of my tongue!

3. Explorers by Sea: The West Coast

VICTOR G. HOPWOOD

TWO CENTURIES before James Cook arrived in 1778 at Nootka, the wave of Renaissance exploration broke just south of what is now British Columbia, leaving the northwest coast of America to be wrapped in myths as thick as its own fogs. The nearest authentic approach was Drake's in 1579, recorded both in Hakluyt's *Voyages* and in *The World Encompassed by Sir Francis Drake* (1628), the latter written by Drake's nephew of the same name and based on the notes of Francis Fletcher, the chaplain on the voyage.

After discovering Cape Horn and pillaging Spanish ports and shipping in the Pacific in one of history's most successful voyages of piracy, Drake explored north in the *Golden Hind*, hoping to return to England by the fabled Northwest Passage, safe from pursuit. The westward trend of the land led Drake to conclude that there was no Northwest Passage, and bad weather added the corollary that if it did exist, it was unnavigable. Here is Francis Fletcher's account:

> The very roapes of our ship were stiffe, and the raine which fell was an unnatural congealed and frozen substance. . . . there followed most vile, thicke and stinking fogges against which the sea prevailed nothing. . . . Adde hereunto, that though we searched the coast diligently, even unto the 48 deg., yet found we not the land to trend so much as one point in any place towards the East, but rather running on continually North-west, as if it went directly to meet with Asia.

The *Golden Hind* therefore returned south and then sailed west across the Pacific, to make the first English circumnavigation of the world and to introduce a pattern for real and fictional voyages in English literature, echoing from its own time down to the character in T. S. Eliot's "Sweeney among the Nightingales" who leaves the estuary of "the River Plate," passes through "the hornèd gate" and reappears, leaning in through branches which "circumscribe a golden grin."

Purchas published in 1625 Michael Lok's story of the apocryphal or semi-apocryphal voyage in 1592 of a Greek, Apostolos Valerianos, usually called Juan de Fuca, supposedly a pilot in the service of Spain. De Fuca claimed to have been searching the Pacific coast for the Straits of Anian when he entered a broad inlet between 47° and 48°, "sayling therein more than twentie dayes" before arriving at a "very much broader Sea." At the entrance of his strait, De Fuca said, there was "a great Hedland or Iland, with an exceeding high Pinacle, or spired Rocke, like a piller thereupon." De Fuca thus added a new myth to geography—the Sea of the West, which turned out in the end surprisingly like the Gulf of Georgia and Puget Sound.

For the next century and a half, the west coast has its epics in fictitious voyages and its poems in the works of imaginative cartographers. As late as 1761, Thomas Jefferys republished a map by De l'Isle, showing the Sea of the West with the fabulous city of Quivira on its eastern coast, which almost touches the sources of the Mississippi. North of the Sea of the West, De l'Isle drew the strait supposedly discovered by Bartholomew de Fonte for Spain, according to a letter published in 1708 as his in the London *Monthly Miscellany*. De Fonte's maze of imaginary lakes and straits eventually led back to Hudson Bay. De Fonte's letter itself is probably a straight-faced imitation, such as Defoe might have written, of a traveller's tale. Amid such fantasies and speculations, it is only natural that Jonathan Swift should place his land of Brobdingnag in the neighbourhood of Vancouver Island and that the following parts of *Gulliver's Travels* should be located in the North Pacific. For those who like to see mysterious correspondences, the Indian myth of giant men, Sasquatches, in southwestern British Columbia, should prove intriguing.

About the middle of the eighteenth century, information began to reach western Europe of the explorations and trade of the Russians across Siberia and the North Pacific to Alaska. The great story is that of the expeditions under Vitus Bering (1725–30, 1733–42), including the tragedy of his death in 1741. The naturalist on the last expedition, the German G. W. Steller, wrote an account that stands out for lively and sympathetic description of animals, and especially for the earliest description of the sea otter, "a beautiful and pleasing animal, cunning and amusing in its habits, and at the same time ingratiating and amorous," copulating "in the human manner." The story of the shipwrecked expedition on the Commander Islands rings like a prophecy of the role of the sea otter in the international commercial struggle to come. The castaways lived in a savage state of disorder and misery

on account of envy and ill-will, making the animals shy by constant pursuit both day and night, and from the beginning driving them from the neighborhood. In the chase of these animals everyone tried to defraud everybody else and in every way and manner to cheat the more the nearer spring approached and the hope rose of being able to transport the skins to Kamchatka with great profit.

Reviving European interest in the unknown North Pacific was indicated by an article published in 1761 by the French sinologist, De Guignes, translating an ancient Chinese account by a priest Hui Shan of a voyage in the fifth century A.D. to what was identified as the North Pacific coast from Kamchatka to Mexico. The date of the possible but unauthenticated voyage is about the same as that of the legendary but not impossible voyage of the Irish priest Brendan across the Atlantic.

Spanish exploration, which had been dormant north of California for a century and a half, was renewed in answer to the rumours of the Russian challenge. On July 18, 1774, the missionary Fray Juan Crespi, who accompanied Juan Perez on a voyage to the northern end of the Queen Charlotte Islands, became the first European to record a view of any part of British Columbia. Two days later, a few miles farther north, near the northern tip of the Queen Charlotte Islands, a canoe came out from shore, giving white men their first sight of the Haida Indians.

While they were still some distance from the bark we heard them singing, and by the tone we knew them to be heathen, for they sing the same song as those from San Diego to Monterey. They drew near the frigate and we saw there were eight men and a boy in the canoe, seven of them rowing, while the eighth, who was painted, was standing up in the attitude of dancing, and, throwing feathers on the water.

A translation of Crespi's journal for this voyage is included in H. E. Bolton's book, *Fray Juan Crespi* (1927).

In 1778, James Cook (1728–1779) arrived from the Sandwich Islands (Hawaii), which he had discovered, to conclude his third great voyage of world exploration. Cook's explorations, in contrast to those of the Spanish, were made public. His two previous voyages had brought much of Oceania out of the dark of speculation into the light of knowledge. For Australians and New Zealanders he has become a national and literary symbol. It is surprising that he has not been given the same recognition in Canadian literature, since his historical role was similar, and his connection with Canada prolonged. He made his name as a surveyor in the estuary of the St. Lawrence River and in Newfoundland, after taking part in the captures of Louisbourg and Quebec.

Cook's narration is plain and modest, tending to conceal the fact that his voyages were adventures continually probing into the unknown areas of the world, more remote and difficult of access than Robinson Crusoe's island. In an age when the seamen were customarily flogged for even small offences, Cook maintained discipline with relatively few and mild punishments. Instead of keel-hauling sailors who undressed during the long voyages, he encouraged his crews to change and wash their frequently damp and filthy clothing— clothing which he was careful to see was adequate to the exposures of his voyages. He also first introduced the systematic use of foods that prevented scurvy. He won the loyalty of his crews, and men and officers enlisted for voyage after voyage. They created a legend about their captain, saying he could smell land when asleep and leap out of bed to appear on deck to meet some peril of the sea. Add his improvements in navigation and map-making, and we can realize that the west coast of Canada was brought into the light of modern knowledge by one of the geniuses of the modern world, a Newton or Darwin of geography.

In spite of matter-of-factness, Cook's narratives of his explorations caught the imagination of Europe. Coleridge's response to them is well known; their influence upon the writing of "The Ancient Mariner" is evident from a passage from *A Voyage to the Pacific Ocean . . . in the Years 1776–80* (1784), occurring as Cook on his third expedition was making his first approach to the shores of western North America, off the coast of Oregon:

Some parts of the sea seemed covered with a kind of slime; and some small sea animals were swimming about. The most conspicuous of which, were of the gelatinous, or *medusa* kind, almost globular; and another sort smaller, that had a white, or shining appearance, and were very numerous. Some of these last were taken up, and put into a glass cup, with some salt water, in which they appeared like small scales, or bits of silver, when at rest, in a prone situation. When they began to swim about, which they did, with equal ease, upon their back, sides, or belly, they emitted the brightest colours of the most precious gems, according to their position with respect to the light. Sometimes they appeared quite pellucid, at other times assuming various tints of blue, from a pale sapphirine, to a deep violet colour; which were frequently mixed with a ruby, or opaline redness; and glowed with a strength sufficient to illuminate the vessel and water. These colours appeared most vivid when the glass was held to a strong light; and mostly vanished, on the subsiding of the animals to the bottom, when they had a brownish cast. But with candle light, the colour was, chiefly, a beautiful, pale green, tinged with a burnished gloss; and, in the dark, it had a faint appearance of glowing fire. They proved to be a new species of *oniscus*, and, from their properties, were, by Mr. Anderson (to whom we owe this account of them), called *oniscus fulgens*; being probably, an animal which has a share in producing some sorts of that lucid appearance, often observed near ships at sea, in the night.

Proceeding up the coast, Cook found the harbour of Nootka, whose name was soon to be world famous. He described the mountains and forests of Vancouver Island, and the Indians of Nootka. After their first greeting of the ships, the natives

lay at a little distance from the ship, and conversed with each other in a very easy manner; nor did they seem to shew the least surprize or distrust. Some of them, now and then, got up, and said something after the manner of their first harangues; and one sung a very agreeable air, with a degree of softness and melody which we could not have expected; the word *haela*, being often repeated as the burden of the song. . . . the canoes began to come off in greater numbers; and we had, at one time, thirty-two of them near the ship, carrying from three to seven or eight persons each, both men and women. . . . One canoe was remarkable for a singular head, which had a bird's eye and bill, of an enormous size, painted on it.

Leaving Nootka, Cook went north up the coast, passing through Bering Strait and crossing back and forth between the northern coasts of Siberia and Alaska, trying to find a way through the Arctic ice. These explorations in the Bering Sea almost, but not quite, wrote finished to the geographic myth of the Northwest Passage. They also contributed further to Coleridge's poetic myth, for the account tells of the ice-blink, the fog and snow, the surrounding of the ship by pack ice, and the tacking back and forth to escape.

Cook's death in a fight with the natives of Hawaii in 1779 meant that the conclusion of this third voyage was told by James King. The voyage as a whole, like the second, was edited for official publication by John Douglas, later Bishop of Salisbury. Probably for political reasons as well as problems in editing and producing the lavish volumes, the official version was not published until 1784. Although all of the officers and crew had been commanded to surrender any private diaries of the voyage, private accounts were also published because of public interest, including those by John Rickman, William Ellis, and John Ledyard. Between 1955 and 1967, an edition of Cook's journals based on his unedited manuscripts was published by the Hakluyt Society under the editorship of J. C. Beaglehole.

The immediate effect of the publication of Cook's explorations was to open up the pursuit, almost to extinction, of the sea otter. The beauty of the gentle and sociable animal's fur made it a fitting garment for mandarins and wealthy merchants, and established a trade triangle of Northwest America, China, and Europe or the United States. Nootka Sound for a brief quarter of a century became a crossroads of trade and the centre of a major international political struggle. The world attention on Nootka meant that accounts of a considerable number of west coast voyages were published and records of many others preserved, of which a number have either some literary quality or the potential of becoming legend.

Cook's third voyage also established the structural pattern of the literature on British Columbia immediately following. Numerous accounts tell of a voyage from Europe or the eastern United States into Oceania, often touching at Hawaii, of bartering for furs on the northwestern shores of America, to be exchanged in China for luxury goods for the home market. Most voyages ranged the world, with the crux of the venture in the North Pacific. None of the wanderers settled in the New World, and most returned to tell their story and realize their profits in the original metropolis.

France was among the nations most stimulated by the publication of Cook's explorations, but the French Revolution and the following wars prevented many actual voyages to the Northwest Pacific. The first and most famous was in 1786, recorded in *Voyage round the World by La Pérouse* (1798, from the French original of Milet-Mureau); there is a brief part on the British Columbia coast. Like other French voyages, its structure follows that of

Cook's. C. P. C. Fleurieu compiled a description of the first French venture into the maritime fur trade in *A Voyage round the World Performed during the Years, 1790, 1791, and 1792 by Etienne Marchand* (English translation, 1801), written after Marchand's death. The book is remarkable for Marchand's perception, expressed rather loquaciously, of the aesthetic qualities of the Haida buildings and sculptures on North Island:

Can we avoid being astonished to find them so numerous on an island which is not perhaps more than six leagues in circumference, where population is not extensive, and among a nation of hunters? And is not our astonishment increased, when we consider the progress this people have made in architecture? What instinct, or rather what genius it has required to conceive and execute solidly, without the knowledge of the succours by which mechanism makes up for the weakness of the improved man, those edifices, those heavy frames of buildings of fifty feet in extent by eleven in elevation?

Mémoires du capitaine Péron (1824) tells the adventures of a French officer on an American ship, among them the rescue from the penal colony at Botany Bay of a number of prisoners, one of them Thomas Muir the Scottish reformer. The description of trading for sea otter skins is enlivened with anecdotes, including that of the sole survivor of a Boston ship seized by the Haida.

The first traders were usually British. The associated captains, Portlock and Dixon, published voyages independently in 1789, valuable for the historian, although pedestrian as writing (Portlock, *A Voyage round the World, but more particularly to the North-West Coast of America*; Dixon's book bears the same title). For literature, Nathaniel Portlock's voyage is significant because his crew included the seaman John Nicol.

The Life and Adventures of John Nicol, Mariner was set down from conversations by John Howell, an editor of more than ordinary literary tact, in 1822 and published by W. Blackwood in the same year. The story has the immediacy of first-hand experience, combined with an aptness of expression and a narrative speed which indicates that the old sailor had polished it through many tellings. It is a unique forecastle prose Aeneid of what is now the British Commonwealth of Nations. After visiting Quebec, Newfoundland, and the waters of Greenland, and serving against American privateers during the Revolution, Nicol sailed for the northwest coast in 1795 as a cooper and brewer with Captain Portlock. He observed that the Indians thought the captain a lesser man than the smith, who

was a smart young fellow, and kept the Indians in great awe and wonder. They thought the coals were made into powder. I have seen them steal small pieces, and bruise them, then come back. When he saw this, he would spit upon the anvil while working the hot iron, and give a blow upon it; they would run away in fear and astonishment when they heard the crack.

After returning to England, Nicol sailed in the crew of a ship to Botany Bay, Australia, carrying women prisoners, by one of whom he had a son. For years Nicol wandered the sea, in trade and battle, striving to return to his Sarah, only to find that she had escaped from the penal colony and could not be traced.

George Dixon's *Voyage* is livelier than Portlock's and makes some pretensions to style, not altogether successful, by taking the form of a series of letters signed by the initials of Dixon's supercargo, William Beresford. The letters describe trade in the Queen Charlotte Islands, which were named after Dixon's ship. They also describe the wretched condition in which Portlock and Dixon found John Meares and his crew on the Alaska coast, asserting that scurvy had been assisted by drunkenness, a statement which provoked a war of pamphlets betwen Dixon and Meares, notable for their virulence.

John Meares's *Voyages Made in the Years 1788 and 1789 . . . to the North West Coast of America . . .* (1790), ghosted by William Combe, is lively in description and forceful in argument, although these qualities are diluted with bombast, promotional rhetoric, and sentimental cliché. The narrative played a significant part in the struggle over Nootka which brought Britain and Spain almost to war. Meares was stronger on the persuasive lie and wily stratagem than on the truth, and when all else failed him, he used violence if he could get away with it. Thus there is both a detective and a human interest in the documents which surround him, particularly the polemics with Dixon and the differing accounts of how his ships were seized by the Spaniards in 1789. The version of this incident to be found in the diary of the Spanish commandant at Nootka, Martinez, is as partisan as Meares's.

Where his own interests were not involved, Meares was among the most perceptive recorders of the people and events of the west coast, and his writing at its best is sharply focussed, as can be seen in his description of the launching at Friendly Cove of the *North West America*, the first ship built in the area for which it was named.

On the firing of a gun, the vessel started from the ways like a shot. Indeed she went off with so much velocity, that she had nearly made her way out of the harbour; for the fact was, that not being very much accustomed to this business, we had forgotten to place an anchor and cable on board, to bring her up, which is the usual practice on those occasions: the boats, however, soon towed her to her intended station; and in a short time the North West America was anchored close to the Iphigenia and the Felice.

Meares tried to appropriate to himself the discovery of the Strait of Juan de Fuca, actually found by Charles Barkley. Captain Barkley was accompanied by his wife, Mrs. Frances Hornby Barkley, the first white woman on the west coast. She kept what is described as a "lively and entertaining diary," which was unfortunately destroyed in a fire; only quotations from and para-phrases of parts of it survive, one of which describes the above-mentioned discovery.

The founding figure for Canada's west coast is George Vancouver (1757–1798), second only to Cook among the explorers and mappers of the North Pacific. Where Cook sketched in bold outline the coast from Oregon north, Vancouver methodically filled in the details and mapped, named, and described many of the intricate waterways, islands, and headlands of the British Columbia, Washington, and Alaska coast. Vancouver's prose in his *Voyage of Discovery to the North Pacific Ocean*, 1790–95 (1801) is clear but rather ponderous and uneconomical, based on accurate observation but lacking in drama and imagination. Its pace is slowed by sentences such as "Little remains further to add respecting the station we had just quitted, but to state the general satisfaction that prevailed on leaving a region so truly desolate and inhospitable." Whereas the Renaissance accounts of voyages treated geography and nautical detail boldly, Vancouver, even more than Cook, dwelt upon them to the point of wearying the ordinary reader. As a result, stories such as those of John Nicol or John Jewitt have greater imme-diacy than Vancouver's officially authorized narrative.

Vancouver's narrative does have its moments of excitement, for example, when he was sailing up Howe Sound, thinking for a few hours that he had breached the barrier of the coast mountains; but, in general, his story is interesting because of the massiveness of his achievement and because its events are surrounded by an aura of later history which makes his progress a succession of significant moments. By far the most interesting and human parts of Vancouver's story are those dealing with his meetings with the Spaniards. The warm friendship between Vancouver and Quadra, representa-tives as they were of contending powers, shines through the impersonal account.

Senr. Quadra had very earnestly requested that I would name some port or island after us both, to commemorate our meeting and the very friendly intercourse that had taken place and subsisted between us. Conceiving no spot so proper for this denomination as the place where we had first met, which was nearly in the center of a tract of land that had first been circumnavigated by us . . . I named that country the island of QUADRA and VANCOUVER.

The first half of the name has been lost, and thereby more than half of the namers' intention.

The pleasant impression that Vancouver gives of his relations with the Spanish is confirmed by the narrative usually attributed to Espinosa of the surveying expedition of the two small schooners, the *Sutil* and the *Mexicana*, commanded by Galiano and Valdes. The expedition made outstanding contributions to the mapping of the waters inside the Strait of Juan de Fuca and left many Spanish names in British Columbia waters. The narrative contrasts very favourably with Vancouver's in its freedom from non-essential detail, and its observation and description of Indian life.

A number of unpublished and unofficial logs and narratives of Vancouver's ships, the *Discovery* and the *Chatham*, give a more human account of the expedition and a less Olympian and more choleric picture of its leader. There is a lively and uninhibited anonymous *Chatham* narrative, which includes a description of natives at Tahiti connected with the *Bounty* mutiny (Bligh was with Cook on his third voyage) and an account of the exploration up the Columbia River by the boats of the *Chatham*. Thomas Manby's journal gives a facile and flowery account of the pleasures of Tahiti and the Sandwich Islands, and an outspoken version of Vancouver's actions.

Archibald Menzies, the naturalist of the expedition, emerges from the multiple references of the various accounts as a most likable character, testy at times with Vancouver's arbitrary commands, but ordinarily a kindly and attentive surgeon. Menzies' own journal has been published in part by the British Columbia Archives (1923). Other naturalists have given Menzies' name to many of the plants which he first observed and described, notably the beautiful broad-leaved evergreen, the Menzies arbutus or madrona.

A naturalist with Quadra, José Mariano Moziña, wrote one of the most interesting descriptions of the west coast of Vancouver Island, *Noticias de Nutka*, only available in English since 1970. His account of the events and flora and fauna of the area are valuable, but his insight into the life of the Wakashan tribes of the west coast is probably the deepest of any early observer. Moziña emphasizes the importance of music in their rituals:

Their natural voices create the harmony in unison on the octave. They are accompanied, in place of bass, by a noise which the singers make on some boards with the first solid object they find, and by some wooden rattles whose sound is similar to that of the Mexican *ayacaztles* [Aztec gourd rattles]. One of the singers constantly gives the tone and all the others follow it successively, forcing their voices unevenly, in almost the same manner customary in the Gregorian chant of our churches. From time to time one of the musicians abandons the chant and gives enormous shouts, repeating the theme of the song as if in summary. . . . Up to now I have used the word poetry because I am convinced they actually have it, although I have not been able to understand the kinds of meters of which their verses are comprised. They certainly have several.

Moziña also describes the arrival by ship on the Pacific coast of rats and venereal disease.

Against Vancouver's great accomplishments must be placed his failure to recognize the mouth of the fabled River of the West, passing it in April 1792 with the comment, "not considering this opening worthy of more attention". Within two weeks Robert Gray in the *Columbia* entered the estuary and named the river for his ship, making the outstanding American discovery on the west coast of America.

There are a number of accounts connected with the *Columbia*, and these have been collected into one volume, *Voyages of the "Columbia" to the Northwest Coast*, by F. W. Howay (Massachusetts Historical Society, 1941). In one way or another, each version reflects the heightening strife between traders and Indians. John Boit's log reveals that even the *Columbia*'s great discovery was marred by the particularly intense piracy of the American maritime fur trade:

At length a large Canoe with at least 20 Men in her got within ½ pistol shot of the quarter, and with a Nine pounder, loaded with langerege and about 10 Musketts, loaded with Buck shot, we dash'd her all to peices, and no doubt kill'd every soul in her.

The narrative of John Hoskins, the supercargo, tells how in 1789 Captain Kendrick of the *Columbia*'s consort, the *Lady Washington*, provoked an attempt at revenge by a reckless affront to the proud people of the village of Ninstints in the Queen Charlotte Islands: "He took Coyah, tied a rope round his neck, whipt him, painted his face, cut off his hair, took away from him a great many skins, and then turned him ashore." Two years later a Haida attempt to seize the returning vessel was turned by the firearms of the Americans into a massacre of the villagers. A New England ballad of the time, "Come All Ye Bold Northwesternmen," records the triumph of the "Boston-men." Christie Harris' *Raven's Cry* (1966) tells the Haida version of this atrocity and subsequent events for the people of the Queen Charlotte Islands in an admirable children's historical novel.

The discovery of the Columbia River marks dramatically the increasing participation of the Americans in the sea fur trade. Accounts of their voyages published at the time are few, and tend to be unofficial, since each captain was interested in keeping his source of furs to himself. One account is that of John Jewitt, a British blacksmith, one of the two survivors of the *Boston*, whose crew was massacred in 1803 by the Nootka Indians led by their chief, Maquinna, who appears in many accounts, beginning with Captain Cook. While a captive, Jewitt secretly kept a diary which was published in a small edition in 1807. This was later edited for him by Richard Alsop of Connecticut into a longer work, *Narrative of the Adventures and Sufferings of John R. Jewitt* (1815). Jewitt's narrative belongs with those of Radisson and Henry in telling a story of survival by adoption. The story itself is fast moving and dramatic, the observation sharp, and the writing vigorous. When Maquinna's harpoons several times failed him, Jewitt made one of steel, with which the chief succeeded in taking a whale:

The bringing in of this fish exhibited a scene of universal festivity. As soon as the canoes appeared at the mouth of the Cove, those on board with them singing a triumph to a slow air, to which they kept time with their paddles, all who were on shore, men, women, and children, mounted the roofs of their houses to congratulate the king on his success, drumming most furiously on the planks, and exclaiming *Wocash—wocash, Tyee*!

The various Indians emerge clearly and distinctly from Jewitt's narrative, which, under the circumstances, shows considerable understanding of and liking for his captors. There is more than a hint in the story that Jewitt actually found life with the Indians pleasant. Perhaps some of his disparaging comments were made for the benefit of his New England public. Jewitt's own outlook is indicated by his editor's statement some years after the book was published that "he feared he had done Jewitt but little good in furnishing him with a vagabond mode of earning a livelihood, by hawking his book from a wheel barrow through the country." These impressions of Jewitt are confirmed by Indian traditions related by Gilbert Malcolm Sproat in *Scenes and Studies of Savage Life* (1868), according to which Jewitt made himself well liked among his captors. Towards the end of his captivity Jewitt wore only a cedar-bark cloak, and there was also a story "of Jewitt's courting, and, I think, finally abducting the charming daughter of the Ahousaht chief." Clearly Jewitt was no longer a captive but an initiated Nootkan.

Another unofficial record of a trading voyage was kept by a seaman, Stephen Reynolds. His log for 1810–14 was expertly edited by F. W. Howay and published in 1938. The *Voyage of the New Hazard* is a forecastle view of the sea-otter trade in its decline. Predatory from the beginning, and conducted among a warlike people, it became increasingly violent and piratical as the competition increased, the furs became scarcer, and the Indians more hostile and better armed. The condition of half war, half trade emerges starkly in entries such as the following: "A canoe came alongside; the captain threw a billet of wood at her and stove her"; "Sold all shrowton [oolichan oil] and two slaves: one slave five skins, one three"; "fired a volley of musquetry, blunderbusses, and a broadside of large guns"; "tried to run them [two canoes] down with vessel, but wind light they got in shore safe."

If the relations with the Indians were near open war, the life aboard ship was brutal to a state of near civil war. Reynolds's log records a continuous series of arbitrary blows, floggings, cattings, puttings in irons, deprivings of rations, and mastheadings. The violence combined with the abbreviated ship's log style gives an essentially illiterate book something of the compelling power of art.

Mr. Gale ordered reef out trysail. Jack and Pace not hearing did not go aft. Gale jawed them, called them sons of bitches, etc., was very censorious. Jack said he was neither son of bitch nor boozer upon which Gale struck and clinched him.

Jack made his defense and soon got the better, when Gale called on the boatswain, who took Jack away, who ran forward, Gale after him, got a handspike and struck him two or three times. Pace took the handspike away; he got it again and after Pace with it. The captain hearing the noise came up; struck Jack and Pace several times with the end of a rope and his fist. After the trysail was hoisted the criminals were sent to the mastheads till eight o'clock, when Gale called them down, made them take off their jackets and gave them a severe rope's-ending.

As the massacre of the sea otter came to its end, the ships deserted Nootka and other centres of the maritime fur trade, leaving no permanent mark save a cluster of legends. Between the voyages of the traders and the explorations of Cook and Vancouver, it had become certain for the ships of the times, in the words of Earle Birney:

> that there is no clear Strait of Anian
> to lead us easy back to Europe.

Ahead was rediscovery from the land and the "long endeavour to be joined" to the settlements slowly spreading west from the St. Lawrence up to and through the mountains, a story already outlined in the previous chapter.

PART II

The Transplanting of Traditions

4. Overture to Nationhood

ALFRED G. BAILEY

LONG BEFORE there were any people of English speech in what is now Canada, Englishmen had begun to frequent the coasts of North America. The fishery in the New-found-land and the northwest passage to Cathay had engaged the attention of Elizabethans, especially those of the West Country, in that legendary age of voyagings overseas. It has been the custom to think of maritime enterprise as the most characteristic aspect of the history of the period. It comes then as something of a surprise to learn, as we do from Professor Galloway in a preceding chapter, that the new world beyond the western ocean had so slight an impact upon the literature of the period. Hakluyt's compilation, of course, did something to bring the narratives of voyages to the attention of those who shared an interest in exploration with the navigators themselves. Yet valuable as these narratives are from this point of view, not all were possessed of sufficient merit to warrant consideration as literature.

Just as monastic chronicles grew from Easter tables, it is evident that the narratives of the seafarers often represented a development from the ship's log. Details of the new lands and of the people who inhabited them are generally meagre. In part this seems to be because of the limitations of current prose style. But it was also because the contest with Spain engrossed the attention of the age. Not until the early decades of the seventeenth century were permanent colonies established in the New World. Even then Virginia was more often the subject of minutes of trading companies, and of reports of propagandists, than it was an inspiration to the poets, and, with some exceptions, it did not itself become, during its first century, the seed plot of an indigenous literature. In this regard the contrast with the New England colonies was sharp. There the Pilgrims and the Puritans, stirred to the depths by the spiritual crisis of the time, wrote histories and theological treatises with the eye of God upon them. Whether in simple narratives such as Bradford's account of the founding of Plymouth or in the doctrinal disputations of John Cotton, Peter Bulkeley, and Roger Williams, the consciousness of being engaged in the building of a new heaven and a new earth was a constant factor.

All these developments were outside the territories that go to make up the present Canadian Dominion. Yet it is an illusion that literary and other cultural phenomena can be fitted to a procrustean bed of territorial nationalism. We make no concession to this illusion when we note the relevance of the New England achievement to the religious and literary stirrings of the Nova Scotian Yankees, much later, in the era of the Revolution.

These pre-revolutionary settlements did not take shape until long after the English had established outposts and colonies in Newfoundland and on the shores of Hudson Bay. The English began to frequent the coasts of Newfoundland in increasing numbers after 1550, in pursuit of the dry fishery, that nursery of seamen and source of "England's treasure by foreign trade." The technique of this method, in contrast to that of the green fishery, required the formation of semi-permanent settlements. Gradually these became more numerous, and eventually permanent. It is germane to the processes of literary history to remark that we would scarcely be concerned with the case of Newfoundland but for the stroke of a politician's pen that in 1949 brought that island in as the tenth Canadian province. By this fortuitous and, in some senses, irrelevant event the content of Canadian literature was increased, slightly enriched, and partially altered. The confederation of the island with the Dominion may serve to remind us of the degree of artificiality characterizing what we are accustomed to refer to as "Canadian" literature.

Canadians must nevertheless accept with gratitude the four centuries of living in Newfoundland, and the writing that came out of it, with which they are now most properly identified. They must equally regret the prolonged dearth that followed upon a remarkable succession of early seventeenth-century governors of literary tastes, notably Hayman, and other learned persons, products of the Mother Country, who happily engaged in the promotion of colonization in those days. Settlement might have borne fruit in a transference of creative effort if exploitation by rapacious merchants and the tyrannous rule of the admirals on the station had not debased the inhabitants, frustrating the normal growth of institutions, prolonging illiteracy, and isolating them from all humanizing influences except those that they could engender for themselves. The growth of balladry, and of new and distinctive forms of speech, is a testimony to the ability of man to improve upon adversity.

Twentieth-century scholars, in looking back upon the early history of Canada, may find it difficult to draw an inference of inevitability from what they see. The Dominion as we now know it could not have been predicted by the generations of men, both French and English, who began the task of laying its foundations in the seventeenth century. That it might have turned out to be quite a different thing, with ethnic and territorial components at variance with those of the present, may serve to warn us against the habit of reading back the modern mystique of Canadianism into earlier epochs in which it must of necessity be quite alien. The reader will therefore not be asked to join in pursuit of the *ignis fatuus* of the "distinctively Canadian" in the writings of the Scots who gave their name to Nova Scotia, but touched only momentarily upon the course of its early history. Neither, for identical reasons, will the narratives pertaining to the successive English conquests of Acadia detain us. Samuel Argall in 1613, the Kirkes in 1628, Thomas Temple and William Crowne (father of the playwright John Crowne) in 1654, and Phips in 1690, are indicative of a persistent English, and New England, interest in the region, but they cannot claim our attention as facts of immediate significance to the theme with which we are concerned in this volume. The narrative of the captivity of John Gyles among the Malecite Indians of the river St. John in the 1690's, however, is not without merit and relevance and a time would come when the New Englanders would claim and even occupy the coasts of Acadia in their drive to possess and exploit the wealth of adjacent fisheries, making records of their material and spiritual dispositions which in the proper place must evoke some passing comment.

For the moment a development of equal concern must engage our attention. We must seek for the beginnings of literary effort and activity among the peoples of English speech who by 1670 had begun the attempt to outflank the French in their pursuit of the beaver and other fur-bearing animals across the central reaches of the North American continent. At the moment in 1607 when Champlain and DeMonts forsook Acadia for Quebec, the French became committed to the control and exploitation of the valley of the St. Lawrence and of the tremendous hinterland to which it led. Almost at the same time that the English replaced the Dutch as masters of the Hudson Valley (1664) they began from their posts on Hudson Bay their inroads upon the northern flank of the great route to the interior which the French had developed in the face of almost insuperable difficulties. It all began with the defection of a French *coureur de bois* of romantic memory. In 1668 Pierre Esprit Radisson, enraged at the French governor, Argenson, who "did grease his Chopps" with the trader's hard-earned proceeds, turned up in England, accompanied by Groseilliers, with the proposal that eventuated in the founding of the Hudson's Bay Company. It has not been possible to determine whether Radisson's account of his adventures in the interior of North America was composed in English by himself or was rendered from the French by an anonymous translator. Whether original or not, it cannot be claimed as a representative example of Restoration prose. As Professor Hopwood has noted, its very illiteracy appears to have imparted to it a kind of primitive vitality, and in this regard, though in different degree, it has something in common with the narrative of Henry Kelsey, the boy who, a generation later, was the first writer of English verse on the Canadian mainland, and so far as is known the earliest to see and describe the Canadian prairie. For all its imperfections Kelsey's work, like that of Radisson, is enhanced in value because of the infrequency with which the merchant adventurers took pen in hand for any but the most mundane purposes. Not until 1754 do we encounter another record of exploration, that of Antony Henday, worthy of mention in a literary history; and not before 1795 did there appear a work of positive literary value, Hearne's relation of his journey to the shores of the Arctic sea. Detachment, sympathy with tribal custom, and insight comparable to that of a trained anthropologist, qualities of the man himself, informed his work and made it memorable.

Hearne stands out for his intrinsic merits and not because the contributions made by the men of Hudson Bay are, from a literary standpoint, so few in number. A greater volume of significant work, by contrast, came out of the North Pacific late in the eighteenth century, at a time when official explorations and claims by Russian, Spaniard, Englishman, and American, and the mounting conflict over the sea otter trade, drew men of many backgrounds to hazard their lives and fortunes in those distant waters. The memory of Drake's exploit, and the hope of finding the Strait of Anian leading back to Europe, had never been entirely lost; but something like two centuries divided the voyage of the Elizabethan, and the accounts of his enterprise, from the new men whose names are linked with Nootka Sound, the renewal of imperialist rivalry, and the later trials and excitements of geographical discovery. In his chapter on the literature of exploration in the North and West, Professor Hopwood has clearly revealed to us the pre-eminence over all others of James Cook, the greatness of his achievement and the worth of his narrative. For the writings of Captain George Vancouver one cannot make similar claims, since unhappily they do not match in literary importance the events which are narrated in such painstaking and meticulous detail. Other men who were in no way the equals of either of the two great captains were nonetheless the authors of unforgettable tales of the strife and hardships of the sea, and of the strange ways of the coast tribes, throwing at times a lurid light upon the beginnings of Canada's west coast province.

II

Very different in character from all this was the literary activity that already had begun to be evident in the old provinces of Nova Scotia and Quebec in the wake of the British Conquest. Port Royal, in what the French called Acadia, had in 1710 surrendered to a British force composed largely of New Englanders, a half-century before the final act in the drama of conquest was brought to an end by the capitulation of Montreal. The Treaty of Utrecht had confirmed the British in their possession of Nova Scotia in 1713, but between that event and the Treaty of Paris, which in 1763 transferred the sovereignty of the St. Lawrence to its new masters, the province by the sea had continued to be vulnerable to the intermittent, but always to be feared, hostilities of the French forces detached for operations in that area. The menace of Louisbourg, and the terror of massacre and torture at the hands of France's Indian allies, hindered, if they did not altogether prevent, a movement of people from New England into the northeastern area as a corollary of the expansion of the fishery in Nova Scotian waters. Only with the implementation of Governor Shirley's "Great Plan" for the destruction of French strongholds, and the transportation of the hapless Acadians, were those dangers at last removed. The conquest of such key points as Beauséjour (1755) and Louisbourg (1758), and the scattered military actions that followed, were recorded in such "illiterate" diaries as that of Sergeant Burrell, stationed in 1758 at Fort Frederick at the mouth of the St. John, as well as the more polished efforts of Abijah Willard, Joshua Winslow, and other officers engaged in those campaigns. Neither these nor the diary of Simeon Perkins, valuable as the latter may be as a source for the period of the American War, can compare with the devotional writings of Henry Alline from a literary point of view.

Professor Cogswell has drawn our attention to the need to take into account the pervasive influence of evangelical pietism upon the life of the people of the Maritime Provinces. It was to have been expected that the Great Awakening in the British colonies to the southward, and especially the disturbances created by Jonathan Edwards in his attempt to revive the Puritan theocracy, would have affected in some degree the several thousands of Yankee settlers who had found their way into the province of Nova Scotia by the beginning of the Revolutionary War. The great work of Henry Alline was to free large numbers of them from the fear of eternal damnation. His style is not quite equal to the gospel of charity and loving-kindness that it was his purpose to impart. But sincerity and depth of feeling carried him a long way beyond any other contributor to the devotional literature of the time. The Puritan temper appears to have had the general effect of stultifying rather than stimulating the growth of literary expression in these provinces throughout the greater part of the nineteenth century. Again it would appear that one must make an exception in the case of Alline. That religion was the all-absorbing interest of Maritimers of three and four generations ago is borne out by the large numbers of books devoted to the subject in any libraries which are still to be found in the old houses throughout the countryside.

Less remote from today seem the worldly gentry of the Loyalist migration who came in such numbers to the old province of Nova Scotia at the conclusion of the War of Independence, submerging for the time being, or so it might have appeared, the Whiggish and Puritan Yankees who had already established themselves to the eastward. It seems remarkable that a group containing such a large proportion of university graduates and members of the learned professions should have failed, with a few exceptions, to express in memorable terms something of the cataclysmic experience through which they had passed, especially when their triumphant opponents made such noteworthy contributions to the literature of political science. Perhaps they were left empty by the ruin of the War. Perhaps it was that, as champions of a counter-revolution that failed of its purpose, they looked to a past that had never existed for comfort and illumination. Understandably they could not rejoice in the new world of man-come-into-his-own that to many, on both sides of the Atlantic, seemed heralded by the birth of the Republic. They sought to realize their own ideals in the new areas of settlement into which they migrated. Though they were not all Tories by any means their coming greatly strengthened the conservatism of what remained of the Empire on North American soil. Their social attitudes, formed before and during the Revolutionary War, they brought with them from the old colonies to the new. Thus it is that colonial New York, New Jersey, the Carolinas, and the other lands they left behind them, are a part of the Canadian past, as is seventeenth-century Quebec; more so than Huronia of which hardly a trace remains, except archaeologically, and as a source of alien inspiration, frequently historiographical and sometimes literary.*

There was a sense in which Edward Winslow, Jacob Bailey, James Moody, Jonathan Odell, and other makers of what literature there was in the Maritimes were to have no successors. Reared, as many of them were, in colonies that had grown to something approaching metropolitan status, they were

*If one wished to state the matter sociologically, one could say that modern Canadians of British origin belong to the same "in-group" as the eighteenth-century New York Loyalists. But to all modern Canadians, even the remnants of the Huron-Wyandot themselves, the seventeenth-century Hurons are an "out-group." The Huron language is no longer spoken and the Huron culture is virtually extinct. The United Empire Loyalist is one of the great strands of a continuous Canadian tradition. The Hurons were deliberately selected for comparison in this chapter because they constitute the example *par excellence* of discontinuity in Canadian cultural history. Although the Loyalists originated outside present Canadian territory and the catastrophe that overwhelmed the Hurons in the 1640's occurred on Canadian soil, the territorial impact is not a direct one as it would be on the lower animals, but is experienced by man through the filter of his culture (in the anthropological sense). This is a literary history, and literature is the expression of a culture. The cultural frame of reference is therefore more fundamental than the territorial, and the Hurons are as "exterior" to us as are the medieval Persians. On the other hand it is worth mentioning in passing that there is a sense in which the Huron catastrophe is the most crucial event in Canadian history. They were much more numerous than the few thousand French in the Canada of the 1640's. If they had been left to multiply as did the English and the French, Canada today might well be a largely Indian state as is Mexico.

forced by the exigencies of the wilderness in which they found refuge to revert to the most primitive conditions imaginable. In the Thirteen Colonies a class structure had evolved and a degree of sophistication had come to mark the mental outlook of the educated and the well-to-do. While the majority of the Loyalists were not of this class, attempts on the part of the "gentry" to establish large estates were by no means lacking. The often extensive grants did not encourage the grouping of dwellings into villages and towns. North of the Bay of Fundy, in that part of the back country of Nova Scotia that was in 1784 erected into the province of New Brunswick, "useful men from New England" were fewest in number. Professor W. S. MacNutt, in a recent history of the province, states: "There was nothing to compel a man to live in proximity to and in emulation of his neighbours. The element that explained the remarkable local initiative of New England, the orderly development of townships that thrust responsibility as well as privileges upon individuals, was completely absent in New Brunswick." The hard labour of the frontier, absence of schools, isolation from stimulating contacts, in many cases a stultifying orthodoxy in the spheres of politics and religion, all combined to discourage, if they did not entirely prevent, a recourse to literary expression on the part of the generations immediately following that of the Migration. Not only in this but in other aspects of provincial culture, notably in architectural style, a deterioration was observable, which was not altogether attributable to the taste of the Victorians.

Students of Nova Scotian attitudes and institutions, as these took shape in the two decades that separated the end of the Seven Years' War from the coming of the Loyalists, will always be beholden to the late Professor Brebner for his admirable, and probably definitive, study of the Yankee populations who, in that interval, established their settlements, largely in the southwestern part of the peninsula nearest New England. The Nova Scotian Yankee had emerged as a variant of the New England Yankee by the beginning of the Revolutionary War. Caught between two competing imperial systems, he strove, sometimes ineffectually, for neutrality. His desire not to make irrevocable decisions in the matter of allegiance, together with the substantial material benefits to be derived from forswearing independence of Great Britain, engendered in him the well-known habits of "moderation" and "harmony" in the face of public questions. He was inclined to be a Whig while not being a rebel, and was thus able to accommodate himself, when the time came, to those Loyalists who settled in the parts that remained Nova Scotian when New Brunswick and Cape Breton were set apart in 1784. He exercised a leavening influence upon the Loyalists who themselves were not all political quietists, so that the whole people when the moment came would stand upon their rights without, at the same time, having recourse to extreme measures.

The province of Nova Scotia experienced a fivefold increase in population from 1784 to 1837, a considerable accumulation of capital from a widening range of industrial and commercial undertakings, from privateering on the high seas, and an enlargement of the means of intelligence through the establishment of schools and colleges, libraries and periodicals. Thomas McCulloch cultivated a zeal for education among the Scottish settlers in the eastern part of the province, while King's College at Windsor, serving the Anglican community, awoke among certain of the students, notably Thomas Chandler Haliburton, a taste for literature that was at once detached and urbane. These characteristics of the provincial Tory underlie the satires and caricatures through which Haliburton hoped to spur his countrymen to emulate the enterprise, both industrial and intellectual, of the Massachusetts Yankees. He was making, in essence, a response to a political challenge, an attempt in new and favourable circumstances to vindicate the choice which the Loyalists had made long before in the cataclysmic year of 1776, the choice between conformity with the principles of the Revolution and exile in a strange land. What he could not bring himself to see was that the only solution for Nova Scotia's continuing ills was to find a peaceful substitute for the American Revolution, an equitable middle ground between independence and subordination to a distant metropolis. It was the glory of Howe, with his political acumen, his clear perception of principles, his tact and moderation, that he was able, against bitter political opposition from the Tory oligarchy of Halifax, to bring to fruition an arrangement for provincial self-government, within the framework of the Empire, which accorded with the historic temper of his people. Howe's poems are relatively commonplace, but in the course of the great contest in which he became engaged he drafted a body of political statements that are forthright and terse, trenchant and perceptive. It is arguable that with the achievement of responsible government Howe's work was done, and that the province went forward to face the ordeal of confederation in circumstances that evoked no comparable literary response.

Later in the nineteenth century Prince Edward Island became the home of a poet, John Hunter-Duvar, whom the anthologists of recent decades have not forgotten, but no movement of national significance arose in the small island province. Almost from its founding to the moment of its confederation with Canada in 1873 its people were the victims of an intransigent system of absentee land ownership that depressed all aspects of provincial life.

No such conditions were to be found in New Brunswick but that province experienced an adverse set of circumstances that were peculiarly its own. It was difficult for a sense of provincial identity, or a common purpose, to emerge in a land of which the different parts were so isolated from one another, and among a people who had been so uprooted as were the Loyalist exiles. They had, as we have seen, been compelled to revert to the most primitive conditions of living in the early years of settlement following immediately upon the migrations at the conclusion of the War of Independence. The adoption of policies by the Imperial Government that affected adversely the prospects of the province, was followed, from the first decade of the nineteenth century onward, by the rise of the timber trade that gave New Brunswick almost its first and for a long time its only accession of wealth. But though it brought prosperity it did so at a cost. The trade was unsettling and retarded the growth of stable communities in which schools and related amenities could develop.

Better times for New Brunswick were in the offing when the momentary depression which had ensued as a consequence of the repeal by Great Britain of the duties on foreign timber, which had protected colonial produce, was followed by an attempt to diversify the economy. With railway building, reciprocity of trade with the United States, responsible government, and a series of educational reforms, the society of the province gathered momentum and a spirit of self-reliance began to replace the traditional sense of dependence on the Mother Country that had been so marked a characteristic in previous generations. King's College, New Brunswick, stemming originally from the Fredericton Academy of 1785, was renamed the University of New Brunswick and placed on a broader foundation than had hitherto proved possible. It was this institution more than any other that was responsible for the development of the Fredericton school of poets. The Loyalist satirist Jonathan Odell had been among the founders of the college, and as the century advanced the Anglican and Tory society of Fredericton was found to be congenial to a number of persons of literary tastes. Much poetry and prose —the name of James De Mille comes to mind—was written elsewhere in the province, some of it having been competently done; but most of it is no longer read and is known only to antiquaries. On the other hand the poetry of Carman and Roberts had a seminal influence upon the course of Canadian literature. The scholars of the University provided an intellectual preparation without which it could not have been written. George R. Parkin and Canon Roberts, themselves products of the University, made essential contributions. On his return from Oxford in 1875, Parkin awakened in his receptive pupils a love of Keats and the Pre-Raphaelite poets. The father of Charles G. D. Roberts instilled in his son a pride in the new land that the Fathers of Confederation had, in the face of formidable odds, succeeded in bringing into being. It was no accident that the son was the first to celebrate the birth of the new Dominion in memorable verse. Graduating in the year of triumph of Sir John Macdonald's National Policy, he first tried his hand at school teaching in Chatham and Fredericton. When in 1883, at the request of Goldwin

Smith, he moved to Toronto to edit the new periodical, *The Week*, he took a step which was to hasten the growth of a literary movement that can be seen in retrospect to have embodied an impulse reflective of the new nationality.

III

The province of Ontario in which Roberts was to find himself in 1883 had, with Quebec, passed through trying circumstances, involving periodic reorganizations not always unmarked by turbulence, in the course of its earlier history. Largely uninhabited at the time of Wolfe's victory on the Plains of Abraham in 1759, it was to have no substantial population of English speech until the close of the Revolutionary War when Loyalists and frontier farmers from western New York moved on to its empty but fertile acres, prompted in some cases more by a besetting land hunger than by any particular desire to alter their allegiance. It was called Upper Canada in 1791. Years before, at the close of the Seven Years' War in 1763, when what are now Quebec and Ontario were an entity, the English were hardly more than a handful of officials who came to administer the newly conquered territory inhabited by some sixty thousand French Canadians. They were supplemented by a few traders, largely of Yankee and Scottish origin, but containing other elements as well, the most influential of whom were intent upon the pursuit of the fur trade. Nowhere, not even in the towns of Quebec and Montreal, could the English-speaking be expected to be numerous enough to form a society for some time to come. Those who celebrated Wolfe's victory in verse in the pages of English periodicals may never have come to Canada at all, and the authors of the logs of the Conquest were mostly transients in alien surroundings, as were almost all of the military and civilian elements who followed them for a generation afterwards. Some were inclined to feel unhappy in the province, like Attorney-General Maseres who wrote with such clarity of insight on the institutions of the colony. Not so the English novelist, Mrs. Brooke, who resided for a time in Quebec and who could write amusingly of social occasions, including the flirtations of the military and seigneurial classes. A striking feature of her work, as noted by Dr. and Mrs. Talman in their chapter on the beginnings of literary activity in Canada, is her sensitive and extended treatment of topography and scenery, which suggests to them almost a work of description and travel. Even the poets who first appeared display a similar bias, and seem related to the travel writers of the period. On the whole, however, it was a literature of information rather than a literature of imagination, concerned with society more than with nature, often embodying statistical compilations of social and economic data relating to the newly acquired territory and its inhabitants.

The traders, on the other hand, must be treated as a class by themselves. Alexander Henry's narrative of the Pontiac rising is touched with the imagination of the artist; and in chapter 2 preceding, Professor Hopwood has reappraised David Thompson at his true worth. By contrast Alexander Mackenzie and Simon Fraser tell plain tales of tremendous feats of endurance. These Nor'westers were trying to achieve on the basis of the St. Lawrence and Great Lakes system an economy that was continental in scope, thus anticipating the territorial limits of the later Dominion. In the end, in the face of competition from Hudson Bay and the American traders, they failed; but long before they were forced into amalgamation with their northern competitors, the old fur-trading metropolis of Montreal had begun to develop the new staples of timber and wheat. By the 1820's it had become evident that canals, banks, an efficacious system of commercial law, and favourable legislation, would all be needed if the possibilities of the new industries were to be realized. In the course of endeavouring to attain their objective the mercantile classes of Lower Canada (as the settled part of what is now the province of Quebec was called from 1791 to 1840) collided with the agrarian party who were largely French-Canadian. Frustration, deadlock, and finally, in 1837, rebellion, all combined to accentuate in the English of Lower Canada their sense of identity with the Mother Country. A self-conscious colonialism became the keynote of their endeavours and was reflected in their newspapers and in the new periodical literature that began to make its appearance in the twenties. The middle-class piety and sentiment of contemporary England, tempered by compatible American influences, were exemplified by the leading periodical of the time. Begun in 1838, Montreal's *Literary Garland* did not consciously encourage a nativist trend, but represented "a detour in the development of a national literature," as Professor Klinck once aptly observed. He characterized Mrs. Traill as having approached slowly, through Nature's door, acceptance of life in Canada West. Susanna Moodie, her more inflexible sister, consciously resisted an idiom, apposite to her North American milieu, that would have required forswearing the standards upon which her life, like that of the class from which she came, had hitherto stood.

Contemporary support from Canada West, lately called Upper Canada, for such periodicals as the *Garland* was limited by the character of that section of the new united province. A low degree of literacy characterized the American farmers, partly Loyalist, who in the first years constituted the bulk of the population. The peaceful absorption of the province into the American union was forestalled by the Americans themselves through their invasion in 1812–1814; but successful resistance meant acquiescing in the rule of an irresponsible oligarchy which thereafter was able to enhance its power by treating its political opponents as enemies of the British connection and by denying reforms that were necessary to the progressive development of the country. The struggle that culminated in rebellion in 1837 was marked by the vigorous journalism of such men as William Lyon Mackenzie, but on the whole there was little forthcoming from either side that is of interest to the student of Canadian literary history. Neither did the great wave of immigration from the British Isles that peopled the wild lands of the province in the thirties and forties contribute much that was immediately favourable to its cultural advancement. Deriving largely from the fringes of British society, and thus containing only a small proportion of persons of learning and cultivation, the immigrants were in addition forced to come to terms with the Canadian back country. This experience accentuated in them a materialistic outlook and bred too often an indifference to education, which were offset only in the course of time through the efforts of such men as Egerton Ryerson, Archdeacon Strachan, and those who aided and applauded them.

In the meantime, apart from the work of several Scottish poet-journalists, and of members of such families as the Moodies, Traills, Stewarts, and Langtons, largely of the Trent valley, the student in search of literary values need not look much beyond the novels of Major John Richardson. Native-born, and on what was still a turbulent frontier, he caught and rendered in literary form the life of the Indian tribes and the pageantry of war; but the indifference which he experienced at the hands of his fellow Canadians in the decade following the Rebellions of 1837 confirms the existence of the limitations already suggested.

Only with the mid-century were the handicaps of the earlier decades at length overcome. Through the occupation of all good arable land by the fifties, together with the building of the railways, the growth of manufacturing, and the accumulation of investment capital, encouragement was given to the formation of a pattern of institutional consolidation and expansion, of which the federation of the provinces in 1867 was the crowning effect. The development of technological skills, evident in many fields including the application of steam power to the printing press, combined with specialized professional knowledge fostered by new university foundations to promote the publishing of books and periodicals for which the demand was suddenly enlarged. The exploration of the Canadian past, and of the French régime in particular, which had been begun with such effect at an earlier day by Mrs. Leprohon, was in 1877 carried to a level of achievement in *The Golden Dog* that brought its author, William Kirby, much popular acclaim. The deliberate fostering of a national spirit by the Canada First movement in the sixties and seventies, under the inspiration of the martyred McGee, helped to focus the aspirations of the time and exerted a quickening influence on all aspects of Canadian writing. Poems published in 1868 by Charles Mair were regarded as embodying the new spirit, and the young poet, Archibald Lampman, while an under-graduate at Trinity, found in the poetry of the New Brunswicker, Charles Roberts, assurance that Canadians were not helplessly situated on the out-skirts of civilization where no art and no literature could be. In actuality much work of literary value had already been achieved in Ontario, but with the advent of the school of Roberts, Lampman, Carman, Campbell, and Scott, the formative period of Canadian literary history may be regarded as having passed into one of a national achievement from which the country has never seriously receded, and from which it has advanced to the ampler perspectives of our own day.

5. Settlement

I. Newfoundland 1715–1880

FRED COGSWELL

THE DEVELOPMENT of literature in the three Maritime Provinces followed a coherent pattern. Writing in the pioneer stage in the eighteenth century consisted mainly of the diaries and journals of soldiers and others. Two movements near the end of the century, the "new light" religion of Henry Alline and the Loyalist migration, provided the impetus and shape for the development of a native literature of substantial proportions in the nineteenth century.

The pattern of the development of literature in Newfoundland was tragically different. Although the first permanent settlement had been established upon the island as early as 1610, the colony in its growth was at least a century behind the Maritimes. The reasons are to be found in the nature of the economy and political control of Newfoundland.

Newfoundland's economy was centred around fishing and fur trading rather than agriculture, and the direction of the colony was controlled by private concerns in Great Britain and by the naval authority. The latter was only interested in the preservation of naval bases, and the former in procuring for their enterprises in the colony the cheapest possible labour from the lowest classes in Great Britain and Ireland. Education and the provision of social amenities, beyond the reach of the colonists themselves, were left to the missionaries, and the eighteenth century was not one in which an evangelical spirit pervaded the Anglican church.

As a result of exploitation and neglect until near the close of the eighteenth century, the Newfoundland colonists sank into illiteracy and barbarism. This illiteracy of most Newfoundlanders had two striking effects upon their culture. It compelled them to preserve and add to the vigorous popular ballad tradition which they had brought with them from the British Isles. Secondly, here alone the English language was not fixed by the printed word, and proliferated into new vocabulary and phraseology extremely interesting to the linguist.

The late eighteenth and early nineteenth centuries brought some amelioration of the social conditions in Newfoundland. The growth of the Methodist missions, their stimulation of the Anglican Society for the Preservation of the

Gospel in Foreign Parts, and the increased activity of Roman Catholic missions all played their part in raising the moral and educational standards among the Islanders. A further impetus was given by the establishment of a local legislative authority in 1832 and by public assistance to the schools in 1843. Nevertheless, the standard of education by 1880 had not reached a sufficiently high level to give rise to and support a native literature.

The literature of Newfoundland from 1715 to 1880 is therefore, with a few exceptions, a continuation of the literature of discovery written by Europeans about the New World.

Cesar François Cassini (1714–1784), of the celebrated Italian family of scientists, visited Newfoundland during the course of a series of experiments to observe the transit of Venus. His observations on the island are recorded in his *Voyage to Newfoundland in 1768* which was translated into English in 1778.

The most important eighteenth-century writer was George Cartwright (1732–1819). Born of an ancient family in Nottinghamshire, Cartwright had fought under Clive in India and under the Marquis of Granby in Europe. Unable to support himself upon his retirement half-pay, Captain Cartwright engaged in trading, fishing, and trapping activities in Labrador from 1766 to 1792.

The literary fruits of Cartwright's enterprise were *A Journal of Transactions and Events of Nearly Sixteen Years on the Coast of Labrador*, published by subscription in three volumes at Newark in 1792, and containing *Labrador: A Poetical Epistle*, later reprinted at St. John's in 1882. Cartwright's *Journal*, much admired by Coleridge and Southey, contains the unvarnished day-by-day jottings of a Pepysian man with a passion for hunting and little sense of discrimination. It is a mine of information about the fur trade, the fisheries, the Indians, the Eskimos, and social conditions on a sordid frontier. It is also an unconscious revelation of a contradictory but powerful personality.

Labrador: A Poetical Epistle condenses into heroic couplets some of the more innocuous material of the *Journal*. Although it does not escape from the dangers inherent in poetic diction, the poem is enthusiastic and charming. It is completely without that sense of bleakness and isolation in the landscape that some critics have seen as characteristic of Canadian writing. The following lines are typical:

> So cutting cold, now blust'ring Boreas blows,
> None can with naked Face, his blasts oppose.
> But well wrapp'd up, we travel out secure,
> And find Health's blessings, in an Air so pure.

Lewis Amadeus Anspach (fl. 1799–1822) wrote two books on Newfoundland, *A Summary of the Laws of Commerce and Navigation* (1809) and *A History of the Island of Newfoundland and the Coast of Labrador*

(1819). The latter book is regarded as the most meritorious of the pioneer histories of the colony. Lieutenant Edward Chappell (1792–1861) of the Royal Navy contributed, in 1818, his *Voyage of His Majesty's Ship Rosamond to Newfoundland and the Southern Coast of Labrador.*

W. E. Cormack (1796–1868) was a native-born Newfoundlander. His father, a prominent St. John's merchant, had him educated in Edinburgh, and Cormack upon his return interested himself in the geography, geology, flora and fauna of the island. Despite opposition occasioned by the reluctance of those in authority to have publicity given to the conditions of the Indians in the interior, he became in 1822 the first white man to make an east to west overland crossing of Newfoundland. His *Narrative of a Journey across the Island of Newfoundland in 1822* first appeared in the *Edinburgh Philosophical Journal* during 1823 and 1824 and has since been thrice reprinted in book form. It is competent narrative containing useful information about the interior of Newfoundland and showing its author's courage, powers of endurance, and humanitarianism. After this exploit, Cormack interested himself in preserving the Beothok Indians, then on the verge of extinction. His "Report of W. E. Cormack's Journey in Search of Red Indians in Newfoundland" appeared in the *New Philosophical Journal* during 1828–29 and is the source of much that is known about that ill-fated race.

Sir Richard Henry Bonnycastle (1791–1847), while commander of the Royal Engineers in Newfoundland, compiled a survey of the island, *Newfoundland in 1842*, published in London in the same year. Far more attractive as a writer was Joseph Beete Jukes (1811–1869). Jukes, one of England's leading geologists, was commissioned to make a geological survey of Newfoundland and incorporated his findings in *Report on the Geology of Newfoundland* (1839). His *Excursions in and about Newfoundland during the Years 1839 and 1840*, published in two volumes in London in 1842, is the most readable nineteenth-century book on Newfoundland. Written in a graceful, easy style, the book abounds in vivid observation and anecdote.

Although one would not expect to find *belles-lettres* flourishing in Newfoundland during the period under discussion, they are represented by two writers, Philip Tocque (1814–1899) and Moses Harvey (1820–1901).

Philip Tocque was born in Carbonear and during his early manhood was an Anglican school-teacher. Past middle age, he studied divinity in Connecticut and was ordained as an Anglican priest in 1864. He is the author of three books, *Wandering Thoughts, or Solitary Hours* (1846), *Newfoundland as it was and as it is* (1878), and *Kaleidoscope Echoes* (1895). *Wandering Thoughts*, written during a short residence on the north coast of Newfoundland, comprises useful information and moralizing addressed to a juvenile audience and grouped loosely under such general topics as "The Past," "The Night Walk," "The Ocean," "Winter," "Temperance," etc. It must have provided much interesting reading to the audience for which it was designed; today it has no value as literature.

Moses M. Harvey was an Irish Presbyterian clergyman who settled in Newfoundland and was for more than twenty years pastor of St. Andrew's Free Presbyterian Church in St. John's. A strenuous local historian and *littérateur*, Harvey produced several books, of which the most important are *Newfoundland* (1883), a rather pedestrian history written in collaboration with Joseph Hatton, and *Lectures, Literary and Biographical* (1864). The latter book consists of lectures delivered to the Literary Institute of St. John's on such subjects as "Edmund Burke and Oliver Goldsmith," "Wit and Humor," "English, Scotch and American," and "Ireland—Her History and People." These lectures evince a wide knowledge and range of reading on the part of their creator but are commonplace in thought and turgidly over-ornate in style.

Newfoundland's sole nineteenth-century writer of verse of any importance was Henrietta Prescott (d. 1875), daughter of Admiral Sir Henry Prescott, Governor of Newfoundland from 1836 to 1841. Her *Poems, Written in Newfoundland* (1839) by their direct simplicity and conventional treatment of domestic themes show her as one of the more attractive followers of Felicia Hemans. Only a half-dozen of her several hundred poems relate to Newfoundland, and these are interesting chiefly for Miss Prescott's whole-hearted appreciation of the natural beauty of the island in all its seasons. In the bleakness of a Newfoundland winter, she can write:

> And let us look upon the snow, as white and pure it lies,
> When the vales are gently sloping, or the hill's tall summits rise;
> Let us mark each branch and twig in the frequent "silver-frost,"
> And confess that, e'en now, the trace of Beauty is not lost. . . .
>
> When we see the smile of peace and health on each beloved face,—
> Oh! *then*, we'll say, "Our lot hath fallen in a goodly place."

II. The Maritime Provinces 1720–1815

FRED COGSWELL

THE MARITIME PROVINCES were principally French settlements throughout the first half of the eighteenth century. Port Royal was garrisoned by English troops after 1710, but it was not until 1749 that the first permanent English settlement was established at Halifax. Eleven years later, a number of New England frontiersmen were settled on lands vacated by Acadians around the shores of Minas Basin and at Sheffield and Maugerville on the St. John River.

Shortly afterward, other emigrants settled in Prince Edward Island, around the Isthmus of Chignecto, and at Pictou. The main impetus for settlement, however, did not come until the close of the American War of Independence. At that time, more than thirty thousand Loyalist refugees tried to establish a new home in the Maritimes, the chief areas of their settlement being Shelburne and Annapolis in Nova Scotia and the valleys of the St. John and St. Croix rivers in New Brunswick.

The coming of the Loyalists transformed what was essentially a scattered frontier of New England farmers, giving it a varied class structure, a multiplication of specialized trades, a temporary influx of capital, and a new political and cultural orientation. Maritime literature between 1720 and 1815 also breaks into two sharply marked and well-defined periods: Pre-Loyalist and Loyalist. The latter, however, was not exclusive. Literature far different in tone from that of the Loyalists was produced between 1783 and 1815, on the one hand by British officials and soldiers and on the other hand by nonconformist religionists.

PRE-LOYALIST LITERATURE (1720–1783)

Early eighteenth-century literature involving the Maritime Provinces was a continuation of the literature of exploration and consisted mainly of the journals and personal narratives of a few individuals who found themselves briefly in that region. These accounts, usually written by semi-literate frontiersmen or soldiers, were simple, unimaginative narratives, interesting for the details which they gave of Indian and French settlements but no more literature than the bulk of the narratives of an earlier period now found in Hakluyt's *Voyages* or Purchas's *Pilgrimes*.

The most interesting of these narratives is the *Memoirs of Odd Adventures* (1736). This is an account of the sufferings and hardships endured by John Gyles (1677–1755) while a captive of the Malecite Indians in the St. John River valley between the years 1689 and 1698. It is noteworthy as a record of the fortitude and endurance of a small boy under hopeless conditions and for the picture which it contains of the perilous and squalid life of the Malecite bands of the late seventeenth century. Skimpier in its details and more articulate in style is the *Journal* of John Witherspoon (17??), which relates its author's experiences as a prisoner of the French and Indians in Acadia during the Seven Years' War.

Although Samuel Curwen (1715–1802), a distinguished Loyalist judge of Massachusetts, did not settle in the Maritimes, his *Journal and Letters* (1864) contains first-hand accounts of the siege of Louisbourg, at which he was present during the years 1744 and 1755. The mediocre verse narratives of George Cockings (d. 1802), *War: An Heroic Poem* (1762) and *The*

American War (1781), also touch upon the naval campaigns in Acadia during the Seven Years' War.

Gamaliel Smethurst (17??–17??), who established a permanent home in Nova Scotia and who ultimately became Controller of Customs and Deputy Surveyor General for that province, was a man of some education; consequently his two volumes, *A Narrative of an Extraordinary Escape out of the Hands of the Indians in the Gulf of St. Lawrence* (1760) and *A Providential Escape after a Shipwreck in Coming from the Island of St. John* (1774), make greater pretensions to literary style than the plain narratives of Gyles and Witherspoon and the laconic notations of Curwen and Cockings.

One other writer who was in Nova Scotia before 1760 deserves mention. John Adams was brought as a boy to Annapolis Royal and lived there until the time of his graduation from Harvard College. After graduation, he was ordained to preach at the Newport, Rhode Island, Congregational Church and remained in New England for the remainder of his life. It is difficult, therefore, to accept the claim of some Nova Scotian authorities that Canadian literature begins with the publication in 1745 in New England of his *Poems on Various Occasions*.

After 1760, prose and verse began to be produced by permanent settlers in the Maritimes. As a child of the New England frontier, Nova Scotia preserved its parent's basic characteristics. Among these was a high degree of literacy. Reading and writing, however, were prized because they were useful in conducting business and because without them an individual was cut off from reading the Bible and the devotional literature which consumed the interest of most of the members of the community during their leisure hours.

The religion of the Nova Scotian Yankee was a Congregationalism that united democracy in church administration with theological tyranny. It was dominated by the concept of a God whose arbitrary will destined each member of the human race irrevocably either to delight or to damnation. In this most important matter affecting existence, the believer was powerless to act on his own behalf. In the scattered rural communities, the minds and spirits of the young were tormented by fear, often for many years, before they accepted finally their preordained positions as members of the elect or the reprobate. Belief in Calvinism was a closed circle out of which few dared to step, guarded as it was by learned tomes liberally garnished with scriptural quotation. The thought of most Nova Scotian divines was, understandably, derivative from the great Calvinistic writers of New England and Scotland, and their sermons, hymns, and tracts are second-rate as theology and literature. One man of genius, Henry Alline, did appear and his work and writings have been more influential than those of any other single individual in shaping the cultural life of the Maritime Provinces.

HENRY ALLINE (1748–1784)

In *The Life and Journal of the Rev. Mr. Henry Alline*, published at Boston in 1806, Alline has set forth, in a tone and spirit remarkably similar to those of Jonathan Edwards' *Personal Narrative*, what is essentially an autobiography of the soul. He is careful, however, to link the spiritual events in his life to the physical details in such a way as to interest the psychologist (part of Alline's *Journal* found its way into William James's *The Varieties of Religious Experience*) and to provide the reader with an adequate picture of his personality. Further evidence of the career, personality, and impact of Alline is provided in many books written by his contemporaries or by those who visited the Maritimes shortly after his death. Most notable of these are *The Narrative of a Mission, to Nova Scotia, New Brunswick, and the Somers Islands, with a Tour to Lake Ontario* (1816) by Joshua Marsden, *Memoir of the Rev. James MacGregor* (1859) by George Patterson, and *A Narrative of the Life and Christian Experience of Mrs. Mary Bradley . . . Written by Herself* (1849) (see below). All these sources concur as to Alline's goodness, the warmth of his personality, and the eloquence and persuasiveness of his preaching.

Henry Alline was born at Newport, Rhode Island, the child of a strict Calvinist household. His formal education ended at the age of eleven when, in 1760, his parents and their seven children moved to a farm at Falmouth, Nova Scotia. For the next fifteen years, Henry Alline was to work with his father on the family farm, but he already kept inside himself a rich and secret inner life.

Alline's inner life began at the age of eight, when through his sister's fears during a thunderstorm, he came to realize that "God" and "death" and "hell" were not mere words but dire facts which at any moment he might be called upon to face. Fear sharpened his zest for religious reading and made keener his understanding of church doctrine. With understanding came an incurable emotional revulsion against a Being who would knowingly damn His creatures as a mere demonstration of the strength of His will. To worship such a God was blasphemy, and young Alline sought through years of prayer and meditation in secret to find a God nearer to his heart's desire. None came, and Alline as a young man abandoned himself to the less carnal forms of worldly enjoyment, becoming a leader in the card parties and frolics of the neighbourhood. One evening when Alline was on the way to a party of pleasure, his God came to him in a dramatic and visual manner. After that, Alline became a pious young man and, receiving a call from God to preach, he hesitated only long enough to assure himself that the voice he heard was not the voice of the devil. He set about preparing to obey the call.

Alline was reluctant to begin preaching because of his lack of a university education, but after an unsuccessful attempt to return to New England to study, he set his hand to the ministry with a concentration that was to take up every waking moment for the rest of his life. From 1776 to 1783, Henry Alline traversed, on horseback and in all weathers, the length and breadth of the then settled areas of the Maritime Provinces, preaching, often several times a day, wherever he could find an audience. Worn out prematurely by his labours but still tireless in spirit, Alline set out to bring the light to New England in August 1783, and at the close of January 1784, he expired of exhaustion in New Hampshire.

The only solace and relaxation which Henry Alline allowed himself was writing on religious themes. The essence of his theology is set out at length in his *Two Mites on Some of the Most Important Points of Divinity,* published at Halifax in 1781, which although not so superficially attractive as the *Life and Journal,* is in aim and execution a far more considerable book.

In *Two Mites,* Alline arranges the results of his meditation and reading into a compact, acutely reasoned, and happily illustrated system of theology. The Bible, the works of Milton, J. W. Fletcher, Edward Young, and William Law are cited to support arguments and positions adopted out of psychological compulsion on the part of the author. Alline's entire theology stems from his conviction that God must be lovable, just, and good. Salvation must come from the free choice of the individual and not by the arbitrary will of God; otherwise, God is a tyrant. It must not come easily; otherwise it would have little meaning. At no time, however, during the life of the individual can it be impossible. With salvation comes union of the individual soul with the Holy Ghost. By this union the soul is strengthened to persevere in good works and gladdened by the restoration of the kind of pristine happiness enjoyed by Adam before the Fall. Each salvation is a deeply felt personal experience, and there is no other way to achieve it, either by good works or by the following of prescribed ritual. A church organization and the rites of the church exist for the mutual sustenance of church members and should be decided by the members collectively, but the form of these rites is not in itself of sufficient importance to cause disunion or lack of charity among church members.

Alline did not lack intellectual daring and ingenuity in setting forth and defending his theology. He believed in Adam's fall from grace. He also believed that it was unjust to condemn a man for any sin but his own. He solved the dilemma by concluding that Adam's wrong choice was made in eternity and concurred in by all the souls of the human race present there with Adam. These souls, as a consequence of sin, became separated from God in eternity into the fallen world of time. As a result of the descent of Christ into that world as mediator, they there enjoy an ever present opportunity of redemption should they avail themselves of it.

Alline's eclectic theology was a disruptive element in the churches of the Maritimes, combatting on the one hand the fatalism of Calvinism and on the other the over-emphasis upon morality and ritual. It did much, however, to release individuals from the grip of fear and to bring a warm-hearted humanity and a more attractive concept of God to religion. He himself founded no church organization, for he felt that Christianity existed through the spirit only. He is, however, the spiritual ancestor of the Baptist church in the Maritimes, and his influence, temporarily eclipsed by the rise of worldliness as an aftermath of the Loyalist migration, reasserted itself in the puritanism of the nineteenth century and lives on today, almost undiminished, in the various evangelical sects that dominate the religious life of the rural Maritimes.

Alline's published sermons, of which *A Gospel Call to Sinners* (1797) is a representative example, are respectable examples of religious homily— marked chiefly by the fervour and eloquence of the joyous passages which occur in them. Alline, however, is more noted as a poet than as a sermon-writer.

His *Hymns and Spiritual Songs* (1802) parallels and exemplifies the theology contained in *Two Mites*. Although cramped by a formal pattern and diction, and marred by the occasional grammatical lapse, Alline's hymns are intense, dignified, and sincere, and often show a depth and originality of thought seldom seen in British hymns of the late eighteenth century. A good example is the opening hymn "On Man's Fall," in which Alline's dogma of the Kabbalistic Adam is set forth in verse:

> When Adam stood in light
> For trial, I was there;
> Between eternal day and night,
> And did my will declare.
>
> For when the choice was made
> I gave my full consent;
> In quest of other lovers stray'd,
> And from my father went.
>
> Then down with him I fell,
> And have no cause to say
> *Imputed guilt sinks me to hell,*
> I threw my self away.
>
> The countless race first stood
> In Adam all as one,
> Nor could a part forsake their God
> While others stood alone. . . .

Alline was a giant among pygmies. His uneducated followers lacked his acuteness of intellect and his sense of proportion. Only one of them deserves remembrance and that for one work. Benjamin Cleveland (1733–1790), of the family from which Grover Cleveland was descended, wrote the hymn beginning:

> O could I find from day to day
> A nearness to my God.

LOYALIST LITERATURE (1783–1815)

The Loyalist migrations ensured the speedy conquest of the frontier in the Maritimes Provinces; they also provided an élite whose Anglicanism, emphasis upon classical education, and conservative political views were in marked contrast to the attitudes of the Puritan farmers. They did not, however, at once provide the Maritimes with a literature. Although many Loyalists had been educated at universities and were fond of literature and although a few had established reputations as writers, they did not easily or readily come to terms with their new environment. The cultural fruits of their presence in the Maritimes did not ripen until the nineteenth century, by which time they were considerably modified by a resurgence of frontier puritanism.

The bulk of Loyalist literature was composed either before the Loyalists settled in the Maritimes or shortly afterward. It falls into two classes. The first of these—the journals, diaries, and letters of Loyalists describing their adventures and exploits during the American War of Independence—resembles the earlier literature of exploration and like that literature is primarily interesting for the light which it throws upon the history of the times. The second and more formal class of literature comprises the satirical verses composed by Tories during the American War of Independence. This is technically superior to the prose narrative and often both ingenious and clever. It is, however, too ill natured in tone and prejudiced in outlook for its appeal to outlast the audience of fellow Tories for which it was composed. In many ways, of course, the literature under discussion in this section belongs more properly to a literary history of the United States than of Canada. It is no accident that the finest poem composed by a Loyalist poet, "To Cordelia" by Joseph Stansbury, was a heart-felt rejection of the Maritime Provinces.

The journals and letters of the Loyalists are fascinating both for the adventures they contain and for the diversity of characters which their autobiographical details disclose. Sometimes, for non-literary reasons and in isolated passages, they approach literature. *The Narrative of Col. David Fanning* is a case in point. It was published posthumously in a mangled form in Richmond, Virginia, in 1862, and restored to its original from the author's Mss. by A. W. Savary in the *Canadian Magazine,* 1907–8. David Fanning (1754–1825), twice wounded and fourteen times taken prisoner in North

Carolina, was a child of civil war and knew no other life than violence until his settlement in New Brunswick at its close. Unimaginative and plodding in style, but doggedly honest, Fanning occasionally produces such a paragraph as Defoe might have envied. The following is a good example:

> . . . my negro took up my rifle and came within ten yards and set himself down and took aim at my head, but luckily the ball missed my head about one inch, but it split my hat. I then got up and went towards him, when he ran at me with the gun and struck at my head. But I fended it off with my arms. He however broke the stock, forward of the lock. I knowing myself weak, I turned and ran sixty yards, but found myself not able to run. I got my feet entangled in some vines and unfortunately fell, and he came to me and with the barrel of my rifle he struck at me many times. I lay on my back and fended his strokes with my heels until he had knocked all the bottoms of my feet to blisters. His great eagerness to kill me put him much out of wind. I accidentally got hold of the gun barrel and he tried to bite my hand for some time. During the time of his trying to bite me, I knocked all his fore teeth out. . . .

Circumstances had made Fanning a vindictive tiger. It is a welcome relief to turn to the journals and letters of older men, who had a recognized place of honour in settled communities, and who had acquired before the outbreak of hostilities a nobler and more civilized outlook than that of the Carolina frontier. One cannot read Lieutenant James Moody's *Narrative of his Exertions and Sufferings in the Cause of the Government since the Year 1776* (originally published in 1782, enlarged 1783) without realizing one's self in the presence of a true hero. Moody settled in Nova Scotia and died there in 1809. Less heroic certainly, but human and attractive are *The Winslow Papers, A.D. 1776-1826* (1901), the edited correspondence of Edward Winslow (1746–1815), a distinguished Loyalist who rose after his exile from the United States to the highest judicial position in New Brunswick. They have the added merit of revealing the feelings and aspirations of the Loyalists after they had settled in their new home.

The most readable of Loyalist documentary literature is *The Frontier Missionary: A Memoir of the Life of the Rev. Jacob Bailey* (1853). Jacob Bailey (1731–1808) is no hero but a timid human being caught in circumstances beyond his control, and the distresses of his last days in an American colony and of his flight to Nova Scotia are movingly related. The editor, William S. Bartlett, includes in an appendix in mutilated form one poem of Bailey's. Its undoubted merit makes one wish that the editor had included others. Bailey's manuscripts are, however, available at the Nova Scotia Archives and deserve editing and publishing at some time in the future.

Although Mather Byles, Jr. (1734–1814) was considered by his contemporaries to have possessed much of his father's poetical skill, the most celebrated Loyalist poets who settled in the Maritimes were Joseph Stansbury (1750–1809) and Jonathan Odell (1737–1818). Their work is most readily available in *The Loyal Verses of Joseph Stansbury and Doctor Jonathan Odell* (1860).

Both Stansbury and Odell were educated in a convention of strict adherence to a set poetical vocabulary and a traditionally sanctioned mechanical form. As a result the poems of one could as easily have been written by the other, despite the extreme differences of temperament that existed between them. They are of four kinds: public songs in the tradition of James Thomson's "Rule Britannia"; satires within a narrative framework; squibs and epigrams; and occasional poems. Both Stansbury's and Odell's patriotic songs are respectable verse within a now-dead tradition; the justice and cleverness of the satires do not outweigh the difficulties presented to the modern reader by the numerous local and contemporary allusions which must have been the chief reasons for their popularity in their own time; the squibs and epigrams, particularly Odell's upon Benjamin Franklin, are cold-bloodedly clever. The most readable and living work of Stansbury and Odell are the few occasional poems which they wrote primarily for the consolation of their own families. Odell's lines in celebration of his daughter's fifth birthday, and Stansbury's plaintive letter to his wife from Nova Scotia,

> —another way
> My fondest hopes and wishes lay,

are all that remain today of human interest out of many hours of meditation and careful composition on the part of two above-average late eighteenth century craftsmen.

OTHER WRITERS (1715–1815)

Although the Loyalists, through their numbers and the preponderance of educated professional men among them, imposed a new cultural pattern upon the Maritime Provinces, they by no means account for all the writers nor did they succeed in establishing a complete hegemony.

Many colonial officials and their families and many soldiers, quite independent of Loyalist influence, were stationed in the Maritimes between 1780 and 1820, and some of these occasionally produced work which can be regarded as literature. Among the Mss. of Lord Dalhousie (1770–1838) preserved at Register House, Edinburgh, are several graceful and witty occasional verses composed during his governorship of Nova Scotia between 1816 and 1819. A generation earlier may be noted the work of Griselda Tongue, the daughter of William Cotnam Tongue, a prominent late eighteenth century Nova Scotian official. Miss Tongue passed her short life at Windsor,

Nova Scotia, and left behind a small sheaf of verses that, despite their sentimentality and narrow range, have something of the charm of the work of William Cowper that inspired them. These verses were preserved by Beamish Murdoch in an appendix to his *History of Nova Scotia* (1865–67).

Little is known of Thomas Daniel Cowdell apart from the autobiographical data which appear in his first book of poems, *The Nova Scotia Minstrel*, first published in Dublin in 1809. From this we learn that he was born in Ireland, orphaned at an early age, emigrated to America, and there married a Scottish woman. After the couple had had eight children they returned to Great Britain where Cowdell published an account of his life in Nova Scotia and of the places visited in Great Britain on his return journey. The poems, written for the most part in octosyllabic couplets, have little to recommend them except the charm that comes of naïveté. By far the best of Cowdell's verse are "Indian Hymn" and "The Contented Indian," two dialect poems expressing what the author conceives to be the sentiments of the Micmac Indians.

Cowdell's second book, *A Poetical Account of the American Campaigns of 1812 and 1813* (1815) is a jingoistic survey of events during the War of 1812, reflecting the partisan spirit and the anxiety of contemporary British colonials. The following lines are representative:

> Thus Canada, with coarse inflated strain,
> The Yankees brawl and threaten thy domain,
> Would fain their dregs, with thy pure worth unite,
> To their equality thy sons invite.
> Thou know'st, when men are equal, 'tis in crime.

In Fredericton, Lieutenant Adam Allan (1757–1823) occupied much of his leisure in translating into standard English Allan Ramsay's Scots pastoral comedy "The Gentle Shepherd." Allan's translation was published as *The New Gentle Shepherd* in London (1798). Allan added to this translation an original poem in heroic couplets descriptive of the Grand Falls on the St. John River. This poem, unpolished and rough in versification, has a vigour and a fidelity to observation which is refreshing.

The most important non-Loyalist writer who lived in the Maritimes during this period was William Cobbett (1766–1835). Between the years 1784 and 1791, Cobbett was stationed with the British garrison at Fredericton. There he rose to the rank of Sergeant Major, and there he engaged in that course of self-education which was to bear such celebrated literary results in later life. Cobbett's reminiscences of his years in New Brunswick are scattered through his writings but occur most notably in *The Life and Adventures of Peter Porcupine* (1796) and in *Advice to Young Men* (1830). They are by far the most readable sketches now extant of life in the Maritimes during the late eighteenth century.

Less important as literature than the writing of officials and soldiers but more symptomatic of the future development of the Maritime Provinces was the continuation of religious writing. Although dimmed by the coming of the Loyalists, the light kindled by Henry Alline and his Baptist followers did not die out. At the turn of the century, it was to be augmented by the activity of British missions.

The Anglican missionaries for the most part remained in the areas settled by the Loyalists, with whom they were akin in spirit. The Presbyterians were most successful in the Scottish colonies of Pictou, Prince Edward Island, and Cape Breton. The Baptists and Methodists vied for the spiritual allegiance of the areas colonized by pre-Loyalists and of the non-Roman Catholic portions of the growing frontier settlements throughout the Maritimes. Their success ensured the continuity of the puritanism of the original Yankee settlers— a puritanism which despised all other forms of literature than those of moral and devotional tracts and verse. During the nineteenth century, these non-conformists were to challenge the political and cultural supremacy of the Anglican Tories and were to modify Maritime secular literature in the direction of their prejudices without, unfortunately, adding to it the fervour and intensity which they gave to their religious devotions. *A Narrative of the Life and Christian Experience of Mrs. Mary Bradley* (1849) recounts the experiences of a young woman (b. 1771) on a frontier where the chief source of interest, apart from daily routine, was the sermons preached by such men as Henry Alline, James MacGregor, and Joshua Marsden. *A Narrative* is the product of a sentimental and limited mind, but it demonstrates graphically the pre-eminent place held by religion in a pioneer community and the perplexities caused by the conflicting dogmas of its travelling exponents.

The sermons and religious tracts of James MacGregor (1759–1830) were preserved by posthumous publication in 1859. The major literary figure among Maritime missionaries, however, was Joshua Marsden.

JOSHUA MARSDEN (1777–1837)

Joshua Marsden was one of five missionaries sent out by the Methodist Church in England to the Maritime Provinces. He remained there from 1799 to 1807, travelling by water and upon horseback to the remotest districts. A detailed account of his mission is given in a series of letters entitled *The Narrative of a Mission, to Nova Scotia, New Brunswick, and the Somers Islands, with a Tour to Lake Ontario* (1816). Joshua Marsden was a man of good family and education. He must have been possessed of considerable personal charm since, during his sojourn in the Maritimes, he married, in the teeth of family hostility, the niece of the redoubtable Bishop Samuel Seabury. His letters, obviously composed from a running journal, reveal an initial sense of inadequacy and of antipathy to the frontier gradually yielding to confidence and love. Here and there in his work, striking sentences like the following occur:

There is, sir, a solitary loneliness in the woods of America to which no language can do adequate justice. It seems a shutting out of the whole moral creation. . . .

Interspersed among the letters are poetical effusions which, although metrically skilful, are stereotyped in thought and expression. The best of these is "A Farewell to Nova Scotia and New Brunswick," of which the following stanza is a sample:

> The spring just peeps upon thee and is fled,
> Short-liv'd thy summers are, severe thy clime,
> And frost and sea-fog bind around thy head
> A chaplet, this of snow, and that of rime;
> Yes, all the landscape terribly sublime
> Displays the rigours of a wintery wild;
> Yet I in thee hath cheerly past my time,
> Around my cot, the snow-clad season smil'd
> For I was preaching *Him*, who every care beguiled.

In 1815, Marsden published in England *The Backslider, a Descriptive Moral Poem, in Four Books*, in heroic couplets of considerable polish. Before embarking upon his theme, a sharp analysis of the psychological processes in the corruption of a good man, the poet describes the land where the poem was written:

> In this cold climate, where rough Boreas blows,
> Pours his fierce hail, and spreads his dazzling snows,
> Disrobes the green-wood, chills the solar beam,
> And shakes his icy-sceptre o'er the stream,
> Let me beguile stern winter's frigid ire,
> With books divine, a friend, and maple fire;
> Or cheat the night-storm terrible and fierce!
> With purest sweets of fancy-pleasing verse.

Joshua Marsden must have cheated many night-storms, for his other published books, most of them obviously composed during his residence in the Maritimes, include: *Leisure Hours; or, Poems, Moral, Religious & Descriptive* (1812); *The Mission* (1816); *Amusements of a Mission; or, Poems, Moral, Religious, and Descriptive, Interspersed with Anecdotes, Written during a Residence Abroad* (1818); and *Poems on Methodism* (1848). There are also two moral prose narratives: *Grace Displayed: An Interesting Narrative of the Life, Conversion, Christian Experience, Ministry and Missionary Labours of — —* (1813) and *Sketches of the Early Life of a Sailor, Now a Preacher of the Gospel* (1820).

Marsden's verse is superior to his prose and shows considerable talent; it fails to achieve its potential excellence mainly because Marsden kept it ever subordinate to his primary calling as a publicist for the Methodist church.

III. The Canadas 1763–1812

JAMES J. AND RUTH TALMAN

The period 1763–1812 saw little English writing in those parts which in 1792 became Upper and Lower Canada. For this dearth there are several explanations. Obviously, at first, the English-speaking population was small and almost entirely without pretensions to literary attainment. Indeed, if we are to believe Francis Maseres, whose letters represent some of the earliest writing in the period, the province was a "very dull and disagreeable place to live in."

The Loyalist migration, while adding greatly to the English-speaking population, did not add anything to its literary capacity. The immigrants did not come from those elements in society which wrote creatively. Indeed, many could not write, and those who could were too busy to do so, or did not have the inclination or competence to put their thoughts on paper. Most writing took the form of petitions to the Government. Non-Loyalist English-speaking immigrants differed from their Loyalist contemporaries only in their inability to secure land as Loyalist claimants.

With the large part of the population made up as it was, writing was left to the few literate immigrants and visitors from the United Kingdom. This writing took the form of one novel, a few poems, some printed sermons, travel accounts, diaries, and at least a couple of morbid items—broadsides purporting to present the confessions and last words of those about to be hanged. A few diaries and letters, not intended at the time for publication, have come down to us as representative of what people were thinking and saying.

The first English writer of note in Canada, after France ceded Canada to Great Britain, was Francis Maseres (1731–1824). He was born in London of Huguenot ancestry. After a distinguished career at Clare College, Cambridge, he graduated in 1752. In 1753 he published the first of a series of mathematical works he produced throughout his life. A year later he entered the practice of law. This profession led him to Quebec, as Attorney General, in 1766, where he remained until 1769. Before his arrival in Canada he wrote a pamphlet entitled *Considerations on the Expediency of Procuring an Act of Parliament for the Settlement of the Province of Quebec* (London, 1766). This was his first publication on Canadian affairs.

As Attorney General, Maseres drew up several reports for the Lieutenant-

Governor and Council on judicial and economic matters in the colony. His most significant report was that "concerning The State of the Laws and the Administration of Justice in that Province." This report and others, published by Maseres in *A Collection of Several Commissions* (London, 1772), are invaluable records of their time.

In the courts Maseres was less successful than he was as a writer. By May 1768 he was thoroughly discouraged with the country. The climate troubled him and he did not admire the scenery. But, he concluded: "What is worse than all, there are few agreeable people here to converse with." He left Canada in 1769 and never returned. In spite of his strictures, he did not lose his interest in the country. A bibliography of his writings, limited only to those items clearly attributable to him, for he wrote much anonymously, reveals a thorough-going knowledge of the country. His letters, edited with an excellent biographical introduction by W. S. Wallace in 1919, provide an early sample of Canadian literature.

One of the strong qualities of Maseres as a writer was his ability to enable his readers to see people as he saw them. For example, his description of a visiting official: "He is a well-bred agreeable man but not a lawyer; and he has a pompous way of talking that seems borrowed from the house of commons cant about the constitution &c, without having precise Ideas of what he would say." As Dr. Wallace has written, Maseres' letters give a "fresh and vivid picture of Canada" during the years 1766–68. Maseres died in England in 1824.

The only novel of the period is *The History of Emily Montague* by Frances Brooke (1724–1789), which was published in England in 1769. *Emily Montague* may truly claim to be the earliest Canadian novel—and, indeed, the earliest novel emanating from the North American continent, as nothing that can be described as a novel had appeared up to this time in the American colonies. Although published in England, the novel was undoubtedly written in Canada and most of its action takes place in a Canadian setting.

Frances Brooke, born Frances Moore, in Stubton, Lincolnshire, married the Reverend Dr. John Brooke in 1756 and joined him in Quebec in 1763 after he became chaplain of the garrison and Deputy to the Auditor General. There she resided for five years and came to know well both the French seigneurs of the city surroundings and officers of the British garrison and British officials.

Mrs. Brooke was peculiarly fitted to write of English–French Canada. Already she had published several novels and plays in England and had established a position in the English literary generation that followed Richardson and Fielding; also she was well acquainted with France, and had published a translation of a French romance. She was thus prepared to give a sympathetic portrayal of both facets of the Canadian scene.

Emily Montague is written in the epistolary style popular in the period.

It consists of 228 letters, written among a group of friends in Canada and England, which unfold the gentle and not very eventful love story of the principal characters, Emily Montague and Colonel Ed. Rivers. Two subordinate pairs of lovers, one in Quebec, one in England, add variety of character. Emily and her Colonel are interesting enough examples of the high cultural and moral "sensibility" much prized by novelists of that time. Emily's friend, Arabella Fermor, a coquette, shows a more sprightly wit. The letters are pleasing, written in an easy, lively style, and give a vivid picture of the society of the small provincial capital, with its afternoon drives and evening parties, balls, and one unforgettable sketch of a sleigh-ride over the ice and snow of the frozen St. Lawrence.

In one respect *Emily Montague* differs from all other novels of its genre. Here we have no violence—none of the abductions, seductions, duels, highwaymen, or ghosts that we find in other such romances, and, indeed, in Frances Brooke's English-based novels. In *Emily Montague,* except for the stumbling blocks in the course of true love, the story runs smoothly and unsensationally. Its sensation is provided by its setting: Canadian forests and rivers, Indians and habitants, waterfalls and snows. Is it a novel only, or might it be classed also with description and travel literature?

More popular than fiction, apparently, was poetry, for the period provides at least four long descriptive poems. The first of these, *Abram's Plains*, by Thomas Cary (1751–1823), was printed privately in Quebec in 1789. The poem, 568 lines in rhyming couplets, was patterned, according to its Preface, on "the harmonious Thompson [James Thomson, author of *The Seasons*]." Cary expressed admiration for Pope but could not help feeling a preference for Thomson "so strikingly unparalleled and inimitable" were the beauties of his numbers. At the same time Cary admitted that before he began his poem he re-read "Pope's *Windsor-Forest* and Dr. Goldsmith's *Deserted Village*, with the view of endeavouring, in some degree, to catch their manner of writing."

Abram's Plains, although derivative in style, is truly Canadian in content. Beginning with an invocation to the Plains "Where . . . I sit and court the Muse," Cary goes on to a description of the whole St. Lawrence system: "cold Superior"; Huron, "distinguish'd by its thund'ring bay"; Michigan; Erie; "thy dread fall, Niagara"; Montreal, with a reference to the fur trade; Quebec, with a description of its surrounding forest and mention of the ship-building industry; and so on, through the Gulf to the coasts of Labrador. In passing, Cary describes the settlers, with their fields and villages; Indians, Eskimos; buffalo, carriboo [*sic*], wolf, otter; fish, with a neatly sketched picture of the fishing through the ice of the St. Lawrence. In short, an epitome of the Canadian scene as it appeared in his time, though it is doubtful if Cary could actually have seen Eskimos.

Cary came to Quebec from England before 1787 and was working as a clerk in a government office when he published his poem. In 1797 he established a subscription library and later, in 1805, he founded the *Quebec Mercury* in the columns of which he continued his literary activity. He died in Quebec in 1823.

Another poem, similar in type, was *Canada, a Descriptive Poem*, written at Quebec in 1805, and presumably published in 1806. Heretofore this poem has been described as anonymous, but it now appears to have been written by Cornwall Bayley (1784–1807), a precocious undergraduate of Christ's College, Cambridge, who left England for Quebec in 1804, evidently travelling via the United States. His preface is dated Quebec, February, 1806. The author entreats "the candid reader to make allowances for the inexperience of a youth." He thoughtfully supplies a Plan of the poem, a useful device as its references are fairly obscure. The Plan gives an idea of what the poet attempted to describe:

The view from Cape Diamond . . . —The animal and vegitable [*sic*] productions of the Country—The Indians with some conjectures upon their origin and former state—The colonization of Canada by the French Missionaries—Its conquest by the British in 1759—The Death of Wolfe—The repulse of the American army under Montgomery—Reflections upon Democracy—and the usual evils of a Revolution—Illustrated by France—The Contrast presented in the innocent manners of the Canadians—Their Civil and Religious liberties—Their manners and customs described, as varying according to the seasons—Upper Canada introduced—Lakes —Falls of Niagara—Reflections upon Great Britain and her Colonies—Address to the St. Lawrence—its rivers—towns and villages—Panegyric upon Quebec—Its General Hospital—The Nuns—Their amusements &c. The poem concludes with a tribute of praise to the females of the Province.

This seems a comprehensive effort for a youth of twenty-one.

Another poet writing in, and of, Quebec was Stephen Dickson (b. 1761?), a graduate of the University of Dublin, who came to America apparently after being implicated in the Irish rebellion of 1798. He spent only a few months in Quebec, but published there early in 1799 *The Union of Taste and Science, a Poem: to which are subjoined a few Elucidating Notes*, a poem in praise of Governor Prescott and his wife, written in heroic couplets, in stanzas of irregular length. The poem represents Mrs. Prescott as Taste and the Governor as Science, and is filled with fulsome flattery toward its subjects, classical and current allusions, elaborate figures of speech and imagery. Dickson took the precaution of adding notes to explain his allusions. This small volume is, incidentally, a fine example of early Canadian printing.

A fourth descriptive poem, published in England, almost took on the attributes of a traveller's guide in verse. This was *Quebec Hill; or, Canadian Scenery: A Poem in Two Parts* (London, 1797). The author, J. Mackay, is an unknown. He does say, however, "By far the greatest part of the Poem was written in Canada, where the Writer has spent a considerable portion of his time." He adds, "The Author is sensible that the Poem might have been rendered, what some men of learning term, more poetical, if less attention had been paid to veracity; but, to lovers of truth, no apology is necessary on this head, and, to those of a contrary disposition, none is due."

The poem includes, among other subjects, a description of Niagara Falls, an account of the death of Wolfe, and lines on the fever and ague of Upper Canada. Some moralizing is thrown in. In the end the author admitted that he had not been won over by Canada:

> Now, having sung Canadian woods and vales,
> Its Summer's heat, and Winter's frigid gales,
> Let me remark, as climates I compare,
> And manners note, 'tis Britain I prefer.
> Dear isle! where temp'rate years their empire hold,
> Free from extremes of ardent heat or cold.

Beyond these four longer poems very little verse remains, except for fugitive items in the newspapers. One commonly recurring form of doggerel was the annual carrier's address, bringing New Year's greetings from the newspaper carrier or the printer's boy to the customers. These verses appeared yearly in the *Quebec Gazette* and other Canadian newspapers. The first in English was printed in the *Quebec Gazette* in January 1781. The verses, which have no literary merit, are sometimes comparable to the modern greeting-card verse; sometimes satirical; sometimes an undisguised hint for a New Year's tip. Similar verses were published to celebrate special occasions, such as the opening of a theatre in Quebec.

Of poetic drama we have one example, by Barnabas Bidwell (1763–1833), who came to Upper Canada from Massachusetts in 1810. During his senior year at Yale in 1784 he published a tragedy, *The Mercenary Match*, which was acted by his fellow students. According to the *Dictionary of American Biography*, the work was distinguished by the general smoothness of its blank verse and the felicity of its phrasing, qualities seldom found in eighteenth-century American plays. This work can scarcely qualify Bidwell as a Canadian playwright. He is said also, however, to have contributed eleven sketches to Robert Gourlay's *Statistical Account of Upper Canada* (London, 1822). These surely would stamp him as a Canadian writer.

Two writers of sermons deserve mention: Alexander Spark (1762–1819) and Jacob Mountain (1749–1825). Spark came to Quebec from Scotland in 1780 and officiated for many years at the Scotch Church (St. Andrew's Presbyterian Church). Though a profound scholar and an excellent writer, Spark left only a few sermons and orations, typical of their class and period in their figurative and rhetorical language. Mountain, born in England, where he held several livings, was appointed first Anglican bishop of Quebec in 1793. In England he wrote poems and sermons. His sole Canadian publication was a thanksgiving sermon published in Quebec in 1799.

Spark, besides his pastoral duties, engaged in journalism. From 1792 to

1794 he supervised the *Quebec Gazette,* and during this period he also edited the *Quebec Magazine,* a monthly journal which was devoted mainly to reprinting papers, alternately in English and French, from European and American periodicals, and contemporary classics. Its original material was mostly on agricultural matters.

Since Canada was a country new to English writers accounts of travel comprise a large part of its early literature. One early travel writer was the Montreal merchant Alexander Henry (1739–1824). His book *Travels and Adventures in Canada and the Indian Territories between the Years 1760 and 1776* (New York, 1809) has become a Canadian classic. This exciting story, besides offering a great deal of valuable geographical information and many curious details of the customs and manners of the Indians, provides an autobiography of the writer, describing his "intrepidity" when placed in "many trying and perilous situations."

Travel literature is represented also by the journal of John Lees. Lees (fl 1764–1775), a Quebec merchant, born in Scotland, was engaged in the fur trade in the upper country. He wrote a journal describing his travels in 1768 from Boston to Detroit and back by the Great Lakes and St. Lawrence to Montreal. His journal (published only in 1911) is a tightly packed storehouse of information about the country he traversed, the people he met, distances, prices, and other such straightforward material. With nothing imaginative about it, and not much grace of style, it is nevertheless of value to the historian of the period.

A similar journey, some years later, was described by George Heriot (1766–1844) in his *Travels through the Canadas* (London, 1807). It provides an account of the topography, climate, scenery, and settlements of both provinces. Heriot's descriptions are careful, detailed, and exact—pedestrian rather than evocative. He dealt with economic conditions, agriculture, and colonial administration, and showed himself a thoughtful observer. His book is not a mere tourist's diary, but a comprehensive picture of the country and its inhabitants. It is copiously illustrated with plates made from his own drawings, which show charm and considerable skill.

Heriot came to Canada from England and served as a clerk in the Ordnance Department at Quebec. From 1800 to 1816 he was Deputy Postmaster General of British North America. He wrote also a *History of Canada,* published in London in 1804. This work was largely based on Charlevoix and is not significant.

Probably the best-known description of Upper and Lower Canada was written by Irish-born Isaac Weld, junior (1774–1856), whose *Travels through the States of North America and the Provinces of Upper and Lower Canada, during the years 1795, 1796, and 1797,* was first published in London in 1799. Several other editions followed, and the work was translated into Dutch, Italian, French, and twice into German.

Weld spent from July to the end of October of 1796 in Upper and Lower Canada, and managed to travel as far west as the Detroit River, with the purpose of obtaining information as to the state of those provinces, and of determining from his own immediate observations "how far the present condition of the British dominions in America might be inferior, or otherwise, to that of the people of the States." His work is in the form of thirty-eight letters, of which sixteen deal with Canada. Weld's descriptions are graphic but do not present as intimate a picture as those of Lambert, who followed him.

He scarcely seems to have become enamoured of America, for his concluding words were, "my thoughts are solely bent upon returning to my native land, now dearer to me than ever . . . I shall speedily take my departure from this Continent, well pleased at having seen as much of it as I have done; but I shall leave it without a sigh, and without the slightest wish to revisit it."

By far the most comprehensive travel account written during this period was *Travels through Lower Canada and the United States of North America in the years 1806, 1807 and 1808,* by John Lambert. Its popularity in Britain was evidenced by the number of editions it went through. The first edition, in three volumes, was published in London in 1810; the second, in two volumes, in London and Edinburgh in 1813, and again in London in 1814; and the third, also in two volumes, in London and Edinburgh in 1814.

Lambert, about whom little is known, arrived at Quebec in the autumn of 1806 and "after residing a twelvemonth in Canada" visited the United States. He returned to Montreal early in May 1808, before he sailed for England. In his account of his tour through Lower Canada and part of the United States his object was to describe the people as he found them; "to remove the veil of unjust prejudices and the gloss of flattery."

In a style discursive and anecdotal he gave an intimate picture of life and manners in Quebec, not always in flattering terms. His account of the Canadian theatre shows something of the cultural development of the colony.

There is, indeed, a building at Quebec called a Theatre, and also one at Montreal; but the persons who perform, or rather attempt to perform there, are as bad as the worst of our strolling actors; yet they have the conscience to charge the same price nearly as the London theatres. Sometimes the officers of the army lend their assistance to the company; but I have seen none, except Colonel Pye, and Captain Clark of the 49th, who did not murder the best scenes of our dramatic poets. It may be easily conceived how despicably low the Canadian theatricals must be, when boys are obliged to perform the female characters: the only actress being an old superannuated demirep, whose drunken Belvideras, Desdemonas, and Isabellas, have often *enraptured* a Canadian audience.

The quality of literature, in his opinion, was little better. "The state of literature and the arts," he said, "did not improve very rapidly after the conquest of the country by the English. The traders and settlers, who took up their abode among the French, were ill qualified to diffuse a taste for the arts and sciences, unless indeed it was the *science* of barter, and the *art* of gaining cent. per cent. upon their goods."

A morbid type of broadside seems to have been popular in Quebec. The *Quebec Gazette* on November 21, 1783, announced that the dying speech and confessions of two convicted murderers and robbers were to be published on the following Saturday. Again, in 1785, the confession of another criminal, hanged for stealing, was published. This type of literature was reminiscent of a type which was popular in Britain earlier in the century. Unfortunately the texts have not been preserved, but undoubtedly they would be similar to others which are extant.

Most of the foregoing literary activity took place in the Lower province as it was a settled community while Upper Canada was still in a much earlier stage of development. One interesting item that appeared early in Upper Canada—indeed, it was the first unofficial publication printed in that colony—was *Thoughts on the Education of Youth* by Richard Cockrel (1783?–1829), a teacher of mathematics at Newark (Niagara-on-the-Lake). This was a pamphlet, "Printed by G. Tiffany, and sold at his Book-Store," 1795. Cockrel shows some surprisingly modern pedagogical ideas, which would not be out of place in a modern P.T.A. meeting. "It behoves every master of a school to become acquainted as early as possible with the disposition of his pupils: soft words are sufficient in order to induce some boys to diligence, some will not do without threats, and others will never make any progress without now and then being brought to the birchen altar." "If masters would also use proper means to gain the affections of children, I am sure they might be successful and more happy in their situations." He made specific recommendations as to the size of classes and methods of presentation; he thought there should be no homework during holidays; rules of politeness should be taught; parents should keep children from the streets; and lastly he queried, "Do parents interest themselves as they ought?"

Contemporary for a time with Cockrel, Elizabeth Posthuma (Gwillim) Simcoe (1766–1850), the wife of Lieutenant Governor John Graves Simcoe, kept a diary which ran from September 17, 1791, to October 16, 1796. This was a day-to-day record from the time the Simcoes left England until they returned. The diary gives a great deal of information on travel, and on the life and people of Upper Canada. The first edition of the diary, edited by John Ross Robertson, was published only in 1911.

The name of D'Arcy Boulton (1759–1834) is not well known in the history of Upper Canada. Boulton was born in England and came to Canada about 1797. He was successively Solicitor General, Attorney General, and judge of assize. Service as Judge of the Queen's Bench was not as likely to lead to fame as other activities, but Boulton's *Sketch of His Majesty's*

Province of Upper Canada (London, 1805) shows the author to have been a lucid and well-qualified writer. He began with a general account of the colony and its political organization and divisions, and followed with a particular account of each township. His views may be appreciated when it is stated that rather than rhapsodizing over the beauties of Niagara Falls he remarked on the mills which the falls might be used to operate.

In 1890 Lady Matilda Edgar edited the Ridout Letters covering the years 1805 to 1815, under the title *Ten Years of Upper Canada*. The greater part of the collection consists of letters between Thomas Ridout (1754–1824) and his sons, George (1791–1871) and Thomas G. (1792–1861). The volume, consequently, is by way of being the work of a composite Ridout author. All were careful observers and could write with facility. Thomas Ridout, born in England, had led an eventful life. He migrated to Maryland and engaged in trade there during the American Revolution, after which he was captured by Indians and spent several months as their prisoner. On his escape he settled in Upper Canada, where he became Surveyor General and a member of the Legislative Council. He thus was closely associated with the early history of the colony. The letters printed range over many subjects —events, people, business, agriculture, and battles. A brief but well-written narrative of Thomas Ridout's captivity among the Shawanese in 1788 was included by the editor.

Canadian writing between 1763 and 1812 may not bulk large in quantity or high in quality. Small, however, as the output may have been our information regarding the country would be sorely depleted were it not for the writers mentioned above. Without them Canada would surely be the poorer.

6. Haliburton

FRED COGSWELL

IN THE TWO DECADES following 1815, the Maritime Provinces underwent a prolonged period of social and economic crisis. The emigrants from New England and Great Britain were hard put to it to maintain their old ways of behaviour and system of values in an economy that was going to pieces before their eyes. For with the close of the Napoleonic Wars, the artificially stimulated markets in timber and agricultural produce collapsed. With the deflation of a temporarily thriving economy, the unspectacular but steady revenues of officialdom became a prize to be fought for, and the resultant political agitation—behind the fine phrases in which it was cloaked—was in reality a naked struggle for assured economic survival on the part of its participants.

Nova Scotia, the most advanced colony and the one which had most benefited by the struggle in Europe, felt most keenly the altered circumstances, and at least two individuals in Nova Scotia possessed some insight into the nature of these pressures which were convulsing their society. Thomas Mc-Culloch in the 1820's saw the thriftlessness and immorality increasing upon the frontier as a threat to the maintainance of religious values. A decade later, Thomas Haliburton shared McCulloch's vision, and added to it his discovery of the underlying motives of the political struggle, whose outcome in his opinion could not possibly solve the colony's ills. Both writers attempted to convert their neighbours to their ways of thinking by putting the situation as they saw it before them in fictitious but realistic terms. Out of their efforts, the first serious realistic Canadian prose fiction was born.

That this fiction did not take the form of the contemporary novel is understandable. The contemporary novel was regarded as a vehicle of escape from life, either to the medieval past of glamour or terror, or to the sentimental intrigues of a hypothetical European aristocracy. Consequently, McCulloch and Haliburton turned backward in time to the eighteenth century and modelled their work essentially upon the essay form as perfected by Addison and Steele.

Each letter in *The Letters of Mephibosheth Stepsure*, each chapter in *The Clockmaker*, is a selection of incidents from rural or urban Nova Scotian life designed to illustrate a moral or a social vice. The continuity between chapters is not arrived at through an over-riding unity of plot, as in the novel proper, but by a continuation of character and tone from chapter to chapter as in the essays of *The Spectator*.

Thomas McCulloch (1776–1843), a Scotsman, became Presbyterian minister at Pictou, Nova Scotia, in the early days of the nineteenth century. For more than forty years he was to play a leading role in the educational and theological life of Nova Scotia. He also found time to write fiction of limited, but genuine, talent. His collection of historical sketches, *Auld Eppie's Tales*, was designed as a counter-blast to the anti-Presbyterian bias of *Old Mortality*, but William Blackwood, the Edinburgh publisher, was too timid to publish it in competition with Sir Walter Scott. McCulloch's *William and Melville* was published in Edinburgh by Oliphant in 1826. Although its two novelettes contain accurate, if unsavoury, accounts of life in contemporary Halifax, they are basically temperance tracts, and their leading characters are wooden and unprepossessing. McCulloch belongs in a literary history for one book, *Letters of Mephibosheth Stepsure*, printed serially in the *Acadian Recorder*, and declined in 1828 by the timid Blackwood on the grounds of the coarseness of its humour. It was reissued in book form in Halifax in 1860.

In sixteen letters, Mephibosheth Stepsure—in his youth a lame orphan—describes his plodding rise to respectability and affluence in the community of Pictou by a combination of hard work, abstinence, religiosity, and cunning. Akin to Mephibosheth in ideology, practice, and prosperity are his wife, Dorothy, and her mother; his son, Abner; his cousin, Harrow; and a hard-featured Scots emigrant, Saunders Scantocreesh. Favoured by God, these devout Presbyterians listen to the spiritual admonitions of Dr. Drone. Against these faithful sheep of the congregation are the goats—all who succumb to the lure of a gambling economy and to the thriftlessness and dissipations of the frontier. In letter after letter, the rake's progress of the local citizens is described and their ultimate hardships are recounted.

There is much to repel the modern reader in *The Letters of Mephibosheth Stepsure*. Christian ethics, one feels, ought to be an end in themselves and not a means of making money, and to a healthy nature cold-blooded gloating over the misfortunes and failures of others is never pleasant. The book also has technical flaws. The characters—Trot, Whinge, Sham, Clippet—are, as their names suggest, caricatures; the episodes are often farce; and the use again and again of the same plot situations is monotonous. To compensate for these defects, *The Letters of Mephibosheth Stepsure* possess a marvellously unified tone and sensibility, a robust realism, a lack of prudishness, and a sustained, almost Swiftian, irony.

Besides being a creditable pioneer attempt at literature, the *Letters* had a seminal importance. They suggested the idea for the letters which Joseph Howe wrote in the *Novascotian* a few years later. They also showed Thomas Chandler Haliburton the possibilities for literature that lay in the local scene. Haliburton's debt to McCulloch has been greatly exaggerated recently; nevertheless *The Letters of Mephibosheth Stepsure* was one of many avenues that led to *The Clockmaker*.

By birth and education, Thomas Chandler Haliburton (1796–1865) was completely representative of early community leaders in the Maritimes. His father, William H. O. Haliburton, the son of a pre-Loyalist and staunch Tory, was clerk of the peace for Hants County, Nova Scotia, and afterwards a judge of the Inferior Court of Common Pleas. His mother, Lucy Chandler Grant Haliburton, was the daughter of parents who had given their lives for the Crown during the American War of Independence. The family was Anglican, and Haliburton attended King's College, Windsor, then the training ground for the Tory and Anglican professional men who dominated the social and economic life of the Maritimes.

From his father Haliburton acquired the philosophic basis of his Tory politics. He received from his mother the emotional prejudices connected with them and a violent dislike of the United States. During his early years at the Bar and as a member of the Nova Scotian Legislative Assembly between 1826 and 1829, Haliburton nevertheless intermittently indulged impulses radically at odds with his position and training. Among causes which he championed were the removal of the disabilities preventing Roman Catholics from holding office, common school education at state expense, and a permanent grant for Pictou Academy. All these were anathema to his Tory friends.

Gradually Haliburton found his position in the Legislative Assembly becoming untenable. Tactlessly outspoken and possessing a great gift for ridicule, he threw all his strength into any issue he supported and gored his friends and foes in turn. He had, however, too great a sense of worldly advantage to go over irretrievably to the party of Reform. His political friends accordingly took the first opportunity to get rid of a troublesome ally by offering him the judgeship that fell vacant upon his father's death in 1829. Haliburton was a judge of the Court of Common Pleas until its abolition in 1841. He then became a Supreme Court judge of Nova Scotia until retirement in 1854. Haliburton neither disgraced nor adorned the judicial office. Removed from direct contact with parliament, the fires of radicalism in him died, and in his old age he condemned the very causes which as a young man he had supported so eloquently.

Haliburton had visited England several times, and decided in 1856 to settle there permanently. From 1859 to 1865, the year of his death, he was

Tory M.P. for Launceston and opposed in the British parliament both the "little England" policy of William Gladstone and the aspirations of the British North American colonies for greater independence.

A complete hedonist, Haliburton was the uxorious husband of two wives, and a connoisseur of good drink, good food, good conversation, pretty women, and fast horses. His bluff heartiness, however, concealed a cold eye to personal profit in any friendship. Like the eighteenth-century country squires he resembled, he saw little but absurdity in any religion that went beyond Sunday attendance at the Anglican church, and like Joseph Howe he was completely out of sympathy with the emotional glories and sectarian disputes that characterized the religious life of contemporary Nova Scotia. Haliburton had little faith in abstract pretensions to virtue and enjoyed exposing the wolf of self-interest that lurked behind the sheep's clothing of idealism in private and public life. As free from prudishness as Smollett, he had an indecorous sense of humour which he indulged in conversation and sometimes allowed to creep into his writing.

Although successful in his private life, Haliburton in his later work developed a vein of melancholy that cannot be entirely accounted for by the inroads that he made upon his constitution. It stemmed paradoxically from a frustrated idealism. Although cynical of the ideals of other men, Haliburton himself was tied emotionally to a cause that was doomed. Haliburton believed passionately in the Toryism of Edmund Burke, and it was his misfortune to live through its decay in both Britain and America—partly from the onslaught of Liberal opportunists but mainly because of an inner loss of conviction on the part of the Tories themselves. Haliburton mistrusted Sir Robert Peel. He found the word "Conservative" merely the word "Liberal" writ large, and he hated it accordingly. He saw himself become an anachronism in a world where even gentlemen preferred *laissez-faire* to *noblesse oblige*; his despair only made him become more stubborn and extreme in the statement of his views. There runs throughout Haliburton's career a supreme irony; men read him for his humour and disregarded what to him was the *raison d'être* of everything he ever wrote.

Haliburton began his writing to make Nova Scotians and the rest of the world aware of the heritage and resources of the colony. He partly accomplished his purpose with the publication of *A General Description of Nova Scotia* (1823) and *An Historical and Statistical Account of Nova Scotia* (1829). Both books are praiseworthy pioneering ventures, well proportioned in arrangement and dignified and straightforward in style, and they represent a vast amount of individual research. They brought Haliburton only a local reputation, although *An Historical and Statistical Account* was, many years later, to provide the theme for Longfellow's poem *Evangeline*. It was *The Clockmaker; or, The Sayings and Doings of Samuel Slick, of*

Slickville, which began serially in the *Novascotian* in 1835 and was published in book form in three series (Halifax, 1836; London, 1838, 1840), that launched Haliburton upon his literary career.

The circumstances behind the writing of *The Clockmaker* are as follows. During Haliburton's years as a member of the Legislative Assembly, he had belonged to the Literary Club of Halifax and there had become a friend of Joseph Howe, then editor of the *Novascotian* and only just beginning his political career. Howe's local pride led him to publish Haliburton's *An Historical and Statistical Account of Nova Scotia* at a loss. Howe also, taking an example from the popularity of the *Letters of Mephibosheth Stepsure,* had ridden the length and breadth of Nova Scotia on horseback, examining the state of the colony and its people and reporting his findings to his own newspaper. A common love of Nova Scotia and a common concern over its lack of prosperity united Howe and Haliburton. One of the results of this concern was the publication of *The Clockmaker* in Howe's paper despite the difference in political opinions which had by 1834 begun to cloud the relations between the two friends.

As early as 1776, Hector St. Jean de Crèvecœur had commented in *Letters of an American Farmer* on the undue reliance of Nova Scotians upon government patronage rather than upon their own industry. Throughout the period of the Loyalist emigration and the Napoleonic Wars, this attitude in Nova Scotia had deepened into a set way of life. With the close of twenty years of speculative prosperity, Nova Scotia found herself in 1815 without capital or markets and with a population which had acquired habits ill suited to a life of meagre income and sober farming. The economic distress of the 1820's culminated in political agitation. Haliburton saw the Reform movement as a cloak for the ambitions of those who wished to supplant the present office-holders in their revenues. The salvation of Nova Scotia could only come, he felt, through a marked change in the habits of its people. He would have them emulate the thrift, hard work, and ingenuity of their Yankee neighbours, and his principal reason for writing *The Clockmaker* was to persuade them to do so. Although Howe disapproved of Haliburton's politics, he was sufficiently in accord with the main purpose of the book to give it his enthusiastic support.

Haliburton was particularly well qualified to comment upon Nova Scotia. He had spent seven years in doing research for *An Historical and Statistical Account.* As a judge on circuit, he observed large areas of the colony and became thoroughly acquainted with the conditions and the people of the county towns. All that remained was to determine the form into which his knowledge and observation were to be poured. That the appeal would be humorous was certain. Haliburton's most effective weapon in the Legislative Assembly had been ridicule, and he had noted the sensation caused a decade before by the *Letters of Mephibosheth Stepsure* and the even greater sensation being produced currently in New England by Seba Smith's *Life and Writings of Major Jack Downing, of Downingsville, Away Down East, in the State of Maine* (1833).

Haliburton borrowed from McCulloch the device—really as old as the Greeks and the Romans—of coining names suggestive of character; from Seba Smith he borrowed that of using vernacular speech and of exploiting the eccentricities of Yankee character. In *The Clockmaker,* however, he surpassed both McCulloch and Smith in imaginative conception and execution.

The Clockmaker, like a picaresque novel, is episodic. The narrator, a thinly disguised Haliburton, and Sam Slick, a Yankee clockmaker, travel about Nova Scotia, and their seemingly chance encounters and observations provide the material for anecdote and conversation. There is no development of plot within the work as a whole, but each chapter is unified in that its incidents and comments exemplify a theme. Each chapter is a lay sermon illustrated by pointed anecdote and often culminating in a homely but original and apt epigrammatic text. With no rising curve of suspense to attract and hold attention, *The Clockmaker* has nevertheless gone through at least seventy editions since the first was published in 1836, and has appeared in the United States, in England, and on the Continent. It has done so as a result of its author's brilliant use of characterization, anecdote, language, and point of view.

Only one of the characters in *The Clockmaker* really counts. The Squire and Mr. Hopewell are either foils to Sam Slick or pegs on which to hang Tory arguments, and the characters met intermittently are types who can usually be summed up in a surname. Human interest is sustained in chapter after chapter of a very long narrative by the vanity, resourcefulness, and linguistic ability of that Yankee jack-of-all-trades, Sam Slick.

The character of Slick has been objected to on the grounds that his attitude and actions are not consistent throughout Haliburton's several works about him, that his speech reflects the dialects of many localities rather than one, that he is in fact paste rather than diamond, a stage character and not a credible human being. It is quite true that the Sam Slick of *The Clockmaker* is not the Sam Slick of *The Attaché; or, Sam Slick in England* (1843), intended for a different audience. In the latter book, the peaceful Yankee pedlar has become a thin-skinned, pugnacious braggadocio. Perhaps critics of the change have not sufficiently noticed that Americans abroad are not always the same as Americans at home. Both Sam Slicks are consistent within the limits of the books in which they appear. In point of fact, Sam Slick's versatility is an artistic reflection of the spirit of New England. The Yankees were the Greeks of the New World, and Slick is a folk hero, an Odysseus of their commercial frontier. In their excursions by land and sea, the Yankees not only acquired knowledge of men and affairs, but they also picked up their language where they found it, appropriating picturesque phrases much as they appropriated ideas that could later be turned into dollars and cents. In Haliburton's time, Slick was a credible New Englander; if he is a stage character today, he is one at least in the same brilliant sense as the characters of Molière and Dickens.

By his use of Sam Slick in *The Clockmaker*, Haliburton preserves a fine balance in assessing Americans, British, and Nova Scotian colonists. His judgments, like those of most great humorists, are essentially ambivalent. He admired the British for their institutions, achievements, and because he was of their stock. He disliked them because they refused to alter traditional ways of doing things and because they patronized colonists. He disliked the Americans because of their bragging, their opportunism, and because they had beaten the British. He admired their thrift, industry, shrewdness, and practicality. Haliburton saw in the Nova Scotians a people of essentially British virtues. They were, however, ruining themselves by extravagance and by sacrificing their private affairs to the pursuit of pleasure, politics, and religion. Sam Slick serves both as an unconscious example of American crudity and as a model to demonstrate to Nova Scotians how they should employ themselves. His praise of Britain is usually confined to secondhand accounts of the opinions of his clergyman and is often qualified by his own disagreement. Out of Sam Slick's comment and action in *The Clockmaker* emerges an ideal Nova Scotian life founded upon Burkean principles and unified by practicality and common sense. The satire becomes universal because individual and local personalities are kept subordinate to the central theme.

Whether of character, situation, or language, the humour in *The Clockmaker* depends upon the reader's enjoyment of the exposure of human weakness or incongruity. Although often coarse, it is not savage or cruel. Despite its theme, *The Clockmaker* is an essentially happy book. At this stage in his life, Haliburton was secure in his enjoyment of life and in his faith that his gospel for Nova Scotia would ultimately prevail.

Haliburton united two incongruous elements in the style of *The Clockmaker*. The narrative parts are written in the formal English of eighteenth-century prose. In Sam Slick's conversations, Haliburton becomes a prose poet, daring in metaphor, building up adjectival climaxes without fear of barbarisms, and utilizing all the local resources of dialect. The use of dialect did for Haliburton what the use of lowland Scots did for Burns. It gave him his crowning touch of individuality and lifted him above the ruck of popular writers like Theodore Hook and Charles Lever whose works superficially resemble his own.

The Clockmaker was Haliburton's most popular book. He followed it in

1843 with *The Attaché; or, Sam Slick in England,* which contained much hard-hitting criticism of English society. Haliburton's British audience proved much less disposed to laugh at themselves than they had been to laugh at Nova Scotian colonists and Yankees. Less popular still, but deservedly so, were the final Sam Slick books: *Sam Slick's Wise Saws and Modern Instances; or, What He Said, Did, or Invented* (1853) and *Nature and Human Nature* (1855).

All four books keep the same structure and for their interest depend upon Sam Slick, the freshness of their anecdotes, and the justice of the viewpoint displayed in them. Few readers can absorb more than sixteen hundred pages of almost continuous monologue by one character without becoming weary of his mannerisms. Few writers can fill up as many pages with humorous anecdote and remain fresh and funny. Haliburton told his best stories first, and after *The Attaché* there is a considerable decline in the quality of the anecdotes presented. Still worse, Haliburton gradually lost the perspective necessary to the humorist. In *The Clockmaker,* he could allow himself to be worsted by Sam Slick and laugh. In less than ten years, his consciousness that his political ideals were doomed prevented Haliburton from further self-laughter. The more strongly the forces of history turned against Toryism, the more extreme became his satire in its favour until the effect of his humour was vitiated by partisan distortion. *The Attaché,* good as it is, is marred by extreme statement. Worst of all, in the last two Sam Slick books, Haliburton shows signs of exchanging the role of social critic for that feeblest of vaudeville roles—the mere teller of funny stories.

Although the Sam Slick books made Haliburton's reputation, they do not comprise all his fiction. Two books in which the professional humorist triumphs over the deeper satirist of human society are *The Letter-Bag of the Great Western; or, Life in a Steamer* (1840) and *The Season Ticket* (1860), the latter published after his move to England.

The first of these reminds one of Smollett's *Humphrey Clinker* and Galt's *The Ayrshire Legatees.* It is a collection of letters purporting to have been written by passengers aboard the *Great Western* en route from Liverpool to Halifax. Haliburton's avowed purpose was to popularize steam travel between England and Nova Scotia, but he completely fails to bring his imagination to this task, so that *The Letter-Bag* throughout remains as crude propaganda. He spends his ingenuity instead on rather juvenile "high jinks" and on burlesquing the national and religious mannerisms which Anglo-Saxons of a certain type automatically assign to "foreigners." Although it contains some fine comic passages, *The Letter-Bag* is too extreme in its caricature and too gross in its humour to rank very high as literature.

Railway travel in the British Isles is the matter of *The Season Ticket.* Here the subject is treated with more understanding and depth and is enlarged to include the whole subject of transportation within the British Empire. Haliburton saw improved transportation as vital to the unification and development of the Empire and advocated, among other projects of a far-seeing nature, the building by the British government of a railway to link the isolated British North American colonies. *The Season Ticket* is by far a more considerable book than *The Letter-Bag*. At the same time, neither incidents nor characters are so lively and entertaining as those of the Sam Slick books.

The Old Judge (1849) is Haliburton's valedictory to a Nova Scotia he failed to convert to his own way of thinking. Sombre, realistic, balanced in its judgments, it is the most satisfying of all Haliburton's books although it lacks the surface brilliance of *The Clockmaker*. It is constructed upon a pattern similar to that of *The Clockmaker* but more diversified. Nova Scotia is seen through the eyes of an educated British tourist who visits his friend, the Old Judge, and is squired around Nova Scotia by another friend, Lawyer Barclay. The tourist's observations and encounters are supplemented by the observations and reminiscences of his friends and the other characters who are incidentally introduced. The most interesting of these last is Stephen Richardson, a Nova Scotian eccentric. In the sketches of men and women, in the account of melodramatic events at lonely frontier outposts, and in his background descriptions, Haliburton unveils in *The Old Judge* an unsuspected facet of romantic feeling and talents of a high order for serious fiction. Had he considered it worthwhile, he might have become Canada's first major novelist.

Although *The Old Judge* is not lacking in the political bias and humour that characterized Haliburton's work, it is a sad book—full of regret for a way of life that was passing and masking its bitterness with ironic dignity. In its range, it is easily the best portrait of early nineteenth-century life in British North America; in human insight and interest, it is matched only by Susanna Moodie's *Roughing It in the Bush*.

Haliburton did not confine himself to fiction. He was a vigorous historian and writer of political tracts, publishing in addition to the works mentioned earlier, *The Bubbles of Canada* (1839), *A Reply to the Report of the Earl of Durham* (1839), *Rule and Misrule of the English in America* (1851), *An Address on the Present Condition, Resources and Prospects of British North America* (1857), and *Speech of the Hon. Mr. Justice Haliburton, M.P., in the House of Commons, on Tuesday, the 21st of April, 1860 on the Repeal of the Differential Duties on Foreign and Colonial Wood* (1860). *Rule and Misrule of the English in America* is a good thesis history; none of the other publications mentioned above are of more than specialist interest.

Haliburton is also important as an anthologist of American humour. He collected unusual stories and articles from United States newspapers, journals, and books, and published the results of his work in two books, *Traits of American Humour by Native Authors* (1852) and *The Americans at Home; or, Byeways, Backwoods, and Prairies* (1854). The prestige of his name made them popular in Great Britain and enabled many readers to sample for the first time a wide variety of New World writing. For these pioneer anthologies as well as for his own writing, Haliburton deserves the title given him by Artemus Ward, "the father of American humour." His labours prepared a reading public for the work of Mark Twain and Stephen Leacock.

Much of Haliburton's work is dated. Many of his favourite mannerisms, like the pun, have gone out of style. The smart Yankee is no longer a novelty to readers. There are, however, in his best work enough humour and wise comment of a universal nature to make it worth reading today. Haliburton must continue to vie with Stephen Leacock as Canada's greatest humorist.

In his own time, there was no question of Haliburton's greatness. For a decade he rivalled Dickens in popularity, and he was the first colonial to be honoured by Oxford University (1858) for literary merit. It is typical of colonial diffidence that Haliburton's work was thought of much more highly in both Great Britain and the United States than it was in his own province of Nova Scotia.

7. Literary Activity in the Maritime Provinces

1815 - 1880

FRED COGSWELL

I. GENERAL INTRODUCTION

WRITING IN THE MARITIMES between 1815 and 1880 is more significant when considered as history or sociology than it is when considered as literature. Literature, like a tree, is an organic growth and dependent for its size and configuration upon soil and climate. Both environment and cultural heritage were powerful limiting factors in the shaping of Maritime literature.

The environment was that of a few cities and many towns, strategically located with respect to transport; each was surrounded by a slowly growing hinterland of clearings where were provided the sinews of their economic life: lumber, farm produce, fish, and a few minerals. Each city or town was dominated by one or two leading families, but within its economic and social structure, it was amazingly diversified. Craftsmen and local industries supplied the homely demands of the rural areas and the luxury demands of the town magnates. There was a pride in craftsmanship and a self-sufficiency which remain in the Maritimes as attitudes although the social patterns which supported them have for the most part passed away.

The effect of the population distribution for literature was to hold down the numbers of those who would normally be expected to respond to or create it, and to restrict them to the members of a particular class. Pioneer conditions circumscribe life within a struggle for material possessions, and most Maritimers spent the nineteenth century in the shadow of the frontier. With few exceptions, education outside of the towns was limited or non-existent, and the literacy of the rural population was of a functional kind. Outside written literature, a vigorous oral tradition of folk literature in English, French, and Gaelic and the hymns of the various churches gave some spice to leisure hours and neighbourhood gatherings.

In the cities and towns most inhabitants—whether professional men or artisans—were more literate. Education was higher in calibre and more readily available. Publishing facilities existed, for the presses of local newspapers were always glad to print tracts and books of verse at their authors' expense. Both Halifax and Saint John made contacts, by means of public lectures and the drama, with the more sophisticated centres of the United States and Great Britain. Nevertheless, most inhabitants—whether professional men or artisans—spent their time in making money. The uncertainty of an economy where demand and price were fixed by fluctuating foreign parliaments and markets made constant attention to the acquiring of capital essential. This meant that only a very small segment of the population had the education, the interest, and the leisure to write. Literature was almost exclusively the property of lawyers, schoolteachers, clergymen, journalists, and their wives and daughters.

This narrow base for the creation and support of literature explains the almost complete absence of dramatic compositions, the scarcity of *belles-lettres*, and the paucity of Maritime prose in general. Other factors, however, must explain the great volume of poetry published by Maritime writers throughout the nineteenth century. For example, at least 108 books of verse were published between 1825 and 1880 in the Maritimes, and 32 books were published elsewhere by Maritime authors. Practically every newspaper had its poetry corner, containing verse little inferior to that currently being published in book form.

To understand the predominance of verse over prose, one must grasp the nature of the Loyalists in their hopes and in their failure. For good or evil, their spirit dominated the cultural life of the Maritimes throughout the century.

The Loyalists desired a stable, pyramidal society. At the top was to be a gentry—officials, great merchants, estate owners, professional men. Supporting the gentry and guided by it were to be, subtly graded, various smaller merchants, artisans, small farmers, tenants, and servants. Every man was to know his place, but there was to be a place for every man. All were to be united emotionally by the twin symbols, the Church and the Crown. Because they had been unwilling to see the spirit of the frontier supplant the spirit of eighteenth-century England, the Loyalists had fled to an even wilder frontier—and found themselves trapped in it.

When the expenses of the French wars forced England to abandon the subsidies which alone would have made aristocracy possible in the Maritimes, most Loyalist families sank into conditions of extreme poverty, and their children reverted to the materialism and illiteracy of the frontier. A few favoured families stood firm by monopolizing the civil appointments in the colonies. But all, whether they had means and education to support their pretensions or not, clung to their traditions. Among continuing values was an admiration—often without understanding—of poetry as a prestige symbol. Prose was common, but only the well-born and the well-educated, as their ancestors had been, could properly appreciate poetry. Unfortunately, the most valued quality of a poetry so conceived and appreciated was apt to be its decoration, conventionally moral and derivative of the fashions in the motherland.

A second prestige symbol among Loyalist families was a classical education. They could not afford much, but as soon as they could, the Loyalists founded academies and small colleges in various centres throughout the Maritimes. Here the élite were to acquire the rudiments of Greek, Latin, rhetoric, and the English classics. A few of them even carried on the habit of translation after their schooldays were done. For example, William Blowers Bliss (1795–1874) issued *Translations from Catullus, Horace, etc.*, from a Halifax press in 1872. The same year, Silas Tertius Rand (1810–1889) published several Baptist hymns turned into Latin verse among the miscellaneous poems of *The Dying Indian's Dream*. So strong was the respect for classical literature in the Maritimes that even Moses Hardy Nickerson, a self-educated radical, fills up several pages of *Carols of the Coast* (1892) with translations from the Latin. Other poets who did not translate directly used the Latin and Greek classics as models for their verse.

This non-utilitarian respect for education and this careful following of models kept Maritime writers from the barbarisms perpetrated by many frontiersmen elsewhere. At the same time, they inculcated the principle of imitation at the expense of originality, leading writers to rely too greatly upon forms of literature designed to meet conditions other than their own.

Cultural borrowing is particularly dangerous when the cultures concerned are disparate. Such Maritime poets as Peter Fisher, Oliver Goldsmith, James Hogg, Joseph Howe, William Martin Leggett, and David Palmer adopted the forms of a poetry already out of date in England. These were the heroic couplet, the public song, and Miltonic blank verse. Of these only the public song—a minor genre at best—proved transplantable. The heroic couplet, designed to express the sensibilities of an urban élite and demanding a professional polish, came off badly when applied to the frontier by amateur poets. Miltonic blank verse had become by the early nineteenth century imitative and mediocre in its own land.

The successors of this generation of Maritime poets borrowed from the great English romantics. Romantic forms and techniques had been developed to resolve the tensions of a complex society going through its time of troubles. Maritime poets fitted them to platitudinous and decorative verse on general themes to satisfy a society whose concepts were narrow and homogeneous.

One cannot help feeling that the emotional drive behind most Maritime poets was neither self nor social realization; it was rather a pathetic attempt to prove that the colonies, although separate in space from the motherland, were still indivisibly one with British culture. Local pride that verse was being written at all led to enthusiastic reviews in the local newspapers. Poets had no incentive to self-examination and improvement, and theme and occasion became the all too sufficient guides for the judgment of poetry.

Professionalism was necessarily absent through the greater part of the century. Prose writers wrote when they felt that they had something useful to say, and poets wrote as a genteel hobby. Not until the late 1860's did two writers, James De Mille and May Agnes Fleming, sit down cold-bloodedly to write for money. Seldom has any literature been so exclusively the province of the amateur.

The great defect of the amateur is that only incidentally is he concerned with form. A classical education had taught both Thomas McCulloch and Thomas Chandler Haliburton how to construct good sentences and proper paragraphs; their greatest defects lie in the larger formal aspects of their work. The form of literature which suffered most from the amateurism of its perpetrators was the novel which, before De Mille, was consistently feeble, wooden, and amateurish.

Most Maritime poets had received a classical education, and contemporary verse forms were straightforward and metrical. These factors kept their work from becoming doggerel, but the blight of amateurism was conspicuously present. A genuine poet achieves the unique expression of his personality through form—a way of putting words together which is the product of intense search and concentration. Maritime poets were too easily satisfied; the result is a sameness of expression which, when joined to a sameness of attitude and theme, makes essentially flavourless verse.

Maritime poets were further limited by the relatively restricted and homogeneous society in which they lived. They wrote in straightforward sentences and did not strain for the unusual phrase or image because their thought was limited. Their world was one of moral and aesthetic blacks and whites. What is most characteristic of their work is that each writer was absolutely certain as to the truth of what he was stating. Such certainty produces rhetoric rather than poetry, and rhetoric is more susceptible than genuine poetry to changes of fashion and taste. When one is certain of truth, one does not torture one's imagination to find fresh ways to express it—the readiest and least ambiguous are the best. The final effect upon the reader of Maritime poetry is one of impersonality—the dominance of a convention beyond which the poets never ventured. Too many poems might quite as easily have been written by other Maritime poets as by their authors.

It is not surprising, therefore, that Maritime poets achieved their best work in light and occasional verse. James De Mille's "Sweet Maiden of Passamaquoddy" springs readily to mind, as do John Hunter-Duvar's "The Emigration of the Fairies" and Richard Huntingdon's "The Memory of the

Red Man." By far the most attractive works of Joseph Howe, Moses Hardy Nickerson, Matthew Richey Knight, and James Arminius Richey are their occasional poems and epigrams.

No society is altogether homogeneous, of course. The most significant writing in the Maritimes sprang from an attempt by Maritime writers to resolve basic conflicts which over a period of years appeared in their society. These tensions are three in number.

The first in time was the conflict between orderly habits of life acquired in Britain and the British colonies in America and the shiftless, gambling economy imposed on the emigrants by their new environment. This tension found its fullest expression in prose in the *Letters of Mephibosheth Stepsure* by Thomas McCulloch, published in the *Acadian Recorder* in 1821 and 1822, in poetry in *The Lay of the Wilderness* (1833) by "A Native of New Brunswick" (Peter Fisher). In their zeal to persuade readers to industry and a more strict application to farming, McCulloch and Fisher gave realistic, if exaggerated, pictures of living conditions in New Brunswick and Nova Scotia.

A similar concern for industry and order in business and agriculture informs the social surveys published in the *Novascotian* newspaper in the 1820's and 1830's by Joseph Howe and *The Clockmaker* (1833) and other writings of Thomas Chandler Haliburton. In the work of Howe and Haliburton, however, the conflict between old ways and new merges with the political struggle for responsible government which from 1830 to 1840 adds a note of one-sided realism to a good deal of Maritime prose. The political polemic of the Maritimes makes intelligent use of the ideological bases provided by British thinkers, but only Haliburton, who saw a naked struggle for power underlying political ideologies, was able to create from this source of tension a literature of lasting value.

The third tension—that between Christianity and the crude hedonism of the frontier—was resolved by a puritanism as extreme as the excesses against which it recoiled. Unfortunately for literature, this puritanism became imbedded in the intellectual life of the Maritimes. The Baptist church, founded by the poet Henry Alline, succeeded in capturing a segment of Halifax intellectuals headed by Edmund Crawley. From the founding of Horton Academy (later Acadia College) in 1828, this religion acquired and maintained a position of leadership in the Maritimes that its sectarian rivals could not ignore. The strongest manifestation of puritanism by mid-century was the rise of the temperance movement which soon expanded to become interdenominational in scope.

The result of attempts to express temperance polemics in literary forms devised by the Romantics and Victorians was incongruity, bathos, and sentimentality. Alexander Kent Archibald's adaptation of the technique of

Byron's *Don Juan* to support the temperance movement in *Poems* (1848) is an excellent example of incongruity. S. C. Fulton's *Red Tarn, or the Vision of the Lake; a Thrilling Temperance Poem in Fourteen Cantos* (1873), in its opening vision of a lake of the alcoholically damned, achieves a turgid grandeur, but it too soon sinks to bathos and puerile rhetoric. The following from *Vesper Chimes* (1872) by Phebe Mills deserves quotation as a sample of the sentimentality that pervades a host of poems on the temperance movement:

> . . . Alas for all her glowing dreams,
> Her new-found joys where are they now?
> Upon her cheek shame's hectic gleams,
> A hot flush mantles o'er her brow.
> What is it rends her feelings so?
> What is it wounds her woman's pride?
> Ah, she has learned the truth to know,
> She is a moderate drinker's bride.

The direct impact of puritanism produced hundreds of prose tracts and several novels, of which the *William and Melville* (1826) of Thomas Mc-Culloch is the most distinguished. All are too extreme in their view of reality and too crude in their form to have more than a functional value.

Not a tension within the society of the Maritimes but an alternate source of culture was the presence of a large Scottish element. The Scottish community delighted in the nostalgic sentiment, the pungent satire, and the radical independence of Robert Burns, and many of its members tried to transfer these qualities to the poetry of their own localities. The result was a body of lowland Scots verse surpassing in realism and pith the achievement of those who clung to the more genteel Victorian colonial tradition.

All these factors were not sufficient in themselves to establish a realistic tradition in Maritime literature. On any frontier, men and women are tempted to use their leisure to escape from what they feel to be harsh and confining conditions; on a frontier in which the community gives its emotional allegiance to another land and another mode of living, they are tempted irresistibly. The first novel and the first book of verse published by native-born writers in the Maritimes demonstrate this truth. Julia Catherine Beckwith made the sub-title of her romance, *St. Ursula's Convent, or the Nun of Canada; Containing Scenes from Real Life* (1824) a misnomer. The book contains merely the day-dreams of a schoolgirl who had read too many British romances. Oliver Goldsmith's *The Rising Village* (1825) describes the pioneer homes of Nova Scotia as if they really were the neat English cottages which the author would have liked them to be. Reading and writing in the Maritimes during the nineteenth century were diversions—the vicarious fulfilments of frustrated hopes.

Apart from a few political pamphlets, the literary impact of Confederation upon the Maritimes was slight. The union ran counter to the spirit of local independence which had been slowly developing throughout the century; it also opposed the spirit of colonialism which was the Maritimer's principal cultural heritage. Confederation was adopted enthusiastically only by those financiers and politicians who had engineered it, and the thirteen years between 1867 and 1880 did not allow more than the tentative growth of a national consciousness. Symptoms, however, of the Canadian nationalism which was later to burgeon in the work of Roberts and others occur here and there in Maritime poetry. Examples are Robert Murray's hymn "From Ocean unto Ocean," V. H. Nelson's "My Own Canadian Home," and Frederick Augustus Dixon's pageant-play, *A Masque, Entitled "Canada's Welcome."*

As has been shown, men and women in the Maritimes did not always write for the right reasons. The society in which they lived and the models that they chose tended to produce at best a respectable mediocrity. Yet their very limitations gave to their work certain positive advantages.

The tone of life in the Maritimes was healthy, optimistic, and remarkably free from cynicism, pessimism, and sensationalism, and the literature reflects the spirit of a people still capable of responding with human warmth to ideal virtues and simple situations—a people whose lives were centred in the home, the occupation, and the church, and who did not require violence to stimulate their appetites. The Maritime writer never questioned that life, love, beauty were enduring gifts of God and that their opposites would be overcome by time and struggle. If the expression of his beliefs was often banal, his sincerity deserves respect.

The very deference which the educated gave to British literature ensured that they read it avidly. There was relatively little cultural lag on this section of the American frontier. Moses Hardy Nickerson sprang to the defence of Lord Byron at the time of the posthumous invasion of that poet's privacy by Harriet Beecher Stowe. A. D. McNeill's "Evolution" is a long poem in very good "In Memoriam" metre in defence of Darwin. In *Poems of Ten Years, 1877–1887*, Matthew Richey Knight, Methodist minister at Boiestown, New Brunswick, defends the British journalist W. T. Stead against clerical attack at the time of his exposure of the "White Slave" traffic in England. In fact, Maritime writers throughout the century dealt with the latest political and intellectual events in Britain with a liberality greater than that which they normally applied to their own *milieu*.

The general respect given to literature in the Maritimes encouraged young men and women to read and to create it. It was only a question of time before writers of genius would transcend, in part at least, the limitations of Maritime environment and cultural heritage. One such writer, as already noted, did emerge in Thomas Chandler Haliburton, whose prose sketches were recognized in Great Britain and the United States as comparable with those created by men of their own nationality. The poets had to wait longer, but the premature death in Fredericton of Peter John Allan was compensated by the development of Roberts and Carman in the 1880's. Throughout the nineteenth century, the Maritime Provinces were the seed-bed where a national poetry might arise if it were to arise at all.

II. THE NOVEL IN THE MARITIMES

No pioneer community has ever produced a major novelist or a major novel. Perhaps the most sophisticated of all literary forms, the novel has been a late-flowering expression of every culture in which it has appeared. It demands a maximum of self-awareness, a differentiated social structure, a demanding and discriminating audience, and a professional attention to technique. The Maritime Provinces lacked these conditions. In fact, many Maritimers as puritans regarded the novel as anathema. The few novels produced were the work of amateurs, and not until after 1810 did professional novelists emerge.

Maritime nineteenth-century works of fiction may be classified into two schools. The first comprises those novels which were written to popularize moralistic doctrines. To this group belong the *William and Melville* of Thomas McCulloch, the work in Halifax of the Herbert sisters, and that in New Brunswick of Sarah French, the pioneer writer of juvenile literature. The titles of the works provide a good indication of their contents. Sarah Herbert (1824–1844) wrote *Agnes Mailard: A Temperance Tale*. Mary Herbert (fl. 1859–1865) produced three novels: *Scenes in the Life of a Halifax Belle* (1859), *Woman as She Should Be; or, Agnes Wiltshire* (1861), and *Young Man's Choice* (1869). Sarah French published *Letters to a Young Lady on Leaving School and Entering the World* (1855) and *A Book for the Young* (1856).

These writers deserve respect for sincerity of intention, and they provide genuine insights into contemporary social conditions. Unfortunately, in their moral and religious zeal they allow their opinions concerning what ought to be to triumph over what in all likelihood would occur were the events of their novels to be transferred to real life. As a result, their plots appear contrived and unnatural. The characters are drawn in too unrelieved whites and blacks to be convincing, and moral earnestness is never leavened by humour.

The second, and far more numerous, group of writers of fiction produced either historical or society novels, more amateurish in technique but as escapist in content as the popular British fiction then being published by Bentley or Colburn.

Julia Catherine (Beckwith) Hart (1796–1867) wrote *St. Ursula's Convent;*

or, The Nun of Canada (1824). This book's sole claim to attention is that it was the first work of fiction to be written by a native-born English-speaking Canadian and the first to be published in what is now Canada. Mrs. Hart, who was Julia Beckwith when she wrote it, was a schoolgirl in Fredericton. She had read about the world of fashionable society in Paris and London, and she had a lively imagination. The best that can be said for her work is that it is no worse than that done by such novelists as Lady Blessington, who certainly had far better opportunities to know and do better. While living in the United States, Mrs. Hart produced a second novel, *Tonnewonte; or, The Adopted Son of America* (1831), slightly better than the first. A third novel exists in manuscript.

Two Saint John writers, John K. Laskey and Douglas S. Huyghue, may be mentioned briefly. Laskey's *Alathea; or, The Roman Exile* (1840) and Huyghue's two novels, *Argimou, a Legend of the Micmac* (1847) and *Nomads of the West; or, Ellen Clayton* (1850), are stereotyped in character, rhetorical in style, and melodramatic in plot.

Agatha Armour (d. 1891) of Fredericton wrote four novels under the direct influence of *East Lynne*. These are *Marion Wilburn* (n.d.), *Sylvia Leigh; or, The Heiress of Glenmarle* (1880), *Lady Rosamond's Secret* (1880), and *Marguerite Verne; or, Scenes from Canadian Life* (1886). *Lady Rosamond's Secret* is of interest to local historians as it contains sketches of Fredericton society during the governorship of Sir Howard Douglas.

Thomas Barlow Smith (1839–1933), a crotchety Nova Scotian seaman, wrote novels after his retirement. Experiences drawn from his own life and travels form vivid but incongruous patches against the romantic façade of *The Young Lion of the Woods; or, A Story of Early Colonial Days* (1889); *Rose Carney, a Story of Ever Shifting Scenes on Land and Sea* (1890); and *Seraph on the Sea; or, The Career of a Highland Drummer Boy* (1891).

Two books deserve mention as exceptions to the moralistic and melodramatic trends in amateur fiction in the Maritimes. The first of these is *The Mysterious Stranger*, published in London in 1817 and afterwards pirated several times in the United States. The book was actually designed as biography rather than as fiction, and it presents an illusion of reality much more vividly than any of the works mentioned above. *The Mysterious Stranger* was written by Walter Bates (1780–1842), Loyalist sheriff of Kings County, New Brunswick, a man with little interest in literature. So amazing, however, were the exploits of Henry More Smith as confidence man, jail-breaker, and horse-thief, that Bates took pen in hand to write his story. Its subject, the simplicity of its style, and the seeming truth of its background make *The Mysterious Stranger* still a readable book. One feels that it achieves its modest success because its author was not sufficiently acquainted with popular British fiction to spoil it by imitation.

The second work in prose fiction produced in the Maritimes before 1880 that contains touches of local realism was the anonymous *Miramichi*, published in Boston in 1863. Despite flaws in plotting, characterization, and style, the book does give some indication of what it was like to be living in New Brunswick during the middle years of the nineteenth century.

All the works discussed above were by amateurs, none of whom produced more than three novels in a lifetime. The term novelist, during the first eighty years of the nineteenth century, can only be applied to two writers in the Maritimes who gave to the novel something of the care and attention which it deserved and who largely depended upon it for their incomes.

The more financially successful of the two was May Agnes Fleming (née Early), a Saint John housewife (1840–1880). During the depression of the 1870's, she earned from the Street & Smith Company of New York as much as $10,000 a year. Mrs. Fleming received this princely income for writing no less than forty-two novels—primarily designed for serial publication—within the space of seventeen years. Undoubtedly she was Canada's first spectacularly successful professional novelist. Fifteen of Mrs. Fleming's novels appeared in book form during her lifetime, and twenty-seven were published after her death, which should constitute some kind of record in posthumous publication.

Apart from facility, there is little remarkable in Mrs. Fleming's work. As professional in her technique as Mrs. Channing, her English counterpart, she introduced into the high-born English society of her novels characters from Canada and the United States, and she was very careful to construct the plot of each novel so that some of the action would occur in Canada. By so doing, she indicates that although her books were designed primarily for United States and British sales, she was mindful of the local pride of a Canadian audience.

Within a very minor convention, Mrs. Fleming's novels are exciting, readable, and remarkably even in quality. A few which may be mentioned as having been very popular in their own time are: *The Dark Secret; or, The Mystery of Fontelle Hall* (1875), *Guy Earlscourt's Wife* (1872), *Lost for a Woman* (1880), *Noreen's Revenge* (1875), *The Actress' Daughter* (1886), and *Estella's Husband; or, Thrice Lost, Thrice Won* (1891).

There is both greater variety and a waste of a very real talent in the work of James De Mille (1833–1880).

De Mille was born in Saint John, educated at Horton Academy, Acadia College, and Brown University (M.A. 1854). He had travelled widely in Europe as a young man before establishing himself as a bookseller in Saint

John. When his bookselling business failed, De Mille turned to teaching and held the posts of professor of Classics at Acadia College (1860–64) and professor of English at Dalhousie College (1864–80). De Mille was, in the opinion of those who knew him, a brilliant and ambitious scholar. He composed a good textbook upon rhetoric and a bad poetical exercise in it, "Behind the Veil," which was published posthumously in 1893. At the time of his death, De Mille was being considered for the chair of rhetoric at Harvard College.

De Mille was a man of extraordinary energy possessed of a wide range of interests. He left behind him a considerable reputation as a host and a teller of witty stories. As a means of supplementing his academic salary, he turned to fiction, and—mainly for the American firm of Harper Brothers—wrote thirty books in less than twenty years.

De Mille's fiction can be classified into five groups: the B.O.W.C. Series, the Dodge Club Series, popular melodramatic novels, historical romances, and the anomalous *A Strange Manuscript Found in a Copper Cylinder*.

Neither the melodramatic nor the historical novels deserve detailed consideration. *Cord and Creese* (1869) and *The Cryptogram* (1871) are representative examples of the first. In these works, lurid incidents and highly coloured characters are woven into plots of great complexity and considerable ingenuity at the expense of the reader's credibility. The stories, however, are related with an energy and verve that are worthy of greater subjects. Typical historical romances are *Helena's Household: A Tale of Rome in the First Century* (1867) and *The Lily and the Cross: A Tale of Acadia* (1874). In these, chunks of undigested history are crudely combined with the typical insipid love affairs of the cardboard heroes and heroines of romance.

The four books of the B.O.W.C. (Brethren of the White Cross) series are *The B.O.W.C.: A Book for Boys* (1869), *The Boys of Grand Pré School* (1870), *Picked up Adrift* (1872), *The Treasure of the Sea* (1873). In this series, books were written for the first time in Canada that appealed to the authentic interests of young people and were at the same time readable and free from overt didacticism. De Mille drew upon his experiences as a schoolboy at Horton Academy for the characters, the background, and many of the incidents, and his lively style and acute sense of humour must have made the B.O.W.C. series a joy for the young people of his time. The writing of books for young people has since become a literary art, and by comparison the B.O.W.C. series now seems dated. It was, however, a commendable pioneer enterprise.

The Dodge Club; or, Italy in 1859 (1869), which initiated the Young Dodge Club series, represents the merging of two influences, *Pickwick Papers* and Mark Twain's work. De Mille took the idea of his plot from Dickens, but it is Twain's humour that dominates the book. Based upon incident rather than upon character, the humour of De Mille is inferior to most of Haliburton's. Occasional passages occur, however, which indicate what De Mille might have done had he been less facile and more careful in his composition. For example, there are few scenes in Canadian literature more delightfully droll than that in which the American Senator and the Italian countess discuss the poetry of Isaac Watts.

De Mille wrote into *The Dodge Club* and its inferior successors experiences gained during his tour of Europe in 1850 and 1851. As a result, the book does convey an authentic picture of travelling conditions in mid-century France and Italy. The characters are stage types, designed not to interfere with the incidents upon which the author depends for the popularity of his work. The love interest is slight, but it is saved from sentimentality by the light-hearted, almost flippant, treatment which De Mille gives to the romantic passages. Much of *The Dodge Club* is in fact a clever parody upon the melodramatic novel in which De Mille was so proficient, and it is mainly for this reason that the book achieves a shallow and superficial success.

A Strange Manuscript Found in a Copper Cylinder was published posthumously. It is indebted to Rider Haggard and to Jules Verne. From Haggard, De Mille took the technical device of telling his story by means of a chance-recovered manuscript; from Verne, he borrowed the method of making the manuscript appear more credible by having an audience of its readers discuss its marvels in the light of contemporary linguistic, palaeontological, and racial theories. This pseudo-scientific commentary is interspersed with the action and is thus designed to make the book more suspenseful as well as more credible. Although ingenious, the commentary is often more boring than convincing and takes up a disproportionate number of pages. The characters are lacking in life. Few readers could become involved in the fate of the hero, Adam More; his sweetheart, Alma; and her rival, Layelah. Despite these flaws, *A Strange Manuscript Found in a Copper Cylinder* is De Mille's most original and powerful work and is by far the most interesting novel to be written in the Maritimes before 1880.

Its greatest virtue is De Mille's imaginative conception of the Kosekin, a society of kindly cannibals who revere darkness, poverty, and death. Few ideas are so pregnant with possibilities for satire. De Mille, unfortunately, does not quite make the most of this one. His ingenious reversal of the values of contemporary Western life enables him to show human nature as a constant, independent of ideology, and he exploits with telling irony man's tendency to reject the absolute in favour of conformity. Nevertheless, he sacrifices an idea that might have produced another *Gulliver's Travels* for the sake of an adventure story. *A Strange Manuscript* is a good adventure story despite the tedious comments upon the manuscript and despite the satirical diversions. De Mille's accounts of bizarre adventure and fantastic landscapes are models of vivid narration. The book fails to achieve greatness only because its author attempted in its composition to do too many things at once.

III. BELLES-LETTRES AND DRAMA IN THE MARITIMES

This section will appear to be disproportionately brief; however, one result of the sparseness and wide distribution of population in the Maritimes was the relative absence of a basis to support dramatic compositions and *belles-lettres*. It is true that Halifax, Saint John, and occasionally Chatham, were visited by many of the great dramatic companies which played in New York and Boston, but the repertoires of these professional companies had no room for the works of local dramatists. Many amateur theatrical productions took place in the towns of the Maritimes, but the local players, none too confident of their acting ability, invariably chose plays whose established popularity was a guarantee of at least a modicum of success. The puritan ethos of the Maritimes also did not encourage the writing of plays. In consequence, all the drama in the Maritimes which found its way into print was designed for reading rather than for acting.

Prose drama, even when not designed for stage production, was almost non-existent. A fragment of a prose play was published in the *New Brunswick Courier* of Saint John for February 23, 1833. This was a crude and vigorous attack upon Sir Archibald Campbell, the Lieutenant Governor, and various members of his government for their conduct in the distribution of Crown lands.

Verse dramatists were scarcely more prolific. All that deserve consideration are a fragmentary romantic play included in *The Poetical Remains* (1853) of Peter John Allan (see below); two closet dramas, *The Enamorado* (1879) and *De Roberval* (1888) by John Hunter-Duvar (1830–1899); and three plays by Frederick Augustus Dixon (1843–1912), the most considerable of which was the wooden *A Masque, Entitled "Canada's Welcome": Shown Before His Excellency the Marquis of Lorne and Her Royal Highness Princess Louise on Feb. 24th, 1879, at the Opera House. De Roberval* is by far the most ambitious of these plays and is the only one that deserves serious literary consideration.

John Hunter-Duvar, who will re-appear in the discussion of poetry below, was a student of Renaissance history and literature and a collector of rare books. Largely for his own amusement he composed closet dramas, of which two only were ever published. In *De Roberval* Duvar tried to present the picture of a strong man marred by pride, to parade his learning of the details of Renaissance life in Europe, and to pay a graceful tribute to Sir

John A. Macdonald, to whom the book in which the play appears is dedicated. Unable to combine these ingredients dramatically, Duvar forces them into his play at the expense of the action. The tedious clowning, imitative of the Elizabethans at their worst, furnishes a further brake upon the development of the plot, and Duvar's mingling of slang and poetic language leads often to bathos:

> Delightful! Write me down a pirate bold.
> Sang dieu! I'll be Rollo o'er again,
> And lay hands on another Normandy.

At the same time, *De Roberval* is one of the first attempts to incorporate into a major literary form the nascent Canadian nationalism, and here and there throughout its pages are scattered passages that in their apt use of language surpass any other blank verse produced in Canada before the twentieth century. No playwright need be ashamed of lines like the following:

> I saw a savage once from Africa;
> Black as a lump of charcoal, kettle black,
> But fat as any high Church dignitary,
> And greasy as a friar mendicant;
> Bohemians bought her for a kind of show,
> As a descendant of the Queen of Sheba. . . .

The scarcity and short life of literary magazines in the Maritimes during the nineteenth century prevented the development of any considerable tradition in *belles-lettres*. A small body of work of seriousness, integrity, and concern for style may be found in *Poems and Essays* (1874) by Joseph Howe (1804–1873), *Thistledown* (1875) by Alexander Rae Garvie (1839–1875), and *Stewart's Literary Magazine* (1867–1872), published in Saint John by George Stewart (1848–1906), a distinguished essayist and journalist and the only Canadian member of the International Literary Congress of Europe.

Maritime literary prose in the nineteenth century was Sunday writing in Sunday clothes. It consisted mainly of essays in which the results of the author's reading and meditation on general topics were gathered together and decorated with lofty language and suitable figures of speech. It is serious, manly, dignified, but at the same time impersonal and inflexible.

Joseph Howe was primarily a politician and orator and secondarily a poet. As these, he will be dealt with elsewhere in this volume. The prose of *Poems and Essays* must, however, be treated as *belles lettres*. It consists of a moral tale, "The Locksmith of Philadelphia," and the text of five lectures, "Shakespeare," "Eloquence," "The Moral Influence of Women," "The Howe Festival," and "The Adornment of Ottawa." Most of the lectures were given to various Mechanics Institutes and illustrate Howe's mastery of a highly allusive rhetorical style—a style in which reminiscences drawn from many literary sources are cleverly combined with personal opinion and experience. They do not talk down to their audience, and their successful reception does credit to the intelligence of the working man in the Maritimes during the nineteenth century. None of Howe's essays is a classic, but all are respectable productions and provide eloquent testimonies to his breadth of learning and intelligence.

The ten essays in Alexander Rae Garvie's *Thistledown* show a keen eye for the details of physical description and a genuine love of Maritime landscape. They also demonstrate by frequent allusion and quotation the breadth of Garvie's reading in the English and French classics. Without being distinguished for originality of thought and style, such essays as "About Plagiarism," "Skating," "A Reverie," and "About Titles" are surprisingly polished productions to issue from a rural manse in New Brunswick in the nineteenth century.

IV. POETRY IN THE MARITIMES

Oliver Goldsmith's *The Rising Village* (1825), to be discussed more fully below, established a vogue in the Maritimes for narrative poetry written in couplets, involving local history and legend, and combining some account of pioneer conditions with a good deal of moralizing about the joys of rural life. This pattern was perpetuated in Peter Fisher's *The Lay of the Wilderness* (1833), and Joseph Howe's "Acadia," also to be discussed below, and continued to be written as late as *Allan Gray and His Doubts* (1881) by "A Lover of the Truth." It produced no masterpieces, but the following representatives are interesting for the light that they throw upon what Maritime poets considered as significant material for literature.

Mrs. I. S. Prowse's *The Burning Forest: A Tale of New Brunswick* (1830) is a graphic description of the plight of human beings caught in a forest fire. William Charles McKinnon (d. 1862) published *The Battle of the Nile: A Poem in Four Cantos* (1844) as an exercise in youthful colonial patriotism. Cassie Fairbanks' *The Long House: A Poem, Partly Founded on Fact* (1859), written in octosyllabic couplets, is a melodramatic account of a local murder. All narrative writers did not, however, use couplets. The Reverend Joseph Clinch wrote his lengthy but dull biblical narrative, *The Captivity of Babylon* (1840), in Spenserian stanzas, and Charles Windsor Hall used blank verse to deal with the expulsion of the Acadians in *Legends of the Gulf* (1870).

Pierce Stevens Hamilton (1826–1893) constructed a more elaborate framework in which to house the tales of Acadian history and legend contained in *The Feast of Saint Anne and Other Poems* (1878). The device is Chaucerian: a picnic party attends a Micmac celebration of the Feast of Saint Anne and its members agree to relate in turn various stories from Nova Scotia's past. Although the stories, composed in ballad stanzas, are vigorous, the framework is clumsily handled and the blank verse in which the balance of the poem is composed is rhetorical and poor.

A more sophisticated pattern for narrative verse was employed briefly by Arthur Sladen in Saint John and by Alexander Kent Archibald (b. 1803) in Nova Scotia. In their most substantial work, both these men adapted the verse form and mannerisms of Lord Byron's *Don Juan* to local themes. "Midnight Rambles" and "Angela" in Archibald's *Poems* (1848) reproduce something of Byron's stanzaic brilliance but fail to preserve the difficult balance between digression and narrative that made his work a success. The two narratives of *The Conflagration* (1838) by Arthur Sladen (mis-spelled Slader on the title-page) suffer from the same defect.

Byron was a short-lived influence upon satire in the poetry of the Maritimes, but throughout the nineteenth century Maritime writers—whether or not they wrote in lowland Scots—drew inspiration from the verses and attitude of Robert Burns. The work of John LePage (d. 1895), *The Island Minstrel*, published in Charlottetown in two volumes, 1860 and 1867, and the many volumes of Andrew Shiels (1793–1879), the Cape Breton blacksmith, are not sufficiently polished in form and phrase to make worthwhile for a reader the detailed study of local and political issues necessary to give them point. William Murdoch (1823–1887), the hermit of Partridge Island, includes in his *Poems and Songs* (1860) many poems of point and polish, of which the following stanza is a good example:

> God pity, then, the poor blue-noses,
> Their cheeks like flour, their nebs like roses;
> They puff they grue, and swallow doses
>   To heat their wame,
> Till oft when night their business closes
>   They hiccup hame. . . .

Although they did not write in lowland Scots, two Nova Scotians, Moses Hardy Nickerson (1846–1943) and David Fleming Little (d. 1881), were satirists in the school of Burns. Nickerson's *Carols of the Coast* (1892) and *Songs of Summerland* (1927) and Little's *Poems* (1881) contain many local satires and epigrams of more than passing interest. Little's verse, sharpened by frustration in love and the shadow of impending death by tuberculosis, exhibits an independence of outlook combined with an intensity of feeling that is all too rare in the poetry of the Maritimes before 1880. One feels that Burns himself would have approved the spirit and execution of "Bunson's Belief," Little's most considerable poem.

Religious satire in verse was too extreme in its outlook to have value in literature. Two exceptions occur. Between 1857 and 1862 James Arminius

Richey published five volumes of scholarly verse which contain many manly and skilful satires constructed in defence of Anglicanism against its more extreme opponents. The anonymous *No Sect in Heaven,* published in Saint John in 1868, is a clever and refreshing attack upon sectarian bigotry in its more absurd manifestations.

By 1850, the lyric had become the dominant literary form in the Maritimes. As stated earlier, Maritime lyric poets were handicapped by the puritan ethos, the uniformity of society, the colonialism, the materialism, and the isolation of a thinly populated frontier. As a result, they initiated no tradition of their own but followed either the Victorian tradition of poetic decoration and moral edification or the lowland Scots tradition of which Burns's "The Cotter's Saturday Night" and "To Mary in Heaven" are exemplars. No Maritime lyricist developed a personal style, and the work of most is a pastiche derived from not necessarily congruous sources. Nevertheless, the work of even the meanest or the most orthodox of Maritime poets holds scattered glints of interest. For example, a Halifax phrenologist, John Salter, published *The Poetical Works of John Salter* (1852). This volume contains as contemptible doggerel as was ever printed, but in it are a few dialect sketches of Negro life in Halifax that are grossly authentic and linguistically exciting. Mrs. J. P. Grant's *Stray Leaves: A Collection of Poems* (1865) is the epitome of Victorian provincialism, but it too contains a few poems, notably "Snowshoing" and "Tobogging" (*sic*), which are unpretentious and exact descriptions of local customs and landscape.

It is difficult for the historian to point out landmarks where all the trees are of nearly the same height. Although certainly not more worthy than others of the name of poets, a few Maritime writers deserve mention for their greater literary knowledge and the higher degree of polish which they gave to their verses.

Amos Henry Chandler (b. 1837) was a New Brunswick physician who, in conjunction with Charles Pelham Mulvany, published *Lyrics, Songs, and Sonnets* (1880). Chandler's contributions show a marked influence of Shelley. His philosophic poems on nature display considerable power of phrase and control over intricate metrical form. They also make use of the Westmoreland landscape to a limited extent. Unfortunately, they lack the intensity of inner conviction required to save them from rhetoric.

Matthew Arnold and Thomas Carlyle are the principal influences upon the work of Matthew Richey Knight (b. 1854), of Boiestown, New Brunswick. Knight's *Poems of Ten Years, 1877–1887* (1887), contain a few good sonnets, several Landor-like epigrams, and a fragment, "Thomas Carlyle," happily conceived in the style and spirit of its subject.

The best of the sentimental followers of Burns were John Murdoch Harper (1845–1919), Robert Murdoch (b. 1836), and John Steele. In his own time, John McPherson (1817–1845) attracted the greatest degree of critical attention. This, however, was more because of his unhappy career as a self-educated farm labourer than because of his verses. *Poems, Descriptive and Moral* (1852), although competently executed, are disappointingly banal in subject, language, and sentiment.

Cursory mention may perhaps be given to the following Maritime lyricists and their works: John S. Allen (1841–1923), *From Apollyonville to the Holy City: A Poem* (1880); Margaret Gill Currie (b. 1843), *John Saint John and Anna Gray: A Romance of Old New Brunswick* (n.d.) and *Gabriel West and Other Poems* (1866); Archibald Gray, *Shades of the Hamlet, and Other Poems* (1852) and *Bubbles from the Deep* (1873); James Haynes, *Poems* (1864); James Hogg (1800–1866), *Poems, Religious, Moral, and Sentimental* (1825); Clotilda Jennings (d. 1895), *Linden Rhymes* (1854) and *North Mountain Near Grand-Pré* (1883); William Martin Leggett (1813–1863), *The Forest Wreath: A Collection of Lyrics* (1833); David Palmer (1780–1866), *New Brunswick and Other Poems* (1869); and Hiram Ladd Spencer (1829–1915), *Poems* (1850), *A Song of the Years, and a Memory of Acadia* (1889), and *The Fugitives* (1909).

Oliver Goldsmith

Although Oliver Goldsmith (1794–1861) only briefly wrote poetry, two circumstances have given him a disproportionate importance in Canadian literature. In the first place, he was the namesake and grand-nephew of the Anglo-Irish poet, Oliver Goldsmith; secondly, his *The Rising Village: A Poem* was the first volume of verse ever published in Canada by a native-born Canadian to receive serious attention at the hands of critics and literary historians.

The son of a Loyalist official, Goldsmith was born in Saint Andrews, New Brunswick, but within two years the family moved to Halifax. After teaching his son the rudiments of reading, writing, and arithmetic, Oliver Goldsmith's father destined him to a variety of occupations in turn. Goldsmith was employed successively in the naval hospital, an ironmonger's shop, a bookseller's shop, a lawyer's office, and a wholesale firm. In 1809, his father decided to send him to the Halifax Grammar School, but within a year he had procured for his son an ensigncy in the Nova Scotia Fencibles. Before Oliver could join that regiment, his father again changed his mind, made him resign his commission, and entered him in the Commissariat at Halifax as a volunteer.

This last choice proved fortunate, and Oliver Goldsmith followed until his death in 1861 the career of a successful colonial administrator. During a year spent in England in 1817 and 1818, Oliver Goldsmith became conscious of the deficiencies of his education, and upon his return to Halifax set conscientiously to work to repair them by reading and study. Although he never mastered Latin and Greek, he did manage to learn French and Spanish and to read widely in English literature.

In 1822, the Halifax Garrison organized a theatrical company, and Goldsmith was chosen to play the part of Tony Lumpkin in his great-uncle's play, *She Stoops to Conquer*. Inspired by the coincidence, Goldsmith composed a successful verse prologue to the play and followed it with a more serious imitation of *The Deserted Village*.

When *The Rising Village: A Poem* appeared in London in 1825, Goldsmith became so disappointed by the invidious comparisons that English critics made with his great-uncle's work that he lost all further interest in poetic composition. He did, however, re-issue the poem, along with a few occasional pieces, in a volume entitled *The Rising Village, with Other Poems*, published in Saint John in 1834. Goldsmith's only other work in literature was a manuscript autobiography, published for the first time in 1943 by the Ryerson Press.

The 570 lines of *The Rising Village* fall into three divisions. The first third of the poem traces in general terms the growth of a colony from the hardships of the early settlers to the settled calm enjoyed by their descendants. The final section paints an illusory picture of contemporary Nova Scotian prosperity. Sandwiched between and bearing little organic relation to either part is the pathetic story of Flora and Albert.

In his skilful use of balance and antithesis, Goldsmith demonstrates how carefully he had studied his great-uncle's work. Unfortunately, he borrowed tamely every conceivable trite phrase and hackneyed rhyme that had found its way into the eighteenth-century British couplet. As a result, his otherwise respectable lines are studded with clichés. Only in a few excursions into local description does his verse become more than a literary mosaic. The following is an example of his style at its best:

> Here, nails and blankets, side by side, are seen,
> There, horses' collars, and a large tureen;
> Buttons and tumblers, fish-hooks, aprons and knives,
> Shawls for young damsels, flannel for old wives;
> Woolcards and stockings, hats for men and boys,
> Mill-saws and fenders, silks and children's toys;
> All useful things, and joined with many more,
> Compose the well-assorted country store.

Goldsmith's additions to the 1834 volume comprise a few short occasional pieces and religious exercises in verse and a handful of love lyrics. All are undistinguished and make the reader view Goldsmith's early retirement from verse-making without regret.

Peter   Fisher

A comparison of subject-matter and attitude in three rare anonymous books—*Sketches of New Brunswick* (1825), *Notitia of New Brunswick*

(1838) and *The Lay of the Wilderness: A Poem in Five Cantos,* by "A Native of New Brunswick" (1833)—would indicate that they were written by the same author. The first two are known to be the work of Peter Fisher of Saint Anne's (Fredericton), New Brunswick's pioneer historian.

The son of Ludovic (Lewis) Fisher, a New Jersey Loyalist of German descent, Peter Fisher (1782–1848) was born at Staten Island where the family were awaiting evacuation to New Brunswick. Fisher, who received a good education from the distinguished pioneer schoolmaster, Bealing Stephens Williams, combined great powers of observation and a good memory with commercial shrewdness and tremendous physical strength. While operating an extensive lumber business and raising a large family of distinguished sons, Fisher found time to gather materials for his histories and to incorporate into them and into his verse accurate descriptions of the social conditions of a New Brunswick in the grip of a lumbering economy. Although they are too unpolished to be significant as literature, his poem and his histories provide the best insights we have into living conditions in New Brunswick in the first forty years of the nineteenth century.

The Lay of the Wilderness is less literary than *The Rising Village.* Lacking the devices of balance and antithesis, Fisher's lines often degenerate into doggerel. Nor is the narrative intrinsically more interesting or better managed than that in Goldsmith's poem. *The Lay of the Wilderness* does, however, contain two ingredients conspicuously lacking in Goldsmith's work. One is an awareness of the democratic difference between life in a North American colony and life in Great Britain; the other is the uncompromising bluntness with which Fisher depicts the degeneracy of the Loyalist officers who attempted to settle on the upper St. John River. The failure of their settlement is sharply contrasted with the spectacular success achieved at Woodstock by a settlement of disbanded N.C.O.'s and privates.

Joseph Howe

Joseph Howe (1804–1873) was the greatest of all Maritimers. The self-educated son of a pioneer Nova Scotian printer, he won his way upward in society by unflagging energy and superior intelligence. A lustful, healthy, many-sided individual, Howe rivalled Benjamin Franklin in the versatility of his achievements. His career as a politician, orator, and prose writer is dealt with elsewhere in this volume. Howe himself was fondest of writing poetry. "Poetry," as he put it, "was my first love, but politics was the hag I married."

Howe's poetry, composed at odd moments snatched from a busy life, was published posthumously in *Poems and Essays* (1874). Its longest poem is the incomplete narrative, "Acadia," dealing with the perils of early settlement in Nova Scotia. The moralizing at the beginning and end of the poem is conventional and dull, but the central narrative differs from those of

Goldsmith by its vigour and fast pace. Howe's couplets are technically superior to Fisher's but less polished than Goldsmith's. They are, however, forthright and straightforward and bear more distinctly than the work of the other poets the marks of a personality.

Howe's other poems include heavy moralizing on "poetic" themes in a diction old-fashioned even for his time, occasional poems, and songs. The occasional poems are surprisingly effective. Howe could turn a graceful compliment or a clever epigram when the occasion offered. His finest verse is contained in the songs. These have the dignity, balance, and fine phrasing that characterized the public songs of England in the days of "Rule, Britannia." Few better patriotic poems have been written in Canada than "Song for the 8th of June" and "The Flag of Old England." Unfortunately, these have lost their magic since the spirit of British colonialism to which they appealed has given place to the spirit of Canadian nationalism.

Peter John Allan

Most of Peter John Allan's brief life (1825–1848) was spent in Fredericton, where his father was chief medical officer. Of commanding physique and endowed with unusual beauty and intellect, Allan embodied in his personality the romantic temperament at its best, and his death by fever at the age of twenty-three was a loss to the cause of poetry in the Maritimes. Had he lived, he might have established thirty years earlier the kind of poetic renaissance that Roberts and Carman were to create in the 1880's and 1890's. The posthumously published *Poetical Remains of Peter John Allan* (1853) indicate that Allan had begun to imitate his British models in the same spirit and with the same concern for technical perfection as Roberts was later to do. The book is a more immature and chaotic *Orion*.

Byron, Shelley, and Tennyson were Allan's masters, and he had learned their lessons with respect to the construction of stanza, line, and phrase although he had not, however, even begun to master the archetectonics of a long work. His major faults, however, were those of a young man to whom reading had brought more vivid experiences than had life. He is too ready to create literature out of other literature rather than out of his own experience, and there is little of his local background embodied in his work.

Alexander Rae Garvie

Of Scottish ancestry, Alexander Rae Garvie (1836–1875) was born in Demerara in British Guiana and died at Montreal. The greater part of his life, however, was spent in the Maritimes—mainly New Brunswick—as a Presbyterian clergyman. Garvie was shy and retiring by nature but an omnivorous reader and such a delightful companion to his intimate friends that George Stewart, Jr., likens him to Charles Lamb.

Garvie's essays in *Thistledown* (1875) have already been dealt with. His verse is largely lyrical, sober, reflective, and moralistic. Although skilful in its handling of metre, it is undistinguished in its phrasing. Exceptions are the sonnet, "Best of All Trees I Love the Stately Sombre Pines," a dignified expression of the stern grandeur of his religion, and the stoic "An Epitaph":

> How went my youth? Alas! bitter truth!
> It waned like the moon into clouds uncouth,
> Which hung over dawning dark omens of rain.
>
> How went my age? Turn thou the torn page,
> And read, writ in blood, Death's final mortgage—
> Signed, sealed and delivered in presence of Pain.

Garvie's most interesting poem is his narrative, "Allan Gray," the story of a love between two boys which ends in the tragic death of one of them. "Allan Gray" in some respects foreshadows the much greater treatment of this theme contained in Earle Birney's *David*. The tone of the poem is right throughout, but the effect is partly muffled by commonplace diction.

John Hunter-Duvar

John Hunter-Duvar (1830–1899) was a Scotsman of French ancestry who, after having been stationed for most of his life in the army in British North America, finally settled at "Hernewood, Fortune Cove, Prince Edward Island." There he commanded the Prince County battalion of active militia and for ten years served as Supervisor of Fisheries for the Government of Canada.

Like his drama, which has already been dealt with, Duvar's poems are the exercises of the leisure of a gentleman and are distinguished more for grace of execution than for any relevance they possess to the environment of Prince Edward Island at the time of their composition.

De Roberval, a Drama (1888) contains scattered songs and also two longer poems, "The Emigration of the Fairies," and "The Triumph of Constancy, a Romaunt." The latter is a moral fable in verse on a medieval theme. It is consistent in subject, sensibility, and language, and were it placed within the frame of *The Earthly Paradise*, it might easily pass as the work of William Morris.

"The Emigration of the Fairies" is Duvar's poetic masterpiece. The conception of this poem is original and happy. A bit of earth on which fairies still exist is washed from its native England during a storm, drifts across the Atlantic, and comes to rest at Hernewood, where Duvar gives the little people a second home. This device enables Duvar to describe the beauties and dangers of an Atlantic crossing, to contrast the old land with the new while paying graceful tributes to both, and to indulge his bizarre fancy with descriptions of objects upon a liliputian scale. By truncating Byron's *ottava rima* to a six-line stanza, Duvar found a form to fit his theme perfectly. Although the poem lacks modulation and possesses wit and fancy rather than feeling and imagination, "The Emigration of the Fairies" is the most technically successful and the most aesthetically satisfying poem to be published in the Maritimes before 1890.

In addition to the plays *The Enamorado* and *De Roberval*, and the very rare *John a' Var: His Lays* (n.d.), Duvar left behind in newspapers and periodicals a good deal of fugitive verse. One poem, "Making an Acadian Farm," deserves rescue for the clarity with which it expresses the division in the Maritime soul between colonialism and frontier pride:

> Here dwelt the Squire . . .
> Self-reliant, as became his race,
> He set himself to see what he might do.
> And summing up his knowledge, found he knew
> Of trading nothing, and of farming little,
> But much of the great glory of the woods;
> So mainly fancy-led he took a stretch
> Of forest land, full of acclivities,
> With winding brooklets running at the base;
> And in the process of his clearing laid
> By bit and bit his English knowledge by;
> Saw zig-zag fences, without hate, and learned
> The science of the handling of the hoe,
> The handy shift and rude Colonial ways,
> And watched so long the swinging of the axe,
> He almost learned himself to chop a tree;
> He made himself a roughish kind of farm
> And called it by a fond ancestral name.
>
> Where once the stumps had been grew apple trees,
> And grass and grain and a rude garden place,
> And in the course of time the orchard fruits
> Grew red-cheeked in the sun; and specimens
> Of planted trees for landscape—beech and elm—
> And some imported—lime and sycamore,
> Became umbrageous, and lent dignity;
> While round the circuit of the whole domain
> Was left a margin of the old rough woods,
> Wherein the intersecting timber-roads
> Were under-brushed and trimmed to bridle-paths,
> At which the Squire—a setter at his heels—
> Would frequent take his rides in Spring or Fall,
> Beneath the red flame of the maple bush,
> Or in the yellow rain of beechen leaves;
> And musing, with full heart, would grateful say,—
> "Dear Lord! the land is fair to look upon,
> Although it is not like my English home!"

8. Literary Activity in the Canadas

1812-1841

CARL F. KLINCK

"A CANADIAN," Arthur L. Phelps has said, "is one who is increasingly aware of being American in the continental sense without being American in the national sense." The story of literary activity in the Canadas (Upper and Lower) from 1812 to 1880 supplements the social and political history of a period during which this part of North America absorbed settlers, largely from Britain, and ensured separation from the United States, at first by war and later by the formation of a new Dominion (1867). Among the factors making for cultural independence in this North American country were the presence of the co-operating *canadien* French, local solutions to local problems, the waves of new, direct British immigration, and closer ties with Britain than the United States had desired after the Revolution.

Literary activity had a part to play in the positive development of a separate people, with much that became characteristically their own in attitudes, sensitivity, turns of thought and phrase, subject-matter, allusions, symbols, myths and legends. Many such images will be mentioned in chapters 8 and 9, and the composite image is of no small importance. The literary sources of this inheritance will now be traced in this chapter under two divisions, (I) Lower Canada: Quebec city and Montreal from the War of 1812 until the Union of the provinces (1812–1841) and (II) Upper Canada during the same period. In chapter 9 there are two more divisions, (I) Genteel colonialism in Canada East (Quebec) and Canada West (Ontario) (1841–1855) and (II) the Confederation era in central Canada (1855–1880).

I. LOWER CANADA: QUEBEC CITY AND MONTREAL (1812–1841)

At the time of the American War of 1812–1814, when naval and military forces supplied a temporary increase, the normal English-speaking population of the cities of Quebec and Montreal was estimated at about three thousand in each centre. As John Lambert saw them in Quebec (*Travels through Lower Canada and the United States*, 2nd ed., 1814), these people were the British and North American English who dominated the colony, consisting principally of government officials, military officers, and legal and ecclesiastical dignitaries, along with merchants, practitioners in medicine, shopkeepers, and traders. In Montreal there were fewer officials and more traders, especially those in the business of furs. These, of course, made up only a fraction of the population, for the British had not come fifty years earlier into an empty land. Lower Canada (in our day the province of Quebec) was almost wholly French in language, culture, religion, and laws. The term "Canadian" was equivalent to "*canadien*," that is North American French, and the image of Canada was made up of seigneurs, habitants, black-clothed clergy, advocates, *coureurs de bois, voyageurs*, French Hurons at Lorette, Gallic gaiety, rides in *calèches* or sleighs, folk singing, farm labour, lumbering, church-going, and villages scattered along the banks of the St. Lawrence. The English image, significant of power but also picturesque, included vice-regal display, military colour and bustle, polite sport, harbours full of transatlantic ships, vast stores for continental trade and development, political quarrelling, and high social life.

From the outside it was customary to regard Quebec and Montreal as subjects for literature in terms of war because of Wolfe and Montcalm; of age because of memories of the *ancien régime*; of primitivism because of the proximity to sublime scenery and harmless Indians; of forest adventure because of the visible product of furs; and of pleasurable "roughing it" because of Thomas Moore's "Canadian Boat Song" ("Faintly as tolls the evening chime"), published in 1806. From the inside the continuous involvement of two languages and peoples was more obvious. This complex internal situation can be illustrated from the journalistic works of John Neilson (1776–1848), who succeeded his uncle as editor of the venerable and influential Quebec *Gazette*. In Montreal a half dozen newspapers and journals, and at least two books of verse, *The Charivari* (1824) and *Jean Baptiste* (1825) showed a growing interest in the local affairs of this part-English, part-French city.

Jean Baptiste was the work of Levi Adams of Henryville, L.C., who went to Montreal to study law. His reputation as a minor poet rests upon this book and upon "Poetry Run Mad" in the *Herald* (November 1825). *The Charivari* was attributed in an advertisement to "Launcelot Longstaff." In an introduction to a recent reprint of *The Charivari* (Golden Dog Press, 1977), Mrs. Mary Lu MacDonald has satisfactorily identified "Longstaff" as Captain George Longmore, a native of Quebec City, stationed in Montreal in the early 1820's as a Captain of the Royal Staff Corps.

My references, here and elsewhere, to Adams as the *Charivari*-poet are, therefore, incorrect. Yet there are many unexplained similarities between

The Charivari and Adams's *Jean Baptiste*. Both are comic, but sympathetic, narratives of the wooing and wedding of elderly French-Canadian bachelors. The treatment of the subject "after the manner of Beppo" is explicit in Longmore and certain also in Adams. The Captain, indeed, attempted adaptations of the whole of Byron's poetic cycle: the melodies, the Eastern tales, the dramas, and the burlesques. The local reviewers, then beginning their own careers, congratulated this poet, as David Chisholme said in *The Canadian Review* (1824), on portraying "the domestic habits and social pastimes of a virtuous people."

Several claims for priority among the poets of the Canadas may be made for Longmore. Contributions from his pen appeared frequently in Chisholme's *Canadian Magazine* and *Review* between December 1823 and December 1824. Many of these poems were republished in 1826 in *Tales of Chivalry and Romance*, a book of 306 pages of verse issued anonymously in Edinburgh and London. In its pages one can find Longmore's metrical romance "Tecumthé" occupying a third of the book. The *Tales* of this Canadian expatriate stands with Oliver Goldsmith's *The Rising Village* (London, 1825) and Major John Richardson's *Tecumseh* (London, 1828) among the first books of poetry published in the United Kingdom by native-born British North Americans.

If Mrs. Anne Cuthbert (Rae) Fleming (d. 1860) had been born in Canada, full claims for priority could have been made for her. The author of *A Year in Canada, and Other Poems* (Edinburgh, 1816) came to this country from Aberdeen, Scotland, in 1815 or 1816, after she had separated from her first husband, a Mr. Knight. The book gave her name as Anne Cuthbert Knight. She later became a resident of Montreal when she married James Fleming, brother of the financial celebrity John Fleming (1786?–1832). Her Goldsmithian poem, "A Year in Canada," deserves recognition as a very early and most thoughtful, if somewhat condescending, treatment of rural life and manners in Lower and Upper Canada (especially in Glengarry). In many ways she anticipates (but not in prose) the later works of Mrs. Traill, Mrs. Anna Jameson, and Mrs. Moodie. When she became a teacher in Montreal, Mrs. Fleming published chiefly school books, including *Views of Canadian Scenery for Canadian Children* (1843).

Official literature, of course, operated on a pretentious level, especially in Quebec city; name, rank, British background, and political connections received unusual respect. Yet even here there was a strong dash of North Americanism, illustrated neatly in the career of the Hon. William Smith (1769–1847), author of a *History of Canada*, printed in Quebec in 1815 but not issued until it was enlarged in 1826. Smith's father, from whom he inherited a position in the ruling class, had been a Loyalist from the American colony of New York. The son collected early records of Quebec—a special interest centred on this side of the Atlantic, although not resulting, Mrs. Leprohon asserted in her *Antoinette de Mirecourt* (1864), in a due respect for the French upper classes and habitants. Smith's correspondence with the Earl of Dalhousie shows that he helped the Governor General to plan and establish in 1824 the Literary and Historical Society of Quebec, an organization still in existence today. British paternalism had one of its better moments when the Earl called for "the formation of a Society, not entirely 'Antiquarian' but Historical rather and Canadian." The term "Canadian" was here formally baptized into the English realm of letters.

The Society's charter members, "men, eminent for rank, erudition and genius," included François-Xavier Garneau, who later interpreted Canadian history for his own people, and Joseph Bouchette (1774–1841), the native-born Surveyor General and famous author of *A Topographical Description of the Province of Lower Canada* (1815). But French-Canadian participation, except in the case of Bouchette, was infrequently realized, even after partial union with a rival society in 1829. Bouchette, however, and his fellow scientists, particularly the Army and Navy's practical professionals, skilled in mathematics, physics, geology, and hydrography—the explorers of this era—dominated the Society and its early *Transactions*. They are given credit for encouraging the official geological survey of Canada.

The first of the Society's *Historical Documents* did not come out until 1838. It is possible to read in them the literary efforts of the gentlemanly amateurs, who made certain that Canadian poets would know the local robin better than the foreign nightingale. Mrs. William Sheppard of Woodfield wrote papers on shells and song birds; her husband and the Countess of Dalhousie on Canadian plants; John Wilkie on the grammar of the Huron language; and Dr. Walter Henry on the ways of the salmon. Outside the Society, Robert Christie (1788–1856) also illustrated this tendency to treat the familiar, the practical, and the immediate. His history of Lower Canada was printed in instalments, eventually in six volumes, covering chiefly periods through which he himself lived; he presented in it an invaluable collection of copies of despatches, speeches, newspaper articles, and the like regarding matters as important as the events leading up to the rebellion of 1837, the coming of Lord Durham, and the achievement of responsible government.

Military men were the spice of Quebec society, and, after the Napoleonic and American War, the colony received some liberally educated half-pay officers who contributed to the vast store of British campaign literature. *Haverhill; or, Memoirs of an Officer in the Army of Wolfe* (London, 1831), by the American James Athearn Jones, is an example of the persistence of the earlier Conquest material and the deliberately bookish treatment of stock situations. Dr. Walter Henry, the salmon expert, however, in *Trifles from my Portfolio* (1839), "by a staff surgeon," showed himself to be the "Tiger" Dunlop of the lower province. Henry was a stylist and perhaps a conscious romantic, for he built up a picture of himself as officer, young lover, traveller, participant in historic events, physician, and naturalist. He had indeed been at St. Helena when Napoleon died; he had also had twenty-nine years of military service in the Peninsula, France, the East Indies, and Nepal. In addition, he was able to make a vivid report of the rebellion years in Upper and Lower Canada. Like Dunlop, Henry gives the reader a strong sense of being present at great events beside a remarkable companion.

Quebec was not the place to expect philosophical radicalism, but there was at least one man whom European upheavals had sent to the city and its reading public. *The Enquirer*, a periodical which began in May 1821 and lasted one year, was edited by "C.D.E.," whom W. Kaye Lamb has identified as Chevalier Robert-Anne D'Estimauville de Beaumouchel (1754–1831), author also of *Cursory View of the Local, Social, Moral and Political State of the Colony of Lower Canada* (1829). C.D.E. was a native Canadian, long a resident abroad, who returned to Quebec in 1812 in his fifty-eighth year. His series on "My Own Life" in the rare files of the *Enquirer* should be his claim to remembrance; Samuel Hull Wilcocke printed part of it in the *Scribbler* of December 18, 1823. This man, Wilcocke said, was "no bad writer himself." The Chevalier gave an account of his experiences in London "in the latter end of 1779 and in 1781" when he was "intimately acquainted with the respectable family of the three Brothers Sharp, with Dr. John Jebb and the celebrated Thos. Holcroft." But he was converted, he said, from the "alluring rights of man" to "Heavenly philanthropy," discovered through the "gospel." Captain George Longmore shared the romantic enthusiasm of Lord Byron for the oppressed people of Europe, especially in Greece and Spain. In "The Fall of Constantinople" he celebrated the "former fame and freedom" of Greece; and in "The Guerilla Bride" and "Ode to Spain" he deplored the lost "soul of honour" among the modern Spaniards. In a preface there was a reference to his own "sojourn" in their country.

The Church of England had its stalwarts in Quebec in the persons of its first three bishops, the Right Reverend Jacob Mountain, Charles James Stewart, and George Jehoshaphat Mountain (Bishop of Montreal, 1836–50, and of Quebec, 1850–63). The second two deserve to be remembered for their literary works, Bishop Stewart for his missionary reports of Upper and Lower Canada, and the younger Bishop (G.J.) Mountain (1789–1863) for his many published sermons, and his later unaffected account of his canoe trip in 1844 from Lachine to the church's mission at the Red River, in Prince Rupert's Land. This cultured traveller, following the route of the fur traders, gave his report with humility, accuracy, and vividness in his *Journal* (1845) and *Songs of the Wilderness* (1846). The "songs," written by "one whose habits of poetry were formed only in youth," give the impression of a Bryant actually in the wilderness. Few colonial versifiers were more sincere in describing native flowers, waterfowl, *voyageurs*, Indian life, fireflies, and mosquitoes ("mementos of the fall!"). The preface to the *Songs* expressed this churchman's opposition to currently fashionable verse which, he professed, ran "counter, in many particulars, to my own tastes and to my own predilections—perhaps I should say, my own prejudices." A generation earlier, he had been opposed by prejudices on the fashionable side, for his father and he had been criticized by an irresponsible, temperamental, but clever young Irishman, Adam Kidd, who liked Stewart and hated the Mountains.

Kidd (1802–1831), evidently a friend of the Percevals at Spencer Wood, had been no model student in the church's school of instruction for candidates for holy orders. For a life of this kind he had been ill prepared by his own romantic travels in the wake of Thomas Moore and perhaps by a weakness for Indian girls. Kidd's rebellion took the form of the first consciously symbolic narrative by a Canadian, explained—or obscured—by his own note printed in *The Huron Chief* (Montreal, 1830). He said that he had suffered "an accidental fall from the cloud-capped brows of a dangerous Mountain, over which I had heedlessly wandered, with that open carelessness which is so peculiarly the characteristic of poetic feeling." This seemed for a long time to refer romantically to Slievegallin in his native Ireland! Sufficient proof is now available to show that the mountain was one of the episcopal Mountains, whom Kidd then proceeded to compare in a long Indian idyll—heavily documented from Heckewelder and other "Indian" authorities—with Skenandow, chieftain of the Hurons, whose home was a natural mountain. The episcopal father-image suffers in Kidd's comparison with the father-image of the pagan sage Skenandow, and missionary activity is regarded as supererogatory for those who are by nature good.

The Montreal *Gazette* of May 30, 1830, reported entertainingly how Kidd, a year before his early death, solicited subscriptions for his book from door to door, asking half a crown before publication and another half a crown on delivery. If Kidd's preface may be trusted, he sold 1500 copies in advance; the total would have been nearly £190, and again as much on delivery. Many persons must have subscribed in ignorance of the "Mountain" reference; the *Gazette* reviewer did not allude to it.

Indians were known to Kidd in their very persons at Lorette, near Quebec city, but another poet, William Fitz Hawley (1804–1855), author of *Quebec, The Harp, and Other Poems* (Montreal, 1829), appears to have prepared himself for *The Unknown, or Lays of the Forest* (Montreal, 1831) by reading Campbell, Moore, and Byron, perhaps confusing Indians with characters in Mediterranean metrical narratives—a risk one took with romance in those days. Hawley's lays are located in Italy, Persia, Arabia, and Greece. The "forest" of the sub-title belongs only to the framework (the introduction and conclusion) of the tales; and the inhabitants of this forest near Three Rivers, a noble old man, a lost Leonie, and a mysterious stranger, are stock figures drawn from Eastern or Indian romances. Hawley confessed in his first book that he had not reached "the polished strains of Campbell, the wild energy of Byron, nor the magic wand of Moore, wreathed with flowers, and glittering with gems." In "To Maia," one of his "Other Poems," he did achieve the magic he desired, but in general he proved that foreign muses did not, or did not yet, rest comfortably on the slopes of Mount Royal.

Society verse with an eighteenth-century, and timeless, flavour was written with great success by Adam Kidd in poems like his address to Miss———— (whom he loved "for a minute"), his "Epitaph" on a drunken parson, and his lines "To the Countess of D——e" (undoubtedly Dalhousie):

> Oh! do not curse the humble bard—
> He's poor enough without it—
> For if he said your heart is hard,
> There's very few will doubt it.

Gustavus William Wicksteed, a charter member of the Literary Society, lived longer and also achieved a reputation for polite versifying. Quebec had often received tributes for its gay, social life: from Peter Kalm in 1749, Frances Brooke in the 1760's, John Lambert in the early 1800's, and John Galt in 1827. In that last year Galt wrote a piece for the amateur theatre and "Tiger" Dunlop "performed the Highlander beyond anything [Galt] ever saw on the regular stage." The festivities of the vice-regal court, the military, and the wealthy families of Quebec were rivalled in Montreal by the feasts of the kings of the fur trade. The hospitality accorded Washington Irving by some partners in the North West Company in 1803 was remembered as evidence of the "perfect romance" of the life of a trapper or fur trader when he wrote *Astoria* in 1836. Irving had, in turn, provided hints for Canadian writers who knew the gay and witty *Salmagundi* (1807), a series of Addisonian essays set in New York and written by Irving, Irving's brother William, and James Kirke Paulding. *The Charivari* (Montreal, 1824), by Captain George Longmore, employed a Salmagundian pseudonym, "Launcelot Lo[a]ngstaff." Another name from these New York essays, "Jeremy Cockloft," had been used in 1811 on a title-page to stand for the author of *Cursory Observations Made in Quebec*, probably the work of a Bermudian, who, as William Toye has recently pointed out, also published a minor epic, *Britannia, a Poem*.

Cultural criticism in Lower Canada may have been encouraged by the example of *Salmagundi*, the influence of the Philadelphia *Port Folio*, and especially by the second series of *Salmagundi*, edited by Paulding in 1819–20. Witty discussion was by no means everyone's forte; didacticism always has stalwarts, and not only among old men like the Chevalier D'Estimauville, who wrote *Cursory View*. Edward Lane, a younger man, introduced his "few remarks . . . on the religion, manners, customs, etc. of the Canadians" into a conventional and contrived romance of a Byronic hero who seeks a runaway wife and a lost son in Canada. This was called *The Fugitives; or, A Trip to Canada* (London, 1830), and the author described himself as "formerly a resident of Lower Canada." Lane has not been securely identified; perhaps he was the Edward Lane who served as a catechist (1833–34) at Rivière du Loup en Haut, near Sorel and Three Rivers, in the diocese of Quebec during the episcopate of Charles James Stewart. If this is so, one must indeed reckon with the literary influence of the Society for the Propagation of the Gospel in Foreign Parts. On the S.P.G.'s roll as teachers for a short time were Lane and the poet Adam Kidd, and as priests for longer periods the poet Adam Hood Burwell, Bishop G. J. Mountain, and the Rev. Joseph Abbott (1789–1863), who turned his memoranda for emigrants into a kind of novel, entitled *Philip Musgrave* (1846).

Yet another effort in social criticism, supplementing the newspapers, was a semi-monthly magazine in Montreal, *The Literary Miscellany*, edited by Henry John Hagan, which began in November 1822 and disappeared in June 1823. It had a "pedagogical air," said Samuel Hull Wilcocke of the *Scribbler*, who was himself a Salmagundian of a coarse variety, tempered not in New York but in the arena of British journalism. The issues of his ephemeral rival, the *Literary Miscellany*, Wilcocke explained, "were too much occupied with newspaper controversy, and newspaper criticism, both objects that are, in most cases, beneath the dignity of an essayist."

The great contemporary literary journals, the *Edinburgh Review,* the *Quarterly Review* (London) and especially *Blackwood's Edinburgh Magazine,* proved that Scots could be Salmagundians, on every level from academic wit to outrageous practical joking. David Chisholme and Dr. A. J. Christie, however, Wilcocke's other rivals as editors of Montreal literary journals, were not graduates of the Wilson-Lockhart-Maginn-Hogg-"Tiger" Dunlop school. These immigrants, recently arrived in Canada (Chisholme in 1822 and Christie in 1817), were courageously, and perhaps naively, determined to make the large and handsome issues of their magazines not unworthy Canadian parallels of the Edinburgh models. They were practical and sober men; it was no mean achievement to get these issues printed. Chisholme (1796–1842), a protégé of the Earl of Dalhousie, subsequently published *The Lower Canada Watchman* (Kingston, 1829) and was editor of the *Montreal Gazette* (1837–42). It was he who edited *The Canadian Magazine and Literary Repository*, a monthly, through seven numbers, from July 1823 until February 1824. Then he left this project and edited *The Canadian Review and Literary and Historical Journal*, which had a history of five numbers, appearing irregularly and ending in September 1826. Dr. A. J. Christie (d. 1843) had practised medicine, edited the Montreal *Herald* from 1819 to

1822 and the Montreal *Gazette* from 1823 to 1824; he had also published *The Emigrant's Assistant; or, Remarks on the Agricultural Interest of the Canadas* (1821). Christie succeeded Chisholme as editor of the *Canadian Magazine* in February 1824 and carried it into 1825.

These two editors wished to avoid giving their journals a colonial appearance. They reprinted, as North American editors habitually did, from British publications (the *New Monthly Magazine* is acknowledged), but they did so with more discretion than later Victorian editors displayed in seeking decorative fillers. The *Canadian Magazine*, for example, printed in its first numbers extracts from an account of Captain William Parry's expedition into the Arctic regions, a review of Captain John Franklin's *Narrative of a Journey to the Shores of the Polar Sea*, and chapters from Scott's *Quentin Durward*, along with "Original Papers" on the fur trade of Canada, the Lachine Canal, the history of Montreal from the time of Cartier, the establishment of an English Theatre in Montreal, and "The Fall of Constantinople" by Longmore. The *Canadian Review* began in July 1824 with articles on the Quebec Literary and Historical Society, the settlement of the townships of Lower Canada, the influence of literature, the education and duties of a Canadian merchant, the wars of Canada, the history of the aborigines, and the fur trade; there were also reviews of John Howison's *Sketches of Upper Canada*, of *St. Ursula's Convent*, and of *The Charivari*, together with at least three poems which may be attributed to Longmore. The *Review* was kept, as Carl Ballstadt has estimated in an unpublished thesis (Western Ontario, 1959), 77 per cent Canadian in content.

The *Magazine* and the *Review* offer a parallel to *Salmagundi*, principally to ideas in the second series, because Paulding gave the impression that authors in the United States were as self-conscious, as eager to establish local identity, and as defiant of some British fashions as Chisholme and Christie— and Wilcocke—were. Paulding's essay on "National Literature" is the show-piece for this attitude. He opposed fiction which offended an American sense of decency and reality. There was no need for literary reliance upon superstition or ghosts, fairies and goblins; wonder could be excited and feelings aroused by struggles and situations within the experience of Americans.

"Real life is fraught with adventures," Paulding wrote, "to which the wildest fictions scarcely afford a parallel." On the basis of such convictions the *Canadian Magazine* of April 1824 approved of *The Widow of the Rock* (1824), a book of poems by Mrs. Margaret Blennerhasset, and the *Canadian Review* praised Longmore's *Charivari*. For similar reasons, *St. Ursula's Convent* (1824) by a Canadian woman, Julia Catherine Beckwith (Mrs. Hart) (1796–1867), was denounced as a "Quintessence of Novels and Romances." Wilcocke turned to this same book as one of the "miseries" of a reviewer and expressed the wish that the author had made a novel of the true story of six Canadian nuns from Sandwich, in Upper Canada, who were captured by pirates off Cuba, retaken by a British cruiser, and forwarded to New Orleans by an American vessel!

The maturity and shrewdness of Samuel Hull Wilcocke (1766?–1833) were coupled with the audacity to descend into the blackest depths of gossip and vilification. His pseudonym, "Lewis Luke MacCulloh, Esquire," was a very thin disguise. The weekly *Scribbler* (1821–27), his "blasted blue book," along with its companion, *The Free Press* (at first, published in Burlington, Vermont, 1822–23), had the notoriety of a scandal sheet in its own time; it was fated for oblivion after that during a century and a half, and now for professorial resurrection. Wilcocke could be painstaking enough to record acceptably the debates of the Lower Canada legislature for 1828–29, but he could also employ the tactics of vicious English journalism. "Tiger" Dunlop's paper, the *Telescope* (1825), published in London, England, in this lawless period of the *Age*, did not sink so low, even (apparently) with some efforts by his helpers, Lockhart and Maginn. Dunlop had not suffered as Wilcocke had.

The latter had been brought to Montreal about 1817, at the age of fifty, to support Edward Ellice, the "Bear" (pseud. "Mercator"), a partner in the North West Company, in a major "contest between the Earl of Selkirk and the Hudson's Bay Company, on one side, and the North-West Company on the other." More than thirty books on this controversy (which resulted in the supremacy of the Hudson's Bay Company) were published, and Wilcocke edited at least four of them. Either his own company turned against him, or he stole from them—as was alleged—and he claimed that he was "infamously used, grossly oppressed, and falsely accused." Illegal capture of him by the company's agents on United States territory caused an international incident, and resulted in Wilcocke's living precariously just over the United States border while he edited the Montreal *Scribbler* and the *Free Press*. These uninhibited vehicles criticizing Montreal officialdom, business, and society exposed and terrified the inhabitants of the city, who could expect to be recognized in ludicrous or compromising situations under names like Sir Frederick Brute, Lord Goddamnhim, the Hon. Tory Loverule, Rev. Moral Police, and McRavish, McKilliway & Co.

Although it was very uneven, the *Scribbler* functioned as a literary review, exhibiting Wilcocke's unusual background of reading and his flexible style. It demanded weekly issues from its harassed editor, yet it ran through ten volumes while other periodicals grew up and collapsed. Wilcocke could claim to be "the first that regularly assumed the critic's chair in Canada" and his journal to be the first to acquire "the dignity of appearing bound in volumes on the shelves of a library." Chisholme and Christie gambled on the existence of a cultivated reading public; Wilcocke scratched the surface of what he found.

An American colony in Montreal—recently identified by Lawrence M. Lande in *Old Lamps Aglow* (1957)—served as a North American influence. Harman and Margaret Blennerhasset, who had come originally from Ireland, had turned from the United States to this Canadian city for refuge and employment during the years 1819–22; Aaron Burr's wild expedition to fight the Spanish, conquer Mexico, and found a southern empire had failed, leaving the Blennerhassets disgraced and deprived of their great paradisal mansion on an island in the Ohio River near Parkersburg, Virginia. Mrs. Blennerhasset (1778–1842) gave expression to her sensations of exile and loss in *The Widow of the Rock and Other Poems, By a Lady* (Montreal, 1824). "A Negro's Benevolence" and other poems were presumably additions by her husband. Her title-poem was typically a frontier idyll of vanished happiness—of a young pioneer wife who went mad when her husband was killed by rattlesnakes. This remains as an instructive example of a process worth observing in early North American verse, the conventional tale or lyric hides and sublimates a real-life history similar in feeling although different in detail. Margaret Blennerhasset's heart, it is clear, was back in her own happy mansion, described in "The Desert[ed] Isle," a poem which concluded (in the Canadian version) with lines attacking Jefferson and anarchic Democracy.

In this American group there were also Charlotte Sweeny of Vermont and her husband Robert Sweeny, who had emigrated from Ireland about 1820 and who in December 1840 lost his life duelling with a Major Ward, while defending, so the legend goes, the honour of his beautiful wife. His epigrams and poetic "trifles light as air" were published in *Remnants* (Montreal, 1835) and in *Odds and Ends* (Montreal, 1836), the latter "a Canadian reprint" of a New York edition (1826). Of "A. Bowman," publisher of *Hours of Childhood and Other Poems* (Montreal, 1820), little is known; he was probably also the author, and therefore the hard-working American patriot described in the Preface. He may be identified with the Ariel Bowman who was a bookseller and started the *Canadian Times* in Montreal in January 1823, with Edward V. Sparhawk, a local publisher, as editor. The paper gave offence to the French-Canadians and was stopped by order of the Assembly at Quebec in October of that year. Even less is known about John H. Willis, who may also have been of American origin. Lawrence Lande reports that he was "a civil servant by profession, and an artist by inclination." His talent for sentimental social verse was described as "making my Muse beseem a Harlequin" on the title-page of his book, *Scraps and Sketches; or, The Album of a Literary Lounger* (Montreal, 1831).

Irish wit and story-telling which might have enlivened the literary society of Quebec or Montreal may be found in *The Emigrant, a Poem, in Four Cantos* (Montreal, 1842) by Standish O'Grady (b. 1793), a farmer near Sorel. He was the very image of a displaced person: an Irishman who had had no real desire to emigrate, as he did in 1836; a Protestant in French

Canada who regretted that he could not live in Upper Canada; a clergyman and graduate of Trinity College, Dublin, who made no success of farming. "A Canadian stud horse," he said, "with one miserable cow were the only remnant of my stock which survived the winter." His poem, *The Emigrant*, shows, therefore, less adaptation to life in the Canadas than appears in other immigrant "epics," Adam Hood Burwell's "Talbot Road" (1818), William Kirby's *The U.E.* (written 1846), and Alexander McLachlan's *The Emigrant* (1861). The theme of exile or homesickness for the Old Land was not as common in Canadian colonial writing as one has been taught to believe. David Moir ("Delta"), who wrote the famous "Canadian Boat Song" for *Blackwood's Magazine* (September 1829),

> Fair these broad meads—these hoary woods are grand;
> But we are exiles from our fathers' land,

had never been in Canada. Among the early immigrants themselves, the theme was exploited mainly in the works of the small minority who had lost more by coming than they had gained by staying in this country.

O'Grady employed the heroic couplet of Pope or Goldsmith with facility in discursive, satiric, mournful, or sententious passages. His copious, gossipy notes make one wish that he had rounded out an essay in prose. Mr. and Mrs. Sawtell, friends of his in Sorel who were kind to him in sickness, had a some-what more fashionable taste in verse; Mrs. M. Ethelind Sawtell's *The Mourner's Tribute; or, Effusions of Melancholy Hours* (Montreal, 1840) suggests the more sentimental tendencies of Cowper, Moore, Thomas Campbell, and Mrs. Hemans. In her solemn moods, idealistic elevation, and occasional felicitous references to the scenes about her, she belonged with the ladies who dominated the *Literary Garland*, the Montreal journal which first printed her title-poem (1839). For cultured people like her, in the towns as well as the cities, the emergence of the *Garland* marked the beginning of a new period.

II. UPPER CANADA (1812–1841)

West of Montreal, north of the St. Lawrence, Lake Ontario, and Lake Erie, there were many more Americans, or North Americans, living beside British immigrants and a very few Frenchmen in the separate British colony known since 1791 as Upper Canada. Here the waves of continental population movements were strongly felt and the cultural situation was far less stable. At the time of the War of 1812, the Loyalists of the post-Revolution era were still loyal, but they were North American in origin and not all of British stock. Moreover, they constituted, as Michael Smith pointed out in his *Geographical View of the Province of Upper Canada* (1813), only one-fifth of the 80,000 inhabitants; another three-fifths were non-Loyalist natives of the United States or their children; only one-fifth were direct British immigrants or their children. The early settlement of Upper Canada was clearly a part of the continental push westward. To the south, Americans had moved before 1800 from Virginia and the Carolinas into and beyond Kentucky. Farther north, there was a movement from Kentucky and Pennsylvania into southern Ohio, Indiana, and Illinois, and, still farther north, from New York and New England into northern Ohio, Michigan, and Upper Canada along the Great Lakes.

In his *Literature of the Middle Western Frontier* (1925), Ralph Leslie Rusk has named Lexington, Kentucky, from about 1779 to the 1820's, and after that Cincinnati, Ohio, as the cultural capitals. Detroit and Chicago were still small forts vulnerable to Tecumseh's Indians in the War of 1812; the town of Buffalo, on the way to the port of New York, stood nearest the early Upper Canadian towns of Niagara, Dundas, Hamilton, and York (Toronto after 1834). Cobourg and Belleville were farther to the east, as was Kingston, the most populous of these centres until the enormous burst of British immigration came in the 1830's and effected significant changes. When that decade ended, the settlers from Britain would outnumber those of North American origin, and the English-speaking residents of the combined Canadas would match the total of those who spoke French. By resisting invasion in war and subsequently becoming a goal of British emigration, Upper Canada remained a unique island in the American "Old Northwest"—retaining British rule, keeping up cultural relationships with the Old Land, and possessing a governmental system which would be adjusted (after a small rebellion) to provincial responsibility and the complexion of a non-aristocratic society.

When the period began, during the War of 1812, reality on the Niagara and Detroit borders offered literature some Indian–frontier imagery exceeding romantic fancies. Canadian writers (except Major John Richardson) and British readers generally have neglected this surfeit of the spectacular, this almost incredible profusion of New World "Gothic" material. Historical documentation has taken none of the storybook lustre from the gallant General Brock, the wise and brave Tecumseh, redcoats attempting forest warfare, American invaders, sharp-shooting mounted Kentuckians, sturdy Canadian militiamen, harassed settlers, navies battling on Lake Erie, and particularly Indians capable of strategic fighting or brutal massacre. The best treatment of this material is in Major Richardson's *War of 1812* (Brockville, 1842), enhanced by A. C. Casselman's editing in 1902. This autobiographical and documented history of the campaigns around Detroit is much better reading than Richardson's uninspired effort in fiction, *The Canadian Brothers* (1840) or his early metrical romance, *Tecumseh; or, The Warrior of the West* (written about 1823; published in London, 1828). This Byronic poem's only rival was Longmore's "Tecumthé," which was printed in the *Canadian*

Review in December 1824 and occupied about a third of the pages in *Tales of Chivalry and Romance* (Edinburgh, 1826).

Richardson's masterpiece, *Wacousta* (London, 1832) was not directly about this same war of 1812–14, of which Richardson was a veteran. Instead, he exercised his instructed fancy upon an earlier Indian struggle, Pontiac's siege of Detroit (1763), in which his grandfather Askin had played a part along with Major Robert Rogers, author of *Ponteach* (1766). Richardson (1796–1852), born at Queenston and reared at Fort Malden, was taken into Colonel Procter's 41st Regiment at the age of 15 or 16, fought in Procter's, Brock's, and Tecumseh's battles, and was captured at Moravian-town, where the great chieftain died. As a British officer, during the following twenty years in England, Barbados, Spain, and probably Paris, he learned the art of writing and published his experiments in a metrical romance (*Tecumseh*), a pseudo-moral exposure of sin in Paris (*Ecarté*, a novel, 1829), and a witty verse satire on fashionable moustaches and beards (*Kensington Gardens in 1830*).

After he returned to Canada, early in 1838, as a temporary correspondent for *The Times*, he rehashed his quarrels with military officers in a number of books, and produced a remarkably valuable autobiography, *Eight Years in Canada* (1847). Canadians seemed to be forgetting Richardson's boyhood war, while the United States was experiencing a revival of interest in the 1812–14 struggle, as old Indian fighters campaigned for the vice-presidency (Colonel Richard M. Johnson, 1836–40) and even the presidency (General William Henry Harrison, 1840–41). Hopeful of a better reception on the American side of the border, Richardson prepared some of his romances as thrillers for the cheap paperback market, where a few of them lasted until the 1880's. *The Canadian Brothers* was Americanized into *Matilda Mont-gomerie*, and two new ones, *Hardscrabble* (1850) and *Wau-nan-gee* (1852), gave an account of the fall and the massacre of Chicago. In 1847 or 1848 Richardson had moved to New York City, where he died in 1852, destitute and neglected.

Wacousta remains his best work: a Gothic tale of a feud carried by Englishmen from the Old to the New World. Wacousta is no Indian, except in acquired Indian habits, but the savages—nothing like Cooper's symbolic creatures—are there as they had impressed themselves on Richardson's soul. The book is poetic and a romance in a sense which does not belong to Cooper, for *Wacousta* is essentially a complex of vivid external equivalents (shrieks, surprises, terrors) for the outrages of mind and heart experienced by Richardson when he was a boy at war in the forests of the Canadian border.

In spite of such evidence, early English-speaking Upper Canada must be seen in proper perspective not as a vast hunting-ground of beyond-the-law frontiersmen, but as the home of settlers, *canadiens*, Loyalists, Mennonites, British colonists, New Englanders, and other North Americans. While in practice the system of land tenure was open to abuses and contradictions until well beyond the Rebellion era, the beginnings of law and order had been introduced after 1791 under principles laid down by Governor Simcoe and his able Surveyor General, D. W. Smith. The axe-and-plough pioneers are not without interest; they deserve something better than the caricatures often drawn of them. The first distinction to be made is between the early North American settlers and the British immigrants of the 1830's, 1840's, and 1850's. Richardson belonged to the early group and was one of those who felt lost in the deluge. Colonel Thomas Talbot, however, the baron of the Lake Erie shore, immortalized by Mrs. Anna Jameson in *Winter Studies and Summer Rambles in Canada* (1838) and Edward Ermatinger in *The Life of Colonel Talbot* (1859), breasted the waves. Closely associated with Talbot was Mahlon Burwell, the surveyor, and Mahlon's brother, Adam Hood Burwell (1790–1849), native-born (at Fort Erie) of Loyalist parents.

Adam Burwell began publishing poems in Upper Canadian newspapers as soon as these were revived after the American invasions. Wilcocke's *Scribbler* and the *Canadian Review* also accepted his offerings from 1821 to 1825. Among his poems dating back to 1816–18, and therefore slightly earlier than Oliver Goldsmith's *The Rising Village*, is "Talbot Road," a long, vigorous account of the Lake Erie barony. The elegance of neo-classicism, so conspicuously lacking in this world of forest homes, was curiously and uniquely supplied by the stock phrases and "poetic diction" of Thomas Campbell, James Thomson, Gray, and Goldsmith. Henry Scadding, indeed, was reminded of Drayton's *Polyolbion*. Burwell devised no native idiom for the natural scenery which he enjoyed and which spoke to him of God and man in the manner of the evangelical tradition. Elegance gave way in his later work to raw emotion and finally to Irvingite mysticism. It was either religion or politics which occupied the pioneer when his axe and plough were at rest.

The first ripples preceding the waves of British immigration brought adventurers, fanatics, and sometimes martyrs. Cawdell, Gourlay, and Mackenzie are, respectively, examples vivid enough to become lasting pioneer images. All were writers, James Martin Cawdell (1781?–1842) being so obscurely, because *The Wandering Rhymer* (York, 1826) and *The Roseharp* (1835) were only vague promises of performance. As he drifted down the various levels of decadent gentility, Cawdell lampooned Francis Gore, the lieutenant governor, and then in 1818 addressed to Gore's successor, Sir Peregrine Maitland, a *Memorial* which is a *tour de force* of autobiography, a pathetic joke, a serious burlesque of requests for easy preferment. The *Memorial* exists, far from public view, in the Public Archives of Canada and in a reprint by Adam Shortt in the *Canadian Historical Review* (1920). While Cawdell was lackadaisical in promoting schemes for colonization, Robert Fleming Gourlay (1778–1863) went too far, too fast, in his campaign against evils. His famous trial at Niagara in August 1819, in his second year in Upper Canada, yielded John Charles Dent a remarkable opening chapter for his book (1885) on the Upper Canadian Rebellion. Gourlay carried his own trouble back and forth across the Atlantic. His *Statistical Account of Upper Canada* (1822) and *The Banished Briton and Neptunian* (1843) are miscellanies of pamphlets, letters, petitions, and exhortations.

William Lyon Mackenzie (1795–1861) emigrated to York, Upper Canada, at the age of 24, and edited *The Colonial Advocate* first at Queenston in 1824 and then at York until 1834. He became unquestionably one of the major figures in colonial history, a complex man who could be pictured as a martyr or a fanatic, certainly a reformer, no less a "firebrand," a self-made man, an unwilling rebel, an ineffective leader, a blessing to Canadians in spite of himself. The *Selected Writings* of this man, recently (1960) edited by Margaret Fairley, reinforces the opinion that his early training, vast reading, alert observation, passion for facts, and powerful, popular style made him a Canadian William Cobbett. His essays on education, public works, agriculture, and publishing, as well as on politics, recreate vividly the early life of the settlements and rising towns.

A review of the newspapers is impossible in this limited space; Upper Canada had eight weeklies in 1825, thirty-eight in 1836, and its first success-ful dailies in the early 1850's. Out of the newspaper print-shops came the first pamphlets and books. Charles Fothergill at York published almanacs and James Lynne Alexander's poem, *Wonders of the West* (1825). At Kingston, Hugh C. Thomson of the *Herald* was very enterprising; Mrs. Hart's *St. Ursula's Convent* (1824) came from his press. At Ancaster, near Hamil-ton, George Gurnett (1792?–1861), who had lived in Richmond, Virginia, when Edgar Allan Poe was there as a boy in his teens, set up the *Gore Gazette* (1827–28), which printed some native poetry. The *Gore Gazette* led in 1833 to the short-lived *Canadian Literary Magazine* (York), of which Gurnett was the publisher. Three fortnightly publications attempted at nearby Hamilton failed between 1831 and 1833. A monthly *Canadian Magazine* at York ran into only four numbers in 1833; its publisher was Robert Stanton, and its editor was William Sibbald, "Late of the 1st or Royal Reg't," son of Mrs. Susan Sibbald, who later lived at "Eildon Hall," near Jackson's Point. The *Christian Guardian,* founded at York by the Rev. Egerton Ryerson as a weekly journal for the Wesleyan Methodists, began in 1829 its century-long honourable career.

The most interesting publication of the thirties was certainly Gurnett's *Canadian Literary Magazine* (three issues, 1833), expertly edited by John Kent under conservative, perhaps vice-regal, auspices. His contributors were promising *littérateurs* such as Mrs. Susanna Moodie, Dr. "Tiger" Dunlop, and Robert Douglas Hamilton, all British-trained authors who had published before arriving in Canada. Young Henry Scadding, whom he was teaching at Upper Canada College, impressed Kent. The "Editor's Address" sounded a hopeful note: "I did not expect to find the Canadians an ignorant people. . . . I find them advanced in civilization, beyond my expectations."

The population of Upper Canada rose between 1823 and 1840 from approximately 130,000 to 450,000 persons. Most of the increase must be attributed to immigration from Britain, which added to the total number of agricultural settlers, but also to that of the half-pay officers, gentlewomen, officials, younger sons, clergymen, lawyers, and especially young journalists— people like John Kent and the contributors to his magazine. Along with them came—and went—travellers, men and women of similar standing in society, some of whom enjoyed reputations and status in the great British journals, notably John Howison, Captain Frederick Marryat, Captain Basil Hall, Thomas Hamilton, Mrs. Anna Jameson, and Sir Francis Bond Head (a lieutenant governor). Less prominent (but equally interesting now) were Sir George Head, Lieutenant Francis Hall, Edward A. Talbot, John Mactaggart, Adam Fergusson, Isaac Fidler, John MacGregor, Andrew Picken, Patrick Shirreff, Thomas William Magrath, Thomas Need, and Alfred Domett. All of these and others of special note, William Lyon Mackenzie, John Galt, Dr. Dunlop, and Mrs. Traill wrote travel and emigrant books to the total of approximately one hundred dated between 1815 and 1840. With one exception—Thomas Rolph's *A Brief Account* (Dundas, U.C., 1836)—these were not published in Canada but in Britain. If these volumes reached Canada, they arrived chiefly—as Mrs. Moodie pointed out—in the baggage of emigrants who had purchased them before leaving the home ports. The market was in the British Isles among people hungry for useful details about the colony; realism was preferred above romanticizing.

Travel books may be called literature of quality if they perform the higher literary functions of fiction and achieve something of form, that is, if they go beyond "statistical accounts" and settlers' handbooks to create the myth of the new country, and at the same time show affinity with journals, sketches, essays, autobiographies, extended anecdotes, and other ordered narratives. Such fiction led to novels of manners in this age and place, when North American matter-of-factness was paralleled in Britain by a rising middle-class distrust of exotic romances. The vogue of Dickens was yet to come, but Scotland had an earlier writer, John Galt (1779–1839), who exhibited brilliantly what the novel could be if it did not become aristocratic, Gothic, historical, or even sentimental. His *Annals of the Parish* (1821) and *The Ayrshire Legatees* (1821) were in the long tradition of the Addisonian essay, of Defoe, Smollett, and Maria Edgeworth. Galt's intimate realistic descriptions of lowland Scottish characters (not without malicious touches) made fiction, as Mrs. Margaret Oliphant alleged, "of facts scarcely modified at all save by the machinery of story-telling."

By a rare coincidence, Galt came to Upper Canada in 1826 to be superintendent of the Canada Company's colonization scheme, and stayed until 1829. *Lawrie Todd* (1830) and *Bogle Corbet* (1831), his "Canadian novels," written after his return to England, were addressed to the British and American public as well as the Canadian. The action of *Lawrie Todd* is set in northern New York state, near enough to Guelph and Goderich to make Galt's Canadian experiences serve the text. He had his era's flair for large-scale planning; in some ways this was to be the comprehensive emigrant and travel book for this broad band of the American-Canadian Northwest. All the "forms" of travel literature were to coalesce in a novel. His habit of using "familiar models" accounted for his creation of Zerobabel L. Hoskins, a dialect-speaking Yankee character (five years before Sam Slick), and his use of Grant Thorburn's autobiography, which he literally purchased from Thorburn for exploitation ("a little poetical") in *Lawrie Todd*. *Bogle Corbet*, a sequel demanded by publishers, was meant to be more directly helpful to Canadian immigrants. Half of it was set in Glasgow, London, and Jamaica and the rest in Upper Canada near the Debit (that is, the Credit) River. Some of the Scottish passages rank with Galt's best efforts in witty description. Observation, ingenuity, humour, the right tone, reliable detail, and general applicability made these novels popular, though only for a few decades. No one has attempted to annotate their many allusions. Yet, as long as *Lawrie Todd* had a vogue, it advanced the cause of realistic fiction in the Canadas.

The Scots, Irish, English, and Yankees thronging Canadian ports, roads, forests, and villages included many "stage" types, whose living images can be recovered from the voluminous travel literature. Among these Dr. William "Tiger" Dunlop (1792–1848) was a prime character, willing to pose or to put himself on paper. His "Recollections of the American War" in the *Literary Garland* of 1847 excelled all such memoirs except Walter Henry's, and far surpassed Henry's in humour and charm. His own gifts for entertainment, combined with conscious employment of the manners of the *Blackwood's* circle (he played tiger to their leopard, scorpion, and boar), made him the most celebrated conservative literary man in Upper Canada. Coarse, candid, and realistic, he liked the frontier, and turned his merry bachelor life at "Gairbraid" into a legend. His *Statistical Sketches of Upper Canada* (1832) was famous for its sections on climate, "field-sports," cookery, and the like. This array of topics, impishly planned to suggest an Old Countryman's polite inquiries, was handled with an unspecified amount of buffoonery and burlesque. Dunlop thus persuaded his old friends, the Scottish reviewers, and, no doubt, a host of emigrants that Canada was a pleasant place. Admiration outlived him, and two women, Robina and Kathleen Lizars, revealed their love affair with his memory in a book, almost a novel, *In the Days of the Canada Company, 1825–1850* (1896). The "almost-novel" is precisely his place, for the good-natured sketch-cum-novel is the principal indigenous contribution to the literature of manners from Dunlop and Mrs. Traill to Stephen Leacock.

Dunlop was the untamed male in the backwoods; Mrs. Anna Brownell Jameson (1794–1860), a distinguished visitor, was the sophisticated feminist. *Winter Studies and Summer Rambles in Canada* (London, 1838), a remarkable book of travel, observation, and research, exhibited Mrs. Jameson's extra-curricular entertainment while she was attempting to make a settlement with her estranged husband, Robert S. Jameson, head of the legal profession in Upper Canada. She was always the accomplished European gentlewoman, the popular British author of *Loves of the Poets* (1829), *Memoirs of Celebrated Female Sovereigns* (1831), and *Characteristics of Women* (1831), the last of these being a contribution to Shakespeare criticism. She saw Colonel Talbot, colonial housewives, the Schoolcrafts of Mackinaw, and the squaws with a discerning feminine eye. "Few European women of refined and civilized habits" had taken such risks as she had in the northern waters, and none had recorded them. Her controlled sentiment, shrewd comments, delightful style, and an "impertinent leaven of egotism" gave Upper Canada one of the masterpieces of North American travel literature and a remarkable document of womanly independence.

For Mrs. Catharine Parr Traill (1802–1899) and Mrs. Susanna Moodie, refined ladies who adopted the life of settlers' wives, the problem of describing the country was not so easy. Their traditional idiom of ideas and words did not fit daily marginal living in the bush near Cobourg and Peterborough. A defence could be set up by use of stock words with inflexible interpretations, or surrender could be announced by a change of idiom with the risk of unpredictable responses. In the latter direction lay a fresh North American literature, but also, they felt, the destruction of their social order. Mrs. Traill, who lived thirty years in England and sixty-five years in Canada, gave in slowly because she suspected that the law and order of her new world was founded in a sublimely regulated nature rather than, as at home, in a fully regulated society. She began her report in *The Backwoods of Canada* (London, 1836), a book which became so popular that N. P. Willis extracted fifty-eight large pages from it to accompany the W. H. Bartlett prints in *Canadian Scenery* (1842). She continued her description in "Forest Gleanings," published serially (1852–53) in the *Anglo-American Magazine* of Toronto. And she won distinction as a naturalist in such books as *Canadian Wild Flowers* (1869), *Studies of Plant Life in Canada* (1885), and *Pearls and Pebbles* (1894).

Mrs. Traill brought a sense of immediacy, cheerful realism, controlled sentiment, shrewd comment, and a delightfully honest style to the series of autobiographical letters (addressed to her mother and friends in England) which made up the *Backwoods* volume. She established the image of the settler in the bush. Her chapter headings alone suggest some details: "the ocean voyage/ majestic and mighty river/ up the river to Montreal/ impressions of city and country/ first problems of backwoods/ Peterborough and environs/ journey through the woods/ settling on the land/ building a log-house/ winter in Canada/ problems of new settlers/ clearing the land/ Indian neigh-bours/ Canadian wild flowers/ Canada, the land of hope/ summer and its visitors/ some ills and troubles/ increasing home comforts/ the Mackenzie rebellion/ bush weddings."

Mrs. Moodie's *Roughing It* (London, 1852) belonged to the same period; Susanna lived in the bush near Cobourg and on the Otonabee, in eastern Ontario, from 1832 to 1840. She wrote occasional "Canadian" poems and sketches at least as early as 1838, and published the first of these sketches in the *Literary Garland* of 1847. She took more time than Mrs. Traill in making literature of the backwoods life, although she was personally less patient. *Roughing It* was primarily the result of nursing her tensions. This she did while she celebrated her escape (after 1840) and became a social critic. Her ideal was the home she had known in Suffolk, where she, Elizabeth, Agnes, Sara, Jane, Catharine, and Samuel Strickland—six sisters and one brother—had practised polite living and instructive writing in an evangelical and sentimental atmosphere not yet called "Victorian." Agnes had become the most famous of them, with *Lives of the Queens of England* (1840–48).

Susanna (Mrs. Moodie) advocated and illustrated such an English life for Canadians in a series of "English" novels in *The Literary Garland* (1838–51) of Montreal; in the *Victoria Magazine* (1847–48), "a cheap periodical for the Canadian people" which she edited with her husband at Belleville; and summarily and explicitly in *Life in the Clearings* (1853). So much experience with the craft of story-telling prepared her to carry emigrant fiction a step beyond John Galt's *Lawrie Todd* in the direction of the apprenticeship novel, a record of personal development rather than a survey of other people's lives. There are indeed many characters in *Roughing It* but they are all revealed as they rub against Mrs. Moodie, and as they add something to the image of herself—the suffering, learning author-heroine. Her liveliness, guileful humour, crafty rhetoric, mimicry of dialogue, polite "roughing," and romancing about herself were almost too successful. The settlers themselves resented her stubborn superiority, and thought that she exaggerated and distorted the truth for gullible outsiders. Her books were not popular in the Canadas until she publicly adopted all Canadians, and Canada itself, in a preface to her first edition in this country (in 1871, after Confederation). Since then she has been regarded, much too uncritically, as the typical settler's wife.

9. Literary Activity
in Canada East and West
1841-1880

CARL F. KLINCK

I. GENTEEL COLONIALISM (1841–1855)

MONTREAL WAS THE NATURAL CENTRE for literary activity about 1840. The rebellion of 1837 was over, the two Canadas were united politically in 1841, and in December 1838 the Montreal *Literary Garland* had begun publication. A decade of transatlantic immigration toward the near west (Upper Canada) had strengthened the British foundation of literary endeavour. In the United States, especially in the eastern cities, there was a vogue of gentility, not unaptly described as English and Victorian, upheld by a polite reaction against the cruder aspects of western expansion. It was a world for women. John Lovell published *The Literary Garland*; John Gibson was editor; and men of the literary clubs, even rugged souls like Dunlop and Richardson, contributed. But the substance and tone were set by invincible ladies of Old British or Bostonian origin upon the pattern of the popular annuals or gift-books of the 1820's and their inevitable consequence, monthly journals, of which Godey's *Lady's Book*, begun in 1830, was the most famous.

The Montreal *Garland* bore a typical gift-book title, barely escaping a name like *Amulet, Iris,* or *Dew-Drop,* and the contents were consistently described as "gems" or "flowers." Every "boudoir from the Atlantic to Lake Erie" was to have them. In such precious pieces American *mores* allowed some eroticism. Sentimental romance had been taken over by female authors who were beguiling their sisters with wishful excitement, captivating menfolk by delicate attitudes, teaching good conduct by suggesting and deploring seduction, and thus delaying the rise of serious fiction. Poets like Letitia E. Landon served a similar popular demand, yet L.E.L. was copied in the respectable journals almost as much as Mrs. Hemans and Mrs. Lydia H. Sigourney. In Hemans and Sigourney the *Garland* probably found suitable models of taste, writers who could measure out excitement and instruction in acceptable proportions. This the editors also attempted to accomplish through fiction and verse in terms of middle-class morality, evangelical religion, superior status, high fashion, and English modes of thought.

The *Garland* kept up its own supply of didactically charged society tales, together with the inevitable biblical narratives, dramatic sketches and poems. The temptation to be English in the aristocratic or upper-gentlefolk manner was, of course, especially strong in the British colonies, where class distinctions lived a precarious life among only the favoured few. W. D. Howells would have seen much positive harm being done by literature catering to the dreams of this minority. The life portrayed was obviously foreign to most Canadian readers, who had shared in these things neither before nor after emigration. As the expression of a social goal or as a palliative it was deplorable. In literature, idealism must clothe itself in a certain dress, and the *Garland*'s garments wafted a strong perfume of artificiality to men and women on the farms and in the towns. The settlers were too literate and practical to be content with condescension or escapism; and the exotic was not well calculated to affect their religious lives. As a cultural experiment, the *Garland* had the commendable purpose of overcoming colonial rawness, of being a genteel supplement to the popular education which W. L. Mackenzie and the Rev. Egerton Ryerson demanded. As an aid to the development of a national literature, it taught certain skills, but it was a parlour game. It encouraged amenable native talent, but it made only feeble attempts to discover a native norm in content, treatment, or quality.

It was Anglo-Bostonian rather than Anglo-Canadian. "We were certain," the editor wrote in January 1843, "that the seed of Old England and of New England, which had been sown in Canada, could not be unproductive." The Old English tone was supplied by Mrs. Moodie, who had published *Enthusiasm and Other Poems* (1831) before leaving her homeland in 1832, and by Mrs. McLachlan, wife of a colonel of the Royal Engineers. But Eastern American contributions in the same mood were made by two Bostonian ladies living in Montreal. These two were, by a happy chance, daughters of Hannah Webster Foster (1759–1840), one of the earliest exponents of the sentimental novel in America, author of *The Coquette; or, the History of Eliza Wharton* (1797). The daughters had published New World historical romances in Boston in the 1820's, before they came to Canada. Their names and works were spread all over the pages of the *Garland*: Mrs. Eliza L. Cushing (1794–1886) contributed at least seventy varied items and finally became editor; Mrs. Harriet V. Cheney wrote poems and prose sketches in the early and the late period of the *Garland*'s existence. Another sister, Miss T. D. Foster (Mrs. Henry Giles), sent in, probably from Boston, her valuable articles on the culture of the Latin countries of Europe. The *Garland* was almost "entirely the produce of Canadian talent," but it was only rarely, as in Mrs. Moodie's "Canadian" poems, devoted to distinctively native subject-matter.

The *Literary Garland* was "done to death" in 1851 by the competitive American journals which it imitated; it was also ready for death because of something insecure in its British connections. The contemporary English period which it reflected had an "interim" quality; it favoured minor writers and period pieces. No one knows what a rejuvenated *Garland* would have become in the 1860's, when strong political nationalism in Canada found corresponding vigour in the major Victorian literary forces of George Eliot; Tennyson the Poet Laureate; Longfellow, the American more than half adopted by Britain; Keats, reborn in Tennyson and the Pre-Raphaelites; and Arnold, whose serene "culture" promised support against the excesses of North American republicanism, of which even Emerson and Whitman seemed to bear the marks.

Cultural tenacity was the clue to everything in the *Garland*. "The literature of a country," James Holmes wrote in August 1840, "is the *measure* of its progress towards refinement." Literature was also a *means* to that end. The *Garland's* programme was not meant to be nostalgic; it was optimistically designed to build a better North American world along lines of evangelical middle-class piety prevailing over any relics of Jacobinism, Regency licentiousness, or unschooled behaviour. Whether these authors began with home thoughts, fashionable manners, foreign history, biblical situations, war, Indians, love, loss, sacrifice, flowers, or illimitable works of God, they ended up with lessons in religious and social propriety. The monotony of the *Garland* poems, which were admirable enough in execution, was due to lack of tension, to a strategy concerned less with word-structure than with making the ideas come out right in cadences nicely adjusted to resolution in the purposes of God and Anglo-Bostonian society. The clergy, ranking also as cultural and religious arbiters, lent their support as the Rev. Edward Hartley Dewart (1828–1908) did in *Selections from Canadian Poets* (Montreal, 1864).

His excellent critical introduction was in effect a summing-up of genteel principles. Yet Dewart searched for more than Canadian talent in the generation of the 1860's; he gathered verses on Canadian themes inspired by incipient nationalism. His *Selections*, the first and last general anthology compiled before Confederation, represented Canadian poets alone, without any admixture of borrowed song. Collectively, these poets described their country's scenery, seasons, and weather with more love than realism, and they presented human beings responding ideally to typical situations. The book is panoramic, charming, and promising, indicative of considerable talent and craftsmanship at work during the last decade of colonial status.

Charles Sangster and Charles Heavysege, two of Dewart's major poets, were capable of winning recognition from a few genteel reviewers in the eastern United States and in Britain—and therefore in Canada. Both were lonely writers, self-made, striving hard for excellence in style which they knew was above them, Sangster looking to Byron, Scott, Milton, and Tennyson, and Heavysege looking to the Bible and Shakespeare. Sangster (1822–1893), born in Kingston, Upper Canada, lived in humble circumstances all his life, whether he worked in the Ordnance Office at Kingston, in newspaper establishments at Amherstburg or Kingston, or in the civil service department at Ottawa. During the 1850's he produced at least 450 pages of poetry; *The St. Lawrence and the Saguenay* was published at Kingston in 1856, and *Hesperus* in 1860 at Montreal. Sangster was not content with the world he viewed around him; he insisted on idealizing and ornamenting it:

> And so I love my art; chiefly, because
> Through it I rev'rence Nature, and improve
> The tone and tenor of the mind He gave.

Only in some sonnets "written in the Orillia Woods" and in occasional stanzas did his stock diction happily subside. Generally it is the echoes (managed by something more than dilettantism) and not Sangster's elaborations of ideas that reach toward profundity and power. Dewart's period piece of criticism made these claims for Sangster: "the richness and extent of his contributions, the originality and descriptive power he displays, the variety of Canadian themes on which he has written with force and elegance, his passionate sympathy with the beautiful in nature, and the chivalrous and manly patriotism which finds an utterance in his poems." This statement, by omission, emphasizes Sangster's deficiencies—he lacked a fresh approach and fresh human interest.

Charles Heavysege (1816–1876), an immigrant from England to Montreal in 1853, displayed in his *Revolt of Tartarus*, a Miltonic epic (published in England, 1852), the uncertainties of solitary, bookish, high-brow poeticizing in an English, and (soon) a North American, plebeian environment. Reliance upon the Old Testament and Shakespeare was part of the tradition. Chatham's Abraham Holmes, a satirist, could refer humorously to his Belinda "whose neck was like the tower of David, and head like Mount Carmel," but Heavysege would incorporate such a reference into impassioned imagery. Heavysege was solemnly in earnest, without the range and humour of his contemporary Herman Melville, whose American *Moby Dick* (1851) was biblical and Shakespearean in its own way, and showed its author, as Heavysege's works also did, at odds with God. For such an interpretation of Heavysege—appealing to criticism in our own day—one must remain indebted to Thomas R. Dale and his unpublished thesis on Heavysege (Chicago, 1951).

This poet did his best work in a single decade, while he was a cabinetmaker in Hilton's factory in Montreal (1853–60) and in his first years as a reporter (after 1860) on the Montreal *Transcript* and the *Daily Witness*. His books consisted of *The Revolt of Tartarus* (reprinted in Montreal, 1855);

Sonnets (1855); *Saul*, a Shakespeare-like closet drama of 135 scenes based on the biblical account of King Saul (1857 and 1859); *Count Filippo; or, The Unequal Marriage*, an "Italian" five-act tragedy of love and intrigue (1860); and *Jephthah's Daughter*, again a poetic narrative full of long speeches (1865). *Saul* was his best and representative work, and it was the one around which Coventry Patmore in the *North British Review* (1858) consolidated the view that Heavysege's theme was, as the angel said, "Faith lacking, all his [Saul's] works fell short." In all of Heavysege, however, Thomas Dale finds guarded "suggestions of divine injustice," of God's will as "a capricious and vindictive power." There is "not a grand denunciation in the manner of Blake or Shelley, nor an appeal from Christianity to Paganism in the manner of Swinburne or Hardy." But Dale draws attention to "the careful selection of damaging incident in the Biblical poems, and the complete silence maintained on such matters as divine mercy and happiness in a future life; the psychological truth of his tortured human characters, and the stony bleakness of the natural and supernatural forces which hem them in." Such an understanding of Heavysege is scarcely available to readers who see only anthologies containing a few of the very good sonnets and some extracts from the rhetorical speeches of the fallen angel Malzah, the evil spirit of Saul, a character creation which Patmore thought was equalled in our language only in Caliban and Ariel.

The genteel writers did not have it all to themselves. Before leaving the period from 1841 to 1855, one must look at some Victorian rebels, and at some others who thought they were only old-fashioned, or merely "down to earth." The latter, of course, were close to the bulk of the population, for most colonists read nothing if they did not scan newspapers in shops and taverns. One work which originated in the political world of journalism, *How I Came to be Governor of the Island of Cacona* (Montreal, 1852) by "the Hon. Francis Thistleton"—properly William Henry Fleet of the Montreal *Transcript*—qualifies as satiric fiction ridiculing a vulnerable foreign aristocrat, Lieutenant Governor Sir Francis Bond Head, himself an essayist of considerable charm and author of *A Narrative* (1839).

At least one journal, *The Magic Lantern* of Montreal (1848), attempted overt opposition to the *Garland*'s "romantic young ladies" who "expended their sentimentality upon the public." There were rumblings even within the pages of the *Garland*. Carl Ballstadt has drawn attention to the contributions of "W.P.C." of Williamstown (the town of the Northwesters near Cornwall). In an article on "Our Literature, Present and Prospective" (May 1848), W.P.C. regretted that "of late, our manner of reading has, I fear, included too much of the ideal and romantic, and too little of the real and practical." He recommended, as an antidote to foreign sentimental literature, more devotion to native historical writing and national songs; W.P.C. is thus in the line leading to Thomas D'Arcy McGee. Another significant line may be called the popular-academic, emerging in the 1850's with *The Canadian Journal*, and leading to *The British American Magazine, The Canadian Monthly*, and *The Week*. An uncertain beginning had been made as early as the 1840's through the efforts of the Rev. Dr. John McCaul, Vice-President and Professor of classics, logic, rhetoric and *belles-lettres* in King's College, Toronto (and later Vice-Chancellor of the University of Toronto). He thought in terms of twining lovely flowers with the maple leaf when he edited *The Maple Leaf; or, Canadian Annual, a Literary Souvenir* (1847–49). Although he relied upon European subject-matter, he insisted upon text and engravings which were the "produce" of Canada: "the only hands, which should weave the garland, should be those of her children by birth or by adoption."

Belinda; or, The Rivals: A Tale of Real Life (Detroit, 1843) sprang from a radically different environment. This burlesque of sentimental fiction was prepared in the west, at or near Chatham, where fashionable life, if there was any, was exposed to frontier irreverence and Wesleyan reproof. So few copies are extant that one may suspect confiscation of the rest by irate neighbours whose "real life" found its way into the book. The anonymous author, Abraham S. Holmes, a young law student and journalist, was the son of a well-known Wesleyan preacher and teacher of American origin. It is likely that both Holmes's coarseness and his polish were deliberately assumed. Excuses could be found for poor taste on the part of this author; the American Old Northwest (north and west of Cincinnati) had produced scarcely any native books of fiction except Mrs. Caroline M. Kirkland's *A New Home* (1839), published in Philadelphia. But Holmes may need no excuses. His creation of one of the rare true coquettes in North American fiction since Arabella Fermor (Emily Montague's friend in Frances Brooke's novel, 1769) looks like originality. Holmes's Belinda was not one of the many young ladies seduced by their own feelings and by unscrupulous men— to teach moral lessons, of course—in the hundreds of sentimental novels which were an American fad from Mrs. Foster's time until the Civil War. Miss Marilyn Davis, in a thesis on *Belinda* (University of Western Ontario, 1963), has pointed out that Holmes's heroine is not a victim, but an aggressor—seducing even her creator.

Coquetry is one of the lively arts: capturing it in words, as Holmes has done, requires Belinda's or Eve's own skill. Burlesquing it and, at the same time, standing up as a Methodist took a good deal of doing. Holmes's main equipment consisted of a flair for language, an uneasy conscience about rhetoric, a sophomoric delight in mimicry, a hodge-podge stock of quotations, a sharp eye for misconduct, and enough objectivity (legal and/or journalistic) for ironic dramatization. The disappearance of all but two copies has denied a host of posthumous admirers to a coquette who "at church . . . had the indescribable pleasure of seeing all her beaux together." Chatham's gift to the fiction of the early wild West, who got half a dozen men without a gun, lost the fame her sins deserved because of her author's literary promiscuity.

The *Anglo-American Magazine* (Toronto, 1852–55) may be reckoned among the folksy, rather than the genteel, forces. Its editor was the Rev. Robert Jackson MacGeorge (1811?–1884), known as "Solomon of Streetsville" because of his popular exposure of follies in the *Streetsville Weekly Review*. Associated with him editorially was Gilbert Auchinleck, author of a *History of the War of 1812* which, along with Mrs. Traill's "Forest Gleanings," was the magazine's principal contribution to formal literature. The rest of it was gossipy in the old-fashioned Scottish way of "Noctes Ambrosianae" and other *Blackwood's* articles. MacGeorge spoke out against "twaddle," "slip-slop romances," and "the gentle insipidity of the *Ladies Magazine*," and put his extensive knowledge of literature at the service of his public. *Uncle Tom's Cabin; or, Life among the Lowly*, in the year of its appearance (1852) transcended all his prejudices.

This American novel by Harriet Beecher Stowe affected all levels of literature just when the railroad expansion of the 1850's was linking Upper Canadian cities closely and rapidly with the great American centres. Little more than a half century had brought this change from the small-boat economy of Thomas Moore's time. British immigration to Upper Canada was subsiding. Everything favoured an immense extension of the cultural influence of the United States, if war between the states could be prevented. *Uncle Tom's Cabin* broke the high-middle-class monopoly which Mrs. Moodie and Mrs. Cushing stood for, and brought evangelical piety and sentiment into a broad, popular literary domain. Dickens's novels alone could not have effected this literary revolution in the Canadas.

It should be noted also that here another humanitarian force had been operating, especially on the level of the newspaper poets, among the Scots devoted to the school of Robert Burns. Of these, the acknowledged master was Alexander McLachlan (1818–1896), whom Dewart praised as "the sweetest and most intensely human of all our Canadian bards." The author of *Lyrics* (1858), *The Emigrant and Other Poems* (1861) and (later) *Poems and Songs* (1874) had come as a poor young man from Glasgow in 1840 and had committed himself to rural life in central Canada West. Dewart's selections from McLachlan seem calculated to show that this poet was not ungenteel, but his popular reputation depended upon such songs as "Acres of His Own," "Up, and be a Hero," "Young Canada, or, Jack's as Good as his Master," and "The Man Who Rose from Nothing." Not all Scots were or remained humble, but there was a poor man's Scottish tradition integrated with the earlier equalitarian tradition of the North American pioneer. It was given support by *Uncle Tom's Cabin*, the story of persons much more "lowly."

The "dialect" versifiers had long been active, with the help of fraternal societies and the local newspaper editors, in strengthening real or mystic bonds of nostalgia for either Scotland or Ireland and in fostering rather deliberate literature of exile which can be mistakenly interpreted as indicating dissatisfaction with Canada. Rightly understood, their verses were hymns of Scottish and Irish conquest, signs that Canada was theirs (and, they might have said, not Mrs. Moodie's). Many of them were prospering, going up in the world, and, if they were at times understandably homesick, they could share their sentiments. There were many of them, too many to name; but a sense of their variety and their enterprise may be gained by reference to three men who formed a bridge between those who repeated verses from home but wrote nothing, and the later generations who echoed sentiments in verses about ancestral lands which they had never seen.

Old Country "idiom" is a step beyond simple "dialect" and the term describes best what men like Stephens, Menzies, and MacQueen brought into the seedbed of Canadian writing. William A. Stephens (1809–1891) of Owen Sound, an immigrant from Northern Ireland in early boyhood, became a public phenomenon by the ease and frequency with which he composed impromptu verses in an eighteenth-century manner. When the "Hamilton mountain" was set as a poetical "task" for him by a lady about 1840, he opened on a description of Creation with unmated primeval creatures seeking companions. George Menzies (1796?–1847), who established the *Woodstock Herald*, had published verses when he was a gardener in Scotland; his *Poems*, containing a record of sorrowful thoughts, were published posthumously in Woodstock (1850) and in Aberdeen (1854). Thomas MacQueen (1803–1861), editor of the *Bathurst Courier* before he founded the *Huron Signal* in 1849, published three books of verse in Scotland and only one poem, "Our Own Broad Lake," in Canada. One of his books described him as "The Cottage Philosopher," since he was greatly given to "observations on morals and politics"; he had been a mason in Barkip, near Beith, and had dedicated himself to elevating the minds of the working classes.

II. THE CONFEDERATION ERA (1855–1880)

In Toronto, late in 1855, during "boom times," a great Railway Festival was held, which J. M. S. Careless in *Brown of the Globe* (p. 212) has called "really a public jubilee for the railway god himself." "And in the summer of 1856," Professor Careless continues (p. 229), "as a group of Toronto business men took active steps to open communications with the North West, Brown and his journal began a powerful campaign to awaken Canadians to the value and potentialities of the great Hudson's Bay territories." A travel book of the time, William H. G. Kingston's *Western Wanderings* (London, 1856), described Toronto as a city of colleges, public buildings, and polite society, and the home of the artist Paul Kane.

Not as apparent, but also very significant for literary vision was a shift in the policy of *The Canadian Journal: A Repertory of Industry, Science and Art*, founded in Toronto in August 1852, under the editorship of Henry Youle Hind, by the Canadian Institute as "a publication devoted to the Arts and Sciences of practical life." The journal in itself had been an important step in communication between those engaged in scientific and in industrial pursuits: to "assist, lighten and elevate the labours of the mechanic" and to "afford information to the manufacturer." The universities had had a place in the scheme; eight new institutions had been founded in the Canadas since the American War: McGill in Montreal (1821), Queen's in Kingston (1827), Victoria in Cobourg (1841), Bishop's in Lennoxville (1843), Ottawa in Ottawa (1848), and three Toronto colleges, King's (1827), Trinity (1851), and St. Michael's (1852). The University of Toronto was given its name in 1850 and reconstituted in 1853.

In January 1856 the *Canadian Journal* began a new series with a new purpose; the university men had taken over, to help to give recognized or independent existence to the sciences of Canada, to provide "a medium of communication" for subjects which could not be "profitably treated of in a popular form." In effect it became a learned, not a "mechanical," journal, with "departments" served almost wholly by Toronto professors, E. J. Chapman, James Bovell, Daniel Wilson, H. Y. Hind, Henry Croft, J. B. Cherriman, and the Rev. G. C. Irving. Other scholarly contributors were also welcome: in September 1857, for example, the Rev. A. Constable Geikie made a detailed survey of neologisms in "Canadian English." In February 1856 a similar journal, restricted more narrowly to science, was born in Montreal under the name of *The Canadian Naturalist* (later called *The Canadian Naturalist and Geologist*), sponsored by the Natural History Society of Montreal and supported chiefly by McGill professors. The leading authors in the early days were Elkanah Billings (the editor), Principal (later Sir) William Dawson, Sir William E. Logan (head of the Canadian Geological Survey, organized in 1842), T. Sterry Hunt, and Charles Smallwood. The Earl of Dalhousie's dreams for learned societies and publications were coming true. In content and style, of course, these journals were wholly different from the *Literary Garland*.

The *Canadian Journal* (Toronto), did not disregard the humanities. Daniel

Wilson (1816–1892) (later Sir Daniel, and President of the University of Toronto) dealt with English literature, but also history, ethnology and archaeology, since he was expert in these matters, having written a notable book, *The Archaeology and Prehistoric Annals of Scotland* (1851), two years before he came to Toronto. Many years later he put all these things together, along with Shakespeare's *The Tempest*, in *Caliban, the Missing Link* (1873). Meanwhile, he commented upon current British and American books, with one eye open for Canadiana. In a few learned reviews he established academic literary criticism in the Canadas.

It was a significant moment when, in January 1858, Wilson devoted a long article to Charles Sangster's *The St. Lawrence and the Saguenay,* McLachlan's *Poems,* Carroll Ryan's *Oscar,* and Professor E. J. Chapman's *A Song of Charity.* Wilson was fair, not snobbish, when he found most of Sangster's and Chapman's words and "music" to be regrettably "old worldish." For these men, no less than for Tennyson, he said, the nineteenth century could be "as fresh an *el dorado* as America was to Cortes or Pizaro." He believed that "its politics, its geology, its philosophy, its utopian aspirations, its homely fashions and fancies, all yield to his [Tennyson's] eye suggestive imagery rich with pregnant thought." These would come to the New World poet, he believed, if the poet would see "things as they are." "It is not," he added, "a 'Hiawatha' song we demand." Nor, another review indicated, was it *Leaves of Grass* by a Canadian Whitman that he desired. The *Canadian Journal* had little more to say in this period about the country's *belles lettres,* but Wilson's vision for the Canadian poet was not lost in the universities.

The *British American Magazine* (Toronto, 1863–64) was evidently planned to bring scholarly perception in matters of Canadian literature to a public broader than the restricted membership of the Institute. Henry Youle Hind (1823-1908), a noted explorer, chemist, geologist, and professor at Trinity College, Toronto, who had been first editor of the *Canadian Journal*, now joined Graeme Mercer Adam (1839–1912), an enterprising publisher, in founding the *British American*—a learned-popular magazine. The table of contents looked as if Hind and Adam had possessed, four years before its time, Henry J. Morgan's *Bibliotheca Canadensis* (1867)—an impressive 400-page volume of bio-bibliographical sketches of pre-Confederation authors —and had solicited contributions from the most promising among them. The best-known among those represented were Mrs. Moodie, Mrs. Traill, Mrs. Leprohon, the Rev. Dr. Scadding, Daniel Wilson, Thomas D'Arcy McGee, and Charles Mair.

Along with conscientious surveys of general literature, including the broad range of contemporary British and American journals, the *British American* printed original writings which reveal that the awakening of Canadian cultural life generally assigned to the 1870's and 1880's was actually under way in the 1860's. Looking backward and forward, one can see this complex of Canadian literary interests in existence even before Confederation. Mrs. M. J. H. Holiwell's serial novel, "The Settler's Daughter" (1863), a step from immigration literature toward the commonplace small-town novel, and Thomas D'Arcy McGee's pleas for "British American Nationality," both published in the *British American* (August and October 1863), are examples of what had become articulate since the demise of the *Garland*.

Thomas D'Arcy McGee (1825–1868) was the chief orator and literary man, as Sir John A. Macdonald was the leading politician, among the founding "Fathers of Confederation," who brought Ontario, Quebec, New Brunswick, and Nova Scotia into a national union by the British North America Act of 1867. "Our next census—in 1870—will find us over 4,000,000 souls," McGee told the Montreal Literary Club on November 4, 1867, in an address on "The Mental Outfit of the New Dominion" (the "incipient new nation"). He did not live until the census total was announced, a half million below his guess, but he raised the spirits of Canadians as he had never failed to do since he had settled in Montreal ten years before. On May 2, 1860, "standing before an enchanted legislature," as the Right Honourable Arthur Meighen later described it, McGee had spoken of the Northern Nation:

I look to the future of my adopted country with hope, though not without anxiety; I see in the not remote distance one great nationality bound, like the shield of Achilles, by the blue rim of Ocean. . . . I see a generation of industrious, contented, moral men, free in name and in fact,—men capable of maintaining, in peace and in war, a Constitution worthy of such a country.

McGee's phrases have become part of the Canadian language. His own accents were Irish. Ireland, which had given him life, also in a sense gave him a martyr's death, for he was shot down in Ottawa in April 1868 by a lurking assassin because he had denounced the Fenians, those of the American Irish who had turned the quarrels of their Old Country into a movement threatening the peace of Canada. McGee's whole-hearted adoption of the cause of Canadian nationalism during the last ten years of his life never quite freed him from his ties to Ireland itself. There too he had passionately wished a new nation to be born, and he had taken his place in the famous "Young Ireland" group of the 1840's, which replaced the Repeal Association of Daniel O'Connell and included Charles Gavan Duffy, Thomas Davis, John Mitchell and Samuel Ferguson (who became a link with the Irish Literary Revival of Yeats's generation). Most of them were literary men, and literature played an important part in their programme. They were the founders of the *Nation*, a Dublin newspaper (1842–48). McGee was associated with them from 1846 to 1848, and for a time edited the *Nation*. Like Duffy, he was driven into exile; the former had a notable public career in Australia, and McGee in

Canada, after a spell of vigorous Irish and Roman Catholic journalism in the United States (1848–57).

McGee's efforts on behalf of his people in the United States are generally understood, but his earlier leadership in the "Young Ireland" group of 1846–48 has not been sufficiently emphasized with regard to Canada's literary history. McGee, the young journalist who came to the Dublin *Nation* prepared to become a historian of the Irish people, learned from Duffy and Davis (who died in 1845) the theory and practice of "national poetry" which he later adapted to Canadian needs. In an unpublished thesis (University of Western Ontario, 1956), Miss Kathleen M. O'Donnell has demonstrated the existence of a programme devised by these men, calling for the use of literary works, principally historical works and ballads, in reviving or creating a nation and in giving it a "mental outfit." They said this in many ways: "to advance the cause of Nationality by all the aids, which literary as well as political talent could bring to its advocacy"—"to create and foster public opinion in Ireland, and to make it racy of the soil"—to teach "the native muse to become English in language without growing un-Irish in character."

For national ballads they had a formula, which Miss O'Donnell finds employed in McGee's own *Canadian Ballads* (Montreal, 1858), dedicated to Duffy in Australia, "in memory of Old Times." Duffy had published in 1845 *The Ballad Poetry of Ireland*. Fifteen of McGee's poems were ready after a year of his research into Canadian life and history; and, as if to justify his Irish formula, a number of them became immediate and lasting favourites, especially "Sebastian Cabot to his Lady," "Jacques Cartier," "The Arctic Indian's Faith" and "Our Ladye of the Snow!" McGee's ballads became the fashion. They evidently suited nicely the temperament of the Montreal Irish such as Mrs. Leprohon (Rosanna Mullins). It is interesting to speculate how much he did by such ballads about storm and ice to let the world form exciting or unfavourable opinions about the climate of British North America.

The ballads were only part of his programme, for he threw himself into public life as editor of *The New Era* (1857), member of the legislature for ten years, Father of Confederation, lecturer, orator, and advocate of Canadian culture. Meanwhile, he completed and published in New York, Toronto, Quebec, and London a half-dozen books on Canadian or Irish subjects, including a two-volume *Popular History of Ireland* (1863). He frequently gave lectures on literary topics—such as Shakespeare, Milton, Burke, Thomas Moore, Irish literature, Scottish poets, and the Robert Burns Centennial; these have been gathered into a collection of his *Speeches and Addresses* (1937) by the Honourable Charles Murphy. A large volume of his poems was issued in 1869 by Mrs. Mary Anne Sadlier (1820–1913), wife of James Sadlier, McGee's New York publisher. The editing was done *con amore*, since Mrs. Sadlier was bound by many ties to McGee's Canada. As Mary

Anne Madden, she had emigrated from Ireland to Montreal about 1847 and had written verses for the *Literary Garland* under the initials "M.A.M." This was only the beginning of her career; in the United States, after 1850, she became a prolific novelist, famous for stories of Irish emigration, especially *The Blakes and Flanagans* (1855).

The personal note is appropriate because Montreal gave opportunities for literary men to meet and encourage one another. This point is made in an otherwise undistinguished volume, *Poems by George Murray* (Montreal, 1912), prepared by John Reade, literary editor of the Montreal *Gazette* and author of *The Prophecy of Merlin, and Other Poems* (1870). Murray (1830–1910), classical master in the Montreal High School, was a graduate of King's College, London, and of Oxford. The selections in Murray's *Poems* opened with "How Canada was Saved" (written according to McGee's formula), which in 1874 had won the *Montreal Witness*'s prize for "the best ballad on any subject in Canadian history." In the "biographical sketch" Reade wrote about a literary club on Cathcart Street, of which Murray was secretary; the membership included D'Arcy McGee and Charles Heavysege, and probably the latter's friend George Martin. On the day of McGee's funeral, the club marched in a body to the grave, "each member wearing a badge of suitable device." Murray was also a leading spirit in the Athenaeum Club (begun in 1876), the Shakespeare Club, the Pen and Pencil Club, and the Royal Society of Canada (of which he was a charter member in 1882).

Rosanna Eleanor Mullins (Mrs. J. L. Leprohon) (1829–1879), by virtue of her best books, *The Manor House of de Villerai* (1859) and *Antoinette de Mirecourt* (1864), belongs to the 1860's, although she joined the contributors to the *Literary Garland* in 1846 and her *Poetical Works* were published posthumously in 1881. If she was born in 1829—the date accepted by Brother Adrian (Henry Deneau) in his unpublished thesis (University of Montreal, 1948)—then her fifteen poems, one sketch, and five serial novels appeared in the *Garland* while she was between seventeen and twenty-two years of age, the bright hope for a second generation of sentimental *Garland* romancers. Melodrama and tugging heartstrings she learned too well, but she also learned to write dialogue that was rarely lengthy, tedious, or pompous. And she found subject-matter ideally suited to her desires, re-creation of the life of the "oldest aristocracy" in the land, the French-Canadian seigneurs of the Conquest era—French society in Montreal, as it were, supplementing Mrs. Brooke's English society in Quebec. Rosanna's family was wealthy; her command of French was perfect; and J. L. Leprohon, whom she married in 1851, knew those people who preserved French family traditions.

She was able to give Canadian historical fiction new life and a richer social content, so that Heavysege imitated her (*The Advocate*, 1865) and William Kirby (*The Golden Dog*, 1877) profited by her success. This result was almost wholly due to *Antoinette de Mirecourt*, written and published in English, and also popular in French translation. *Le Manoir de Villerai* became virtually a French book because the *Family Herald*, in which it appeared, was discontinued, while Edouard L. de Bellefeuille's translation (1861), frequently reprinted in French, remained. Like *Antoinette, Mrs.* Leprohon's poems (in the posthumous edition by John Reade) have the mid-Victorian tone and diction of the *Literary Garland*, Dewart's selections, Tennyson, and Long-fellow. They also have unmistakably the accents of Montreal and the new nation. Very few of the themes one associates with D'Arcy McGee, Charles Mair, Isabella Crawford, and Wilfred Campbell were left without a parallel tribute by Mrs. Leprohon; the transition from the pioneer verse of Mrs. Moodie to that of the early "Dominion" poets is nowhere more clearly shown than in Mrs. Leprohon's "Jacques Cartier's First Visit to Mount Royal," "A Canadian Summer Evening" "The White Canoe," "Red Rock Camp: A Tale of Early Colorado," and "An Afternoon in July."

William Kirby (1817–1906), also a romancer and poet, seems old-fashioned by comparison; his dedication to Canadian subject-matter was combined with literary manners derived from Goldsmith, the Tennyson of the *Idylls*, Sir Walter Scott, and Dumas the elder. Although he was an immigrant from England, he was temperamentally a Loyalist of the Niagara border, intent on making neo-Loyalists of British Canadians of the second or third generation, for whom nationalism rather than antiquarianism could raise an interest in pre-immigrant history. Kirby married into a Loyalist family, edited the Niagara *Mail* (1850–63), indulged in local historical research, became a public figure, corresponded with great men, and kept his eye on Tennyson, the Poet Laureate. Kirby came to Canada when the *Literary Garland* began, but he never contributed to it. *The U.E.: A Tale of Upper Canada in XII Cantos* was written in 1846, but published at Niagara in the *Mail* office in 1859. The cantos were in rhyming couplets, as were some of the idylls collected with others in blank verse in *Canadian Idylls* (Toronto, 1881, and enlarged later). On taking up *The U.E.*, one wishes Kirby well; one tries to read again; and one is still disappointed. The historical material of the Niagara Loyalists failed to find an appropriate form. The idyll had no life to lend this Canadian antique material, and even Isabella Crawford's near-genius was defeated by this genre in *Malcolm's Katie* (1884).

Scott and Dumas provided models more readily suited to North American history, as every writer of Wild West stories knows. Kirby, of course, turned toward the east, and found subject-matter more spectacular and popular than that of the Niagara frontier. In *The Golden Dog* (1877), a romance of Quebec in the days of Louis XV, Kirby pre-empted the history of the *ancien régime*, in which Mrs. Leprohon had set her *Manor House of de Villerai*. Kirby spread his net wider, painted on a broader canvas, produced an eventful story rather than a social period piece, and addressed readers in whom the nationalism of the Confederation period had instilled more regard for history. He had kept his eyes open for glamorous material; there were historical details concerning the Chateau of Beaumanoir, the Castle of St. Louis, the Intendant Bigot, Peter Kalm, Philibert, de Repentigny, de la Galissonière, La Corriveau, and "Le Chien d'Or." Parkman noted in a letter to James MacPherson Le Moine that Kirby had "*well* read" Le Moine's series of *Maple Leaves* (1863 and later). The romancer had also gained information from a young Niagara girl, who was the "living model," as Lorne Pierce said in his biography of Kirby, for Amelia de Repentigny. Kirby did not fail in telling a lively story, happily full of realistic detail. Images of Canadian life piled up rapidly under such auspices. But the development of anything native in Canadian romance was probably hindered by this example given by Kirby of ready success with European models.

While Kirby was reporting the past of Quebec, Charles Mair (1838–1917), born at Lanark in the Ottawa valley, was stepping westward, toward the far reaches of the continent. It was chiefly in the period after 1880 that he contributed to the historical and descriptive prose of the West, although his own experiences began with the first Riel rebellion of 1869–1870. Fascinating accounts of travel in the territories west and north of Ontario had been written before this time, especially between 1845 and 1860 by Bishop George J. Mountain (1845), Henry Youle Hind (geologist and explorer), Paul Kane (*Wanderings of an Artist*, 1859), and Robert Michael Ballantyne, the Scottish author of *Hudson's Bay; or, Life in the Woods of America* (1848) and many other boys' books upon which generations of young Britons built their ideas of greater Canada.

Mair's youthful verse in *Dreamland and Other Poems* (1868), a year after the founding of the Dominion, had promised nothing but a bookish career, begun in the grammar school at Perth and at Queen's University: here he was under the spell of Keats. Mair's important relationship with the men of the "Canada First" Movement at Ottawa—William A. Foster, Robert G. Haliburton, George T. Denison, and Henry J. Morgan—was too recent to affect *Dreamland*. Critics have justly found, as A. J. M. Smith has done, "a good deal of accurate observation and precise description" in these verses, but Mair's early stock diction is roughly like Sangster's in the 1850's, without Sangster's carefulness or taste. Mair might have been expected to begin where the popular poets of Dewart's *Selections* (1864) left off, moving tentatively toward Canadian authenticity, although still overwhelmed by popular English models. For Mair, however, the models were academic.

There must have been other young men in the 1860's fired at school or college by a study of Keats, Shelley, Shakespeare, Poe, perhaps Coleridge —especially the Keats of "Flora, and old Pan" happily linked to classical learning and undomesticated by Victorian accretions. Mair's *Dreamland* is evidence of what the universities could do for the poets; academic poetry, superficially at first a hindrance to Canadian literary emancipation (threatening loss of identity and a cultural lag), brought a new and inspiring freedom to Mair at Perth and Kingston before 1868. But Mair was not the man to make brilliant adaptations born of poetic insight. So *Dreamland* remains an item of literary history, throwing light, incidentally, upon the meaning of an often-quoted passage from one of Lampman's essays, in which the latter reported the excitement he experienced at Trinity College on first reading Charles G. D. Roberts's *Orion* (1880). The study of classical and English literature in more than one college in Canada was leading young men to Keats as an emancipating influence. New Brunswick's Roberts taught Lampman nothing in 1881 that Mair had not applied more explicitly to Canadian scenes before 1868: Roberts only overcame Lampman's reluctance to try his wings.

In other respects also the "immigrant" colleges of central Canada were as progressive and poetically inspiring as the Loyalist colleges of the Maritime Provinces. The infectious spirit of "Canada First," which was still strong in Toronto when Roberts sojourned there in 1883, had swept Mair off his feet in 1868, and this also was at the outset "an intellectual movement." Claude Bissell has drawn attention to William A. Foster's "Address to the Canadian National Association" (1875) (see Foster's *Canada First*, 1890, p. 77). Foster quoted with approval a "recent reviewer" who saw the "Canada First" movement as "a direct product, in some measure, of that higher culture which the universities and colleges of our land are steadily promoting." In Toronto not only the colleges were a leaven, but Mr. Goldwin Smith, a former Regius Professor at Oxford, had the stature of a Matthew Arnold. Even Isabella Valancy Crawford, who had not attended college, was warmed by the glow.

The impact of the new culture upon the poets was not confined to dipping Canadian details in Keatsian diction or to constructing national songs. British North American anti-republicanism was strong and many were ready to echo Daniel Wilson's "Not *Hiawatha*!" as well as "Not Whitman!" But the border was open, and influences from the United States freely contributed to another, more complex, growth of Canadian poetic imagery which could cope simultaneously with neo-Greekish myths and concepts of nature, Indian lore, theories of evolution, liberal theology, and primitive religion. Wilfred Campbell (1858–1918) finds his place in Canadian literary history as the exemplar of this development. Thoroughly imbued with Longfellow while he was a youth in Wiarton, Campbell moved on to University and Wycliffe Colleges in Toronto (1880–82), the city in which Daniel Wilson had recently prepared an adventure into the areas of poetic anthropology in *Caliban, the Missing Link* (1873). For two years thereafter, Campbell studied at the Episcopal Theological School in Cambridge, Massachusetts, near Harvard

University. Twenty years later, in his book *The Dread Voyage* (1893), the fruits of his preparation were fully evident, for *Hiawatha, Caliban,* (Sir) Edward B. Tylor's *Primitive Culture* (1871), and John Fiske's *Myths and Myth-makers* (1872) had led to Campbell's experiments in imagery of primitive nature and primitive religion; this was several generations before Sir James Frazer's *The Golden Bough* (1890–1915) enriched the poetry of the McGill group of the late 1920's. It is instructive to observe the similarity of Campbell's "The Mother" (*Harper's,* 1891) and "The Mother's Soul," also called "The Butterfly" (1883), of Isabella Crawford, who lived only in the environs of the Toronto colleges.

Very near was also the home of Goldwin Smith (1823–1910), a former professor at Oxford and Cornell, a great journalist and an indefatigable commentator, who settled in Toronto in 1871 at the age of forty-seven and after 1875 lived at "The Grange." A succession of literary-political magazines were taken under his wing. The first of these was the *Canadian Monthly and National Review* (1872–78), planned by the "Canada First" group before he arrived. Until late in 1874 he was its principal support in money, articles, and prestige; its editor, Graeme Mercer Adam, adopted Smith's unpopular, but yet influential, ideas on national independence. In poetry, however, Smith was definitely not radical. He indulged in verse translations from the Latin poets or the *Greek Anthology,* and he probably helped the universities to draw readers to the classics, which were undergirding the poetry of the young academic poets. His own taste in poetic selections stopped short at Tennyson, perhaps later at Matthew Arnold. It was in the first volume (May 1872) of the *Canadian Monthly* that William Dawson LeSueur described the spirit of the times:

If Mr. Arnold were wholly Greek, of what interest would he be to us? He could be but the echo of that original inspiration the direct products of which are yet in our hands. But if, with that breadth and calmness of manner which distinguished the great minds of Greek antiquity, he can present to us the living ideas and issues of today, then indeed is there food for the mind, as well as for the aesthetic sense, in his writings.

In performing the "function of criticism," Smith did not match Arnold's "disinterestedness," but his magazine *The Canadian Monthly* was, as Elisabeth Wallace has said in *Goldwin Smith, Victorian Liberal* (1957), "the nearest equivalent to such British periodicals as the *Fortnightly* and *Contemporary Review.*" He wrote better than any one of his contributors, but their level, in prose, was high. Smith's own breadth was reflected in sections on "Current Literature," "Book Reviews," and "Literary Notes"; the reader could feel that Toronto shared in the culture of contemporary Britain, even in its fine art and its music. Generally speaking the young Canadian Greeks were not yet ready to publish in the 1870's. Native commonplace realism, however, happily demonstrated its persistence in the works of "Fidelis," Miss Agnes Maule Machar (1837–1927) of Kingston, who began her career with good history and readable fiction in *For King and Country: A Story of 1812* (in the *Canadian Monthly* and in book form in 1874).

The thin showing of *belles-lettres* by native authors was offset by a lively presentation of the nation's history and current affairs, for this was the magazine's true purpose. "*The Canadian Monthly* owed its existence," Smith said, "to the shortlived glow of national feeling which passed through the veins of the community on the morning of Confederation. . . . Then, as the movement in which it had originated flagged, the shadow of doom began to fall upon it . . . against English and American competition, patriotic feeling alone could hold its ground, and of this the limit has been seen." This obituary for the *Canadian Monthly* appeared in *The Bystander* of January 1883. In the late 1870's the *Monthly* had become *Rose Belford's* (1878–82). Smith kept on writing, always with a journalistic vehicle, and typically as "Bystander." From time to time in the 1880's he had his own journal with that very title (1880–81; 1883; 1889–90). In the meantime he founded *The Week* (1883–96).

The 1870's, therefore, may be seen as a period of transition, a time for gathering strength. Early in the productive decade which followed, before *The Week* began publication, the Royal Society of Canada was founded (1882) at the suggestion of the Marquis of Lorne (afterwards Duke of Argyll), Governor General of Canada. Smith, Dawson, Kirby, George Murray, Le Moine, Reade, Sangster, and Daniel Wilson were among the charter members. Almost sixty years had passed since the Earl of Dalhousie had organized the Literary and Historical Society of Quebec. The English literature of the Canadas had played its part in the building of the country's culture. A regional character had been formed and a national character was emerging out of trial and error, tradition and independence, observation and insight, during years of preparation.

10. Folktales and Folk Songs

EDITH FOWKE

FOLKTALES AND FOLK SONGS are our unwritten prose and poetry: they are handed down orally from generation to generation, exist in many different forms, and tend to lose their folk quality once they are frozen in print. As the literature of an unlettered people, they often reflect more clearly than printed literature the culture and development of a country in its early stages.

I. THE FOLKTALE

"Folktale" is a general term used to include all types of traditional narrative—myth, legend, fairy tale, animal story, and fable—and Indians, French Canadians, and English Canadians alike have delighted to tell them.

The Indians and Eskimos were particularly prolific story-tellers, and thousands of their tales have been collected and published. Certain stories were common to tribes all across the continent, while others were found only among the tribes of one region: for example, among the Eskimos of the far north, or the Indians of the Pacific Coast, the Plains, the Great Lakes, or the Maritimes.

Most of the Indian tribes have some "creation myths" or sacred legends in which they tell tales of their beginnings. Usually these are built around a culture hero: Glooscap of the Micmacs, Manabozho of the Algonkins, the Raven of the Pacific tribes, or the Old Man of the Plains. The most common myth tells how the culture hero, floating on a raft on primeval waters, sends down some animal, usually the muskrat, to bring up a few grains of sand, and out of that he makes the earth. Most tribes also have tales about the origin of light, fire, the seasons, the winds, the sun and moon. Usually the hero steals fire and light from some enemy who is keeping them from mankind.

There are also many stories about calamities that destroy the world. The most frequent is a great flood, but other tales tell how the world was destroyed, or almost destroyed, by fire, blizzards, or drought and a very widespread one tells of the efforts of various animals to free the sun, which has been trapped by some hostile power. In another tale the hero, like

Phaeton in Greek mythology, is permitted to carry the sun and almost burns up the earth.

The Indians also like to tell of trips to other worlds. The most famous tale is of a girl who finds herself in the upper world and marries a star who forbids her to dig in a certain place; when she disobeys, she sees her old home below and is seized with a longing to return; secretly, often with supernatural help, she prepares a rope and descends. Other stories suggest the European tales of Cupid and Psyche and the Swan Maiden, telling of a hero who climbs to the upper world in search of his supernatural wife, and finds her only after surviving many perils. Less common is the tale of a descent to the land of the dead, which closely parallels the Greek myth of Orpheus and Eurydice.

Many Indian stories remind us of familiar European fairy tales: one from the west coast, "The Deserted Children," resembles "Hansel and Gretel," with elements of "Jack and the Beanstalk." However, many Indian tales are very un-fairy-tale-like, for they deal both realistically and imaginatively with the processes of procreation and evacuation. So frequent are such themes that most anthologists find it necessary to note that they have eliminated them from the tales they publish. The anthologists prefer the more romantic legends that account for famous landmarks or that explain the various characteristics, of birds and animals.

The first to note the Indian tales in Canada were the Jesuit Fathers. During the second half of the seventeenth century they recorded a number of Huron and Algonkin tales in the *Jesuit Relations*. Later, priests such as Father Lacombe and Father Petitot noted tales of the western and northern tribes. The first to record any tales in English was Henry Rowe Schoolcraft who served as Indian agent among the Ojibwas of the Great Lakes between 1812 and 1842. His tales inspired Longfellow's *Hiawatha*, although the actual Ojibwa culture hero was not Hiawatha but Manabozho; Hiawatha was a historical Iroquois leader of the sixteenth century.

In the half-century after Schoolcraft many others followed his example. Indian agents, missionaries, doctors, and teachers noted down the tales they heard and printed them, sometimes translating the narratives literally, more often retelling them in a style they thought would be of greater interest to the reading public. The most important of these early collectors was the Rev. S. T. Rand, whose *Legends of the Micmacs* (1894) is still a basic reference.

Then towards the end of the nineteenth century, the amateur collectors were succeeded by the specialists: anthropologists, ethnologists, and folklorists, who published literal translations of the tales they collected from particular tribes. Among the important regional collections are James Teit's *Traditions of the Thompson River Indians of British Columbia* (1898), *Folk-Tales of Salishan and Sahaptin Tribes* edited by Franz Boaz (1917), *Sacred Stories of the Sweet Grass Cree* by L. Bloomfield (1930), *The Micmac Indians of Eastern Canada* by W. D. and R. S. Wallis (1955), and several volumes by

Canada's foremost folklorist, Dr. Marius Barbeau, notably *Haida Myths Illustrated in Argillite Carvings* (1953) and *Huron-Wyandot Traditional Narratives in Translations and Native Texts* (1960).

Using the tales actually collected from the Indians as raw materials, many authors have published books in which the tales are rewritten or adapted for popular consumption. Pauline Johnson's *Legends of Vancouver* (1911) gives a rather romantic treatment of the ancient tales, and Cyrus Macmillan's *Canadian Wonder Tales* (1918) and *Canadian Fairy Tales* (1922) emphasize the fanciful elements. More representative are such general anthologies as *The Corn Goddess and Other Tales from Indian Canada* by Diamond D. Jenness (1956) and *Indian Legends of Canada* by Ethel May Clark (1960).

The second largest group of Canadian folktales was brought to New France by the seventeenth-century colonists. Along the St. Lawrence the medieval "romans de la Table Ronde" were handed down from generation to generation, and until recent times it was the custom to engage good story-tellers to entertain the men who spent the winter working in the lumber camps along the North Shore. Many of the old European tales—such as "The Seven-headed Dragon," "John the Bear," "Little Poucet," "The White Cat," "Cinderella," "Jack the Trickster," and "The Master Thief"—were picked up by the Indians who retold them in their turn. Especially popular were the tales of Petit Jean (or Ti-Jean, or Bon-Jean) whose cunning and trickery made up for his puny size: these may have inspired the lumberjack tales of Paul Bunyan.

Naturally most of the French-Canadian tales have been printed in French, and there are few literal English translations. However, various authors have given their versions of the most popular tales. Early samples appeared in W. P. Greenough's *Canadian Folk-Life and Folk-Lore* (1897) and in J. M. Le Moine's *The Legends of the St. Lawrence* (1898). Sometimes the tales were retold in simulated "habitant" dialect, as in P. A. W. Wallace's *Baptiste Larocque* (1923) and in some of W. H. Drummond's poems.

A good sampling of the European inheritance preserved in French Canada is found in *The Golden Phoenix* (1958), Michael Hornyansky's adaptation of eight tales collected by Dr. Barbeau. Some of these originated in the Orient, with roots that go far back in history.

Of the legends that have taken root in Quebec and acquired a local flavour, Dr. Barbeau felt that the best were: "The Handsome Dancer" or "Rose Latulippe," in which the Devil attends a dance; "The Black Hen," about a soul for sale at a crossroads; "The Witch Canoe" or "La Chasse-Galerie," which flies through the air with a gang of shanty boys; "The Black Horse," in which the Devil helps to build a parish church; "The Buried Treasures of Portneuf County"; "The Church Bell of Caughnawaga"; "The Midnight Mass of Père de la Brosse"; and "The Great Serpent of Lorette" or "Wolverine." All of these he has retold in *The Tree of Dreams* (1955), and the same themes turn up repeatedly in other collections such as *Legends of French Canada* (1931) by E. C. Woodley, *Legends of Quebec* (1966) by Hazel Boswell, and *The Magic Fiddler and Other Legends of French Canada* (1968) by Claude Aubry.

Although the early British settlers also brought many European tales to Canada with them, they did not preserve them nearly as well as the French. Dr. Helen Creighton, a prolific Nova Scotia collector, notes that traditional tales in English are very scarce in that province, and W. J. Wintemberg, who collected various forms of folklore in Ontario in the early part of this century, noted that "folk tales are mostly of the noodle variety": that is, anecdotes about stupid fellows. However, a few storytellers still preserve the old-world folktales; Helen Creighton and Edward D. Ives recorded *Eight Folktales from Miramichi as Told by Wilmot MacDonald* (1962).

Of the more localized tales, Nova Scotia has many telling of buried gold and phantom ships, of ghosts and haunted houses, which Dr. Creighton drew upon for her *Bluenose Ghosts* (1957). Although the Americans claim Paul Bunyan, Canadian shanty boys from the Maritimes to the Pacific told tales of the mighty lumberjack and his Blue Ox, and Dr. J. D. Robins retold some of the Ontario yarns in *Logging with Paul Bunyan* (1957). In western Canada, the *Alberta Folklore Quarterly*, which flourished briefly in 1945 and 1946, published some local legends and characteristic tall tales; an American, Robert Gard, published some of these in *Johnny Chinook* (1954).

Some folktales found their way into other literary forms. William Kirby's historical novel of old Quebec, *The Golden Dog* (1877), incorporates various elements of French-Canadian folklore, and the legend of the *corriveau* plays an important part in his plot. In *Mountain Cloud* (1944) Dr. Barbeau gives a fictional account of an Indian brave, based on the ritual and folklore of the west coast Indians. In the Maritimes, in the early nineteenth century, Thomas Chandler Haliburton made free use of many New England tales in his stories of the Yankee peddler, Sam Slick, and in Alberta in the twentieth, the redoubtable Bob Edwards localized and embroidered many tall tales to enliven the columns of his *Calgary Eye-Opener*. Poets have also borrowed from folklore, the most widely known example being Pauline Johnson's "Legend of the Qu'Appelle"; in a different idiom, Anne Wilkinson's "A Folk Tale" uses the traditional form to achieve a strikingly modern effect. However, on the whole our poets tend to draw their mythology from classical rather than Canadian sources.

II. THE FOLK SONG

Before the white man came to Canada our great plains and forests resounded to the chants of the Indians, and in the frozen north the Eskimos sang in their dance-houses during the long Arctic nights. Indeed, song entered more intimately into the life of the Indians than into that of any white nation, for they believed that the invisible voice could reach the invisible power that permeates nature and thereby bring them success in their undertakings. Thus song was an essential part of everything they did, entering into every important personal experience and every social ritual. As Miss Alice Fletcher, one of the earliest collectors of Indian songs, put it: "In his sports, in his games, when he wooed, and when he mourned . . . the Indian sang in every experience of life from the cradle to the grave."

Indian songs were very short and were usually made up either of a few words repeated again and again or of meaningless syllables. Usually they were not complete in themselves but formed part of a story or a ceremony: for example, prayers for rain, warriors' songs, dirges for the dead, songs of welcome, and hymns of victory. They are very important to an understanding of Indian culture, but as they largely defy translation, they have little bearing on Canada's literary history.

With the founding of New France, the Canadian wilderness echoed to the many songs which the pioneer settlers brought from their homeland and made part of their daily lives on this continent. In the words of Marius Barbeau, "Threshing and winnowing in the barns moved to the rhythm of work tunes, as did spinning, weaving, and beating the wash by the fireside."

The *coureurs de bois* and the fur traders sang as they pushed their way across the new continent, adapting the stately ballads of the French court to the rhythm of their paddles, and their singing made a strong impression on all who heard them. European visitors, explorers, traders, and early settlers frequently referred to the *voyageurs'* songs: Mrs. John Graves Simcoe describes them in her *Diary* (1792–96), as does John Mactaggart in *Three Years in Canada* (1829), Mrs. Anna Jameson in *Winter Studies and Summer Rambles in Canada* (1838), R. M. Ballantyne in *Hudson's Bay* (1848), and John J. Bigsby in *The Shoe and Canoe* (1850). Captain George Back noted some *voyageur* songs while on an Arctic expedition to the Coppermine River, and these were printed in London in 1823 as *Canadian Airs*, the first Canadian folk songs ever published.

Another early collector of French folk songs on this continent was Edward Ermatinger, who noted eleven typical paddling songs while working for the Hudson's Bay Company between 1818 and 1828. These indicate that the songs of the *habitants* along the St. Lawrence and of the *voyageurs* in the west alike belonged largely to the common stock of traditional songs brought over by the early colonists in the seventeenth century—an impression confirmed by the first substantial collection of French-Canadian songs published by Ernest Gagnon in 1865. Indeed, Dr. Barbeau estimated that nineteen out of twenty of all French-Canadian songs are ancient.

Two well-known poems, both known by the title of "Canadian Boat Song," are the direct result of the *voyageurs'* songs. The first, composed by the Irish poet Thomas Moore after his visit to Canada in 1804, was inspired by a song the boatmen sang when rowing him down the St. Lawrence; the other, sometimes known as "The Lone Shieling," was published anonymously in *Blackwood's Edinburgh Magazine* for September 1829, under the title "Canadian Boat-Song (from the Gaelic)," although it is not a translation of any known Gaelic song and is not really a boat song but a lament. There has been considerable debate about its authorship, but it was probably written by David Macbeth Moir as a result of letters sent to him by John Galt when he visited Canada in 1827.

One of the earliest New World songs was the Indian carol, "Jesous Ahatonhia," which Father Brébeuf wrote in 1641 for the Hurons attending the Jesuit mission at Fort Ste Marie. A century later it was translated into French and sung in Quebec, and in 1926 J. E. Middleton wrote his own English interpretation which has become widely known as "The Huron Carol." This is perhaps the most truly Canadian of our songs, for it is the only one known to have been sung in Indian, French, and English.

The earliest song about a Canadian incident is said to be "Petit rocher de la haute montagne," sometimes known as "La plainte du coureur-de-bois." Its hero was a trapper, Cadieux, who died in saving his family from an Iroquois ambush on the Ottawa River in 1709. Soon afterwards the legend of Cadieux became widely popular among the *voyageurs* both as a tale and as a song, and many narratives of the fur trade mention it.

Occasionally the French Canadians composed new words to traditional tunes, the most familiar being "Vive la Canadienne!" a lively toast to the Canadian girl, and "Un Canadien errant," which A. Gérin-Lajoie wrote to express the feelings of a Canadian lad who fled to the United States after the Papineau rebellion of 1837. Other native French-Canadian songs catch the flavour of rural Quebec, for example, "Le Bal chez Boulé" which describes a country dance; "Youpe, Youpe sur la rivière," which tells of a *habitant* lad who goes to call on his girl and is rebuffed for being too fickle; and "Dans les Chantiers" and "Les Raftsmen," which describe life in the lumber camps.

In western Canada the Métis produced a prairie bard, Pierre Falcon, who composed songs that were very popular with the *voyageurs* throughout the nineteenth century. The most famous, usually known as "Falcon's Song," describes the Battle of Seven Oaks in 1816. Louis Riel also composed a number of verses, some of which have come down to us, as have also a few other Métis songs reflecting the early days on the prairies. Samples of these appear in Margaret Arnett MacLeod's little volume, *Songs of Old Manitoba* (1960), and Barbara Cass-Beggs' *Seven Métis Songs of Saskatchewan* (1967).

The heritage of French-Canadian songs is incredibly rich: some 40,000 songs are now in the collections of the National Museum at Ottawa and the Archives de Folklore at Université Laval, and more are being added yearly. Naturally most of the published collections are in French, but a good sampling of the most popular French songs have appeared in English translations. Two nineteenth-century Canadian poets produced small volumes: G. T. Lanigan's *National Ballads of Canada* (1865) and William McLennan's *Songs of Old Canada* (1886). More recent books which give the songs in both French and English include *Canadian Folk Songs Old and New* by John Murray Gibbon (1927), *Folk Songs of Quebec* by Fowke and Johnston (1957), *Chantons un peu* by Alan Mills (1961), and four of Dr. Barbeau's numerous collections: *Folk Songs of French Canada* (1928), *Folk Songs of Old Quebec* (1935), *Roundelays* (1958), and *Jongleur Songs of Old Quebec* (1962). The last volume contains a detailed bibliography of French-Canadian songs.

When the English, Scots, and Irish began to settle in Canada they brought with them thousands of the songs then current in the British Isles, and most of these continued to be sung well into this century. Many of *The English and Scottish Popular Ballads* catalogued by Francis James Child have survived in Newfoundland, Nova Scotia, and Ontario, the most popular being "Barbara Allen," "The Gypsy Laddie," "The Cruel Mother," "Young Beichan," "Sweet William's Ghost," "The Sweet Trinity," "Lady Isabel and the Elf Knight," "Hind Horn," and "Little Musgrave and Lady Barnard." Sometimes ballads have been preserved here that have disappeared in their homeland: for example, in Nova Scotia Dr. Helen Creighton collected "Robin Hood's Progress to Nottingham" of which the American folklorist Phillips Barry wrote: "Not a trace of this ballad has been found anywhere for three hundred years," and of her "False Knight upon the Road" he said: "Your version may be one of the oldest versions of any traditional English or Scottish ballad."

In addition to the medieval ballads, hundreds of the more recent broadside ballads were brought over from Britain and lovingly handed down in Canada: tales of highwaymen ("Brennan on the Moor" and "Bold Turpin") and pirates ("The Flying Cloud" and "Bold Manan"), of true love ("Burns and His Highland Mary" and "Pretty Polly Oliver") and false love ("The Girl I Left Behind" and "The Butcher Boy"), of famous battles ("The Plains of Waterloo" and "The Heights of Alma") and cruel murders ("The Ship's Carpenter" and "The Wexford Girl"). Again, many have survived in oral tradition here that have been forgotten in their homeland, as have also some beautiful versions of Old Country love songs such as "The Morning Dew," "She's Like the Swallow," and "The False Young Man."

Of the native English-Canadian ballads, two of the oldest describe General

Wolfe's victory and death on the Plains of Abraham. Then the United Empire Loyalists brought some songs to Canada, including "Revolutionary Tea" which pictures the outbreak of the American Revolution as a scrap between mother and daughter. The War of 1812 inspired a boastful ditty, "Come All You Bold Canadians," which describes General Brock's victory over General Hull at the Battle of Detroit, and two songs celebrate the victory of the British *Shannon* over the American *Chesapeake* in 1813. When William Lyon Mackenzie's American supporters raided Canada in 1838, the troops who routed them composed another boastful ditty, "The Battle of the Windmill," which was sung around Cornwall for many generations, and the Fenian raids of 1866 produced a Canadian parody of "Tramp, Tramp, Tramp, the Boys are Marching"—a song which later Canadian soldiers adapted for use in the Saskatchewan Rebellion, the Boer War, and World War I.

While such songs give the reactions of those who took part in colourful or dramatic events in Canada's history, the larger number of native Canadian songs reflect the daily lives of the ordinary people. Few of these rate high as poetry: at best they are vivid and lusty pictures of the rustic life; at worst, pedestrian doggerel. However, all those that have survived had something that appealed to the unlettered men and women who preserved them: they lived on because they said something that these people felt to be worth repeating. Some were humorous ditties about jails or sprees or local incidents; some told of murders or tragic accidents or riots. They were, in effect, a form of local history that gained more than local currency by being spread through the lumber camps or the fishing fleets. For example, the Nova Scotia ballad of the *Saladin* mutiny is still remembered in Ontario, as is a "Come-all-ye" describing a Twelfth of July riot that took place in Montreal in 1877. The Miramichi fire of 1825, the Birchall murder case of 1890, and the Halifax explosion of 1917 are still vivid in the folk memory. As a group these native songs are inferior to the older British ballads which have been polished by their passage through the centuries, but they are a significant expression of life in early Canada.

Many of the native songs were inspired by occupations. For some three hundred years the inhabitants of the small coastal villages of Newfoundland and Nova Scotia have been singing, adapting, and composing sea songs: sailors' shanties, accounts of whaling, sealing, or cod-fishing trips, and ballads about shipwrecks or brave deeds upon the high seas. Some are humorous, like "We'll Rant and We'll Roar like True Newfoundlanders"—a fisherman's adaptation of an old British sea song—and some are tragic, like "The Loss of the *Eliza*" or "The Ghostly Sailors," but all reflect the feelings of a people whose life is shaped by the sea.

Lumbering has also played a big part in Canada's history ever since the British navy ordered Canadian timber for its ships during the Napoleonic

Wars. All through the nineteenth century gangs of roving shanty-boys were spending their winters in snow-swept camps where they had to make their own entertainment. The songs they sang were numerous and varied, but the most characteristic fell into three groups: those describing the life and work in the camps ("Hogan's Lake" or "Turner's Camp"), those telling of death in the woods or on the rivers ("The Jam on Gerry's Rocks" or "Peter Emberley"), and those telling what happened when the shanty-boys headed for the bright lights in the spring with their winter's pay in their pockets ("The Grand Hotel" or "When the Shanty-Boy Comes Down").

Farmers produced fewer songs because their work was more solitary, and folk songs need an audience. However, the early settlers did compose some verses describing their life, usually couched in the form of complaints. In Ontario "The Scarborough Settler" longed to leave "Canada's muddy creeks" for "auld Scotia's glens," and out west "The Alberta Homesteader" complained that he was "starving to death on a government claim."

Cowboy songs were popular in Alberta, but most of them were merely borrowed from the United States: the early Canadian ranches were stocked with cattle driven up from Texas along the Old Chisholm Trail, and with them came American cowboys and their songs.

The gold-seekers of the Cariboo and Klondike also sang of their hopes and disappointments, but few of their songs have survived. Some verses that may have been traditional are included in *Sawney's Letters and Cariboo Rhymes* (1869) and *Rhymes of the Miner* edited by E. L. Chicanot (1937). The most popular ditty to come out of the Canadian north, "When the Ice Worms Nest Again," apparently originated with the Klondike balladeer, Robert Service, but it was transformed by the prospectors and trappers who sang it in varying forms all across northern Canada.

Two other poems by known poets were taken over by the folk and turned into songs: "The Wreck of the *Julie Plante*" by W. H. Drummond, and "The Walker of the Snow" by C. D. Shanly. Reversing the process, some authors have borrowed snatches of folk songs to add colour to their fiction or historical narratives, as in Kirby's *The Golden Dog*, or Slater's *The Yellow Briar*, and the old ballads play a leading role in Thomas Raddall's fine short story, "Blind MacNair."

Songs in the folk-song idiom are still being written, and some of them are passing into oral tradition. The best modern examples are "The Squidjiggin' Ground" which Arthur Scammell wrote in 1928 and which quickly became Newfoundland's favourite song, and "The Blackfly Song" written by Wade Hemsworth in 1949, which is increasingly popular in Ontario.

Samples of the different kinds of English-Canadian songs may be found in various volumes in addition to those that have already been mentioned. The earliest published collection appears to be James Murphy's *Songs and*

Ballads of Newfoundland, Ancient and Modern (1902), which gives an interesting assortment of the local songs composed by island bards. More significant is the work of Dr. W. Roy Mackenzie, a Nova Scotia–born English professor who collected a rich variety of Maritime songs during the early part of this century. In 1919 he described his adventures in a delightful book, *The Quest of the Ballad*, and in 1928 his collection appeared as *Ballads and Sea Songs from Nova Scotia*—a volume so well annotated that it is still a major reference for British and American folklorists.

After Dr. Mackenzie's pioneer work, collection in Nova Scotia was taken up by Helen Creighton of Dartmouth, who continued to glean a rich harvest there for over forty years. The best of the four-thousand-odd songs in her collection have appeared in four books: *Songs and Ballads from Nova Scotia* (1932), *Traditional Songs from Nova Scotia* (1950), *Maritime Folk Songs* (1962), and *Folksongs from Southern New Brunswick* (1971). The other important Maritime collector, Louise Manny of Newcastle, published a book of New Brunswick lumberjack songs, *Songs of Miramichi* (1968), and Edward D. Ives of the University of Maine has published books about New Brunswick's famous traditional singer, *Larry Gorman: The Man Who Made the Songs* (1964) and *Lawrence Doyle: The Farmer-Poet of Prince Edward Island* (1971), as well as *Twenty-One Folksongs from Prince Edward Island* (1963).

The first major collections in Newfoundland were made not by Canadians but by visiting folklorists from the United States and Britain. In 1929 two young Americans, Elisabeth Bristol Greenleaf and Grace Yarrow Mansfield, visited the island as "the Vassar College folklore expedition" and published *Ballads and Sea Songs of Newfoundland* in 1933. They included songs of both British and New World origin, but when Miss Maud Karpeles of the English Folk Dance and Song Society visited the island in 1929 and 1930, she was interested primarily in the old British songs to be found there, and published these as *Folk Songs from Newfoundland* (1934 and 1971). Gerald S. Doyle, a St. John's businessman, helped to preserve many of the native Newfoundland ditties by publishing several editions of a small paper-backed booklet, *Old-Time Songs and Poetry of Newfoundland*, in which verses about the adventures of the local fishermen were interspersed with advertisements for patent medicines. More recently, Kenneth Peacock, an Ottawa-based musician, spent a number of summers on the island recording songs for the National Museum, and published his collection as *Songs of the Newfoundland Outports* (1965). Dr. MacEdward Leach, a leading American folklorist, also collected in Newfoundland and Labrador and published *Folk Ballads and Songs of the Lower Labrador Coast* (1965).

Collecting started later in Ontario, but that province also has had a lively singing tradition. Edith Fowke published some of the old British ballads preserved there in *Traditional Singers and Songs from Ontario* (1965), and some of the native songs in *Lumbering Songs from the Northern Woods* (1970).

In addition to these regional collections, a broader selection of songs from across the country may be found in *Folk Songs of Canada* (1954) and *More Folk Songs of Canada* (1967) by Edith Fowke and Richard Johnston, *Canada's Story in Song* (1960) by Fowke, Mills, and Blume, and *The Penguin Book of Canadian Folk Songs* (1973) by Fowke.

Although books help to preserve the words and melodies, they cannot adequately convey the way our traditional songs were sung. They were normally sung solo and unaccompanied, and the melody was adapted from stanza to stanza to accommodate variations in the metre. Fortunately it is now possible to hear folk songs as they were actually sung by the folk on an increasing number of records. Most of these have been issued by the Folkways Record Corporation and include: "Folk Songs of Ontario" (FM 4005), "Folk Music from Nova Scotia" (FM 4006), "Irish and British Songs from the Ottawa Valley" (FM 4051), "Lumbering Songs from the Ontario Shanties" (FM 4052), "Songs of the Miramichi" (FM 4053), "Maritime Folk Songs" (FE 4307), "Songs of the Great Lakes" (FE 4018), "Folksongs of Saskatchewan" (FE 4312), and "Songs from the Out-Ports of Newfoundland" (FE 4075).

In pioneer days, and in rural areas until quite recently, traditional storytellers and folk singers were the main source of entertainment, and their tales and songs were cherished. With the coming of radio and television, their audience has been lost, and the old lore is fast disappearing. Many songs and stories still remain to be gathered from those who learned them in their youth, but the number who remember them is growing smaller each year. However, those that have been collected already and those that may still be garnered will provide a rich store upon which our future novelists, poets, historians, and sociologists may draw. The things that made the folktales and folk songs dear to many generations of our forefathers have much to tell us about our people and our past.

11. Literary Publishing

H. PEARSON GUNDY

AS EVERY CANADIANA COLLECTOR soon discovers, a much larger corpus of literary work has been produced in Canada than is generally known to the common, even well-informed reader. Much of it, to be sure, is now unread and all but unreadable, for the dross greatly outweighs the fine ore. Wilfrid Eggleston, in *The Frontier and Canadian Letters* (1957), sums up Canadian writing of substance before 1900 as comprising "a few collections of poetry, three or four historical works, a few humorous sketches, an essay or two, but not a single novel or play." The rest he dismisses as "crude, derivative, imitative, dull and stodgy"—a harsh indictment which, as the present work shows, leaves out of consideration much that merits critical attention. No objective reassessment of our literary past, however, can transform low-lying plateaux into mountain peaks.

Was Canada, then, so devoid of talent, or were latent literary gifts thwarted before they had a chance to mature? Why, in a country which had printers and publishers for a hundred and fifty years before the present century, were our inglorious Miltons mute? Explanations and excuses have been multiplied: the harshness of pioneer times, the struggle to push our frontiers westward, our long and lingering colonial status, the overshadowing influence of a dynamic and powerful neighbour, our ingrained sectionalism, our retarded sense of identity, our sparse population, our indifference to the fine arts and, by contrast, the homage we have paid to wealth as a measure of success and social prestige. These are among the familiar reasons given for the paucity of our national literary heritage. Canadian publishers have also been made a convenient scapegoat. "Authorship without publishers is like the voice of one crying in the wilderness," cried William Kirby, in 1883. Timid, unadventurous, intent only on big names and safe markets, so we are told, our publishers have been content to promote popular British and American authors to the impoverishment of authorship in Canada.

There is doubtless some measure of truth or half-truth in all of these points, but too often they have been offered as airy generalizations based on insufficient or inconclusive evidence. In this chapter we shall examine the publisher–author relationship as it developed in Canada to determine, if we can, whether the conditions of publishing advanced or retarded Canadian literary expression.

For the first half-century after 1751, when the printing press was established in what is now Canada at Halifax, all printing and publishing was done by weekly newspaper offices and by the government which made use of them. Even after the government established its own printing offices, much work was let out on contract, and the King's (or Queen's) printers did private printing as well. When bookstores made their appearance in the early years of the last century, the more enterprising of them combined bookselling with publishing in the English tradition. The actual printing might still be done in a newspaper office, but the bookseller assumed the financial risk of publication, normally protecting himself by an advance subscription list. By the third decade of the century some of the larger bookstores had their own printing departments and were in lively competition with the newspaper presses.

With a later start than Montreal as a centre of English-language publishing, Toronto by mid-century was already overtaking the larger metropolis and was soon to become the publishing capital of English-speaking Canada. Maritime publishers supplied local needs but never succeeded in competing for the central market. In the west, apart from newspaper and job printing, there was little attempt at literary publication before the present century.

Newspaper offices, government printing departments, and bookstores were thus the direct forerunners of Canadian publishing houses which emerged in the latter years of the nineteenth century, commonly combining book publishing with the wholesale book trade, magazine publishing, or the manufacture of stationery. The development of publishing was, in broad outline, slow and unspectacular from 1751 to 1900; it was a relatively small, dispersed industry, gradually centring in Toronto, but without great capital behind it, hampered in its growth by severe business depressions in the 1850's and 1870's and, as we shall see, by copyright anomalies which so trammelled publishing houses that even the fittest found it hard to survive.

In her *Bibliography of Canadian Imprints, 1751–1800* (1952) Marie Tremaine describes over 1,200 separate publications of Canadian presses in the eighteenth century. Official government documents form the great bulk of this output, followed by ecclesiastical and legal works, almanacs, and a wide range of pamphlets, but very little that could be classed as *belles lettres*. As the English traveller, John Lambert, wrote in 1809, in his *Travels through Lower Canada and the United States* (1810), "The state of literature, the arts, and science in Canada can scarcely be said to be at a low ebb, because they were never known to flow."

Our first literary awakening is commonly attributed to Howe, Haliburton, and their coterie in Halifax during the late 1820's and 1830's. There were, however, unmistakable earlier signs of literary interest, even if the results were meagre. Some early Maritime verse had been published in Boston and Albany, and a narrative poem on the War of 1812 by Thomas Cowdell was issued from the newspaper press of John Howe in Halifax in 1815. Five years later a Montreal bookseller, Ariel Bowman, brought out a slim volume of his own verse, *Hours of Childhood and Other Poems*. In Upper Canada, Hugh C. Thomson, editor and proprietor of the *Upper Canada Herald*, published two booklets of verse in 1822, *Poems* by "Peter Pindar" (of which no copy seems to have survived) and a rhyming defence of the jury system grandiloquently addressed "To the Liege Men of Every British Colony and Province in the World" by "A Friend to his Species." Forsaking verse for prose fiction, Thomson published in 1824 the first novel by a native-born Canadian, *St. Ursula's Convent; or, The Nun of Canada*, whose anonymous author, Julia Catherine Hart (née Beckwith) was the wife of a Kingston bookbinder.

Two periodicals had appeared before 1800, the *Nova Scotia Magazine* (1789–92) and the *Quebec Magazine* (1792–94) though both were essentially miscellanies of reprinted articles and extracts. John Strachan's *Christian Examiner* (1819–20), first published in Kingston, then transferred to York, was an early attempt at an indigenous literary magazine not confined in content to religious themes. Equally transitory were two other early journals, the *Enquirer* (Quebec, 1821–22) and the *Literary Miscellany* (Montreal, 1822–23).

The founding by Lord Dalhousie of the Quebec Literary and Historical Society in 1824 stimulated a flurry of literary interest in the lower province. Some minor volumes of verse had already appeared in addition to the periodicals above mentioned. Then followed two new literary magazines edited by experienced journalists and published by two rival Montreal bookstore proprietors, Joseph Nickless and H. H. Cunningham.

The *Canadian Magazine and Literary Repository* was the first to appear, in July 1823, printed on the newspaper press of Nahum Mower for Nickless the bookseller. The editor, whose name is not given, was David Chisholme, a young Scotsman with legal training and a flair for writing, a *protégé* of the Earl of Dalhousie who brought him out to Canada in 1822. In a long introduction he outlined his editorial policy: ". . . it shall form one of the most prominent parts of our labours to select and transfer into our pages . . . such articles as we may deem of importance, in promoting the diffusion of useful knowledge throughout this country. . . . Besides selected articles from other publications, we intend that this work shall also contain *original* matter of such a local and general character as shall render it at once useful and entertaining to all classes of society. . . . A due proportion of our pages shall be allotted for the selection of published and unpublished verse. . . ."

There was no noticeable change in this policy when Chisholme was superseded, in February 1824, by Dr. A. J. Christie, the editor of the Montreal *Gazette*. The educational mission of the magazine was re-emphasized in volume II:

Ignorance is the means of perpetuating national antipathies, of keeping alive the remembrance of unreasonable jealousy and suspicion. Let light arise among the people, and these bitter animosities will die. Why should the inhabitants of Canada consider themselves as of two distinct nations? Though their ancestors were descended from different originals, have not they themselves, the most serious reasons for unanimity and concord? Do they not breathe the same air? Are they not nourished by the same benignant soil; and all enriched by the commerce of the same River? Are they not protected by the same Government? Have they not the same laws, the same rights, and one common interest? The happiness of one cannot be injured without impairing that of the other. The welfare of both is promoted by the same means. Though their languages are different, their interests cannot be separated. (P. 136)

In July 1824 a rival publication made its appearance, Cunningham's periodical, the *Canadian Review and Literary and Historical Journal* (shortened after the first issue to *Canadian Review and Magazine*). Closely resembling the *Canadian Magazine* in format, the *Review* was edited by Christie's predecessor, David Chisholme, whose leading article was on the newly formed Quebec Literary and Historical Society, "so similar in its objects," he observed, "to our own pursuits."

This innocent comparison roused the ire of Dr. Christie—"The meridian sun to a farthing rushlight!" In a corrosive review of the new journal in his own volume III ("the public as well as ourselves will be woefully disappointed when they come to read this work") he read Chisholme a lecture on the pitfalls of conducting a literary journal in Canada:

That there are men of genius and talent in this country will not be denied; but it is no less true that they seldom devote much of their time to literary composition. Deeply engaged in other avocations, although good judges of what they *read*, but few of them can spare time for *writing*. From this cause the conductor of a periodical publication in Canada has a heavier task to perform than in older countries . . . [and] is more dependent upon his own talents and resources. (P. 113)

Ironically, however, Chisholme succeeded in drawing more widely on native contributors than Christie, and was able to keep the *Canadian Review and Magazine* going for a full year after his rival's publisher had been forced to suspend publication. The final issue ran an article (intended to be continued) on "Writers and Literature of Canada," a pretentious title which, the author wryly admits, would "at first view excite a smile . . . if confined to the productions of native talent"; instead, it dealt with accounts of explorations and the *Jesuit Relations*.

Unimpressive as were the results of this early, self-conscious urge to launch

Canadian literature, it is worth noting that its promoters in widely separated parts of the country were newspaper and bookstore publishers. With little or no prospect of financial gain, they attempted to provide an outlet for writers on a higher literary level than that of the common weeklies. What was lacking were sufficient subscribers, and, above all, an author whose gift of imagination was matched by fresh and vigorous powers of expression. Such a man Joseph Howe was soon to discover in Halifax.

Among the lively young writers whom Howe gathered about him as editor of the *Novascotian* in 1828, was Thomas Chandler Haliburton, eloquent member of the House of Assembly for Annapolis. His first important work, *An Historical and Statistical Account of Nova Scotia* (1829) was published by Howe in two formidable octavo volumes at a heavy financial loss. Readers of this work could scarcely have foreseen the exuberant creator of Sam Slick. But Howe knew his author, and persuaded him to contribute some light sketches to "The Club," a regular feature of the *Novascotian*. Haliburton warmed to the task and produced something new in Canadian journalism. The sayings and doings of the Yankee clock pedlar, Sam Slick of Slickville, for the first time brought international popularity and acclaim to a Canadian writer. Howe re-published the original series as *The Clockmaker* in book form in 1836, now a rare edition much sought by collectors. The success of this book helped to offset Howe's loss on the earlier publication, but there was no possibility of copyright protection. There were, indeed, at that time no imperial or colonial copyright acts, and no vestige of international agreement. Moreover Howe's small newspaper press was not equipped to meet the demands of a "best seller" or even a second best. Subsequent volumes in the Sam Slick series were first published in the United States, in England, and in France.

Howe's other literary publications fell short of his own contributions in verse and prose to the *Novascotian* which, curiously enough, he never re-issued in book form.

Oliver Goldsmith, Howe's fellow townsman, found an English publisher, John Sharpe of London, for his *Rising Village* (1825). The poem was reprinted in its entirety in the *Canadian Review and Magazine*, February 1826, but not until eight years later was it re-issued with additional poems. This first Canadian edition was published by a Saint John bookseller, John McMillan, in 1834. The firm of J. & A. McMillan was soon to become the leading bookstore publisher in New Brunswick, and a close rival to the newspaper press of Henry Chubb, the publisher in 1825 of James Hogg's *Poems, Religious, Moral and Sentimental*. Other Maritime poets and prose writers appeared in the pages of various short-lived literary periodicals: the *New Brunswick Religious and Literary Journal* (Saint John, 1829–30), the *Halifax Monthly Magazine* (1830–31), *The Bee* (Pictou, 1835–38) or the *Colonial Pearl* (Halifax, 1837–40).

There were several bookstore publishers in Halifax during this period, the most active of which was the firm of A. & W. Mackinlay, whose bookshop on Granville Street was well stocked and well patronized. The Mackinlays, however, were less interested as publishers in *belles-lettres* than in school texts, theological tracts, and works of practical reference on the geology and geography of the province. For literary achievement in such subjects, Alexander Monro, in a work on *New Brunswick* (1855), commends the Nova Scotians, but adds a caveat against the circulation of "novels and other light trash of literature," calculated, he believed, "to corrupt the morals and retard the intellectual advancement of the people."

The publishing trend in the Canadas up to mid-century was similar to that of the Maritimes. In Upper Canada two literary journals made brief appearances at York in 1833. The *Canadian Literary Magazine*, published by George Gurnett, was well edited by John Kent, a teacher at Upper Canada College lately arrived from England, who, according to his "Editor's Address" in the first number, found Canadians "advanced in civilization beyond [his] expectation" and who invited "the support of every individual who feels a desire that Canada should possess a literature of its own"—support evidently not forthcoming. The other periodical, also stillborn, was the *Canadian Magazine*, printed and published by the King's Printer, Robert Stanton, and edited by W. Sibbald. It was to be a forum for writers on religion, science, literature, morality, agriculture, and was also to include fiction. Too ambitious for a small provincial capital, the journal expired before the end of 1833.

The following year, when York was incorporated as Toronto, two bookstores were established which soon became the largest in Upper Canada, the one run by a reformer, James Lesslie, the other by a Tory, Henry Rowsell. The Lesslie family, long established as booksellers in Dundee, Scotland, had come out to Canada in the 1820's and settled in Kingston and Dundas. When the father died, James Lesslie consolidated the family business in Toronto. He set up a printing department as well, issued a good many miscellaneous books and pamphlets, but threw most of his energy into a reform newspaper, the *Examiner*, finally bought out by George Brown of the *Globe*. Henry Rowsell, who enjoyed the patronage of Sir Francis Bond Head, Bishop Strachan, and the governing clique, was also a prolific publisher of pamphlets, tracts, yearbooks, law journals, and occasional volumes of minor verse. His chief excursion into *belles-lettres* was *The Maple Leaf; or, Canadian Annual* (1847–49) a literary annual under the editorship of the Rev. John McCaul, Professor of Classics in King's College (later the University of Toronto). The only Canadian feature of the first issue was the title and the fact that all the contributors were Canadians "by birth or adoption." There were articles on the Coliseum, the castles of Europe and Asia, on Val D'Ossola, interspersed with poems which betrayed their Canadian origin only by their limping metre. In format the volume was handsome in the ornate taste of the times, with a maple leaf design heavily printed in gold leaf on the hard covers, an engraved title-page in red and black, and ten full-page engravings to illustrate the text. In a preface to the second volume, 1848, the editor confessed to a miscalculation. He had supposed colonial readers would be most interested in "the scenes and subjects of the Old World," but in point of fact "both near and distant friends regretted the absence from the volume of the characteristics of 'the maple leaf.' " In the next, and final volume, editor and publisher sought, with some success, to produce a distinctively Canadian annual.

One of the verse contributors to the *Maple Leaf* was the bookseller-publisher Samuel Thompson, whose autobiography, *Reminiscences of a Canadian Pioneer* (1884), throws some revealing light on writing and publishing in the middle of the last century. Thompson was a friend of the Todd brothers, Alfred and Alpheus, and brought out the latter's *The Practice and Privileges of the Two Houses of Parliament* (1840), the first such work by a Canadian to be accepted as authoritative not only in the colonies but in Great Britain. Later Thompson became Queen's Printer, suffered bankruptcy, and was bought out by two of his employees, Robert Hunter and George M. Rose. The Hunter, Rose firm became one of the earliest fully-fledged publishing houses in Canada. (The firm was taken over in 1948 by Sir Isaac Pitman & Sons (Canada) Limited.)

More venerable in years than Hunter, Rose & Co. was the Methodist Book and Publishing House (now the Ryerson Press) which had its origin in the hand-press on which Egerton Ryerson in 1829 published the *Christian Guardian*. From the beginning this church press issued secular as well as religious books, and did much to encourage Canadian writing, but up to the period of Confederation it was essentially a periodical rather than a book-publishing house.

Two Montreal firms which began in the mid-1830's provided outlets for Canadian writers and did a good deal to extend literary interest in the two Canadas: Armour & Ramsay, booksellers, stationers and publishers, and John Lovell, printer and publisher.

Andrew Armour and Hew Ramsay conducted a large business with branches in Kingston, Hamilton, and Toronto. One of their shrewdest strokes was to persuade English magazine publishers to issue special colonial editions at a discount, after their normal runs were off the press, in order to compete with cheap American pirated reprints. They did so at some risk as a letter from them to Messrs. Blackwood & Sons, Edinburgh, of March 7, 1843, indicates (National Library of Scotland Ms. 4063); the letter concludes: ". . . have the goodness not to use our name, as it might lead us into unpleasant altercations both with the press here who are greatly in favour of the United States cheap editions as well as the agents who dispose of them." In 1838 Armour & Ramsay published Major John Richardson's *Personal*

Memoirs, the first of his works to appear under a Canadian imprint. The author then projected a revised subscription edition of his novel *Wacousta*, advertising himself as "the first and only writer of historical fiction the country has yet produced." But although his advertisements ran in the provincial press from May to November 1838, the response was too meagre to tempt Ramsay and Armour or any other Canadian publisher. The revised edition of *Wacousta* was set aside until a New York publisher brought it out in 1851. (Lovell finally issued a Canadian edition in 1868.) Meanwhile, however, Armour & Ramsay published a subscription edition of *The Canadian Brothers; or, The Prophecy Fulfilled* (2 vols., 1840). Richardson then determined to become his own publisher by setting up a press in Brockville from which he issued a weekly, the *New Era or Canadian Chronicle*; in this he published serially a new novel, *Jack Brag in Spain*, and the first series (all that was published) of *The War of 1812*. Publication of the latter in book form was made possible by a grant from the government. Richardson was disappointed in his hope that it would be used as a school text, and in the apathy of the reading public. He reported that only thirty copies were sold and when he sent the remainder to be auctioned off in Kingston a bidder was found for only one copy at sevenpence halfpenny. H. H. Cunningham, however, had sufficient confidence in the author to bring out two more of his works, *Eight Years in Canada* (1847) and *The Guards in Canada* (1848).

Another publisher who provided an outlet for Richardson and other writers was John Lovell of Montreal and Toronto. An Irishman by birth, he had come to Canada in 1820 at the age of 10, served his apprenticeship as a printer in Montreal, and in 1835 became an independent job printer. He then branched out into newspaper and periodical publishing, obtained government printing contracts, opened an office in Toronto, and specialized in the publication of gazetteers and directories for which there was a ready market.

In 1838 Lovell and his brother-in-law, John Gibson, launched the *Literary Garland*, the first successful Canadian literary journal, which lasted for thirteen years until 1851. One of Lovell's innovations was to pay his contributors. Susanna Moodie, in a familiar passage of *Roughing It in the Bush*, records her astonishment on receiving an invitation to contribute articles, short stories, and verse, with the promise of remuneration. "Such an application," she wrote, "was like a gleam of light springing up in the darkness. I had never been able to turn my thoughts toward literature during my sojourn in the bush. . . . I actually shed tears of joy over the first twenty-dollar bill I received from Montreal."

Other contributors to the *Literary Garland* included Major John Richardson, Mrs. Anna Jameson, Catharine Parr Traill, Charles Sangster, Mrs. Leprohon, and Mrs. Elizabeth Cushing (who edited the final volume after the death of Gibson). At a time when book publication in Canada was costly and hazardous, Lovell provided a forum for writers both native and immigrant in the pages of the *Garland* without which the literary record of the 1840's would have been even more arid than it is. Although neither publisher nor editor can be said to have discovered major literary talent, their journal maintained a respectable standard in the genteel tradition of the times.

Lovell was, perhaps, the only Canadian publisher of the last century who commissioned an author to write two novels for publication. The writer was Ebenezer Clemo, an impecunious English inventor who was then stranded in Montreal, and his novels (if such they may be called), both published under the pseudonym "Maple Knot" in 1858, were *The Life and Adventures of Simon Seek*, and *Canadian Homes; or, The Mystery Solved*. But as neither has any claim to literary merit, Lovell's gesture savours more of philanthropy than the encouragement of promising talent. There can be no doubt, however, that John Lovell did try to stimulate an interest in Canadian letters. Over a period of some fifty years he sought to bring before Canadian readers short stories, novels, and verse by Canadians. A dozen or more writers of fiction and a score of poets and poetasters appeared under the Lovell imprint. The very names of most of them are now forgotten—J. A. Phillips, A. L. Spedon, G. B. Chapin, H. S. Caswell, Frank Johnson, Augusta Baldwin, H. F. Darnell, Mrs. J. P. Grant, Henry Patterson, Kate Douglas Ramage and others. The more successful Canadian writers of fiction at the popular level, such as James De Mille and May Agnes Fleming, published all their work in the United States. The one Lovell author (apart from such public men as Thomas D'Arcy McGee and Joseph Howe) to achieve prominence in Canadian literary annals was William Kirby, the first edition of whose *Golden Dog* was published by the Lovell firm in 1877 at Rouses Point, N.Y., shortly before this American branch of the publishing house went bankrupt. But for a literary harvest so meagre after a lifetime of publishing, John Lovell cannot justly be blamed. On his part there was neither lack of critical discernment nor failure to provide financial incentives for creative writing. A publisher may encourage but can scarcely be expected to create writers.

After the demise of the *Literary Garland*, other efforts were made in the second half of the century to revive interest in Canadian letters. Six or eight literary magazines appeared in the Maritimes, in Quebec, and in Upper Canada, all of them short-lived. Typical of these was Thomas Maclear's *Anglo-American Magazine*, 1852–55. A Toronto bookstore-publisher, Maclear, in the prospectus for his new journal, deplored the flood of American magazines which were "little calculated to form or improve the literary taste" of Canadians. What was needed was a national, literary monthly, written by Canadians for Canadians. The *Anglo-American* scaled no literary heights, but it introduced Sangster to its readers, published some lively articles and stories, and impressed the English visitor to Toronto, W. H. G. Kingston, as "a very creditably conducted periodical" (to quote his *Western Wanderings; or,*

Pleasure Tour in the Canadas, London, 1856). It was soon to fall a victim to a severe financial depression, however, and its epitaph was "many subscribers but few subscriptions." The Maclear firm was later bought out by two former employees who, in 1869, formed the Copp, Clark Publishing Co.

The largest wholesale bookdealer and publisher in Toronto in the 1860's and 1870's was James Campbell & Son. The firm had a contract with the Department of Education to supply Canadian school texts written or edited by Canadians. Campbell's general line included a series of religious biographies, sermons, travel books, and an occasional volume of verse. The James Campbell & Son imprint became well known from Toronto to Halifax; their books were neat, well-printed volumes, superior in format and presswork to the average book published in Canada at the time. But as the firm regularly advertised that they were "prepared to furnish estimates to authors for the publication of their Mss.," it may be assumed that at least some titles on their list were published at the risk not of James Campbell & Son but of the aspiring authors.

This attitude towards native writers on the part of a large and respected publishing house bears out the contention of Rev. E. H. Dewart in his Introduction to *Selections from Canadian Poets* (Montreal: Lovell, 1864) that Canadian authors were under a severe disability:

There is probably no country in the world, making equal pretensions to intelligence and progress, where the claims of native literature are so little felt, and where every effort in poetry has been met with so much coldness and indifference, as in Canada. . . . Our mental wants [are] supplied by the brain of the Mother Country, under circumstances that utterly preclude competition. . . . Booksellers, too, because they make sure sales and large profits on British and American works, which have already obtained popularity, seldom take the trouble to judge of a Canadian book on its merits, or use their influence to promote its sale.

For publishers the problem was not merely promotion of their Canadian authors but the impossibility of obtaining effective copyright protection as the law then stood. American publishers, if they so desired, could reprint any book published in Canada without compensation to the author or the original publisher. With equal impunity they regularly reprinted British books in cheap editions for the home market and for export to Canada. Against this piratical practice there was no redress.

Canadian copyright was based on the Imperial Copyright Act of 1842, as amended in 1847. This forbade the reprinting of British books in the colonies but permitted the import of American reprints on payment of a duty of 12½ per cent as compensation to British authors in lieu of royalties. Moreover an American author, by establishing temporary residence in Canada and sending a few advance copies of his latest book to England for "first publication," could obtain full protection under the Imperial Act against the reprinting of his work in Canada. A Canadian author's copyright in Great Britain, however, was forfeited if the original form of publication in Canada was deemed to be inferior to British standards.

Naturally this discriminatory legislation was considered intolerable by Canadian publishers who bent every effort to seek federal protection. The difficulty was, however, that the British Act took precedence over any colonial copyright law. Thus a Canadian Copyright Act of 1872 which legalized the reprinting of British authors on payment to them of 12½ per cent of the wholesale price was reserved by Westminster and never became law. This prompted John Lovell and Graeme Mercer Adam, a Toronto publisher, to go to London and place before the Board of Trade their case in seeking an amendment to the Imperial Copyright Act. Although they received a sympathetic hearing, British publishers effectively blocked any action.

The next stratagem was to devise a Canadian Act which would not contravene the provision of the Imperial Act but would specify the conditions under which American authors could obtain copyright in Canada. They had to be "domiciled" (not merely "resident") in Canada, and their books had to be printed (normally from imported stereotyped plates) in Canada. This Act, which obtained royal assent in 1875, was a half-way measure which still left Canadian publishers at a disadvantage in competition with British copyright publishers and with the American publishers of piratical reprints. The whole situation might have been rectified if the United States and Canada had signed the Berne International Copyright Convention of 1886, but neither country saw fit to do so. The United States Chase Act of 1891 made provision for limited reciprocal copyright, but in order to qualify for more than temporary copyright, foreign books had to be wholly manufactured in the United States. It was this requirement that prevented the United States from subscribing to the Berne Convention.*

The depressing effect of copyright restriction on Canadian publishing in the nineteenth century can readily be documented. George MacLean Rose, head of the Hunter, Rose Publishing Company, stated in 1884, in a letter to the Editor of *Books and Notions* (Toronto):

After many years' experience in the publishing business I have come to the conclusion that it is almost useless to attempt building up a large and profitable publishing trade in our country, unless our government takes the matter of copyright in hand. . . . As the British Copyright Act is at present understood and worked it is all one sided, that is, it gives the United States author and publisher entire possession of our markets.

*The British Copyright Acts of 1842 and 1847 were superseded by the 1911 Act which enabled Canada to formulate her own copyright laws. In 1952 a new Universal Copyright Convention was sponsored by the United Nations. The United States became a participating member in 1954 (the manufacturing requirement still holds for her own citizens or domiciliaries), and Canada, after a long delay, in August 1962.

In the same year and in the same periodical, Mercer Adam had, a few months earlier, made the following observation:

The ethical influence of literary piracy on the book trade of America would be a subject for curious enquiry. Not the least of its evil effects is to be seen in the shrivelling up of native literature, and in the degeneracy of the modern publishing firms, who from preying upon British authors have descended to preying upon one another. Another harmful result is the lowering of public taste in the mechanical artistry of bookmaking. . . .

Adam's own career as publisher was frustrated by the British surrender of the Canadian book market to the United States, yet he persevered in advocating a literary revival in Canada with all the fervour of an evangelist. As J. E. Collins said of him in *The Week* (Aug. 28, 1884): "Mr. G. Mercer Adam has always been identified with our literature, saying good words for it when it hardly deserved good words, and blowing breath into its nostrils when it looked so like a corpse."

A Scot by birth, Adam had come to Toronto in 1858 at the age of 19 to enter the retail book trade. Seven years later he established the *British American Review* (after the failure in 1863 of the *British Canadian Review* in Quebec). It ran for two years but then folded up for lack of support. Meanwhile Adam had entered the book publishing field, and in 1867 formed, with J. H. Stevenson, the publishing house of Adam, Stevenson & Co. Together they launched an ambitious programme of bringing out Canadian books and acting as agents for British publishers. Almost single-handed, in 1872, Mercer Adam edited and published a trade journal, the *Canada Book-seller,* the twelve issues of which supply much information on the book trade and publishing industry of the time.

Adam saw encouraging signs that the intellectual and material progress which had led to Confederation would create a new national literature. To provide an incentive for native talent, he proposed to inaugurate a national review. He spoke, cautiously, about it in the *Canada Bookseller* for March 1872:

There has been of late a general awakening of national life, which has probably extended to the literary and scientific sphere. . . . To deal with Canadian questions and to call forth Canadian talent will be the first aim of the *Canadian Monthly.* . . Mr. Goldwin Smith has consented both to contribute regularly and to assist in conducting the magazine.

The initial success of the *Canadian Monthly and National Review* surpassed Adam's expectations; it soon became the most influential periodical of its kind to have appeared in Canada. Adam, Stevenson & Co. expanded their business to become what the *Toronto Directory* for 1873 described as a "great publishing house . . . a monument of the reading and literary ability of the Dominion." The partners had over-reached themselves, however, and in 1876, the firm was forced into bankruptcy. The *Monthly* was taken over by another publisher and continued, with Mercer Adam as editor (after a year's absence in New York), as *Rose-Belford's Canadian Monthly* until 1882.

C. P. Mulvany in *Toronto: Past and Present* (1884) attributed the demise of the *Canadian Monthly* to the indifference of Rose, Belford, the publishers, who ceased to pay the contributors. "With scant appreciation and no reward, Mr. Adam laboured for years to keep life in the *Canadian Monthly* whose publishers showed little inclination to second his efforts. . . . Owing to the course pursued by the publishers, the contributions were unpaid for. . . . "

When a new journal, *The Week*, appeared in 1883 under the editorship of Charles G. D. Roberts, Mercer Adam became a regular contributor. His disenchantment is reflected in an article he wrote for the issue of June 12, 1884, entitled "An Interregnum in Literature," commenting upon the decline of literary interest in the country and the decay of the better-class book trade. "The colonial status and the anomalies of the literary copyright law which surrenders the native book-market to the American publisher, are further obstacles to literary progress." Nevertheless *The Week* lasted for thirteen years and published some of the earliest verse of Roberts, Carman, Lampman, Duncan Campbell Scott, and many others.

William Kirby raised his voice in protest against the copyright laws in a paper read before the newly formed Royal Society of Canada in May 1883. Up to 1842, he maintained, authorship and publishing in Canada had as fair a chance of success as in the United States, but the Imperial Act put an end to all possible competition in Canada with American pirates. "Thus," he says, according to the report in the Quebec *Morning Chronicle* of February 1–4, 1884, "between the upper and lower millstones of British copyright publishers and American piratical publishers of British books, the business of book publishing in Canada has been ground to powder. . . . I say our clever men and women are waiting impatiently for the restoration of literary work in Canada by a due and needful encouragement of our publishing industries. . . . When that is done we shall see what forces are at work among us."

Without doubt Kirby over-simplified the problem and its solution. What was needed was not only untrammelled publishers but a literary climate of opinion and an interested public response, both of which were lacking at the time and could scarcely be produced by legislation.

One Canadian publisher who refused to be daunted by the prophets of gloom was the Reverend William Briggs. Appointed Book Steward of the Methodist Book and Publishing House in 1878, he determined to master a new vocation for which his theological training had scarcely prepared him. A man of great organizing ability, he had sound business instincts and an unlimited faith in Canadian enterprise. He soon belied Adam and Kirby by making publishing pay. At the same time he trained a succession of energetic young bookmen, several of whom later left the mother house to establish their own publishing firms, thus broadening the base of the publishing industry in Canada. In the same year that Kirby reported Canadian publishing "ground to powder," Briggs reported in *Books and Notions* for July that his house had printed during the year 245,023 books and pamphlets (i.e., copies), representing 31,071,070 pages; the number of books bound was 211,714. This placed the Methodist Book and Publishing House well ahead of other book publishers in Canada.

No other Canadian publisher in the closing decades of the last century did as much as William Briggs to stimulate literary talent and promote Canadian literature from coast to coast. Year after year, for the forty years he was in office (he retired in 1918), literary works by Canadian writers, especially the poets, appeared under the William Briggs imprint. William Kirby, Thomas O'Hagan, Sir James Edgar, Charles G. D. Roberts, Frederick George Scott, J. W. Bengough, Theodore H. Rand, Charles Mair, Catharine Parr Traill, and many others of lesser note were represented on the Briggs' lists by the turn of the century, and the real harvest was yet to come in the years of the Ryerson Press. This was a remarkable achievement for a Methodist minister in charge of a church publishing house at a time when other publishers were going bankrupt or barely managing to survive.

What, then, can be said in conclusion about the publisher-author relation in Canada up to 1900? We have seen that in the early period printer-publishers sought to provide outlets for native writers in newspapers, periodicals, and occasional subscription books. In this there was little thought or expectation of financial gain. Production costs were high and potential readers few and scattered. Literary journals appeared and disappeared but succeeded in producing a not inconsiderable body of Canadian writing, much of it uneven in quality. Book publication was a dubious financial risk which few publishers, whether newspaper proprietors or booksellers, could afford without the safeguard of a subscription list. The onus was usually on the author to produce this guarantee, a condition which doubtless discouraged all but the most determined writers.

From the mid-forties onward an increasing flood of cheap American books and pirated reprints of British authors further depressed the writing market in Canada. The reading public was content with the standard British and American authors of the day and showed little interest in supporting a native literature.

In the third quarter of the century, an expanded and more literate public provided a potential market for Canadian books, but copyright restrictions gave little or no protection to authors or publishers in Canada, and remedial legislation was reserved. Publishing increased in volume but was largely confined to non-literary productions. *Belles-lettres* continued to lag behind.

Confederation brought about a new access of patriotic and national senti-ment and encouraged publishers to expect the first fruits of a literary harvest, a harvest which largely failed, however, to mature. Journals continued to provide a forum for literary talent, but Canada's ablest writers, with a few notable exceptions, became expatriates and had their work published outside of Canada.

William Briggs, Hunter, Rose & Co., Copp, Clark, W. J. Gage, and a few other houses with specialized publishing interests survived into the present century; others well known in their day were forced into bankruptcy. Under adverse conditions they did what they could to encourage and foster a native literature, and cannot be held accountable for the lowly estate of Canadian letters in these years.

To what extent copyright reform a century ago would have revolutionized Canadian book publishing, created markets for Canadian writers, and produced a golden literary harvest may be debated but never resolved.

PART III

The Emergence of a Tradition

12. Confederation to the First World War

ROY DANIELLS

THE YEAR 1885 saw the failure of Louis Riel's second rebellion and the completion of steel on the Canadian Pacific Railway's transcontinental line. These were outward signs of the growing strength of the Canadian nation. Nationalism as a sentiment found expression in the Canada First movement whose aims had been made explicit when in 1871 W. A. Foster spoke to a Toronto audience on "Canada First; or, Our New Nationality," urging them to believe that "all the requirements of a higher national life are here available."

In the late eighties, nevertheless, the air was filled with debate which produced, not clarification, but further confusion. A strong sentiment for commercial union with the United States provoked violent reaction from convinced imperialists. Assertions of French nationalism, sharpened by resentment at the execution of Riel, were countered by the British nationalism of Ontario, which spread to Manitoba. The prime minister of Nova Scotia openly advocated the secession of his province from the Dominion. American pressures upon Canada led to a reiteration of Macdonald's National Policy, the protection of Canadian independence by tariffs and railways. "A British subject I was born, a British subject I will die" was the substance of his manifesto before the Conservative electoral victory of 1891.

What gave pattern and purpose to the confused drama was the desire in almost every segment of Canadian opinion to achieve national unity. Though good commercial reasons existed for reciprocity with the United States, and though Goldwin Smith confidently anticipated annexation, the sentiment of national independence inevitably prevailed. Both Quebec and Ontario desired a viable Canadian nation though with very different ends in view.

The desire for national unity was, in terms of economics, a desire to weld together the visibly diverse regions of this northern half of the continent in which uniquely abundant natural resources could support a full-scale economy if transport were made available. Independence of the United States and association with Britain in the Empire were generally and increasingly regarded as essential to the realization of this plan. A sure instinct for national survival led to the ideological suppression of elements of discord. The concept of reciprocity was never clarified but allowed to disintegrate under the pressure of Macdonald's National Policy. The provinces established in 1884 the fact that their legislatures had sovereign powers in those matters which had been put within their jurisdiction, but at the time concessions of this sort served to strengthen federal unity. The disruptive opposition of capital and labour never came to a head until after the First World War, nor to the majority of middle-class nineteenth-century citizens did it appear more than the greedy outcry of workmen for what they had not earned, or as *Grip*, Canada's equivalent of *Punch*, saw it in 1877, "Hooray for general suffrage, Communism, free lunches, free drinks, free everything, general distribution of property. . . ."

As the century drew to a close, Canadians became increasingly absorbed by the effort of economic expansion. The old National Policy, of eastern industrialization and western settlement held together by a transcontinental railway, was at last realized as a heartening actuality. Even the northwest prairies were opening to the wheat farmer and from still farther north and west came news of Pacific gold rushes. The economic strength and future potential of Canada were becoming obvious just when the Boer War and the Alaska boundary dispute accentuated Canadian desires for independence, under the Crown. The cloud which was to grow into a world war was still small upon the horizon.

Economic progress in the early twentieth century did not bring with it a commensurate growth of Canadian sensibility. The carefully nurtured, rather self-conscious, English-language culture of Ontario, built up with loving devotion in the 1870's and 1880's, held its ground. In Quebec, however, Henri Bourassa, the clerical leaders, and the editors of *Le Devoir* were uniting to promote quite another version of nationalist sentiment. An immigration of continental Europeans flowed into the Canadian prairies. British immigrants, knowing nothing and caring nothing about Ontario, came by tens of thousands to the far West. Throughout the West the Ontario tradition was becoming diffuse and attenuated. And in the East labour movements began to preach a social gospel of a new and potentially explosive kind.

The World War of 1914–18 evoked and absorbed the energies of Canadian patriotism as nothing else could have done, and of necessity the full effect of its strains became apparent only after the armistice. It was in August 1919, in the year of the Winnipeg general strike, that a Liberal convention, in Ottawa, selected as the new party leader William Lyon Mackenzie King. His victory in the election of 1921 was the beginning of a new set of tactics in the ceaseless effort to realize that national unity which had been implicit in Confederation.

There is no simple correspondence between an objective record of political, social, and economic events, on the one hand, and on the other, a criticism of the arts, whose creation and appreciation are suffused with subjectivity. Keats overheard and passed on the revelation that whatever the imagination apprehends as Beauty is also Truth; Coleridge's remedy for public grievances was "Let us become a better people." It is hard to forge direct links between such assertions and the Battle of Waterloo or the Reform Bill. In Canada, during the four decades following 1880, poetry is the supreme art, yet a direct connection between the best poems and contemporary events hardly exists. Some readers who care about Canada are disturbed by this apparent anomaly; they would like to have the poems spring from significant social thought. Lampman invites brief consideration in this context. He was a reader of Ruskin, Morris, and Mill; he believed in socialism as the ultimately desirable, though not immediately feasible form of government for Canada; he debated with his friends such problems as women's rights, George's single tax, and the conflict between science and religion; his distaste for party politicians and routine church-going he took no pains to conceal. But it has been observed that his poems of social criticism were "constructed rather than conceived," and that upon his best verse his secular liberalism had "directly, no bearing whatever." There remains an understandable and un-dispelled regret that Lampman did not move on to more modern poetic techniques, that he was denied the resources of radicalism or naturalism, and that his intellectual capacities and social insights were affected accordingly. But it can be argued that Lampman should not be expected to employ the selective literary sensibility of the late nineteenth century and simultaneously to act as a cutting edge of socio-political ideology. Lampman, furthermore, really did find peace, happiness, and renewed strength in nature: it seems certain that in nature, during the nineteenth century, strength, peace and happiness were to be found. The concluding lines of "An Old Lesson from the Fields" deserve to be accepted as his testament:

> O Light, I cried, and heaven with all your blue;
> O earth with all your sunny fruitfulness,
> And ye tall lilies of the wind-vexed field,
> What power and beauty life indeed might yield
> Could we but cast away its conscious stress,
> Simple of heart, becoming even as you!

(A creative mind expanding to achieve engagement with the full range of practical issues in its contemporary world is not likely to produce a memorable art-form: Augustine had no strategy for raising the siege of Hippo; Dante wrote in exile, Milton in defeat; neither Chaucer nor Shakespeare nor Wordsworth could envisage what their societies needed in the way of institutional reform.)

It is unfashionable at the moment to oppose the argument that culture appears by extrusion from everyday communal living. Sociological and political preoccupations obscure the concept of culture as a body of experience based upon traditional standards. The phrase "literary culture" has almost ceased to have a meaning. It is therefore natural to praise the "socially significant" poet at the expense of other levels of sensibility, intuition, or vision. What needs to be reasserted in any study of nineteenth-century Canada is the primacy and autonomy of cultural tradition at that time.

The *Canadian Monthly* of 1874 took the trouble to reprint, from the *Contemporary Review*, Mr. Gladstone's article on the Shield of Achilles. This piece, glowing with Gladstone's enthusiasm for the ancient world, was written by a lover of Homer for other lovers of Homer needing no introduction to the delights of wrestling with a difficult passage. The Ontario reader is therefore revisiting a *locus classicus* in the company of an eminent Englishman, an ex-prime minister, and a known scholar. The continuity of cultural tradition is abundantly apparent, as Gladstone's mind ranges over the Mediterranean scene "full of all things glorious, beautiful, and strong."

Wölfflin has observed that "Anyone who concerns himself exclusively with the subject-matter of works of art will be completely satisfied with it; yet the moment we want to apply artistic standards of judgment in the criticism of works of art we are forced to try to comprehend formal elements which are unmeaning and inexpressible in themselves." In an analogous way the student of Canada after Confederation will encounter a great deal of politics, many economic considerations, and a sequence of personalities and events sufficient to engage his whole attention. But he will need other avenues of approach if he is to reach the centre of Canadian consciousness.

A small group of periodicals published in Toronto furnishes a reliable conspectus of the central English literary tradition in Canada. These are the *Canadian Monthly*, the *Week* and the *Canadian Magazine*.

The *Canadian Monthly and National Review* (1872–78) which continued as *Rose-Belford's Canadian Monthly* (1878–82) was edited, with a lacuna of two years, by Graeme Mercer Adam, an ardent nationalist. By his own writing and by his selection of contributors he became one of the founders of the post-Confederation literary renaissance. The *Canadian Monthly* expressed the ideals of the Canada First Movement and was devotedly supported by Goldwin Smith. Its homogeneity over the decade of its life is remarkable; published in Toronto and consciously dedicated to nationalist ideals, it embodied the central sentiment of English-speaking Canada; in the quantity and quality of its ideas and in the range of its interests it had no rivals. Whatever their subject, its pages are never less than lucid, dignified, and persuasive. A small degree of historical imagination or sympathetic rapport will take today's reader of these volumes back into a golden world of high Victorian sensibility.

The ingredient of fiction was small but important. From cautious beginnings in the first volume (a serial story of Irish life and a few translations from French and German) we move to such a full-blown novel as ran from November 1880 to June 1881, crammed with striking incidents and stretched into long dramatic suspense, all in Wilkie Collins's best manner. The selection of this body of fiction shows a consistent regard for literary style and an intermittent desire to escape the local Canadian scene. England and the Mediterranean are preferred settings; romantic sentiment and melodramatic action are desired ingredients. Fairly strong moral and religious overtones make themselves heard, ranging in quality from the pervasive Christian faith of "Fidelis" to the stereotyped scenes of Collins—"the baffled Jesuit turned furiously on the dying man."

History, too, is a repository of exemplary wisdom. An account of George Fox and Quakerism ends with a summary appraisal: "It has exemplified the subtlety, pervasiveness and power of truth and love, and so strengthened all men's faith in their reality and ultimate victory." An editorial in 1872 reviews historical events common to Britain, Canada, and the United States and concludes: "It is possible that the hour of Canadian nationality may be drawing near. If so, let us prepare to found the nation, not in ingratitude but in truth and honour."

How deliberate and conscious were the aims of the founders of the *Monthly* is revealed on their first page. The magazine will deal with Canadian questions and call forth Canadian talent; it will nevertheless seek in all quarters for the means of interesting and instructing its readers; the utmost latitude of subject and expression is to be allowed, with the exception of party politics and party theology, "nor will anything be admitted which can give just offence to any portion of the community." The managers of the magazine have a national object in view and will endeavour to preserve throughout "a tone beneficial to the national character and worthy of the nation."

This desire to preserve, justify, and substantiate national unity imparts to these volumes an extraordinary unity of topic and tone. Criticism is constructive; love of country is everything from deep affection for the terrain itself to patriotic pride over memories of Lundy's Lane; the very book reviews shine like stars in a moral firmament. A world is created, its centre in the Canadian home, its middle distance the loved landscape of Canada, its protecting wall the circle of British institutions, associations, and loyalties. Across this welcome breastwork the United States, now neither menacing nor necessarily hostile, is to be viewed, and more exciting because less familiar, the great outposts of the civilization of continental Europe—France, Italy, Germany, and behind these the splendours of ancient Greece and Rome. It is a world as centripetal as that of Sherlock Holmes and as little liable to be shaken by irruptions of evil. There is recurring acknowledgment but little understanding of the culture of French Canada and of the implications of bi-culturalism; the natural vista from Ontario is into the immensity of the West, extending itself to the Pacific. The Indian is seen through the eyes of paternalism: "The thoughtful treatment of our Indians by the Hudson Bay Company, in the first instance, has tended to make them as peaceful and industrious as they are. It remains now for our Government to keep them strictly to an understanding that their rights will be secured to them as they are to the whites; but that in return for such treatment they must submit to the rule of life which the white man's law prescribes."

The solid agglutinative core of the magazine consists of articles on Canadian scenes and places, Canadian history, and Canadian culture. The direct approach of the writers is wholly delightful and a measure of the practical quality of their patriotism. Canada, one writer argues, is at bottom the creation of the labourer who clears the land for a farm. The merchant appears, to supply him; the magistrate to interpret the law; then the men of science and ministers of religion. Finally the statesman labours to "form his compact community or nation with the least amount of evil." To Canada national sentiment is an absolute necessity and its first principle is patriotism. But Canada needs the power to confer Canadian citizenship. The article concludes with a list of proposals aimed at securing Canadian unity and self-sufficiency; for example, French should be made compulsory in the common schools. The historian and politician J. G. Bourinot contributed a lengthy analysis of Canadian intellectual development up to 1880. It is a highly perceptive bi-cultural review, ending with a vision of "a future full of promise for literature as for industry."

National communities have an inevitable ritual in which the story of their heroes and the tales of their famous battles are rehearsed. A fine instance is the historical sketch of the War of 1812 written by the redoubtable "Fidelis" for the issue of July 1874. It has the true ring of heroic story, rising to its climax with the death of Brock: "Queenston Heights, where his death occurred, and where his memorial column stands, is, no less than the Plains of Abraham, one of Canada's sacred places, where memories akin to those of Thermopylae and Marathon may well move every Canadian who has a heart to feel them."

"Fidelis," or Agnes Maule Machar, was born in Kingston in 1837 and died there exactly ninety years later. She was a prolific contributor to the *Canadian Monthly* from 1873 onward and a superbly representative and summary figure. To the last volume, in 1882, she contributed not only articles on Sophocles but poems (one an Advent Hymn) and a plea for co-education in the universities. Her tenacity of purpose, her consistency of aim, her articulateness, and her ability to fuse religious, patriotic, and cultural interests give her all the force of a legend, and the prolongation of her literary work well into this century is in accord with the persistence of post-Confederation values until the period of the First World War.

The poetic contributions, which were numerous, will be discussed in a later chapter.

The *Canadian Monthly* went out of existence in 1882 and the void left by its passing was partially filled by the establishment, in the next year, of *The Week*, published in Toronto and edited by Charles G. D. Roberts. Its prospectus promised "faithfully to reflect and summarize the intellectual, social and political movements of the day" and, disdaining party leanings, to further "the free and healthy development of the Nation." Goldwin Smith backed the new magazine and contributed to it. G. Mercer Adam, "Fidelis," "Seranus," and other familiar names reappear. The continuity of the tradition is very real, although Roberts was less happy in his editorial office than Adam had been and soon abandoned it. *The Week* went out of existence in 1896 but *The Canadian Magazine*, 1893–1939, was already carrying on the tradition though with less *élan*. Founded and edited by the journalist J. G. Mowat, it too was published in Toronto. Its initial announcement would equally well have suited the old *Monthly*: "While the pages of the Magazine will be open to the expression of a wide diversity of opinions, and opinions with which the Magazine does not agree, the policy will be steadily pursued of cultivating Canadian patriotism and Canadian interests, and of endeavouring to aid in the consolidation of the Dominion on a basis of national self-respect and a mutual regard for the rights of the great elements which make up the population of Canada."

Another landmark of cultural publication is the collection of poems edited by William D. Lighthall as *Songs of the Great Dominion* in 1889. (An English edition appeared in the same year and another English edition, with a change of title, in 1892.) Lighthall's introduction and his choice of poems have a firmness of stance which gave his early readers the shock of recognition and won for his book a wide regard. He begins:

The poets whose songs fill this book are voices cheerful with the consciousness of young might, public wealth and heroism. Through them, taken all together, you may catch something of great Niagara falling, of brown rivers rushing with foam, of the crack of the rifle in the haunts of the moose and caribou, the lament of vanished races singing their death-song as they are swept on to the cataract of oblivion, the rural sounds of Arcadias just rescued from surrounding wildernesses by the axe, shrill war whoops of Iroquois battle, proud traditions of contest with the French and the Americans, stern and sorrowful cries of valour rising to curb rebellion. The tone of them is *courage*. . . .

He goes on to a lyrical praise of the landscape and natural resources of the country. His description of Canada is everywhere superlative:

> Her population is about five million souls. Her Valley of the Saskatchewan alone, it has been scientifically computed, will support eight hundred millions. In losing the United States, Britain lost the *smaller* half of her American possessions; the Colony of the Maple Leaf is about as large as Europe.

There is more, however, to Lighthall's love of Canada than a vision of geographical or material greatness:

> But what would material resources be without a corresponding greatness in man? Canada is also imperial in her traditions. Her French race are still conscious that they are the remnants of a power which once ruled North America from Hudson's Bay to the Gulf of Mexico. Existing English Canada is the result of simply the noblest epic migration the world has ever seen:—more loftily epic than the retirement of Pius Æneas from Ilion,—the withdrawal, namely, out of the rebel Colonies, of the thirty-five thousand United Empire Loyalists after the War of the Revolution. . . . Canada has, of historic right, a voice also in the Empire of today, and busies herself not a little in studying its problems. For example, the question whether the Empire will last is being asked. Her history has a reply to that:—IT WILL IF IT SETS CLEARLY BEFORE IT A DEFINITE IDEAL THAT MEN WILL SUFFER AND DIE FOR; and such an Ideal—worthy of long and patient endeavour—may be found in broadminded advance towards the voluntary Federation of Mankind.

It is hard to imagine a more perfect manifesto, articulating as it does a sense of the magnificence of the landscape, a vision of manifest destiny, an epic feeling for the heroic past, and a shining desire for moral excellence. The relation of English-speaking Canada to Quebec, to the Empire, to the United States, and to native Indian races has an air of being realized with the clarity of a cameo.

In compiling his anthology, Lighthall explicitly disclaims a purely literary aim. He is looking only for poetry that illustrates the country and its life "in a distinctive way." In 1889 he was a young lawyer living in Montreal, thirty-two years of age, a product of McGill University. In due course he became a K.C. and embarked on a long career of public service and of authorship. He exhibits a confidence and an enthusiasm which reflect the powerfully corporate Loyalist sentiment of the period.

The poems are grouped under headings which summarize Lighthall's intention: the Imperial spirit, the new nationality, the Indian, the *voyageur* and *habitant,* settlement life, sports and free life, the spirit of Canadian history, places, seasons. A few pieces by Crawford, Lampman, Carman, and D. C. Scott, filled with an appreciation of nature, stand above the general undistinguished level. Lighthall was fully aware that he was sacrificing poetic quality for representative national sentiment. This latter he perfectly reflects. It is the product of a high colonial culture.

The central concepts of this culture are precisely indicated in Lighthall's introduction. A vigorous spirit of expansion looks out on a magnificent, under-developed, and inviting terrain stretching into the boundless West. The past is a story of intense and successful struggle to conquer, to colonize, and to defend the country. The French have been defeated, the Americans repulsed, and the rebellions quelled. The French exist as remnants of a great power. The Americans have but the smaller half of what was British America. The Indians are a vanishing race. Destiny is at the service of English Canadians, whose epic virtues, derived from the heroism of the Loyalists, are equal to the double effort of creating the reality of national unity "from sea to sea" and clarifying, for the whole British Empire, its task of leading the advance towards a Federation of Mankind.

The formulated attitude towards French Canada, which to say the least imperfectly covered the ambiguities of the situation, is once more exhibited by Lighthall himself, under the transparent pseudonym of Wilfred Chateau-clair, in *The Young Seigneur* (Montreal, 1888). In this slight story he intends "to map out a future for the Canadian nation." He draws an idyllic picture of the grandeur and beauty of the St. Lawrence valley, the virtues of the *habitant,* and the aspirations of those French Canadians who combine hereditary capacities for leadership with liberal politics, progressive ideas, and a firm morality. The idealism of Lighthall and his desire to see Canada become "The Perfect Nation" are simply an intense and poetically clairvoyant variant of the general Canadian hope. To French Canadians he says, "Identify yourselves with a nation vaster than your race, and cultivate your talents to put you at its head." These highlights of his story throw into relief dark shadows of ultramontane clerical bigotry and rampant political fraud.

The Golden Age of high colonialism in Ontario endures for about a quarter-century, from 1871–72, when the Canada First movement took shape, the *Canadian Monthly* began its course, and the first organization of the C.P.R. Company was effected, to 1896–97, when the economic depression came to an end, *The Week* ceased publication, and Laurier took office as prime minister.

The brazen age of prosperity which followed is also conveniently and fairly accurately seen as a quarter-century, terminating with the repatriation of Canadian soldiers after the First World War and the symbolic first publication of the *Canadian Forum* in October 1920. By this time the ideology of high colonialism had suffered marked diminution and decline, though never to the point of disintegration.

Several questions at once arise. Why did the fact of Confederation prove so powerful (though brief) a stimulus to Canada's literary culture? Why does the land, in the sense of terrain, play so dominant a role in Canadian experi-ence? To what extent is periodical publication a reliable guide to cultural sensibility? How may we assess changes in this sensibility between, say, 1880 and the end of the First World War?

Students of English literature are often puzzled by what might be called the Waterloo effect—that is, the enormous but undefinable influence upon British morale and British creativeness induced by the long sustained effort of the Napoleonic Wars. It is plain for all to see yet it can never be properly documented. It is a kind of extra dimension to British life, "As every child can tell." Something similar happened to Elizabethans when the Armada was deflected and defeated.

The fact of Confederation created a field of force in the English-Canadian mind which brought Wolfe, the emigration of Loyalists, "Queenston Heights and Lundy's Lane," the repulse of the Fenians, the defeat of rebels in 1837 (and of Riel in 1870) into alignment. "Fidelis" and Lighthall, in comparing such events to Thermopylae, Marathon, or Æneas leaving Ilion to found another kingdom, were saying literally what they and thousands of others felt. It is the same sentiment as enables a contributor to the *Encyclopaedia Britannica* to say simply that Alfred is the noblest of the English kings.

Such considerations are above party politics or provincial interest; they are above sectionalism of any kind, whether of race, religion, or region. They give urgency, conviction, and a certain vagueness to patriotic utterance throughout the period. Men of all parties were powerfully if imprecisely impressed with the vastness of Canadian territory, the drama of Canada's history, and the potential future greatness of their country. What afflicted Macdonald, who had the stature of heroism, was the discrepancy between the vision of Canada's greatness and the meanness of political manipulation needed to realize it. "Send me better men to work with and I will be a better man."

Typical of patriotic writing in the *Canadian Monthly* is an article in 1874 on "The Massacre at the Cedars." American claims are disproved, American propaganda reprehended: "The publication of the original documents renders it possible to ascertain the real facts as they occurred, and Canadians, the more narrowly they enquire into the doings of their forefathers, will have the more reason to be proud of the early history of their country."

Typical also is a determination not to confuse a commitment to the British cultural tradition with uncritical admiration of British politics and society. The defeat of a strike of English farm labourers in 1874 is recorded in the *Monthly* with the bitter comment, "Combating privation in his industrial war, the peasant has shown something of the same stubborn valour with which, when in arms for his country, he has often held the post of duty upon the blood-stained hillside. . . . But the columns which he encountered on this occasion were columns which could not be rolled back like those which mounted to the attack at Waterloo. . . . Against overpowering wealth and territorial influence, with hunger as their sword, no valour or endurance can prevail."

The desire for Canadian national unity was intense and sustained. This ensured that the rational Goldwin Smith, with his Manchester-school liberalism, would always be odd man out. His eloquent desire to see Anglo-Saxon culture established in Canada brought him into the main stream of criticism and literature. His advocacy of continental union, his scepticism as to the nation-building potential of the C.P.R., his failure to grasp that French Canadians intended to remain French: these lapses kept him out of the main stream of Canadian political thought.

It has often been noticed that in the decades following Confederation the supreme art in Canada is poetry and that the best poems concern themselves with Canadian natural surroundings. This may be thought incompatible with the kind of Canada First aims we have just reviewed; yet, remembering the analogy of Romantic writing in England, we can perhaps concede that the Canadian poets chose with instinctive wisdom. It is not Lampman alone who, believing profoundly in his country, finds in landscape the intuition of its goodness and greatness. "It is in Nature," says one of Lighthall's characters watching the sun rise on the St. Lawrence, "that I can love Canada most, and become renewed into efforts for the good of her human sons." Those who turned to nature were not evading but seeking the true Canada. The only thing Canadians possessed that other people did not was the top half of the American continent. This presented the Golden Age with its most pressing problem, the achievement of transport as a means towards political and economic unity. Wolseley's difficulty was not to overcome Riel but to reach Fort Garry. The industrial problem of Canada was the long haul, for raw materials and for the finished product. The Canadian terrain was an enormous and irreducible fact as Lord Dufferin discovered when he travelled thousands of miles through the United States to reach the western side of his own territory. In ways that are not always rationally clear and through channels of expression often far from logically explicit Canadian feeling about the terrain of Canada made itself powerfully felt. Then, as now, the geological, geographical, topographic, and lyric features of the Canadian landscape were the fundamental facts of Canadian experience.

There are several reasons why the texture of Canada's literary *milieu* in the three decades following Confederation can be reliably sampled in the pages of the *Canadian Monthly*, *The Week*, and the *Canadian Magazine*. Newspapers, preoccupied with party politics, did not hold a clear mirror to national consciousness. Book publication was hazardous and for economic reasons failed to cover the true range of Canadian interests. The small group of Toronto periodicals is therefore peculiarly significant. Toronto was fortunate in having Goldwin Smith, who in turn was fortunate in Adam, the ideal editor. The image they projected upon the pages of the *Monthly* remained in focus for the rest of the century. This simplification of the pattern may appear to ignore not only Quebec but also the Maritimes and the successive frontiers of the West. The influence of French culture upon English was, however, tenuous and destined to become neither dominant nor subservient nor even contributory; the historical clarification has been towards a polarity. As for the prairies and the seaboards, Canadian cultural experience has always declined to follow the American form. The representative attitudes are not realized regionally or on the frontier, they are shaped and conserved at the centre, which in the present context and for the period under review is Ontario. S. D. Clark has shown how centrifugal forces were resisted, as tending towards American continentalism and towards the weakening of Canadian sovereignty. At this time moreover the provincial economies were all vulnerable and could only hope for stability and growth within the concept of national integration. The same was true of the cultural nexus in each of the English-speaking provinces.

To turn from the confused politics and desperate economics of the period to the world of ideas and values projected by Adam and his fellow contributors is a delightful as well as an illuminating experience. Book reviews and critical articles combine into a complex, lucid, and rewarding pattern. The climate of opinion never really changes: Canadian independence, for example, is advocated in terms of cultivating "A strong feeling of patriotism as opposed to mere loyalty," and this shift implies neither radical nor revolutionary thinking.

Moral earnestness is everywhere dominant. The period of pioneer settlement is conceived as Canada's "heroic age." The prospect of political independence brings biblical phrases to the pen: "it does not yet appear what we shall be." The reviewer of a book on Kant wants to keep the intellectual advantages of both Kant and Herbert Spencer. As a consequence of this kind of high seriousness, no real dialectic is allowed to develop. Exposition is a pervasive method of reviewing, but argument—as the whole cavalcade of Victorian problems rides by—is muted by the conscious need to recognize both orthodox Christian piety and the new liberal rationalism. The synthesis achieved is sufficiently liberal and sufficiently moral to make of George Eliot the Canadian reviewers' ideal novelist. A dynamic acceptance of the principle of moral regeneration, a constant realistic insight into character and conduct, a capacity to picture middle-class living: George Eliot had them all in abundance.

It follows that realism, whether in fiction, in drama, or in painting, was felt as a means to realize the ideal. An article on science and art begins with the words of Victor Cousin, "La vraie beauté est la beauté idéale, et la beauté idéale est un reflet de l'infini." Realism in drama is expected to serve other ends than its own. The sensational novel is condemned as untrue to moral and social actuality. In comments upon science, there is the same desire to reconcile objective inquiry with a conservation of ideal values: an article on Darwin praises him as "a reverent believer in the Unknown Power, from whom all Life proceeds" and goes on to say that "if the Church disagrees with Science, so much the worse for the Church."

The ingredients of high colonialism can be assessed fairly accurately. There is a real desire for cultural achievement, to match commercial achievement: "Canadian ships, freighted with the products of Canadian industry, are to be found floating in almost every sea. How many foreign nations know anything of Canadian thought or scholarship?" At the same time the vital necessity of cultural stimulus from outside is eagerly acknowledged. Cultural independence is, with a different time sequence, in the same class of desiderata as political independence. As the monarchical principle had been central to the plan of confederation, had made possible the concept of independence within the Empire, and had provided a safeguard against the "absorptive presence" of the United States, so the principle of loyalty to British cultural tradition provided a *milieu* within which Canadians could hope in time to achieve a national nexus. In the meantime British models were accorded the sincerest form of flattery. The *Canadian Monthly* had before it the example of the *Fortnightly Review*. This visible dependence upon British tradition, however, had no element of subservience. Misrepresentation of Canadian opinion in London journals, failure to guard Canadian interests on the part of British diplomats, ineptitude in the class of immigrant known as the remittance man: all were canvassed without hesitation. British aggression in Afghanistan and acts of brutality in the suppression of the Indian Mutiny were roundly condemned.

French and German literatures are given, on a lesser scale, the same earnest attention. Not only is fiction reviewed or translated; there are serious articles dealing with such key figures as Voltaire, Diderot (whose materialism is attacked), and Goethe (whose sense of the divine is admired). There is a lively interest in the standard American writers—Emerson, Holmes, Howells, and Whittier.

During the four or five decades under review, Romanticism gave ground to Realism; concepts of evolution belatedly permeated the public mind; collectivism gained recognition as a social fact; a pervasive materialism of outlook accompanied the economic boom which, beginning about 1896, lasted well into the war years. Book reviews in the periodicals provide a useful index to cultural change. The *Canadian Monthly*, during 1872, reviewed four biographies, including those of Wesley and Dickens; six books on literature and language, including works of Longfellow, Macaulay, and Aytoun; five historical works, whose subjects ranged from Mary Queen of Scots to the American Civil War; two works on science, including one by Huxley; five books on religion and morals, including Morley's *Voltaire* which is so treated; a few novels and travel books; and a reprint of *Roughing It in the Bush*. The general tone may be judged from the remark, "We begin almost to long for a biography, if it were possible of some one who *did not* rise in life, but, ignobly content with the humble state to which he was called, found happiness in duty and affection." The *Canadian Magazine*, during 1893, offers reviews covering the same general range of interests but reduced in number, truncated to become mere notes and generally inferior in range of ideas and critical style. Biography is represented by a life of Senator John Macdonald, a successful and generous business man. Two travel books, totally unimportant; a history of Bering and one of Columbus; an Ontario biography and the story of the Parliament Buildings in Toronto: these account for history and geography. The best poet reviewed is Edwin Arnold; in fiction we are on the level of Verne, Henty, and Lew Wallace; language is represented by a book on punctuation, science by a report of the Hamilton Association. Nor do critical articles come to any effective rescue of the world of ideas: Roberts is praised for "Ave," Tennyson and Browning for their concept of a future life, Kingsley for the allegory of *Water Babies*. Emerson is noticed twice, once in conjunction with Bacon and Cicero in praise of friendship. Having achieved in its review columns the lowest possible level consistent with its professed aims, the *Canadian Magazine* appears to have found a reliable formula. The books chosen for review continue with few exceptions to be mediocre and the reviews themselves trivial. Without being lost, the tradition is everywhere weakened and cheapened.

For this decline there appears to be no one explanation. The *Canadian Monthly*, when it ceased publication in 1882, gave as its reasons "our inchoate state as a nation," competition from England and America, "the indifference of our people to higher literature," lack of encouragement from the press and from public men, and the loss of steady patriotism in the excitements of "the political game." As the literate public became larger it appears to have become less literary. Though statistics are lacking, it is clear that English-speaking Canadians taking a cultural view of life were at no time very numerous, even in Ontario. Smith, Adam, and their friends made a brave and sustained effort, but never can so much have been owed by so few to so few.

If must be remembered that, although Toronto was the centre of Canadian publishing, a cultural impulse which produced some of Canada's best writing originated in Fredericton, the city memorable for Roberts and Carman. A. G. Bailey has identified this impulse as the second of two "creative moments" of the Maritimes, the first being centred in Nova Scotia, which in the 1830's and 1840's had produced Howe and Haliburton. The development in New Brunswick came a generation later, in Fredericton. Here Loyalist traditions persisted; the very isolation of the community from the expansive and disruptive development of the timber industry was a safeguard of intellectual pursuits and of the values of a class structure. In 1859, the University of New Brunswick was created on the basis of King's College, which had received its charter in 1826 and was in turn based on a college which had been in existence for over sixty years. Charles G. D. Roberts's father and Sir George Parkin, who taught Roberts and his cousin Bliss Carman, were themselves pupils of Baron d'Avray, professor of modern languages, remembered also as founder of the first provincial normal school, editor of a newspaper, and superintendent of education. A continuous tradition reached back to the 1780's when Royal Engineers had laid out the town for incoming Loyalists and Governor Carleton had made it his capital. In Fredericton the conservation of British values and the preservation of a colonial culture were no deterrents to the acceptance of nineteenth-century liberal ideas and Romantic literature.

The emergence of Roberts and Carman, together with others of their group, from the town and countryside of Fredericton in the 1880's has implications relevant to the whole of Canadian literature. It appears that even a small community may furnish the "critical mass" needed for a literary expansion; that preservation of social and cultural forms may be as significant in some contexts as innovation is in others; that when environmental influences have all been acknowledged there remains the fact that like answers to like, that poets are inspired, guided, and given models by other poets: the image of Parkin reading Keats, Rossetti, and Swinburne to his boys can never be effaced. Here was the origin of Canada's "dolce stil nuovo" and the source of our first national literary movement.

The pattern of periodical publication in Ontario appears with equal clarity, though on another scale, if we compare the three New Brunswick periodicals, *Stewart's Quarterly* (Saint John, 1867–72), the *Maritime Monthly* (Saint John, 1873–75) and the *New Brunswick Magazine* (Saint John, 1898–1905).

Stewart's Quarterly has a strong resemblance to the original *Canadian Monthly* and serves to demonstrate how pervasive, throughout the Canadian provinces, was the spirit of high colonialism. It is significant that George Stewart, its editor and proprietor, became in due course, after its demise, the editor of *Rose-Belford's Canadian Monthly* and of a newspaper in Quebec. It must have been difficult for Stewart to strike the right note for his Maritime clientele, as some changes of sub-title indicate, but he strove to preserve a balance among Canadian, British, European, and American elements and to find space for fiction, poetry, articles, and reviews.

Perhaps the most notable feature of his magazine is the sense of historical continuity which it induces. There is a continuous effort to recall the past and to establish tradition. A natural concomitant is an almost unfailing note of practicality and earnestness. There are articles on Canadian archives, on fishing rights, on the old forts of Acadia, on Newfoundland and the far Northwest, on Canadian worthies, on French and Indian wars, on the Canadian army of the future—calling for a uniting of "courage as was displayed by the men who led the Six Hundred at Balaclava, with the hand of science which the chiefs of that fatal yet glorious day failed to grasp." The British connection is tightened by warmly appreciative articles on Scott and Carlyle, Thackeray and Dickens, and minor figures. English literature is covered, period by period, in long and loving accounts. London papers, Oxford colleges, the Royal Family, the beauties of Scotland complete the picture, and the reader, on a tour of the field of Waterloo, is brought to the very scene: "Tread lightly, for beneath your feet is the dust of heroes." American tradition gets more scattered attention, though there is acknowledgment of the great (Columbus, Lincoln) and of the immediately popular (Mark Twain, Bret Harte). Attention to Europe is significant, if sporadic: we are told of Spanish history, Hungarian music, and Paris after the siege. Bach, Handel, and Mendelssohn receive serious attention.

Fiction is less prominent than one would expect, probably from lack of local talent. Brief stories of hazards in the bush or on the ice are interspersed with romantic, moral, or comical tales of local life: all are so slight as to infer no recognition of an art of fiction. Poetry is similarly sketchy: standard Victorian sentiments are versified about the seasons, the names of fair ladies, or historical events. Homer, Anacreon, Pindar appear, translated or adapted. In critical articles such names as McLachlan, Sangster, and Heavysege receive patriotic praise. An interest in science is apparent, though articles on scientific subjects are few. A revealing remark appears in a dialogue: "I have managed to read Lamb, Matthew Arnold, Keats, Longfellow, Browning, Bryant, Tennyson, Sydney Smith, Dickens and Whittier, and they are 'Household Words' by my fireside." But the speaker is now immersed in the reading of science.

There are many literary notices, particularly of English and American periodicals, but few reviews and these painfully restricted in outlook. Stewart, like Mercer Adam, seems to have laboured against difficult odds. Twenty issues appeared, growing from forty pages to ninety, and then he gave up: "The work has been somewhat arduous, as any man of experience knows; and though our labours have not been crowned with pecuniary success, we hope, as a literary venture, our work has not been altogether thrown away. Our aim has been to furnish a good, sound, healthy literature for the people of this 'incipient northern nation.' "

The *Maritime Monthly,* which appeared in 1873, approximated its predecessor in both style and content. Yet there is an indefinable relaxation of the spirit of high colonialism, a loss of centrality, a loss of the formal elements of composition. A Halifax contributor lays down the plan of Canadian literature as it should be: Canada has no aristocracy of blood, no oppression, no revolting forms of vice or corruption; "the delineator of Canadian life must picture the quiet scenes of industry, the simple incidents of ordinary life, the joys, sorrows, hopes, disappointments, successes and failures which are incident to men in the common routine of life."

The *New Brunswick Magazine*, which first appeared in 1898, made the Maritime provinces its special field and admitted that its aim was not a literary one, but the "diffusion of information in respect to the country and its people." Although many of its comments on old military manoeuvres, shipwrecks, history of settlement, derivation of words and the like can still be read with interest, the glory has departed. In the last few issues, even the historical material dwindles, and is replaced by an ever-increasing quantity of light fiction.

Within a decade and a half of Confederation several other journals were thrown up by the rising tide of nationalism; for example, the *Canadian Literary Journal* (Toronto), the *Harp* (Montreal), the *New Dominion Monthly* (Montreal). None, however, created a cultural pattern as significant, as consistent, and (even under abrasive neglect) as durable as the sequences we have discussed. The same may be said of the group established around the turn of the century in the Maritimes and in the West: the *Canada-West Magazine* (Winnipeg), the *Manitoban* (Winnipeg), *Acadiensis* (Saint John), the *New Brunswick Magazine* (Saint John), the *Prince Edward Island Magazine* (Charlottetown). In Toronto, the precarious *Bystander* (1880, 1883, 1889–90) and *Nation* (1874–76) of Goldwin Smith were extensions of his older and more solid enterprise of the *Canadian Monthly*, already discussed. Most other journals were either organs of particular churches or popular magazines or in the academic tradition of the universities.

Political radicalism, during the period under review, found literary expression which will be dealt with in a subsequent chapter.

To turn the pages of the old *Canadian Monthly* is to enter a lost world. Courage and loyalty were its pre-eminent virtues; it demonstrated that liberal views, critical standards, and religious faith could strengthen one another. A handful of people set themselves to form the ideas of a new nation. Inevitably limited by remoteness from great centres, unavoidably prejudiced and in the face of many dangers unable to develop a full dialectic, they achieved a vision of national greatness and an intellectual method more serviceable, more coherent, more beautiful than any other in English-Canadian history. From their record, in the phrase of D. C. Scott, "Rises the hymn of triumph and courage and comfort, Adeste Fideles."

13. Historical Writing in Canada

to 1920

KENNETH N. WINDSOR

IN THE pre-Confederation period the English-speaking community in Canada could not take much satisfaction in the achievement of its historians. In 1866, the year before the publication of his *Bibliotheca Canadensis*, Henry J. Morgan complained that, with the exception of F.-X. Garneau (1809–1866), Canadian historians "have no reason, as a general rule, to plume themselves upon the elaborate nature of their productions." This was also the opinion of J. Castell Hopkins (1864–1923) in his *Encyclopaedia* at the turn of the century. After considering the substantial achievements of French-Canadian historians in the early period, he confessed that "literary progress in English-speaking Canada had been much slower and less productive," and explained that "The competition of other interests and pursuits was keener and the characteristic physical activity of the race greater. The natural result was comparative indifference to anything except political controversy, through the medium of popular journals, or the ever present charm of English standard works."

I

Some of the earliest historical writing is found in those compendia of useful information, the Statistical Accounts, doubtless prepared in imitation of Sir John Sinclair's massive *Statistical Account of Scotland*, which was drawn up, as the title-page indicates, "from the communications of the ministers of the different parishes." There is a historical introduction and a good deal of historical information in Robert Gourlay's famous *Statistical Account of Upper Canada* published in 1822. Convinced that more accurate information about Canada was needed in the mother country, Gourlay (1778–1863) addressed 31 questions "to the Resident Landowners of Upper Canada" and urged each township to reply. Of the same type are the very useful compilations of Joseph Bouchette (1774–1841), culminating in his two-volume *The British Dominions in North America; or, A Topographical and Statistical Description of the Provinces of Lower and Upper Canada, New Brunswick.*

Nova Scotia, the Islands of Newfoundland, Prince Edward, and Cape Breton
. . . published in London in 1831. Bouchette was surveyor-general of Lower
Canada from 1804 to the Act of Union and vice-president of the venerable
Literary and Historical Society of Quebec founded by Lord Dalhousie in
1824. *The British Dominions in North America*, which contains a lengthy
historical introduction, was written "to demonstrate the intrinsic worth of
those vast and flourishing regions of the British Empire" and "to establish
their importance to the mother country, the advantage of the mother country
to them, and consequently the mutual benefits conferred, upon both parts of
the empire, by their union, under a liberal and enlightened system of colonial
policy." Also in English is Pierre de Sales Laterrière's *A Political and Historical Account of Lower Canada with Remarks on the Present Situation of
the People* published anonymously in England in 1830. Dr. Laterrière (1785–
1834) deplores the lack of information in England about the political crisis
in Lower Canada and challenges the policy and pretentions of the oligarchy
as expressed by John Fleming (1786?–1832) in his *Political Annals of
Lower Canada* (1828). Like Gourlay, Laterrière had his remedies, particularly the abolition of the Legislative Council.

The most significant historical work in this rather awkward genre is Thomas
Chandler Haliburton's *An Historical and Statistical Account of Nova Scotia*
which was printed, in two volumes, by Joseph Howe in 1829. The first
volume, a *History of Nova Scotia*, is one of the most impressive pieces of
historical writing produced in Canada in the nineteenth century and it marks,
with the appearance of Howe's "Rambles" in the previous year, a most significant advance in Canadian letters. (See also chapter 6, above.) The *Account*
was compiled while Haliburton was a busy young lawyer and member of the
Legislative Assembly living in Annapolis Royal, without the benefit of public
or private libraries. The motive of compilation was largely patriotic. In
Great Britain, he said later, "this valuable and important Colony was not
merely wholly unknown, but misunderstood and misrepresented. Every book
of Geography, every Gazetteer and elementary work that mentioned it, spoke
of it in terms of contempt or condemnation." About the history, he wrote to
Judge Peleg Wiswall in 1824, "When I . . . called the work I had in hand the
history of the Country, I did not mean to apply it in the usual acceptation as
a narrative of political events, but in a more enlarged sense as an account of
whatever might be found in the Colony." But Haliburton's concept of history
is not so broad as he suggests. It is the picturesque and romantic incidents
which hold his creative attention: the exploration of the country and the
competition for empire. About the latter he said, "These occurrences
resemble duels, for which the parties for political purposes sought our wilderness as the most convenient place of Rendevous." The narrative stops at the
Peace of Paris; as he put it himself, "After that period the 'short and simple

annals of the poor' afford no materials for a continuation, and a history of the province subsequent to that epoch would be about as interesting as one of Dalhousie settlement." Throughout, Haliburton's style is elegant and his comments judicious, as can readily be seen in his discussion of the expulsion of the Acadians. Stopping his narrative as he does in 1763, he has little opportunity to express his intensely Tory point of view. He admitted in his preface, "I have drawn freely, wherever it suited my purpose, and in some instances have copied entire passages" from a "great number of authors," whom he lists. And this, according to the practice of the day, when footnotes were few and far between, was the extent of his acknowledgment to those who had gone before. For Howe the book proved a "ruinous speculation." "It cumbered my office for two years," he wrote, "involved me in heavy expenses for wages, and in debts for paper, materials, binding and engraving. . . . None sold abroad. The Book, though fairly printed, was wretchedly bound, the engravings were poor, and I was left with about 1000 copies, scattered about, unsaleable on my hands."

It should be pointed out, however, that Haliburton's *Historical and Statistical Account* was not the earliest book in this form dealing with Nova Scotia. The honour goes to *A Geographical History of Nova Scotia; Containing an Account of the Situation, Extent, and Limits thereof; As also of the various Struggles between the Two Crowns of England and France for the Possession of that Province* . . . , published anonymously in London in 1749. The information is based, so the preface states, partly on Charlevoix and partly on the author's own observations. It is a modest book of some 100 pages and is generally regarded as the first history in English relating to Canada.

The first book of this kind describing New Brunswick was Peter Fisher's *Sketches of New Brunswick; Containing an Account of the First Settlement of the Province, with a Brief Description of the Country, Climate, Productions, Inhabitants, Government, Rivers, Towns, Settlements, Public Institutions, Trade, Revenue, Population &c.,* which appeared in 1825. Fisher was born on Staten Island, New York, the son of a Loyalist who served in the New Jersey Volunteers, and came to New Brunswick with his father when he was still an infant. It had been his intention to compile a systematic geographical and statistical account for the province, but when this project was taken over by the New-Brunswick Agricultural and Emigrant Society he gave up the idea and presented the material he had already collected with the hope that "these Sketches . . . may serve to give a faint knowledge of the Country, till a more perfect Work is prepared." The title indicates the subject-matter and organization of the book, in which he includes a description, largely geographical, of each county in the province. Fisher was the first to admit that his information was partial and possibly inaccurate; but his *Sketches* are very attractively written. The book was published in Saint John, New

Brunswick, under the pseudonym "An Inhabitant," the name Fisher used for his other publications as well. (See also chapter 7, section IV, above.)

In 1832 Joseph Howe published Robert Cooney's *A Compendious History of the Northern Part of the Province of New Brunswick and of the District of Gaspé in Lower Canada.* In his *Autobiography,* Cooney (1800–1870) tells how he "explored" the district of Gaspé and the counties of Northumberland, Kent, and Gloucester, camping out and losing no opportunity to talk to the Indians, the lumberers, or the Acadian habitants. He did his best to achieve accuracy under very difficult circumstances. ". . . I have carefully weighed the authenticity of every statement, determined, that although there be no merit in the composition, there should be truth in the narrative." Cooney possessed a vigorous, even flamboyant, style and an impressive understanding of the relationship between events. In speaking of the French Revolution he states, "What the French King endeavoured to establish in America, that was he destined to endure at home." But this was Cooney's "first and last effort as a historian." While he was in Halifax seeing the book through the press, he was converted to God and putting aside "all secular pursuits" he soon entered the ministry of the Wesleyan Methodist church.

New Brunswick was the subject of two additional *Accounts.* In 1844, a Presbyterian minister, W. Christopher Atkinson, published *A Historical and Statistical Account of New Brunswick, B.N.A. with Advice to Emigrants.* It is in fact an extension of his very interesting *The Emigrant's Guide to New Brunswick* (1842). Atkinson felt that the contemplation of "the progress of man from a state of nature towards civilization" was a worthy subject, but he provides very little information about the process. Of more significance is the long historical introduction to *New Brunswick; with Notes for Emigrants* (1847) compiled by the geologist, Abraham Gesner (1797–1864), the man who later discovered kerosene oil. Gesner complains that the value and resources of the British North American colonies are too little known in England and, like Gourlay, he finds in these colonies the answer to the problem of the "redundant population and dormant wealth" of the mother country.

In the same period several books of this kind were put together in the mother country. The best of these from a literary point of view is a *Historical Account of Discoveries and Travels in North America . . . with Observations on Emigration* (2 vols., 1829), by that erudite and retiring geographer Hugh Murray (1779–1846). Not only was he a most industrious scholar, but he was aware also of the significance of the expansion of Europe and of the literary possibilities of the phenomenon. He wrote in the advertisement, "The series of bold adventures by which the coasts of North America were discovered and its colonies founded; the daring attempts to find a Northern Passage by its arctic shores; the unparalleled growth and extending power of the United States; with the openings which America affords to our emigrant population,—all these circumstances conspire to render that continent an object of peculiar interest." In 1839 he published *An Historical and Descriptive Account of British America* in three volumes. Done with Murray's usual care, these volumes contain a most impressive and attractive summary of what information was available. Another interesting work of the same kind is John MacGregor's *British America* which appeared in two volumes in 1832. MacGregor (1797–1857) had lived "for several years in America" and travelled extensively in the colonies. Similarly, the third volume of the *History of the British Colonies* (1834–35) by Robert Montgomery Martin (1803?–1868) covers possessions in North America. Just enough historical information is given to make the statistics intelligible. The inscription on the title-page is typical of the spirit of these undertakings, "Far as the breeze can bear—the billows foam— / SURVEY OUR EMPIRE."

II

But not all historical writing in English in the first half of the nineteenth century in British North America was ancillary to statistical accounts and travel books. There are half a dozen other efforts worthy of attention. The authors of these were not much interested in the subtle relationship between events, but rather in recalling the picturesque happening and drawing the appropriate moral conclusions. For them history was very much philosophy teaching by examples. They borrowed freely from their predecessors such as Charlevoix and from one another. They valued fair-mindedness, clarity of expression, and honesty—for these were some of the virtues they were trying to inculcate. "The citizens of Rome," wrote George Warburton (1816–1857) in the introduction to his *Conquest of Canada* (1849), "placed images of their ancestors in the vestibule, to recal the virtues of the dead, and to stimulate the emulation of the living. We also should fix our thoughts upon the examples which history presents, not in a vain spirit of selfish nationality, but in earnest reverence for the great and good of all countries, and a contempt for the false, and mean, and cruel, even of our own."

The first significant historian writing in English on a Canadian subject was George Heriot (1766–1844), the controversial deputy postmaster-general of British North America from 1799 to 1816. In 1804 he published the first volume of *The History of Canada from its First Discovery; Comprehending an Account of the Original Settlement of the Colony of Louisiana.* It is in fact a carefully written condensation of Charlevoix and it stops abruptly without summary or conclusion at 1731, the year in which Charlevoix's connected narrative ends. Heriot's greatest interest was in the manners and customs of the Indians and in the Indian wars. The second volume of his history never appeared but he did publish in 1807 his very valuable *Travels through the Canadas*. It was, in part, an attempt to convey "an idea of some of the picturesque scenery of the Saint Lawrence, at once the largest and most wonderful body of fresh waters on this globe," an enthusiasm not uncommon among Canadian historians.

More important than Heriot's condensation of Charlevoix is William Smith's two-volume compilation, the *History of Canada, from its First Discovery to the Year 1791*, which was printed by John Neilson in 1815 but appeared on the market only in 1826. Son of the historian of New York State and Loyalist Chief Justice of Canada of the same name, Smith (1769–1847) was Clerk of the Legislative Assembly of Lower Canada and later master in Chancery. His *History* is a jumbled and tortuous narrative—Smith admitted that it did not deserve the name of history—but it contains some valuable information. For the period before the Conquest, not covered by Charlevoix and Heriot, and forming one of the more useful sections in the book, Smith copied what he wanted from an unpublished and anonymous manuscript identified only recently as the work of Louis-Léonard Aumasson de Courville. Smith despised the "arbitrary and despotic" government of the *ancien régime* and betrays a particularly low opinion of the political influence of the Roman Catholic clergy among the people. Clearly he considered the introduction of British institutions as providential. Smith put it bluntly; none the less, this was the view which obtained among most English-speaking historians for the remainder of the century.

The War of 1812 was, predictably, the subject of many reminiscences and some significant historical writing. William James (d. 1827), who is best known for his extensive, five-volume *Naval History of Great Britain from the Declaration of War by France in 1793, to the Accession of George IV* (1822–24) had published in 1818 *A Full and Correct Account of the Military Occurrences of the Late War between Great Britain and the United States of America*, in two volumes, which is very largely an attack on the American accounts of the war. James had been an attorney in Jamaica and was for a time a prisoner in the United States during the conflict. As with his other work, his information was impeccable, but he usually managed to show the British cause to advantage. David Thompson (1796?–1868) in his *History of the Late War between Great Britain and the United States of America with a retrospective view of the causes from whence it originated* ... (Niagara, 1832) also complained—and it is a very common complaint among Canadian historians during the nineteenth century, which hardened into a prejudice—that American historians of the war did not tell the truth. Thompson's *History* has few pretensions; but it claims to establish the facts so that "generations yet unborn will trace the footsteps of their ancestors in that glorious struggle for the salvation of their country, and emulate their virtuous example. . . ." It was the first important book to be published in Upper Canada and it was a financial failure. Unable to pay the printer's bill, Thompson was sent to gaol for a time as a debtor.

Much the best written of the early histories of the War of 1812 is Major John Richardson's *War of 1812, Containing a Full and Detailed Narrative of the Operations of the Right Division of the Canadian Army* (Brockville, 1842), which appeared first in the columns of his newspaper, *The New Era*. "No compilation could," he stated in the preface, "with greater propriety or consistency, be placed in the hands of Canadian students, than that which records the gallant deeds performed by their fathers, fighting side by side, with the troops of England in defence of their invaded firesides. . . ." The history is an interesting and reliable guide to the events in which the author as a youth had participated. He had been present at the surrender of Detroit and was taken prisoner at the rout of Procter's force on the banks of the Thames in October 1813. But the history did not increase the sales of his newspaper nor could he induce the district councils to recommend its patriotic message for use in the schools. Rather disappointed by the reception of his account of the war on the western frontier, he left the history unfinished.

Among the early histories the best written and the most sophisticated is *The Conquest of Canada* (1849) by "Hochelaga." Like Richardson, the author, George Warburton (1816–1857), was involved in the Carlist War in Spain. From 1844 to 1846 he served with the Royal Artillery in Canada. In 1846 he published in London an account of his extensive travels in North America under the title, *Hochelaga; or, England in the New World*. Of all the early writers, Warburton is the most interested in ideas and in the complicated relationships between events. He was aware of the influence of the Conquest on the development of an independent spirit in the thirteen colonies and of the significance of the success of the American revolution on European development: "their light has served to illumine the political darkness of the European Continent." Warburton believed that the distinctive aspects in the personality of a nation could be told in the development of its colonies. He was a great admirer of what he called "the Anglo-Saxon empire in America." "New France," he said, "was colonised by a government, New England by a people."

III

In spite of an impressive beginning, little historical writing of any significance was attempted in the Atlantic provinces of British North America for a generation following Haliburton; on the other hand, in the province of Canada there was ambitious and significant activity. Although the object of writing remained very much the same, the history reflected the particular preoccupations of the community. It became increasingly, what it was in other parts of the Western world, the study of past politics, and it was infused, in Canada as elsewhere, with the spirit of nationalism. Furthermore, most of the historians writing in the second half of the nineteenth century in Canada, whether serious or popular in their intentions, possessed that attitude to the historical process which is usually described as the Whig interpretation of history. For those of this sensibility, history is the contemplation of freedom broadening down from precedent to precedent towards an agreeable present. They believe in democracy and in social and economic progress. Their history is Protestant in sympathy and secular in application. It divides individuals, institutions, and movements into those that are for and those that are against progress. This approach, as we shall see, frequently results in misplaced emphasis, vast over-simplifications, and superficial judgments.

In the working out of these political and national objectives, most historians emphasized the significance of the individual as a causative factor in the succession of events. The struggle of the settler against the forest primeval and against uncongenial remnants of his heritage—a landed aristocracy and an established church—presented a situation which could readily be described in terms of individual initiative and protest. Most Canadian historians of the period would have subscribed to Carlyle's great-man theory of history.

The year 1855 was a remarkable one in early Canadian scholarship. It saw the completion by Robert Christie (1788–1856) of a six-volume compilation, *A History of the Late Province of Lower Canada*, and the publication of the first reputable survey of Canadian history, John Mercier McMullen's *The History of Canada from its First Discovery to the Present Time*. In the following year, Charles Roger published the first volume of his survey *The Rise of Canada from Barbarism to Wealth and Civilization*.

In 1846, McMullen (1820–1907) had published in London *Camp and Barrack-Room; or, The British Army as it is*, an interesting guide on how to survive and get ahead in the British army. In 1855, although he had "then only resided for a few years in this country" and was "obliged to attend closely to his business of Book-seller and Printer" in Brockville, he published his *History*, the first large-scale general survey of Canadian history in English. The book rings with unqualified enthusiasm for the prospects of the province of Canada. "The present condition of Canada points to a future national greatness of no ordinary magnitude. Her inland seas and noble rivers, have already become the highways of a vast and rapidly increasing commerce. The silent forest of by-gone days has disappeared before the progress of civilization, and the matin voice of a mighty nation resounds over a scene as varied as it is beautiful." McMullen assumed that "wise legislation" and "identity of interests" would overcome the difficulties arising from diversity of race. The Canadian future was better than the American: "With us the sun of fierce party antagonism, there is every reason to hope, has set forever; in the United

States it rapidly ascends towards the meridian of bitterness." While he recognized that separation from Great Britain was very likely, "a result heralded by the very progress of the race itself," he perceived that the imperial connection "is our true line of policy. . . . it secures to us an independent national existence." He possessed most of the prejudices of his adopted community: he was for liberty (he thought Canada should "continue to be a land of genuine freedom, and the 'city of refuge' to the oppressed man of color"), he regretted the "torpid repose" of the French Canadians and he despised the Family Compact.

McMullen knew what he was about. "To infuse a spirit of Canadian nationality into the people generally—to mould the native born citizen, the Scotch, the English, and the Irish emigrant into a compact whole, a purely Canadian literature . . . is a most important element. A popular history of Canada, issued at a price which places it within the reach of every working man, is a step in this direction." His book was carefully worked over and brought up to date in a second edition published in 1868 and again in a two volume edition which appeared in 1891–1892. McMullen did no research himself; but he was a competent journalist. His was the standard guide to Canadian history in the second half of the nineteenth century.

In the following year, Charles Roger of Quebec City (b. 1819) issued the first volume of his survey of Canadian history which he called *The Rise of Canada from Barbarism to Wealth and Civilization*. Like McMullen he was a recent arrival in the country and a journalist by profession. As the florid analogies he constructed between Canadian development and the history of the Jews might suggest, he had for a time studied for the ministry; but this interest did not produce in his case anything like McMullen's very impressive *The Supremacy of the Bible and its Relations to Speculative Science, Remote Ancient History, and the Higher Criticism* (1905). Roger wrote in a vigorous and entertaining style; but he was careless in points of fact and superficial in judgment. The tone of his history is strongly nationalistic and the point of view crudely Whiggish. Only the first volume, which carried the narrative down to the first departure of Lord Dalhousie in 1824, appeared; he later put together several books on local history including various editions of *Quebec: As it was, and As it is* and *Ottawa Past and Present* (1871).

The degree of interest in the War of 1812 is always a fair indication of the intensity of national feeling in Canada at any particular time. In 1855, Gilbert Auchinleck, one of the editors of the *Anglo-American Magazine*, put together the articles on the war which he had written for the *Magazine* and published them as *A History of the War between Great Britain and the United States of America during the Years 1812, 1813, and 1814*. A decade later, in 1864, with the dangers to Canadian interests resulting from the American Civil War very much in mind, a Canadian soldier and civil servant, William F. Coffin

(1808–1878), published *1812; The War, and its Moral: A Canadian Chronicle*. He begins: "1812—like the characters on the labarum of Constantine—is a sign of solemn import to the people of Canada. It carries with it the virtue of an incantation. Like the magic numerals of the Arabian sage, these words, in their utterance, quicken the pulse, and vibrate through the frame, summoning, from the pregnant past, memories of suffering and endurance and of honorable exertion. They are inscribed on the banner and stamped on the hearts of the Canadian people—a watchword, rather than a war-cry." He was determined "to invest the story told, as far as possible, with a Canadian character; to present the war in Canada in a Canadian point of view; and . . . to impart . . . a Canadian individuality to this Canadian Chronicle of the War." Coffin possessed an excellent style. Unfortunately, he was able to produce only one volume which carried the narrative as far as de Salaberry's victory at Châteauguay.

The charismatic event of Confederation and the problems of the early national period produced a succession of patriotic glosses on Canadian development. "Everyone who can write an article in a country newspaper thinks he is competent to give the world a history of our young Dominion in some shape or other," complained John G. Bourinot in *The Intellectual Development of the Canadian People* (1881). One of the more active and most able was H. H. Miles (1818–1895), professor of Mathematics in the University of Bishop's College and, after 1867, secretary of the Council of Public Instruction in the province of Quebec. Shortly after Confederation he produced *A School History of Canada* (1870) and *The Child's History of Canada for the Use of the Elementary Schools and of the Young Reader* (1870). In 1872 he published *The History of Canada under the French Régime 1535–1763*, a sober, extensive, and well-written survey of the political and military history of the French period. Miles complained that the treatment of the French régime in English had been too brief and too biased and suggested that something more was necessary in the interests of national objectives.

That most active young journalist Charles R. Tuttle (b. 1848) published in 1877 *An Illustrated History of the Dominion 1535–1876*. It was, he says, in the field of history, "the first popular work illustrated and sold by subscription" in Canada and was written so that Canadians "might be awakened to the inculcation of a higher and nobler sentiment of patriotism,— a greater love for that country which our beloved sovereign has named the 'Dominion of Canada.' " A second volume, *The Comprehensive History of the Dominion of Canada with Art Engravings*, appeared in 1879 and covered the period from Confederation to the close of 1878. In 1878 he published in Boston a *Short History of the Dominion of Canada, from 1500 to 1878; with the contemporaneous history of England and the United States*. But these books were not written solely for the creation of Canadian national feeling; they were the first Canadian histories written expressly for American readers, "to intensify the admiration for Canadian industries and institutions, which the Dominion exhibits at the Centennial Exposition awakened."

Born in Nova Scotia, Tuttle spent most of his adult life in the United States, although he was in Winnipeg long enough to found a conservative newspaper there, the *Times*, in 1879. Of all the popularizers of the period, including J. Castell Hopkins, he was the most prolific. As a young man he embarked on the ambitious project of writing a one-volume history of each of the states of the American union and got half a dozen of these done. His industry was prodigious. By the time he was thirty, he seems to have written at least eleven books of history and two novels. In 1878, on the appointment of the Marquis of Lorne as Governor-General, he wrote *Royalty in Canada; Embracing Sketches of the House of Argyll, The Right Honorable the Marquis of Lorne . . .* , a book of over two hundred pages, in the space of four days. Needless to say Tuttle did no original research. He merely gathered and arranged, copying whole sections from official documents and from other historians. He could, however, write well and his ideas are always interesting. He accompanied the Hudson Bay Expedition of 1884 and wrote it up in *Our North Land* (1885). He was convinced of the "unerring north-westerly trend of human progress" and held that "the highest latitudes produce the greatest men." He found it strange that "the north is always underrated." Like many others, he was convinced that a distinctive French community was destined to disappear in North America: "Anglo-Saxon civilization," he said, "cannot be circumscribed." He was much interested in religion and predicted that the Methodists would form "the future great church of Canada" becoming ultimately the national church. He was a strong promoter of the myth of Canadian educational superiority. He thought that the common school system had reduced the animosity among the sects and it was "so perfect" that Canadians need have no fears about their ability to develop the country.

In the same year that Tuttle's *Short History* appeared, W. H. Withrow (1839–1908), the cultured and industrious editor of the *Canadian Methodist Magazine*, published *A Popular History of the Dominion of Canada from the Discovery of America to the Present Time*. Believing that "the essential prerequisite of a rational patriotism is an intelligent acquaintance with the history of one's country," Withrow put together with great care a compendious survey of the political and military history of Canada. It was well written and, like his many other books of history, biography and fiction, it was marked, as his obituary in the *Proceedings and Transactions of the Royal Society of Canada* indicated, "by high patriotism and intelligent piety."

Another talented author who attempted a general survey of Canadian history was the distinguished Presbyterian clergyman and educator, George Bryce (1844–1931). He had previously, in 1882, published *Manitoba: Its*

Infancy, Growth, and Present Condition to provide information for the immigrant. He admitted that "a description of the country, its resources, and prospects will be found shining through all the discussions." In 1887, *A Short History of the Canadian People* appeared. Clearly Bryce wanted to give rather less space to political and military history and he indicates that, while he sympathized "with movements for wide extension of true freedom," he could appreciate another set of values. His history is better organized and better written than most; but its contents and point of view are decidedly conventional.

In 1897, John G. Bourinot (1837–1902) contributed *Canada* to Putnam's "The Story of the Nations" series. Clerk of the House of Commons of Canada, Bourinot succeeded Alpheus Todd (1821–1884) as an international authority on comparative government and parliamentary procedure. In his short history, space is given to those events which exercised "the most influence on national development." An interesting chapter on French Canada is included. Although Bourinot is the most sober and level-headed of this group of historians, he radiates a real satisfaction with Canadian parliamentary institutions and with Canadian achievements in the arts and in science.

At the turn of the century, a flurry of patriotic histories from the hand of J. Castell Hopkins (1864–1923) appeared from the presses of Canada, the United States, and Great Britain. In 1899, he published *The Story of the Dominion: Four Hundred Years in the Annals of Half a Continent* and in 1900 the *Progress of Canada in the Nineteenth Century*. He took the position that "Canada only needs to be known in order to be great." These histories were prepared at the same time that he was putting together his extensive and very useful *Canada: An Encyclopaedia of the Country* in six volumes. The variety of information which he collected for the *Encylopaedia* made it possible for him to deal more adequately with such topics as the development of transportation, education, and religion. Hopkins was the biographer of Sir John Thompson (1895) and was frequently an apologist for the Conservative party; none the less, his work represents the first serious attempt to revise the conventional interpretation of the Family Compact.

The list of patriotic surveys would not be complete without the mention of *A History of Canada* by Charles G. D. Roberts (1860–1943) which was published by Morang in 1902. The book was prepared for use in the secondary schools at the instigation of the Dominion Educational Association and submitted in what was called the Dominion History Competition. The sum of two thousand dollars in prizes was contributed by the various provincial governments and by the time the competition closed in 1895 fifteen manuscripts had been received. Roberts did not receive the prize; nor did George Bryce, who also entered the competition. It went to Judge W. H. P. Clement

(1858–1922) for an incredibly dull and fact-ridden volume which was published in 1897 and authorized for use in six provinces and the territories. When Roberts' *History* appeared, the august *Review of Historical Publications Relating to Canada* conceded that it was "from a literary standpoint the most attractive history of Canada which has yet appeared." But the reviewer noted an unseemly patriotism which reminded him of the "prejudiced, boastful spirit, quite in the vein of some of the jingo school-books of the United States." Roberts' book was certainly the most readable general survey of Canadian history produced in the whole period under discussion and it reflects the general tone of these books clearly. It reflects not only the Whig interpretation of Canadian history but suggests the Whig interpretation of Canadian literature: "The real beginnings of a literary spirit in Canada may be said to date from the triumph of Responsible Government. That struggle had broadened men's minds and taught them to think for themselves."

IV

The more serious and specialized historical writing in the second half of the nineteenth century was less obviously nationalistic. The research was done both more intensively and more carefully. Nevertheless, it possesses the same general set of values which are apparent in the more popular and general treatments. History is essentially political history and most of the emphasis is on the extension and development of British parliamentary institutions in the various provinces of British North America or of the Dominion.

Perhaps the earliest of these more specialized political histories and certainly one of the most important is the extensive six-volume *History of the Late Province of Lower Canada* of Robert Christie (1788–1856) which appeared between 1848 and 1855. These volumes incorporate most of Christie's earlier writings which are, in themselves, significant: *Memoirs of the Administration of the Colonial Government of Lower Canada by Sir James Henry Craig and Sir George Prevost; From the Year 1807 until the Year 1815, Comprehending the Military and Naval Operations in the Canadas during the Late War with the United States of America* (1818), *Memoirs of the Administration of the Government of Lower Canada by Sir Gordon Drummond, Sir John Coape Sherbrooke, the late Duke of Richmond, James Monk, Esquire, and Sir Peregrine Maitland* (1820) and *Memoirs of the Administration of Lower Canada by the Right Honourable the Earl of Dalhousie* (1829). *A History of the Late Province of Lower Canada* is an attempt to explain why the constitution of 1791 "modelled upon that of Great Britain, as far as circumstances admitted . . . proved a failure. . . ."

Christie possessed an intimate knowledge of the political situation in

Lower Canada. In 1827 he was elected member of the Legislative Assembly for the County of Gaspé, which has been described as in those days "the nearest thing to a pocket borough in Lower Canada." As chairman of the quarter sessions of the District of Quebec, he complied with the wishes of the Governor and revised the list of magistrates to exclude those who had led the opposition in the Assembly. For this, he was repeatedly expelled from the Assembly. "He was yet a simple and single minded man," wrote a reviewer in the Montreal *Gazette*, "with almost no guile, at times exhibiting that particular kind of courage which led him to butt his head against the stone wall of a superior power. He dressed quaintly—in the style of a former generation; and as in his dress, so in his manners, he never adapted himself to the times."

Christie had few literary pretensions. He confessed in the preface to the fourth volume that readers must find his books "dry and heavy, if not absolutely a penance." His purpose was simply "to record, for future information, the various and important sayings and doings, parliamentary and political, that have taken place in Lower Canada. . . ." Following these objectives at such length, he produced a work of lasting value. It is not surprising that he possessed little sympathy for the reform party; but he tried throughout to let the facts speak for themselves.

A similar kind of book, although much better organized and much better written, is *The History of Newfoundland from the Earliest Times to the Year 1860* (1863) by a minister of the Congregational church, Charles Pedley (1821–1872). It is essentially a political history culminating in the achievement of responsible government in the colony in 1855. In the same tradition is the voluminous and encyclopaedic *A History of Newfoundland from the English, Colonial, and Foreign Records* by Judge D. W. Prowse (1834–1914), published in London in 1895. Prowse's passion for the history of Newfoundland developed from his interest in the North Atlantic fisheries. "The great English historians," he complained, "ignore altogether the part Newfoundland played in the making of England . . . the daring of West Country traders and cod fishers, who began the conquest and colonisation of a greater England in the new world. . . ." And he bitterly protested British policy: "Our treatment by the British Government has been so stupid, cruel, and barbarous that it requires the actual perusal of the State Papers to convince us that such a policy was ever carried out."

A writer who frankly admired Christie and who worked in the same manner, was Beamish Murdoch (1800–1876) for a time the editor of the *Acadian Recorder*. He was, too, an active politician and a distinguished lawyer. In 1832–33, he published an *Epitome of the Laws of Nova Scotia* in four volumes. In his retirement, he compiled *A History of Nova Scotia or Acadia* which appeared in three vast volumes between 1865 and 1867. Like Christie, he faced a real problem in abridgement, for he was determined to "preserve everything of genuine interest." He loved Nova Scotia, "a happy, free and intelligent province, progressive and prosperous," and felt that its history, "the courage, the endurance and generosity that are the attributes of the early adventurers and settlers" possessed a moral relevance for his own day. He wanted to "transport the reader . . . back to the actuality of past times" and he thought that this could best be done "in its own forms and colors and language." For Murdoch as for Christie, this meant the inclusion of numerous documents within the body of the narrative and the compilation of endless appendices. Writing in the 1860's, he felt that it was necessary to point out the permanent value of colonies. He insisted on the loyalty of the province to the mother country and suggested that the skills of the population might be very useful to the Royal Navy in times of danger.

Murdoch's great volumes on Nova Scotia were followed shortly by one by Duncan Campbell (1819?–1886), *Nova Scotia, in its Historical, Mercantile and Industrial Relations*. Murdoch's *History* closes with the year 1827. Very conscious of this, Campbell gives about half his space to the period between 1827 and the death of Joseph Howe in 1873. Although he had come from Scotland as recently as 1860, he achieved an impressive knowledge of the history of his adopted province. Clearly, he wanted to broaden the content of his history; but, in spite of the title, it is essentially a political narrative. Campbell valued style—"readableness" he called it—much more than Murdoch. The book was handsomely printed and published by John Lovell of Montreal in 1873. In 1875, Campbell produced a *History of Prince Edward Island* which, he hoped, "might claim some degree of merit as to conciseness, accuracy, and impartiality." It covers, in some two hundred pages, the period from the Peace of Paris to the entry of the Province into Confederation and, like his history of Nova Scotia, it is attractively written.

What Murdoch and Campbell had done for historical studies in the other maritime provinces, James Hannay (1842–1910), lawyer and journalist, did for the province of New Brunswick. His first important book was *The History of Acadia, from its First Discovery to its Surrender to England by the Treaty of Paris*, which appeared in 1879. Hannay acknowledged his debt to the "industry and research" of Murdoch, but he felt that there was a place for a "consistent narrative." In 1897 he published *The Life and Times of Sir Leonard Tilley, being a political history of New Brunswick for the past seventy years*. In 1909, his magnum opus, a large two-volume *History of New Brunswick*, appeared. His aim was simply "to trace the development of the constitution, and the growth of the laws of New Brunswick from the foundation of the Province down to the present time." The work terminates with chapters on the churches and education; but these are really appendices to an essentially political narrative. Hannay also published, in 1901, a *History of*

the War of 1812 between Great Britain and the United States of America,
which was published in England under the title—should that audience miss
the point—of *How Canada was Held for the Empire: The Story of the War
of 1812.* Like Hannay's other books, it is well written, but unfortunately it is
frequently inaccurate and is intensely biased. Very little can be said for the
Americans: they ". . . invaded our country, burnt our towns, ravaged our
fields, slaughtered our people and tried to place us under a foreign flag."
Hannay was also the biographer of *Wilmot and Tilley* (1907) in the "Makers
of Canada" series.

The Northwest was also the subject of some good history written in the
style of Christie and Murdoch. The most impressive early historian of that
vast region was Alexander Begg (1839–1897). In 1867 he introduced the
Red River settlement to goods manufactured in Canada and for a number of
years he was a leading merchant in Winnipeg. He was a witness to the Red
River Resistance of 1869–1870 and from his very valuable daily journal he
compiled *The Creation of Manitoba; or, A History of the Red River Troubles,*
which appeared in 1871. Years later, when he was living in Victoria, he put
together his *History of the North-West* in three volumes, published in 1894
and 1895. His subject is really "the march of civilization in the North-West,"
which was no longer "a vast hunting ground" but the "home of thousands of
thrifty settlers." Not only was the Northwest "one of the brightest jewels in
the British Crown," but it was, also, a region of great strategic significance,
"one of the most important links in the chain of Imperial unity." The book
is written in an effective style and was handsomely produced by the Hunter,
Rose Company of Toronto. It contains a mass of information, including many
documents, and remains a valuable source of information.

By an extraordinary and confusing coincidence, the best early history of
the province of British Columbia was written by a different man with the
same name—Alexander Begg (1825–1905). Born in Scotland, he taught
public school in Ontario. For a number of years, he was employed by the
Department of Internal Revenue in Ottawa and was, for a time, Emigration
Commissioner in Scotland for the Province of Ontario. He was the editor of
several newspapers in small places in Ontario and publisher of the *Canadian
Lumberman.* In 1887, he arrived in Victoria where he was appointed Emigration Commissioner by the Province to investigate the possibility of settling
Scottish crofters on Vancouver Island. The idea was abandoned; but Begg
appended the initials C.C. (Crofter Commissioner) to his name to distinguish
himself from the historian of the Northwest. In 1894 he published his *History
of British Columbia from Its Earliest Discovery to the Present Time.* The
style is undistinguished and the organization primitive. Like Christie and
Murdoch, he attempts to "gather and compile . . . as full and complete a
record as possible. . . ." This he did successfully.

As might be predicted, the Northwest inspired many less systematic and more popular histories. One of the best was *From Savagery to Civilization; The Canadian Northwest: Its History and Its Troubles, from the Early Fur-trade to the Era of the Railway and the Settler* . . . by Graeme Mercer Adam (1839–1912) which appeared in 1885. It is really "the narrative of three insurrections," the Selkirk massacre and the two Riel Rebellions. From 1860 to 1892 Adam was connected with a succession of distinguished Canadian journals beginning with the *British American Magazine*. He founded the *Canadian Monthly and National Review* (1872–78) and was business manager of *The Bystander* (1880–81, 1883). (See also chapter 11, above.) His history of the Northwest is vigorously written. Even here his Whiggish values did not fail him for he states in the preface that "these revolts, in some degree at least, are the legacy of the days of monopoly and privilege."

The Northwest was also the subject of most of the important work of Agnes C. Laut (1871–1936) and Lawrence J. Burpee (1873–1946). Agnes Laut was a most prolific and energetic writer. Although most of her active life was spent as a journalist in the United States, she never tired of Canadian subjects. In addition to several volumes in the "Chronicles of Canada" series, she wrote a very popular *Pathfinders of the West: Being the Thrilling Story of the Adventures of the Men Who Discovered the Great Northwest: Radis-sion, La Vérendrye, Lewis and Clark* (1904) and *The Conquest of the Great Northwest* . . . , a large history of the Hudson's Bay Company which appeared in two volumes in 1908. At the time, she was the only person who had access to the Company's archives and she consulted them with great industry. In 1909, she published *Canada, the Empire of the North: Being the Romantic Story of the New Dominion's Growth from Colony to Kingdom* written in what the *Review of Historical Publications Relating to Canada* called "her own vivid and picturesque way." She was sometimes careless about points of fact and intolerant of the conclusions of other scholars; but she was always good reading, for she possessed real gifts of imagination and a vivacious style. If anything, her books are over-written.

Lawrence J. Burpee was a distinguished civil servant and an active writer in such fields as history, geography, and bibliography. He brought these varied interests together in his impressive and scholarly *The Search for the Western Sea: The Story of the Exploration of North-western America* which appeared in 1908. Among other books, he wrote a biography, *Sandford Fleming, Empire Builder* (1915) and contributed to the "Chronicles of Canada" series a popular volume based on his extensive researches, *Pathfinders of the Great Plains: A Chronicle of La Vérendrye and his Sons* (1915). He later edited *Journals and Letters of Pierre Gaultier de Varennes de la Vérendrye and His Sons* . . . for the Champlain Society (1937).

V

But it was the western half of the old province of Canada, later the province of Ontario, that saw the greatest achievements of the Whig school of Canadian historians. There, because of the personalities involved and because of the lively memories of '37, the interpretations were frequently partisan, sometimes resembling extensive political tracts. However undesirable this tendency might be from a scientific point of view, it frequently produced good literature.

One of the most important books produced by this group was by Charles Lindsey (1820–1908), *The Life and Times of Wm. Lyon Mackenzie, with an account of the Canadian Rebellion of 1837, and the subsequent frontier disturbances, chiefly from unpublished documents*, which appeared, in two volumes, in 1862. Born in England, Lindsey came to Canada in 1841. He was an editor of the *Examiner*, a reform newspaper founded by Francis Hincks in 1838, and later was editor-in-chief of the conservative Toronto *Leader*. In 1852, the same year in which the *Leader* was established, he married a daughter of William Lyon Mackenzie and was confronted with the "vast mass" of the reformer's papers. Lindsey got to know Mackenzie well; he admired his energy, courage, and fierce honesty. But he felt that the rebellion was a mistake, "unfortunate and ill-advised." He perceived that "the amelioration which the political institutions of Canada have undergone would probably have come in time," but he argued that change "would not have come so soon" nor would the province "yet have reached its present stage of advancement." The book is as exciting as the events which it describes, although the language is curiously florid. As was the fashion, it contains extended footnotes and the inevitable appendices. Always a strong supporter of the voluntary principle, Lindsey was the author of *The Clergy Reserves— their History and Present Position* . . . (1851). In 1877, he published *Rome in Canada: The Ultramontane Struggle for Supremacy over the Civil Power*, a book of almost 400 pages given to an examination of what Lindsey thought was a papal and Jesuit conspiracy against the institutions of a liberal and democratic society.

Of all the Whig historians, the most controversial and the greatest stylist was John Charles Dent (1841–1888). Although he was born in England, he was educated in Canada. He was called to the bar of Upper Canada in 1865, but earned his living as a journalist in London, England, and in Toronto where he was on the editorial staff of the *Globe*. In 1880–81 he published, in four volumes, *The Canadian Portrait Gallery* and in 1881 a political history in two volumes, *The Last Forty Years: Canada since the Union of 1841*, written from the point of view of the Reform party. In 1885 *The Story of the*

Upper Canadian Rebellion, two volumes, appeared. It began with a discussion of the "slow crucifixion" of Gourlay and is throughout a sustained diatribe against the Family Compact. For Dent, the rebellion was "the fitting sequel to a long course of oligarchical tyranny and oppression," the natural result of "a succession of military lieutenant-governors who had no knowledge of or sympathy with our local institutions" and of the interference of a colonial minister "thousands of miles away." With this interpretation many would agree. But he created a furor in his determination to exalt the character and accomplishments of Dr. John Rolph and denigrate the memory of William Lyon Mackenzie. To Dent's way of thinking, Rolph was "unquestionably one of the most extraordinary persons who have ever figured in the annals of Upper Canada"; while Mackenzie was "a creature of circumstances" driven by an "itch for notoriety."

"*The Story of the Upper Canadian Rebellion*," the *Dominion Annual Register* stated soberly for the record, "called forth more favourable and more adverse comments than any Canadian history, excepting, perhaps, Mr. B. Sulte's *Histoire des Canadiens-français*" (8 vols., 1882–84). The father of W. L. Mackenzie King, John King (1843–1916), quickly compiled *The Other Side of the "Story"* (1886), a collection of unfavourable reviews of the first volume and of damaging documents. Most writers agreed with the reviewer in the Toronto *Daily Mail* who suggested that Dent had attempted to make "a hero out of the most unpromising material, the most unheroic of men." The *Story* appeared in two handsome red volumes bearing quantities of gilt. Like *The Last Forty Years*, it is elegantly and lucidly written in a style which the writer in *Canada and Its Provinces* compared, not unfavourably, with that of the great Macaulay.

The most prolific of this group of historians was William Kingsford (1819–1898). Born and educated in England, he came to Canada with his regiment in 1837. He remained and qualified as a civil engineer. Outspoken and hot-tempered, he had an uneven career as an engineer. In 1873 he was appointed engineer in charge of the harbours on the Great Lakes and the St. Lawrence, a post from which he was suddenly dismissed by Sir Hector Langevin in 1879. At this point, at the age of sixty, he began his serious historical studies and writing. In 1886 he published *Canadian Archaeology, an Essay*, which is, in spite of its title, "a history of the first printed books in the provinces of Quebec and Ontario." It also contains titles of early newspapers and a survey of manuscript collections in the various archives and libraries. This was followed, in 1892, by *The Early Bibliography of the Province of Ontario . . .* the first careful and critical, but by no means definitive, list of publications on the early history of Ontario.

Between 1887 and 1898, Kingsford published *The History of Canada* in ten large volumes running in all well over five thousand pages. It is the most extensive general history of Canada ever attempted by a single author and it was thought at the time to achieve in the English language what Garneau had done earlier in French. But Kingsford was no artist and his volumes were written in haste, almost at the rate of one a year. He could not match Garneau as a stylist, and his sentences are long, involved, and infelicitous. Nevertheless, his *History* represents a remarkable achievement especially for a man of his years.

The purpose of Kingsford's great study was "to trace the history of British rule in Canada since its Conquest from the French, and to relate . . . the series of events which have led to the present Constitution under which the Dominion is governed." After giving four volumes to the old régime by way of introduction, he proceeded with a most detailed constitutional and political history of Canada in which colonial liberty and imperial authority were ultimately reconciled by the device of responsible government. He was determined that his *History* "should not fail from any insufficiency of fact." But there is little else and the range of interest is very limited. The *Review of Historical Publications Relating to Canada* complained that "There is scarcely an allusion to the social or industrial life of the people, the condition of agriculture, the increase of commerce, or the development of the fur trade. The tide of immigration that set in from and ultimately flowed back to the United States is unnoticed." Kingsford insisted that he never strained the evidence. But that is not the impression most readers have received. A startling example is his determination to prove that the first and perhaps greatest hero of the narrative, Champlain, was a Protestant. But, whatever its defects, his work does represent a summary of the Whig position and a source of information and inspiration for other works with that point of view.

The greatest achievement of this school of historians was the "Makers of Canada" series. With the possible exception of the historical articles in J. Castell Hopkins' *Canada: An Encyclopaedia of the Country* (6 vols., Toronto, 1897–1900), it was the first co-operative venture in Canadian historical writing. "Each of the great figures in our history will be dealt with in a single volume," J. Castell Hopkins wrote to Sir John Willison (1856–1927), editor of the *Globe*, on the subject of the "Makers," "and each will be treated by a writer who is best fitted, by study and taste and eminence, to discuss the particular topic. Some of the writers already arranged with are N. E. Dionne, . . . Principal Grant, . . . Rt. Hon. Sir Wilfrid Laurier. . . ." Principal George Monro Grant (1835–1902) did not live to expand his excellent essays on Joseph Howe and Laurier could not find time to write a biography of A. A. Dorion; but the list indicates the level at which the work was conceived.

The publisher was George N. Morang (1866–1937) of Toronto who used to refer to the "Makers" as "my great enterprise." "The printing, paper and binding . . . ," proclaimed the *Review of Historical Publications Relating to*

Canada, "are beyond praise." The books were sold in sets by subscription; Morang agreed with Mark Twain that selling "through the trade" was like "printing for private circulation only." It was his sales experience with this series which attracted Robert Glasgow to a career of similar publishing. By 1910, Morang had already sold 3,500 sets and the series was still going at the rate of 40 sets a week. At this point, he brought out two less expensive editions (the eleven-volume two-volume-in-one editions) with the hope of selling 10,000 more sets. These are remarkable figures for the period when it is considered that a most significant and well-advertised biography, the *Memoirs of the Right Honourable Sir John Alexander Macdonald* by Sir Joseph Pope (1854–1926) (2 vols., 1894), had over several years sold less than 600 copies.

The original edition was published in twenty volumes between 1903 and 1908. The editors were the poet, Duncan Campbell Scott (1862–1947), and Professor O. Pelham Edgar (1871–1948) of Victoria College. Later William Dawson LeSueur (1840–1917) was added and he did most of the serious and constructive editing. The series comprised biographies of *Lord Elgin* (J. G. Bourinot), *Egerton Ryerson* (Nathanael Burwash, 1839–1918), *Sir Frederick Haldimand* (Jean Newton McIlwraith, 1859–1938), *Papineau, Cartier* (A. D. DeCelles, 1843–1925), *Joseph Howe* (J. W. Longley, 1849–1922), *General Brock* (Lady Edgar, 1844–1910), *Wolfe and Montcalm* (Abbé H. R. Casgrain, 1831–1904), *Mackenzie, Selkirk, Simpson* (George Bryce), *John Graves Simcoe* (Duncan Campbell Scott), *Bishop Laval* (A. Leblond de Brumath, 1854–1939), *Count Frontenac* (W. D. LeSueur), *Champlain* (N. E. Dionne, 1848–1917), *George Brown* (John Lewis, 1858–1935), *Wilmot and Tilley* (James Hannay), *Lord Dorchester* (A. G. Bradley), *Baldwin, Lafontaine, Hincks* (Stephen Leacock, 1869–1944), *Lord Sydenham* (Adam Shortt, 1859–1931), *William Lyon Mackenzie* (Charles and G. G. S. Lindsey), *Sir John A. Macdonald* (George R. Parkin, 1846–1922), *Sir James Douglas* (Robert Hamilton Coats, 1874–1960, and R. E. Gosnell, 1860–1931). An index volume was added in 1911 and a supplementary volume on *Sir Charles Tupper* in 1916 by J. W. Longley who had already done the volume on *Joseph Howe.*

Although the workmanship was always impressive, the quality of writing varied considerably. The best books in the series were *Lord Sydenham* by Professor Adam Shortt and Jean Newton McIlwraith's *Sir Frederick Haldimand.* In both cases, the authors were able to draw upon extensive collections of documents which had recently been made available by the Public Archives of Canada.

In 1926, a new edition of the "Makers" with extensive alterations was brought out by the Oxford University Press with W. L. Grant (1872–1935), the principal of Upper Canada College, as editor. Lindsey's *William Lyon*

Mackenzie was dropped. A new life of *Bishop Laval* by the Abbé H. A. Scott (1858–1931) replaced the one by A. Leblond de Brumath and J. G. Bourinot's *Lord Elgin* was removed in favour of a new treatment by Professor W. P. M. Kennedy (1880–1963). There were several additions to the original selection. A much-admired book, Sir John Willison's *Sir Wilfrid Laurier and the Liberal Party: A Political History*, which was originally published by Morang in two volumes in 1903, was included. It was described in 1926 by the editor of the *Canadian Historical Review*, W. S. Wallace (b. 1884), "as perhaps the most distinguished example of political biography in Canadian literature. . . ." Also added were *The Life and Work of Sir William Van Horne* by Walter Vaughan (1865–1922) which had first appeared in 1920 and a new life of *Lord Strathcona* by Professor John Macnaughton (1858–1943).

It is not surprising that Morang's "great enterprise" was conceived as a series of biographies. As William Buckingham (1832–1915) and George W. Ross (1841–1914) put it in the first sentence of *The Hon. Alexander Mackenzie His Life and Times* (1892): "The history of an individual is often the history of a nation." The influence of Carlyle was pervasive and to the heady nationalism of the turn of the century the physical environment suggested opportunities not limitations, a challenge to human ingenuity and moral purpose not a range of restricted possibilities. Doubtless because of the achievements of the period, biography has persisted as an unusually popular and successful form of expression for Canadian historians. Although less critical and analytical than the monograph, it possesses great literary possibilities and is probably the most accessible form of history from the point of view of the general reader.

The point of view of the writers was consciously Whiggish. This can be seen in the very selection of the "Makers." Egerton Ryerson is included, but not Bishop Strachan; William Lyon Mackenzie, but not John Beverley Robinson. The politics of the editor is abundantly demonstrated in the long altercation in the courts over the volume on William Lyon Mackenzie. The author was one of the editors, W. D. LeSueur, who had already written a very readable biography of Frontenac for the series. This choice was most offensive to William Lyon Mackenzie King and LeSueur wrote to Sir John Willison that Rodolphe Lemieux, who was successively solicitor-general and postmaster general in Laurier's government, "warned me that I had better take care how I wrote it." None the less, LeSueur received permission from Charles Lindsey, the previous biographer, to use the Mackenzie papers which were in the possession of the family and for five months in 1906 LeSueur lived in Lindsey's house where the papers were kept.

The biography was written with unusual care. Robert Glasgow (1875–1922), who knew a good book when he saw one, insisted as late as 1914 that it was "the best book of history yet done by any Canadian writer." It is clear that LeSueur had wanted for some time to revise the traditional evaluation of Mackenzie. Later, he wrote to John Willison, "I will never ask you to expend much admiration on the so-called 'family compact,' but don't you think it probable that, if a thing has been steadily abused for a couple of generations, the condemnation might have cumulatively become too strong. I suppose that, theoretically, you might paint a fence till there was less fence than paint." LeSueur, whose interests and sympathies were unusually catholic, treated Mackenzie with respect and affection; but he took the position that Mackenzie had a "retardatory" influence on Canadian political development. "Others emerge from my pages in a guise which will disappoint many," he wrote to John Lewis, author of *George Brown* in the same series. "Colonial secretaries, lieutenant-governors, judges, office holders under the old system have been ruthlessly robbed by me of those repulsive features under which an enlightened posterity has loved to contemplate them. They were all, or nearly all, decent old-fashioned folk doing their duty in the several stations to which they had been called in an honest old-fashioned way—not entirely unsuited to the comparatively undeveloped situation of the country. Morang no doubt rolled up his eyes to heaven and held up his hands in horror as he dictated to his type-writer the words (addressed to me): 'You have defended the Family Compact!' "

Morang refused to publish the book and LeSueur was prevented from publishing it elsewhere by an injunction obtained in the courts by the Lindsey family. In 1914, Robert Glasgow offered to publish it under the title, *William Lyon Mackenzie and the "Family Compact": A Political History*, provided the author could remove all the information obtained directly from the Lindsey collection. But G. G. S. Lindsey (1860–1920) argued in a letter to LeSueur that "It is now impossible for you to write a *Life of Mackenzie*, after five months continuous research among his private papers, and after many more brooding over them, without tincturing your manuscript throughout with color thrown into it by material from these sources." This position was upheld by the courts and LeSueur's best book was never published. Its place was taken in the series by a hasty abridgment by G. G. S. Lindsey of his father's two volume biography of the reformer.

The achievements of this group of historians are obvious; but some of the large deficiencies of the Whig point of view, as they apply to Canadian history, should be discussed more fully. In the first place, the Whig interpretation resulted in a vast over-simplification of Canadian development. This came in part from a preoccupation with two particular periods, the conquest of New France and the struggle for responsible government, almost to the exclusion of other vital and interesting areas. One of the signally neglected subjects was the movement for the union of British North America. This is indeed curious in the light of the rampant nationalism of the period. But it seems clear that the Whig sensibility looked upon the confederation movement as a corollary to responsible government, a natural outcome of the achievement of internal colonial liberty which barely needed explanation.

But after all one subject is as legitimate as another. The real criticism of the Whig historians is that they failed to understand adequately even those periods to which they gave so much attention. The fact is that these writers were not really interested in writing about what happened; but rather in demonstrating the truths of their political and social philosophy as they worked themselves out in congenial periods of the country's history. In the French period, they were so anxious to tell the story of the triumph of English over French imperialism, of Protestantism over Roman Catholicism, of liberty over authority, of enterprise over paternalism that they took little note of the complexities of the colony's development and society. For the purposes of their system, a caricature was more manageable than the real thing. And Francis Parkman (1823–1893), in *The Old Régime in Canada* (1874), for all his artistry and meticulous attention to detail, was probably the greatest offender.

Nor did the Whig fixation with the struggle for responsible government result in real understanding. In the first place, thinking of the political transition of the 1830's and 1840's as a struggle misrepresents those complex and vastly creative decades. It confuses the true relationship between the mother country and the colonies and takes little notice of the fact that British political institutions were also in a state of violent flux. To the Whigs everything was simple. "The rebellion, then," wrote John Charles Dent, "though it failed in the field, was very far from being an utter failure. It accelerated the just and moderate constitutional changes for which the Reform party had for years contended, and which, but for the Rebellion, would have been long delayed. It led to Lord Durham's mission, which brought everything else in its train. From Lord Durham's mission sprang the union; from the union sprang the concession of Responsible Government, the end of the Family Compact domination, the establishment of municipal institutions, reform in all the departments of state."

It is astonishing that most of these historians did not seem to know when responsible government actually came into existence. Kingsford seems to have thought that it was achieved with the Act of Union in 1841. In 1907, Stephen Leacock, who had just been through the documents for his book *Baldwin, Lafontaine, Hincks* in the "Makers," felt that it was necessary to point out in an article which he wrote for the first volume of the *American Political Science Review*, that "the interpretation of the principle of responsible government now prevailing was not present in the minds of imperial statesmen at the time of the adoption of the Act of Union of 1840, commonly assigned as the date of the inception of self-government." Nor did these writers understand how responsible government worked. Not until Shortt's *Sydenham* were they aware of Sydenham's administrative reforms and the significance of these changes usually escaped them. They showed little comprehension of the nature of political parties in the 1840's and the process by which responsible government was worked out and put into practice.

Furthermore, the rigidities of the Whig point of view made the evaluation of the individual in the historical process very difficult. There were "good guys" and "bad guys" and there was no difficulty in telling the one from the other. There were those who were for the extension of colonial liberty and those who were against it; there were those who wanted a liberal, rational, democratic, and secular society and those who for one reason or another were wedded to an unenlightened traditional position. This kind of history possesses all the moral subtlety of a cowboy and Indian movie. It is not surprising then that some very significant names just will not fit conveniently into the usual Whig categories. Egerton Ryerson is an example. His ideas on education were, from the Whig point of view, sound; but his support of the reform movement was uneven. So it was largely as an educational reformer that he was included in the "Makers" in the biography by Nathanael Burwash, the president and chancellor of Victoria College. The perplexities of the Whig position are well illustrated just at the end of the first volume of Dent's *The Last Forty Years* where he attempts an evaluation of the work and personality of Sir John A. Macdonald. And Sir George Parkin is really no more successful in the volume he did on Macdonald for the "Makers" series.

VI

The deficiencies of the Whig point of view were in no way corrected by the influence of the two most distinguished foreign historians ever to give their attention to Canadian studies: Francis Parkman and Goldwin Smith (1823–1910). The seven epic volumes of Parkman's *France and England in North America* (1865–92) completely dominated the interpretation of the old régime, especially among English-speaking Canadians, throughout the period under discussion and for a long time afterwards. Parkman laboured under almost incredible physical and mental handicaps, but his research was most carefully done and his volumes were beautifully written in an elaborate and heroic style. He proved definitively that Canadian history need be neither provincial nor dull. It is possible even that the erudition and elegance of the great Bostonian discouraged some able Canadian scholars from working in an area where their efforts might be compared or might seem redundant; but he was a boon to the journalists and popular historians who plundered his magnificent volumes without restraint.

Yet the interpretation was strictly Whiggish. To Parkman, the machinations of rival imperialisms represented simply the struggle between "Anglo-Saxon Protestant liberty—which was the hallmark of Progress—and French Roman Catholic absolutism." As he put it in the final volume of the series: "This war was the strife of a united and concentrated few against a divided and discordant many. It was the strife, too, of the past against the future; of the old against the new; of moral and intellectual torpor against moral and intellectual life; of barren absolutism against a liberty, crude, incoherent, and chaotic, yet full of prolific vitality." Within this frame of reference, as Professor Eccles has pointed out, "Parkman regarded the final war not as a war of conquest, but as a war of liberation. The Canadians were not conquered, they were finally liberated from Absolutism." "A happier calamity never befell a people," wrote Parkman in the concluding paragraph of *The Old Régime in Canada*, "than the conquest of Canada by the British arms."

To this general interpretation of Canadian history, Goldwin Smith also lent his extraordinary talents and international reputation. From 1858 to 1866 he had been Regius Professor of Modern History at Oxford and in 1868 he crossed the Atlantic to become Professor of English History at Cornell. In 1871 he settled in Toronto where he took a lively interest in Canadian political and intellectual life. He had no higher opinion than Parkman of the Indians, the French Canadians, Roman Catholics or the old régime and to this considerable catalogue he added a very real prejudice against the Irish.

But from this distance, Goldwin Smith is most interesting because of his ideas on, to use the title of one of his famous papers, "The Political Destiny of Canada." In a series of lectures and periodical articles, he took the view that Canada was merely "a political expression," "that the movement in favour of Canadian nationality had only political motives on its side." "The Union of the Canadian Provinces resembles, as a wit said in the [Confederation] debate," he stated in his *Reminiscences* (1911), "not that of a bundle of rods, gaining strength by their union, to which a confederationist had complacently compared it, but that of seven fishing-rods tied together by the ends." It was impossible to write even a decent history of the country, he wrote to Professor George MacKinnon Wrong (1860–1948), because of "the difficulty of running the histories of several Provinces abreast and imparting anything like unity to the whole." For reasons "geographical, racial, social, and commercial," he became convinced of Canada's "continental" destiny much to the annoyance of the Canadian nationalists and to the abhorrence of those infected with the enthusiasm for Imperial Federation. He felt Canada had nothing to fear from the United States. As he argued in an important essay, "The Schism in the Anglo-Saxon Race" (1887), "If political union ever takes place between the United States and Canada, it will not be because the people of the United States are disposed to aggression upon Canadian independence, of which there is no thought in any American breast, nor because the impediments to commercial intercourse and to the free inter-change of commercial services will have been removed, but because in blood and character, language, religion, institutions, laws and interests, the two por-tions of the Anglo-Saxon race on this continent are one people."

In 1891, with the question of unrestricted reciprocity before the electorate, Goldwin Smith summarized his position in *Canada and the Canadian Ques-tion*. Opinionated and brilliantly written, it is very probably the most exciting interpretative treatment of Canadian development ever written. Although he recognized the operation of other factors, *Canada and the Canadian Question* was the first extensive environmentalist interpretation of Canadian develop-ment by a historian.

It should be pointed out, however, that Alexander Monro (1813–1896) had reached the same position in *The United States and the Dominion of Canada: Their Future* which had appeared in 1879. Like Smith, Monro was born in Britain; but he came to New Brunswick as a youth. He was a sur-veyor and an amateur statistician, and his approach was statistical rather than developmental. Earlier he had published *New Brunswick; with a Brief Out-line of Nova Scotia, and Prince Edward Island: Their History, Civil Divisions, Geography, and Productions* (1855), *Statistics of British North America* (1862), and *History, Geography and Statistics of British North America* (1864). These books have more affinities with the old statistical accounts than with history as it was being written at the time. But, on the basis of this information, and having seen a good deal of the country as a land surveyor, he decided that Canada did not possess an independent national destiny. It was his opinion "that the United States and Dominion of Canada belong as it were to each other—that they are the geographical and commercial comple-ment of each other. . . ." He thought that it was "necessary that the branches of the Anglo Saxon and other families in North America, should unite with each other. . . ."

VII

Fashions in history do not change overnight. But by the first decade of the twentieth century, the history which had been written for the preceding half-century seemed to many people inadequate. It was the kind of history which had taken shape with Christie, McMullen, and Murdoch and had culminated in the achievements of Dent, Kingsford and "The Makers of Canada" series. The change which now took place was not so much one of basic values, but rather one of technique. The writing of history became less the hobby of journalists and lawyers and increasingly the province of professional histori-ans, scholars trained in the graduate schools of the United States or Europe and employed as teachers—at one level or another—or as archivists. Although many wrote history who were not professionally trained, they were influenced by the standards and techniques which were being introduced and against which their own efforts were judged.

There were notable changes in emphasis. In the first place, the professional historians insisted on greater accuracy. In the first volume of the *Review of Historical Publications Relating to Canada* (1897), covering publications for 1895 and 1896, E. A. Cruikshank (1853–1939) tore into the seventh volume of Kingsford's *History*, complaining particularly of the "many errors and inaccuracies" and pointing them out much to the annoyance of the historian's friends and admirers. Secondly, they deprecated what the English historian J. R. Green had called "drum and trumpet history" and insisted that history must describe more accurately the development of the total experience of the community. "In my opinion," wrote Robert Glasgow to Professor Adam Shortt, "there should be a severe penalty imposed upon any writer in this day, who would begin his history of Canada with a mention of Columbus or the Northwest passage." "It never occurred to me before," wrote Laurier's future biographer, O. D. Skelton (1878–1941), to Professor Shortt, "how completely and absolutely & inexcusably wanting all the histories of Canada are on the side of trade & commerce & industrial life generally." Professor Shortt suggested to the Canadian Education Association "the desirability of simplifying the treatment and broadening the scope and subject matter of elementary histories, thus getting into touch with primary elements in the life and growth of our social and economic life, from the first breaking into the wilderness to the present day structure of our cities. This involves tracing the gradual stages in linking up the life and interests of the people throughout the Dominion. Such a field of treatment and line of approach would put the facts of history in touch with the life of the children in any part of the Dominion, and prepare their minds for a more intelligent study of constitutional issues on these primary foundations."

In the attempt to find out what actually happened in so many areas of human development and under pressure resulting from the conviction that history, particularly Canadian history, was an essential subject in the educational programme of a democratic society, some historians were quite prepared to surrender any claims which history might possess to be considered as a branch of *belles-lettres*. Professor W. F. Ganong (1864–1941), who was a biologist as well as a historian, told the Royal Society of Canada in his paper "A Plan for a General History of the Province of New Brunswick," read in 1895: "Every man tends to write that kind of book which he likes best to read. A history of mine would be coldly scientific, precise, classified, complete; but it would lack the life and form and colour which should distinguish a history for the people." But most historians were reluctant to abandon the ancient claims of their craft. Some of the professional historians such as Professor G. M. Wrong in his *A Canadian Manor and Its Seigneurs:*

The Story of A Hundred Years, 1761–1861 (1908), *The Rise and Fall of New France* (2 vols., 1928), and *Canada and the American Revolution: The Disruption of the First British Empire* (1935), combined the highest professional standards with literary excellence.

In any case, the collection of books and documents made research very much easier and a good deal more productive. It is easy to forget the difficulties under which the earlier historians laboured. When Charles Lindsey reviewed Kingsford's *Bibliography* in *The Week* (December 9, 1892), he was able to add "several" titles to the list from his own library. In 1851, the government of the Province of Canada sent G. B. Faribault (1789–1866) to France to obtain copies of documents relating to the old régime. In 1857, T. B. Akins (1809–1891), who had helped Murdoch with his *History*, was appointed Commissioner of Public Records by the Province of Nova Scotia and in 1865 the government provided money for the publication of a volume of documents of "moderate size."

But the great break-through came with the systematic organization of a federal collection which was begun in 1872. Under the direction of Douglas Brymner (1823–1902) and his very able successor Arthur Doughty (1860–1936), a most extensive collection of invaluable documents was acquired and put in order, an undertaking which Professor Chester Martin (1882–1958) described as "perhaps the most impressive achievement for historical scholarship in this country." Beginning in 1872, as supplements to the reports of the Minister of Agriculture, the Archives Branch issued an annual *Report* (1872–1905), which summarized sections of the growing collection. Under Doughty's direction, the Archives ceased, for a time, to issue calendars and began, in 1907, to issue documents starting with Shortt and Doughty's *Documents Relating to the Constitutional History of Canada*. In 1917 the federal Government set up the Historical Documents Publication Board which was soon known as the Board of Historical Publications. ". . . the object aimed at by the Board," Adam Shortt wrote to Sir Robert Borden, "is to put at the immediate and convenient service of all persons in any way interested in Canadian History, the most essential documents bearing on the development of the vital interest of the Canadian people."

In 1903 the Province of Ontario established a Bureau of Archives and from the beginning issued an annual *Report* (1903–1933) in which a great number of documents were printed. In 1908 the Province of British Columbia appointed a historian, R. E. Gosnell, as archivist. He was joint author, with R. H. Coats, of *Sir James Douglas* (1908) for "The Makers of Canada" series and wrote, with his successor E. O. S. Scholefield (1875–1919), *A History of British Columbia* (2 parts, 1913).

In the dissemination of documents several provincial and local historical societies did excellent work. From time to time, the venerable Quebec Literary and Historical Society, founded by Lord Dalhousie in 1824, had published important documents. Both papers and documents were printed in the *Collections of the Nova Scotia Historical Society* which started to appear in 1878. In 1899, the Ontario Historical Society, previously known as the Pioneer and Historical Association, began to issue its valuable *Papers and Records* (1899–1946). Some of the local historical societies published important holdings. Under the direction of the Lundy's Lane Historical Society, Lieutenant-Colonel E. A. Cruikshank edited *The Documentary History of the Campaigns upon the Niagara Frontier* (1896–1908), a collection of documents relating to the War of 1812, which ran to nine volumes. The London and Middlesex Historical Society made the best of the William Proudfoot papers available.

Of all the societies dedicated to the publication of documents, the most distinguished was the Champlain Society. It was organized on May 17, 1905, in the board room of the Canadian Bank of Commerce in Toronto. The moving spirit and first president of the Society was Byron Edmund Walker (1848–1924), general manager of the Bank. James Bain (1842–1908), librarian of the Toronto Public Library and indefatigable collector of Canadiana, was the treasurer. The secretaries were Professor G. M. Wrong of the University of Toronto and Professor Charles William Colby (1867–1955) of McGill University. "In the past, while much has been done by local societies for local history," said a letter announcing the existence of the Society, "there has been no society on the lines of such organizations as the Surtees Society, the Hakluyt Society, the Prince Society, etc., which has devoted itself to the task of publishing or republishing important material relating to Canada's history as a whole. The consequence has been that this material has received more attention in the United States than in Canada." "The Society was not to be conducted for profit," wrote W. S. Wallace in 1937 (he was then an honorary secretary), "but was to undertake the publication of rare books or unpublished materials relating to Canada that the ordinary commercial publisher would not accept for publication; and it was understood that its volumes would be published in a form attractive to book-lovers and would be edited by competent scholars, with the necessary critical apparatus." "The books . . . are splendid examples of book making and the historical criticism is the best Canada can afford," Walker wrote to Lord Beaverbrook. They were printed in the United Kingdom and bound in red buckram which was thought more durable than leather. "It will not do to have the Ballantyne name on the title page," wrote Professor Wrong to W. L. Grant. "We shall possibly get into trouble anyhow for having the volumes printed in Edinburgh rather than in Canada, and we do not wish to obtrude our iniquity upon the public gaze."

At first, membership in the Society was limited to 250 persons, who paid a sustaining fee of $10.00 a year. Later, the membership was extended to 500 and 250 memberships were offered to libraries. It was decided to issue two volumes a year. Considering the fee and the fact that each edition was a limited edition, a membership was thought to be an excellent investment— "very valuable from a mere money point of view," as the president put it to an official of the National Trust Company.

As a beginning, the Society brought out the edition (3 vols., 1907–14) of Lescarbot's *History of New France* under the direction of W. L. Grant and H. P. Biggar (1872–1938) and W. F. Ganong's edition of Nicolas Denys's *The Description and Natural History of the Coasts of North America* (1908). In 1908, the Society decided to bring out a definitive edition of *The Works of Samuel de Champlain*, which ran to six volumes (1922–36) and was edited by H. P. Biggar. Other early volumes were: W. B. Munro (1875–1957), *Documents Relating to the Seigniorial Tenure in Canada, 1598–1854* (1908); Lieutenant-Colonel William C. H. Wood (1864–1947), *The Logs of the Conquest of Canada* (1909); and J. B. Tyrrell (1858–1957), an edition of Samuel Hearne's *A Journey from Prince of Wales's Fort, in Hudson's Bay, to the Northern Ocean* (1911). In 1916, Tyrrell edited David Thompson's very valuable and very scarce *Narrative of his Explorations in Western America 1784–1812* (1916).

In the same years, other important documents were made available. In a magnificent effort, of which the founders of the Champlain Society were all too aware, R. G. Thwaites (1853–1913), secretary of the State Historical Society of Wisconsin, issued a scholarly edition of *The Jesuit Relations and Allied Documents 1610–1791* in 73 volumes (1896–1901). Both the original documents and an English translation were printed. Also significant were the collections compiled by J. G. Hodgins (1821–1912), Deputy Minister of Education for Ontario, 1876 to 1889, and "historiographer" to the department until his death. He published a *Documentary History of Education in Upper Canada from the Passing of the Constitutional Act of 1791 to the Close of the Reverend Doctor Ryerson's Administration of the Education Department in 1876* (28 vols., 1894–1910); *Historical and Other Papers and Documents Illustrative of the Educational System of Ontario 1792–1853* (5 vols., 1911–12) and *The Establishment of Schools and Colleges in Ontario 1792–1910* (3 vols., 1910).

Another phenomenon which greatly assisted the professional historians was the proliferation of local histories in the period following Confederation. Indeed, in 1929, Dr. A. R. M. Lower (b. 1889) complained that local histories "are as the sand on the sea shore." This was the golden age of local history in Canada. The community was young enough to remember its early experiences with some precision and old enough to contemplate them with a certain nostalgia. It is true that the local historians seldom possessed the larger picture; but they were generally accurate. They knew what they were writing about and they preserved a vast amount of information which otherwise would most certainly have been lost. In fact, at this distance, their work is frequently more useful than that of their more ambitious and theoretical contemporaries. It is impossible to mention all the good and useful work done. Only a few books, typical of the better efforts, can be listed.

One of the more important of the earlier writers was James MacPherson Le Moine (1825–1912). Antiquarian, sportsman, ornithologist, he wrote, in both French and English, a series of books and papers mostly about the St. Lawrence River and Quebec City. Alexander Ross (1783–1856), fur-trader and adventurer, produced a valuable history of *The Red River Settlement* (1856). Edward Ermatinger (1797–1876) wrote a *Life of Colonel Talbot, and the Talbot Settlement* (1859) and those remarkable sisters Kathleen (d. 1931) and Robina (d. 1918) Lizars put down the legend of "Tiger" Dunlop in *In the Days of the Canada Company* (1896). Every county had to have its history written up. Good ones include the Reverend James Croil (1821–1916), *Dundas; or, A Sketch of Canadian History, and More Particularly of the County of Dundas* (1861); the Reverend George Patterson (1824–1897), *A History of the County of Pictou* (1877); Robert Sellar (1841–1919), *The History of the County of Huntingdon and of the Seigniories of Chateaugay and Beauharnois* (1888), and Norman Robertson (1845–1936), *The History of the County of Bruce and of the Minor Municipalities Therein* (1906), which was issued under the auspices of the Bruce County Historical Society. There were important regional histories such as those by A. G. Morice (1859–1938), *The History of the Northern Interior of British Columbia, Formerly New Caledonia* (1904) and W. G. Gosling (1863–1930), *Labrador: Its Discovery, Exploration, and Development* (1910). Municipal histories flourished. Among the better are books by Dr. Thomas W. Poole (1831?–1905), *A Sketch of the Early Settlement and Subsequent Progress of the Town of Peterborough* (1867); the Reverend Henry Scadding (1813–1901), *Toronto of Old* (1873); T. B. Akins, *History of Halifax City* (1895) and Agnes M. Machar (1837–1927), *The Story of Old Kingston* (1908).

The fact is that this was a period rich in the production of histories of all kinds and on all subjects. William Peter Smith (dates ?) wrote a humorous history of Canada called *The Victoria Diamond Jubilee History of Canada* (Toronto, 1897), which is very good. Among other things, he poked fun at the frantic industry of J. Castell Hopkins and the *Review of Historical Publications Relating to Canada*, assailing its pretensions and pointing out the imprecision of its language. Denominational histories flourished. Probably the best was by the Reverend William Gregg (1817–1909), *History of the Presbyterian Church in the Dominion of Canada from the Earliest Times to 1834* (1885). But it is impossible to leave out the Reverend John Carroll (1809–1884), *Case and His Cotemporaries; or, The Canadian Itinerant's Memorial:*

Consisting of a Biographical History of Methodism in Canada (5 vols., 1867–77). Also impressive is Father A. G. Morice's *History of the Catholic Church in Western Canada from Lake Superior to the Pacific (1659–1895)* (2 vols., 1910).

A related form of writing, which, like local history, was sometimes heavily genealogical, were the ethnic histories which flourished in the same period. They were a reflection, in part, of a consciousness of race—racial origins, differences, potentialities and disasters—a feeling which became increasingly intense towards the end of the century. One of the earliest and best known of these works is *The Irishman in Canada* (1877), by Nicholas Flood Davin (1843–1901). Born in Ireland, he came to Canada in 1872 where he was both a lawyer and a journalist. In 1887 he was elected Conservative member for West Assiniboia in the House of Commons. Davin identified strongly with the national aspirations of his adopted country. His *History* is developmental in approach, indicating at each stage what the Irish contributed to the growth and well-being of the community. He was conscious of the vituperations of Goldwin Smith and wanted to "raise the self-respect of every person of Irish blood in Canada." He was a real stylist and his books are all vigorously written.

The same house, Maclear of Toronto, also published, by William J. Rattray (1835–1883), *The Scot in British North America* in four volumes (1880–84). The work is divided into five sections: The Scot at Home; The Scot across the Sea; The Scot in Public Life; The Scot in Professional Life; and The Scot in the North-West. The tone is intensely nationalistic. Rattray took the position that "attachment to the land from which we or our fathers came is not only compatible with intense devotion to the highest interests of the country where we dwell, but is a necessary condition of its birth, its growth and its fervour. The dutiful son, the affectionate husband and father, will usually be the best and most patriotic subject or citizen; and he will love Canada best who draws his love of country in copious draughts from the old fountain-head across the sea." Rattray was an able journalist, but his books on the Scot were written in a period of declining health. The final volume was completed by "another hand" and was published posthumously. His real interest was in problems of religion and philosophy. His best work is scattered in his regular contributions to the Toronto *Mail*, with which he was connected as an editor, and in his articles published in the *Canadian Monthly* (1872–78).

The best books in this genre are the two volumes of *The Scotsman in Canada* published by Musson in 1911. The volume on eastern Canada was done by the poet W. Wilfred Campbell (1861–1918) and the one on the west by George Bryce. This was Campbell's only significant effort in the field of historical writing. It was "a labour of love" and the research was very carefully done. He begins with a history of the significant Scottish settlements in eastern Canada and then attempts a broad description of the relationship and the contribution of Scottish people to various areas of Canadian life. Dr. Bryce's book is also an interesting and scholarly one. He was able to draw upon his considerable knowledge of the area as already demonstrated in *The Remarkable History of the Hudson's Bay Company* (1900) and *Mackenzie, Selkirk, Simpson* (1905), which he had done for "The Makers of Canada" series.

There were, of course, histories of other groups in the community which did not share a common ethnic background, but rather a particular experience. A whole literature, for example, grew up around the United Empire Loyalists. The historians contributed abundantly to the revival of interest in the Loyalists which marked the last quarter of the century particularly in Ontario. Here the pioneer work, which supplied much of the information, was by William Canniff (1830–1910), the excellent and carefully researched *History of the Settlement of Upper Canada, (Ontario), with special reference to the Bay of Quinté* (1869). The most extensive treatment of the whole subject by a Canadian was in two ponderous volumes by Egerton Ryerson (1803–1882), *The Loyalists of America and Their Times: From 1620 to 1816* (1880). The first volume carries the Thirteen Colonies down to the Declaration of Independence; the second deals with the Revolutionary War, the migration, the settlements, and the problem of claims. The second volume concludes with a blow by blow account of the War of 1812. "The war between Great Britain and the United States, from 1812 to 1815," wrote Ryerson by way of introduction, "furnishes the strongest example of the present century, or of any age or country, of the attachment of a people to their mother country, and of their determination, at whatever sacrifice and against whatever disparity, to maintain the national life of their connection with it. The true spirit of *the Loyalists of America* was never exhibited with greater force and brilliancy than during the war of 1812–1815." Another valuable local history which was inspired by the Loyalist revival and in turn contributed a good deal of information to it, was by Judge J. F. Pringle (1816–1901), *Lunenburgh or the Old Eastern District, its Settlement and Early Progress: With Personal Recollections of the Town of Cornwall*, which appeared in 1890.

Not only was more information available in these years, but there would shortly be more scholars as well. This resulted largely from the recognition of history as a subject of instruction in the Canadian universities and the creation, at a somewhat later date, of chairs and departments of history. In 1895, the chair of history and English literature at the University of Toronto was divided and G. M. Wrong became the first full-time professor of history. In the same year, Dr. C. W. Colby, who had taken his Ph.D. at Harvard (1890), was appointed Kingsford Professor of History in McGill University. Most of these teachers wrote Canadian history, but this does not mean that Canadian history had achieved a place in the curriculum. As Professor Preston has pointed out: "Soon after Wilson began teaching at Toronto in 1853, the Vice-Chancellor called his department 'really ridiculous' because he only taught the history of Egypt to Cleopatra, of Spain to Ferdinand and Isabella, and of England to Henry VII. Ridiculous or not, this was the prevailing pattern of that time." Although J. B. A. Ferland (1805–1865) had been teaching Canadian history at Laval as early as 1854, no lectures were given in Canadian history in an English-speaking Canadian university until the last decade of the nineteenth century. In 1895 Adam Shortt, of the department of political science, gave the first lectures in Canadian history at Queen's University. In 1898, Professor G. M. Wrong indicated that his department would emphasize the history of England, the United States, and Canada. The trend is clear, but, generally speaking, not much Canadian history was taught in the universities in the period under discussion.

Undoubtedly the most important event in the development of the professional study of history in Canada was the appointment of George MacKinnon Wrong. Born in Elgin County, Canada West, he was educated at University College and Wycliffe College in the University of Toronto. In 1883, he was ordained a priest of the Church of England. From 1883 to 1892 he taught at Wycliffe College and from 1892 to 1894 he was lecturer in history at the University of Toronto. Two years after his appointment as professor, in 1897, he brought out, at his own expense, the first volume of the *Review of Historical Publications Relating to Canada* (1897–1919) in which the growing literature on Canadian history was judged by the standards of the emerging profession. Although Wrong was, in the words of Lionel Curtis, "the kindest man I know," the *Review* could be otherwise. "No hesitation has been shown in pointing out defects," wrote the editor in a preface to the first volume. In fact the reviews were sometimes brutal. E. A. Cruikshank largely demolished Kingsford's reputation and J. G. Bourinot wrote of Joseph Pope's *Confederation: Being a Series of Hitherto Unpublished Documents bearing on the British North America Act* (1895): "Out of the three hundred pages of this volume there are not a dozen which can be fairly considered useful or important." Some readers were disturbed at such ungentlemanly candour, but Professor W. J. Ashley (1860–1927), formerly professor of political economy and constitutional history in the University of Toronto, wrote from Harvard: "I am glad you have not shirked your duty to Kingsford. And you have said something that needed saying about Parkman, whom I cannot regard as a great historian. . . . The philosophy in the *Old Régime* has always seemed to me identical with the narrow bourgeois Liberalism of the '60s & '70s."

The contributors to the *Review* were "free to sign their names or not as they prefer" and the reviews were long enough to give an accurate impression of the book and for the reviewer to develop an idea or two of his own. Starting with the second volume (1898), H. H. Langton shared the editorial duties and the *Review* was organized in five sections, which in themselves indicate the more inclusive definition of the subject which now obtained: Canada's Relations to the Empire; The History of Canada; Provincial and Local History; Geography, Economics and Statistics; and Law, Education and Bibliography. Later, an additional section, Archaeology, Ethnology and Folk-Lore, was added. Both books and articles were noticed. In 1920, the *Review* was reconstituted as a quarterly, the *Canadian Historical Review* (1920–   ) containing both scholarly articles and critical reviews.

In his own books, of which *The Crusade of MCCCLXXXIII, known as that of the Bishop of Norwich* (1892) was the first, Wrong combined the highest professional standards with a pleasant narrative style. As in his lectures, his main purpose was to be "interesting." Most of his work, in one way or another, was a contribution to an examination of the Imperial connection. When he sent André Siegfried's *Le Canada: les deux races* (1906) to Professor W. L. Grant for the *Review*, he suggested, "Dwell as much as you can on his view of Canada's relations to Great Britain. I want to keep that subject before the public mind, in view of the coming Colonial Conference. We must, in some way, get control of our foreign affairs—that Alaska business has sunk deep into the hearts of the Canadian people." He regretted that "Canada has the nondescript title of 'Dominion' instead of being a kingdom" as Sir John A. Macdonald had intended. But he was critical of the position taken by J. S. Ewart (1849–1933) in his *The Kingdom of Canada . . . and other Essays* (1908). "With great skill and ingenuity the author works up an elaborate case against Great Britain. She has checked Canada unduly in the past; she is checking her unduly still, and resisting her assertion of the privileges of the grown-up. Canada has a long list of grievances. Mr. Ewart has read widely, not, one fears, so much to see his subject as a whole, but to make points against Great Britain." But much as Wrong loved English values and society, he realized increasingly that Canada was essentially different from the United Kindom. "The Canadians are becoming indeed a people quite different from the English," he wrote in *The Nineteenth Century* (LXVI, 1909). "The saying of Horace, now trite enough, *coelum non animum mutant, qui trans mare currunt*, is, in this relation, profoundly untrue . . . environment counts for something." On the other hand, he felt that "Canada is not becoming Americanized, if this means that she is drawing closer politically to the United States. On the contrary, just because she has a growing confidence in her own self, she is daily growing farther away from any thought of political union with that country."

Year after year, the *Review of Historical Publications Relating to Canada* chronicled and criticized new achievements in the field of Canadian history.

It can only be described as a kind of creative and scholarly explosion and it culminated in two great co-operative undertakings, *The Chronicles of Canada* (32 vols., Toronto 1914–1916), edited by Professor Wrong and H. H. Langton, and *Canada and Its Provinces: A History of the Canadian People and Their Institutions by One Hundred Associates* (23 vols., Toronto, 1914–1917) edited by Adam Shortt and A. G. Doughty. The publisher in both cases was Robert Glasgow and the books were printed by T. and A. Constable at the Edinburgh University Press.

Glasgow had been involved in selling "The Makers of Canada" and he was convinced of the considerable potential of the market. He left "facts and historical accuracy" up to the professional scholars, but "as to the organization or construction of the books," he wrote to Professor Wrong, "I have never found anyone who could handle this as well as I can myself. On nearly every manuscript I request the author to reorganize his work to some extent and as he nearly always agrees with me, I have come to believe that I understand this phase of making a book." He was a remarkable man. "I don't know whether you know anything about Glasgow," wrote Professor Wrong to J. S. Willison. "He is a coming man in the publishing world, with good ideas, and a high integrity that will always make him respected. He knows how to sell books and to make them pay." In the production of these books, *The Chronicles* and *Canada and Its Provinces*, he worked day and night. In 1918, he moved to the United States, where he brought out *The Chronicles of America* series edited by Professor Allen Johnson (1870–1931), (50 vols., New Haven, 1918–1921). About this series he wrote to Professor Wrong, who contributed a volume on *The Conquest of New France* (1918), "We are getting some great books, and everyone says that the series is going to have great value in cementing the entente of the English-speaking peoples. If so, and I think it is so, this will ease my conscience for not doing direct work for the war." In fact, he gave his life in this cause. Exhausted, he died of a heart attack on April 5, 1922, at the age of 47. He was the greatest publisher in the history of historical writing in Canada.

The Chronicles of Canada were written for the general reader; but most of them were written by professional scholars. Professor Stephen Leacock wrote three volumes and O. D. Skelton two. W. S. Wallace did a revisionist volume on *The Family Compact* (1915); he also wrote the one on *The 'Patriotes' of '37* (1916) although it appeared under the signature of A. D. DeCelles. Glasgow did not think the book would sell under the real author's name in the province of Quebec. A. G. Doughty did *The Acadian Exiles* (1916) and Professor W. B. Munro, *The Seigneurs of Old Canada* (1915). Glasgow believed that the "portraits of men" were "the best thing in history" and a number of biographies were included. Professor C. W. Colby did sketches of Champlain (1915) and Frontenac (1915) and W. L. Grant wrote *The*

Tribune of Nova Scotia: A Chronicle of Joseph Howe (1915). William C. H. Wood, author of *The Fight for Canada* (1904), did six volumes of military history. The books were illustrated and most attractively printed and bound.

But the monument to the professional study of history was *Canada and Its Provinces*. It, too, was the product of "Glasgow's fertile brain." The idea was to cover all the country's history—political and constitutional, economic and social, intellectual and ecclesiastical. The project was intimidating in its scope. "I haven't yet made up my mind about that big history plan," wrote Professor O. D. Skelton to Adam Shortt, "it seems over ambitious." But the publisher and the editors brought the combined resources of the profession to bear on the problem. "The range of facts is so wide and the topics so various and complex," explained the editors, "that no one author could possibly compass them. The work, therefore, has been apportioned among many writers each of whom has some special sympathy and aptitude for the topic with which he deals." The approach was developmental, topical, and regional; the subject was divided into twelve "main divisions": I, New France, 1534–1760; II, British Dominion, 1760–1840; III, The United Canada, 1840–1867; IV, The Dominion: Political Evolution; V, The Dominion: Industrial Expansion; VI, The Dominion: Missions, Arts and Letters; VII, The Atlantic Provinces; VIII, The Province of Quebec; IX, The Province of Ontario; X, The Prairie Provinces; XI, The Pacific Province; XII, Documentary Notes, General Index. Behind the careful scholarship stood an insistent patriotism. ". . . a sound knowledge of Canada as a whole, of its history, traditions and standards of life, should be diffused among its citizens, and especially among the immigrants . . . ," wrote the editors in the introduction to the first volume, ". . . mere wealth-making is not the chief essential of citizenship. Good citizenship grows out of a patriotic interest in the institutions of one's country and a sympathy with the people who dwell there."

The real editor of *Canada and Its Provinces* was Adam Shortt. He also wrote more of it than any other contributor. Born near London, Ontario, he was educated at Queen's University and in the universities of Glasgow and Edinburgh. In 1885, he returned to Queen's as an assistant in the department of philosophy and, in 1891, he was appointed Sir John A. Macdonald Professor of Political Science. He was also the University librarian. Although he possessed a rather low opinion of most politicians, he went to Ottawa in 1908 to become Canada's first Civil Service Commissioner. He greatly admired Lord Acton whom he regarded "as having much the truest conception of history among modern writers" and possessed always a profound respect and persistent enthusiasm for original sources. Much of his early work was concerned with the early economic history of the country and with the nature and influence of the frontier, studies which did not escape the notice of Frederick Jackson Turner. Between 1896 and 1906, he published thirty-two articles on the history of Canadian banking in the *Journal of the Canadian Banker's Association*, and in 1898 a series of these papers came out under the title, *The Early History of Canadian Banking*. "I think most of us appreciate the work which you have done for Canadian economics," wrote Harold Adams Innis (1894–1952), "and I have thought at sometime in the near future of writing an appraisal of your position as the founder of the subject."

The professional historians, like their colleagues of the older school, gave what seems like an exorbitant amount of attention to the seventeenth and eighteenth centuries. But, in combination with such American historians as Parkman, H. L. Osgood (1855–1918), R. G. Thwaites, C. M. Andrews (1863–1943) and G. L. Beer (1872–1920), to mention only the most distinguished, they did a good deal to recover the unity of North Atlantic experience and civilization. From the distance of the early twentieth century and fortified, as they were, with a substantial dose of Anglo-Saxon racism, the disruption of the First British Empire seemed to them more like an unfortunate incident than a cataclysmic event. It had been unpleasant but not fatal to British interests, while in the New World it signalled the birth of not one but two communities—the American republic and English-speaking British North America. In this era of good feeling all parties to the imperial altercation of the eighteenth century looked like winners—all, that is, except the French. And even France had her revenge in the Revolutionary War. But not so the French colony on the St. Lawrence. To most English-speaking historians, French Canada was an unfortunate remnant unredeemed by time. Very few could identify with its history or its aspirations. "Of course Parkman has done the early period," wrote A. H. U. Colquhoun (1861–1936) to Professor Wrong, "but we Canadians of the 20th century cannot live on a past that is really not our own. To me there is much to inspire in all the chief episodes of our history since 1759. . . ." The *Review of Historical Publications Relating to Canada* had to remind G. T. Denison that Canadian history did not begin, as he had assumed, with the arrival of the United Empire Loyalists. This is the kind of thing one would expect from Colonel Denison, but it was a notion widely held in the English-speaking community. The Canadian historians writing in English contributed brilliantly to the integration of the North Atlantic community, but they contributed little to the understanding of the internal cultural dilemma.

Although many of these historians deplored what Goldwin Smith called "the schism in the Anglo-Saxon race," they did not possess any simple answers as to how this unfortunate condition might be healed. The professional historians, for the most part, condemned the Imperial Federation movement or any other system for the political or military integration of the Empire. Many were simply expressing what O. D. Skelton called his "incurable Canadianism." But for most their opposition was more profoundly and rationally based. Discussing his work on the American Revolution with Adam Shortt, Professor Wrong wrote: "What I have feared is blaming the people in England. Their benevolent intentions cannot be doubted and they certainly took abundant pains to find the facts. What they lacked was insight. This lack of insight only shows that people on one side of an ocean can't govern, because they can't understand, the people on the other side of the ocean living in a wholly different environment." "If we are true to ourselves in a broad-minded way we shall not injure the Empire," wrote Shortt to J. S. Willison in 1904. But Imperial Federation, he told E. R. Peacock, would be like pasting "millstones to each others necks."

VIII

As was pointed out, in the nineteenth century the nation state or the inter-action of nation states was the usual unit of historical study and this was doubly so in Canada. Canadians were preoccupied with building a nation and most Canadian historians felt that they—if anyone—had something to contribute in the quest for a national identity. Very few overcame the national fixation and fewer still contributed anything of much significance to the literature or the knowledge of the larger world.

Probably the most successful of these scholars was Alpheus Todd (1821–1884) and he was more a political scientist than a historian. His career, as the English historian Spencer Walpole intimated in the preface to the third edition of his *Parliamentary Government in England*, was a paradigm of Victorian self-help. Born in England, he came to Canada with his family when yet a boy. He went to work as a librarian to the Legislative Assembly of Upper Canada and developed an "addiction to parliamentary studies." Although self-educated, he produced, at the age of nineteen, *The Practice and Privileges of the Two Houses of Parliament*, a book of over three hundred pages, which he described as "a Manual of Parliamentary Practice for the use of the Legislature." In 1854 he became the librarian of the Legislative Assembly of Canada and in 1870 he took charge of the Parliamentary Library in Ottawa. At the time of Confederation, he published *On Parliamentary Government in England: Its Origin, Development, and Practical Operation* (2 vols., 1867, 1869), an elaborate discussion of the British constitution, a system of government "so often admired, but never successfully imitated." "There is nowhere to be found," he stated in the preface to the first edition, "a practical treatment of the questions involved in the mutual relations between the Crown and Parliament, or any adequate account of the growth, development, and present functions of the Cabinet Council." He felt that "the great and increasing defect in all parliamentary governments, whether provincial or imperial, is the weakness of executive authority" and insisted that a "political system based on the monarchical principle must concede to the chief ruler something more than mere ceremonial functions." In 1880, he published *Parliamentary Government in the British Colonies*. The work, he admitted, dealt "largely with questions that have arisen out of the working of the new constitution conferred upon Canada in the confederation of the various provinces in 1867"; but he hoped the discussion would be relevant to other British colonies as they moved in the direction of political unification and self-government. In 1881, owing to the intervention of the Governor-General, he was made a C.M.G., but many felt that he did not receive sufficient recognition for his contributions to the study of British institutions. It was on the subject of Todd's deserts that Kingsford, who admittedly was irascible, remarked in connection with the American revolution: "The real grievance was not the Stamp Act, and all the misrepresentation which has been written about the tyranny of the home government. It was the misapprehension and the failure to do justice to the colonial intellect which estranged men like Jefferson, Samuel Adams, and Madison, who learned from personal sentiment to entertain an unextinguishable hatred to England."

Another distinguished scholar, who, like Goldwin Smith, did some of his important work in Canada, was Daniel Wilson (1816–1892), professor of history and English literature in University College, Toronto, from 1853 until his death. In addition to a multitude of scholarly papers, he published while in Canada a greatly revised edition of his *Prehistoric Annals of Scotland* (2 vols., 1851), a work of enormous erudition. The book established Wilson as "the pioneer of scientific Scottish archaeology" and was admired so widely that the word "prehistoric," employed for the first time in the edition of 1851, entered the language. It is a curious combination of information and interests —antiquarian and archaeological, historical and anthropological. On coming to Canada, he turned his attention to the North American Indian and in 1862 his *Prehistoric Man, Researches into the Origin of Civilization in the Old and the New World* appeared. Although inferior as a systematic treatise to his *Prehistoric Annals of Scotland*, it, in the words of his biographer H. H. Langton, "laid the foundation of archaeological study in Canada."

There were other important books. Andrew Bell (1838–1866), who translated Garneau into English and took so many liberties with the text that it is very properly known as "Bell's Garneau" (1860), earlier published *Historical Sketches of Feudalism, British and Continental, with Numerous Notices of the Doings of the Feudalry in All Ages and Countries* (1852). Thomas D'Arcy McGee (1825–1868) produced *A Popular History of Ireland: From the Earliest Period to the Emancipation of the Catholics* (2 vols., 1863) which was very well received both in Canada and in the United States. In 1863, the Reverend John McCaul (1807–1886), president of University College, Toronto, published *Britanno-Roman Inscriptions, with Critical Notes* a book of little literary significance, but a very great scholarly achievement. Also important is the most scholarly of W. H. Withrow's many books, *The Catacombs of Rome and Their Testimony Relative to Primitive Christianity* (1874). Withrow was, in addition to his other talents and achievements, a linguist and he was able to use the results of Continental research. Although scholarly, his book was also polemical. It was written with the conviction that "the testimony of the Catacomb exhibits, more strikingly than any other evidence, the immense contrast between primitive Christianity and modern Romanism. . . ." The work of John Foster Kirk (1824–1904) cannot go unmentioned. Born and educated in the Maritimes, he was for many years private secretary and amanuensis to the great American historian William H. Prescott (1796–1859). At Prescott's suggestion, he undertook a *History of Charles the Bold, Duke of Burgundy* of which two volumes were published in 1864. A third volume appeared in 1872 after he had examined the archives in France and Switzerland and had visited the scene of Charles's defeat. The style is elaborate, even extravagant; but that was the fashion of the day. The *Saturday Review* stated: "Mr. Kirk has produced a work which is quite entitled to take rank with the writings of his two predecessors [Prescott and Motley] with whom he has, both in his merits and his faults, a certain family resemblance."

Books by Canadian historians on non-Canadian subjects did not become much more numerous in the later period under discussion. Colonel George T. Denison (1839–1925), one of the founding members of the Canada First movement, published an impressive *History of Cavalry* (1877), which won a prize offered by the Tsar of Russia. Goldwin Smith wrote three histories of the survey kind: *The United States: An Outline of Political History, 1492–1871* (1893); *The United Kingdom: A Political History* (1899) and *Irish History and the Irish Question* (1905). William Robinson Clark (1829–1912), who was professor of mental and moral philosophy in Trinity College, Toronto, was the author of *Savonarola, His Life and Times* (1890), *The Anglican Reformation* (1897), and *Pascal and the Port Royalists* (1902). James Mavor (1854–1925), Scottish-born professor of political economy in the University of Toronto (1892–1923), published in 1914, *An Economic History of Russia* in two large volumes. "I got the other day a copy of your prodigious work on Russia and was struck with wonder," wrote Sir William Van Horne to the author. "How the devil did you find time to do such a thing?" In fact it was the labour of seventeen years. The first part was based on V. O. Kliuchevski's *History of Russia* and the value of Mavor's work was somewhat reduced by the translation of Kliuchevski's volumes into English (1911–1930). Also important is J. S. Ewart's *The Roots and Causes of the Wars (1914–1918)*, an elaborate revisionist interpretation which appeared in two volumes in 1924.

This has been a chronicle of development and achievement. And yet, in 1932, Professor Chester Martin, writing in *Fifty Years Retrospect*, an anniversary volume put together for the Royal Society of Canada, said "Sir John Bourinot's verdict fifty years ago is still substantially true: 'the history of Canada, as a whole, has yet to be written.' " By this he meant that the ambitions and pretensions of the professional historians had not yet been realized. At the same time, there was a general deterioration in historical writing as literature. In 1926, W. S. Wallace, then editor of the *Canadian Historical Review*, using De Quincey's categories, insisted that the history being written belonged almost exclusively to the "literature of knowledge" rather than to the "literature of power." "One finds it difficult to think of any book published by a graduate student in British, American or Canadian universities," he wrote, which "the world will not willingly let die." This resulted partly from the choice of subject-matter and partly from attitudes of mind. The rigid constitutionalism, the theoretical environmentalism, the touchy nationalism of the inter-war period were not the stuff of which great history is made. It was not until later, until the English-speaking community in Canada felt threatened, that historical writing in English became what it had always been in French, a literature of survival, and history reclaimed its position as an ornament of Canadian literature and culture.

14. The Growth of Canadian English

M. H. SCARGILL

IT IS IN ITS VOCABULARY that Canadian English is most distinctive; and it is in its varied names that Canadian English is most appealing, something which Canadian authors, such as Pratt in poetry and Hutchison in prose, have not been slow to recognize.

> Ottawa, Toronto, Montreal,
> Wetaskiwin, Pembina, Thrums, St. Paul;
> Skookumchuck, Chilcotin, and Heart's Ease,
> Wintering Hills, Swan Hills, Hills of Peace.

This profusion of colourful names, American Indian, French, Scottish, English, was noticed early by travellers. Writing about the Northwest in *Ocean to Ocean* (1873), almost one hundred years ago, G. M. Grant of Nova Scotia commented that "The name of almost every river, creek, mountain, or district is French or Scotch" (p. 183). And he deplored that "custom of discarding musical, expressive Indian names for ridiculously inappropriate European ones" (p. 31).

But it is not names of places alone that the English language in Canada has borrowed and then made its own. Although, as is the case with American English, the greater part of the vocabulary is shared with British English because it is derived from that source, hundreds of words of various origins have made their way into the Canadian language, either directly or through the United States. New names for new conditions of life, for new flora and fauna, for new peoples, new politics, new weather, all have joined the vocabulary of the New World to that of the Old in Canadian English and given it a vitality and variety that few other languages know.

From the French have come such words as *habitant, voyageur, portage, prairie, gopher, cache, snye*. From native languages have come *shaganappi, pemmican, muskeg, igloo, kayak, manitou, tepee, skookum,* and those numerous "translations" such as *pale face, pipe of peace, bury the hatchet, and happy hunting grounds*. From Spanish America, through American English, have come *coyote, stampede, corral, ranch, rodeo, bonanza, chaps, nosey along*. From British English, but with new meanings and in new combinations, and from English dialects have come words like *reeve, Outside, Confederation, York boat, by acclamation, concession, warden, Seaway, separate school, tickle, droke.* And from various languages and peoples come such words as *hoodoos, Doukhobor, Nisei, wiener, cookie, bush,* and *chop suey.*

These borrowings, new uses, and, in some cases, outright coinings (*Splake* from *speckled* and *lake* trout) are found in almost every area of the life and thought of English-speaking Canadians, as the following brief sampling will show. (The parentheses enclose the earliest date for a Canadian use of the words.)

ANIMALS: *caribou* (1672), *carcajou* (1760), *buffalo* (1635), *prairie dog* (1823), *ground hog* (1789), *wolverine* (1743), *loup cervier* (1784), *moose* (1744)

BIRDS: *Acadian owl* (1868), *fool hen* (1760), *whisky jack* (1743), *snow bird* (1749).

FISH: *oolican* (1877), *muskellonge* (1825), *inconnu* (1789), *gaspereau* (1760).

GOVERNMENT: *by acclamation* (1827), *fishing admiral* (1620), *fence viewer* (1793), *hog reeve* (1825), *path master* (1822), *improvement district* (1841), *warden* (as presiding officer of a county council, 1842).

INDIAN LIFE: *Algonquin* (1665), *Huron* (1665), *calumet* (1665), *lacrosse* (1760), *Manitou* (1703), *wampum* (1791), *lodge* (1789).

POLITICS: *Anti-Unionist* (1823), *Clear Grit* (1849), *Radical Reformer* (1833), *Durhamite* (1840), *Family Compact* (1849).

GENERAL: *corduroy bridge* (1824), *Métis* (1816), *arpent* (1703), *sault* (1665), *homestead* (1765) *seigniory* (1703), *York currency* (1799), *Brock copper* (1819), *batture* (a gravel flat in a river, 1815).

It was vocabulary that first caught the attention of early commentators on what was to become Canadian English. Heriot, the "Deputy Post Master General of British North America," in his *Travels through the Canadas* (1807) notes *planters* in Newfoundland: "These are not properly seafaring men and are distinguished by the name of *planters*" (p. 10). He gives us an erroneous derivation of *Quebec* as from the French "Quel bec" (p. 27); and he derives *Eskimaux* from the "Abinaquis language" meaning "an eater of raw flesh" (p. 11). Heriot records *habitant, voyageurs, coureurs de bois, watape* (root fibres), *cahots* (ridges in the snow), *carriole,* and the *King's Posts* (settlements on the northern shores of the St. Lawrence). W. S. Moorsom, an observant English officer, in his *Letters from Nova Scotia* (1830), calls attention (wrongly) to the *freshet*: "This is a word peculiar to America and is expressive of the extraordinary rise of rivers and streams, after either thaws or heavy rains" (p. 185). He also notes *aboiteau* as "a term introduced by the Acadian French" (p. 187); the *loup cervier,* "pronounced Lucifee," he says

(p. 125); the frost "coming out, as it is termed" (p. 165); and a few localisms such as "the marsh frog, the Nova Scotia Nightingale as he is sometimes termed" (p. 163); the "Digby chicken" (p. 254); and "a regular Kenty-cooker . . . a term used to express a native Nova Scotian of the true breed" (p. 317).

An excellent book on Nova Scotia is T. C. Haliburton's *An Historical and Statistical Account of Nova Scotia* (1829). It contains a most interesting list of names of birds, fish, flowers, with such entries as *Whore's egg, Labrador tea, Indian pipe, Old Wife, Boblincon, Whip Poor Will*. He records *moufle* (II, 392) and *intervale* and *cradle* as "a machine of American invention . . . composed of a scythe, and its handle, with the addition of a few light bars of wood . . ." (II, 365). *Intervale*, he says, "is a term peculiar to America and denotes that portion of land which is composed of the alluvial deposit of large brooks and rivers . . ." (II, 362).

A fascinating book, written about the same time as Captain Moorsom's, describes Upper Canada in the early 1800's through the letters of two families of Irish settlers. *Authentic Letters from Upper Canada* (1833) offers correspondence from the Magraths, who settled near York, and the Radcliffs, who settled in Adelaide. They seem to have been very practical persons, with a real appreciation of all things new, particularly those to do with getting a living. There is much ado about the *Bush*, explained as "the wild forest" (p. 12), the *Bush-road*, the *log-house*, the *clearing*, the *Concession line*, the *maskanonge, windrow chopping*, and the *shanty*, described as the "first and most contracted habitation a settler forms" (p. 13). These Irish people had a strong sense of humour, and one letter contains an amusing account of the speech of an Irish servant (invented for the purpose, but doubtless typical), who talks of *maypole sugar*, the *squawl* (squaw), *porpus* (papoose), and of *bumpkin pie*.

Mrs. Susanna Moodie, writing in *Roughing It in the Bush* (1854), is a rather different commentator, not at all happy with herself or with her neighbours. She seems to think of the inhabitants of Upper Canada as English (like herself), Yankees (anybody not born in England), and Irish. One gets the impression that what was different she condemned; and she is the first commentator I know of to distinguish (wrongly) a form of speech which she calls "Vulgar Canadian." She describes *pritters* as "Vulgar Canadian for potatoes" (p. 245). "What is a charivari?" asks Mrs. Moodie (p. 288), rather impatiently one gathers. *I guess* and *to hum, fixings* and *sace* (sauce) are "Yankee." It is interesting to note that Mrs. Moodie does not feel it necessary to explain *habitant, corduroy bridge, wigwam, squaw, papoose, wolverine, mocassin, or maskinonge*. But she does give a note on *logging bee, blazing* (trees), and "to make garden, as the Canadians term preparing a few vegetables for the season" (p. 376).

Canadian English has sometimes been unlucky in its commentators. For example, Anna Jameson was in Upper Canada around 1836, when the population was about 375,000. But she was most uninterested in what she saw and heard. "These streams," she writes in *Winter Studies and Summer Rambles in Canada* (1838), "have the names of Thirty Mile Creek, Forty Mile Creek, Twenty Mile Creek, and so on; but wherefore I could not discover" (p. 21). However, she does explain for us *corduroy, cat-a-mountain* (as the "American tiger"), *bush, lumber, cutter, town line, traverse, kinnikinic,* and *wattup* ("split ligaments of the pine-root").

Bonnycastle, in his *Canada and the Canadians in 1846* (1846), notes the Irish influence in pronunciation and gives a number of words which he records as Canadian: "shops or stores as they are universally called in America and Canada" (II, 53); "keeping tavern, as it is called in the backwoods of Canada West" (II, 207); "his lot, for so a property is called in Canada West" (I, 176).

John Bigsby tells his readers in *The Shoe and Canoe* (1850) that "the French Canadian has brought one remarkable custom—the charivari" (I, 34). He defines a *bee* and says that *chop-cabbage* is a "Canadian by-name . . . applied to the peasantry" (I, 176).

By the middle of the nineteenth century, the English language in Canada was so different in vocabulary from British English that a would-be settler, reading the various "immigrant's guides," must have wondered just what kind of country he was going to. If he picked up, as many did, Mrs. Traill's *The Canadian Settlers' Guide* (1855), he would find a bewildering array of new terms, some with an explanation, some without: *the Bush, logging bee, blazed line, ground-hog, chitmunk* (sic), *Indian summer, mowkowks* (birch baskets). And what pictures he must have formed of the *Whisky jack*, the *whip-poor-will*, and the *chickadee*. Mrs. Traill, quoting from her brother, carefully explains *plan-heap, chopper's shanty,* and how to *log* and to *underbrush*. This latter is so vital that it is explained twice. W. Dunlop, in *Statistical Sketches of Upper Canada* (1832), and J. B. Brown, in *Views of Canada and the Colonists* (1846), also writing for settlers, add to the strangeness of the new land with *Indian Reserves, Crown Lands, Huron Tract, bois-brule* (defined as a half-Indian), and *batteau* (or flat-bottomed boat).

In pronunciation, Canadian English has not pursued quite the same line of independent development as it has in vocabulary. In general, it is closer to northern British English than it is to that variety of English cultivated by B.B.C. announcers and called "Received Pronunciation" even though it is received only by a minority. Some of the differences in pronunciation between Canadian English and British Received Pronunciation, such as the Canadian preservation of *r* in words like *card*, the preference for a short vowel in words of the *grass* type, the presence of an almost unrounded vowel in words like *cot,* may be due to the influence of American English. Other differences, or even all, are due to three causes: the fact that many settlers left England for Canada when all dialects of British English were changing and Received Pronunciation had not developed; the presence of many settlers from areas in England where Received Pronunciation is not common; the fact that many settlers brought with them a variety of Irish or Scottish English.

The Irish and Scottish influences on the pronunciation of Canadian English were early noted and often despised, especially the Irish. And such frequent late eighteenth-century and early nineteenth-century English pronunciations as *sarce* (sauce), *darter* (daughter), *deef* (deaf), *arter* (after), *bile* (boil), *git* (get), *wrastle* (wrestle), *critter* (creature), *varmint* (vermin), were often falsely labelled as "Yankee" in origin.

Mrs. Moodie notes as "Irish": "yer too particular intirely; we've no time in the woods to be clane" (p. 402). And Anna Jameson comments on the "Irish" *iligant, nate, clane.* We do not have these ladies' views on Pope's rhyming of *tea* with *obey.* Captain Moorsom, writing of New Glasgow and Arisaig, says, "Gaelic is the language of this part of the country,—I mean it is the tongue which you hear in every cottage" (p. 332). And of Pictou he writes, "Keen-looking fellows . . . discussing in broad Scotch or pure Gaelic the passing topics of the day" (p. 353). *Sarce* or *sace* (sauce) seems to have fascinated all observers, both as a pronunciation and as a dish. In *Authentic Letters from Upper Canada* we read, *"Sace* is everything you could name—potatoes, vegetables, butter, pickles, and sweetmeats—they're all *sace*—only mustard, pepper, and vinegar is not" (p. 135). But pronunciation never attracted from early observers the same amount of attention as did vocabulary.

As population began to spread, thinly it is true, observers seem to have become more and more aware that the English spoken in Canada was by no means identical with that of England and, moreover, that more than one kind of English was spoken in Canada. But it is not until the latter half of the nineteenth century that much attention is paid to regional differences in speech, although the observant Moorsom had noted, in addition to "Gaelic and broad Scotch," instances of distinctive "Lunenburg talk": "Fy don't you make the vimen vork?" (p. 77). And he writes that the "settlers of German extraction throughout Nova Scotia are commonly called *Dutch,* although there are but few to whom that national appelative is strictly appropriate" (p. 306). Much earlier than this, Cartwright's *Labrador Journal* (1792) offers an interesting glossary containing such words as *caplin, flakes* (for drying fish), *loubscouse* (a sea-food dish), *lolly* (soft ice floating in water), *tilt* (a small hut), and *tickle* (a passage between two masses of land).

Students of Canadian English would wish that there had been more observers of the calibre of G. M. Grant, who crossed Canada in 1872 with Sandford Fleming. He had the makings of a true dialect geographer. Writing in *Ocean to Ocean* about the Prairies, he says, "The Saskatoon are [sic] simply what are known in Nova Scotia as Indian pears, and the kinni-kinnick creeper is our squawberry plant" (p. 164). He notes that *scrub pine* is called "cypress" in the West and that in Victoria "the smallest silver piece is what is called a bit" (p. 342). On the Pacific slope, writes Grant, Indians are called *Siwashes* and farms are called *ranches*. An enclosure for cattle is a *corral*. Among what he calls "slang terms of the Pacific," Grant notes *Doc.*, *git*, *Cap.* (captain), and the *Rockies*. "Every adjective and article that could be dispensed with was rejected from their English . . ." (p. 264). And he tells us that *creek* is universally pronounced "crick" in the Northwest. Grant defines for us (wrongly) *Chinook jargon* as "a barbarous lingo of one or two hundred words, first introduced by Hudson's Bay agents" (p. 242). He explains *lobstick* as "the Indian or half-breed monument to a friend or man he delights to honour" (p. 202). The *Red River cart*, says Grant, is "a clumsy-looking but really light box cart with wheels six or seven feet in diameter and not a bit of iron about the whole consern" (p. 129). *Shaganappi* he defines as "raw buffalo hide" (Miss Pauline Johnson in *The Shagganappi* (1912) says that it is really the name of a creamy-brown colour and spells it with two g's); and he gives *spell* as "the length of the journey between meals and stopping places" (p. 126).

Grant also edited a book called *Picturesque Canada* (1882), which is valuable for scholars interested in dialects. The chapters on Quebec record a variety of terms such as *arpent*, *bonne* (a lumberman's boat), *censitaire*, *caleche*, *seigneur*, and *Canadienne*. Among lumbering terms are *head-swamper* (or roadmaker), *bush superintendent*, *slide master*, *river driver*, *on the cruise* (spotting likely trees). Chapters on the Northwest have *bluff of woods*, *Red River cart*, *prairie schooner*, *tump lines*, *North canoe*, *prairie chicken*, *brigade* (or caravan), *York boat*. Ontario offers *tulip-tree*, *Queen City*, *Soo*, and *Six Nations*. From the Maritimes are entered *Blue nose*, *Digby chicken*, *steam drivers*, *intervale*, *gaspereau*.

A. P. Silver, writing about the Maritimes in *Farm-Cottage, Camp and Canoe in Maritime Canada* (1908), has some interesting words: *ouananiche* [Lake St. John region] (pronounced "wonaneesh," he says); *bog-sucker* (wood-cock); *liveyeres* (as settlers on the Labrador coast); *squaw bushes*; *bogan* (or cove). As pronunciations, Silver offers *pizen* (poison); *wexed* (vexed); *sarve* (serve); *kiver* (cover).

Viscount Milton and W. B. Cheadle, in *North-west Passage by Land* (1865), were impressed by some of the terms of the West, particularly by miners' talk; and they record from Lilloet "bully for you," "caved in," "you bet," "pay dirt." Many miners were from California, and from them our two travellers learned that "a grass widow in America is a woman who has separated or been divorced from her husband" (p. 389).

Among other writers who note terms from the Northwest is Charles Mair in *Through the Mackenzie Basin* (1908), his account of a journey into the Athabasca and Peace River areas in 1899. Mair gives such examples as "small barges, called sturgeons and the old York or inland boat" (p. 32); *snies*, described as "tortuous, narrow channels"; *Klondikers*; *umiak*; *babiche*; *old timers*.

An interesting book by J. T. Bealby, *Fruit Ranching in British Columbia* (1909), describes life in the Kootenays around the year 1907. Bealby is a keen observer of language although he is not able to distinguish regionalisms in speech. To him, anything new is simply "Canadian." But he notes several expressions: "a bunch (of cattle), to use a Canadian idiom" (p. 53); "car being Canadian for a passenger carriage or coach" (p. 21); "squatted on the land or, in the Canadian language, staked it" (p. 66); "and, in the Canadian phrase, might be shipped any day" (p. 71); "one of his [the Canadian's] favorite phrases is up against it" (p. 136).

H. J. Parham, author of *A Nature Lover in British Columbia* (1937), was a member of an English family which settled in the Okanagan valley about 1905. A keen naturalist, he records such words as *kokanee, squawfish, skunk cabbage* (wild arum lily), *coho, tyee, cutthroat*.

So far, I have dealt almost entirely with those writers who were observing the English language in Canada rather than using it creatively. What of our creative writers as distinct from travellers and commentators? Are they Canadian in language? Certainly when they are writing of things Canadian, they are distinctively Canadian, although a man like Galt belies this statement. But when Canadians are writing of "universal" matters, then they draw on that vast stock of English which is common to all English-speaking peoples and to which no special label can be attached. But to an Englishman, the works of Pauline Johnson, for example, reveal an entirely new world of language: *Shagganappi, cayuse, tepee, Reserve, gopher, potlatch, ollallies, snow snake, tillicum*. So do the works of R. J. C. Stead: *colonist car, wolf willow, rampike, pea-vine, Chinook arch*. Thomas H. Raddall's Nova Scotian characters are stamped as Nova Scotian by their speech. There may be an objection here that these are regional varieties of Canadian English. But Canadian English includes its regionalisms; and a Canadian author is as free to draw on them as the British writer is free to imitate Cockney or Lancashire speech in his writings.

A novel that exploits speech differences to the full is John Campbell's *Two Knapsacks* (1892), the tale of a summer holiday in Ontario. The publisher's note to the novel praises "its extremely clever dialect, representing Irish, Scotch, English, Canadian, French, Southern, and Negro speech." It is most interesting to see what Campbell considers to be "Canadian speech." His two heroes, one a lawyer and the other a teacher, are simply represented as speaking a form of English devoid of any pronunciations or phraseology which are used in the book to mark the two Englishmen, one uncultivated and the other cultivated, who say such things as "back to Hold Hingland" (uncultivated), "dawg" (cultivated), and "thanks awfully" (cultivated). But Campbell also offers another variety of Canadian speech which he puts in the mouths of lower-class Canadians, and this is quite different from that of his lawyer "of Osgoode Hall." These uneducated speakers come from the neighbourhood of Barrie, Ontario, and offer such statements as these: "thay's a crick away down the track"; "I guess I've pooty nigh paralyzed his laigs"; "the hull consarn."

Such examples are, of course, conscious. But Campbell himself shows his Canadianism in speech by offering without comment or explanation such words as *lot, concession, township, bee, dug-out canoe.* That is, since he is writing about Canada, he has to employ Canadian English. What else?

One of the most amusing of Canadian novelists is Mrs. Everard Cotes, "Canada's Jane Austen." Although a great lover of England, she is well aware that neither her thinking nor her language are British. In *Cousin Cinderella: A Canadian Girl in London* (1908), she concentrates on emphasizing that "We are not Americans: we are Canadians." Unfortunately, in this book, she avoids Canadian speech, having given her comments on this subject in *An American Girl in London* (1891). Here she does note differences between British and American English, well aware that Canadian English shares these differences with American English. Her heroine asks for *crackers,* to be told that "biscuits is what you mean." She is severely criticized for using *rubbers* instead of "goloshes," *bangs* instead of a "fringe" (of hair), *valise* instead of "portmanteau," and *elevator* instead of "lift."

I have called this chapter "The Growth of Canadian English"; but it should really be called "Recognition of the Growth of Canadian English." Canadian English emerged some time ago; and English-speaking Canadians have been using it for many years. But recognition of a language is always long in coming; and, strangely enough, the people who are slowest to recognize a distinctive form of a language are often the ones who use it. It is really only within the past decade or so that much attention has been paid to the recognition of Canadian English by scholars interested in dictionaries, historical surveys, and so on. Indeed, in 1954, when the Canadian Linguistic Association was formed, one of its immediate aims was to investigate the possibility of a *Dictionary of Canadian English on Historical Principles.**

A historical survey of evidence such as I have given would be incomplete

---

*In 1967 the Lexicographical Centre for Canadian English at the University of Victoria produced and had published by W. J. Gage a *Dictionary of Canadianisms on Historical Principles.*

unless brought into the living present; and, to conclude my chapter, I give the views of a distinguished Canadian author on the nature of the language in which he gives expression to his thoughts and feelings. Here is what Earle Birney has written to me:

As a poet, I like to think I am an heir to the total vocabulary of the English-speaking world, but I know that in reality many of the words I think I choose are supplied by complex subconscious processes which are themselves in part determined by my Canadianism. The particular blend in my verse of what I elect to say and what, in a sense, is elected for me, constitutes whatever I have of a "voice," that unique "saying" of a personality which it is a poet's hope to achieve. My deliberate vocabulary ranges from Chaucerian archaisms like "mappe-mounde" to such coastal words as "clambake," and includes words like "coyote" and "chickenhawk" used to symbolize forces of destruction. But someone else has to point out to me that "lassooing," a word so much a part of me I never had to think to write it, must be a provincial distortion since it is unrecorded, in this spelling or pronunciation, in either the Oxford Universal or Webster's.

As a novelist attempting to create contemporary Canadian characters and make them talk, I have naturally tried much more consciously to catch whatever I feel to be essentially Canadian in speech rhythms and locutions. A novelist is not, however, a linguistic geographer, and must contrive to suggest, as by an occasional spelling device, the highly complex variations in speech he could not possibly record without resort to the IPA and consequent loss of all his readers (except perhaps the members of the Canadian Linguistic Association). In *Turvey*, especially, I tried to call up something of the really considerable range in speech levels and the rich variations in slang, localism, jargon and bawdry which swirled together from 1939 to 1945 to create an original stew of language, neither quite British nor quite American, though borrowing blandly and by right from both—the speech of the Canadian Army. But I am aware how far my characters talked short of the reality, and I wait hopefully for the Canadian novelist who will succeed, before it is too late and we are all talking like American radio announcers, in transporting into art the subtle, challenging distinctiveness and variety of our native speech.

15. New Forces: New Fiction
1880-1920

GORDON ROPER

THE CANADIAN FICTION LANDSCAPE was bleak to the Canadians who wrote about it in the early 1880's. Spring and the growing season seemed very slow in coming. In 1884, in *The Week*, J. E. Collins concluded that "in fiction, Canada makes a wretched showing," and many contemporaries would have agreed. Even in 1893, John Bourinot wrote in his *Our Intellectual Strength and Weakness*: "But if Canada can point to some creditable achievement in history, poetry, and essay writing . . . there is one respect in which Canadians have never won any marked success, and that is in the novel or romance." But the unfreezing of the imagination had begun as Bourinot wrote. Thomas G. Marquis looked back from 1912 in his essay on "Canadian Literature" in *Canada and Its Provinces* (vol. XII):

A new movement took place in Canadian poetical literature about the year 1880; some ten years after this date Canadian fiction entered upon a new stage of its development. It would be quite within the mark to take the definite year 1890 as the dividing line between the early writers, more or less provincial in their art, and the modern school, influenced by world standards.

After 1890 the number of Canadians who wrote fiction increased rapidly. The number of volumes of new fiction doubled in the eighties and quadrupled in the nineties. Technical competence became common. Subjects, tone, and treatment became more diversified. The work of a number of Canadian writers became well known in the English-speaking world, in American, British, and Canadian editions, and through translation in many other countries. Canadian writers created images of Canadian life that still linger in Canada, and persist even more firmly abroad.

Our knowledge of the fiction of those years has become fragmentary, partly because with the passing of time almost all of it has disappeared from library shelves, and partly because historians of Canadian literature, judging by literary standards current in mid-twentieth century university departments of English, have dismissed all but one or two books as less than first rate. Reading them in the spirit in which they were written, their contemporary readers judged differently. This chapter and the following two do not quarrel with either judgment; their primary aim is descriptive, not judicial. They present information and perspectives which may help us recover our lost knowledge of that fiction and of the Canada in which it was written. This chapter essays a description of the conditions which shaped the writing of fiction from 1880 to 1920. Chapter 16 continues with a panorama of the kinds of fiction written then, and chapter 17 concludes by presenting a small gallery of portraits of the writing careers of the most prominent fiction writers of the period. The generalizations they suggest are tentative, since they are based on a reading of only about two-thirds of the volumes published in those years, all that is at the moment available in Canadian and American libraries.

The remarkable increase in the writing of fiction in Canada during these years can be seen clearly when the figures for publication of fiction in book form up to 1880 are placed against those for the years 1880 to 1920. Up to 1880 about 150 Canadians published over 250 volumes of fiction. Almost two-thirds of these volumes appeared in the sixties and the seventies; about 100 of them were written by five writers: James De Mille, Thomas Chandler Haliburton, Mrs. Agnes Fleming, Mrs. Susanna Moodie, and Mary Anne Sadlier. In contrast, during the years 1880 to 1920, more than 400 Canadians published over 1,400 volumes of fiction. Charles G. D. Roberts, Gilbert Parker, Robert Barr, James Oxley, Theodore Roberts, and Margaret Marshall Saunders together accounted for more than 200 of this total, and fifteen other writers published from nine to twenty volumes each. These bare figures are for fiction published in book form in a day when most fiction saw the light of day first in magazine form, and many stories never reappeared in book form.

One of the reasons for this striking increase in the number of Canadians writing fiction was that in the years after 1890 the North American market for fiction expanded rapidly, and it became more feasible to add substantially to one's income, or even to make a living, by writing fiction. Of the very few who had earned some kind of living from fiction before 1880, the most widely read and most successful Canadians probably were May Agnes Fleming and James De Mille; both died in 1880. Mrs. Moodie had stopped writing fiction earlier. In the earlier eighties the only prolific Canadian writers of fiction were Agnes Machar, Margaret Murray Robertson, Mary Anne Sadlier, and her daughter Anna Teresa Sadlier. The picture began to change radically in the late eighties. From 1888 to the First World War years, about 50 Canadians established themselves as professional or semi-professional writers, and much of their work was fiction. About two-thirds of the fifty were men. A few of the fifty made comfortable livings by their pens; more supplemented incomes from journalism, editorial work, or free-lancing by writing fiction; some were ministers who wrote fiction to extend their ministry; some were wives of ministers or professional men; a few were teachers, lawyers, or doctors.

In almost every year from 1888 to 1914, one, two, or three young Canadian writers published his or her first volume of fiction. To list them is to present a roster of the most prolific Canadian writers of the period. In 1888 Roger Pocock and Clive Phillipps-Wolley published their first fictions in book form; Margaret Marshall Saunders, James Oxley, and Emily Weaver followed in 1889; Sara Jeannette Duncan in 1890; Lily Dougall, William McLennan, and Robert Barr in 1891; Gilbert Parker in 1892; Charles G. D. Roberts and Joanna Wood in 1894; Edward William Thomson, Cy Warman, and Jean McIlwraith in 1895; Ralph Connor (the Rev. Charles Gordon) and Ernest Thompson Seton in 1898; William Fraser, Virna Sheard, and Winifred Reeve in 1899; Arthur Stringer and Basil King in 1900; Norman Duncan and Adeline Teskey in 1901; Alice Jones and Ridgwell Cullum in 1903; John Price-Brown, Susan Jones, and Theodore Roberts in 1904; Robert Knowles, Marian Keith (Mrs. Mary Esther MacGregor), Marjorie Pickthall, Harvey O'Higgins, and Peggy Webling in 1905; Archibald McKishnie and Francis Pollock in 1906; Frederick William Wallace in 1907; Lucy Maude Montgomery, Nellie McClung, Frederick Niven, and Bertrand Sinclair in 1908; Stephen Leacock, Samuel Alexander White, and Hiram Cody in 1910; Robert Service and Frank Packard in 1911; Hulbert Footner and Alan Sullivan in 1913; and Robert Stead in 1914.

This list of those who began writing careers in these years represents only about an eighth of the number of Canadians who published volumes of fiction from 1880 to 1920. About 200 of the some 400 who published wrote only one or two volumes. Some of these were men or women in small communities who published one volume at their own expense, and then no more. Many of these solo flights were more earnest or ambitious than skilful, but among them are a few of the more interesting Canadian fictions of the period: Kathleen Blackburn's *The Dagmar Who Loved*, Frances Beynon's *Aleta Dey*, Margaret Brown's *My Lady of the Snows*, Martin Allerdale Grainger's *Woodsmen of the West*, the Lizars sisters' *Committed to His Charge*, Henry Cecil Walsh's *Bonhomme*, and *In the Village of Viger*, the single volume of tales Duncan Campbell Scott published before 1920.

Changing social, economic, and literary circumstances—inside and outside Canada—produced this wave of fiction writers. They differed primarily from the earlier fiction writers in that they were native born and bred. Almost all the earlier writers had been born and had grown up in England, Scotland, or Ireland before they had migrated to British North America. A few, and they were the most prolific, were native: the Nova Scotian Thomas Chandler Haliburton; May Agnes Fleming and James De Mille of New Brunswick; and Agnes Machar of Kingston. Most of those who wrote after 1880 were native born. Of those listed above, William Alexander Fraser, James Oxley, Alice Jones, Susan Jones, and Margaret Marshall Saunders were Nova Scotians. Charles G. D. Roberts, his brother, Theodore, and Hiram Cody were born in New Brunswick. Basil King and Lucy Maude Montgomery were born in Prince Edward Island. Lily Dougall, Anna Teresa Sadlier, William McLennan, Frank Packard, and Alan Sullivan were born in Montreal. Gilbert Parker, Sara Jeannette Duncan, Norman Duncan, Virna Sheard, Jean McIlwraith, Edward William Thomson, Marian Keith, Arthur Stringer, Harvey O'Higgins, Archibald McKishnie, Nellie McClung, Samuel Alexander White, Ralph Connor, Robert Knowles, Adeline Teskey, and Robert Stead were born in southern Ontario. Stephen Leacock, Robert Barr, Joanna Wood, Emily Weaver, Marjorie Pickthall, Bertrand Sinclair, and Ernest Thompson Seton were born in Great Britain, but were brought to Canada by their families while they were young. Among the few who came from Great Britain after schooling were Roger Pocock, Clive Phillipps-Wolley, Peggy Webling, and Robert Service. Cy Warman was born in Illinois, and Frederick Niven in Chile.

The earlier writers had migrated from the Old Country to one of the separate colonies in British North America. The new writers, however, were born in the Canadian provinces just before or after Confederation. The frontier had been pushed back earlier in the localities in which they grew up, and by the turn of the century being a writer in Canada had become, in Henry James's phrase, a much more "complex fate" than being a writer in a colony, or even in the United States. Most of the new writers grew up in a time of talk and writing about the need of a native literature to body forth a new nation. This had its influence on some of them. But from the subjects and values they expressed in their fiction, it appears that much the strongest influence was that of being native to a small town or rural community, in Nova Scotia, or New Brunswick, or Prince Edward Island, or southern Ontario.

The forces at play on a growing boy or girl in these small communities were not simple. There life focussed upon individuals and what they did, said, and felt, and how they did these things. Story telling was a natural way of talking. Homes were peopled not only with the living generations, but also with the forefathers, and strong filaments of feeling ran back to "the Old Country" and often south to "the States." The village yards and street ends ran out into the country or the woods, or down to water, greatly extending the imaginative world.

The young, imaginative individual also was apt to grow up in a world of print. Families in these small towns and on the adjacent farms often subscribed to one or more newspapers, church papers, or American or British magazines. Books were advertised in these periodicals, and were obtainable by mail order or from travelling book agents. George Doran, who left Canada early in these years to become a publisher, recalled in his *Chronicles of Barabbas* that in the eighties "good bookshops were to be found in every town of more than one thousand inhabitants. Toronto with a population of about 150,000 had at least a score of real book-stores owned and operated by highly intelligent booksellers." It has fewer now. He also estimated that in Canada "the book consumption was higher per capita than in any other country of the world with the possible exception of Australia." Moreover, literacy was particularly high in the homes in which Canadian writers grew up. Their fathers were ministers, lawyers, teachers, or doctors; a few were journalists; frequently their mothers had been school-teachers. Characteristically, their environment was one in which the power of the word—spoken and written—was taken for granted.

They grew up in a world of print, and much of that print was fiction. Daily and weekly newspapers, weekly story papers, religious publications, monthly magazines, and books, at all prices from 5 cents to $1.50 and up, provided the Canadian reader with short stories, fictional sketches, romances, and novels. The quality ranged from serious fiction (in hard covers, and paperback editions at 20 cents or less) by writers as different as George Eliot, Henry James, Thomas Hardy, and Zola, through high romance, historical romance, tales of everyday life, local colour stories, domestic sentimental fiction, boys' adventure books, girls' stories, pious moral tales, stories of detection, crime, Indians, and the West and Northwest. What was not sentimental was apt to be sensational, and often fiction was both sentimental and sensational.

The newspapers sometimes printed short stories in their daily editions, and ran serials along with short stories and the news in their weekly editions. They carried the work of well-known American and British writers, for the syndicates, which supplied stereotypes on a subscription basis to newspapers and magazines, often paid writers more for their work than the magazines which, in turn, often paid more than book publishers.

During the seventies and the eighties, the popularity of the English penny weekly, and the even more ubiquitous American counterpart, the story weekly, had declined very little. These mass-produced fiction papers were published in newspaper or smaller format, and sold for about 6 cents in Canada. They had been developed to appeal to the great mass audience which had grown steadily throughout the Victorian years. Even in the mid century, the three English penny-weeklies, the *Family Herald*, the *London*

Journal, and *Reynolds Miscellany* together issued over a million copies a week, and probably were read by some three million people. Hundreds of periodicals imitated them in format and content, ranging in appeal from the pious to the lurid. In the United States, the most successful of the story weeklies was Bonner's *New York Ledger,* and it too had its hundreds of competitors and imitators. These story papers advertised themselves vigorously and they also boasted of how highly they paid their name authors. Their circulation spread throughout the Canadian provinces. The Montreal *Family Herald and Weekly Star,* founded in 1869, and the Toronto *Saturday Night,* founded in 1887, were Canadian versions of these mass-circulation fiction papers. Nellie McClung, in her autobiography *Clearing in the West,* recalled what the *Family Herald and Weekly Star* fiction meant to her and members of her family when she was young on a new Manitoba farm:

But I was telling about our enjoyment of the weekly newspaper. The continued story was really the high point of interest for we had a whole week to speculate on the development of the plot. There was one story that shook our neighbourhood to its foundation. It was called *Saved, or the Bride's Sacrifice,* and concerned two beautiful girls,—Jessie, fair as a lily, and Helen with blue black hair, and lustrous eyes as deep as the night. They each loved Herbert, and Herbert, being an obliging young fellow, not wishing to hurt anyone's feelings, married one secretly and hurriedly by the light of a guttering candle, in a peasant's hut, (Jessie), and one openly with a peal of organ and general high jinks, at her father's baronial castle, (Helen).

This naturally brought on complications. There were storms, shipwrecks, and secret meetings in caves, with the tide rising over the rocks and curlews screaming in the blast, there were plottings and whisperings; a woman with second sight and one with the evil eye. And did we love it?

I can remember staggering along through the snow behind the sleigh reading the story as I walked, and when I drew near home, members of the family would come out to shout at me to hurry.

Most of the fiction in these story paper weeklies was in the great popular tradition of the sentimental romance, laced with sensationalism. The black and white characters, humble or high, pure or villainous; the dying scenes, the orphans, the lost heirs, the seductions, betrayals, the lost wills, the high confrontations, the tears; the elegant language that was spoken only in fiction of this kind or on the mid-century melodramatic stage; the fine moral sentiments—all were designed to produce a series of strong emotional responses in the willing reader. Some of the young Canadians who later wrote fiction themselves learned about life in fiction from these weeklies.

A wide variety of quality monthly magazines also brought the work of skilful and complex fiction writers into Canadian homes. From England came magazines such as *Blackwood's, Chambers's Journal, Cornhill, London Illustrated News* (weekly), *Macmillan's, Temple-Bar, St. James,* or *Belgravia.* And from the United States came, among many others, *Harper's*

Monthly, Atlantic Monthly, the *North American Review, Lippincott's,* the old *Scribner's Monthly,* and the *Century.* The new issues of these monthlies were advertised in Canadian periodicals, and often were reviewed as if they were new books, since much of the finest fiction and non-fiction appeared in their pages before appearing in book form.

Although both British and American magazines circulated in Canada, the American were more to the taste of the Canadian reader. Sara Jeannette Duncan wrote in *The Week* in 1886 that "the British magazines could not compete in numbers, liveliness, variety, and price with the Americans," and another writer in *The Week* asserted that the American magazines out-sold the British 100 to 1 in Canada. This preference for the North American way of seeing things and saying things is manifest later in the fiction written by Canadians who were growing up in the seventies and eighties. But the preference for American magazines does not mean that they rarely read the fiction of British writers, for the American magazines published the fiction of all the prominent British writers, frequently simultaneously with its appearance in British magazines. The quality American magazines also were rich in local colour stories and sketches of New England, the Midwest, the South, and the far West, and the obvious popularity of these stories must have encouraged young Canadian writers to use their own native experience in the fiction they submitted to the editors of American magazines. The young Canadian also could have learned from the pages of the quality American magazines of the literary personalities, the literary trends, and the critical battles in the literary centres, for they contained excellent book reviews, news about the literary great, and critical essays about the warfare beween the new Realists and the old Idealists, about the nature of fiction, and about nationalism in literature. Literature mattered in these pages, and in them an author was a man of high consequence.

Although in the seventies and eighties readers read much of their fiction in periodical form, books also were available easily. Few volumes of new fiction came directly from Great Britain, since the British publishers were mono-polistic and maintained high prices, and their cheaper reprints were anti-cipated and undersold in Canada by American reprints. New fiction, including the new work of the popular British writers, was published in the United States at about $1.50, and quickly went into reprints at a dollar and less. Consequently the Canadian provinces were flooded by books from the United States, at prices from $1.50 down to the 5 cents and 10 cents of the Beedle dime novels and their imitators. One of the results was that very few volumes of fiction by Canadians were published first in Canada, other than those published by Lovell in Montreal—except, of course, for those published at the writer's own expense by his local publishers.

The importation of fiction in book form from the United States increased greatly after 1875 when unorthodox new publishers disrupted the American book trade by publishing mass editions of fiction, including the best recent English fiction, at 5 cents, 10 cents, or 20 cents, in paper covers. This publishing revolution was led partly by young men who had come from Canada to the greener fields of the United States: the Belford brothers and James Clarke from Toronto, John W. Lovell from Montreal, and George and Norman Munro from Halifax. Their cut-rate competition caused a rush among established American publishers to build competing ten-cent libraries. The low price of these libraries was made possible by mass printing, by new means of distribution, and by the use of foreign books unprotected by copyright. The established publishers also drew on their backlog of old fiction. When the publishing of foreign books not protected by copyright in the United States was reduced greatly by the Chace Act in 1891, and when the industry over-extended itself, the cheap libraries declined. Meanwhile, in the late seventies and throughout the eighties they placed fiction from the highest to the meanest quality within the price of all readers. Sara Jeannette Duncan once won a school literary prize of ten dollars and spent it all on 10 cent books, and many of the young Canadians who later would write fiction must have spent their money in the same way. This publishing warfare made book publishers most reluctant to risk the work of new writers, unless that work had appeared first in magazines and had received some critical notice. On the other hand, the magazines were on the hunt for manuscripts and paid well for them. So the young writer fashioned his stories primarily for the magazine editors and readers.

This world of print provided the early reading and fictional models of the Canadians who began to write fiction in the late eighties. But their writing also was moulded by their years of schooling and professional training. One of the forces which moved them out from their native communities was the desire for more education. Of the writers before 1880, De Mille and Haliburton were among the few who had university training. But a striking number of the writers from 1880 to 1920 were university graduates. Of the group of some fifty listed early in this chapter, twenty were graduates of universities, mostly of Canadian universities. Four were graduates of Normal School, two of art academies, and six had private school education. It may be that the university years inhibited as much as encouraged them as writers, for the standard Canadian university training then was classical, from alien professors who were steeped in the past of other lands, and usually were above such sub-literary things as romances and novels. The university student often learned more outside a classroom than in it. At least the university years were further years of training in a world where the word, written and spoken, was a natural and powerful instrument.

Their more intensive and practical training in writing came after their formal education. Many of them moved on from the universities into apprentice work on Toronto, Montreal, Halifax, or Detroit newspapers. There they made a mark as they began to freelance, and then they moved on again. Like their contemporaries from the villages and the small towns of upper New York state, Ohio, Indiana, Michigan, Illinois, and the West, they were pulled to the great centres of publishing and writing, New York, Boston, or London, to work on newspapers and magazines as reporters, correspondents, or editors. Most of those who became prolific professional writers migrated: Robert Barr, Norman Duncan, Charles G. D. Roberts, Theodore Roberts, Sara Jeannette Duncan, Gilbert Parker, Arthur Stringer, Harvey O'Higgins, Edward William Thomson, Roger Pocock, Frederick Niven, Agnes Laut. A few, like Lucy Maude Montgomery or Robert Stead, worked only on Canadian papers. Others left the universities for the ministry— Ralph Connor, Hiram Cody, Basil King, and Robert Knowles—and moved about the country widely in their work as missionaries and ministers. Many of those who wrote only two or three books also were journalists, or ministers, or ministers' wives or daughters.

The forces which caused this migration of young Canadians to New York and London were multiple, but probably the most powerful came from the radical changes in the magazine world in the closing years of the century. New editors, Edward Bok, S. S. McClure, Frank Munsey, and George Lorimer in the United States, and George Newnes and William T. Stead in Great Britain, used the invention of photoengraving, the rapid increase in commercial advertising, and mechanical improvements in rapid, cheap printing to develop a new journalism for various segments of the mass audience. They realized that with large circulation they could make more money by selling advertising space than by selling individual copies of the magazine. They launched 15 cent and 10 cent weekly magazines such as the *Ladies' Home Journal, Munsey's, Cosmopolitan, McClure's, Collier's, Scribner's Monthly, Everybody's, Outdoors,* or *Saturday Evening Post.* These new editors broke through the unwritten rules of taste set by the editors of the genteel *Century* or *Atlantic Monthly,* or by the narrowly moral denominational press. They filled their magazines with vigorous action fiction of politics, life in the slums, labour strife, the plains and mountains of the West, high finance, along with muckraking articles exposing the sore places in North American life. They hunted out writers and manuscripts; frequently they commissioned special articles and stories, and they paid excellent prices In the nineties the competition from the new magazines raised prices for contributions, and increased greatly the number of places where one could place manuscripts. It encouraged a writer's market.

In Great Britain comparable new magazines also invited more worldly and masculine fiction. New magazines such as the *Strand, Windsor, Pal*

Mall, or *The Idler* competed with the established magazines and appealed to wider audiences. The stir in the magazine world was reflected on the Canadian scene by the establishment of somewhat similar (although quieter) magazines, *Dominion* (1888), *Canadian Magazine* (1893), which made it a special policy to publish Canadian writers, *Maclean's* (1896), or *Westminster* (1897), which added a more liberal tone to the denominational press.

Revolution was stirring also in the book world. In Great Britain a demand for the triple-decker at a high price had come from the great circulating libraries, and had led publishers to confine their fiction publishing largely to the work of well-known popular writers favoured by the libraries. They risked publication of an unknown, young writer only if his manuscript seemed to promise exceptional popular success. In 1894 the subscription libraries dropped their demand for the triple-decker, and publishers began to issue new fiction at six shillings, a price stabilized shortly after by the adoption of a net system of pricing. A wave of young publishers appeared on the scene to hunt out and develop new writing talent. In the United States the passage of the Chace Act in 1891, and the decline of the cheap book industry, enabled the American writer to compete equally with British writers. New techniques of production and distribution were adopted, and new life ran through the publishing houses.

Book production increased greatly in these years. Helmutt Lehmann-Haupt in his *The Book in America* states: "There was not too great difference in the total number of titles published in 1869 and, again, in 1880. But by 1890 the annual output was about doubled, and tripled by 1900, statistical proof of the enormous increase in volume which American publishing experienced at the turn of the century." The publishing of fiction in book form increased even more sharply, until in 1901 more fiction in book form was published in the United States than in any one year before—or since: 2,234 titles out of a total of 8,141 titles of all books. Total annual production for all books climbed until 1910, although the percentage of fiction fell off. The war years ended the boom. But throughout the 1890's and the 1900's, publishing was profitable. George Doran estimated that in the mid-nineties "it was possible to publish fiction, pay 10% royalty, and make a little profit on a 1,200 to 1,500 copies sale; at 5,000 the publisher was in clover." Publishers were on the hunt for books to print. In the book world, as in the magazine world, it was a writer's market in these years.

So the ambitious Canadian writer was attracted to the great fiction markets in the United States or Great Britain. The copyright situation after 1891 in those countries made it most advantageous for him to contract either for first publication in the United States or first publication in Great Britain with "simultaneous publication" in the United States. Many of the great Anglo-American publishing houses had offices on both sides of the Atlantic, or had working arrangements with trans-Atlantic firms. With British and American copyright secured, the British or American firms usually arranged for publication in Canada through an agent in Toronto or Montreal, and so also secured Canadian copyright protection.

The pull to New York or London was a strong one; there was little in the Canadian literary or publishing scene to counter it. Big publishers were few in Canada, and they were concentrating in Toronto. They published little fiction on their own initiative; what they did issue often was printed at the writer's expense, just as small local firms in the various provinces usually printed books at the local author's expense. The large Toronto publisher, William Briggs of Toronto, served the Methodist connection well with sermons, lives of the church fathers, travels by missionaries, and non-fiction of more general or technical interest. But up to 1895 it published only about one Canadian novel or romance a year; from 1895 to 1920 it published on the average three or four a year, mostly of a religious or moral tone. Concurrently, however, as the agent of New York or London firms, it imported stereotypes or sheets of Anglo-American successes and issued Canadian editions under the Toronto imprint. From 1896 to 1917, as agents, Briggs, Copp Clark, Morang, and Revell's Toronto branch of their Chicago–New York firm together issued, under their imprints in Toronto, from 250 to 300 volumes of fiction by some fifty of the best-selling British, American, and Canadian writers. Few contemporary fiction writers of any merit or popularity were overlooked. Thus the Canadian editions of the work of the most prolific Canadian fiction writers from 1880 to 1920 usually were reprints of an earlier edition published in New York, Boston, or London. As Robert Barr said in an article "Literature in Canada" in the *Canadian Magazine* (November 1899): "Toronto will recognize the successful Canadian writer when he comes back from New York or London, and will give him a dinner when he doesn't need it."

Canadian firms occasionally did take the initiative in publishing the work of Canadian writers. The Westminster Press of Toronto issued *Black Rock* and *The Sky Pilot* by Ralph Connor, after they had requested him to write the first as a serial for their magazine, to stir up interest in Western missions. After the turn of the century, Canadian firms became more enterprising, especially the new firm of McClelland and Stewart. But the market for book fiction in Canada was not large. The editor of the *Westminster Magazine* in the November 1902 issue wrote:

"Four thousand copies is a good sale for a novel in Canada," said Mr. Copp, "and I gather that the average is quite under two thousand. Of course, there are a few books that have passed the twenty thousand mark. Gilbert Parker's *The Right of Way* in cloth last season and in paper this summer was one; and Ralph Connor's *The Man from Glengarry* in cloth only passed twenty-five thousand in Canada within ten months of its publication. But that is a rare experience with a publisher."

The market for magazine fiction in Canada also was small. Apart from the numerous religious periodicals, the Canadian writer could look only to a few secular Canadian magazines such as the *Canadian Magazine, Maclean's,* or *Saturday Night,* and a few weekly newspapers like the Montreal *Family Herald and Weekly Star.*

The relative smallness of the book and magazine market for Canadian fiction was primarily the result of the size and composition of the Canadian population. In the nineties the population of Canada was approaching the five million mark. But of those five million, about a third were not English-speaking. Of those who were English-speaking, in spite of a relatively high literacy rate, a number were illiterate or barely literate. Many, literate and illiterate, were completely occupied in making their living in a new land. Among the literate, some assumed that any new fiction by a Canadian was apt to be less interesting than one by a New York or London writer. Because of the sectionalism of the new country, many a Nova Scotian reader naturally looked east or south for his reading, not hinterland to Ontario or the West, while the Ontario reader was apt to ignore Nova Scotian writing as he looked east or south.

Moreover, among the Canadian reading public, two influential elements looked down upon fiction with attitudes varying from aloofness to abhorrence. To many of the most highly educated, trained in the classical tradition, fiction at best was merely popular entertainment, or at worst something that debased public taste. In his *Our Intellectual Strength and Weakness* (1893), John Bourinot wrote:

I do not for one depreciate the influence of good fiction on the minds of a reading community like ours; it is inevitable that a busy people, and especially women distracted with household cares, should always find that relief in this branch of literature which no other reading can give them; and if the novel has then become a necessity of the times in which we live, at all events I hope Canadians, who may soon venture into the field, will study the better models, endeavour to infuse some originality into their creations and plots, and not bring the Canadian fiction of the future to that low level to which the school of Realism in France, and in a minor degree in England and the United States, would degrade the novel and story of every-day life.

Bourinot was addressing the Fellows of the Royal Society of Canada and probably few of them would have disagreed with his high view that the end of fiction was to elevate rather to entertain, that a good history was much more valuable than the best of fiction, that no Canadian had written good fiction, that if and when one did he would be an imitator of a great English (or American) writer. They might also have shared his apprehension that a sub-literary jungle of cheap fiction, fertilized by the commercialism of publishers, was growing up around Canadian readers.

These views, however, were more tolerant than those expressed hotly in many evangelical newspapers and magazines, and delivered from pulpits. A fiction was a lie, inspired by the Father of Lies, unless, of course, it was a "parable" or "allegory" to inculcate moral views. Popular fiction was denounced because it made vice attractive, and made violence seem natural. It spread irreligious, free-thinking, or undemocratic (or democratic) sentiments in seductive form. Many lay members of the fundamentalist flock were equally suspicious of fiction. Some would open a new book to the title-page, and if the title included the word "romance" or "novel," would read no further; if the title claimed the book to be a "tale of real life" or of "everyday life" they might venture on. Some parents prohibited the reading of all fiction to their children; some permitted the reading only of what came from church-sponsored presses and libraries. Some permitted it only on weekdays. When the Toronto Public Library opened in 1882, the guardians of public morality and the public purse tried to prevent fiction from being placed on the shelves. They argued that fiction led readers into sloth; it gave them irresponsible notions about life; it sapped the moral fibre. Or they argued that since it was mere entertainment, public money should not be squandered on providing it free for library readers.

From the fervent evangelical, the idealistic, or the intellectual view, there was cause for concern; for fiction had become endemic in the English-reading world. Some of it did express new and disturbing ideas. Some of it was "cheap and nasty." But the soaring production and sale of fiction in North America and in Great Britain make it clear that those who feared fiction were not the majority of the reading public, not even in what H. L. Mencken later called the North American "Bible Belt." The audience for fiction in Canada had been expanding in the years before 1900, and with the influx of some three million immigrants into the country around the turn of the century, with a wave of prosperity and expansion, with the growth of cities, with the greatly increased numbers of Canadians writing about the Canadian scene, the market for fiction in Canada grew rapidly. Fiction was placed on the shelves of the Toronto Public Library, and on the shelves of Canadian town libraries as they opened under the Carnegie sun. Fiction-printing newspapers and magazines increased in numbers and circulation, and the publication of fiction in book form, inside Canada and outside, rose markedly.

The nationalistic mood which led Prime Minister Sir Wilfrid Laurier to predict that the twentieth century would belong to Canada led a number of Canadians to make special demands on Canadian fiction writers. In Canadian periodicals and in public speeches they called for the creation of a unique Canadian literature which would promote a national consciousness.

A few Canadian fiction writers attempted to respond to this patriotic call. But it is one thing to call for the writing of the Great Canadian Novel, and another thing to write it. The patriotic demand for a national literature may also have been influenced by the campaign for a nationalistic American literature in American periodicals earlier in the century. But even at mid-century Hawthorne had pin-pointed the difficulties of North American literary patriotism when he wrote "We have so much country that we have no country," and added that when a writer attempted to make a land with "no limits and no oneness . . . a matter of the heart, everything falls away except one's native State."

By the end of the century, young Canadian writers could have learned from their American contemporaries in American magazines that a literature should be literature first and only then "national" by being at once local and universal. Certainly in this period, for most Canadian writers everything fell away except the different localities in which they had been born and raised; for the limits of their newly formed political union were much less clear, and their confederation had much less "oneness" than the American Union. Moreover, there was no market for "Canadian" nationalism in the great publishing centres in New York or London, although there was a lively market for stories about the past or present in French Canada, maritime Nova Scotia, New Brunswick, domestic Prince Edward Island, rural Ontario, or the various localities of the great West.

Growing up in this complex of international and domestic circumstances, the Canadian fiction writer naturally assumed concepts of the nature of fiction then common in the English-speaking world. Most British and American fiction writers in the later nineteenth century assumed that the first end of fiction was either to entertain or to instruct. If it instructed, it did so most effectively by entertaining, that is, by engaging a reader emotionally. Consequently the writer had to establish and maintain a close relation with his reader. Trollope had said: "It is the first necessity of the novelist's position that he make himself pleasant." Wilkie Collins's precept was: "Make 'em laugh; make 'em cry; make 'em wait." Even a writer as deeply concerned with the fine art of fiction as Henry James felt a primary obligation to be interesting to his reader.

To be entertaining, a fiction above all had to be a "good story." Readers wanted a moving account of "what happens," told in a way that made them feel part of that happening. They liked the "strong situation," and they liked episode after episode of "telling incidents." They wanted characters (their reviewers said) who were "life-like," by which they meant characters who were much larger, simpler, more ideal, than in life—characters with whom they could identify strongly. They wanted a setting which gave them the pleasures of the exotic and unknown, or the pleasures of recognition of the familiar; in either case, the function of setting was to reinforce the emotional effect of the action. They wanted a structure that engaged them fully, that aroused suspense, that had sudden, surprising turns, and an exciting pace. They wanted a conclusion that resolved the conflict and rewarded the good with fortune and happiness, or, occasionally, with the pleasure of renunciation or atonement. They liked a style that brought out their emotional response.

If one can judge from the prefaces of authors and the reviews and the articles on fiction in contemporary magazines, few late nineteenth-century readers were concerned with the art of the fiction they read—nor are most readers today. What they were concerned with was the qualities of the book; the vitality; the morality, especially the "purity"; the nobility and the villainy; the heroic and the pathetic or the comic; the variety, pace, contrast, and intensity. They judged a fiction by how strongly and frequently it moved them; in a word, they liked melodrama—sentimental or sensational, or a fusion of both. When the term "melodrama" is used in this chapter it is not intended to demean but to describe a literary form in which all elements are organized to produce intense emotional effect in the reader. Melodrama was an all-pervasive art form in the nineteenth century. The sub-structure of much of even the most serious fiction was melodramatic. It was a strong element in nineteenth-century painting, music, opera, sculpture, architecture, and the graphic and decorative arts. The views of God, man, and the universe—with emphasis upon sin, guilt, judgment, hell and damnation—which nineteenth-century churchgoers heard from their pulpits were often melodramatic. Political feelings (such as the emotion about "Greater Britain" and "Soldiers of the Queen," or President Roosevelt's "bully little war" with Spain) were apt to be melodramatic. The contemporary battles between rugged individualism and social conscience were expressed in melodramatic form.

Some fictions were simple melodramas, composed of exciting, fast-paced action, performed by black and white characters, each with a limited set of stock feelings, and occurring in front of an appropriate setting. Melodrama also was used to heighten the other basic modes of the fiction of the day, the "romance" and the "novel." The titles of most fictions then were double-barrelled; the second half of the title often told the reader whether he should expect a "romance" or a "novel," or a "tale of everyday life." The term "romance" promised the reader he would get a picture of life unencumbered by the way things occur every day. It presented life as one would like it to be, or as it ought to be—life reconstituted to satisfy one's fantasies. It often was set in the past, or in the future, or in some glamorous level of society or in some far-away land. Its language was more elaborate, more elegant, or more lyrical than everyday speech. Its characters were much larger than life, and its action usually was erotic in that it concentrated on the mating process, opening with the meeting of a young hero and heroine, emoting with them through the difficulties which inevitably separated them, and ending by their union.

The "novel," on the other hand, tried to present a faithful picture of everyday life, of the here and now, to offer a fictional world where places, people, and events were recognizably like the life the writer and reader knew. What the writer thought life really was like, of course, determined the "realism" of his fiction, and many a tale of domestic tribulation, of put-upon piety sentimentally conceived, was labelled and passed with sentimental readers as a "novel." To the more sophisticated writer and reader a novel meant a fiction in which the author analysed human behaviour and its motivations, and discussed the moral and social consequences of such behaviour. Or it might embody some moral or social concept. Usually in a novel the narrator told his story in a quiet, middle style, often with a tone of detachment or even of irony. It usually contained passages of dialogue in which the writer tried to catch the diction and rhythm of actual speech. While the romance usually focussed on a central group of hero, heroine, and villain (or villainess), the novel more often had a wide range of central characters, and although the action often centred on the mating process, it also was apt to concern itself with other human activities—the process of growing up, of making a living, of achieving success; or it portrayed the clash between generations, the iniquity of institutions, or a growth in spiritual awareness. The end of the romance was to entertain, either by superficial excitements or by appeals to the deeper fantasies. The end of the novel was sometimes to please by stirring the sense of recognition; more often it was to instruct, by embodying some religious or ethical truth, or by dramatizing some social evil, or in the hands of writers like George Eliot, Meredith, William Dean Howells, or Henry James by enlarging the reader's awareness and understanding of the complexities of the human condition.

The modes of romance and novel often mingled in one fiction, especially in the work of the unpractised writer and in the work of the sophisticated professional. Romancers dominated the field of Anglo-American fiction, and novelists coloured their views of ordinary life with sentiment or heightened it with melodrama. The prevalence of what George Meredith called the "rose-pink" and the "blood and glory" pictures of life led to the biggest literary battle of the last quarter of the nineteenth century. The opposing forces were the "realists" on one side and on the other the romanticists and several varieties of "idealists," with a few under the banner of "Art for Art's Sake" skirmishing against both sides. Reviews and articles on fiction in the magazines in the late seventies, eighties, and nineties identified William Dean Howells and Henry James as the leaders of the realists among Anglo-American writers. Howells and James both felt that the reading public was being debauched by fiction that collectively could be published under the title *Slop, Silly Slop.* They believed that fiction could and should be one of the high forms of literature. Howells' credo was that fiction ought to picture ordinary life, and that it must picture that life truthfully, without rhetoric, without melodrama, and without preaching. James was in fundamental agreement with his friend, although he had a different feeling for what was "interesting" in life. Both of them had an intensely moral concept of art in that they believed that its end was to heighten the quality of living. Both believed that a writer could be truthful only by writing out of his own experience of the life he had observed. They encouraged young writers to rely on personal experience—local as it might be—by the example of their own stream of fiction and of reviews and articles on fiction. Howells played a vital part in encouraging regional writing in North America by his preference for local colour and realism in the fiction he chose for the *Atlantic Monthly* during his editorship from 1871 to 1880, and by his influence on the editorial taste of *Harper's Magazine* from 1885 to 1920. As the dean of American letters he gave personal encouragement to young realists as diverse as Hamlin Garland, Stephen Crane, Harold Frederick, Frank Norris, and Theodore Dreiser. This campaign for truthfulness in fiction inclined some young Canadian writers to be anti-romantic and more self-reliant. The fiction of Sara Jeannette Duncan in particular, and in varying degrees of Robert Barr, Frances Beynon, Arthur Campbell, Francis Grey, William Fraser, Arthur Stringer, Robert Stead, Harvey O'Higgins, and Bertrand Sinclair was liberated by the work of earlier British and American realists.

The realists were strongly opposed by a large, diverse, and influential force of writers, reviewers, and readers who denounced the view of life presented by the realists as narrow, mean, pessimistic, and degrading. They argued that the realists looked down, not up, that they showed the animal in man rather than the angel. They feared that Howells and James were opening their optimistic, genteel, middle-class, provincial Anglo-Saxon world to a flood of French realism by Balzac, Flaubert, the de Goncourt brothers, De Maupassant, and Zola, with all its "cynicism," "decadence," and "nasty emphasis" upon sex. An unsystematic sampling of the reviews and articles on fiction in Canadian periodicals during these years suggests that the bulk of Canadian opinion was on the side of the conservatives. Canadian writers like Gilbert Parker and the Protestant ministers who wrote fiction championed romanticism and "idealism," as they understood "idealism."

Comprehension of the feelings and concepts expressed in this literary battle is essential to an understanding of what made the Canadian fiction of this period acceptable to its readers. For idealism—the habit of judging things in the light of how they ought to be—was pervasive among writers and most segments of the Anglo–North American audience. It had many forms, not all compatible, ranging from a raw "Boost; Don't Knock" western attitude at one extreme to various codes of Christian perfectibility or Brahmin moral tone at the other. Both Howells and James were realists because they were idealists in the old American grain of tough-minded, pragmatic humanism. They believed in the self-reliance of the individual, but they believed also that the individual achieved stature through his relation with other individuals in a social milieu. Along with their opponents, they assumed that art is communication—a social matter—not self-expression. Civilized men (and the artist to them was the most civilized of men) willingly inhibited their writing to avoid giving needless offence to others. They accepted the fact that the reading audience, especially of the quality magazines in which most of their work first appeared, was home-centred, and therefore in addressing their readers certain decencies were to be observed as one would observe them in a dinner-table or fireside conversation. One limitation that many English and American writers accepted was that of never bringing a blush to the cheek of that finest flower of the genteel tradition, a young lady.

The quality family magazines and the old-established publishing houses in Boston, New York, and London were dominated by editors and publishers of the genteel tradition, who had a paternalistic attitude towards their readers. The denominational presses dominated another large segment of the publishing world, especially in Canada. The inhibitions of publishers added to the personal inhibitions cultivated in the individual writer by his own particular brand of idealistic upbringing, and wove a network of restraint through much of the fiction of the day. The general feeling was that this was the way it should be; for "the more smiling aspects of life"—in expression as well as in material—to most Americans truly represented life in North America, where they believed life goes so much more "unterribly" than it does in the countries of the Old Land. But life in North America and in Great Britain was changing rapidly during this period, and here and there strands of this network loosened as new publishers and new magazines began to compete for the mass markets. More freedom in attitude, theme, and range of expression is evident in the work of Canadian writers after 1900.

These major assumptions about the nature of fiction were the guide-lines within which Canadians wrote. The matter and manner of their fiction were shaped by the kinds of fiction that were prominent, and waxed and waned in popularity, during these years in the Anglo-North American world. Among the books still widely read in their formative years were the various kinds of fictions by Scott, Cooper, Thackeray, Hawthorne, Charlotte Brontë, Dickens, Bulwer-Lytton, Collins, Reade, and George Eliot; for whenever a fiction achieved popularity in the nineteenth century it was read by more than one generation and by more than one segment of the reading public.

Among the ingredients that sustained the popularity of the fiction of these

English and American writers was their sentimental and sensational melodrama. These melodramatic qualities were singled out and amplified in the work of many British and North American writers in the fifties, the sixties and the seventies. Some of the most widely known books of those decades— and they remained in print in cheap editions into the twentieth century—were the sentimental melodramas of the hearth, or the more sensational melodramas of high life. Hundreds of thousands of readers shed tears over the simple pieties of Elizabeth Wetherell's *The Wide, Wide World* and Maria Cummins' *The Lamplighter*, or the more elegant pieties of Augusta Jane Evans's *Beulah* or Elizabeth Phelps's *The Gates Ajar*; and hundreds of thousands thrilled to the feverish passion and sensation in Mrs. Wood's *East Lynne*, Miss Braddon's *Lady Audley's Secret*, Mrs. E.D.E.N. Southworth's *The Fatal Marriage, Ishmael*, and *Self-Raised*, Ouida's *Under Two Flags*, Miss Evans's *St. Elmo*, or E. P. Roe's *Barriers Burned Away*. These domestic sentimental melodramas and the sensational tales of higher society were written largely by women, and read largely—but certainly not only— by women. Their sensationalism contributed to the mistrust of fiction by the more sober-minded, and led religious publishing houses in Great Britain, the United States, and Canada to encourage the writing of pious fiction to jam the inflow of such unnerving romances into the homes of the faithful. By the mid-eighties this sensational kind became embroidered with more sophisticated elements. A number of Canadian women had considerable success with these melodramas—notably May Agnes Fleming, the Sadliers, mother and daughter, and Margaret Murray Robertson. The sensational kind was imitated most by Canadian writers in the seventies and eighties, and faded out in the nineties into other forms; the pious kind in various sublimations goes on forever.

The early sixties also saw the proliferation of simpler action melodramas for the adolescent and older male audience who had learned of the frontier from Cooper and Simms and Davy Crockett, when the new Beedle dime novels included in their earlier numbers Anna Stephen's *Malaeska; or, The Indian Wife of the White Hunter*, and Edward Ellis's *Seth Jones; or, The Captives of the Frontier*. The yellowbacks not only made scouts, redskins, outlaws, and Indian hunters ubiquitous, they also made bandits and detectives popular with the enormous success of their "Old Sleuth," "Old Cap Collier," and "Nick Carter" series. Books like Wilkie Collins's *The Woman in White* or *The Moonstone*, and Dickens's *The Mystery of Edwin Drood* offered more complex mystery stories. The mystery structure probably had become the most common structural pattern for nineteenth-century fiction, serious as well as light. Sinister characters from the mysterious East were frequent. By the eighties the Pinkerton man and the amateur detective often appeared as minor characters. The detective moved into the centre of the stage with the blaze of popularity of Conan Doyle's Sherlock Holmes stories in the late eighties and early nineties. In the late nineties Ernest Hornung's Raffles, the gentleman-cracksman, became a familiar character. The popularity of specialized forms of crime fiction—suspense stories of the underworld, of private detectives, and of international intrigue—increased in the first years of the twentieth century. The Canadians Arthur Stringer, Frank Packard, and William Fraser were major contributors of mystery and crime stories to the popular magazines, and after their stories appeared in book form they were reprinted frequently in Burt or Grosset & Dunlap cheap reprint editions.

The novel of social protest or problem novel was another kind of fiction widely read in the third quarter of the nineteenth century by the more serious-minded, and by many others also, for it was often as melodramatic as a romance of high life or as exciting as a crime story. This fiction, written to trouble the reader's complacency and his conscience, was as various in theme as Disraeli's *Coningsby*, Thackeray's *Vanity Fair*, Newman's *Loss and Gain*, Kingsley's *Alton Locke*, Dickens's *Bleak House* or *Hard Times*, Mrs. Stowe's *Uncle Tom's Cabin*, Mrs. Gaskell's *North and South*, Reade's *It's Never too Late to Mend* or *Hard Cash*, T. S. Arthur's *Ten Nights in a Barroom*, Mark Twain's *The Gilded Age*, or George Eliot's *Middlemarch*. Controversial fiction often went into edition after edition. Probably more than six and a half million copies of *Uncle Tom's Cabin* in book form alone were sold on both sides of the Atlantic and in translations. *Ginx's Baby* (1870), an attack on English complacency about slum conditions by the Canadian born and bred John Edward Jenkins, appeared in more than thirty-six editions.

Fiction with a purpose was more widely written and read in the socially troubled years from 1880 to 1920. One of the most influential books of the late nineteenth century was Henry George's treatise *Progress and Poverty* (1879) on the relation of capital, labour, and production to land, and its arguments were debated in many fictions. Edward Bellamy's *Looking Backward* (1888) was one of the most successful of more than one hundred Utopian fictions. The strikes that erupted in the mounting struggle between capital and labour were dramatized in stories such as John Hay's *The Breadwinners*, or, more effectively, in *The Mutable Many* by the Canadian Robert Barr, or *A Hazard of New Fortunes* by William Dean Howells. Problems of faith became insistent for many under the pressure of social and intellectual changes, and created an appetite for fiction on religious themes. Among the most widely read and imitated of the religious fictions were General Lew Wallace's historical melodrama of Christians and circuses, *Ben Hur* (1880), Mrs. Humphry Ward's much more intellectual study of loss of faith, *Robert Elsmere* (1888), and one of the most popular fictions ever published in the United States, the Reverend Charles M. Sheldon's *In His*

Steps (1897). *In His Steps* was followed in the next year by Ralph Connor's first success, *Black Rock*, and in the year after that by the equally popular *The Sky Pilot*. Connor's stories were only the most popular of many fictions on religious themes by Canadians.

Another area of disturbing social change was that of the status of women and the relation of the sexes. Henry James's young American girl, Daisy Miller, was discussed widely as a disagreeable (or agreeable) new phenomenon in the early eighties. The "New Woman" began to appear in British and American fiction in the late eighties. The appearance of Ibsen's Nora in *A Doll's House* in the early nineties in England and America intensified the discussion. Varieties of the New Woman appeared in Hardy's *Tess of the D'Urbervilles*, Sara Jeannette Duncan's *A Daughter of Today*, more notoriously in *The Woman Who Did* by the Canadian-born Grant Allen, and in Edith Wharton's *The House of Mirth*. One of the most widely read fictions about female emancipation was Sarah Grand's *The Heavenly Twins* (1893).

Even the leaders of the parade of romances, Marie Corelli and Francis Marion Crawford, stirred currently fashionable ideas about women, love, philosophy, religion, and spiritualism into their successes. Interest in psychic phenomena and spiritualism rose in the late eighties and the nineties and was reflected in the popularity of romances by Corelli, of Rider Haggard's *She*, and Robert Louis Stevenson's *Dr. Jekyll and Mr. Hyde*. Henry James's serial for *Collier's Magazine* in 1898, *The Turn of the Screw*, was only one of the most disturbing of hundreds of ghost stories in the periodicals of the nineties.

In the late nineties new magazines in the United States and Great Britain encouraged the writing of "muckraking" fiction to expose particular political, social, and economic evils; a number of these, particularly Winston Churchill's *Coniston* (1906), *Mr. Crewe's Career* (1908), and *A Far Country* (1915), and *The Jungle* (1906) and others by Upton Sinclair, became best-sellers. Fictions written to advance the cause of temperance had been steadily growing even before Arthur's *Ten Nights in a Barroom* (1855). These crusading books increased greatly in numbers in the closing years of the century as the Prohibition movement gathered strength. Many volumes of domestic fiction or of out-of-door adventure had a strand of anti-drink propaganda woven intemperately through them. The denominational presses, Canadian as well as British and American, published most of the temperance fiction.

The international theme of the innocent from the New World in the Old runs like a thread through North American fiction from Cooper to the present. The theme was early treated humorously or satirically in Thomas Chandler Haliburton's *The Attaché; or Sam Slick in England* (1843) and De Mille's *The Dodge Club; or, Italy in 1859*. Mark Twain made his first real success with *The Innocents Abroad* in 1869, followed by *A Tramp Abroad* in 1880, both of which were immediately reprinted in pirated editions in Toronto. Henry James's *Daisy Miller* and his *The Portrait of a Lady* (1880) and William Dean Howells's *The Lady of the Aroostook* (1879) took up this theme in a different mood, and were also popular. As tourism increased in the eighties and as more American heiresses married into the Old World aristocracy, more fictions explored the international theme. To it Canadians with transatlantic experience—Sara Jeannette Duncan, Gilbert Parker, Lily Dougall, Alice Jones, and Susan Jones—made a contribution.

Europe also meant to the Anglo-North American reader the liberating world of art and the artist, on which Henri Mürger first had opened a window in his *Bohemians of the Latin Quarter* (1848, 1851). The artist was romanticized in fiction in the late seventies and the eighties, and Bohemianism became a fad in clubs, magazines, and fiction in the late eighties and the nineties. The romance and mystique of art, embodied in a young painter, singer, musician, or sculptor (rarely a writer), appeared in fiction like Henry James's *Roderick Hudson*, Jessie Fothergill's *First Violin*, Ouida's *Tricotrin*, or Francis Marion Crawford's *A Roman Singer*. The more intense interest in Bohemianism came with Marie Corelli's *A Romance of Two Worlds* (1890), Kipling's *The Light that Failed* (1890), and the Trilby craze that followed Du Maurier's story (1894) of the Latin Quarter artists, artists' models, and the hypnotic Svengali. The glamour of the world of the artist in Europe probably was enhanced for some Canadians by the career of Madame Albani, the Quebec girl who became a well-known opera star and friend of Queen Victoria in the 1870's.

One of the most striking phenomena of the literary taste of the period was the upsurge in popularity of historical romance between 1886 and 1904. The peculiar mixture of spirited romance, local colour, history, and idealism in Scott and Cooper had elevated historical romance to a higher level of respectability than most other kinds of fiction. It had risen and fallen in vogue during the century, but books by Bulwer-Lytton, Ainsworth, G. P. R. James, Dumas, Reade, and Dickens's *A Tale of Two Cities* and Hugo's *Les Misérables* were widely read in the formative years of Canadian writers. Interest in new historical fiction rose with the success of Wallace's *Ben Hur* in 1880 and Robert Louis Stevenson's romances in the late eighties. The deluge, however, came in the nineties; the pace-setters were tales like Stanley Weyman's *Under the Red Robe*, Gilbert Parker's *The Seats of the Mighty*, Sienkiewicz's *Quo Vadis*, S. Weir Mitchell's *Hugh Wynne, Free Quaker*, and *The Adventures of François*, Charles Major's *When Knighthood was in Flower*, and Winston Churchill's *Richard Carvel*. After the publication of Mary Johnston's *To Have and To Hold*, Thompson's *Alice of Old Vincennes*, and Hewlett's *Richard Yea-and-Nay* the vogue diminished. The matter of these romances was Rome in the early Christian days, Elizabethan England, the days of Bonnie Prince Charlie and of Louis the Sun King, colonial North America, the American Revolution and the French Revolution. Some, like Mitchell's *Hugh Wynne, Free Quaker*, were more novel than romance; others were rapier and cloak melodramas. The enormous popularity of historical romance led Canadian writers to write of their own local history or of the romantic days of England, France, or the Thirteen Colonies, or of the early Christian era. A variant of historical romance—the romance of the imaginary kingdom—also had its great vogue in the nineties and early 1900's, with Stevenson's *Prince Otto*, Anthony Hope's *Prisoner of Zenda* and *Rupert of Henzau*, and George McCutcheon's *Graustark*, but this form seems to have offered little to Canadian writers.

The other striking phenomenon of the literary taste of the period was the appetite for local colour, or regional fiction. It was the fashion that affected more Canadian writers of this period than any other. The purpose of the local colourist was to capture in a short story or in a book made up of related sketches the particular flavour of his chosen locality. Some tried for the utmost accuracy—like Mrs. Stowe, who said she had attempted to "make her mind as still and passive as a looking-glass" so that she might reflect in her stories "New England life and character." Others, like Bret Harte, heightened their local scenes with humour and pathos. Although they had earlier British counterparts such as John Galt in his *Annals of the Parish* or Mrs. Gaskell in *Cranford*, and the current work of the Kailyard School, Canadian writers were most impressed with the stories of the American writers that filled the family magazines of the day. After magazine publication, stories often were collected in book form—Bret Harte's *The Luck of Roaring Camp* (1870), Mrs. Stowe's *Oldtown Folks* (1869), and work by Rose Terry Cooke, Mary Wilkins Freeman, William Dean Howells, or Sarah Orne Jewett picturing the New England scene. Edward Eggleston's widely read *The Hoosier Schoolmaster* (1871), Mark Twain's *The Adventures of Tom Sawyer* (1876) and *Adventures of Huckleberry Finn* (1884), and Hamlin Garland's *Main Travelled Roads* (1891) showed different aspects of the Midwest, and George Washington Cable's *Old Creole Days* (1879) pictured the South. Local colour was in demand, and Canadian writers were encouraged to write out of their own experience of their own localities.

The popularity of fiction of the out-of-doors and of the frontiers, related in many ways to the popularity of local colour and regionalism, grew rapidly after 1900 as the enormous popularity of historical romance declined. From Cooper's time, one main stream of North American fiction had been that of frontier adventure. Sometimes, as in the dime novels, the setting was used only as a backdrop for adventure; sometimes as in Cooper it was used to communicate the mystical redemptive quality of Nature. John Burroughs expressed in the seventies a widespread feeling that the progress and salvation of New World society depended "upon the great teachers and prophets, poets and mystics who gain their enlightenment ultimately from the Great Out-of-Doors, God's Nature." The opening of the West had become a matter of fiction in the magazines in the closing years of the century; the Gold Rush in the north and President Roosevelt's publicity for the "virile" life dramatized the out-of-doors to a people who, in spite of the growth of big cities, were still close to it themselves in their daily lives. Charles G. D. Roberts, Ernest Thompson Seton, and Ralph Connor published their first out-of-doors books before 1900. The great wave of popularity rose just after 1900, with Jack London's stories, Owen Wister's *The Virginian* (1902), and stories by Stewart Edward White, Rex Beach, James Oliver Curwood, Zane Grey, and many others. Even the popular domestic sentimental fiction moved out-of-doors with Gene Stratton Porter's *Freckles* and *The Girl of the Limberlost*. Out-of-doors fiction became one of the great staples of Canadian writers. Canadians also became pace-setters in creating the popularity of animal stories during these years.

Before concluding this brief sketch of the fiction current in the Anglo–North American world during the years 1880 to 1920, it is necessary to note the striking popularity of the shorter forms of fiction. In North America before 1891, magazine editors bought much more short fiction than long fiction from native writers. With the increased activity in the magazine world at the close of the century, editors demanded more short stories and serials. During these years several hundred volumes of short stories were published in book form, in spite of the publisher's rule of thumb that books of short stories rarely pay their way. Some of the most esteemed writers—Robert Louis Stevenson, Rudyard Kipling, Conan Doyle, Henry James, O. Henry, and Jack London to name only a few—were known as much for their short stories as for their longer work. Most writers, British, American, or Canadian, began their careers by contributing stories to magazines; most of them continued to write short stories or serials while they published book-length fiction. Many of the Canadian writers noted in these pages formed a first book by collecting together the best of previously published short stories. It is not surprising to find that the qualities of the short story form—emphasis upon situation, action, static character, and atmosphere—predominate in much of their long fiction.

16. The Kinds of Fiction

1880-1920

GORDON ROPER, RUPERT SCHIEDER

AND S. ROSS BEHARRIELL

WRITING WITHIN THE SOCIAL AND LITERARY MILIEU described in chapter 15, more than 400 Canadians published over 1,400 volumes of fiction. In their work seven or eight kinds of fiction predominate: the local colour story; the historical romance; the action or adventure story; the animal story; the mystery, detective, or crime story; novels of ideas or of social criticism; and the sensational and sentimental society story. Like their American and British fellow writers, they wrote most of their society stories in the eighties, and most of their local colour fiction in the nineties and 1900's. They wrote historical romances of various kinds in growing numbers in the eighties, in a flood in the nineties, and fewer after 1904. Their writing of action stories increased greatly after 1900. Throughout the period they wrote romances and novels dramatizing the interplay of religious faith and doubt. Their mystery stories increased in numbers after 1900. They wrote a variety of problem novels during these forty years: some deal with the political scene; some with labour strife; some with education. Forty or fifty present aspects of the artist's life, or of "the New Woman." Many moral melodramas depicting the ravages of drink were written by occasional writers.

These were the popular kinds. Along with them a few philosophical novels appear; a half-dozen Utopian romances in the vein of Bellamy or the train of Donnelly; some fantasies in the manner of Jules Verne, H. Rider Haggard, or H. G. Wells. Other fictions picture farm life, lumbering camps, horse-racing, railroading, college life, and even banking. A number deal with missionary life in the Northwest or in the Orient, and the interest in religious fiction led to the writing of more than a dozen biblical or classical historical romances. The highly emotional atmosphere of the Great War appears in the closing pages of several dozen fictions in the last years of the period. A few—surprisingly few —fictions carry on the comic tradition of Sam Slick, although comic minor characters in the Haliburton-Dickens tradition turn up frequently in other kinds of fiction.

Some of this fiction was written obviously for a local audience; much of it was written for the New York-Boston-London publishing world, and the various segments of the Anglo-North American audience it catered to. Probably few of these writers thought of their work as literature in the sense in which that term was used in the universities. They practised a popular art; they addressed the widest audience; they wrote for the here and now, and they expected to have their writing judged in this light.

There is little in the structural patterns of their fiction or in the views of human nature which moulded the characters and situations they created to mark their work off from that of the British and American fiction writers of their day. But when their work as a body is placed against that of their British and American contemporaries, differences are apparent.

What most distinguished the fiction written by Canadian writers from that written by their British and American contemporaries is their writers' experience of place, and, to a lesser degree, their experience of time. The fiction written by Canadians before 1880 presents scenes of Canadian life in only a few isolated spots in an unknown country. One cleared patch lies along the St. Lawrence, centring on a Quebec City and a Montreal of the Old Régime. Another smaller patch includes the Minas Basin of the Evangeline country, and a vaguely adjacent Louisbourg and Halifax. Another small patch is around Saint John; other, unrelated patches are the bush clearings of the Ontario Front. A few English writers, R. M. Ballantyne, Kingston, and Henty, put Hudson's Bay and the wilds of the Northwest on the fictional map. Canadian critics in the 1880's had good reason to feel strongly that Canadians had not awakened to the possibilities of using their own localities in fiction. An editorial in *The Week* for September 29, 1887, reprinted a note from the *Boston Literary World*, entitled "A Field for Romance," which suggested that American writers ought to exploit the Canadian scene, since little use had been made by Canadians of "the abundant and rich material for fiction afforded by the scenery and history of these neighbouring lands."

In the following thirty years, Canadian writers did use the abundant and rich materials of their own land to a remarkable degree. The panorama of their fiction which follows below is representative, not exhaustive. In these years, the fictional map of Canada expanded as quickly as the physical map had in 1867. By the time of the First World War, the whole known area of Canada had been sketched in, and the scarcely knit, pluralistic localness of Canadian life in those years had been mirrored directly or obliquely in hundreds of short stories, romances, and novels.

The most prominent eastern region on the new literary map is the French-Canadian country along the Upper and Lower St. Lawrence, along the Ottawa, in the Eastern Townships, and in the Gaspé. The Maritime part fills out. The Minas Basin country is explored in greater detail; so is the North Shore, Cape

Breton, and land on both sides of the Bay of Fundy, and the New Brunswick woods. Prince Edward Island appears as a large area centring on Green Gables. The southern Ontario part expands greatly; life there is pictured in settled rural areas and villages, along the Ottawa, in Glengarry County, on the Bay of Quinte, around Orillia, in the Grand River and the Thames valleys, and along the north shore of Lake Erie. Some fictions picture college life in Cobourg and in Toronto; a few picture city life in Toronto and Ottawa.

The fictional opening of the West paralleled the physical opening with only a few years' lag. Winnipeg was also a fictional gateway for settlers and adventurers who spread out on to homesteads to the southeast and southwest, and on over the prairies, into the foothills of the Rockies. In the Rockies and along the Coast, writers exploited the discovery of gold, lumber, and salmon fishing. The "Northwest," or "North of 53," was filled by fiction with trappers, Métis, outlaws, mounted police, exiled young English lords, remittance men, squaws, and beautiful half-breeds. The latest fictional discovery was the Yukon country in '98; fiction came out with the gold.

The French-Canadian scene was widely used by Canadian writers—and others—from 1890 to 1915. It provided a setting for more than seventy-five volumes of historical romances, of local colour stories, and of tales and legends published during these years, most of them between the years 1895 and 1902. Many of these fictions first appeared in American, British, or Canadian magazines. The picturesqueness of the scenery and the culture had been well known to American writers, readers, and travellers since the 1840's. This transplanted version of Old Europe on their northern doorstep had attracted Americans to Montreal, Quebec, and the trip down the River. Longfellow's *Evangeline* (1847) was read in innumerable editions in North America and Great Britain. William Dean Howells had presented a charming sketch of the St. Lawrence and the Saguenay trip in his *The Wedding Journey* (1871). The rich past of French Canada had been made widely available by the volumes of Francis Parkman's history of France and England in the New World, beginning with his *Conspiracy of Pontiac* in 1851, and culminating with *The Old Régime* (1874), *Count Frontenac and New France under Louis XIV* (1877), *Montcalm and Wolfe* (1884), and *A Half-Century of Conflict* (1892). These provided a great warehouse of story and fact for the historical romancers at the turn of the century. Concurrently, information and story were provided by the writings of a group of French-Canadian literary men, Garneau, Ferland, Gérin-Lajoie, Casgrain, Taché, and LaRue. Philippe Aubert de Gaspé had preserved his own memories for later writers to borrow—in his *Les Anciens Canadiens* (translated in 1864, as *The Canadians of Old*, and in 1890 by Charles G. D. Roberts; reissued as *Cameron of Lochiel* in 1905). Sir James MacPherson Le Moine had retold legends of the past and provided information about historical scenes and events in his *Quebec Past and Present* (1876),

The Chronicles of the St. Lawrence (1879), and the seven volumes of his *Maple Leaves* (1863–1906). It was from the sketches of "Chateau Bigot" and "The Golden Dog" in *Maple Leaves* (I and IV) that William Kirby laid the groundwork for his Chien d'Or romance, started in 1865 and published in 1877.

When the tide for romantic historical fiction began to flow strongly in the eighties in Great Britain and North America, and reached its height in the nineties, the French-Canadian past was one matter which American, British, and Canadian writers exploited. Some used it merely as backdrop for sensational romances; others used it to celebrate great men and events; some Canadians deliberately wrote to make a heroic past for their new country. William Kirby had worked long on his *The Golden Dog* to stir his fellow countrymen with a sense of their past. William Douw Lighthall's hero in his *The False Chevalier* (1898) comes out of the French-Canadian countryside into the Guard at Versailles and dies a "real" chevalier to demonstrate native nobility. Andrew Macphail's *The Vine of Sibmah* (1906) dramatizes the 1670's in England, Boston, and Quebec with some historical responsibility. William McLennan and Jean McIlwraith's *The Span of Life* (1899) also used the England, New England, Louisbourg, and Quebec scene in those crucial years, with some sense of historical accuracy. Robert Sellar's *Morven: The Highland United Empire Loyalist* (1911) is a faithful chronicle of settlement in the eastern provinces, and his *Hemlock: A Tale of the War of 1812* (1890) is in the Scott and Cooper tradition of verisimilitude to historical event and physical scene. One of the most graphic reconstructions of a historical situation was made also by Sellar in his "Summer of Sorrow" in *Gleaner Tales* (II, 1895) in which he told in journal form of the immigration from Lord Palmerston's Irish estate in 1847, ending in the tragedy of the quarantine sheds at Grosse Ile.

But the writers who attempted deliberately to stimulate the patriotic sense of their countrymen were relatively few. More used the French-Canadian past as backdrop for costume dramas of mystery, chase, sword-play, and crossed loves. Although Gilbert Parker used historical documents in writing his *The Seats of the Mighty* (1896) the book is more high romance than history. A feeling for the actual men and events plays even less part in Mary Alloway's romance, *Crossed Swords: A Canadian-American Tale of Love and Valor* (1912), which purports to deal with the American invasion. Blanche Macdonell's *Diane of Ville-Marie* (1898), is an equally romantic love story of the 1690's, and Mabel Clint's *Under the King's Bastion* (1902?) is less a story of Quebec in the Spanish-American War than a fictionalized guidebook. John Burnham's *Marcelle* (1905) is a crude melodrama of Frontenac's time. Jean McIlwraith used Quebec as background for a charming, lively romance in the 1770's (in which the young Nelson figured) in *A Diana of Quebec*

(1912). Thomas G. Marquis wrote a wooden romance of the days of Jacques Cartier in *Marguerite de Roberval* (1899), and William Douw Lighthall went further back to present a romance of the pre-French days of Hiawatha in *The Master of Life: A Romance of the Five Nations* (1908).

Thanks to the great popularity of Longfellow's *Evangeline* (1847), Acadian history offered materials for an easy appeal to the romantic sensibility of readers in these years. Charles G. D. Roberts wrote four very light action romances based on the country he knew around the shores of the Bay of Fundy; the titles tell their tale: *The Raid from Beauséjour* (1894); *The Forge in the Forest, being the Narrative of the Acadian Ranger, Jean de Mer* (1896); *A Sister to Evangeline* (1898), reissued as *Lovers in Acadie* in 1924; and *The Prisoner of Mademoiselle: A Love Story* (1904).

Other writers used local scene and legend for sentimental and melodramatic historical romances: the Reverend Daniel Hickey in *William and Mary: A Tale of the Siege of Louisburg* (1884); Edward Payson Tenny, *Constance of Acadia* (1886); A. J. McLeod in a long short story, *The Notary of Grand Pré* (1901). Alice Jones's spy romance, *The Night Hawk* (1901) is set in Halifax during the American Civil War. Percy W. E. Hart's *Jason—Nova Scotia* (1903) is a melodramatic tale of Annapolis in the time of Bonnie Prince Charlie. Theodore Roberts spun even lighter historical romances than his brother in his *Brothers in Peril* (1905), *Captain Love* (1908), *A Cavalier of Virginia* (1910), *A Captain of Raleigh's* (1911), and others. Amelia Fytche's *The Rival Forts; or, The Velvet Side of Beauséjour* (1907) is a sentimental costume drama. The coming of the Loyalists to Saint John is narrated in a boy's book, *Roger Davis, Loyalist* (1907) by the Reverend Frank Baird. By 1910 the popularity of historical fiction was ebbing in Great Britain and the United States, and the tide of Canadian historical fiction receded with it.

The fictional form that rivalled historical romance in popularity in these years was the local colour story or sketch. Travel sketches of picturesque foreign lands and atmospheric stories of local American communities filled the *Atlantic Monthly* or the *Century*, and, after 1893, their emulator in Canada, the *Canadian Magazine*. Most of these magazine stories were handsomely illustrated with sketches by skilful artists. A similar taste for the local and the everyday was current in the painting of the day, typified by Millet's canvases, or the work of Horatio Walker or Homer Watson. The growing demand by magazine editors in the eighties and nineties for local colour stories encouraged Canadians to write fictional sketches of French-Canadian life. Many of these stories later were collected in book form. William McLennan, a well-known Montreal lawyer, published a group in *As Told to His Grace, and Other Stories* in 1891; some of the stories included in his *In Old France and New* (1899) also picture *habitant* life, and painstakingly reproduce *habitant* dialect. Edward William Thomson's *Old Man Savarin and Other Stories* (1895) contains some lively stories of the Ottawa River French-Canadians. Duncan Campbell Scott published one of the most skilful collections in his *In the Village of Viger* (1896), and in his later collection, *The Witching of Elspie* (1923). Frank Clifford Smith collected a group in *A Lover in Homespun* in 1896; Louis Fréchette translated some of his stories into English in *Christmas in French Canada* in 1900. Henry Cecil Walsh's *Bonhomme: French-Canadian Stories and Sketches* (1899) is less hazed with sentiment than Fréchette's stories, and includes a few character studies of poor French-Canadian city people. Honoré Beaugrand told more fantastic tales in his *La Chasse-Galerie, and Other Canadian Stories* in 1900. George Moore Fairchild's *A Ridiculous Courting, and Other Stories of French Canada* (1900) stands alongside Scott's in sureness of touch and artistic economy. The tales in Annie Jack's *The Little Organist of St. Jerome and Other Stories of Work and Experience* (1902) probably first appeared in Sunday School papers. James Edward LeRossignol, who published his first book *Little Stories of Quebec* in 1908 and his more impressive full-length story *Jean Baptiste* in 1915, became one of the most prolific writers about the French-Canadian scene.

Most of these writers were visitors to the *habitant* scenes they told about. Their tone is bucolic, as if they are remembering with some quiet pleasure the village scene and the people with whom they had spent some pleasant hours while on a vacation. The sentiment is marked, but not usually heavy; the humour and pathos equally light. They show life centring in individual people in their family roles—the father, the mother, the young son and daughter, the curé. The actions are those of growing up, of courting, or rivalry in the field or village, of leaving home and returning. The characters are animated with devotion to the simpler virtues, to piety, fidelity, to the old ways, resistance to the machine and the city. Money is scarce, and is hoarded. Food is plain and not abundant, until the feast days, when community life boils up in *habitant* homes. Most story-tellers did not attempt to reproduce French-Canadian speech directly, but rather tried to catch the flavour of it through cadences and the odd word of French.

The local colour story was content to picture the local scene for the sake of its own interest. Other writers used the French-Canadian village or seigniory as picturesque background to reinforce romantic melodramas. Gilbert Parker placed his historical fantasy, *When Valmond Came to Pontiac* (1895), in an appropriately romantic French-Canadian village scene, and he returned to the Pontiac scene in his *The Lane that Had No Turning and Other Associated Tales Concerning the People of Pontiac* in 1900. The French-Canadian village during the troubles of 1837 is the setting for his *The Pomp of the Lavilettes* (1896), and he created a mythical parish of St. Saviour for his more contemporary romance *The Money Master* (1915). Contemporary Montreal and a near-by imaginary parish of Chaudière provided the background of one of his most popular books, *The Right of Way* (1901). Parker summed up what many of these writers found attractive in the French Canadian when he wrote: "I think the French Canadian one of the most individual, original, and distinctive beings of the modern world. He has kept his place, with his own customs, his own Gallic views of life, and his religious habits, with an assiduity and firmness. . . . He is essentially a man of the home, of the soil, and of the stream; he has by nature instinctive philosophy and temperamental logic."

The French-Canadian background is even more subordinated to sentimental and sensational foreground in Maud Ogilvy's *The Keeper of Bic Light House* (1891) and her *Marie Gourdon* (1890). Susie Frances Harrison did the same in her *The Forest of Bourg-Marie* (1898) and *Ringfield* (1914). Lily Dougall set part of her religious novel *What Necessity Knows* (1893) in the Matapedia valley, with some care for authenticity. Fashionable Murray Bay and the trip up the Saguenay River form part of the setting in Agnes Maule Machar's romance *The Heir of Fairmount Grange* (1895). Frank Clifford Smith's *A Daughter of Patricians* (1901), although romantic and sensational, does centre on some of the social forces in French-Canadian life.

The novel which achieves the greatest success in presenting unromantically and perceptively a study of French-Canadian life is Francis William Grey's *The Curé of St. Philippe: A Story of French-Canadian Politics* (1899).

Maritime writers were more active in writing about the Maritime localities of their own day than of the past. Arthur Wentworth Eaton and C. L. Betts pictured the Halifax scene in their *Tales of a Garrison Town* (1892). Susan Jones's *A Detached Pirate* (1903) shows the gayer side of garrison life. Grace Dean Rogers published her local colour *Stories of the Land of Evangeline* in 1891. Alice Jones set part of her sensational romance *Bubbles We Buy* (1903) in Nova Scotia. Basil King placed *In the Garden of Charity* (1903) along the lower Nova Scotia coast, and took his heroine from a good Halifax family into Boston society in *The High Heart* (1917). Halifax also afforded some of the background for his *The City of Comrades* (1919). John Alexander Cameron set the early part of his *A Colonel from Wyoming* (1907) in Cape Breton, and made a Cape Breton smuggler captain his chief character in *The Woman Hater* (1912). William Albert Hickman wrote a journalistic epic of icebreakers in the Northumberland Strait in his *The Sacrifice of the Shannon* (1903). Frederick McKelvey Bell fictionalized contemporary history in his *A Romance of the Halifax Disaster* (1918). What appears to be the Annapolis valley scene forms the background for Grace Dean Rogers's *Joan at Halfway* (1919). Margaret Marshall Saunders began her *Rose à Charlitte* (1898, also entitled *Rose of Acadie*) with excellent local colour, but like so many other book-length romances in these years, it turned into romantic melodrama. Carrie Jenkins Harris wrote *A*

Modern Evangeline (1896) and several other light romances of the Windsor area. J. M. Oxley set his *Bert Lloyd's Boyhood* (1892) in Nova Scotia. The life of Nova Scotia fishermen was dramatized most effectively by Frederick William Wallace in his *Blue Water* (1907), *The Shack-Locker: Yarns of the Deep Sea Fishing Fleets* (1916) and later volumes.

The Gaspé country appears in *Marcus Holbeach's Daughter* (1912) and *Flame of Frost* (1914) by Alice Jones. The New Brunswick woods and country form the background for Hiram Cody's *The Fourth Watch* (1911), *The Unknown Wrestler* (1918), *The Touch of Abner* (1919) and others. Half of Theodore Roberts's thirty-four books are set in the Maritimes, many of them in the New Brunswick woods. *Tales of the St. John River and Other Stories* (1904) by Ernest Kirkpatrick, the earlier *Charlie Ogilbie: A Romance of Scotland and New Brunswick* (1889) by Leslie Vaughan, and *Marguerite Verne; or, Scenes from Canadian Life* (1886) by Agatha Armour are New Brunswick stories. The coast of Prince Edward Island provides the local colour for Lily Dougall's mixture of ideas and melodrama, *The Mermaid* (1895); the numerous Anne books made Avonlea famous.

One of the few books of Newfoundland local colour is the Reverend John O'Reilly's loosely knit sketches and anecdotes, *The Last Sentinel of Castle Hill* (1916). The Newfoundland and Labrador background also was used by Ralph Graham Taber in his *Northern Lights and Shadows* (1900); by Theodore Roberts, notably, in his *The Harbor Master* (1913); and by Norman Duncan in his *The Way of the Sea* (1903), *Dr. Luke of the Labrador* (1904), *Harbour Tales Down North* (1918), and his Billy Topsail boy's stories. The medical missionary Wilfred Grenfell proselytized for better living conditions for seamen in his *The Harvest of the Sea* (1905), *Off the Rocks* (1906) *Down to the Sea* (1910), *Down North on the Labrador* (1911), and others.

After the turn of the century the Ontario scene became even more prominent on the Canadian literary map than the Quebec scene. The Ontario that emerges from the fiction of these years is predominantly a projection of the countryside in which its writers grew up. It centres in some locality north of Lake Ontario, or Lake Erie, or along the Ottawa, either in a small town, a crossroads village, or on a near-by farm. The tone of many of these fictions is that of the narrator recapturing his or her past, usually with some affection. In the short story this tone provides a unity; in a book-length story, the narrator frequently, after establishing the tone of his scene, felt the need for stronger interest. His patterns of strong action were the popular melodramas of the late nineteenth century—story or stage—and so what promised in the opening chapters to be an authentic local colour story becomes often an action story, a mystery, or a sentimental romance.

The native scene pictured in most of these stories has a close counterpart in the local colour fiction of New England, and an even closer one in the fiction of village and rural life coming out of the American Midwest: Ohio, Indiana, or Michigan. The centre of this fictional world is the individual, in a family, on a farm or in a small town. Home, school, church, the village store are focal points. The conflict is often between the generations, the old values held by those who have brought them from the Old Country, against those of the young who grow up in the local community. The typical actions are those of growing up, of school and play, of leaving the community, and of returning. Few narratives move out with the protagonist into the outer world. Most of them are romances about the finding of love. They contain little sense of old-world caste; what sense of difference between people there is arises from racial or clan background, or from moral or religious difference. Unconsciously values in them are individualistic, and democratic. What binds people together in these communities is first of all a sense of love; what separates is hate, selfishness, isolation, malicious gossip, and un-Christian lack of charity. The doctor, the father, the mother, the minister are strong figures. Society is assumed to be friendly, and Nature is beneficent, and often inspiring. The characters (and the author) respond to the natural beauty of a winter's night, or a June mid-day, or the changing weather of April or mid-October. For the most part, these fictions present a springtime view of their world. Few were written in the vein of what William Dean Howells called "critical realism," or expressed the "revolt from the Village" which began to appear more frequently in American fiction in the first decades of the twentieth century and culminated most strikingly in Sinclair Lewis's *Main Street* in 1920.

Some of the best stories in Edward William Thomson's *Old Man Savarin* (1895; revised, 1917) picture aspects of life in the Scots communities in Glengarry and along the Ottawa, and Ralph Connor called up his own memories of growing up in Glengarry for the earlier part of *The Man from Glengarry* (1901), in *Glengarry School Days* (1902), and in several of his later books. Robert Lorne Richardson's *Colin of the Ninth Concession* (1903) recaptures similar memories in the first half. His later *The Camerons of Bruce* (1906) also opens with a local Scots scene. The English journalist G. B. Burgin wrote three books about the Hawkesbury locale: *The Only World, The Dance at Four Corners*, and *The Judge at Four Corners.* In a tone of simple piety, the Reverend Bertal Heeney's *Pickanock* (1912) recalls affectionately early days near Ottawa and in the lumbering country of the Gatineau. Moving westward in southern rural Ontario, Marian Keith (Mary Esther MacGregor) began her pleasant and sometimes charming imaginative reconstructions of the Scots settlement in Oro Township (near Orillia) in *Duncan Polite* (1905), and most of her subsequent thirteen volumes are of Oro. Stephen Leacock recreated Orillia in his *Sunshine Sketches of a Little Town* (1912), with a touch of nostalgia mixed into his human comedy. Village life somewhere north of Lake Erie provides the scene for May Wilson's sensitively remembered story of family feuds, *Carmichael* (1907). Small village characters are sentimentalized in Adeline Teskey's volumes of tales which began with *Where the Sugar Maple Grows* (1901). The Reverend Archibald McKibbin's mildly didactic story *The Old Orchard* (1903) takes place in Middlesex County, and several of the Reverend Robert E. Knowles', from his *St. Cuthbert's* (1905) on, are of the Grand River valley. One of the stories in Alice Maud Ardagh's *Tangled Ends* (1888) tells a tougher-minded story of life on a Grand River farm. Another story about people in the Grand River valley, *The Untempered Wind* (1894) by Joanna Wood, and *The Unexpected Bride* (1895) by "Constance McDonnell" (Mrs. J. B. Hammond) set near Toronto, are candid pictures of rural Ontario life. Eric Bohn (John Price-Brown) set his scene in a western Ontario village in *How Hartman Won* (1903). The curiously powerful psychological drama *The Dagmar Who Loved* (1904) by Kathleen Blackburn also is set in a western Ontario village. Arthur Stringer wrote in *Lonely O'Malley* (1905) a Tom Sawyerish tale from his own boyhood experiences in Chatham; Archibald McKishnie told a more sensational tale in his *Gaff Linkum: A Tale of Talbotville* (1907). E. E. Sheppard used the Ontario rural scene in his *Dolly, the Young Widder up to Felder's* (1886), written for a farm magazine. Sydney Preston's pleasant *The Abandoned Farmer* (1901) and *On Common Ground* (1906) are set near Clarkson. Not all writers recalled growing up in Ontario villages with pleasure; E. E. Sheppard pictured the old deacon father, leading his family at prayers, with a cold fury in the opening chapters of his *Widower Jones* (1888), and much in the rest of the volume fulfils the promise of the sub-title: "A Realistic Story of Rural Life." W. A. Fraser's *The Lone Furrow* (1907), set in a town much like his own Georgetown, presents with some complexity and insight a group of central characters besieged by villagers with little charity and some viciousness. Kathleen and Robina Lizars' *Committed to His Charge* (1900) pictures effectively the gossip and the meanness which oppresses the life of more sensitive characters in a village like Stratford. The excitement of small town political life and of election day are treated lightly in Kate Carr's *Cupid and the Candidate* (1906), and with much more complexity and realism in Sara Jeannette Duncan's *The Imperialist* (1904), which takes place in Elgin (Brantford). The Reverend LeRoy Hooker's *Baldoon* (1899) has a little of Miss Duncan's satirical touch in depicting village life in Lambton County. Henry Mainer's *Nancy McVeigh of the Monk Road* (1908) is a more sentimental story of a local ministering angel, the old widow who keeps a tavern on the Monck Road in Haliburton County.

Almost all of these fictions of small community life in southern Ontario reveal little awareness of the existence of the Ontario cities of Toronto, Hamilton, London, or Ottawa. Rarely does the action of the book follow a village character who "goes away" from his home; and characters who do leave are more apt to go away to a vague area to the south called "the States." The exception to this self-centredness is the departure of the young man or woman to the city for his or her college years. But only a few narratives accompany the character. Ralph Connor showed his Man from Glengarry going to Varsity, and his central characters in his later *The Doctor* and *The Prospector* also are shown at college. The Reverend William Withrow sent his hero to Victoria in Cobourg in *The King's Messenger* (1879). Maud Petitt sent her heroine from a small western Ontario town to Victoria after it had moved to Toronto, in her *Beth Woodburn* (1897). Harvey O'Higgins's realistic *Don-A-Dreams* (1906) presents a fuller picture of Varsity life before his characters leave for New York. A. R. Carman's *The Preparation of Ryerson Embury* (1900) is set in a college town. And Robert Barr used his memories of the Toronto Normal School for his satire on education in the lively *The Measure of the Rule* (1906).

But college life in these books is not city life, for these undergraduates usually have little awareness of the city lying around the campus. The earliest stories of the city scene were by women writing in the sensational society fiction vein of Mrs. Fleming or Mrs. Sadlier. They sketch a fantasy world of "society" in which their characters intrigue and contend. The most gauche of these is *A Heart-Song of Today Disturbed by Fire from the 'Unruly Member'*, by Mrs. Annie Gregg Savigny in 1886. Her book *Lion, the Mastiff* (1895) places its Humane Society story in Toronto, and her *A Romance of Toronto* (1888) is set in Rosedale. However, these fripperies could have been set in any North American city; the mention of Mr. Eaton's store or of Toronto street names seems to be the only local touch.

Some fictions exploited the widerspread belief that virtue lived in the village and vice in the city. Toronto, as a big city, where crookedness reigned in high places, is depicted in E. E. Sheppard's sensational *A Bad Man's Sweetheart* (1889), and much more skilfully in the detective thriller with society and psychological overtones, *Geoffrey Hampstead* (1890) by a prominent young Torontonian lawyer, Thomas Stinson Jarvis. John Charles Dent exploited city crime in his semi-fictional *The Gerrard Street Mystery and Other Weird Tales* (1888). Isabel Ecclestone MacKay's view of the city is more sophisticated in her *Mist of Morning* (1919), in which a country boy encounters an aristocratic young city girl. R. S. Jenkins's overloaded mixture of society romance and murder mystery, *The Heir from New York* (1911), is set in Hamilton and the surrounding countryside.

Several women writers in the Fleming and Sadlier vein also used the Ottawa social scene for sensational and sentimental romances; their books are noted below among the fiction about the federal political scene.

In these years Ontario writers also began to create an imaginative past for their communities. George Millner in his *The Sergeant of Fort Toronto*

(1914) set his strong Cooper-like tale around Toronto and Niagara during the mid-eighteenth century. The Reverend William Withrow narrated a fictionalized history of the establishment of Methodism in Ontario in the 1790's in his *Barbara Heck* (1895). In *Neville Trueman, the Pioneer Preacher* (1880) he attached his young minister to the Canadian forces at Queenston, and constructed a fictionalized history of the Niagara campaign in 1812, and the death of Brock. William Wilfred Campbell in his *A Beautiful Rebel* (1909) pictured the crossed loyalties which sprang from a heroine from a rebel family and a hero in the loyal forces. His dramatization of the battle of Queenston Heights is text-bookish. John Price-Brown was more successful in dramatizing his material in *In the Van; or, The Builders* (1906) which describes the heroic march in 1813 of a British regiment from Nova Scotia to Penetang to build a fort. Graeme Mercer Adam and Ethelwyn Wetherald attempted to fuse two love stories set around Lake Simcoe and York in the 1820's in their *An Algonquin Maiden* (1887) but their romance is overladen with genteel sentiment, intricate plotting, and historical essays. Archibald McKishnie dramatized the conflict between the man of the woods and encroaching "civilization," embodied in a Colonel Talbot-like character, in his *Love of the Wild* (1910). Samuel Mathewson Baylis overwhelmed his story with lecturing and stiff dialogue in "Rebel or Patriot: A Story of '37" in *Camp and Lamp* (1897). John Price-Brown evoked forcefully the drama of Mackenzie's flight from Markham in the middle section of his *The Mac's of '37* (1910). May Wilson ("Anison North") presented the Rebellion from the viewpoint of the rebels in the first half of *The Forging of the Pikes* (1920) and from the viewpoint of the loyalists in the second half, but unfortunately she permitted her love story to overshadow her sense of the past. One of the most vigorous, entertaining stories of pioneer Ontario is Percival John Cooney's *Kinsmen: A Story of the Ottawa Valley* (1916). Daniel Clark's *Josiah Garth* (n.d.) also dealt with the Rebellion.

In *Candlelight Days* (1913), Adeline Teskey told gentle, sentimental tales of the time of the building of the Welland Canal. Marjorie Pickthall's semi-juvenile *Dick's Desertion* (1905) pictures a young boy growing up in a bush clearing near Peterborough, before he responds to the mystical pull of the North. Robert Barr wrote a lively comic treatment of the battle of Ridgeway (Fenian Raids) in his *In the Midst of Alarms* (1894). The description of Ridgeway which appears among the simple sketches of early Ontario rural life in *The Dear Old Farm* (1897) by "Malcolm" (Coll MacLean Sinclair) reads like a non-partisan, first-hand account. In *The Old Loyalist* (1908) Allan Ross Davis wrote "a plain, unvarnished tale" to provoke a greater interest in "our grand old Loyalist ancestors." His amateurish melodrama is a family story of from 1865 to 1884 around Adolphustown, in which Sir John A. appears to make Tory speeches. Sir John A. also is a force in R. E. Knowles's picture of new settlers coming to Glen Ridge, north of Hamilton, in *The Handicap* (1910), and plays *deux ex machina* in what is essentially a sentimental romance.

Probably the part of North America that has most stirred the popular imagination in the Western world has been the West. In the United States it has been the West of the mountain men, the Indian, the covered wagon and the Pony Express, the cowboy, and the miner. In Canada it was first the Northwest Territories, or "North of '53." In 1880 the Northwest Territories included the vast stretch of land north of the St. Lawrence River basin and Lake Superior, the land north of the northern Manitoba border of 52.50', and west of Manitoba to the Rockies and the British Columbia border. The adventure stories of R. M. Ballantyne, W. H. G. Kingston, G. A. Henty, and other English writers had established before 1880 the picture of a great lone land, ruled by the Hudson's Bay Company and inhabited by half-breeds, Indians, Scots factors, or farther north, a white land explored adventurously by men like Franklin. In the early nineties, Gilbert Parker and others turned popular notions about the Northwest into material for stories in English and American magazines. Parker's melodramatic northern stories appeared in *The Chief Factor: A Tale of the Hudson's Bay Company* (1892), *Pierre and His People* (1892), *An Adventurer of the North* (1895), *A Romany of the Snows* (1896), and *Northern Lights* (1909). James Macdonald Oxley wrote more than twenty boy's adventure stories of the North in the nineties and early 1900's. John Burnham's juvenile *Jack Ralston* (1901) is set in Ungava. Susan Jones's *A Girl of the North* (1900) is romantic melodrama. W. A. Fraser centred his excellent tale *The Blood Lilies* (1903) in Fort Donaldson. The second half of Robert Lorne Richardson's *The Camerons of Bruce* (1906) moves to a melodramatic West, and Edwyn Sandy's *Trapper Jim* (1903) is similarly melodramatic. Samuel Alexander White published the first of a number of western action stories, *Empery: A Story of Love and Battle in Rupert's Land*, in 1913 (also published as *Law of the North*). George Ray showed a strong feeling for authentic setting (and sensational melodrama) in *Kasba: A Story of Hudson Bay* (1915). Hiram Cody combined the didactic and the Northwest adventure tale in *If Any Man Sin* (1915) and later stories. W. D. Flatt wrote an even more exemplary tale of two boys making good with the Hudson's Bay Company in *The Making of a Man* (1918). Agnes Laut emphasized the epic quality of the days of discovery and exploration in *Lords of the North* (1900) and followed it by the Radisson story in *Heralds of Empire* (1902).

A different and much more varied West began to emerge in the seventies when settlers moved into what became Manitoba. The transcontinental railroad was completed in 1885, and opened the great plains, the foothills of the Rockies, and the river valleys of British Columbia to the flood of migration which poured westward and northward in the closing years of the old century and the opening decade of the new. The old Northwest Territories shrank in 1905 when the provinces of Saskatchewan and Alberta were carved out of it, and the districts around Hudson Bay became parts of Quebec, Ontario, and Manitoba in 1912. The new West offered many themes for fiction— migration, homesteading, farming, ranching, railroading, mining, timbering, the mingling of cultures, acclimatization, the breakdown of Old World patterns and the forging of new. Smuggling and outlawry and policing were natural subjects for theatrical embroidery. Moreover, the opening of the Canadian West coincided with a rapidly expanding market in American and British magazines for red-blooded, outdoor fiction. This outdoors fiction appealed strongly to a generation conscious of the growth of cities and the swelling complexity of urban and national life. Consequently the Canadian western literary map expanded almost as explosively as did the West itself.

The Manitoba scene first appeared in the memoirs and reminiscences of those who participated in the opening of the West. The first fiction, Alexander Begg's *"Dot-It-Down"* (1871) is partly a satire on men involved in the Red River Rebellion ("Dot-it-down" is the note-taking Charles Mair). Christopher Oakes sketched some vivid scenes of Winnipeg in the boom days of 1882 in the first part of his *The Canadian Senator* (1890). Mrs. M. J. Frank ("A.L.O.M.") gave a semi-fictional, sentimental account of early settlement in *The Brock Family* (1890). A most improbable Manitoba forms the background of James Morton's temperance melodrama *Polson's Probation* (1897), but Ridgwell Cullum's *The Hound from the North* (1904) contains, besides its Yukon melodrama, some realistic scenes of farm life in south-eastern Manitoba. Probably the first fiction to be really concerned with the relation of the land and the people who come into it is Ralph Connor's *The Foreigner* (1909) which dramatized the problems of immigration. Mrs. Elizabeth Covey's *Comrades Two: A Tale of the Qu'Appelle Valley* (1907) is more idyllic than realistic; Nellie McClung's stories, *Sowing Seeds in Danny* (1908), its sequel *The Second Chance* (1910), and *The Black Creek Stopping-House* (1912) try to present faithfully the everyday life of small town and farm. The Reverend Edward Anthony Gill's *A Manitoba Chore Boy: The Experience of a Young Emigrant Told from his Letters,* and his *Love in Manitoba,* both published in 1912, deal with immigration and homesteading with some realism. In W. H. Jarvis's amusing exemplary *Letters of a Remittance Man to his Mother* (1909?) the young writer discovers in two years in Winnipeg and on nearby farms why the English "remittance man" (who appears in many western fictions) is held in contempt by Canadians and by Englishmen who are making good. Elinor Marsden Eliot's *My Canada* (1915), in diary form, is description and apologia to outsiders. *The Heart of Cherry McBain* (1919) by Douglas Durkin is a romance of love and action, set in a railroad construction camp near the Saskatchewan border, with considerable feeling for the country. Cy Warman included some tales of early railroading days in the Canadian West in his *Frontier Stories* (1898),

Snow on the Headlight (1899), *The White Mail* (1899), and *The Last Spike* (1906). The best novel to come out of the Manitoba scene before 1920 is Frances Beynon's *Aleta Dey* (1919), although its Winnipeg and Brandon backgrounds play little organic part in the story.

The Rebellion troubles are fictionalized in the highly melodramatic *Annette the Métis Spy: A Heroine of the N. W. Rebellion* (1886) by the journalist J. E. Collins. More romantic and less sensational treatments were published by John Mackie in *The Rising of the Red Man* (1902), and by Joseph Kearney Foran in *Tom Ellis: A Story of the North-West Rebellion* (n.d.). F. D. Reville's *Rebellion: A Story of the Red River Uprising* (1912) is an unskilful mixture of fiction with material from a private journal and an eye-witness account of the earlier troubles.

The early stories of the opening of the Plains and the foothill country stress the dangers and the adventure. General William Francis Butler's *Red Cloud: The Solitary Sioux* (or *Red Cloud: A Tale of the Great Prairie*) (1882) is in the Ballantyne-Kingston-Henty manner. Campbell Shaw's *A Romance of the Rockies* (1888) and Roger Pocock's mixture in *Tales of Western Life, Lake Superior, and the Canadian Prairie* (1888) are simple adventure stories. Love and temptation complicate the outdoor adventure in *The Devil's Playground* (1894), *Sinners Twain* (1895), *They That Sit in Darkness* (1897), and *The Prodigal's Brother* (1899) by John Mackie, the popular Scottish romancer who had been a Mounted Policeman in the eighties. Mounted Police had appeared earlier in Pocock's stories, and in the "Pierre" stories by Gilbert Parker. Cowboys and "Sky Pilots" are central characters in the short stories and sketches of John Maclean's *The Warden of the Plains* (1896). The missionary hero became much more widely known through the success of Ralph Connor's *Black Rock* (1898), and the equally successful *The Sky Pilot* (1899). The North West Mounted Policeman became the hero of full-length romances in Connor's didactic *Corporal Cameron of the North West Mounted Police* (1912) and Hiram Cody's *The Long Patrol: A Tale of the Mounted Police*, published in the same year. An inside picture of the Mounted is presented in Ralph Selwood Kendall's *Benton of the Royal Mounted* (1918) and *The Luck of the Mounted* (1920), since Kendall himself had been one of the force. The most effective stories of the early days of the Force are not found in fiction, but in the personal narratives of Sir Samuel Steele, *Forty Years in Canada: Reminiscence of the Great North-West* (1915) and the other men who were its first commanders.

A fictional stereotype of the Mountie became one of the standard figures in the wave of western action stories which followed the innovators early in the century—the American writers Jack London, Stewart Edward White, Owen Wister, and the more commercial Rex Beach, Zane Grey, and James Oliver Curwood. Some Canadians were prolific producers of these formula westerns which appeared first in men's magazines, then in book form, then in cheap reprints issued by A. L. Burt and others. Ridgwell Cullum's first western, *The Story of the Foss River Ranch*, appeared in 1903. His *In the Brooding Wild: A Mountain Tragedy* (1905) dramatizes in epic terms the pre-ranching-trapping-and-trading frontier. Samuel Alexander White's first was *The Stampeder* (1910); and Hulbert Footner's first, *Two on a Trail*, was published in the same year. William Amy, writing under the name "Luke Allan," published his first western, *The Blue Wolf: A Tale of the Cyprus Hills*, in 1913. Some of the most skilfully told western tales appeared in William Alexander Fraser's *Bulldog Carney* (1919), a set of stories about a Robin-Hood-like smuggler in the Alberta foothills.

Other Canadians, native to the Western scene, attempted to portray different aspects of Western life with greater fidelity to what they themselves had experienced. Frances Herring's *On the Pathless West* (1904) was an early attempt to picture life on the plains in romance form, and she followed it with *Nan and Other Pioneer Women of the West* (1913). Frank Robinson's *Trail Tales of Western Canada* was published in the following year. Gilbert Parker tried to picture a situation in the big new West "where destiny is being worked out in the making of a nation" in his *You Never Know Your Luck* (1914), *The World for Sale* (1916), and *Wild Youth and Another* (1919). But Parker knew his Saskatchewan towns only from the outside, and what insight he had into the conflict between races in *The World for Sale* was buried under rhetoric and melodrama. Another exotic, Arthur Stringer, had the advantage over Parker of ranching in Alberta. His trilogy, *The Prairie Wife* (1915), *The Prairie Mother* (1920), and *The Prairie Child* (1922) depict with honest realism some aspects of ranch life, but are marred by being mixed with *Saturday Evening Post* journalism. When his work is compared with that of Harold Bindloss, the popular English writer who had spent a few years in the West before beginning his writing career in England, Stringer's unevenness of intention is apparent. In able romances like his *Ranching for Sylvia* (1912) or *The Girl from Keller's* (1917), Bindloss manages to convey a living sense of his farm environment and the moulding effect of that environment on his pleasant but unheroic characters. The native novelist who developed the realistic portrayal of his Alberta country and his people was Robert Stead. His first fiction, *The Bail Jumper* (1914) reveals his effort to portray his material honestly, although frequently his form was borrowed from the action western. In his *The Homesteaders* (1916) his sense of fidelity to his scene is less distorted by melodramatic form. His range and perception increased in *The Cow Puncher* (1918), and reached the peak of effectiveness in *Grain* (1926), set in Manitoba in the nineties—one of the ablest studies of the transition from pioneering life in the West written by a Canadian. Isabel Paterson's first two novels, *The Shadow Riders* (1916) and *The Magpie's Nest* (1917), also are able pictures of Alberta life.

British Columbian fiction, like British Columbia itself, for outsiders, began with the Cariboo gold rush days of the late 1850's and the early sixties. Anecdotes and tales of the early mining days appeared in Campbell Shaw's *A Romance of the Rockies* (1888), and Arthur Hodgkin Scaife's ("Kim Bilir") *Three Letters of Credit and Other Stories* (1894) and *As It was in the Fifties* (1895). Bret Harte, Mark Twain and other American writers and dramatists had provided the popular forms for fiction about miners and mining. Clive Phillipps-Wolley mined this lode in *Snap: A Legend of the Lone Mountain* (1890), and *Gold, Gold, in Cariboo!* (1894). Ralph Connor combined didacticism, sentiment, and melodrama in his tale of later mining life in *Black Rock: A Tale of the Selkirks* (1898), and he followed this success with *The Sky Pilot: A Tale of the Foothills* (1899), *The Prospector: A Tale of the Crow's Nest Pass* (1904), *The Doctor: A Tale of the Rockies* (1906), *The Sky Pilot at Swan Creek* (1905) and others. Francis Pollock's first books were *The Treasure Trail* (1906) and *The Frozen Fortune* (1910); Bertrand Sinclair's first was *Raw Gold* (1908), and Frederick Niven's was *The Lost Cabin Mine* (1909). Roger Pocock published his *Jesse of Cariboo* in 1911. Julia Henshaw's extravagant melodrama, *Why Not, Sweetheart?* (1901) includes mining scenes, and the heroine of Lily Dougall's *The Madonna of a Day* (1895) sleepwalks from a Pullman in the Rockies into a melodrama of action and ideas in a mining camp. R. E. Knowles followed the pattern of his fellow-minister's *The Sky Pilot* in *The Singer of the Kootenay* (1911). Bertrand Sinclair's hero goes gold-prospecting in his *North of Fifty-Three* (1914), but Sinclair was more concerned with the theme of the redemptive qualities of wilderness living than with exciting action.

Most of these fictions of mining life are action stories. But other fictions are more concerned with communicating the excitement of life in the new British Columbia Eden, an open, awesomely beautiful land which promised the good life to the venturesome, the courageous, and the flexible. Here in farming, ranching, lumbering, or fishing—in the river valleys, in the mountains, and along the coast—the individual could free himself from the pressures of life in the East or the Old Country where social conformity, class structure, and the pursuit of money and status confined the human spirit.

Probably the most effective picture of life on the West Coast is the single volume written by Martin Allerdale Grainger, *Woodsmen of the West* (1908). Grainger knew his lumbering community; his characters are complex and obviously drawn from firsthand acquaintance. His book should remain a minor classic of Coast life. Roger Pocock's *Man in the Open* (1912), although less successful as a whole, has scenes which capture vividly the feel of mountain life, and is peopled with characters who often come alive for some pages. Bertrand Sinclair's novel of the lumbering world, *Big Timber* (1916) and his *Poor Man's Rock* (1920) of the salmon fishing industry, are honest pictures of complex characters in locales which Sinclair knew well. Gilbert Parker early in his writing career worked into part of his novel *Mrs. Falchion* (1893) the conflict between salmon fishermen and lumbering men in a British Columbia coastal village, but the locale seems an incongruous part of the book as a whole. Robert Watson in his *My Brave and Gallant Gentleman* (1918) and *The Girl of O. K. Valley* (1919) used the coast and mountain country more effectively. Like Watson's books, Robert Allison Hood's *The Chivalry of Keith Leicester* (1918) is most occupied with the difficulties of courtship of well-born young English people; the actions of his hero and heroine—both Oxford graduates—take place in the Fraser River farm country and Vancouver. Evah McKowan wrote an engaging book in *Janet of Kootenay* (1919) in which, in letter form, a young "new woman" recounts her adventures in setting up a fruit farm in the Okanagan valley. Minnie Smith's *Is It Just?* (1911) is a unhappier tale of a wife who, after she has to follow her husband from her flourishing Manitoba farm to the Okanagan valley, is deserted and suffers from British Columbia law.

The sensation caused by the gold strikes in Alaska and the Yukon in the nineties immediately led to journalism, anecdote, and fiction about the Gold Rush. Three semi-fictions came out in the year 1898: T. M. Ellis's *Tales of the Klondike*, Thaddeus Leavitt's *Kaffir, Kangaroo, Klondyke*, and Edward Roper's *A Claim on the Klondike: A Romance of the Arctic Eldorado*. The real literary Gold Rush, however, followed the success of the Alaska stories of Jack London and other popular American writers, and even though a Canadian writer might have had some experience of the North, his fiction usually copied the formulas of action fiction. Robert Service's well-known *The Trail of '98* (1911) had woven into it his own experience, but his book imitated the crudest action stories in its characterization, situation, and dialogue, touched up with Service's own literary Bohemianism. Hiram Cody's *The Frontiersman* (1910) and *The Chief of the Ranges* (1913) also derived partly from personal experience, but lost any uniqueness they might have gained from this by their use of stereotype characters, situations, and language. The first part of his later *Glen of the High North* (1920), set in the post-war depression years, gains more power from its originality. Ridgwell Cullum's *Way of the Strong* (1913) and *The Triumph of John Karrs* (1917) are effective action tales, with less of the complexity of the human element sometimes found in his other work. William Henry Jarvis's *The Great Gold Rush* (1913) has more authenticity. Although it is a romantic melodrama, one of the most effective pictures of Dawson City life is caught in Madge Macbeth's *Kleath* (1917). But the Canadian "Northwest" familiar to a world-wide audience in the 1910's and the 1920's was not primarily the Yukon, the Rockies, or the Coast; it was the Peace, Athabaska, and the Mackenzie country. Of the Canadians who wrote of this last of the pre-1920 frontiers, the most popular were Hiram Cody, Hulbert Footner, Samuel Alexander White, Arthur Chisholm, and Ridgwell Cullum. Harold Bindloss, who had travelled in the West before returning to England to begin his prolific writing career, set some of his romances there. The most widely read writer about the Northwest, however, was James Oliver Curwood, a Michigan man who spent many seasons in "God's Country." Following the patterns of the red-blooded and the nature fiction writers of the turn of the century, he achieved a large international following by the melodramatic vigour of his work. His thirty-one romances sold well over four million copies in English, and many more copies in translation in eleven other languages; most of his stories also were converted into popular moving pictures.

The fictions listed above were among the primary agents which during these years established in the minds of the Anglo–North American reading public images of life in the different regions which made up the political entity "Canada." Not all of them were concerned directly with creating a sense of a particular locality; many were more concerned with depicting some aspect of the quickening social, political, economic, religious, and ethical conflicts of their times. The 1880's and early 1890's were periods of intense economic depression in various parts of North America; the later 1890's and the first decade of the twentieth century were boom years. They were the years of the rapid growth of the cities, of the movement of millions of people into North America and from one part of North America to another. They were the years of bitter struggle between capital and labour, and the rise of protest parties and dreams of democratic Utopias. Although Canada was still predominantly rural, some Canadian fiction reflected the growth of industrialization and its social impact. Agnes Maule Machar's *Roland Graeme, Knight* (1892), John Galbraith's *In the New Capital* (1897), A. R. Carman's *The Preparation of Ryerson Embury: A Purpose* (1900), H. P. Blanchard's *After the Cataclysm* (1909), and Mabel Burkholder's *The Course of Impatience Carningham* (1911) deal with the various aspects of labour unrest or industrial social injustice. Robert Barr's novel of labour conflict in an English factory, *The Mutable Many* (1896) is the most effective full-length study of labour–capital strife. William Henry Moore's *Polly Masson* (1919) presents in several of its scenes the conflicting interests of Canadian farmers, union leaders, and business men.

Few Canadian writers presented transcendental schemes for social reform in their fiction; their typical position was that of the middleman, discomforted by pressures from the right and left, feeling that if only capital and labour would stop pushing and behave as decent Christian small-town neighbours, social problems might go away. This middle position is expressed by various narrators in some of Stephen Leacock's sketches, although Leacock, an admirer of Veblen, more frequently took as his mark the pretensions of the plutocracy.

The fiction which reflects some picture of Canada as an entity was built on political themes. Some writers like Christopher Oakes in his *The Canadian Senator* (1890) made fun of pomposity and incompetence in high places. Blanchard's *After the Cataclysm* and Galbraith's *In the New Capital* are more sweeping in rejecting the current political ways. Like Galbraith and "Ex-Journalist" in his *They Two: or, Phases of Life in Eastern Canada Fifty Years Ago* (1888), Moore organized his *Polly Masson* in an omnibus fashion so that he could present a wide range of Canadian political topics: the opening of the West; the building of the C.P.R.; the treatment of the Indians; reciprocity; free trade; Roman Catholic–Protestant tensions; Canadian relations with the United States and Canadian feeling for the Mother Country. Sara Jeannette Duncan wrote *The Imperialist* (1904) to show how ordinary Canadians really felt about Imperial relations. Her delightful irony plays around the colonial-minded in *Cousin Cinderella: A Canadian Girl in London* (1908). Three of her Indian books, *His Honour and a Lady* (1896), *Set in Authority* (1906), and *The Burnt Offering* (1909) are concerned with the tragic consequences of political power. Her novel *The Consort* (1912) pictures the struggle for power between a philanthropist wife and her writer-politician husband in England. Other Canadian women used the political scene to embroider their light society romances: Kate Bottomley's *Honor Edgeworth; or, Ottawa's Present Tense* (1882), Helen Bogg's *When the Shadows Flee Away: A Story of Canadian Society* (1891), and Kate Carr's *Cupid and the Candidate* (1906). Apart from Sara Jeannette Duncan, the only other Canadian woman to write a serious novel on political ideas was Margaret Adeline Brown in *My Lady of the Snows* (1908); unfortunately her intellectual idealism exceeded her art.

One of the subjects most prevalent in Canadian fiction in this period is religion. In 1909, in one of a number of conflicting articles in the *Canadian Magazine*, the Reverend John Paterson Smyth, rector of St. George's, Montreal, discussed "the wide influence which novel-reading exerts in our day in the field of morals and theology." Far from protesting against this influence, he contrasted the advantages of the popular novel, whose circulation might reach 1,000,000 copies, with the limitations of the pulpit. In most sections of the country, as in the United States and parts of Great Britain, the church was the centre of community life, and the clergyman often was an arbiter of culture. In Canada in these years, the ministry, along with journalism, provided more fiction writers than any other profession; more than thirty Canadian ministers published fiction. They were encouraged to do so by religious-minded publishers such as Briggs, Westminster, Copp Clark, and Hunter Rose, and by religious societies abroad. A receptive public, predominantly rural or small town, middle-class and church-going, and largely fundamentalist in training, gave religious fiction its share of the great boom in fiction at the turn of the century.

Religion was presented in a wide variety of ways in these fictions. It was used merely as sensationally different plot material in the Reverend Albert de Long's *A Wolf in Sheep's Clothing* (1905); as part of the historical scene in Gilbert Parker's fiction set in Quebec, or in W. W. Campbell's *A Beautiful Rebel* (1909); or as incidental critical comment in *They Two: or, Phases of Life in Eastern Canada Fifty Years Ago* (1888) by "Ex-Journalist" (Richard Lanigan) and *Tales of a Garrison Town* (1892) by A. W. H. Eaton and C. L. Betts. In *Widower Jones: A Faithful History of his "Loss," and Adventures in Search of a Companion* (1888), E. E. Sheppard in an early scene attacked religiosity and hypocrisy; at one critical point in Robert Stead's *The Cow Puncher* (1918) the hero, revolted by cant, walks out of church.

Pietism predominates in much of the domestic sentimental fiction written largely by women. Mrs. M. J. Frank's *The Brock Family* (1890), Mrs. Emma Wells Dickson's *Miss Dexie: A Romance of the Provinces* (1895), and Rosa Portlock's *The Head Keeper* (1898), are representative. They stress Christian virtues and individual morality in the family and among neighbours. Maud Pettit's *Beth Woodburn: A Canadian Tale* (1897) is unusual in treating the problem of the aspiring young artist, but once the heroine's decision to channel her art to the purposes of religion has been made, it conforms to the general pattern. Not all domestic fiction is sentimental; *Committed to His Charge* (1900) by R. and K. M. Lizars presents the human problems of a young Anglican minister in a small Ontario town, with some complexity of tone.

Less sentimental and more active are the stories in a group whose subject is the clergy. Although some of the best were written by clergymen, they are not particularly sectarian. Much of the material is familiar: the evangelical purpose, the old hymns, the plea for temperance, the repetition of the "prodigal son" story. Related to adventure and frontier fiction, set in the outdoors and packed with physical activity, many of them illustrate the personal influence of one strong man, often the oversized muscular Christian, on the fallen and the stragglers. Outstanding examples are Ralph Connor's *Black Rock: A Tale of the Selkirks* (1898) and *The Sky Pilot: A Tale of the Foothills* (1899), Norman Duncan's *The Measure of a Man: A Tale of the Big Woods* (1911), and, from numerous stories of this pattern by the Reverend Hiram Cody, *The Frontiersman: A Tale of the Yukon* (1910), *The Fourth Watch* (1911), and *The Unknown Wrestler* (1918). Ernest Thompson Seton's *The Preacher of Cedar Mountain: A Tale of the Open Country* (1917) presents the conflict in a minister torn between the call of the city and the frontier ministry.

A number of fictions, written chiefly by ministers, attempted to proselytize by portraying life in a specific religious community. They range in form from a simple presentation of faith, through the tract or sermon, to the arena where differing views contend. *Philip Hazelbrook; or, The Junior Curate* (1886) by the Reverend H. F. Darnell was intended "faithfully to portray the Church of England of to-day as she really is"; the contributions of the extremely popular and prolific Basil King present general moral problems within the framework of the Episcopal church. *Duncan Polite: The Watchman of Glenoro* (1905) by Marian Keith and *St. Cuthbert's* (1905) by the Reverend R. E. Knowles centre in the Presbyterian manse and settlement. Although they are not primarily "religious," W. A. Fraser's *The Lone Furrow* (1907) and Sara Jeannette Duncan's *The Imperialist* (1904) dramatize the importance of the church and church-going in sections of Ontario that are predominantly Presbyterian. *The King's Messenger; or, Lawrence Temple's Probation: A Story of Canadian Life* (1879), *Neville Truman, the Pioneer Preacher: A Tale of the War of 1812* (1880), and *Barbara Heck: A Tale of Early Methodism in America* (1895), represent the Reverend W. H. Withrow's devoted contribution to his particular church.

More closely related to English religious fiction, the battleground for rival sects earlier in the century, are attacks or defences of the Roman Catholic cause. Emily Weaver in *Soldiers of Liberty: A Story of Wars in the Netherlands* (1892) recalled the Spanish persecutions to express her fear of Catholicism. Frank Clifford Smith in *A Daughter of Patricians* (1901) attacked the marriage laws of Quebec and the power of the Catholic clergy over their credulous people. The Roman Catholic cause was defended and advocated by W. J. Fischer's *Winona and Other Stories* (1906), Elizabeth Gagnieur's *Back in the Fifties; or, Winnings and Weedings: A Tale of Tractarian Times* (1907), and the Reverend E. J. Devine's *The Training of Silas* (1906). Lily Dougall, always quick to profit from strange materials, portrayed Mormon struggles sympathetically in *The Mormon Prophet* (1899). J. P. Buschlen's Mormon story, *Peter Bosten: A Story about Realities* (1915) is more partisan. The Amish way of life in their central Ontario settlements is described with understanding by Clyde Smith in his *The Amishman* (1912). The most topical and most controversial of these partisan works was *Looking Forward: The Strange Experience of the Rev. Fergus McCheyne* (1913). Here, using the method of Edward Bellamy, the Rev. Hugh Pedley looked forward to the time when Church Union has been achieved, making Canada "better because a little more of heaven has entered into its life."

These works deal with firm convictions and determined positions. There are several, however, that are more closely linked with contemporary religious uncertainty. These, a mere handful in contrast to the large output in Great Britain and the United States, reflect the dissolution of traditional beliefs, the intellectual problems that result from the impact on traditional religion of science and "Higher Criticism" and the growth of scepticism and agnosticism. The emphasis falls on one central character, around whose spiritual biography the plot is built. The novel traces his doubts, loss of faith, and his search for a new religious position, unorthodox and undogmatic, or for some substitute "religion." The chief problems are the inspiration of the Bible, the presence of pain and evil in the universe, and the divinity of Christ; solutions are found in Pantheism, Universalism, and a belief in "Brotherhood," "true Christianity," the "living Jesus of the Gospels."

An incongruous mixture of current ideas and sensation, mystery and sentiment mars Watson Griffin's *Twok: A Novel* (1887), A. E. Greenwood's *The Light and the Lure* (1897), and James Algie's *Houses of Glass: A Philosophical Romance* (1898). Algie's *Bergen Worth* (1901) is more successful, through his realization of two characters that embody his central idea: the superiority of a religion based on the promptings of the individual conscience, expressed in charitable action, over that based on authority. Lily Dougall, strenuously intellectual, and at the same time sensitive to the requirements of the public, included the search for a new, more tolerant faith in *What Necessity Knows* (1893). In *The Zeit-Geist* (1895) she traced the central character's discovery of what he calls "Pantheism," when he finds himself "alone in the world with his new ideas."

Roland Graeme, Knight: A Novel of Our Times (1892) by Agnes Maule Machar and *The Preparation of Ryerson Embury: A Purpose* by A. R. Carman have much in common. Both heroes, brought up by fundamentalist parents, lose their dogmatic faith at college, but through the dual influence of Henry George and a good minister, come to a new faith that solves the problems of labour by the example of the life of Christ. While Agnes Maule Machar placed her emphasis on external events and direct statement, Carman came closer to finding a suitable form, concentrating on the internal struggle of Ryerson Embury. Reading Paley, Paine, Strauss, and Ingersoll, and disturbed by the problems raised by science, he loses his faith. It is Carman's steady focus on Embury's spiritual odyssey through a significant pattern of events, against a solidly realized social background, that makes *The Preparation of Ryerson Embury* stand out among this group of religious novels.

A number of ministers and their parishioners, militant against drink, used fiction to preach cautionary tales. The titles usually tell the story: the Reverend James Seymour's *The Temperance Battlefield and How to Gain the Day: A Book for the Young of All Ages, full of Humorous and Pathetic Stories* (1882); Austin Potter's *From Wealth to Poverty: or, Tricks of the Traffic: A Story of the Drink Curse* (1884); Lance Bilton's *"Guilty": Forgiven—Reclaimed; "Truth is Stranger than Fiction": A Canadian Story from Real Life* (1906) or the two stories in one volume, *A Fragment of*

Ontario's Scott Act: or, A Ruined Life, by "W.C.T.U." (Mrs. DeWolf) and *Lawyer Robert Streighton's Discovery at a Mineral Spring*, by "Carlton" (Mrs. C. A. Baird). Episodes dramatizing the evils of drink, along with little sermons and tableaux, appear in a number of the longer fictions of the day, such as H. A. Cody's *The Frontiersman* (1910) or Stephen Cureton's *Perseverance Wins* (1880). Some of the realistic novels used alcoholism as one of the grimmer facts of everyday life, such as Frances Beynon's *Aleta Dey* (1919). Temperance reformers are derided in a few fictions, such as E. E. Sheppard's *A Bad Man's Sweetheart* (1889). One of the most spectacular scenes involving drink occurs in James Dunlop's melodrama *Forest Lily* (1898) when a drunkard curses and immediately is snatched up.

Missionaries and their wives wrote fiction to attract support for their work in spreading the gospel. Some missionaries wrote of the Far East: Janet McKillican published her *The Tragedy of Paotingfu* in 1902; the Reverend James Gale wrote of Korea in *The Vanguard* (1904); the Reverend William Walker did the same in *Occident and Orient* in 1905; in 1914 the Reverend Thurlow Fraser published his *The Call of the East: A Romance of Far Formosa*. Other missionaries wrote of the home missionary fields; the romances of Ralph Connor, Robert Knowles, Hiram Cody, and Dr. Grenfell have been noted. The Reverend Egerton Ryerson Young directed his missionary story *Oowikapun; or, How the Gospel Reached the Nelson River Indians* (1895) and five others to young, impressionable readers; his son, of the same name, carried on his work. Christian evangelism welled over into missionary endeavour for animals. Margaret Marshall Saunders is said to have given most of what royalties she received for her many animal stories to Humane Societies; her most famous book, *Beautiful Joe* (1894), published originally by the American Baptist Publishing Society, sold over one million copies in fourteen languages. Miss Saunders' story is not as sentimental as the many animal tales by other Canadian women writers. The men who wrote animal stories—Roberts, Seton, Fraser, and McKishnie—wrote in a different vein; their work is considered elsewhere.

The demand for historical romance led some Canadian writers to write of the past of lands other than their own. Elizabethan and Jacobean England seems to have attracted the more sentimental romancers, such as Emily Weaver in *My Lady Nell* (1889) and *Prince Rupert's Namesake* (1893), Virna Sheard in *Trevelyan's Little Daughters* (1898), *A Maid of Many Moods* (1902) and *By the Queen's Grace* (1904), and Marjorie Pickthall in the more private *Little Hearts* (1915). John A. Copland's *A Meteor King* (1899) is of Richard III. The Spanish Catholic suppression of religious liberty in the Netherlands was used for propaganda by Elizabeth Walshe in *Within Sea Walls; or, How the Dutch Kept the Faith* (1881) and in Emily Weaver's *Soldiers of Liberty* (1892). William McLennan told swashbuckling tales in his *Spanish John* (1898) and *In Old France and New* (1899). Gilbert Parker's romance of the Jersey Islands, *The Battle of the Strong* (1898), was considered by many readers his best historical romance.

Historical romances of biblical, Greek, and Roman times enjoyed a steady success in the nineteenth century. In 1882 the Reverend William Withrow constructed a romantic story *Valeria: A Tale of Early Christian Life in Rome* out of his earlier history of the Catacombs. The Reverend P. J. Harold wrote another romance of female Christian martyrdom in his *Irene of Corinth: A Historical Romance of the First Century* (1884). The journalist and actor William Thorold told a story of Nazareth and Rome in his *Zerola of Nazareth* (1895); the Reverend LeRoy Hooker published *Enoch, the Philistine: A Traditional Romance of Philistia, Egypt, and the Great Pyramid* in 1898. Emily Weaver's *The Rabbi's Sons: A Story of the Days of St. Paul* appeared in 1891. L. O. Loomer used the Amos story in his *The Prophet: A Story of the Two Kingdoms of Ancient Palestine* in 1911. Edgar Maurice Smith exploited the violence and rapine of Hannibal crossing the Alps in *Aneroestes the Gaul* (1898). James Miller Grant's *The Mother of St. Nicholas (Santa Claus): A Story of Duty and Peril* (1899) is a melodrama of lions, Christians, and coliseums in the third century in Asia Minor.

The religiosity of some found outlet in pseudo-spiritual fiction. Canadian versions of the popular kinds of psychic fiction appear in Julia Henshaw's *Hypnotized; or, The Experiment of Sir Hugh Galbraith* (1898), Ida May Ferguson's *Tisab Ting; or, The Electric Kiss* (1896), Flora Macdonald's *Mary Melville, the Psychic* (1900), Benjamin Fish Austin's *The Mystery of Ashton Hall* (1910), and "Q, A Psychic Pstory of the Psupernatural!" in Stephen Leacock's *Nonsense Novels* (1911).

A characteristic part of the experience of a number of Canadian writers during these years was that of "going away" from their small, native communities to alien lands. The three broad movements were westward to the plains, foothills, and the Coast (manifest in the fiction listed above in the description of the literary map of Canada); southward to large American cities, particularly New York or Boston; and eastward across the Atlantic to London or the Continent. Those who used their encounter with the Old World in their fiction possibly followed the success of earlier Canadian writers who had pictured provincials abroad—Thomas Chandler Haliburton in his *The Letter Bag of the Great Western* (1840), his *The Attaché; or, Sam Slick in England* (1843), or De Mille's *The Dodge Club; or, Italy in 1859* (1869), or else they followed the success of American books about innocents abroad, passionate pilgrims, and other international themes. Mrs. Carrie Jenkins Harris pursued the comic vein of her Maritime predecessors in her lamer *Mr. Perkins of Nova Scotia* (1891). Sara Jeannette Duncan was much more successful in her spirited social comedies of international manners, *An American Girl in London* (1891), and its sequel *A Voyage of Consolation* (1898). Her central character, Lorne Murchison, in *The Imperialist* (1904) is affected strongly by the vision of imperialism during his visit to England, and one part of the book deals with the political and social consequences of this vision. In Miss Duncan's fullest canvas of the Canadian in England, *Cousin Cinderella* (1908), the young narrator and her brother, sent to England as cultural ambassadors, are conscious of being colonials no longer; "home" is not London but the small Ontario town and countryside. In *Those Delightful Americans* (1902), Miss Duncan pictured the innocent young Englishwoman's encounter with American culture. L. S. Huntington similarly brought a group of English people to America in his *Professor Conant: A Story of English and American Social and Political Life* (1884), with less acuteness than Miss Duncan.

The innocent Canadians abroad in Alice Jones's *Gabriel Praed's Castle* (1904), *Marcus Holbeach's Daughter* (1912), and *Flame of Frost* (1914) are beset by the corrupt forces of the Old World. Miss Duncan had followed faithfully her mentors Howells and James in trying to present the truth as she saw it; Alice Jones highlighted the aspects of the Old World which brought out her romance and melodrama. Susan Jones did the same in *A Girl of the North* (1900); in *A Detached Pirate* (1903) she brought her gay young divorcée from London to Halifax, and narrated through letters her romantic adventures in the garrison set. The spirit and the form make it an amusing contrast to that first of Canadian fictions, Frances Brooke's *The History of Emily Montague*, published 134 years before.

Gilbert Parker (later Sir Gilbert, and a London spokesman for Imperialism) used the theme of the young person from the province in "At the Sign of the Eagle," *The Translation of a Savage* (1893), and *The Trespasser* (1893), some of his earliest work while he himself was assaulting the London literary world. His stories of the people from the periphery in England are of struggle for power, and recognition. Beverley Baxter's *The Parts Men Play* (1920) is the story of an American idealist in wartime England, and suggests a bright young writer's strenuous effort to conceal the fact that he is a Canadian.

Canadian writers had one more dimension to their international experience than their American contemporaries, for they could go south or east. The move to Boston is central to Basil King's *The High Heart* (1917) and *The City of Comrades* (1919), and appears incidentally in some of his other books. Arthur Stringer's ambitious first novel, *The Silver Poppy* (1903), is about a young literary graduate from Oxford who moves to New York to write his great novel. Thomas Stinson Jarvis's *She Lived in New York* (1894) deals in part with New York Bohemia, as his earlier *Dr. Perdue* (1892) had dealt in part with an international smart set. The second half of Harvey

O'Higgins' *Don-A-Dreams* (1906) brings three young Canadian undergraduates to New York to storm the heights. These fictions were written from first-hand experience of the American cities; the second half of Robert Lorne Richardson's *Colin of the Ninth Concession* (1903) was derived apparently from Horatio Alger's stories of the country boy who comes to the big city and achieves financial success by pluck and luck. Susie Frances Harrison's *The Forest of Bourg-Marie* (1898) contrasts the ways of life in provincial Quebec and in a godless American city (Milwaukee).

Although the central character in stories of young Canadians in New York may aspire to be a writer, the great good place for young Canadians with raw talent in the arts was Europe. Jane Conger's *A Daughter of St. Peters* (1889) is the story of young artists in Rome. In Maud Ogilvy's *Marie Gourdon* (1890) a Canadian girl becomes a famous singer, and a boy an artist. In Thaddeus Leavitt's *The Witch of Plum Hollow* (1892) a young Canadian girl becomes a famous artist. Sara Jeannette Duncan sent her "new woman" from Illinois to study painting in the Latin Quarter in *A Daughter of Today* (1894), and after failure in Paris, to free-lance in London. Amelia Fytche's *Kerchiefs to Hunt Souls* (1895) is a melodrama of a young woman who goes to Paris to paint, marries a Frenchman, and is deserted by him. Joanna Wood's heroine in *Judith Moore; or, Fashioning a Pipe* (1898) flees from a great singing career in the outside world to the Ontario village of Ovid, where she finds love. The power of music plays a major part in the romances by Clifford Smith, *A Daughter of Patricians* (1901) and Lilla Nease, *In Music's Thrall* (1903). The title of Albert Richardson Carman's book tells enough of its tale: *The Pensionnaires: The Story of an American Girl who Took a Voice to Europe and Found—Many Things* (1903). Europe as an art world is the background for Alice Jones's *Gabriel Praed's Castle* (1904). The ineffectual heroine in Harvey O'Higgins' *Don-A-Dreams* (1906) fails to achieve a musical career in Europe. Robert Service's *The Pretender* (1914) is a romance of bohemian life in the Latin Quarter. Winifred Reeve's *Marion* (1916) is the story of an artists' model. The hero of John Murray Gibbon's *Hearts and Faces* (1916) moves from Aberdeen, through Soho in London, to Paris in search of his creative soul. Gibbon's *Drums Afar* (1918) also is concerned, in part, with artists. Very few Canadian fictions pictured the writer or artist as indigenous; in W. A. Fraser's anti-romantic *The Lone Furrow* (1907) the narrator is a novelist; in Susie Frances Harrison's *Ringfield* (1914), the heroine acts in a small Montreal theatre. The young heroine in Maud Petitt's *Beth Woodburn* (1897), living in a small western Ontario community, has the ambition to become a novelist, but sacrifices it to become a missionary; Miss Petitt's book is a rare example of the mingling of the worlds of art and religion; in most of the books noted here the world of art is indifferent, or hostile, to the world of religion.

In the last few years of this period, the First World War, chiefly in its domestic aspects, appeared in some Canadian fiction. A few writers wrote as did Nellie McClung in her semi-fictional *The Next of Kin* (1917) to make the home fires burn brighter. Others wrote to capitalize on or commemorate aspects of the war, as Frederick Bell did in *A Romance of the Halifax Disaster* (1918), or Gertrude Arnold in *Sister Anne! Sister Anne!* (1920), or Captain S. N. Dancey in *The Faith of a Belgian: A Romance of the Great War* (1916). Some sentimentalized the home front, as Jean Blewett did in *Heart Stories* (1919).

Other writers used the War as a force to help them express certain themes in their novels. Robert Stead in *The Cow Puncher* (1918) closed his story of his hero's search for identity by having him die at the Front and thus become initiated into the "Order of Suffering." Basil King used the tensions created by Canada's entering the War earlier and for different reasons than the United States in his *The High Heart* (1917) and *The City of Comrades* (1919). Beverley Baxter in *The Blower of Bubbles* (1919) depicted the conflicts in an idealistic pacifist in wartime England and New York, who eventually joins the American army and finds his problems resolved in action at the Front. In the closing section of Frances Beynon's *Aleta Dey* (1919) the heroine loses her man to the War and campaigns for the pacific cause in Winnipeg, is arrested, and dies with a noble pronouncement. Bertrand Sinclair in his equally anti-romantic *Burned Bridges* (1919) made the personal choice of enlistment one of the bridges his hero must burn behind him. The heroine of Evah McKowan's *Janet of Kootenay* (1919) finally joins her fortunes with those of a wounded returned officer. The disenchanted returned man in John Murray Gibbon's *The Conquering Hero* (1920) takes to the woods as a guide. Ralph Connor's *The Major* (1917) is a sentimental romance, set in a small Alberta community, as the world moves into war. His *The Sky Pilot in No Man's Land* (1919) takes a young Alberta chaplain to active service at the Front and to a sacrificial death. It is the epitome of a prevalent Anglo-Saxon Canadian view of the War—idealistic, Protestant evangelical, and British tribal—and probably more prevalent among non-combatants and officers than among Other Ranks.

One other major kind of fiction written by Canadians between 1880 and 1920 is that of mystery and crime melodrama. Many of the books noted above, although not mystery or crime melodramas, open with some mystery —the problem of unknown parents, hidden relationships, inscrutable motives, lost wills, inexplicable disappearances, or the arrival of unknown strangers; and many of them conclude with the solution of the initial mystery and the heroine in the hero's arms. But more than fifty fictions during these years are mystery or crime stories in the stricter sense. Some of them are semi-fictitious accounts of actual happenings, such as the highly melodramatic *The Four*

Canadian Highwaymen; or, The Robbers of Markham Swamp (1886) by Joseph Collins, or John Charles Dent's *The Gerrard Street Mystery and Other Weird Tales* (1888). Some play with supernatural or psychical elements: Thaddeus Leavitt's *The Witch of Plum Hollow* (1892), James Algie's *Bergen Worth* (1901), or Benjamin Austin's *The Mystery of Ashton Hall* (1910). Others mix mystery or crime with local colour, humour, and sentiment, as does E. E. Sheppard's *A Bad Man's Sweetheart* (1889) or the second half of his *Dolly: The Young Widder up to Felder's* (1886), or Isadore Asher's *An Odd Man's Story* (1889). After the turn of the century the fashion changed to the mystery or suspense story of the underworld or of international intrigue. The typical hero became the master-mind, either within or outside the law. One of the pacesetters of the new fashion was Arthur Stringer in his *The Wire Tappers* (1906), *Phantom Wires* (1907), *The Gun Runner* (1909), *The Shadow* (1913), and *The House of Intrigue* (1918). Some of the earliest stories in Frank Packard's long and prolific career are suspense stories of moral and sentimental dilemmas, *Greater Love Hath No Man* (1913), *The Miracle Man* (1914), and *The Beloved Traitor* (1915). Packard produced the first of his widely popular master-mind mysteries in *The Adventures of Jimmy Dale, Detective* in 1917. Harvey O'Higgins published his *The Adventures of Detective Barney* in book form in 1915. Guy Morton's *The Enemy Within* (1918) is the first of his ten mystery stories. Hulbert Footner and W. L. Amy interspersed mystery fiction in the publication of their steady streams of western action tales.

Between 1880 and 1920 few Canadian fiction writers revealed in their work any awareness of the various kinds of "new fiction" which appeared in Great Britain and in the United States as these years rolled by, from writers as diverse as James, Conrad, Crane, Norris, Dreiser, Wells, Forster, Ford, Mackenzie, Lawrence, Joyce, Anderson, Virginia Woolf, and Willa Cather. Often experimental in form, the "new fiction" frequently explored the darker side of human experience. Usually it was written to express the writer's private vision, not to please the tastes of the comon reader. Canadian writers, however, like most of their British and American contemporaries, lived and worked on another floor in the house of fiction. As this panorama of roughly two-thirds of the Canadian fiction published during these years has shown, they wrote in the varieties of fiction read by the great middle band in the spectrum of the reading public. Panoramas of their values, their forms, their characters, and their fictional techniques would show similar community. What did distinguish their work, as a body, was the remarkable extent to which they used their own native grounds as material in their stories.

17. Writers of Fiction
1880-1920

GORDON ROPER, S. ROSS BEHARRIELL
AND RUPERT SCHIEDER

ANOTHER PERSPECTIVE of the contours of Canadian fiction between 1880 and 1920 can be obtained by placing, side by side, sketches of the fiction-writing careers of the more skilful Canadian writers of these years, in order of their first appearance in book form.

John Bourinot's opinion of the barrenness of the Canadian fiction field, quoted at the beginning of chapter 15, was also held by other Canadian commentators on the arts in Canada. In his essay, however, Bourinot did express some hope that the first books recently published by the young Gilbert Parker, Sara Jeannette Duncan, and Lily Dougall marked the end of the barren period. That he did not name two other writers of Canadian background, Grant Allen and Robert Barr, who already had made places for themselves on the London literary scene, suggests that Bourinot shared the uncertainty of other Canadians in the early nineties about who and what was a "Canadian" writer.

Grant Allen (1848–1899) was Canadian in the sense that he had been born near Kingston, Ontario, and had spent his first thirteen years there before his Irish clergyman father moved the family to Connecticut, then to France, and finally to England. Allen graduated from Oxford in 1871 with a keen interest in science. He threw himself into a writing career in London to support his scientific studies and to advance his ideas. Out of a stream of magazine writing on evolution, biology, botany, religion, and human relations, he published some seventy books, including over forty fictions. His fiction often dramatizes new scientific and social ideas; he had a vigorous imagination; his work was controversial, and it was widely read in England and in North America. His fiction includes *Philistia* (1884) which satirized fuzzy Utopianism; the sensational *The Devil's Die* (1888), and the more notorious *The Woman Who Did* (1895) which embodies his ideas about the value of sexual freedom.

Grant Allen's fiction contains little that reflects his Canadian birth and early education. His books were discussed in Canadian journals, but few Canadians, for whatever reasons, thought of him as "one of ours."

More readers thought of Robert Barr as a Canadian writer. Barr (1850–1912) was born in Glasgow, Scotland, but had been brought to Canada by his family when he was five. He grew up on a farm near Wallacetown, Ontario, and after a year at the Toronto Normal School taught near Windsor. He began his professional writing career on the *Detroit Free Press*, and moved permanently to England in 1881 when he was thirty-one. In London he became one of the more successful of those who wrote for the English and American magazines; he also was co-founder with Jerome K. Jerome and editor of *The Idler* magazine in 1892. Among his many literary and journalistic friends he numbered Stephen Crane, with whom he collaborated in writing a picaresque tale, *The O'Ruddy* (1903). His more than thirty volumes of fiction include examples of almost every kind of fiction popular in the Anglo-American literary world at the turn of the century: adventure romances in the Richard Harding Davis vein; costume dramas and historical romances in somewhat imaginary kingdoms; detective tales; tales of the supernatural; and "muckraking" novels of political, social, and labour strife.

Unlike Grant Allen, Robert Barr drew on his Canadian experience in some of his short stories and longer fiction. *The Woman Intervenes* (1895) has an Ottawa interlude, and his study of political corruption in New York, *The Victor* (1901), has a Montreal episode. Much more fully Canadian was one of his first books, *In the Midst of Alarms* (1894), whose central action is a comic treatment of the battle of Ridgeway during the Fenian Raids. In one of his last books, *The Measure of the Rule* (1906) Barr used still-vivid memories of his Toronto Normal School experience to attack the stuffiness of Ontario life, and, in particular, the Ontario educational establishment, subjects which he must have known would not command universal international attention.

It is understandable that Grant Allen, concerned primarily with the discovery and propagation of new truths, found little or nothing in his Canadian past of use in his writings. Nor is it surprising that Robert Barr, concerned primarily as he was with entertaining the sophisticated Anglo-American reading public, drew little on his Canadian experience. What is odd is that he did write two books so largely concerned with particulars of the Canadian scene.

Like Allen and Barr, Sara Jeannette Duncan (1861-1922) was attracted to literary London, made her début there in book form, achieved an international literary popularity, and never returned to live in her native country. But unlike Allen and Barr who assimilated themselves abroad, Sara Jeannette Duncan made much of her work out of her acute sense of the distinctions between Canadians, Americans, and the English. Even her novels of British India have an angle of vision that is non-English and anti-colonial. Miss Duncan was born and grew up in Brantford, Ontario, and, after a little teaching, sailed into a remarkably successful journalistic career with the Washington *Post*, the Toronto *Globe*, and Goldwin Smith's *The Week*, as correspondent and columnist. Her first book, dedicated to Mrs. Grundy, was published in London in 1890, as *A Social Departure: How Orthodocia and I Went Round the World by Ourselves*. British, American, and Canadian reviewers welcomed it for its freshness and cleverness. She capitalized on this success by writing the first of a number of international comedies, *An American Girl in London* (1891) in which Mamie Wick, a lighter-hearted Daisy Miller from Chicago breezily comments on her English social experiences. This Jamesian heiress of all the ages tells of her later matrimonial and travel adventures on the Continent in *A Voyage of Consolation* (1898). The device is reversed in *Those Delightful Americans* (1902), in which a young English married woman makes her first trip to America. The device was varied again in 1908 in *Cousin Cinderella: A Canadian Girl in London*, where Mary Trent, a young Canadian, narrates her story of a visit to England with her brother as cultural ambassadors for their senator father. Mary is a more natural and more complex character than Mamie Wick; her brother, Graham, has an idealism about Empire similar to Lorne Murchison's in the earlier *The Imperialist*, and the book, for all its comedy, touches serious chords of thought and feeling. The last book in the international vein, *His Royal Happiness* (1914), is a romantic fantasy, expressing a dream of stronger British-American unity.

Meanwhile in 1891 Miss Duncan married Everard Cotes, whom she had met in India, and much of the rest of her life was spent there. Her early experience had given her the materials for her international comedies; her Indian life gave her the experience for nine more books. Her first Indian book was *The Simple Adventures of a Memsahib* (1893), a quiet, charming comedy of a young English girl who goes out to India to marry, and of her day-by-day experiences in adapting herself to her exotic circumstances—a man, an Indian life. Mrs. Cotes used the migrant pattern in a broader vein in *Vernon's Aunt: Being the Oriental Experiences of Miss Lavinia Moffat* (1894). In the same year she published a juvenile, *The Story of Sonny Sahib*.

In 1894 Mrs. Cotes also opened the more serious vein she was to pursue in her later Indian books and in *The Imperialist*, with *A Daughter of Today*, the story of Elfrida Bell, an independent young woman from Sparta, Illinois, who goes to the Left Bank to express her soul. There she finds her talent inadequate, and she moves to a bachelor flat in Kensington to earn a living by journalism and to storm the heights of the literary world. Mrs. Cotes dissects the egotism of this "New Woman" with cool and sustained analysis. No Canadian had ever written a book like this in subject or in tone.

Two years later she pursued this darker vein in one of her finest books, *His Honour and a Lady*, a novel of the English ruling classes in India. It is a tragedy of misplaced love and betrayal, presented in dramatic scenes, with much less author-analysis. *The Path of a Star* (*Hilda*, in the American edition) followed in 1899. This story of two parallel and tangled love affairs, involving a very independent young actress with an Anglican missionary, and a young Englishman with a fanatical Salvation Army girl, was granted "the reality and the force" the critics had found in Mrs. Cotes's earlier work, but some complained of her growing love for tortured metaphor, an element which declined in her later work.

Her interest in the rising controversy over the possibility of a "Greater Britain" led her to write her next serious novel, *The Imperialist* (1904). This is her one novel set in an Ontario town, Elgin (Brantford), with a full cast of hometown people. She wrote it to correct the impression about Canadian enthusiasm for Imperialism spread in England by over-heated oratory at Toronto banquets, by showing how the issue appeared to "the average Canadian of the average small town . . . whose views in the end count for more" than those of banquet speakers. The book reflects her strong feeling for the various aspects of southern Ontario town life, and is touched with humour and indulgent irony.

In 1906 she published *Set in Authority,* a tense drama caused by the zeal of an Indian governor who, with stern idealism, tries to enforce equality of justice to Indian and Englishman alike, and brings tragedy to those close to him. The uglier realities of Anglo-Indian relations underlie the story, and the tone is darker than in the earlier Indian novels. Even closer to immediate unrest in India is *The Burnt Offering* (1909), in which a zealous, idealistic socialist M.P. comes from England to see the social wrongs that are leading Indians to open revolt. With him comes his suffragette daughter; she marries an Indian who has, unknown to her, dedicated himself to the assassination of the Viceroy. This is the most quietly violent of Mrs. Cotes's books; it ends with an unspoken curse on both houses.

Politics also forms the background of Mrs. Cotes's next, and in some ways, most interesting novel, *The Consort* (1912). But the foreground of the book is the moral drama of Mary Pargeter, an assured woman of immense inherited wealth who lives for its stewardship. She has been married by an ambitious literary man who finds himself smothered by his wife's high sense of duty, and by her money. The book is written with power and clarity, and has moments of deep insight.

Mrs. Cotes's last two books are much lighter in weight. *Title-Clear* wa published just before her death in 1922 in Surrey, England, and *The Gold-*

Cure (unfinished) was published two years later. She also published earlier in her career four novelettes under the title *The Pool in the Desert* (1903), of which the second "A Mother in India," shows her at her cleverest.

Sara Jeannette Duncan Cotes is of the small company of Canadian writers who, like Leacock and Haliburton, had a sharp eye for the human comedy, but who also, like Henry James and George Meredith, were concerned with what underlay the comedy. Canadian fiction had before her no woman writer of such literary skill and range, and has had only two or perhaps three since.

Horatio Gilbert Parker (1860–1932), like Sara Jeannette Duncan, achieved a career as a popular writer after leaving Canada. About half of his thirty-six romances and novels are set in a Canadian scene, but, unlike Sara Jeanette Duncan, he used his scene as romantic atmosphere to enhance melodramatic action. Gilbert Parker was born in Camden East, a crossroads village northeast of Napanee, Ontario; he was educated locally and at Ottawa Normal School, studied theology at Trinity College where he gave instruction in elocution, and, later, also at Queen's University. After serving as a deacon in Trenton, he set off for the South Seas and Australia. Four successful years of newspaper work and writing plays allowed him to establish himself in London as a writer of short stories about the South Seas and the Canadian Northwest. His first book, *Pierre and His People* (1892), collected seventeen Pretty Pierre stories, and twenty-two more were published in book form as *An Adventurer of the North* (1895 in England, and as *An Adventurer of the North* and *A Romany of the Snows* in the United States). These and the first five tales collected in *Northern Lights* (1909) present a theatrical picture of the Northwest before the railroad came, and, as he said, are full of "poignant mystery, solitude, and big primitive incident." Parker later claimed that they opened up a new field of fiction, but the milieu was hardly new to those who had read Ballantyne, Kingston, or Henty, while the manner seems a mixture of Bret Harte, R. L. Stevenson, and Parker's own strong melodramatic flair and elocutionary rhetoric. Some Canadian readers resented the tales as misrepresentation of the Canadian Northwest.

The other twelve stories collected in *Northern Lights* deal with the changing Northwest as the railroads opened up the country in the eighties. In three later books, *You Never Know Your Luck* (1914), *The World for Sale* (1916), and *Wild Youth and Another* (1919), Parker wrote stories of Saskatchewan town life in the early years of the twentieth century, based on some first-hand knowledge of the scene but more impressive for their action than their fidelity to the local scene or people.

Parker had not seen the Northwest when he wrote his Pierre tales, but had visited French Canada, and his romantic imagination responded to what he felt to be its picturesqueness, and its hierarchical traditional quality. He used French Canada, past and present, for the background of eight of his books before 1920: *The Trail of the Sword* (1894); *When Valmond Came to Pontiac* (1895); *The Pomp of the Lavilettes* (1896); *The Seats of the Mighty* (1896); *Born with a Golden Spoon* (1899); *The Lane That Had No Turning* (1900); *The Right of Way* (1901); and *The Money Master* (1915). His "story of a lost Napoleon," *When Valmond Came to Pontiac*, dramatizes the "pathetic—unutterably pathetic—incident of a man driven by the truth in his blood to impersonate himself," and he looked back upon this as his finest work. This historical fantasy has a unity of tone, action, and character that his better-known *The Seats of the Mighty* lacks, and it has a *panache* that his other work does not have in so sustained a fashion. In *The Seats of the Mighty* he used the fall of Quebec as background for a costume drama that fails to catch the flavour of the times as Kirby had done in the first half of his *The Golden Dog* (1877), or as Francis Parkman had in the historical narratives which Parker used for source materials. The French-Canadian countryside of his own day served Parker much more effectively as atmosphere for his best-selling *The Right of Way*, the mystery of the dipsomaniac Charley Steele who lost his memory and assumed another personality.

Parker once wrote: "Whatever may be thought of my books, they represent nothing but the bent of my own mind, my own wilful expression of myself, and the setting forth of that which seized my imagination." Although he tended to romanticize himself as a writer, the French-Canadian stories probably throw light on Parker's own temperament. Two other early stories, *The Translation of a Savage* (1893) and especially *The Trespasser* (1893), throw a stronger light on their author. Both books have the theme of the impact of an unsophisticated young person from the wilds of Canada upon the "complicated orderly life of England." Unlike Henry James's "passionate pilgrim," Parker's avenging son in *The Trespasser* wills to become a power in the Old Land. In other guises in Parker's stories, this Young Man from the Provinces is a dynamic force, and suggests a self-projection of the writer. For Parker himself moved on from his early writing success to marry a New York heiress, to become a member of the British parliament, and a figure in Imperial affairs in England. He moved in court and upper social circles, was knighted in 1902, made a baronet in 1915, and a member of the Privy Council. During the First World War he was in charge of British propaganda for North America. It was a long way from Camden East.

As he became more involved in the English and Imperial scene, he found new matter for his romances. One of his strongest historical romances, *The Battle of the Strong* (1898), is set in the Jersey Islands during the Napoleonic Wars. *Donovan Pasha* (1902) was a study for a longer Anglo-Egyptian political drama, *The Weavers* (1907). His concern for South African affairs resulted in *The Judgment House* (1913); his political interest in land settlement is reflected in the Saskatchewan stories *You Never Know Your Luck,* and *The World for Sale.* His best work, with the possible exception of *Tarboe* (1927), was done before 1920.

In 1912 his collected work began to appear in the Imperial Edition (1912–1923, 23 volumes), published by Scribner's in a format similar to that of their handsome editions of Dickens, Turgenev, Meredith, Kipling, and Henry James. Like Henry James, Parker wrote a preface to each volume. James's prefaces were searching explorations of the art of fiction; Parker's prefaces seem more concerned with self-justification and self-enhancement. Against the charge that his work lacked vital relation to life, he stated that he cared more "for truth and beauty than he did for fact," and that an "inner vision permitted him to see life as it really was." Replying to the criticism that his work was badly structured, he claimed that he worked instinctively, not methodically, and that many of his books seemed to write themselves as he worked in a continuous trance-like state. Countering the stricture that he saw character only as a series of melodramatic gestures, he asserted that "in my mind the episode was always the consequence of character." And against the criticism that his attitudes and his style were over-inflated, he answered that he "feared being led into mere rhetoric," and had to curb "a natural yet rather dangerous eloquence." Perhaps he was most just to himself when he wrote "I was a born dramatist." For, in spite of his aggrandizement of his work, he was a successful writer of fiction of strong effect. His strength lay in his power of creating spirited action, and enhancing it with romantic atmosphere.

When *Beggars All,* the first of eleven novels by Lily Dougall (1858–1923), appeared in 1891 it was warmly praised for its success in combining an entertaining story for the ordinary reader and metaphysical discussion for the thoughtful reader. A native of Montreal, and a graduate of classes for women at Edinburgh University, an LL.A. from St. Andrews, and the first editor of *The World Wide,* Lily Dougall lived most of her life in England. Fiction was for her a medium for conveying ideas, and one which she abandoned after 1908 for religion and philosophy. Although often obscured by other elements, the centre of her characteristic novel is religious and philosophical discussion. Her action presents a struggle to overcome doubts, or a conflict between two codes of ethics, or a search for the ideal life, and contains discussions of such subjects as individual responsibility, the Mormon and Adventist religions, and mesmerism. She was against the intolerance and persecution that spring from narrow sectarianism, and she advocated faith in "an eternal and beneficent purpose," tolerance, and Love. To present these ideas she adopted the framework of the mystery novel, with plots overladen with melodramatic incident, coincidences, disguises, hidden pasts, and endings in which threads are pulled together conveniently and miraculously, and good triumphs over evil.

At her best, she could tell a lively story with well-defined plain characters in a graphically described setting—the Rockies in *The Madonna of a Day* (1895), the coast of Prince Edward Island in *The Mermaid* (1895), the lonely backwoods region south of the Ottawa valley in *The Zeit-Geist* (1895) or the isolated farms of the Matapedia valley in *What Necessity Knows* (1893). But by adopting the formulas of sensational fiction, by disconcertingly sudden shifts from the world of realism to a world of sensationalism, and by employing a highly "literary" style, her fiction often fails to be as impressive as it obviously was intended to be.

London had been the great literary magnet in the eighties and the early nineties for ambitious young Canadian writers. The force of the American centres—Boston, Philadelphia, and especially New York—was stronger for the young Canadians who began writing in the mid-nineties. Some moved to New York or Boston as journalists and then became free-lance writers; others remained in their native localities. The alignment with the American centres was less alienating for most than the alignment with London. In the American centres they were accepted as natives, or near-natives, while in London, as Sara Jeannette Duncan pointed out, they often were half-accepted as colonials. The American publishers were nearer, easier of access, and more numerous than the British. American publications had a much greater market in Canada than had British publications. The American publisher was apt to regard fiction about the Canadian scene as an extension of American local colour writing or of American historical romance, and both were extremely popular in the nineties. The British publisher, on the other hand, was apt to find more saleable the exotic and wild aspects of the Canadian scene.

But not all Canadian writers were émigrés. Just before Sara Jeannette Duncan, Gilbert Parker, and Lily Dougall published their first books, two Canadian writers who remained within their native Canada began prolific, semi-professional careers. Margaret Marshall Saunders (1861–1947), author of one of the most widely read books written by a Canadian, *Beautiful Joe*, was born in Milton, Nova Scotia, and educated in Edinburgh and in Orléans, France. She began her career with a pleasant romance *My Spanish Sailor* (1889; enlarged and republished as *Her Sailor* in 1900). Her great success came when she visited some friends in Meaford, Ontario, saw Joe, and wrote his story. *Beautiful Joe* (1894) eventually sold over one million copies in English and in translation in numerous languages. Miss Saunders hoped to do for dogs what *Black Beauty* had done for horses. She shrewdly allowed Joe to tell his own story in a relatively unsentimental way, and Joe told the story well. Most of her twenty-six books are about animals, and follow the didactic pattern and sentiments of her great success. A few, such as *Rose à Charlitte: An Acadian Romance* (1898), reveal in their unencumbered storytelling and feeling for character (at least in the opening pages before the story becomes melodramatic) the qualities which made her animal stories so appealing to millions of young and old.

James Macdonald Oxley (1855–1907) became one of the most popular of the Canadian writers of boy's adventure stories. He was born in Halifax, and educated in the Maritimes and at Harvard. Apart from his literary activities, he had a distinguished legal and business career. He began writing while still in the Maritimes, contributing articles and stories with Canadian themes and settings to a great number of American periodicals. After moving to Ottawa, he turned almost exclusively to juvenile stories. In the twenty years after 1885, he published more than two dozen books. A few of his works are historical novels, usually with a teen-age hero; a few are set in the Maritimes; most of his books are stories of adventure in the remote and more romantic parts of Canada. His books were popular in England and the United States, and undoubtedly spread or reinforced the widespread notion of Canada as a land of simple-minded, exciting adventure.

There was little of the juvenile in the work of Thomas Stinson Jarvis (1854–1926), a member of a prominent Toronto family, who established an international reputation as a criminal lawyer, travelled widely, and distinguished himself as an international yachtsman. In 1890, Jarvis published *Geoffrey Hampstead*; set in Toronto, it is a study in criminal psychology in the form of a detective thriller which makes use of the author's knowledge of economics, criminal law, science, yachting, and upper class "society." The popularity of the book in the United States led him to a new career in letters. Moving to New York, Jarvis became a professional novelist, editor, and dramatic critic.

His second novel, *Dr. Perdue* (1892) is a sequel to *Geoffrey Hampstead*, picking up the criminal's career several years later, after his prison term, and after he has become a famous surgeon. The setting is Paris and England; the characters include both Canadians in Europe and the international yachting set.

The psychology of love is the central theme in Jarvis's final novel, *She Lived in New York* (1894). Daring, but delicately done, the book contains many pictures of the gay life in New York's high society, as well as some realistic description of its bohemia and less attractive *demi-monde*. Liberal and anti-puritan in its view, the novel has a journalistic, sometimes almost documentary flavour; the frankness with which it discusses love and sex is unusual for its time.

Jarvis's novels reflect the wide experience and the wide range of his interests; his urbane style, and his use of the novel as a vehicle for ideas, mark him as one of Canada's more sophisticated authors in the early 1890's.

Charles G. D. Roberts (1860–1943) wrote about fifty volumes of fiction during an unusually prolific writing career. All but a few of his fictions are animal stories, and are discussed elsewhere in this volume. His domestic romance, *The Heart That Knows* (1906) is largely biographical of his own family. His historical romances, *The Raid from Beauséjour* (1894), *The Forge in the Forest* (1896), *A Sister to Evangeline* (1898), and *The Prisoner of Mademoiselle* (1904) are of the *Ancien Régime*, and are located in or near the countryside he knew. *Barbara Ladd* (1902) is a historical romance of New England during the Revolution. *By the Marshes of Minas* (1900) collected a number of Acadian stories. Roberts's writing probably is at its weakest in these historical romances. The actions are episodic and repetitious; the emotional atmosphere is that of the light historical romance so popular in the nineties. The animal characters in his woods stories are more human than the puppets in these costume dramas. The freshest elements in such bread-and-margarine books are the passages describing the Bay of Fundy settings which Roberts obviously recalled with affection.

Edward William Thomson (1849–1924) was one of the most skilful story-tellers of the Canadian writers of his day, and it is a distinct loss that he published so few stories for adults. He was born in Peel County, Ontario, educated at Trinity College School, and, after volunteer experience in the American Civil War and the Fenian Raids, became an editorial writer on the Toronto *Globe* (1879–91), and then editor of the famous *Youth's Companion* in Boston (1891–1901). His first collection of short stories was published as *Old Man Savarin, and Other Stories* (1895). It contains tales, humorous and grave, of French Canadians and of Scotch settlements along the Ottawa, of war experiences and of U.E. Loyalists. "The Privilege of the Limit" has been a favourite of Canadian anthologists. The Canadian tales in this volume were reprinted, with new ones, in his expanded edition *Old Man Savarin Stories: Tales of Canada and Canadians* (1917). These tales are vigorous, dramatic, unsentimental, and economical in style. His other books, *Walter Gibbs, The Young Boss, and Other Stories* (1896), *Between Earth and Sky and Other Strange Stories of Deliverance* (1897), and *Smoky Days* (1901), were for a juvenile audience.

The sudden success of Ralph Connor (Rev. Charles William Gordon, 1860–1937) was phenomenal. His first book *Black Rock* (1898) was a collection of sketches which the young Presbyterian minister had written for his church magazine, to help raise funds for the church's missions in western Canada. *Black Rock* and its sequel *The Sky Pilot*, published the following year, captured the imagination of a vast reading public in Canada, the United States, and England which liked vigorous religion dramatized in story form. *The Man from Glengarry* (1901) sold almost as well. Within a few years the combined sales of his first three books were well over five million. Ralph Connor had become the most widely read Canadian writer, a distinction he was to enjoy for the next twenty years.

In all, Connor wrote more than a score of novels, as well as another half-dozen religious, biographical and autobiographical books. All of his fictions deal with Canada; most are tales of the ranges and timberlands and frontier settlements of the West. In addition to *Black Rock* and *The Sky Pilot*, the western books include *The Sky Pilot at Swan Creek* (1905), a collection of short stories; *Corporal Cameron* (1912) and *The Patrol of the Sun Dance Trail* (1914), North West Mounted Police stories; *The Gaspards of Pinecroft* (1923), a British Columbia romance. *The Prospector* (1904) and *The Doctor* (1906) both start in Ontario, but the stories move to the western frontiers. Early immigration in Winnipeg and the pioneer settlements provide the background for *The Foreigner* (1909); post-war labour problems in Winnipeg provide the theme of *To Him That Hath* (1921). Most of these western stories, particularly the early ones, capitalize on the romance, adventure, and physical beauty of the early West. Connor was writing here about his own experience. "I knew the country," he later wrote. "I had ridden the ranges. I had pushed through the mountain passes. I had swum my bronco across its rivers."

Connor was most at home, however, in his books which dealt with another, earlier aspect of the Canadian scene, the Ontario which he had known in the sixties. The two Glengarry books, *The Man from Glengarry* and *Glengarry School Days* (1902), both record Connor's boyhood experiences of pioneer life, as do the opening sections of *The Prospector, The Doctor,* and *Corporal Cameron.* It was in these books that Connor did much of his most effective writing; here are to be found his fine descriptions of many varied phases of the life of the early settlers, ranging from the logging bee to the wake, from the barn-raising to the revival meeting, from the bear hunt to the Dominion Day games. In the tradition of the local colourist, Connor portrayed the manner of life and the characters of an earlier age; in this type of writing, he displayed a skill and an artistry that he was not able to sustain through the larger narrative unit of the novel. Two of the later novels return to this same period, *Torches through the Bush* (1934), and *The Girl from Glengarry* (1933); but only the former succeeds in a limited way in catching the spirit of the earlier works.

The two wartime books, *The Major* and *The Sky Pilot in No Man's Land,* revived Connor's slightly waning popularity. After the war he wrote little that can compare with his earlier work: three historical novels, and three modern romances of the Maritimes and Ontario complete the canon.

Ralph Connor's melodramatic parables are shaped to make the reader identify strongly with the Good, usually simple-hearted Christians, relentlessly oppressed by scoffers and non-believers. After much violence, physical and emotional, Good redeems all. The world he created in these books is a projection of the emotional world of crisis, suffering, and overcoming of an evangelical Protestant minister. He wrote for, and helped to create, an audience that wanted fictionalized morality, and did not care much about artistic standards so long as the morality was pure and simple, the spiritual issues clear and strong, and the action exciting. However, his otherwise undistinguished romances contain many forceful passages. For Ralph Connor could be very effective when he wrote as a local colourist recording life in the early West and in pioneer Ontario.

The thirty or so books by Ernest Thompson Seton (1860–1946) are almost entirely about animals or woodcraft, and are discussed elsewhere in this volume. His books made Seton famous as a story-teller, illustrator, and naturalist. His rare excursion into fiction about adults, *The Preacher of Cedar Mountain: A Tale of the Open Country* (1917), is, in the vein of Ralph Connor, about a young man who goes to divinity school and becomes a minister in a new western town. But Seton's world is more complex than Ralph Connor's. His young minister is pulled from one side by a mystique about Nature, and from the other by his sense of duty to his townsmen. This conflict is complicated when he responds to a call of the city, and goes to South Chicago to start an undenominational worker's club. In the end the Nature mystique proves stronger, and he turns west again to God's country.

William Alexander Fraser (1859–1933) also established his early reputation as a teller of animal stories, *Mooswa and Others of the Boundaries* (1900), *The Outcasts* (1901), and *The Sa'-Zada Tales* (1905). What he called the first, a "simple romance of a simple people, the furred dwellers of the Northern Forests," is true of all three, for the animals speak as humans and take on human traits, good and bad. He also spun tales of Crees, Blackfeet, and white settlers in three tales in his first book, *The Eye of a God and Other Tales of East and West* (1899), and in *The Blood Lilies* (1903). Burma and India provide the setting for the other mystery stories in *The Eye of a God*, *Thirteen Men* (1906), and *The Three Sapphires* (1918). These incident-packed tales supply excitement through the devices of stolen jewels, spies, spells, drugged wine and opium, and murder, but they are told with a humorous touch that makes the scarcely hidden clues and the far-fetched improbabilities acceptable. He is most successful in his more sophisticated mystery and adventure tales about horse-racing, *Thoroughbreds* (1902), *Brave Hearts* (1904), and *Delilah Plays the Ponies* (1927), where thefts, disguises, crooked trainers and jockeys, doped horses, are ancillary to the effective races. One of his most amusing and exciting racing stories is included in *Bulldog Carney* (1919), a thoroughly entertaining collection of tales about a Robin Hood of the Rockies, who gambles, smuggles, bootlegs, and races, and has a big heart of gold.

The wide variety of people and scene in his stories came from Fraser's varied experience. He was born in Pictou County, Nova Scotia, educated in Boston, New York, and India, and worked in India, Burma, and the Canadian Northwest. He settled in Georgetown, Ontario, and it provided him with the background for the most serious of his fourteen books, *The Lone Furrow* (1907). Setting out to teach the importance of love and tolerance, he traces the career of a minister and his wife in Iona, a small Scottish settlement in Ontario. The frame and some of the materials are melodramatic. The enduring parts of the novel are those in which Iona is evoked: the community gatherings, the vicious local gossip, the religious bigotry, the interior of the houses, and the complex emotions of the central characters.

Fraser was one of the more effective magazine story-writers of his day, and generally he succeeded in doing what he set out to do, to entertain by a lively story, with a number of sharply realized characters, accurate dialect economically handled, and a lack of sentimentality.

Probably most fully professional of all the Canadian writers of the period was Arthur Stringer (1874–1950). In volume of publication, variety, and popularity of appeal, he ranked with Charles G. D. Roberts and Gilbert Parker. All three addressed most of their work first to magazine audiences. Stringer's magazine work reappeared in book form in over forty volumes of fiction, fifteen volumes of poetry, and three plays. He also wrote several biographies, a study of Shakespeare's *King Lear,* and plays and moving-picture scripts for several successful feature films. He was born in Chatham, and educated in London, Ontario. He contributed to Canadian and English magazines while he was at the University of Toronto and at Oxford, and gained his first popular success while working as a journalist for a large New York syndicate. His first volume, *The Loom of Destiny* (1899), had appeared originally in a New York periodical as a series of sketches of boy life in New York's East Side. His first novel, and in some ways one of his most interesting, was *The Silver Poppy* (1903), an ambitious study of a young man, fresh from Oxford, aspiring in New York's Bohemia to express life in a novel. *Lonely O'Malley* (1905) is a lively story of an orphan boy growing up in a Chatham-like town; it is a Canadian *Tom Sawyer*, without Mark Twain's anti-romantic undertone or his fine ear for speech.

Dividing his time between a southern Ontario fruit farm, New York, and travelling on the Continent, Stringer produced a long line of thrillers. The first of these, for which he carefully gathered facts, was *The Wire Tappers* (1906), followed by *Phantom Wires* (1907), *The Under Groove* (1908), and *The Gun Runner* (1909). These underworld adventures were interspersed by volumes of poetry, which he regarded as his serious literary work.

After 1914 he took up ranching in Alberta, and out of his western experiences came *The Prairie Wife* (1915). He achieved immediacy and vitality in this novel by having his gay-spirited, highly educated young New England girl tell in diary form of her arrival at an Alberta ranch as a young bride. In spite of some embarrassingly intimate slang, and some smart *Saturday Evening Post* situations, the underlying anti-romantic tone of the story often is convincing. The prairie wife continues her diary in *The Prairie Mother* (1920), and gives a wry account of the break-up of her marriage in *The Prairie Child* (1922). Stringer moved to New Jersey in 1919, and there wrote more ambitious novels, *The Wine of Life* (1921), *Power* (1925), and *The Mud Lark* (1932), in between new thrillers and stories of adventurous romance in the Canadian Northwest.

Stringer was one of the most competent and popular magazine writers of his day; he wrote a story that was fresh-spirited, fast-paced, dramatically told, with a sophisticated tone. His success in the popular field may have choked out the talent for more serious work that he revealed occasionally in a few of his books.

In contrast to the stream of fiction from Arthur Stringer, Francis William Grey (1860–1939) wrote only one novel, *The Curé of St. Philippe: A Story of French-Canadian Politics* (1899); its quality makes it regrettable that he wrote no more. Grey was English-born and educated, taught English at the University of Ottawa, and later worked in the Archives Bureau. He was a poet, playwright, and a contributor to Canadian periodicals. In his novel, Grey presented current native political and religious issues in the manner of the most finished Victorian novelists. His Trollopian narrator, the most interesting voice in the book, relates a plain narrative of facts about the new parish of St. Philippe des Bois in the Richelieu county. Undramatically and unromantically, he reflects the local elections, the intrigue for political rewards, the creation of the new parish, the building of the church, the business dealings, the social relations of the older generation and the love affairs of the younger. Grey's intelligence and his craftsmanship enabled him to depict the appearance and the forces shaping the appearance of the political, religious, and racial problems of this part of French Canada in the last years of the nineteenth century.

One of the more sophisticated popular novelists of his day, the Reverend William Benjamin (Basil) King was born in Charlottetown, Prince Edward Island, and educated at King's College, Windsor, Nova Scotia. After some years at St. Luke's, Halifax, he became rector of Christ Church, Cambridge, Massachussetts. Forced to retire in 1890 because of ill health, he turned to the writing of fiction; in the next twenty-eight years, he published two dozen novels and several other books. From the beginning, he was competent and successful. His *The Inner Shrine* was first on the American best-selling list in 1909, and his next two books, *The Wild Olive* (1910) and *The Street Called Straight* (1912), also became best-sellers.

Many of King's novels are international in the Jamesian tradition, exploring moral problems, such as divorce or family honour, in the light of the differing cultural conventions of France, England and the United States. But in most of his books he used American themes, settings, and characters.

In the Garden of Charity (1903), one of his earlier works, is wholly Canadian, and although it lacks the polish of his later novels, it is one of his most interesting. It is a story of love, loneliness, and charity in an isolated section along the lower Nova Scotia coast, worked out against a fully realized setting, and through local characters who are sensitively interpreted.

In two of King's later novels, Canadian characters play leading roles. Frank Melbury, in *The City of Comrades* (1919), is a young Canadian architect who dreams of developing a distinctively Canadian architectural style. Although the action takes place largely in the United States, Melbury goes to war for his native country, and the author's strong patriotic feeling is apparent. King's patriotism is as strong in *The High Heart* (1917), but his treatment of Canadian-American relations is more comprehensive. Alexandra Adare, a Halifax girl from a good family, finds that she is not accepted by Boston society because she is Canadian and thus of a lesser breed. In telling the story of her conquest of her suitor's Boston family, King presents one of the few detailed studies of Canadian and American attitudes written in this period.

Although he was a deeply moral and religious man, Basil King avoided the heavy didacticism and sentimentality common in much of the fiction of the day. Unlike many of his contemporaries, he was more concerned with tracing the complex relations between human beings than he was with providing exciting entertainment. In addition, he was a disciplined craftsman, well aware of the structural possibilities of the novel, and at his best, he achieved a high level of technical competence.

Another Canadian who placed Canadian characters under international pressures was Alice Jones (1853–1933). The daughter of a wealthy Halifax business man (later lieutenant-governor of Nova Scotia), she was educated in Europe and knew a more cosmopolitan society than most Canadian novelists of her time. She published short stories and three novels before settling in Mendone, France, in 1905, where she wrote two more novels.

Her first novel, *The Night Hawk* (1901), is a conventional historical romance of the adventures of a Southern girl who becomes a Confederate agent in Halifax during the American Civil War. *Bubbles We Buy* (1903), a thriller set in Nova Scotia and Europe, makes use of her knowledge of the international set. Her most forceful book is *Gabriel Praed's Castle* (1904). The action is melodramatic; Gabriel Praed, a Montreal business man who is purchasing paintings for a new Gothic castle in Montreal, is duped by a villainous Parisian art dealer, but Praed's unsophisticated young daughter, aided by American friends, saves her father. The treatment of the action, and the depiction of the characters, however, are somewhat reminiscent of the early manner of Henry James.

In *Marcus Holbeach's Daughter* (1912) the chief contrast is between a young girl reared in the wilds of the Gaspé and the corrupt aristocratic English society into which she is introduced. *Flame of Frost* (1914) deals with a similar contrast: the unspoiled girl from the woods is moved into corrupt European society.

Alice Jones's work is uneven, and has elements of sensationalism, but her fiction does have an awareness of the complexities of international experience.

Although Norman Duncan (1871–1916) produced such successful books for children as *The Adventures of Billy Topsail* (1906) and its several sequels, and some fifteen other fictions, it is only in a handful of short stories, particularly "The Chase of the Tide," "The Strength of a Man," "The Raging of the Sea," and "The Fruits of Toil," included in *The Way of the Sea* (1903), that he reached a high level of story-telling. In these he limited himself to a representation of the lives of fishermen and seal-hunters of the bleak shores of Newfoundland and Labrador in their fight with the merciless forces of nature.

When he was at his best, Duncan set the scene with precision and economy, and with a vividness of general impression. He allowed his people to demonstrate their qualities by their own actions, and in their own dialect stories. At his best he was an effective regional writer. But even within these particular short stories, he failed to maintain objectivity. His admiration for the prototypes of his characters led him to idealization and platitudinous interruption that recalls the work of Bret Harte rather than that of the serious regional writers. He often forsook the directness and biblical simplicity of the best portions of "The Fruits of Toil" for rhetoric loaded with apostrophe and grandiose generalization.

His few years of experience with Newfoundland and Labrador life provided him with feeling and material which brought out his best writing. Born in Brantford, and a graduate of the University of Toronto, he had become a journalist in New York, in the course of which he had been sent to write about Newfoundland. He returned to further journalism in the United States, and later to college teaching. His American journalism unfortunately seemed to encourage the sentimental and the didactic in his work, especially when he dealt with "mother love" and family relations in *The Mother* (1905), *The Suitable Child* (1909), *Finding His Soul* (1913), and *The Bird Store Man* (1914), or when he dealt with the strong and flawless missionary in *The Measure of a Man* (1911).

Norman Duncan found he had to warn readers of later editions of *Dr.*

Luke of The Labrador (1904) that he had not modelled his hero on Dr. Wilfred Thomason Grenfell (1865–1940) of the Royal National Mission to Deep-Sea Fishermen. Dr. Grenfell wrote his fiction to proselytize. *The Harvest of the Sea* (1905) came from his own medical missionary work aboard the fishing boats, and dramatizes the appalling conditions of that life, and the improvements which could be brought about by the United Fisherman's Christian Association. In *Down to the Sea in Ships* (1910) and *Tales of the Labrador* (1916) his "parables" are straightforward sermons. His writing is similar to Duncan's in its direct didacticism, its black and white characters, the familiar rhetorical adjectives and author's comment, and the episodic and melodramatic structure. His writing differs from Duncan's in its driving Christian and humanitarian evangelism.

Theodore Goodridge Roberts (1877–1953) was a more prolific popular journalist than his elder brother Charles G. D. Roberts. After his education in New Brunswick, he did editorial work on a New York newspaper, acted as a war correspondent during the Spanish-American War, and edited a magazine in Newfoundland before returning to Fredericton to pursue free-lance fiction-writing. His historical romances, adventure stories in the New Brunswick woods and on the Atlantic Coast, and his juveniles appeared first in the magazines; many of them appeared later in book form, starting with *Hemming, the Adventurer* in 1904. His romances reached a total of some twenty-four before he went overseas in 1914 with the Canadian army. After the war another ten appeared in book form. His fiction is largely light and fast-moving action, peopled with conventionally romantic characters, and with only occasionally a glimpse of setting which conveys some of the felt truth of good local colour.

The seven novels of R. E. Knowles (1868–1946), published between 1905 and 1911, are didactic and moralistic. Knowles, a Presbyterian minister, wrote largely about life in a small Ontario town. His first and best book, *St. Cuthbert's* (1905), is the story of a young Presbyterian minister who takes over a new parish. The plot is sentimental, melodramatic, and ragged. But the author has a pleasing prose style, a quiet sense of humour, and an insight into many facets of human nature. The book presents an interesting if prosaic picture of church-centred life in a small Scottish community. *The Undertow* (1906) and *The Attic Guest* (1909) also use a Presbyterian minister as a central figure, the latter novel extending his service to the southern United States, where he takes a stand on the race problem. In *The Handicap* (1910) Knowles turned to pioneer Ontario, and to an even more melodramatic plot. *The Web of Time* (1908) follows Presbyterian morality into the big city; *The Singer of the Kootenay* (1911) uses British Columbia for a sentimental and moralizing tale in the *Black Rock* manner. *The Dawn at Shanty Bay* (1907) is a slight, sentimental

Christmas story set in a northern Ontario lumber camp. Only occasionally do any of these later books come close to the style or the quiet effect of *St. Cuthbert's*.

Knowles's purpose was didactic; he is always the cleric; the artist seldom emerges. But though he never succeeded in creating a coherent narrative structure, he, like Ralph Connor, could be quite effective in short descriptive and non-dramatic passages. His otherwise conventional novels are relieved by some scenes of mild humour and faithful local colour.

The early novels of Marian Keith (Mrs. Mary Esther MacGregor, 1876–1961) are records of life in a small Ontario community. Her writing was heavily influenced by her Presbyterian background, and many of her stories are about ministers and churches; all have a moral appended. Her plots were derived from Victorian melodramatic and sentimental fiction; she had little sense of structure; her characters, except for some fine minor vignettes, were thinly developed and unconvincing. But she wrote about a subject which she knew well: the Scottish settlements of central Ontario in the late nineteenth century. In her books *Duncan Polite* (1905), *The Silver Maple* (1906), *Treasure Valley* (1908), *'Lizabeth of the Dale* (1910), she sketched an authentic and charming picture of rural Canadian life. Some of her scenes are reminiscent of Ralph Connor's kind of Ontario local colour: village life with its Dominion Day picnics, its general store, its church socials, its interchurch and Scotch-Irish rivalries, is all here.

Marian Keith was at her best when dealing with humorous anecdotal material. For example in *The Silver Maple* she related skilfully an incident in which the Glencoe MacDonalds decide to compete with the Orangemen's parade. They stage a "walk" of their own; led by a Highland piper they arrive at the village's only hotel just ahead of the Irishmen; they commandeer all the refreshments, and provide an unexpected anticlimax to the Orange celebrations. In her early works, there are many similar charming, unexaggerated incidents which are typical of the times and the people. These, along with her quieter pictures of family and manse life, enliven her otherwise conventional stories, and lend them an importance and an interest which far exceeds their literary merit. In spite of her shortcomings as a novelist, Marian Keith was an able chronicler of life in rural Ontario.

One of the first writers to make use of the western prairie scene was Nellie McClung (1873–1951), who, although she had been born on an Ontario farm, grew up on a Manitoba homestead. Her first book, *Sowing Seeds in Danny* (1908), tells of everyday life in a small town in southern Manitoba. It is made up of a series of short stories and sketches about Pearlie Watson, a twelve-year-old daughter of a section-hand, who goes into domestic service to help pay off the family debts. Pearl's story is continued in *The Second Chance* (1910), as the family moves out to a homesteading farm a few miles from town. Nellie McClung had resolved from the first to write about life as she saw it around her. She saw life directly, but her crusading spirit led her often to present what she saw in the forms of the Methodist and temperance literature of the day. But her books contain many excellent pictures of the drab and frustrating life of homestead days, relieved by happier scenes of communal gaiety at parties, picnics, or lacrosse games. Here and there in her third book, *The Black Creek Stopping-House* (1912), stories of early life on the Prairies are presented with a clarity and a penetrating understanding of human nature, and also with a charming sense of humour. Her writing was directed by a necessity for telling the truth, by a moral zeal, and by a strong Christian purpose; she had little use for any other artistic standards. However, many of her pictures of the early settlements of the West are deeply felt and effectively drawn.

Lucy Maude Montgomery (1874–1942) was born and raised in Prince Edward Island. She attended various Maritime colleges, and after graduation worked as a reporter and columnist for the Halifax *Echo*. She gave up a promising career to return to Cavendish, Prince Edward Island, to care for her aging and ailing grandmother. Living here under trying conditions, she began writing poetry and short stories for American and Canadian periodicals. In 1906, she began working on her first novel, expanding a short story which had originally been designed for a Sunday School weekly. She described it as "merely a juvenilish story, ostensibly for girls"; accepted by an American publisher, the story *Anne of Green Gables* (1908), turned out to have an appeal far beyond the local and juvenile level. At the request of her publishers, she wrote a sequel the next year, and then continued the story through a series of six Anne books; eventually she carried the story on into another generation. Most of the later books are less successful than the original; for as Anne grew up, she lost many of the charms of childhood and adolescence which had endeared her to the hearts of millions. In 1911 Miss Montgomery married a minister, and moved to southern Ontario, where she spent the rest of her life. She continued writing fiction, usually with a Prince Edward Island setting; but turning for the most part to adult fiction where her talents did not lie, she never came close to the standard or the popularity of the early Anne books. Miss Montgomery's letters reveal an intellectual depth and a speculative mind which is seldom evidenced in her fiction, where her successes are largely to be found in her description of the Prince Edward Island scene, and in her sensitive creation of an imaginative little girl, Anne of Green Gables.

One of the most original stories of the period is *Woodsmen of the West* (1908) by Martin Allerdale Grainger (1874–1941). It is not surprising that it is his only full-length work, for Grainger, born in England, spent a full life on the West Coast: as placer miner and logger; in the service of the province as Chief Forester; and in private business. What is surprising is his high level of technical proficiency. Every element of the narrative serves Grainger's purpose: a factual depiction of the life of the West Coast logger. The events are few and simple, but through Grainger's narrative art the reader is directly plunged into them: the hardships of logging, the trips up and down the Inlet, battling the waves and the weather, and above all, the central dramatic tension between Carter and Mart, the narrator. Mart, built upon Grainger himself, is skilfully and economically presented as the sensitive, perceptive amateur woodsman. But Grainger's finest achievement is the complex character of Carter, the logging boss. Although morbidly vain, pig-headed, maliciously egotistical, with a lust for power over men, Carter assumes heroic proportions in the narrator's eyes. "For among the clinkers and base alloys that made up much of Carter's soul there is a piece of purest metal, of true human greatness." Beside him and the rest of the characters, the loggers of Gilbert Parker, Hiram Alfred Cody, and Ralph Connor stand like stereotypes of fiction transferred to the backwoods or coast. Figures like Carter could only survive such a romantic treatment when placed against a solid background of materials obviously gathered from actual experience, and narrated in an appropriately varied style. With his sense of proportion, his feeling for appropriate pace, Grainger found a unified and flexible structure admirably suited to his own needs. He combined an accurate, detailed factual picture of the woodsmen of the West with a close analysis of complex men to produce, in a gripping narrative, one of the finest pieces of local and psychological realism in Canadian writing.

Although he was less grasping in imagination and often handicapped by undistinguished style, the writer who most closely approached Grainger's success in transmuting West Coast life into fiction was Bertrand William Sinclair (b. 1878). Sinclair was born in Edinburgh, Scotland, but grew up in the eastern foothills of the Rockies and developed a love of the western out-of-doors which later led him to travel extensively out from his home in Vancouver through the mountain and coast country from California to the Arctic Circle. His first books, *Raw Gold* (1908) and *The Land of Frozen Suns* (1910), although "Western" and "Northern" action stories, foreshadow his later emphasis upon the relation of character to environment. *North of Fifty-Three* (1914) dramatizes the corruptive force of Eastern city life, and the redemptive power of love in the British Columbia mountain country. Evidently set in the Harrison Lake area in British Columbia, Sinclair's *Big Timber* (1916) centres on the conflict between big timber interests, run by men in a hurry and careless of employees and nature, and small timber men of integrity and with a deep affinity with their woods. In his next novel, *Burned Bridges* (1919), he structured his work by facing his hero with a series of moral dilemmas and choices. The unconventional Wesley Thompson first fails as a missionary to the Crees, backtrails to the cities, looking for a job and for his identity; works his way to success in the motor industry in California; establishes himself in Vancouver at the head of a sales agency; confronts the personal moral dilemma of enlistment in the First World War, and finally finds himself and his love. Sinclair changed his locale and his focus of interest in *Poor Man's Rock* (1920) which depicts from the inside the fight for supremacy in the fishing industry in Puget Sound. Here, as also in *The Hidden Places* (1922) and *The Inverted Pyramid* (1924), he made effective use of his first-hand knowledge of the localities and the conditions he chooses to write about. *The Inverted Pyramid*, based on the Dominion Trust failure in Vancouver, and probably Sinclair's most ambitious novel, is a narrative of how the fifth generation of an influential British Columbia family meet their responsibilities when the oldest son brings financial and moral disaster upon them. Sinclair returned to the Vancouver scene in a story of rum-running days, *Down the Dark Alley* (1936).

Hiram Alfred Cody (1872–1948), like Ralph Connor, used the matter and manner of popular action fiction to achieve his primary aim of teaching Christian principles. He himself had been a missionary in the Yukon and a rector in New Brunswick parishes; each of his early novels is dominated by a Christian hero who also is either a missionary in the North or a minister in New Brunswick. Keith Stedman, the medical missionary hero of Cody's first romance, *The Frontiersman* (1910), is the traditional noble, lone traveller, the fearless fighter, and the chaste lover. The action is set in the Yukon, and is a series of attacks by wolves, gold thefts, floods, accidents, and coincidences. One of the early tasks of the hero is to overcome the vicious, cowardly villain who is corrupting the Indians by drink. *The Fourth Watch* (1911) presents another commanding figure in Parson John Westmore—somewhat older than Stedman, and under suspicion of theft for most of the story—who demonstrates Christian love in action among the loggers of the St. John River. *If Any Man Sin* (1915) offers both the young medical missionary and the older disgraced clergyman who has fled to the Mackenzie River to escape the church and religion. His faith finally is restored. The hero of *The Unknown Wrestler* (1918) is a farmhand, oversized and powerful, who represents "the spirit of adventure." He not only runs, wrestles, plays the violin, but also reveals himself at the end of the story as the new rector.

The R.C.M.P. officer who is the hero of *The Long Patrol* (1912), the newspaper reporter of *Glen of the High North* (1920), and the central figures of the later historical romances stand and fight for the same Christian principles, and are marked by the same characteristics as the heroes of the early stories. It is only in the titular hero of *The Touch of Abner* (1919), a shrewd local wag, and the townspeople of *The Fourth Watch* that Cody attempted any sharp individualization. Nor did Cody depart from the action tradition in his use of setting or of style. In spite of his first-hand knowledge of the North and his native province, he was content to use the standard idealized mountains, forests, waterfalls, log cabins, or farms merely as a background for his dramatic events. The conventionality is increased by his unnatural diction, by frequent rhetorical questions, and the repetition of stock adjectives and epithets. Cody and his readers, however, were not concerned with originality in these matters. His strength lay in his story-telling drive, and the appeal of his simple, strong-hearted, evangelical heroes.

The writer who was the most skilful humorist of his day and who also embodied in his writing most fully a spirit critical of his place and times was Stephen Leacock (1869–1944). In his attitude towards himself as a Canadian writer he also is representative of a significant difference between the earlier and the later writers of this period. As he wrote in his article "Exporting Humour to England," "I am a Canadian, but for the lack of any other word to indicate collectively those who live between the Rio Grande and the North Pole, I have to use 'American.' If the Canadians and the Eskimos and the Flathead Indians are not Americans, what are they?"

Leacock was born in England, and, after his family migrated to Canada when he was six, grew up on a farm near Lake Simcoe, in Ontario. He was educated locally, at Upper Canada College, and at the University of Toronto. He gave up school-teaching to study at the University of Chicago where Thorstein Veblen was lecturing. With his doctorate from Chicago, he joined the McGill University staff as a full-time lecturer in political science. His career as humorist was achieved concurrently with a distinguished academic career at McGill, during which he published almost one hundred scholarly articles in his own and allied fields and more than two dozen serious books on political science, economics, history, literature, and a variety of other subjects.

But it is as a humorist that Leacock became widely known in the English-speaking world. In 1894, when humour was one of the most popular kinds of writing in North America, he began his career as humorist by contributing sketches to American and Canadian magazines. He collected a number of his early pieces in his first book, *Literary Lapses* (1910), published privately in Montreal, republished in the same year in New York and London, and subsequently reprinted in some twenty editions. From 1910 until after his death in 1944, Leacock's new humorous volumes appeared year by year with almost unbroken regularity: *Nonsense Novels* (1911); *Sunshine Sketches of a Little Town* (1912); *Behind the Beyond* (1913); *Arcadian Adventures with the Idle Rich* (1914); *Moonbeams from the Larger Lunacy* (1915); *Further Foolishness* (1916); *Frenzied Fiction* (1918); *The Hohenzollerns in America* (1919); and *Winsome Winnie* in

1920. Eight more collections of sketches, burlesques, parodies, and stories followed in the twenties, eleven or so more in the thirties, and five in the forties. He not only maintained this steady stream of book publication, but also theorized about humour and anthologized it. His fullest examination of the art appeared in *Humour: Its Theory and Technique* in 1935, and in *Humour and Humanity: An Introduction to the Study of Humour* in 1937. In the thirties he published personal appreciations of his two favourite humorists, Charles Dickens and Mark Twain. Of them he wrote: "Charles Dickens stands at least as eminent as a humorist, if not higher. But Mark Twain was beyond anybody else in the world a technical humorist. He combined the basis of the matter—the inspiration—with the mechanism of it."

Leacock's own art was patterned after the traditions of North American humour which Mark Twain had brought to full flower. The early "Down Easterners," Haliburton and Seba Smith, had derived much of their humour from a hoss-sense view of human nature, expressed by shrewd native characters like Sam Slick or Major Jack Downing. Later the professional "funny men" of the post–Civil War years—Artemus Ward, Josh Billings, Bill Nye, Mark Twain, and others—had developed the verbal arts of humour, in print and on the lecture platform, to the delight of an ever expanding North American and British audience. They made their living (some of them very handsome livings) by making people laugh.

Like them, Leacock often spun nonsense; frequently his nonsense was interspersed with epigrams or afterthoughts which flicked the pretensions of the sophisticated or of the plutocracy. As they did, he used a multiplicity of forms: the dialogue, the memoir, the letter, the travel sketch, the tall tale, the anecdote, the literary burlesque and parody. He had the same bag of highly developed tricks as they had: the pun, chop-logic, the sudden juxtaposition of levels of speech, the mixed metaphor, the absurd coupling of words, the malapropisms, and the apparently witless flow of free association. He did not indulge in the wild spellings which some of them used; his taste for sudden violence was not as over-developed as it was in some of them; but like the best of them he was a master of lean, fresh native speech, and seemed to talk—whether he spoke from the lecture platform or the printed page. Like Mark Twain particularly, Leacock often adopted the persona of an innocent, either a native lunkhead, or a simple outsider (like Twain's Westerner), who with an irreverent spirit and hoss-sense observed the strange world of the city, with its acquisitiveness, its political struggle, its boarding houses, its millionaire clubs, its churches, or the even stranger world of England and the Continent.

Only a few of Leacock's thirty or so humorous books have an over-all unity. *Sunshine Sketches of a Little Town* (1912) and *Arcadian Adventures with the Idle Rich* (1914) are portraits, respectively, of a small Ontario town and of life in the big city. Each is made up of independent sketches, held together only by a common locale and some interlocking characters; neither makes pretensions of having a central plot or structure. The portraits emerge from a series of vignettes, rather than as a single canvas. A few other books have a unity of theme: *My Discovery of England* (1922) and *College Days* (1923) deal with one subject; *Nonsense Novels* (1911) is a collection of literary burlesques.

But these are exceptions; most of Leacock's books are collections of separate, brief comic writings on a variety of topics. *Literary Lapses* (1910), his first and still one of his most popular books, is a good example of the form and subject-matter of all his work. It contains forty-two unrelated sketches, essays, burlesques, parodies, letters, monologues, dialogues, and stories. Leacock himself referred to his writings as "pieces," which is perhaps the only term inclusive enough to describe the many similar but distinct forms in which he cast his comic treatment of a great variety of topics, ranging from economics to barbers, from education to Chinese laundries, from the financial affairs of the Doogalville parish church to the deliberations of the House of Lords.

Literary Lapses, which includes pieces published in magazines as many as sixteen years before, clearly shows that Leacock was already master of the comic craft. It contains examples of every comic technique he would use in his later books. His comic spirit, although still youthful, was already at its height, and was not to grow or decline significantly in the next thirty-four years. Already his sense of the incongruous could evoke laughter through irony or pathos, exaggeration or satire, nostalgia or verbal fun—or sometimes through an undefinable but distinctly Leacockian amalgam of sheer nonsense and deep wisdom.

This is not to suggest that his work is uniformly good. In his off moments, he could try much too hard to play the funny man. Leacock was not a good judge of his own work; as J. B. Priestley has pointed out, Leacock was better in practice than in theory, for Leacock's two books and many articles on humour do not add much to our understanding of his own craft. There is some strained, mechanical material in the canon; but considering that he turned out almost a book a year for thirty-four years, it is remarkable that there is not more.

Leacock has been regarded as a displaced eighteenth-century squire viewing the maddening scene of modern science and industrial organization with a benign eye from his country estate outside of Orillia. He also has been seen as an irascible, embittered, witty satirist with many double-edged axes to grind. Both views have some truth in them; there are, perhaps, two Leacocks.

One could be sharp and cutting; he was against shams and pretensions of all kinds, and he tried to destroy them by making fun of them. He lashed out, sometimes without mercy, against all forms of hypocrisy; spiritualists, doctors, lawyers, utopias, efficiency experts, statisticians, and faddists of all kinds were his special targets. He opposed socialism, prohibition, enforced retirement, misuse of language, and pretentiousness in any form, particularly in writing. When he went after this kind of opponent, he could be bitter, sharp, and satirical. He was bitterest when he attacked a Kaiser or a Hitler or a Mussolini, or anyone who threatened his own Canada or his own Empire. Most often, however, he used his sharpest literary pen against anyone or anything which threatened his sense of human dignity. There are enough pieces with a bitter flavour to suggest that Leacock was not always without malice. And yet it was usually a kindly malice, with the deep recognition of common human failings, and it was usually expressed without any sense of superiority. It is here than Leacock's great charm lies. He never set himself up as an authority on anything. He appears rather as the unspecialized, the unpredictable, the irrational average man whom modern society, modern science, and modern education are attempting to specialize, to predict, to rationalize. From his core, Leacock opposed this dehumanization, and the bitterness which appears in his writing stems from his central view that mankind, imperfect as he may be, is important.

But it is the other, the more purely comic Leacock that is better known. In his lighter moods, he produced his most characteristic and most enduring work. His spontaneous sense of incongruity, touched occasionally with tints of nostalgia, comes from a mellowed vision of human nature, and is combined with a profound human sympathy and understanding. Above all, Leacock's best work is funny; it evokes real laughter.

Leacock and these other twenty-seven writers are only a handful of the Canadians who wrote fiction between 1880 and 1920. But they may be taken as a group large and diversified enough to be representative of the Canadian fiction writers of the day. (The group is unrepresentative quantitatively in that it is made up largely of the more prolific writers of the time. The few more prolific writers not included are Harvey O'Higgins, Archibald Mc-Kishnie, and Frederick Niven, who published their first books between 1905 and 1910, and Samuel Alexander White, Frank Packard, Hulbert Footner, William Amy, and Robert Stead, who published their first books between 1910 and 1915. It does not include many of the some four hundred Canadians who published one, two, or a few more volumes of fiction during these years.) Different as were the twenty-eight we have discussed in place of birth, in nurture, in temperament, and in experience, they did hold in common certain assumptions about the writing of fiction, about the reading public, about the nature of fiction, and about their relation to their local Canadian scene.

For the writers in this group, fiction-writing was an occupation; part-time for most, full time for a few. It was not a way of life. Most of them wrote to gain an income or to supplement an income; but while they wrote for money, some also wrote for the pleasure of entertaining their readers, and more wrote to edify their readers and to support them in certain views of life. They assumed that their reading public was local and international, not national. They addressed their fiction to various segments of the wide, middle range of the reading public, not, on the one side, to "the saving remnant," or, on the other, to the readers of cheap pulp magazines. Most of them scored their first success with magazine stories, then with the publication of a first or an early book. Their later books often were variations on the themes and patterns of their first successes. They wrote in a variety of conventional forms, using conventional techniques, often with considerable skill. Their fiction was not personal, subjective, or inward searching; it was communal, written for an audience for whom fiction essentially was "story," and "story" told within a framework of unexamined, idealistic values.

Most of them placed their work with magazine editors and book publishers in New York and London. But although they often published in markets outside Canada, most of them wrote about the local Canadian scene which they knew, or had known, from first-hand experience. Some spun historical pasts for their localities; some told stories of the opening West and North; some told of Canadians abroad. Some tried to record in fiction the communities in which they lived; some built their fictions out of pleasant memories of the small communities in which they had grown up.

However they pictured life in the outside world, when writing of local Canadian scenes these Canadian writers rarely saw their society as institutional. In their fiction the world centred in the individual and in his relations with a few other individuals. The mainsprings of action were the good and bad in human beings, not in social forces. They pictured a self-contained, fluid world, still close to open country. Characters naturally moved out of their local worlds, sometimes south to the city, more often west or north to unsettled country; when they moved they rarely became deeply involved in their new societies. The dream of success common to most of these central characters is primarily emotional, not social or economic, and almost always the dream is fulfilled in the closing pages of these books. Few of these characters had any quarrel with their world; few felt alienated from it. The feeling expressed with such fine modulation in "L'Envoi: The Train to Mariposa," at the close of Stephen Leacock's *Sunshine Sketches of a Little Town*, is much more prevalent than is the feeling "You can't go home again."

Most of these books are now out of print, and are no longer read by the reading public. They are not regarded as serious literature by the literary critics of our day; the pictures of Canadian life they present have been overlooked by the cultural historians. Yet the Canadian fiction-writers between 1880 and 1920 were read more widely by their contemporaries, inside and outside Canada, than have been the Canadian fiction-writers—collectively—since. Because they wrote in the grain of the dominant feeling of their Anglo-North American world, their fiction had a significant reciprocal relation with their times. It reflects, through direct presentation or through fantasy, many aspects of the pluralistic life in Canada between 1880 and 1920; it also provided images of Canadian life which formed a definition of Canadian identity, at home and abroad.

18. Essays and Travel Books

I. Essays 1880–1920

BRANDON CONRON*

THE ESSAY IN CANADA developed slowly from early collections of speeches, magazine articles, sketches, and newspaper columns, all of which resemble the established form of the essay in relative brevity and discursiveness, but differ from it in purpose. The primary intention of the writer of such pieces was usually either hortatory or descriptive; his central interest lay in his subject, or, if he were in public life, in his opinions, but attention to the theme, a principal mark of the essay, was largely coincidental.

The fact that Joseph Howe (1804–1873) is sometimes considered the first Canadian essayist indicates one source of the tradition in Canada. For although the elaborate oratorical flourishes in his *Poems and Essays* (1874) have little more than historical interest, nevertheless, the political speeches and formal orations included were designated as "essays" and were looked to as stylistic models. This concept of the genre accounts in part for the necessity of considering as essayists later in this survey such figures as Osler, Falconer, and Massey.

The greatest single source of the essay in Canada, however, lies in journalism. The columns of *The Week*, "An Independent Journal of Literature, Politics and Criticism" (Toronto, 1883–96), saw the first appearance of many articles which were later collected as "essays." Though differing widely in interests and style, the writers of these pieces had one quality in common: the assumption, whether tacit or expressed, that their work had literary value, even when their purposes were dictated by politics or religion, and their methods by the editorial, the feature article, or the regular column. This assumption was due in part to the policy of *The Week* itself. In an early issue the first editor, Charles G. D. Roberts, made it clear that the journal was a forum for the expression of individual opinion by requiring every writer to sign his name to his contribution. The paper, though founded by Goldwin Smith, had no specific platform or purpose other than that of most Victorian

*Assisted by Donald Hair.

journals: "stimulating our national sentiment, guarding our national morality, and strengthening our national growth." Its articles discussing questions of the day and its descriptive sketches are the forerunners of the essay in Canada, though they themselves can scarcely be considered as literature. A typical contributor to *The Week* was the Reverend George Jacobs Low (1836–1906), who discussed current issues and described his own life in "Parson's Ponderings" with genial disregard for form and style.

The articles of Goldwin Smith (1823–1910) are far more polished in style than those of Low, but similarly fall short of being essays. Undoubtedly Smith felt that his discussions of current political questions were, like his earlier *Lectures and Essays* (1881), "contributions to Canadian literature," but his opinions on the Canadian constitution, and his methods as a writer, are of far more interest to the historiographer than they are to the student of literature. Similarly, the articles of Sir James Le Moine (1825–1912), some of which were included in the *Maple Leaves* series (1863–1906), are a storehouse of information for the antiquarian, although they have little literary interest.

The numerous contributions of Sara Jeannette Duncan (1861–1922) to the journal may be divided roughly into two groups: feature articles discussing questions of the day, such as "American Influence on Canadian Thought" (IV, 518), or "Our Latent Loyalty" (IV, 418); and more informal pieces which she called "Saunterings," reminiscent in method, intimate in tone, and unpretentious in style. Though journalistic, these pieces stand closer to the essay tradition than do those of the private secretary to Goldwin Smith, Theodore A. Haultain (1857–1941). Of his few articles, most are, like those of his employer, comments on current political questions. One or two of his descriptive pieces, however, foreshadow his later interest in nature (*Two Country Walks in Canada*, 1903; *Of Walks and Walking Tours*, 1914), and hint at his constant theme—the unity of nature and man. Haultain attempted to compensate for the tenuousness of his "speculations, semi-mystical, semi-intelligible" by paying careful attention to his mode of expression, but the result, except in his witty collection of aphorisms *Hints for Lovers* (1909), is often a stilted self-consciousness.

Of all the contributors to *The Week*, only Archibald MacMechan (1862–1933) deserves the title of essayist. Although born in Ontario, he adopted Nova Scotia, the Ultima Thule of his later descriptive books, as his native province. Its scenery and history are the materials out of which MacMechan shaped the essays of *The Porter of Bagdad and Other Fantasies* (1901) and of *The Life of a Little College* (1914). Fantasy, as the title indicates, is the key. Like the Victorian writers in whom MacMechan took more than the scholarly interest demanded by his position at Dalhousie University, he was the heir of the Romantics. The Dreamer, the agent of MacMechan's fancy, transforms purely descriptive pieces into whimsical reveries celebrating the fresh innocent beauty of nature, art, and woman. MacMechan's romanticism, however, is never escapism. Words order and control his experience, and create a formal if fanciful pattern to fix "golden days in memory for the enrichment of less happier times to come" ("Afoot in Ultima Thule"). The simplicity and restraint of the style, on the one hand, and the luxuriousness of the subject-matter, on the other, combine best in pieces like "Ghosts," "The Fence-Corner," and "My Own Country," where a fresh and distinctive lyricism reveals an imaginative but not unreal world of infinite delights for the thoughtful observer.

The decade in which MacMechan's collected essays first appeared may be taken as the period during which the essay emerged as a literary form in Canada. Its late appearance is not surprising. The essay always exalts being over doing, enjoyment over practicality. It demands leisure and meditation and some degree of detachment in order to realize its primary purpose of communicating to the reader a single and distinctive mode of thought, so as to evoke in him a sense of the essayist as an individual with a distinct personality and a distinct vision. This purpose was realized in different ways by Osler's *Aequanimitas* (1904), Carman's *Kinship of Nature* (1903), and Macphail's *Essays in Puritanism* (1905), three books which set a new if not always adequate standard for the essay in Canada. None of these writers was particularly interested in the easy formality and personal intimacy possible in the essay form; each chose the form because it emphasized the theme and was therefore the best vehicle for his own insights. And while these insights were primarily an illumination of life in general, they frequently had a utilitarian relationship with the writer's vocation, a relationship rather different from the *fin de siècle* tradition in England of essay writing as a leisurely activity pursued in retirement from practical life.

Typical are the essays of Sir William Osler (1849–1919), whose achievements in medicine and in medical education were for many years the principal basis of his fame. As a member of the medical faculty at McGill (1874–1884), Johns Hopkins (1889–1905), and Oxford (1905–19), Osler was often called upon to deliver the addresses upon which his reputation now rests. The address from which the title of his earliest volume *Aequanimitas* was taken introduced the theme that occurred again and again in Osler's works. He warned the graduating students that, should they become engrossed in professional cares, they would soon find no place "for those gentler influences which make life worth living." The gentler influences in Osler's own life came from two ministers, his father, and the Reverend W. A. Johnson, headmaster of Trinity College School, the man who first introduced Osler to

Sir Thomas Browne. Like Browne, Osler tried to strike a balance between the rational and the emotional. This "most serious difficulty of the intellectual life" Osler overcame by harmonizing the two conflicting elements of his nature. Of his vocation he wrote: "The practice of medicine is an art, based on science" ("Teacher and Student"); about the "unhappy divorce" between the humanities and the sciences he said: "Humanists have not enough Science, and Science sadly lacks the Humanities" ("The Old Humanities and the New Science"). The vital synthesis that Osler strove to maintain in every-day life had a firm basis in his religious beliefs, which were quiet but perva-sive. He would "rather be mistaken with Plato than be in the right with those who deny altogether the life after death" ("Science and Immortality"). The equanimity of Osler's own mind is reflected in his style. Although his earliest addresses retain a good many oratorical flourishes and rely to a considerable extent on the elaborated aphorism, his later pieces capture the clarity and polish of the best English prose without sacrificing the pithiness of the wise saying. To the best of his essays (and especially to "The Student Life," a model of the form) may be applied what he himself said of Browne: "How pleasant it is to follow his thought, rippling like a burn, not the stilted for-mality of the technical artist in words, the cadences of whose precise and mechanical expressions pall on the ear."

The claim of Bliss Carman (1861–1929) to the title of essayist is a tenuous one, principally because his constant theme of personal harmonizing exhibits a growing tendency towards didacticism, a tendency that Carman himself was fully aware of when, in his *Talks on Poetry and Life* (1926), he added by way of apology that "one is sometimes betrayed into preaching." His first book, *The Kinship of Nature* (1903), remains his best, though many of the pieces in it are vitiated by the constant concern with self-better-ment. Simplicity, grace, and subtle rhythmic patterns enhance the lyrical qualities of his style, but are not sufficient to redeem his prose from a dis-advantageous comparison with his poetry. Carman's limitations as a prose writer are painfully evident when one compares his various pieces on spring ("At the Coming of Spring," "The Vernal Ides," "April in Town") with his better-known "Spring Song." The poem renders the emotion, but the prose never does more than talk about "these rare instants of existence."

Like Osler, Sir Andrew Macphail (1864–1938) was a physician but his literary interests were of a more professional nature. In 1907, while teaching medicine at McGill, he became editor of the *University Magazine*, and remained so until 1920. Macphail's concept of the essay tended towards straight discursive writing, as the titles of his books indicate: *Essays in Puritanism* (1905); *Essays in Politics* (1909); *Essays in Fallacy* (1910). In each of the *Essays in Puritanism*, for instance, the biography of a prominent writer or theologian forms the subject-matter, but it is Macphail's own appreciation of the Puritan spirit, with its emphasis on individualism, progress, and independence of all but God, that forms the theme and makes the pieces essays. Where the reader finds the ideas uncongenial, he is likely to be carried along by the genial vigour of the style. Macphail is a master of the clipped phrase, the pungent statement, the epigram. The compression and frequent distortion involved in such a style, however, may alienate the reader. The *Essays in Politics* fail to keep the balance of the *Essays in Puritanism*, partly because of the nature of the subject (Canada's relation to England), partly because Macphail's interests were turning more and more towards criticism and biography, and away from the essay as a literary form.

Neither Osler, Carman, nor Macphail consciously set about making contributions to literature. Thomas O'Hagan (1855–1939) did. A journalist and a teacher, he failed to distinguish the essay from literary criticism, historical writing, and travel literature. All of his pieces are didactic in intent, superficial in approach, and cursory in treatment, nor does his style ever rise above the journalistic hodge-podge of *Chats by the Fireside* (1911), a collection of his articles from the *Catholic Register*. The fact that O'Hagan's tacit assumption that his journalistic background was the proper one for writing essays went unchallenged is indicative of the particular nature of the Canadian essay.

The fame of Peter McArthur (1866–1924) rests upon his column of farm life which for many years appeared twice weekly in the Toronto *Globe*. The articles, re-arranged and to some extent revised, were collected into several books, beginning with *In Pastures Green* (1915) and ending with *Around Home* (1925). McArthur made his reputation as a humorist and sage; he was also peculiarly suited to be a Canadian essayist of the first importance. After a career as a journalist and editor in New York and England, he retired to his rural Ontario farm, like Montaigne to his tower, to take stock of his experience. But McArthur was too carefree and perhaps too careless to reflect on life either at length or in depth, and consequently his best pieces are only sketches that approach the essay. He believed his pieces had a cathartic effect but no literary value: "No particular merit attaches to writing a book." Yet McArthur's humble lack of pretensions should not blind the critic to his merits. His point of view— perhaps the only genuinely pastoral one in Canadian literature—was by nature contemplative, serious, and contented. It yielded the humble chronicles of farm life that we now most typically associate with McArthur. His humour was a pleasant quality of his point of view; his satirical vein was often an unpleasant point of attack. Of a stray calf he writes bluntly: "After the chores were done I took a pail that was as empty as a political platform and she followed me right back into the pen just like an intelligent voter" (*The Red Cow and her Friends*, 1919). McArthur's pastoral point of view, with all the virtues of simplicity and brotherhood implicit in it, served him best when he came to write on the subject that has plagued most Canadian essayists—Canada's international relations. *The Affable Stranger* (1920) is a fresh approach to the plea for better understanding between Canada and the United States. McArthur's more typical concern, however, was his farm. His themes may be summed up in one quotation from "The Return of Spring": "To me all Nature is as much alive as I am myself and flushed with the same life force. Only man with his egotistic self-consciousness misses its reviving touch." The relation of the character sketch to the essay is often ignored, a fact which may account for the sparse attention that seems to have been paid to *The Red Cow and her Friends* (1919), a collection of sketches of farm animals which is in many ways more satisfying than other more generalized pieces. McArthur's greatest deficiency is his style. At all times rambling, loose, and colloquial, it often lapses into sheer carelessness which cannot even be excused as "homely charm." When his theme is not nature, he reverts to the popular phrase, a practice particularly evident in some of the least successful efforts in *The Affable Stranger*. At his best McArthur is genial and easy, at his worst hackneyed and slipshod. But throughout his writing there is the same unassuming note of *In Pastures Green*: "I like to keep my feet on the earth—in good Canadian mud. . . ."

Very different in style and intent are the essays of William Hume Blake (1861–1924). Laurentian fishing trips provided the experiences out of which the Toronto lawyer produced three books in the Waltonian tradition—*Brown Waters* (1915), *In a Fishing Country* (1922), and *A Fisherman's Creed* (1923). Like Walton, Blake juxtaposes the complex world of "politics, stock-markets, courts, theatres, clubs" and the simple natural world where "the evening and the morning are the first and every following day." Simplicity is the mark of Blake's quiet intellectual approach to the world of nature, an approach complemented by the virtues he admires: appreciation of natural beauty, skill in fishing, the courage of the trout, the hospitality and shrewdness of the French guide. In fact, the reader soon discovers that angling is for Blake, as it was for Walton and later would be for Haig-Brown, one of those activities that epitomizes the good life. Fishing in Canada (and particularly in Quebec) has, moreover, its peculiar virtues, not the least of which is the fostering of mutual comprehension between French-and English-speaking Canadians ("Le Long du Sentier"). Closer to Walton is the gentle statement of faith that appears in *A Fisherman's Creed*—the belief in a divine design which each individual is continually furthering or thwarting. In this design the moral struggle is particularly important: "Salvation and damnation are habits of the soul, slowly acquired by the inner self, becoming inveterate in the passage of time." Choice is the mode of the struggle; for Blake himself fishing is undoubtedly a symbol of the continuing choice of good. Blake's style complements his creed. The careful shape of his sentences, the gentle ebb and flow of the rhythm, the unpretentious yet solid structure of his paragraphs, all are marks of the good workmanship which Blake admired so much in every walk of life.

The title Stephen Leacock (1869–1944) gave to his *Essays and Literary Studies* (1916) is an unusually serious one for a humorist, and suggests a gravity of purpose that is soon dispelled by the robust humour of the essays themselves. Nevertheless, the serious note is important because it marks the difference between those pieces in which humour is used as a structural principle, and those which exist solely for the sake of the humour. The former are essays; the latter are not. "The Devil and the Deep Sea: A Discussion of Modern Morality" is a good illustration of Leacock's contribution to the essay form. Simple in structure, it is basically a series of humorous paragraphs, "the cross sections of the moral tendencies of our time," all of which develop the theme: "The devil is passing out of fashion." Leacock's humour is so boisterous, however, that it often overwhelms the theme, so that even he himself in a serious moment must warn his readers "that though they may be conscientiously unable to digest all that I have told them . . . I shall nevertheless be amply satisfied if they will believe the half of it." The point is, of course, that Leacock's primary interest lies in humour, and not in essay writing; and humour works in a very different way from that literary form of the essay which Lorne Pierce has defined as "an epistle to the world of kindred spirits at large."

The development of the essay in Canada between the years 1880 and 1920 is by no means as steady as the literary historian might wish, but nevertheless some general trends are evident. The early essays spring directly from the writers' vocations, and are consequently didactic in intent and serious in tone. Yet this didacticism is subsumed by writers like Osler and Macphail into an attempt to express the eternal verities of human wisdom, and to express them in a distinctive and individual manner. Other writers mitigated the basic seriousness of their approach with humour, fantasy, lyrical description, reminiscence, and wit. Few had models. Whether their purposes were literary or not, these writers strove honestly and independently to express their own insights, and, with the exception of several contributors to *The Week*, left posterity to judge their literary value. Consequently as the essay emerged from its many related forms, it was characterized by a heterogeneous but vigorous individualism that combined the traditional ideals of civilization with the peculiar reactions to a distinctive physical environment and the peculiar problems of a new nation.

II. Travel Books 1860–1920

ELIZABETH WATERSTON

1860–1880*

WITHOUT DOUBT, the most important Canadian event of the 1880's was the completion of the Canadian Pacific Railway; the linking of this vast country marked the real beginning of its growth into nationhood. The two decades immediately preceding, 1860–1880, which saw the foundations of the nation being laid, were years of immense hope, far-reaching visions, and imaginative westward-dreaming, only momentarily dimmed by such troubling episodes as the Pacific Scandal. And all of this, the new awareness of the vastness of Canada, the promise of exciting days ahead and, in particular, the upsurge of interest in the West, was reflected in the travel literature of the period and epitomized in one outstanding work, George Grant's *Ocean to Ocean* (1873).

A combination of adventure-story and mythic chronicle, this book depicts the chief aspiration of post-Confederation Canada, the fulfillment of its motto, "Ocean to Ocean." Grant, a Canadian scholar-clergyman, was secretary to Sandford Fleming's survey expedition which, in 1872, prepared the route for the new railway. Assuming such narrative stances as that of naïve narrator, Tory propagandist, and prose lyricist, Grant ranges from homely accounts of life around the campfire, at trading posts, and in western hotels, to ardent defences of Macdonald's railway policies, to reverent (and often beautiful) descriptions of the physical beauty everywhere around him.

Before the completion of the CPR, the chief preoccupation of writers traveling in the Northwest was with the "wildness" of the country and they (Englishmen all) were indulging themselves in that soon-to-be-forgotten luxury of having set foot on land through which no other white man had moved. Ballantyne-like, they revelled in that "spirit of adventure" which "roughing it" on the prairies and in fur posts provided. And, in the presence of such graphically depicted experiences as those presented by Francis Butler in *The Great Lone Land* (1872) and *The Wild North Land* (1873), few readers can remain imaginatively uninvolved.

In the first of these, Butler, whose prose style is as entertaining as his anecdotes, describes his hurried departure from England to join Wolseley's troops as they headed to quell Riel's insurrection (1870), his role as advance scout, his lone entry into Red River, his interview with Riel and his subsequent commissioned tour of the prairies. The second recounts an even more daring and

---

* This subsection was prepared by R. Gordon Moyles of the University of Alberta.

dangerous trip northward to Lake Athabasca, the Peace River, and through the mountains, and is enhanced by the frequent philosophic interpolations and critical comments on the white man's influence on the native way of life.

Other major travel books offer further insight into western Canadian society and bring us face to face with the personalities behind such names as Father Lacombe and John McDougall. Henry Youle Hind's *Narrative of the Canadian Red River Exploring Expedition* (1860), though ostensibly a quasi-scientific report, offers excellent descriptions of the people met and the towns passed through. Viscount Milton and W. B. Cheadle's *The North-west Passage by Land* (1865), abounds with personalities and with humour, describing a nation-wide pleasure tour by two equally eccentric young men. The Earl of Southesk's *Saskatchewan and the Rocky Mountains* (1875), "a diary and narrative of travel, sport, and adventure," is an excellent example of travel writing at its best, a blend of description, anecdote, and personal commentary.

Adding depth to these three are some regional travel books: C. E. Barrett-Lennard's *Travels in British Columbia* (1862), with hair-raising descriptions of Indian attacks and interesting comments on the goldrush; Charles Horetsky's *Canada on the Pacific* (1874), a lively account of travels through the Peace River country, through the Rockies and down the Naas River; St. John Molyneux' *The Sea of Mountains* (1877), a Toronto *Globe* reporter's account of Lord Dufferin's conciliatory visit to British Columbia in 1876; and James Trow's *A Trip to Manitoba* (1875), J. C. Hamilton's *The Prairie Province* (1880), and Mary Fitzgibbon's *A Trip to Manitoba* (1880), examples of books resulting from "the Manitoba fever."

In contrast, Horton Rhys's *A Theatrical Trip for a Wager* (1861) shows the new country from the perspective of a happy-go-lucky actor, but somehow misses the real drama of western expansion.

"And I suppose when you get home you'll be writing a book?" The question might be asked of the traveller through Canada with sympathy or with sardonic hostility; the answer was usually "yes." Some travellers came with the intention of writing a report. Others, often at the urging of friends, belatedly scrambled journals, letters-home, or random notes into a holiday record. Most travellers packed some literary preconceptions along with their portmanteaux: phrases from *Evangeline* and Tom Moore's "Boat Song," from Dickens and Howells and Mark Twain; and later from Pauline Johnson and W. H. Drummond and Ralph Connor. All sifted what they saw through their own interests and needs, social and economic, personal and national (A Scottish farmer saw Montreal as "the finest city in Canada" because "The farmers realize £10 per acre for their potatoes there." An ailing lady timidly noted the location and condition of the cemetery in each Canadian town. The first automobilist dismissed Quebec as "a city unfit . . . for a self-respecting touring-car.") The books they produced ranged from slim sketches to ponderous tomes, but there never was a break in the flow of books by travellers who had "done" Canada and were prepared to tell the world what they had found. Peak years in the production of such books occurred in 1885, 1895, and 1911.

Of the hundreds of travel books on Canada published between 1860 and 1920, most were read by a very small audience—the clergyman's flock, the delegate's sponsors, the fellow-suffragists—but a few were very widely read, by both sophisticated and unsophisticated readers: the memoirs of Lady Dufferin and descriptive sketches by Kipling and by Lord Lorne, the Duke of Argyll. These helped fix the picture of Canada for the next generation. Canadian readers probably formed the largest part of this audience, showing early and always an anxiety to know how their country had affected her visitors. Canadian writers also helped supply the demand for books on this country, and in particular exploited the continuing market for books of regional travel and description, mostly panegyric.

Canada challenged her visitors with the unexpected: scenes unimaginably rugged in the early years of railroad travel, a society unimaginably hostile to upper-class Englishmen in succeeding years, and a golden prairie unimaginably cruel still later. The traveller who responded to this challenge by reporting details sharply and by fusing them into a lively yet logical pattern could produce a noteworthy addition to the world's travel literature.

No single book of travel to Canada is as entertaining as Dickens's *American Notes*, or as deeply analytical as Emerson's *English Traits*, but Sandford Fleming's *England and Canada*, Douglas Sladen's *On the Cars and Off*, Walt Whitman's *Diary in Canada*, and Rupert Brooke's *Letters from America* approach the greatest travel books in liveliness and force. Because spaces in Canada were so great, actualities of travel are more emphasized than in books on England or Europe; and in the simpler national texture the rare quaintness of French Canada, of the Indians, of the western homesteader inevitably focuses attention. Compared to books on the United States, these Canadian travel accounts offer less variety in order and organization. In the 1880's, for instance, there was one route only—the Canadian Pacific Railway, and one direction—East to West or, in rare relief, West to East, never such zig-zag itinerary as lured Britons touring the United States. Chapter headings unroll inevitably: "Trip Across," "Maritimes," "Quebec and Saguenay," "Montreal and Ottawa," "The Railway," "Toronto," "Niagara Falls," "The Great Lake Steamers," "Winnipeg and the Prairies," "The Farther West," and "Homeward Bound." Differences in proportion, in accent, in angle of narration, become significant in such a set scheme.

The 1880's

First travel-books of the 1880's were unassuming and informative. Delegations of English and Scottish tenant farmers dutifully published their views on Canada as a field for settlement, beginning a deluge of "Emigrant Guide" books. The range in background of writers of guide books shows how widespread was the interest in Canada as a haven. Thomas Moore, editor of the *Irish Farmer*, offered *A Tour through Canada in 1879* (1880). Hugh Fraser, farmer of Inverness, wrote *A Trip to the Dominion of Canada* (1883). J. E. Ritchie, a journalist, in *To Canada with Emigrants* (1886) reported on politics as well as colonizing. J. G. Holyoake, organizer of the Co-operative movement in England, described his work in *Travels in Search of a Settler's Guide Book* (1884). "S. Scrivener," Secretary of the "Self-Help Emigrant Society," wrote *Off to Canada* (1888) and *With the Self-Help Emigrants* (1888). Tenant farmers published *Reports . . . on the Dominion of Canada as a Field for Settlement* (1880). Henry Tanner, Senior Member of the Royal Agricultural Society, wrote *A Report upon Canada* (1883). All these writers included descriptions of their own travel experiences, as did Peter Mitchell, a Canadian cabinet minister, in *The West and North-West* (1880), "Anglo-Canadian" in *Canada* (1882), "A Retired Officer" in *A Year in Manitoba* (1883), and "Family Man," a British university graduate, now a professional man with a family of sons, who asked *Shall We Emigrate?* (1885). Of all these travel books published in hope of helping would-be emigrants, the most attractive are two ingenuous reports by young men— boys really—who experienced the life of emigrant labourers: J. S. Cockburn's jaunty *Canada for Gentlemen* (1885) and A. J. Church's *Making a Start in Canada* (1889), a cheery account consisting of letters by the sons of a professor of Latin (who solemnly lists his own publications at the end of the book—*Roman Life in the Days of Cicero,* etc.) The boys finally built their own hut out west, "rather like a pig-sty," put up bookshelves and photos, bats, "rackets" and guns, and pronounced the effect "quite jolly." Much more dignified, and more influential, were the volumes produced by the conscientious Marquis of Lorne, *Canadian Pictures* (1884). The Marquis of Lorne incorporated advice to emigrants in his *Canadian Life and Scenery* (1886) along with his account of travels as Governor-General and as holidaying sportsman. The artistic Lorne in his romantic sketches of the wilderness beauty of the West set a visual image often reproduced in later books. His was the most important book of the decade in terms of numbers of readers.

Among "holiday travellers" the range of personalities, professions, and intentions was again wide—much wider than at any time before or after the 1880's. "A. S." wrote *A Summer Trip to Canada* (1885) to induce other ladies to make similar trips; Charles Elliott, F.S.I., Devonshire gentleman and horse-breeder dedicated *A Trip to Canada and the Far North-West* (1886) to Lord Lorne, the Governor-General. Dr. George Bryce bowled along in *Holiday Rambles between Winnipeg and Victoria* (1888) in a "prose idyll," designed to thrill others at the sights he saw: "The Fraser River is not only wonderful, IT IS TERRIFIC in its grandeur." A. S. Hill, D.C.L., Q.C., M.P., self-important partner of the Earl of Latham, described his "autumn wanderings in the North-West" in *From Home to Home* (1885). Few "holiday trippers" could outdo the satisfaction of Hugh Bryce, business man of Paisley, who in *Narrative of a Trip to Canada* (1881) presented "statistics" on wages and prices of haircuts, grapes and the "self-feeding parlour stove"; described the nuns "in a monastery" in Quebec, the churches and schools in Hamilton, the Canadian "language"; and ended "with the gratifying reflection that I had spent no more money during my trip than I had calculated upon."

It is interesting to note how many Englishmen assumed they could "do" Canada and the United States in one holiday trip. Some representative titles strike the jaunty note: M. Jackson's *To America and Back, a Holiday Run* (1886); C. B. Berry's *The Other Side; How It Struck Us* (1880), John Strathesk's *Bits about America* (1887), Rev. John Kirkwood's *An Autumn Holiday in the U.S. and Canada* (1887). Some cut a still wider swath: J. J. Aubertin's *A Fight with Distances, the States, the Hawaian Islands, Canada, British Columbia, Cuba, the Bahamas* (1888); Mrs. E. H. Carbutt's *Five Months' Fine Weather in Canada, Western U.S. and Mexico* (1889). Brevity is flaunted in T. P. Powell's *A Trip beyond the Rockies, 8000 miles in Eight Weeks* (1887); Thomas Greenwood's *A Tour in the States and Canada; Out and Home in 6 weeks* (1883); Sir Henry Edwards' *A Two Months' Tour in Canada and the United States* (1889).

All these "rapid tours" are open to criticism for glibness and rapid generalization. E. Catherine Bates, speaking of Canada in chapter One of *A Year in the Great Republic* (1887), reports that she spoke to two immigrants and found both discontented. Of this group three hold considerable interest: Joseph Hatton, whose *Today in America* (1881) gives sensitive political and social analysis of "Canada and the Union"; Emily Faithful, who in *Three Visits to America* (1884) includes a study of the position of Canadian women; and Thomas R. Rickman, a querulous architect, whose *Notes of a Short Visit to Canada and the States* (1885) takes a sour look at Canadian arts. America, the ladies, and the arts—three topics to remain controversial.

The Americans, for their part, produced a variety of travel books, emphasizing social differences from the United States, as in C. D. Warner's serious *Studies in the South and West with Comments on Canada* (1889), or in "Captain Mac's" humorous *Canada* (1882); colourful scenes for children as in H. Butterworth's *Zig-Zag Journeys in Acadia* and *New France* (1885) and in C. A. Stephens's adventures of *6 Young Men in the Wilds of Maine and Canada* (1885); and sports as in J. A. Knox's *A Devil of a Trip* (1888), on a yachting tour up Lake Champlain via the St. Lawrence to Nova Scotia, and in B. Watson's *The Sportsman's Paradise* (1888).

To this last group, the "sportsmen's guides," we may add three British books: J. J. Rowan's *The Emigrant and Sportsman in Canada* (1881), mostly on New Brunswick, and remarkably readable on both society and sport; G. H. Wyatt's *The Traveller's and Sportsman's Guide* (1880), a brief and practical book; and J. A. Lees and W. J. Clutterbuck, *B.C. 1887* (1888), regional in title, but introduced by a continental travel sequence. In or out of western territory, this book is one of the gayest and most vigorous of all Canadian travel books.

Another kind of traveller is the specialist who comes to a convention, then "at the urging of friends or family" re-works his travel diary into a book. In the 1880's, British scientists who had been treated to a trip along the C.P.R. as a climax to the first Canadian session of the British Association added reports on Canada "as seen from the cars." An anonymous writer in the *Canadian Gazette* prepared the way with *A Tour through Canada* (1884). Commissioner J. G. Colmer followed with *The Dominion of Canada as it will appear to Members of the British Association* (1884); Rev. Harry Jones, chaplain to the Association, wrote *Railway Notes in the North-West* (1884), Gen. Sir J. H. Lefroy wrote *The British Association in Canada* (1885), and Clara Lady Rayleigh, mother of the professor of experimental physics at Cambridge, added *The British Association's Visit to Montreal* (1885). This redoubtable lady outdid the official delegates in vigour and interest.

As well as the emigrant guides, the holiday accounts, the sportsman's digests, and the scientists' memoirs, Canadian travel books in the eighties included some very competent journalists' analyses. Prior to the opening of the C.P.R., Fraser Rae of the London *Times* had "done Canada" very well in *Newfoundland to Manitoba* (1881).

The opening of the transcontinental line of the C.P.R. brought journalists intent on "copy" and C.P.R. publicists into the travel book business. Mrs. Spragge of Toronto rode the first train *From Ontario to the Pacific* and produced a competent little report (1887). *The Times* sent out another special correspondent in 1886 for *A Canadian Tour* (1886). Stuart Cumberland, an Australian reporter, wrote the biggest and liveliest report, a canny, spirited account of the first West-to-East trip on the C.P.R.: *The Queen's Highway* (1887).

Even the Anglican dean of Montreal, Dean Carmichael, in *A Holiday Trip* (1888), produced something suspiciously like a railroad brochure. The Reverend D. V. Lucas got into the act with *All about Canada* (1883) a pocket reference, also heavily featuring the C.P.R. Sandford Fleming's stirring *England and Canada* (1884) is a railway book in a different sense. The great engineer, returning to the Rockies, retraced the steps of locating the last link of the railway through the Illecillewaet gorge. His report, like that of Lees and Clutterbuck, is on a life of action and courage, a Hemingway world of "camping-out." His was the Canada which would appeal more and more strongly to Europe in the years just before the First World War, and again in the distraught 1930's. In organization, Fleming's work is an unusual blend of travel report and memoir. It fuses the account of a routine trip with memories of the dangerous, challenging past. Many later writers would try to enlarge the time-scope of a day-by-day trip, but none have handled the problem of time in a travel book more effectively than Sandford Fleming.

All travellers to Canada in the eighties felt impelled to "do" certain set scenes. There were Montmorency Falls, the Ice Palace in Montreal, the Parliamentary Library in Ottawa, and the University at Toronto. There was Niagara Falls ("The indescribably superb, gigantic, towering flow of the glorious Canadian rapids! Nearer and nearer the billows roll . . . and then the Fall! . . . And this goes on forever!"). There was Winnipeg, a touchstone for the tourist of the eighties, with its astonishing growth from the hamlet in the mud of the previous decade. Then came the prairies, the Rockies, and Vancouver and Victoria, already contrasted.

All tourists commented on the differences between old and new Canada. Farms stood for sale in New Brunswick, and French Quebec dozed in picturesque backwardness. But fabulous harvests in the West brought hope even to the newcomers, the old-country settlers, both the well-born and the ex-waifs, and even to the odd ethnic groups in communal settlements of Mennonites and Icelanders. Beyond this farm world lay the frontier, rough and bare, bringing American visitors a sense of "the ecstasy of freedom," but filling Englishmen with less enthusiasm. Out at the far end of the railway was an odd and colourful world of improvisation and frontier equalitarianism. "When people wants their boots cleaned," said the hotel proprietor at Fort Moody, "they generally in these parts cleans 'em theirselves; but most of 'em don't want 'em cleaned at all."

Everywhere, Canadians seemed to the British "fluent and friendly," democratic ("Zeke eats with the family"), and busy. Politics attracted the best class (in the United States "the best class holds aloof"). Englishmen were bombarded with complaints against British superciliousness and indifference to Canadian trade. On the other hand, American visitors mocked

Canadian social pretensions and the apeing of English customs. "Captain Mac" has an amusing chapter on "The Knighting of J. Muggins Jones in Ottawa." Differences between Canada and the United States were constantly explored. "The further West, the more American do the cities become." Yet the frontier was distinctly different from the American West—"no shooting, no frontier lawyers." The Northwest Mounted Police clanked through the trains, visible symbols of law and order, keeping a particularly benevolent eye on the rather shiftless Indians, and maintaining the liquor laws. (They might even be observed sniffing at bottles marked "lavender water," drawn from old ladies' reticules.)

Sport called out most social gatherings: curling, tennis, football, sleighing ("simply splendid"), skating by torchlight, trotting, ice-boat sailing, hunting the wild ram, the bear, the grouse, the snowshoe rabbit, fishing (including tommy-cod fishing through the ice), hockey, "trabogoening" ("which has its literal drawbacks"). There was less activity in the arts: collections at Laval and in Sir Donald Smith's Montreal home; a few artists at the "scenic spots" (Mr. Lucius O'Brien, President of the R.C.A., was observed at Glacier, painting "in raptures" but rather bothered by bears). Theatre was rarely enjoyed, though a few travelling troupes and private theatricals supplemented the Theatre Royal in Montreal. Book pedlars plied their wares on the trains, and in Toronto a tribe of writers turned out "cheap moral literature" exploiting a demand. The greatest cultural medium was the newspaper, proliferating in small towns, great centres, new villages, even in a frontier shanty where "a village might be expected later." (Of course the great number of journalists among the travellers of the eighties in part explains the constant emphasis on newspaper workers.) Other Canadians accessible to tourists included politicians, business magnates, and a mixed bag of celebrities (Hanlan the great oarsman, Janet Hanning the sister of Carlyle, and Jefferson Davis, "vivacious, fragile, erect," self-exiled leader of the Southern Confederacy).

But most writers of the eighties were less concerned with people, or the arts, more concerned with scenery, with the winter ("Here they measure milk by the yard") and with the facts of emigrant life.

The 1890's

Some of the "news value" of a Canadian tour had vanished by 1890. Indeed, this next decade produced about half as many books of travel as had appeared in the previous ten years. Many Canadians proudly wrote in this decade their own version of their country's charms, her power, her claims to attention. G. R. Parkin's *The Great Dominion* (1895) was very widely read, to judge by references to it in later travel accounts. It was equalled in ponderous pride by J. D. Edgar's *Canada and its Capital* (1898) and in J. L.

Wood's *Canada from Ocean to Ocean* (1899). These are all less books of travel than glorified guide books, as is G. M. Grant's handsome volume designed for American readers, *Our Picturesque Northern Neighbour* (1899). Such publicizing efforts by prominent Canadians outnumbered the travel books by visiting tourists.

The visitors were lighter in touch. The impression of sprightliness in this decade perhaps reflects the fact that so many of the travel-writers were ladies. Sketch-pad in hand, lady's maid (unwillingly) in tow, a succession of English gentlewomen brightly surveyed the Canadian scene. Greatest of these ladies, both socially and aesthetically, was Lady Dufferin. *My Canadian Journal* (1891) is probably little altered from the informal letters-home written by Lady Dufferin during her years as wife of the Governor-General. Her energy and her enthusiasm for Canadian sports, for theatre, for balls and receptions and camping-trips give this book rare charm. But as a report on Canada it presents a puzzling study in influence. The actual scenes described were those of the seventies but the book was printed twenty years after her experiences in Canada. Because of her prestige and position, it was very widely read. But *My Canadian Journal* fixed in its readers' minds the picture of a life already vanished. Another much read and still readable account of vice-regal life is Lady Aberdeen's self-styled "taffy for the Dominion," *Through Canada with a Kodak* (1893).

Most of the ladies' books sport "Kodak" shots, or drawings by the authors, reproduced in sepia tones; the books are bound in artistic shades of mauve or mustard, ornamented with gold line drawings of flowers and leaves.

Botanizing Lady Theodora Guest in *A Round Trip in North America* (1895) and Lady H. J. Jephson in *A Canadian Scrap-Book* (1897) include "illustrations from the author's sketches." Winnifred, Lady Howard of Glossop, adds to the ladies' books a *Journal of a Tour in the U.S., Canada and Mexico* (1897) and Mrs. Howard Vincent a more serious report, *Newfoundland to Cochin China* (1892).

Gentleman travellers usually rely on photographs for illustration. Holiday "shots" enliven William Smith's *A Yorkshireman's Trip to the United States and Canada* (1892) and A. Giles's *Across Western Waves and Home* (1898). Among other holiday travellers Robert Shields, "the Horatio Alger of Toronto," described *My Travels* (1900); J. G. Colmer wrote *Across the Canadian Prairies* (1895), Hugh Bryce, a delegate to a Christian Endeavour convention in San Francisco, wrote *Across the American Continent* (1898), and W. S. Webb, a businessman travelling by "special private train" contributed *California and Alaska and over the Canadian Pacific Railway* (1891).

Many holiday trips still fitted Canada into an American tour: Rudyard

Home's *Columbian and Canadian Sketches* (1895) emphasizes Irish contributions to the New World; W. T. Crosweller reports *Our Visit to Toronto, Niagara Falls and the United States of America* (1898); Alexander Craib in *America and the Americans* (1892) focuses on "home life" and pious Protestant groups like the Y.M.C.A.; Archibald Porteous, *A Scamper through Some Cities of America* (1890), a Scottish business man's account, allots three chapters out of seventeen to Canada, covering Niagara to Hamilton, Ottawa and Montreal. J. Bond's *A Fortnight in America* (1891) reaches the extreme in time limit. Thomas Hughes, popular author of *Tom Brown's Schooldays*, issues his *Vacation Rambles* in 1895 in a late reprinting of travel letters from 1870, perhaps with something of the same effect as Lady Dufferin's delayed report.

Two Australians add records of leisurely trips: J. F. Hogan, *The Sister Dominions* (1896), and J. W. C. Haldane, *3800 Miles across Canada* (1900). Three Americans report: Julian Ralph in *On Canada's Frontier*, gives sketches of sport and adventure in "Nepigon," Hudson Bay, and the "Eldorado" of the new Northwest (1892); H. M. Field, in *Our Western Archipelago*, offers effective analysis by an established author of travel books (1895); and R. H. Davis views *The West from a Car Window* (1892).

Dr. P. E. Doolittle supplements the "railroad" books by an account of Canadian sights of interest to high-perched "wheelmen," *Wheel Outings in Canada* (1895).

Less jaunty are the accounts of immigrant life. These books usually begin with a travel account, then expand the description of life in the new settlements. The best are Wm. Elkington's *Five Years in Canada* (1895), a day-by-day account of farming near Strathclair and later at Qu'appelle; A. A. Boddy's *By Ocean Prairie and Peak*, "some gleanings from an Emigrant chaplain's log" (1896); C. C. Johnstone's *Winter and Summer Excursions in Canada* (1892), case histories of successes and failures designed to offset the over-optimism of official pamphlets; Thomas Moore's *Canada Revisited, 1879–1893* (1893); P. R. Ritchie's *Manitoba and the North-West Territories* (1892), a young farmer's account of travels in search of a new home; and finally a collection of reports on *The Visit of the Tenant-Farmer Delegates to Canada in 1890* (1891). This last is produced in the old small print of the "emigrant guides" of the previous decade.

But the look of most of the travel books in the nineties is impressive. Solid books, in clear big print on glossy paper, most of them were obviously not designed for potential emigrant-farmers. Careful style and structure reflect a changed conception of the aesthetic sophistication of the audience.

In Douglas Sladen's *On the Cars and Off* (1895) and Edward Roper's *By Track and Trail* (1891), the travel book reaches a modest but satisfying height. Both books are energized by the excitement of railway travel (which

provides both a literal and a literary dynamic). Both create attractive
personae as observers, and both add a second dynamic in the interaction
between the observer and his companions. Edward Roper focuses his
whimsical story of settlers' travels through the eyes of "Miss Maud and
Miss Maggie," the two pretty English girls who accompany him west; Douglas
Sladen unifies *On the Cars and Off* by a similar use of "The Pretty Girl"
and "The Matter-of-Fact Woman." Travel is subtilized, humanized, given
artistic unity and structure by these devices. The travel book seems almost
to emerge as a literary genre here.

Kipling's *From Sea to Sea* (1899), while even livelier in treatment of
scenes on the West Coast, seems fragmentary by contrast. It is good Kipling,
but not a great travel book. His tone and themes were already established,
and Canada could not effect a change in his palette.

Egerton Ryerson Young's books for boys, such as *Winter Adventures of
Three Boys* (1899), not strictly travel books, fixed the image of the "great
lone land" in the minds of British schoolboys.

For most tourists of the 1890's people mattered more than in the 1880's.
They recorded meetings with Van Horne, with Laurier, with Dunsmuir in
British Columbia, with Goldwin Smith in Toronto, with Father Lacombe out
west. Scenery mattered less. A sense of re-doing over-worked scenes inhibited
the new observers of Quebec, Montreal, the prairies, the Rockies. They strained
for subtler effects, as when the Saguenay becomes a "sophisticated dream of
death." For Niagara, few raptures: "I duly did the Falls," said one writer.
The iridescent arch seemed "no longer what it was"; the scandal of control
by speculators and the "cockney treatment" of the surroundings appalled.
"No fine scenery, no fine weather—and no fine flowers." At Ottawa there
was "no good *coup d'œil*"; in Quebec, city of romance, there was a sense
of the real world passing by; in Montreal, a charming view from the Mountain, "but oh! the roads, the horrid, rutty, dirty, muddy, dusty roads!"
Disenchantment extended to the hotels. The opulent city establishments like
the Windsor (much praised in previous years) now seemed outbalanced by
the cheerless bush hotels where half-breeds lingered in an airless kitchen.
No blind, no glass, no service in Quebec; no taste, no comfort in Nipissing;
no charm anywhere.

These sophisticated travellers found much to interest them in Canadian
character. It was bustling, a little priggish, resentful of British criticism,
very loyal to Queen Victoria, but hostile to the dissipated British lordlings
now on drunken display in western saloons. Yet Canadians bristled against
being called "American," and had a laughing rejoinder to annexation talk,
"Let them jine us!" There were new concerns too, with "perfidious Russia,"
and with the new Japan.

The new Canadian gospel was "work." Few festivals broke the year; tales were heard of young men marrying widows to get their children as labourers, and there was little sense of a cultural growth to compensate for this grim practicality. Churches flourished, but in mutual antagonism. The new universities, though blessedly open to all, focused on agricultural science. Teetotalism was militant. (The director of the Canadian National Exhibition invited one visitor into his broom closet for a drink.) Women married too early, lost their freshness. Canadian children, boys as well as girls, did domestic chores, but were hard to manage in school. "All speak with a twang unequalled in ugliness."

Yet most of these details were reported with interest rather than disdain.

The 1900's

As Canada moved into the twentieth century, the vision of a "vast reserve of Empire" continued to inflame British imagination, but enthusiasm was checked by Canadian arrogance. Admiration and irritation alternate in most travel books of the decade. The ladies were silent; in their place came a succession of serious, statistic-minded males. R. J. Barrett, editor of the *Financier and Bullionist*, produces *Canada's Century: Progress and Resources of the Great Dominion* in 1907, a confident report, with economic conclusions firmly set in black-face at the end of each chapter. J. A. Hobson, author of *The Evolution of Modern Capitalism and Imperialism*, sets forth *Canada Today* (1906) in similar analytic vein. H. R. Whates, London journalist from the *Standard*, includes excellent chapters on fiscal policy and national sentiment in *Canada, the New Nation* (1906) but contrasts life in exile, on the prairies, with the luxuries of home, friends, theatre, thoroughfares. Less pretentious accounts come from George Bain, *A Run through Canada* (1905); George Briggs, *Recollections of a Visit to Canada: Experiences of a Member of the Corporation of London* (1907); and Herbert Grange, *An English Farmer in Canada and a Visit to the States* (1904), but these pedestrian books sometimes offer rewarding details: a glimpse of a St.-Jean-Baptiste parade in Montreal, ugly telephone wires, Orange Day in the West, Indian schools, a Chinook in the foothills. Other travel accounts lighter in tone include Fr. E. J. Devine's *Across Wildest America* (1905), about a remembered train ride to a far western mission; Harry Brittain's *Canada There and Back* (1908), an uncritical attempt to persuade friends to try a similar tour through "magnificent country"; and Joseph Adams's *Ten Thousand Miles through Canada* (1909), a vigorous narrative of shipboard and train-ride, emphasizing always the links between old country and new—the Boy Scouts on board ship, the suffragist orators bound for new audiences in Ontario, the prairie-bound brides.

J. W. C. Haldane, in *3800 Miles across Canada* (1900), attempted to solve the technical problem of travel narration by giving himself a "split personality"—and referring to himself alternately as the sharp-eyed "Chiel" and the affable "Happy Traveller." But most travel books of the decade differed only in their geographical pattern of organization from the weighty books of general analysis and description in which the period abounds— books not properly travel accounts but rather panegyrics: A. G. Bradley's *Canada in the 20th Century* (1903), F. A. Wrightman's *Our Canadian Heritage* (1908) and W. W. Campbell's *Canada* (1907), H. J. Morgan and L. J. Burpee, *Canadian Life in Town and Country* (1905). All are heavily partisan, handsomely printed; in numbers they equal the travel accounts by British and American visitors of the decade.

Even books designed for English children, such as J. T. Bealby's *Canada* (1909), though lively in spots, were ponderously informative in others, presenting awed summaries of the outputs of mines, of lumber-yards, of wheat fields. Equally solemn, though less complete in coverage, were the books endemic in this period, by "one-track travellers"—the men who came obsessed by a single idea. Kipling, in *Letters to the Family* (1908), pounded imperialism readably, but still obsessively. C. J. Farncombe, Nonconformist preacher, in *My Visit to Canada* (1907), Sir Frederick Young, in *A Pioneer of Imperial Federation in Canada* (1902), J. C. Smith, of the "Soul-Winning and Prayer Union," in *Holidays for Jesus* (1901), and Bailie D. Wilcox, in *With the British Bowlers in Canada* (1906)—each reports only what relates to his obsession. Joseph Pope's *Tour of Their Royal Highnesses the Duke and Duchess of Cornwall and York* (1901) belongs in this obsessed group, as all royal tours must. The Canadian background fades behind the royal couple, their doings, sayings, and posings for photographers. The Duke of Argyll's Canadian scenes continued to be reprinted, always with new pleas appended for Imperial solidarity and for the use of Canadian spaces as receiving ground for the overcrowded British labouring classes.

Very few travellers attempted to describe the panorama of the whole nation in this decade. Walt Whitman's haunting *Diary in Canada*, the account of his trip from London to the Saguenay (1904), is the best of the regional studies. Paul Fountain writes of *The Great North-West* (1904), James Outram of *The Heart of the Canadian Rockies* (1905), F. G. Pauli of *Chibogamoo* (1907), Major Durham of *A Trip from Buffalo to Chicoutimi* (1901), Andrew Iredale of Niagara and the Thousand Islands in *An Autumn Tour* (1901), John A. Walker of the eastern provinces in *Canada: Or the Western Land of Promise* (1902), St. Michael Podmore of Lake Abitibi in *A Sporting Paradise* (1909), F. E. Herring of the West in a series of books, *Canadian Camp Life* (1900), *B.C.* (1903), and *On the Pathless West* (1904).

The author of a regional sketch straining for unity, might organize it by reference to rivers, as in L. J. Burpee's *By Canadian Streams* (1909), or to seasons, as in Theodore Haultain's delightful *Two Country Walks in Canada*

(1903), or to scriptural passages, as in D. V. Lucas's *Canaan and Canada* (1904). (Haultain's book is of interest also for its tone of mildly satiric realism, anticipating Leacock's method and range.) Of all regional studies the most important deal with the crucial Midwest. Brian McEvoy's rapid, colourful *From the Great Lakes to the Wide West* (1902) blends flair for anecdote with patriotic response to the "Boom." James Lumsden, another journalist, in his *Through Canada in Harvest Time* (1903) promises comfort and independence in the golden West. H. A. Kennedy dedicates *New Canada and New Canadians* (1907) to "all who love their country and whose country is the British Empire." All emphasize economic facts rather than moral or social ones: themes of moral disintegration or regeneration by the prairie, and themes of social difficulties in assimilation (valuable to Ralph Connor and other novelists of the period) are unexplored. Two bitter footnotes to the optimism of earlier emigrant guides appear in the works of "Homesteader," *Canadian Life as I Found It* (1908), and of Basil Stewart, *The Land of the Maple Leaf* (1908). Next year Stewart excerpted and reprinted the angriest parts of his report in *No English Need Apply* (1909), a belligerent protest against Canadian boosters, American immigrants, and British emigration pamphleteers.

Inevitably, the more kindly disposed books of this period of "boosting" and independence are Amercan. "There's only one West left, and . . . Young Canada has got that," cried Anson Gard, in a last twist of the old American frontier-worship. Gard, tossing off a series of bright little books, brassy but readable, *The Wandering Yankee* (1902), *The New Canada* (1903), *The Last West* (1906), is an odd partner for the majestic Walt Whitman. Whitman dreamily mused on the Canadian current of life, so strangely separated from "the glorious mid-artery of the great free Pluribus Unum of America," as he dreamily watched Canadian life in a hayfield and on a lake boat. But Whitman united with Gard in sympathy for the new Canada.

All travellers reported now on the new Montreal, of St. James Street, Victoria Bridge, river front, tenement houses, and "foreign Jewry." Toronto was a puzzle of self-conscious culture, of "small-calibred people," of money values, and mealy-mouthed piety. A new Ontario of mines, of the "Soo," and Port Arthur, was emerging. In Winnipeg, the "Canadian Chicago," this raw new world was focused in its shoddiness, its energy, and its anti-British sentiment. The "Great Clay Belt" held promise, and the Far West, exploiting natural resources, "hustled." Everywhere there were comforts, pavements, electricity, telephones, tram-cars. In hotels, a "roughish element" afflicted with superfluous saliva held stations in the uncurtained ground-floor saloons. Rural festivals consisted of Orangemen and lemonade and abuse of the late John A. Macdonald. There were few sports now—baseball, "dreariest and most negative of games," while "cricket flickers but feebly." Football players appeared more warlike than in England, padded and encased.

In contrast with this hustling world of energy and materialism, the natural landscape was filmed over in vapid sentimentalism. Like the pale water-colour illustrations in Campbell's *Canada*, Whitman's descriptions typify this genteel prettiness: Montmorency Falls are "like strings of snowy-spiritual, beautiful tresses."

Englishmen, irritated by the sentimental façade, annoyed by Canadian brashness, disturbed by car-loads of "Galicians"—Russians, Poles, Hungarians—disillusioned by the continuing deterioration of whiskey-laden Indians, uneasy at the "dirty" farming out west and the utilitarian grinding life of wheat-growing, were puzzled and not attracted by twentieth-century Canada. To Kipling, Canada was like the Canadian lady, "powerful, comprehending, vital." Kipling didn't like Canadian ladies.

1910–1920

The great triangle of British-American-Canadian sentiment shifted again in the years around the war. Canadian bragging, intolerable in the raw opening years of the new century, seemed justifiable now that the prairies and the western valleys had been brought to spectacular harvest, not to mention the human harvest of heroism produced by this raw society when war came.

The free new life offered fewer cultural opportunities and no guaranteed reward in wealth, but the sensitive Englishman—Rupert Brooke, for instance —on the eve of European war, was too confused by European troubles to be able to reject the Canadian way as confidently as his predecessors had done. And the survivors of that wave of public school boys, younger sons, remittance men, who had caused so much hostility in the previous decade, were now obviously giving a quality to western Canada very different from the alleged degradation of the American West. British travellers, naturally meeting ex-schoolmates, gained a general impression of the dignity, at least in desire, of the Canadian.

On the other hand, abuse of the Englishman, a staple of conversation in 1910–13, simmered down by the end of the war, doused in part by the war records of the upper-class British soldiers.

Englishmen contributed the majority of the travel accounts of this period. The total number of travel books was growing again. In 1911 the greatest number ever published in a single year appeared, and of these all but four were by Englishmen. In contrast to the previous decade, Canadians now produced about one-fifth of the total number of descriptive accounts. American reports had dwindled to one-tenth of the total.

American influences in Canadian life continued to grow, as every traveller noted. But Americans were no longer completely enamoured with Canada. "America last century—Canada this!" was a phrase often repeated, not designed to win American hearts. Americans in Canada were less likely to be workaday immigrants, more likely to be power figures: wealthy and arrogant tourists, trade union officials, newly nationalized magnates like Van Horne and Charles Hays. The Canadian manner, "semi-tense but friendly," seemed to English visitors an American manner. The new school system in the West with its emphasis on agriculture, the lionizing of scientists like Saunders and Rutherford, all seemed American.

There were still some markedly *Canadian* features, and English and American travellers agreed in enjoying the French-Canadian community (though there was an increasing unease at the extent of Roman Catholic domination evidenced in the Eucharistic Congress of 1910) and the Mounties, "those thousand soldier-dandies, half cowboy, half-dragoon," and the thrill of the far West, Edmonton, Peace River, Athabaska, Okanagon valley—new names for Eldorado. But no longer could the visitors see the great ice palaces (except as a shabby backdrop in a cheap theatre) nor would one hear the old rhapsodies on the railroad. One traveller recounted the legend of a farmer hacking at its rails as at octopus tentacles; and now that the Grand Trunk and the Great Northern rivalled the C.P.R. the romance of that single thread across the great spaces was lessened. There was still the paradox of vast empty spaces plus lack of privacy, in homes, hotels, offices, and stores.

Both English and American visitors recognized in the Canadian woman qualities alien to their own countrywomen: to the American she seemed English in her dress, her colouring, her outdoor life. To the Englishman she appeared American, "bargain-counter haunting, street-car patronizing, hurrying, non-sentimentalizing . . . not a creature of fine bouquet." She antagonized her visitors, but the Canadian woman also aroused admiration and, particularly out west, sympathy.

Similarly, one might be "almost oppressed by the optimism of Canada," the gracelessness, the discourtesy, the "push-pump mentality" of her sections. One might dream of a new-style emigrant poster, reading:

> WANTED for CANADA!
> 300 brainy authors!
> 150 philosophers!
> First-class passage and a good living guaranteed.
> To the right man!
> Also new ideas, plots, scenes, quiet surroundings
> With unlimited nature!

But one recognized the eager support for public libraries, the growth of art galleries and museums, the presence even in rough farm houses of "Scott,

Omar, Schopenhauer, Dickens, de Maupassant," and the rise of Toronto as "fourth among large cities on the continent as a music centre."

All of which balancing of culture and anarchy may be the result of another change in the travellers. In the years just before the war, the ladies returned. Not the aristocrats this time, the specially privileged; instead earnest women with a variety of causes: midwives for the midwest, free land for lady home-steaders, suffrage for all. Mrs. George Cran wrote *A Woman in Canada* (1910), Mrs. B. Pullen-Burry *From Halifax to Vancouver* (1912), Georgina Binnie-Clark *A Summer on the Canadian Prairie* (1910) and *Wheat and Woman* (1914). All are effective writers, competent at anecdote, sprightly in style, and close to fictional technique. Miss Binnie-Clark, for instance, uses the Canadian trip as a background for her own story—a shipboard near-romance, a visit with sister Hilaria to their amiable inefficient brother "batching it" on a homestead, a decision to enter farm management. Mrs. Cran provides "a series of [literary] snapshots, offered with ragged edges," but they are competently finished and communicate a strong sense of her personality. Mrs. Pullen-Burry, interested in politics and especially in the suffragette movement, presents information on Canadian attitudes and problems in eminently readable dialogue. Even the less charming accounts offer welcome relief from the heavy solemnity of turn-of-the-century statisticians. E. C. Sykes's *A Home Help in Canada* (1912), Mary J. Sansom's *A Holiday Trip to Canada* (1916), *Our Lady of Sunshine* edited by the Countess of Aberdeen (1910), and Elizabeth Keith Morris's *An English-woman in the Canadian West* (1913) are all attractively written, and present individual Canadian lives in convincing reality.

The ladies react against old-style travel books, "neat, dowdy things they are, full of facts and figures, written by people with tidy minds, and packed with information." They make a claim for their own impressionism: "The man who rushes out and back has . . . no affections, no prejudices."

Male visitors report their travel findings in livelier fashion too in these pre-war years. Friendly, good-humoured, with an eye to pathos and whimsy, Copping, Yeigh, and Vernède prepared a trio of books attractively illustrated in clear bright colours and printed on thick matt paper, books obviously designed for a reading mood of friendly relaxed interest: A. E. Copping, *The Golden Land of Canada Today and Tomorrow* (1911), Frank Yeigh, *Through the Heart of Canada* (1911), and P. E. Vernède, *The Fair Dominion* (1911). Less lively but similar in pattern are E. W. Elkington's *Canada, the Land of Hope* (1910) and W. E. Curtis's *Letters on Canada* (1911).

Less pretentious travel diaries in the old style include H. P. Scott's *Seeing Canada and the South* (1911), E. G. Busbridge's *Canada, Impressions of a Tour* (1912). J. B. Bickersteth's *The Land of Open Doors* (1914) consists of the vivid and thoughtful letters of a lay missionary at Edmonton. Frank Carrel in *Canada West and Farther West* (1911) reports a one-month journey, from Quebec to Victoria. Some of these old-style travel books reflect colourful personalities: C. J. Sparling, sharp-eyed, opinionated farm hand, author of *The Irish-Canuck-Yankee* (1910), E. G. F. Walker, zestful "Zummerset" farmer, author of *Canadian Trails* (1911), and N. P. R. Noel, likable young job-hunter, author of *Blanket-Stiff* (1911).

Again there are fragmentary regional sketches, most significantly of the new world of big game and adventure North and West. Vilhjalmur Stefansson's important series of Arctic studies begins with *My Life with the Eskimo* (1913). Readers devoted to Jack London and Robert Service were fed Nicholas Everitt's *Round the World in Strange Company* (1915), F. C. Cooper's *In the Canadian Bush* (1914), F. N. Alfalo's *A Fisherman's Summer in Canada* (1911), Grant Hamil's *Two Sides of the Altantic* (1917), and the Earl of Dunraven's *Canadian Nights* (1914). These idylls of camp life fixed the image of Canada as refuge, as wilderness haven, towards which so many nerve-shocked Europeans would turn in the 1920's.

Emigrant guides of the pre-war years differ from these cavalier hunting-tales, but differ also from the pedestrian accounts of the nineteenth century. Descriptive books, hotly focused on economic conditions, on new exploitations of resources, on analysis of fiscal policies and trade, they seem designed to attract the small capitalist rather than the tenant farmer. F. A. Talbot in *Making Good in Canada* (1912) emphasizes the opportunities. Basil Sewart in *Canada as it is* (1910) repeats his tale of disillusionment. F. W. Freier in *Canada, the Land of Opportunities* (1919) gives practical hints and a businesslike analysis of openings for "colonizers." H. H. Fyfe, lightly, in *Shall I Go to Canada?* (1912), E. P. Weaver, heavily, in *Canada and the British Immigrant* (1914) and *Canadian Pictures* (1912), H. J. Boam, fulsomely, in *20th Century Impressions of Canada* (1914), J. F. Fraser, analytically, in *Canada as it is* (1911) add to the survey. In all these, the travel element is subordinated to argument. William Maxwell's *Canada of To-day* (1910) and W. L. Griffith's *The Dominion of Canada* (1911) emerge as social studies rather than travel accounts. One little book is titled to show a typical blend of travel with Imperial thesis: P. Machel's *What is My Country? My Country is the Empire, Canada is my Home* (n.d.).

Finally, three books indicate changes of fact, of taste, of theme. T. W. Wilby, in *A Motor Tour through Canada* (1914) triumphantly tallies history: "The canoe, the steamship, the railroad, and now the touring car." And the car, with its "single centre lever control for the gears, pedals for both brakes, two speedometers, a horn worked by foot . . ." provides high drama when the speedometers read 30 mph and local dogs go crazy. The book, and the car, introduce a new route through Canada.

A Canadian writes the second of the trio. B. B. Cooke's *The First Traveler* (1911) gives nine swift, strong sketches of life along the rail line, deepened into the symbolic level by a vision of the transcontinental railway as "the alternating pulse of the nation." This book is linked with emerging energy in another art form, for it is illustrated by the young J. E. H. Macdonald.

Finally, Rupert Brooke, in *Letters from America* (1916), seals the old range of topics with a fine review of the traditional tour: Quebec and the Saguenay, Montreal and Ottawa, Toronto and the Falls, the Prairies, and "outside"—the sportsmen's wilderness. Here he at last finds value in this "country without a soul":

It awaits the sun, the end for which Heaven made it, the blessing of civilization. Someday it will be sold in large portions, and the timber cut down and made into paper, on which shall be printed praise of prosperity; and the land itself shall be divided into town-lots and sold, and sub-divided and sold again, and boomed and re-sold, and boosted and distributed to fishy young men . . . and given in exchange for great sums of money to old ladies in the quieter part of England. . . . And . . . churches, hotels, and a great many ugly skyscrapers [shall] be built, and hovels for the poor, and houses for the rich, none beautiful, and there shall ugly objects be manufactured, rather hurriedly, and sold to the people at more than they are worth, because similar and cheaper objects made in other countries are kept out by a tariff. . . .

But at present there are only the wrinkled, grey-blue lake, sliding ever sideways, and the grey rocks, and the cliffs and hills, covered with birch-trees, and the fresh wind among the birches, and quiet, and that unseizable virginity.

Brooke's report is the best of that legion of books on tours of the United States in which a swing through Canada is included. Here the Canadian note is carefully sounded, for accent, for contrast, and for the intrinsic interest in the theme of the "Northern Neighbour."

19. Nature Writers
and the Animal Story

ALEC LUCAS

NATURE WRITING is a comparatively recent literary development. Yet its roots lie deep in folklore, the Bible, and the myths, fables, and pastorals of Ancient Greece, for man has always been concerned with his relationship to the natural world. For the Jew of the Old Testament it manifested the power of the Deity and revealed His purpose. For the Greek it stimulated the mind and fed a love of beauty. The growth of the Christian Church, however, set man at odds with nature, which, as the medieval writers saw it, was distinct from and inferior to man, a *massa perditionis* unworthy of his study. The proper study of mankind was God. Even St. Francis loved birds and animals from a sense of love of God, not from one of companionship with them. He had no desire to learn from and to study them for their own sakes, an attitude which, generally speaking, characterizes modern nature writing. As for the natural historians (except Frederick II, Roger Bacon, and Albert of Cologne), they, too, made little effort to observe for themselves and looked on nature as a way of teaching the good life. Depending on classical authority, especially Pliny, for their facts, their books (bestiaries) are marked by the moralizing allegory and unnatural natural history of this description:

> The elephant is so constructed that he has no joints in his knees, which makes it impossible for him to rise if he falls. Because of this he sleeps leaning against the bole of a large tree. . . . In order to catch the elephant, the hunter saws the tree halfway through. When the elephant comes to sleep he falls with the tree to the ground. If other elephants hear the fallen one trumpeting for help, they come and try to raise him, but without success. Finally a small elephant comes and lifts up the fallen one, in the same way that Christ in lowly human form came to save man from the Devil and raise him up again.

Beast fables, a genre exemplified in Chaucer's "The Nun's Priest's Tale," were another of the popular forms of medieval nature writing. They were, however, like *Aesop's Fables*, their model, a commentary on man rather than nature, for the birds and animals that formed their subjects talked and acted as people. Unlike the bestiary, the beast fable has never died out, and as late as 1947 Philip Grove adopted it in *Consider Her Ways*, satirizing human society in the guise of the ant world. Furthermore, the fable would seem to have fathered the highly anthropomorphic children's animal story of the nineteenth and twentieth centuries.

The sportsman's or outdoors book also began in medieval times with Piers Fulham's discussion of fishing (Ms. 1420, Trinity College, Cambridge) and Dame Juliana Berners's *Treatyse of Fishinge with an Angle* (1496), but not until Izaak Walton's *The Compleat Angler* (1653) did the genre of the sportsman book and the form of *belles-lettres* nature writing become established. Although frequently marked by close observation of nature and an appreciation of its therapeutic value, the outdoors book usually centres in personal experience and presents the hunter, not the hunted, as protagonist. Behind this writing is an acceptance of man's dominion over nature—God's never ending bounty for man's benefit, a concept that accounts in part for the descriptions of the merciless slaughter of wildlife that fill early Canadian sportsman's books.

The rise of humanism during the Renaissance marked a change in man's understanding of nature. Although Petrarch complained that it was of no advantage to be familiar with the nature of beasts, birds, and fish, some thinkers disagreed. On the one hand, Montaigne cited examples of the moral and rational in the animal world which denied man his unique and superior place in the chain of being. On the other, Sir Francis Bacon called for the examination of all nature. If man was to advance, he needed to study his environment, not in terms of classical authority and morality but in the light of his own reason.

Under the stimulus of such thinking, expressed most concisely in Descartes' mathematical logic, men sought to discover a rational proof of an ordered universe, and finally in Newton's work saw it set forth, as they thought, in definitive form. The world was ordered, and all things were part of a vast unity. Men could not overlook the relationships of plants and animals in a kinship based on universal reason. For all the impetus that science thus gave to the study of the natural world, there were those, however, and especially churchmen like the influential John Ray, who believed that plants and animals had been placed on earth for their own sakes, not simply as objects for man's use or as cogs in a machine. Thus religion reconciled a feeling for nature with the predominant rationalism of the day and fostered an appreciation of living things in a mechanistic universe, an appreciation that Gilbert White expressed in *The Natural History of Selborne* (1789). This famous book, characterized by accurate observations and a kindly interest in birds and animals, established the scientific-literary essay as a genre that has since become one of the most popular forms of nature writing.

In the eighteenth century, however, forces were acting to produce an attitude toward nature different from White's. Locke's philosophy stressed the importance of environment and Shaftesbury's, that of feeling. Enclosure and the rise of the industrialized city revivified the old dream of a golden age when man supposedly lived in harmony with nature, for as man extended his control over his world, his interest in and longing for the untamed in contrast to the tamed increased correspondingly. To the formal beauty of the garden and the well-kept country seat he now opposed the sublimity of the "horrid" mountain and the grandeur of the wilderness, and to civilization an Arcadian primitivism.

From these influences in large part came the romantic movement of the early nineteenth century. Now man went to nature not to wonder at evidences of rational order. He went, like Bewick, to observe and to draw pictures from nature or, like Gilpin, to enjoy the picturesque. Under the guidance of Rousseau and Wordsworth, the high priests of a new form of natural religion, he might learn also how to dream and so feel the eternal Presence in all things. If the seventeenth and eighteenth centuries had found God through nature, the early romantics found Him in it, and for them it became a source of inspiration, consolation, and moral guidance. As a result, much romantic writing is highly subjective, since even the intimate details of the natural world tend to lose themselves in this same awe, for, if a sunset could become the source of "elevated thoughts: a sense sublime," so, too, could a mouse become "miracle enough to stagger sextillions of infidels."

Related to the romantic is the humanitarian, who preached the rights of animals vis-à-vis the rights of man. He recognized man's dominion, but sought to express it through pity and understanding. Writers of this kind at first selected tame rather than wild animals as subjects, treating them often as if they were members of that favourite Victorian group, "the deserving poor." Ouida's A Dog of Flanders and Anna Sewell's Black Beauty set the fashion, which, in our literature, is best exemplified by Marshall Saunders's work.

By the mid-nineteenth century man's interest in nature took a new turn, for the publication of Darwin's The Origin of Species (1859) and The Descent of Man (1871) re-affirmed rationally the relationship between man and nature, but re-focused man's attention on it for itself and not as a path into an ideal world which it symbolized. Many tended to conclude that if man were a superior animal and not a fallen angel, he ought to study nature for what it could reveal about himself. The proper study of mankind was not God, nor man, but animal. Man and animal, as the romantic held, did differ only in degree; but the link was now not Creator but ancestor. Yet if the romantic had raised the natural up and the Darwinian had brought the human down, many nature writers tried to restore the balance by preaching the merits of animals.

Although science spoke out about man, it remained silent about God. He was again an outsider as He had been for the eighteenth-century rationalists. In their mechanistic universe, nevertheless, He had at least created its parts and established the laws by which it operated. Now the parts were self-explanatory and the system self-contained. Whether God was in His heaven was beside the point. For the naturalist, as for the rationalist, and the pantheist, fact was important; not, however, as evidence of order or of the mystery of being, but as the record of an earthly evolution in which Nature, "red in tooth and claw," recognized survival as the only value.

Aside from this intellectual background of Canadian nature writing, there is the matter of physical foreground, since the greatest single fact of the new country was nature—and a most unWordsworthian nature. Explorers marvelled at the great rivers, forests, and mountains; travellers thrilled to the sublime (the awful Niagara Falls) and the picturesque. Their books, however, lie outside this chapter since it includes only those in which the writers have made nature a central interest and whose approaches to it are not purely factual.

One must turn to the early settlers for our first nature writers. They had to live close to nature, whether or not they wished to. Most did not wish to and saw nature as an obstacle on the road to civilization. The grandeur of lake and river was lost in a concern over floods, portages, sawmills, and steamboats. The sublimity of the forests disappeared in counting the chopping days needed to level them. Man's kinship with the wild creatures was usually expressed with rod and gun. Yet some settlers laid these and the axe aside for their quills. Back home the folks wanted to know what life was like "over there." Was it true that flights of pigeons darkened the sky, that there were snowbanks even in the summer? In response, the pioneers often became amateur field-naturalists and in their writing about land grants, "bees," and crops included observations on the world of tree and beast that obtruded dramatically into all their activities. The same general influence has been responsible for the annual crop of books the Arctic now produces. The frontier has simply shifted back a thousand miles and ahead a hundred years.

The best-known pioneer nature writers belong to the Otonabee School— Major Strickland, Thomas Need, the Langtons, Mrs. Frances Stewart, Mrs. Susanna Moodie, and Mrs. Catharine Parr Traill. Although all wrote of nature, only Mrs. Traill (1802–1899) made it the subject of more than incidental commentary. When she came to Canada, she was thirty and had already written about nature, and in her first Canadian book, *The Backwoods of Canada* (1836), she turned to it again, including among many general comments a full chapter on native flowers. Later she expanded it into *Canadian Wild Flowers* (1869), the first book of the kind in our literature, and *Studies of Plant Life* (1885), with the hope that it might "become a household book, as Gilbert White's *Natural History of Selborne* is to this day among English readers." Mrs. Traill kept a nature diary and from it in her old age drew her last book, *Pearls and Pebbles* (1894), another series of literary-scientific essays, but in this case on the commoner birds and animals.

Mrs. Traill was a fairly accurate observer, but, influenced by the romantics, tended to sentimentalize and moralize her natural history. Disliking "anything ugly or disgusting" such as reptiles and spiders, she looked to nature as a source of inspiration and morality. "We stand," she writes, "beneath the pines and enter the grand pillared aisles with a feeling of mute reverence; these stately trunks bearing their plumed heads so high above us seem a meet roofing for His temple who reared them to His praise. . . . And hark! . . . There are melodies in ocean, earth and air . . . heard by unseen spirits in their ministrations of love fulfilling the will of our Father." (*Pearls and Pebbles*, p. 134.)

When Mrs. Traill moved from contemplation of God's grandeur to observation of the details of His world, she sometimes found in them also a way "to refine and purify the mind," to climb "a ladder to heaven." (For all this, however, she can call some of God's handiwork "wicked" and "horrid," when it is a polecat in her henhouse.) Generally, however, her descriptions reveal a genuine liking for nature and much of her writing is characterized by the intimacy of this little sketch:

Listen to that soft whispering sound. It cannot be called a song it is so soft and monotonous. It is the note of a tiny brown bird that flits among the pine cones, one of the little tree-creepers, a Sitta or Certhia, gentle birds small as the tiniest of our wrens.

They live among the cone-bearing evergreens, gleaning their daily meal from between the chinks of the rugged bark where they find the larvae upon which they feed.

As they flit to and fro they utter this little call-note to their companions, so soft that it would pass unnoticed but for the silence. . . . (*Pearls and Pebbles*, p. 135.)

Since the publication of *The Backwoods of Canada*, the nature essay has grown vigorously. The number of writers in the genre has increased greatly, especially during this century, and includes some of our best-known authors —Peter McArthur (1866–1924), Frederick Philip Grove (1872–1942), Grey Owl (1888–1938), and Roderick Haig-Brown (b. 1908). Over the years, too, its subject has become almost all nature—the general, the specific, the animate, the inanimate. William Lett (1819–1892) describes the deer of the Ottawa valley in *The Antlered Kings* (1884). Samuel Thomas Wood (1886–1917) draws on his field trips in *Rambles of a Canadian Naturalist* (1916), and Stuart Thompson (1886–1961) on his for *Outdoor Rambles* (1958). Egbert Allen (b. 1882) generalizes about nature in *The Out-of-Doors* (1932) and *Our Northern Year* (1937). Hugh Halliday casts his net wide in *Wildlife Friends* (1954), *Wildlife Trails* (1956), and *Adventures among Animals* (1960). Dan McCowan (1882–1956), a regionalist except for *A Naturalist in Canada* (1941), centres, like H. J. Parham in *A Nature Lover in British*

Columbia (1937), on western Canada with *The Animals of the Canadian Rockies* (1935), *From Tidewater to Timberline* (1951), and *Upland Trails* (1955). Lorus and Margery Milne assume an unusual perspective with *The World of Night* (1948). Franklin Russell examines the aquatic world minutely in *Watchers at the Pond* (1961) and M. B. Williams and E. Newton-White turn to problems of conservation in their books.

As for the essay itself its prose style has varied from the lyrical, purple passages of Duncan Armbrest's *The Beech Woods* (1916) to the journalistic of Bruce Wright's *Wildlife Sketches* (1962). The form has ranged from the chatty anecdotal vignettes of Ernest Thompson Seton's *Wild Animals at Home* (1913) and Hubert Evans's *Forest Friends* (1926) to the formal discussions of J. W. Winson's work, especially *Wildwood Trails* (1946); from Richard Saunders's nature diary *Flashing Wings* (1947) and his journal of a birding expedition, *Carolina Quest* (1951) to Kerry Wood's guide books, *Birds and Animals of the Rockies* (1946) and *A Nature Guide for Farmers* (1947). The writers' moods have ranged from the high seriousness of Theodore Haultain's cosmological speculations in *Of Walks and Walking Tours* (1914), the boisterous high spirits of Kerry Wood's *Three Mile Bend* (1945), to the reminiscences of Sherwood Fox's *The Bruce Beckons* (1952). Again, there is on the one hand the naturalism of Grant Allen's series of books that began with *Vignettes of Nature* (1881) and ended, after six more studies of evolution, with *In Nature's Workshop* (1901), and also of Robert McLeod's *In the Acadian Land* (1899) and *Further Studies of Nature* (1910); on the other hand there is the idealism of Bliss Carman's *The Kinship of Nature* (1903) or the whimsical sentimentality of Ernest Fewster's *My Garden Dreams* (1926).

Largely twentieth-century writers, these, for the most part, look on nature neither as evidence of God's law nor as a source of morality, but as a unity in which man is simply another creature. They do not seek "the bird behind the bird." Nature is as it is, and they try to let it be its own commentator, centring their interest in their relationships with the living things of wood and field. Their essays are never quite the depersonalized writing of science. Whether descriptive—even in the expository natural history essay—or narrative and dramatic, their work reveals a human sympathy with the whole natural world.

As an example of descriptive writing, Samuel Wood's *Rambles of a Canadian Naturalist* is excellent, for Wood is a well-informed and enthusiastic field-naturalist and an essayist of literary ability. Like John Burroughs, he is, too, a "natural philosopher" as this characteristic passage (pp. 66–67) illustrates.

The Night-hawk never takes up the white man's burden. He is a missionary from the great outer world—in the city, but not of it. His name is as ill-applied as it is ill-omened, for he is not connected with the Hawks by consanguinity, sympathy, or unity of purpose. He has a grace of flight peculiarly his own, turning, wheeling, and darting hither and thither without apparent effort, or circling on easily extended pinions. The conspicuous white spot under each wing looks like a hole, and may have suggested the modern idea of ventilating yacht sails. Nature paints with a careful touch, and the great spots, bands, and patches carelessly displayed by birds in white, black, or colour are laid on the exposed webs or tips, one feather at a time, so that a plucked quill would be as irregular and meaningless as a fragment from a mosaic.

Among the writers who stress the narrative and dramatic Frederick Philip Grove holds a high position, his reputation resting on *Over Prairie Trails* (1922) and *The Turn of the Year* (1923). The first of these books, a collection of seven essays on trips Grove took through western Manitoba, tries to catch something of his total impression of that vast area. A keen observer, with an almost scientific bent, his attention focuses on the phenomena of land formations and the weather. As Malcolm Ross writes, "Every twist and scar of the land is known and wondered at and claimed. Every freak of fog and drift and frost is a mighty event, to be known . . . to be felt, to be re-created and re-set in the 'interior landscape' of the self." Although descriptive of the same austere land, Grove's second book, *The Turn of the Year*, is written with more feeling and from a greater sense of intimacy. Grove turns from inanimate nature to its living things, frequently also dramatizing rather than discussing his experiences with them. Set against the passage cited from Wood, the following (p. 46) reveals sharply the differences between the two methods.

I go east, along the grade, perchance, to where, a mile from my house, the woods recede on the southside, opening up into a meadow which is fenced for a pasture. The bush to both sides is noisily vocal, of course, with the cawing of crows; and perhaps I now hear quite distinctly and unmistakably the quacking of ducks from the sloughs to the north. But when I reach that meadow, unexpectedly, from quite close by, like a great overwhelming joy, I hear the familiar, cheerfully whistling flute-note of the meadow-lark. I jerk my head about; and truly, there he sits on a low charred stump, right next to the road, or perhaps on a fence-post; and his breast is the brightest of all bright yellows; and like black velvet the crescent lifts itself off from the throat.

Grove goes to nature obviously as neither natural historian nor natural philosopher. He seeks no moral law. He wishes only to enjoy the dynamic force of nature. He manages, also, by arranging the essays in seasonal sequence, a fairly common practice, to catch something of its life-and-death rhythm.

As the writers have adopted various attitudes and methods, so, too, have they addressed themselves to several different classes of readers. Some have published nature essays for children, a type which began with Mrs. Traill's *Afar in the Forest* (1850) and has continued to the present with Mrs. Berrill's *Wonders of the Arctic* (1959) and Paul May's *A Book of Canadian Animals* (1962). The genre has not been very popular, most authors preferring to combine natural history with fiction in the bedtime animal story.

Some, aside from Richard Saunders, who was mentioned earlier, have written for (and as) birdwatchers—the voluminous Sir James MacPherson Le Moine (*Maple Leaves*, 1863–1906), the oologist Walter Raine (*Bird-nesting in North-West Canada*, 1892), Hamilton Laing (*Out with the Birds*, 1913), Louise Marsh (*Birds of Peasemarsh*, 1919, and *With the Birds*, 1935), and Hugh Halliday (*Adventures among Birds*, 1959). Some have written books for (and as) fishermen and hunters in the sportsman's or outdoors book, and some, for (and as) "escapists" in the "back-to-nature" book.

Essentially the sportsman's or outdoors book is "escapist" too and frequently reveals the influence of romanticism as obviously as that which advocates a return to nature. In the old tradition the sportsman's book is implicit about man's dominion over nature, whereby one can simultaneously preach the beauty of nature and assume the right to destroy it. In the romantic tradition the book is often explicit about the therapeutic values of the woods and streams, where, far from that villain, the city, man can find peace and self-fulfillment.

The genre began with the letter-writers and itinerant Englishmen of pioneer days and has been popular ever since, soon becoming a favourite with "Residents." Thomas Magrath described his field sports in *Authentic Letters from Upper Canada* (1833). Frederick Tolfrey, if he can be called Canadian because of five years spent with rod and gun slaughtering the wildlife of Quebec, published *The Sportsman in Canada* (1845). Campbell Hardy recounted his experiences in *Sporting Adventures in the New World* (1855); the Reverend Agar Adamson tried to imitate Walton with *Salmon-Fishing in Canada* (1860); the Reverend Joshua Fraser drew on the events of a hunt for *Three Months among the Moose* (1881); and Arthur Silver described his adventures as sportsman in *Through Miramichi with Rod and Rifle* (1890). Seton (1860–1946) and Sir Charles G. D. Roberts (1860–1943) began their literary careers in sportsmen's and outdoors magazines, a fact that the latter's collection of tales and anecdotes in *Around the Campfire* (1896) evidences. ("Bear vs. Birch-Bark," 1886, which appeared in *Around the Campfire*, was the first story by Roberts to be published in a book—entitled *In Peril: True Stories of Adventure*, 1887.) Since the late nineteenth century, the genre has more than held its own in both book and periodical and has gained considerable importance as Canadiana and as history, for the older books are records, available nowhere else, of one phase of pioneer life.

The subject-matter of the outdoors book varies widely within the limits of the type. Seton's *The Birch-Bark Roll* (1902) and *The Book of Woodcraft* (1912), Paul Provencher's *I Live in the Woods* (1953) and Keith Barnes's *Wilderness Camping and How to Enjoy It* (1956) are little more than manuals. Related to these are books which use anecdote to leaven information about the where and how to fish and hunt and the gear required. Edwyn Sandys's *Upland Game Birds* (1902), David Reddick's *Fishing is a*

Cinch (1950), and F. H. Woodling's *The Angler's Book of Canadian Fishes* (1959), for example, comment on each species and then add an essay on an appropriate experience. Some books in this group, like *Trapper Jim* (1903) and *Sportsman Joe* (1924), emphasize narrative. In these two, Sandys tries to vitalize his programme of studies for the successful sportsman by setting himself up as guide to a boy tenderfoot on innumerable field-trips, a method which in general characterizes Arthur Heming's two books (both grim and unimaginative) about life with Indian trappers in northern Canada, *The Living Forest* (1925) and *The Drama of the Forests* (1947). Here, too, belong "Jack" Hambleton's boisterous *Fisherman's Paradise* (1946) and *Hunter's Holidays* (1947).

Generally, however, books of this kind simply try to communicate the pleasures of good fellowship and life in the open air and the thrill (not the technique) of catching fish and bringing down a creature of the chase. In them the reader can vicariously hunt and fish with Arthur Silver (*Farm-Cottage, Camp and Canoe in Maritime Canada*, 1908), accompany Bryan Williams (*On Game Trails in British Columbia*, 1926), follow Nevill Armstrong (*After Big Game in the Upper Yukon*, 1937), or enjoy killing salmon with George F. Clarke (*Six Salmon Rivers and Another*, 1960). Frequently, the subject-matter is less interesting than the writer's personality, a fact that accounts largely for the attractiveness of Richard Pattillo's *Moose Hunting, Salmon Fishing and Other Sketches of Sport* (1902) and Napoleon Comeau's *Life and Sport on the North Shore* (1909). Usually the books are a medley of tales, tall or otherwise, reminiscences, character sketches of guides and companions (even dogs), and casual comments on natural history, "a collection of incidents and observations," like Austen Peters's *Feathers Preferred* (1951), in which the essay tends to become the article. Although man-centred, like all outdoors books, they usually show some interest in and "sympathy" for (but little empathy with) wildlife, especially game birds and animals *vis-à-vis* predators. Yet their authors can argue (probably as pseudo-Darwinians) that hunting "makes for the preservation and increase of the species" (Sandys, *Sportsman Joe*, p. 156). Again they almost always allude to nature's healing powers—usually in terms of the recreational or entertaining. Although normally not solemn books, only in John Robins's *Incomplete Anglers* (1943) and Sherwood Fox's *Silken Lines and Silver Hooks* (1954), however, does their humour rise consistently above the funny story or farcical event. Outdoors books are relatively numerous and, aside from those discussed, there are the ubiquitous Le Moine's *Maple Leaves*, Sidney Kendall's *Among the Laurentians* (1885), Samuel Baylis's *Camp and Lamp* (1897), Sandys's *Sporting Sketches* (1905), Philip Moore's *With Rod and Gun in Canada* (1922) and *The Castle Buck* (1945), Kerry Wood's *Three Mile Bend*, Clint Fleming's *When the Fish are Rising* (1947), Pete McGillen's *Outdoors with*

Pete McGillen (1955), and Phillip Keller's *Wild Glory* (1961), a book which complements McCowan's *Outdoors with a Camera in Canada* (1945), for Keller also hunted with a camera.

McGillen's book is typical. A collection of forty-two essays, it has something for almost everyone interested in nature—for the fisherman, "Muskie Madness"; the hunter, "Blue Geese at James Bay"; the conservationist, "Wildlife Management" and "A Pox on Gang Hunters"; and for those without special interest in either game or fish, there are "Bells for House Cats," "Winter on the Farm," and "Bird-Watching—a Hobby." McGillen writes in a popular manner, enthusiastically and sometimes humorously in chatty English. He says little of the meaning of what he describes. The outdoors is largely a place of legal sizes and bag limits, where one delights in "God's open air" by means of gun and rod. Controversial subjects such as bounties and predators are discussed but superficially. Snapping turtles are "ugly, vicious predators." Duck hunters are warned that "crows, pike, muskrats, skunks, raccoons, and snakes, not to mention the foxes and the hawks" are "whittling the duck population." McGillen has observed the habits of both fish and fisherman, hunted and hunter with some care, and he knows farm life. His writing is that blend of "human interest" and natural fact which characterizes so many books of the kind.

In the outdoors school, William H. Blake (1861–1924) and Roderick Haig-Brown, the Izaak Walton and the Charles Cotton of our literature, rank among the best. Of the two, Haig-Brown is the more prolific with his series *A River Never Sleeps* (1946), *Fisherman's Spring* (1951), *Fisherman's Winter* (1954), and *Fisherman's Summer* (1959). Haig-Brown lives on Vancouver Island, and his books, except the third listed, which describes a South American fishing trip, relate his experiences on West Coast rivers and lakes. Blake left only two books of the kind, *Brown Waters* (1915) and *In a Fishing Country* (1922), and these are set in Quebec. Moreover several of his essays are given over to people and places rather than sport. Again Haig-Brown is the better-informed ichthyologist, and his book *The Western Angler* (1947) is a recognized authority on Pacific Coast fish. Yet Blake was a keenly observant man and, within the limits he set himself, an excellent naturalist. Haig-Brown is the more meticulously detailed, and his books contain many exact descriptions of taking fish. Nevertheless, at his best, he, no more than Blake, lets fact and theory override him. He does not invest his material with overtones in Blake's manner, being less subjective and less the natural philosopher, but rather develops thoughts that grow out of the experience he relates. If the chief concern of both writers is not so much nature but the sport it affords, their subject is not simply the thrill (or the science) but the art of fishing and the world of lake, river, and forest in which they practise it.

More than subject or attitude, however, their prose style differentiates their work from that of other authors. Both avoid the journalistic. Their diction is neither trite nor unduly technical. Their sentences are rhythmical and varied. Sampling them almost anywhere, one finds writing like this from Blake's *Brown Waters* (pp. 67–68):

> For many a year of free and strenuous life his swiftness and dexterity in stemming rapid streams, in pursuing prey, in avoiding the attacks of enemies had been things that counted, and in this, his final struggle, he used the arts which had availed him. After what seemed to be a very long time, but was not and could not be measured by the watch, the rushes became shorter, and we caught a glimpse of a side glorious with red and orange; then did we first know, of a surety, that here at last was the fish worth toiling and waiting for,—the fish of dreams. Fighting to the end, under the utmost pressure of tackle, he came slowly to the bank where Mesgil performed to admiration the task of netting. One breathless moment there was when it seemed that the capacious landing net would not receive him, but his day had come, the last impulse of his powerful tail sent him home and in he swung to meet the *coup de grâce*.

Related to the outdoors books are those that extol the pleasures of a return to nature—to a nook in the country or the wilderness—not for sport but for freedom from the tensions of city living. Many pioneers of the nineteenth century in southern Canada and of the twentieth in the West and North have described lives spent in such surroundings but not as a voluntary return to nature. They are the Crusoes not the Rousseaus of our literature.

The back-to-nature book developed late and only after the rise of the large city, when nature acquired something of the romance of the unknown or the nostalgic. It owes much to the pastoral tradition and may reveal something of man's longing for his lost Eden. Some books are largely reminiscences— A. C. Wood's *Old Days on the Farm* (1918), Sherwood Fox's *'T Ain't Runnin' No More* (1946), a discussion and history of the Aux Sables River, and Kenneth C. Cragg's *Father on the Farm* (1947), a rural version of life with father. More frequently the writers try to capture something of the immediacy and contentment of living in the country. Haig-Brown's *Measure of the Year* (1950) examines the ways of a farming community. Clark Lock's *Country Hours* (1959) describes the creatures of the woods and fields about his home. McArthur and Kenneth Wells (b. 1905) strike a balance between the two. Their subject is the farm—its "breachy" cattle and pugnacious goats, its friendly woodchucks and springtime crows, its seasonal activities of wood cutting, sugaring-off, sowing, harvesting, and apple-picking. (Here we should mention Orlando John Stevenson, 1869–1950, who edited *Country Life Reader*, 1916, a book of essays and poems on farm life.)

McArthur's books, comprising selections from the columns that he published for years in the Toronto *Globe*, are strong pleas for a way of life, not a way of making a living. McArthur feared that mechanization and "the cash crop" would eventually bring to the farm many of the stresses of the city, where man's life and work are things apart. A rural philosopher, he strove from his first book of the genre, *In Pastures Green* (1915), to his last, *Friendly Acres* (1927), to illustrate and preach the virtues and values of country living and to reveal the forces that threaten to depersonalize it. Now didactic and expository, now humorously dramatic (especially in *The Red Cow and her Friends*, 1919, a series of character sketches of a cow, "Fence-viewer," and other farm animals), now wittily aphoristic or satirical, but always genial, these and McArthur's other books, *Around Home* (1925) and *Familiar Fields* (1925), evoke the feeling of living close to the soil. Sensitive to nature and aware of a fellowship with it, he does not unduly humanize and idealize his subject in order to achieve effect. He writes merely as a man who, living at a leisurely pace, has had time to look about him. He enjoys the countryside, and it is the strength of his essays that they convince one of this fact.

When the quail came right up to the door I might have known that something good was going to happen. It was during the cold spell—the lion spell—in the beginning of March. Everything was buried under the snow and at seven o'clock in the morning the thermometer had touched ten degrees below zero.

I was doing the chores at the stable when I heard the quail whistling in the orchard and fully intended going to have a look at them, to see how they were wintering. I had not set out feed for them for, alas, there are enough weeds on the place and in the neighbourhood to feed them fat. But to resume. When I had finished the chores and was starting towards the house I struck the tracks of the quail, looking like a picture of loosely strung barbed wire on the snow. To my surprise I found that they were headed straight for the house. In growing amazement I followed them until they passed around the corner of the house and then I saw the marks of their wings on the snow where they had taken flight, within ten feet of the front door.

I felt really disappointed when I found that they had paid me a visit and I had not been at home. I do not know of many from whom I would have so thoroughly enjoyed a little call. No one in the house had noticed them, but judging from the excitement of Sheppy, the dog, he must have seen them and perhaps had something to do with their flight. He kept running about nosing their tracks and barking. It made me feel that I am being accepted in the country, now that the quail are so friendly. They are very careful about their neighbours and it is not every one they are willing to chum with. (*In Pastures Green*, p. 66.)

The most recent and, aside from McArthur, the most prolific writer of the rustic school is Wells, whose popular *Owl Pen* (1947) set the stage for *By Moonstone Creek* (1949), *Up Medonte Way* (1951), and *By Jumping Cat Bridge* (1956), all books about the author's little place in the country. Although Wells went to school to McArthur, he lacks the insight, sincerity, and style of his master. Entertaining and informative about country life and appreciative of the natural world, his books are marred by superficiality. They leave the impression that Wells is playing at farming. Too frequently the butt of his own jokes, he is the greenhorn who seems almost to pride himself on being one in his misadventures with his goats, ducks, and chickens. He is irritatingly anthropomorphic. McArthur's animals remain animals; Wells's rarely do. Chickens with names, a drake that becomes a "dapper gentleman," and ducklings, "web-footed babes," that stare with "bulging eyes and gaping bills" when they first see water and "talk" when they dive into it all reveal how far Wells fails to depict rural life. His fault is not, however, that he wishes to idealize it, but that in trying to he only makes it cute and sentimental.

Several writers have recounted the pleasures of a return, not to the humanized nature of the farm but to the nature of forest and river. John Rowland's *Cache Lake Country* (1947) dramatizes his experiences and observations as woodsman-naturalist in the Lake of the Woods area. In the manner of Thoreau's *Walden*, Grant Madison's *River for a Sidewalk* (1953) describes his life as a solitary in the mountain fastness of British Columbia. Setting up the old contrast of city and country, Madison plumps for the latter, since there, freed from all the gadgets that get between life and living, he found himself —building his cabin, making a garden, gathering mushrooms, hiking through the wilderness. Although *River for a Sidewalk* is by no means a *Walden*, it does attempt to examine the deeper significance of the man-nature relationship, and it does have a warm sympathy for the world of bird and beast. (Several other books—Martin Hunter's *Canadian Wilds*, 1907, Harry Macfie's *Wasa-Wasa*, 1953, and Eric Munsterhjelm's *The Wind and the Caribou*, 1953, describe life in the woods, but their authors are trappers and hunters. There are also several "back-to-nature" books by Americans who lived in the Canadian wilderness for a time.)

No other Canadian writer had a greater reputation in the 1930's, both at home and abroad, than Grey Owl, another member of this school. Many knew of his pet beavers, Rawhide and Jelly Roll, the stars of several films. Many knew also of Grey Owl the naturalist and conservationist through his autobiography *Pilgrims of the Wild* (1935), his children's book *The Adventures of Sajo and Her Beaver People* (1935), and his essays, *Tales of an Empty Cabin* (1936). But all knew, if they knew nothing else, that he was an Indian. Here was the romantic's noble savage, the natural man who could depict the natural world with an insight denied other authors. So went the thinking, but it was ill founded. Born in England and christened Archibald Stansfeld Belaney, Grey Owl (Wa-Sha-Quon-Asin) was a hoax. As a young man, he had drifted into northern Ontario, where he had lived as hunter, trapper, and guide (a life he recounts nostalgically in *The Men of the Last Frontier*, 1931) before becoming author and conservationist. If he played Indian all his life, he played his part well, and, even if adopted, the hinterland was his true home; moreover, whether Indian, Métis, or white man, he was a gifted writer and naturalist.

In prose now eloquent, now lucidly precise Grey Owl celebrates "the wonders of the wilderness." The forested solitudes, his "Temple of Nature," have a "sanctity" that makes "not a few theosophies seem weak and tawdry." Yet he does not decry their harshness as Thoreau did when he left his rustic haunts in Concord to visit northern Maine. The wilderness is for Grey Owl both "a land of wild, romantic beauty" and "an austere and savage region," for his imagination is such that he can blend these views and see into the very core of his world, as this passage illustrates.

And as the last dying echo fades to nothing, the silence settles down layer by layer, pouring across the vast deserted auditorium in billow after billow, until all sound is completely choked beyond apparent possibility of repetition. And the wolves move on . . . and the frozen wastes resume their endless waiting; the Deadmen dance their grisly dance on high, and the glittering spruce stand silently and watch. (*The Men of the Last Frontier*, p. 44.)

If Grey Owl preached the grandeur of the wilderness, he was no less enthusiastic over its minutiae. A reformed trapper, he writes of the birds and animals as a convincingly sincere humanitarian, and his books are an impassioned plea for a sympathetic appreciation of wildlife. Despite this attitude, Grey Owl is no sentimentalist. He tries to make his case by recounting his personal experiences and presenting accurately intimate details of the ways of his beaver and the other wild creatures that lived about his lodge. As a result his essays focus on both what he learns about the wild creatures and what he learns from them, and are typified by a passage like this.

The two original whiskey-jacks who were attached to this spot when first I came here, have called in off the endless, empty streets of the forest, all of their kin who resided within a reasonable distance, say about five miles, judging by the number of them. This assembly of mendicants follows me around closely on my frequent tours of inspection, wholly, I fear, on account of what there is in it for them, and my exit from the cabin with something in my hands, supposing it is only an axe or an empty pot, anything at all, is the signal for piercing outcries from watchful sentinels who have been waiting patiently for hours for my appearance. . . . They will go to almost any lengths to gain their ends, and I once saw one of them, dislodged from a frozen meat-bone by a woodpecker (a far stronger bird), waiting with commendable patience until the red-head should be through. However, the woodpecker was far from expert, and using the same tactics on the bone that he would have employed on a tree, he pecked away with great gusto, throwing little chips of meat in all directions, thinking them to be wood, only to find, when he got to the heart of the matter, that he was the possesser [*sic*] of a clean, well-burnished, uneatable bone. This pleased the whiskey-jack mightily, for at once appreciating his opportunities, he hopped around among the flying scraps of meat and had a very good lunch, while the unfortunate woodpecker, who had done all the work, got nothing. (*Tales of an Empty Cabin*, pp. 283, 284.)

As popular as the genres mentioned have been, several other kinds of writing about the animal world have been part of our literature for many years. These are the legend, the nature novel, and the animal story in its various forms of children's story, animal biography, and short story. With the exception of some animal biographies, all are fiction. Paradoxical as it may seem, however, many of their authors, no less than the essayists, pride themselves on the merits of their work as natural history. Yet their method can be explained simply. They select details that are correct and arrange them to suit their purpose and thus seek to have the best of both the naturalist's and the artist's world.

As nature writing, the legend is bound up with folklore, both Indian and Eskimo, and is simply a recording of traditional tales which these people have invented. Sometimes they relate to the mountains, rivers, and lakes as in Pauline Johnson's *Legends of Vancouver* (1911). Sometimes they are accounts of the magical qualities of birds and animals like those retold in Robert Ayre's *Sketco the Raven* (1961). There have been many collections and retellings of legends—Mabel Burkholder's, Charles Clay's, Cyrus Macmillan's, Silas Rand's, and Marius Barbeau's to mention but a few—but only two nature writers have used legends as subjects. Seton, who invented some of his own, published *Woodmyth and Fable* (1905), *Woodland Tales* (1927), and a catch-all collection, *Ernest Thompson Seton's Trail and Camp-fire Stories* (1940). These, however, differ significantly from the native folk tales, for on the one hand they are highly moralistic and on the other they are based on scientifically accurate explanations of natural phenomena. The other author, Haig-Brown, has made the legend a means of organizing his material and presenting natural history. Yet his novel, *Pool and Rapid: The Story of a River* (1932), succeeds in fusing the two without sacrificing the characteristic supernaturalism of Indian lore. His river, the Tasish, is more than a river. It becomes a motif, a way of uniting present and past in his story of lumberman and settlers, a living and constant reminder of the myths and legends by which the Indians explained its existence and the presence of the salmon that ran in multitudes up its waters and the wildlife that dwelt in its forested valley.

The nature novel, the second fictional genre listed earlier, is not simply one with an outdoors setting. A product of both the romantic and the pastoral traditions, it is an amalgam of natural history and a story in which heroes and heroines are veritable children of the wild. Books of the kind are few; it is apparently difficult to turn our rugged hinterlands into Arcadia. An early book, *Panthea, the Spirit of Nature* (1849), by Robert Hunt (1807–1887), author of *The Poetry of Science* (1854), turns Panthea into a Spirit-scientist who warns the hero against the "False" view of nature, in which it becomes "seductive by its poetic associations." The genre really developed from John Murdoch's *In the Woods and on the Waters* (1896), although Joseph Hilts had already introduced natural history into his novel *Among the Forest Trees* (1888). He did so, however, largely through essay-like discussions, whereas

Murdoch makes an organic unity of his story and his knowledge and appreciation of nature. His method is simple. He selects as hero a hunter who spends much time either praising the beauty and bounty of the forest or berating the "falsehood, treachery, and dishonesty" of the city.

As for the other authors of nature novels, Roberts is the most famous but not the most successful. That honour belongs not to his *The Heart of the Ancient Wood* (1902) but to Fred Bodsworth's *The Strange One* (1959). Roberts's book relates the experiences of a young woman—Miranda—a kind of princess-naturalist who becomes a friend of the forest animals and the beloved of a stalwart woodsman. Idyllic and sentimental, its treatment of wild creatures is even less satisfactory than that of its protagonists. With Bodsworth's work, it is otherwise. A study of the habits and life-history of a barnacle goose that in migration has strayed to the Canadian Arctic from Europe, and a story of Kanina, an Indian girl, and Rory Macdonald, a biologist working in the north, *The Strange One* integrates both study and story without injustice to either. If Bodsworth tells two stories, one is always a comment on the other. The hardships that beset the barnacle goose parallel those of the protagonists; in its struggles it becomes for them a symbol of their own aspirations. Yet Bodsworth does not lose the goose in the symbolic—although he may somewhat in the romantic—and surpasses all other writers of the nature novel in combining natural history with fiction.

Between the dates of Roberts's and Bodsworth's books, a few others of the genre appeared—*Willow, the Wisp* (1918), by Archibald P. McKishnie (1875–1946), the eulogy of a heroine (an almost exact duplicate of Roberts's Miranda) who lives on a game preserve in northern Ontario; the same author's *A Son of Courage* (1920), in which the hero seems a Tom Sawyer turned nature student; and John Mantley's *The Snow Birch* (1958), a story of a boy's life among the animals and woodsmen in the far North. These are more melodramatic than Roberts's book, and were it not for their emphasis on nature as foreground would belong with frontier and regional novels like McKishnie's *Love of the Wild* (1910) and Hulbert Footner's *A Backwoods Princess* (1926) in both of which the wilderness is merely a setting for romance and adventure.

The same cannot be said of Haig-Brown's *On the Highest Hill* (1949), although in it, too, nature is largely background. Yet it is always the dominant influence on Colin Ensley's life, conditioning him when as a boy and a youth he roams the forested mountains and luring him back to them after the war. The book is based on the old antithesis of town and country, but Haig-Brown's is not the romantic solution of Murdoch's *In the Woods and on the Waters* and Madison's *River for a Sidewalk*. The hero of *On the Highest Hill* has no place to hide. His valleys have been devastated by lumber companies or closed to him by the government, and when, a fugitive, he falls to his death, he becomes the author's final comment on civilization's ever increasing encroachment on the natural world and its suppression of man's freedom of spirit.

Of the three kinds of animal story in literature, the children's appeared first. Mrs. Traill introduced it with *Afar in the Forest* (1850), which, like her pre-Canadian books, contained several stories of this type since they humanize nature (the animals frequently speak) and aim at teaching natural history and sometimes morals. The children's animal story did not become established until the late nineteenth century, but since then it has been popular and has taken several different forms.

Mrs. Traill published more fable-like tales in *Cot and Cradle Stories* (1895). Seton wrote *The Wild Animal Play for Children* (1900). William A. Fraser (1859–1933) tried his hand at North American Jungle Books in *Mooswa and Others of the Boundaries* (1900) and *The Outcasts* (1901) before submitting even more to Kipling's dominance with *The Sa'-Zada Tales* (1905) about animals of India. Carol Cassidy Cole's *Downy Wings and Sharp Eyes* (1923) and her three similar books of children's adventures with animals, Ralph Sherman's *Mother Nature Stories* (1924), McKishnie's *Dwellers of the Marshlands* (1937), and Edith Tyrrell's *Furry and Fluffy* (1946) are bedtime stories that hint strongly the influence of Thornton W. Burgess. Harper Cory, an Englishman who lived for some years in Canada, also wrote children's books—for example *Wild Life Ways* (1936)—with Canadian settings. Louise de Kiriline's *The Loghouse Nest* (1945), the life of a chickadee, and Mel Thistle's *Peter the Sea Trout* (1954) adapt the full-length animal biography to the children's book. Elizabeth Sanderson's *The Circle of the Year* (1904), James Grant's *On Golden Wings through Wonderland* (1927), and Frances Lloyd-Owen's *The Gnome's Kitchen* (1937) fuse the nature and the fairy story. The genre has also branched off into the boy's book by combining nature study (without cute talking animals) with adventure—as in Seton's semi-autobiographical *Two Little Savages* (1903) and his much less successful *Rolf in the Woods* (1911). (Kerry Wood's *Wild Winter*, 1954, describes the author's life as a boy-naturalist, but is autobiography not an adventure story.) In this category belong also McKishnie's *Openway* (1922), Haig-Brown's *Ki-Yu: A Story of Panthers* (1934), and Muriel Miller's textbookish *Peter's Adventures in the Out-of-Doors* (1940). Books of the kind are not numerous; many that would seem similar, to cite Lloyd-Owen's *The Call of the Cougar* (1941) and "Jack" Hambleton's *Wolverine* (1954) as illustrations, are largely adventure stories with outdoors settings.

The animal biography began as a story of domesticated animals and is exemplified early in English Canadian literature by Mrs. Moodie's *The Little Black Pony and Other Stories* (1850). It was, however, Marshall Saunders's autobiography of a dog, *Beautiful Joe* (1894), the first of her fourteen books about dogs, cats, monkeys, pigeons, canaries, and other pets that gave the animal biography the impetus it has retained to the present; Sheila Burnford's *Incredible Journey* (1961), an account of two dogs and a cat wayfaring in the wilderness, and Carol Pearson's *Brown Paws and Green Thumbs* (1961), a collection of stories about pets (including camels and crocodiles), are only two in a long list of similar books—some by well-known authors—of varying aims, attitudes, and techniques. Mrs. Annie Savigny at once imitated *Beautiful Joe* with a mixture of pity and propaganda in *Lion, the Mastiff* (1895). Mazo de la Roche (1885–1961), who also wrote children's animal stories, paid tribute to her Scotch terrier in a memorial, *Portrait of a Dog* (1930), following it with *The Sacred Bullock and Other Stories* (1939), a book of short stories characterized by a similar sensitive insight into the world of man and his pets. Farley Mowat's *The Dog Who Wouldn't Be* (1957) and *Owls in the Family* (1961) belong in the boy-and-his-pet convention of Louise Rorke's *Lefty* (1931) and *Black Vic, the Story of a Boy and his Pony* (1949), but Mowat's books are far less sober-sided and sentimental. Barbara May's *The Five Circles* (1958) adopts the old technique of Saunders (and Sewell) by having a horse tell its story.

Running counter to these "humane" biographies, which praise the gentle, are those that celebrate the heroic. Typical are Fraser's stories of race horses in *Brave Hearts* (1904), Seton's *Santana, the Hero Dog of France* (1945), and the "lives" of tough alley cats and valiant camp dogs scattered throughout his work. Here, too, belong Roberts's "thriller," *Jim, the Story of a Backwoods Police Dog* (1924), which might well have been the model for Hubert Evans's four books about Derry, a courageous and sagacious Airedale, and those stories that recount the lives of feral animals. Although the latter type is fairly common—Roberts and Seton wrote several biographies of the kind—only Francis Dickie's *Hunters of the Wild* (1937), a story, in the Jack London tradition, of a dog that lives as a wolf, is a full-length book.

Many other writers published books about their pets—F. W. Andrew, Russell Cockburn, Kenneth Conibear, Elizabeth Guelton, Edward Sprang, Major Benson Walker, and the Reverend Egerton Young. Yet only Andrew in *Klinker* (1948) analyses animal behaviour. The rest are content to describe it in terms of actions and anecdotes that win sympathy, or in those of adventures and noble exploits that stir admiration.

Stories about wild animals, like those about tame, may be either biographical tales, which present some episode or life history in simple narrative form, or short stories, and all may be either "true" or fictitious. Yet they differ, for the story about the wild animal has a greater scientific bent. It tries to avoid humanizing tendencies, to "convey an accurate idea of the animal's life and behaviour [and] its mental processes" from "the animal's viewpoint" (Seton,

Famous Animal Stories, p. iv). Man may enter, but only as "accessory or villain." The animal must remain central, for the authors stress and pride themselves on the truthfulness of their animal psychology (Roberts, "The Animal Story," *The Kindred of the Wild* (1902), pp. 15–29). Yet for all that John Burroughs labelled them nature-fakirs, an accusation that may seem justified by Seton's attempt to prove in *The Natural History of the Ten Commandments* (1907) that animals are nomistic.

The genre had a twofold beginning in Seton's "The Life of a Prairie Chicken" (*Canadian Journal*, February 1883) and Roberts's "Do Seek Their Meat from God" (*Harper's*, December 1892), the first of many such stories that they and their imitators were subsequently to write. Although both men used the two forms—the biography and the short story—Seton preferred the former, and Roberts, the latter, and between them they have made the history of the wild animal story almost entirely the history of their work in it.

Although Seton published a typical biography in 1883, he did not make his name until 1898, when *Wild Animals I Have Known* appeared. Seton was no arm-chair naturalist, as his two-volume *Life-Histories of Northern Animals* (1909), *The Arctic Prairies* (1911), and his eight-volume *Lives of Game Animals* (1925–27) prove, and his stories of wild animals he had known—"Lobo," "Silverspot," and other wild creatures—written, like all his work, out of experience, combine narrative and natural history admirably. He repeated the success of *Wild Animals I Have Known* with a similar book, *Lives of the Hunted* (1901). (Seton selected stories from both the *Lives* and his earlier book and published them under the following titles: *Lobo, Rag, and Vixen*, 1899; *Redruff, Raggylug, and Vixen*, each in a braille edition, 1900; *Krag and Johnny Bear*, 1902; *Johnny Bear, Lobo, and Other Stories*, 1935; *Johnny Bear and other Stories*, n.d.) He followed his two early successes with the similar *Animal Heroes* (1905), *Wild Animal Ways* (1916), and *Mainly about Wolves* (1937), a mixture of fact and fancy in a compendium of "true" accounts of "historic wolves." Interspersed among these works were *The Trail of the Sandhill Stag* (1899) and five later book-length animal stories. In the first of these, Seton as Yan, who was soon to become the hero of *Two Little Savages*, recounts his experiences while hunting a great buck in the Carberry hills. Although an animal biography only in part, *The Trail of the Sandhill Stag* became the forerunner of five stories true to type: *The Biography of a Grizzly* (1900), *Monarch, the Big Bear of Tallac* (1904), *The Biography of a Silver Fox* (1909), *Bannertail* (1922), the life of a grey squirrel, and *The Biography of an Arctic Fox* (1937). Seton also published two books of animal portraits: *Pictures of Wild Animals* (1901), and *Bird Portraits* (1901).

As a writer-naturalist, Seton is much less interested in the art of fiction than in telling a true tale (although "Krag" is a fine short story) and imparting knowledge of the outdoors. His usual method is to stress narrative and events. Yet he does tell good stories, for he never lets his natural history override his narrative, and his events are interesting in themselves. Moreover his success depends, too, on the way in which he appeals to his reader for sympathy with the animal world. It was this trait that brought charges of "nature-fakir," for despite all his claims of literal truthfulness his animals, "brave little souls," sometimes "lonely and sad," "stop to think things over." Much less aware than Roberts of the wider implications of events in nature, Seton seldom reveals anything of the cosmological, of the tragic irony, or of the paradox of nature's changing changelessness. Even his long animal biographies are animal adventure stories, unified by having the same creature participate in all events. If there are unifying overtones they are emotional, for Seton writes much as Saunders wrote of Beautiful Joe, as humanitarian and propagandist, "an animal evangelical." Here as an example is the conclusion of "Redruff":

Have the wild things no moral or legal rights? What right has man to inflict such long and fearful agony on a fellow-creature, simply because that creature does not speak his language? All that day, with growing, racking pains, poor Redruff hung and beat his great, strong wings in helpless struggles to be free. All day, all night, with growing torture, until he only longed for death. But no one came. The morning broke, the day wore on, and still he hung there, slowly dying; his very strength a curse. The second night crawled slowly down, and when, in the dawdling hours of darkness, a great Horned Owl, drawn by the feeble flutter of a dying wing, cut short the pain, the deed was wholly kind.

The wind blew down the valley from the north. The snow-horses went racing over the wrinkled ice, over the Don Flats, and over the marsh toward the lake, white, for they were driven snow, but on them, scattered dark, were riding plumy fragments of partridge ruffs—the famous rainbow ruffs. And they rode on the winter wind that night, away and away to the south, over the dark and boisterous lake, as they rode in the gloom of his Mad Moon flight, riding and riding on till they were engulfed, the last trace of the last of the Don Valley race.

Typical of the endings of many of Seton's stories, this passage reveals the cast and limits of their overtones. Or are compassion and kindness such basic truths that Seton can say no more? His animal psychology may be pure surmise, but can we know anything except in our own terms, or express identity with nature in any other way?

Roberts originated the animal short story with "Do Seek their Meat from God" (1892), a "sketch," as he called it, which, with two like it, he published among the fifteen stories of *Earth's Enigmas* (1895). He then dropped the genre. After the success of *Wild Animals I Have Known*, however, he returned to it enthusiastically with *The Kindred of the Wild* (1902), *The Watchers of the Trails* (1904) and went on and on until *Further Animal Stories* (1936) to a total of nineteen volumes. This number does not include nine books, each of a single story selected from the books referred to. He also wrote one magnificent book-length animal biography, *Red Fox* (1905), and a chapter on pre-historic wildlife in a "pre-historic historical romance," *In the Morning of Time* (1919).

The background of Roberts's new genre includes both literature and science. Roberts had already written articles for *Forest and Stream* (in the 1880's) before "Do Seek their Meat from God" appeared. Moreover, the short story was a prominent form at the time, and Roberts simply adapted it to a whole new subject. As for the influence of science, the spread of Darwinism, positing man's evolution from animals, and the increasing number of books on the subject, refocused man's mind on the interrelationship of man and nature.

Roberts's life was also influential on his work. Like Seton, who spent his boyhood, much as Yan had, roaming the countryside near Lindsay and Toronto, Roberts owed his interest in nature to his childhood "passed in the backwoods" in New Brunswick. He was not, however, a naturalist of Seton's stature—was, in fact, not a naturalist but a casual observer. Despite his realism, he did not write his "true" stories like Seton out of his experiences but, in large part, from hearsay and his reading. Consequently, his two hundred or so stories on almost every living creature are often inaccurate and lack something of the attractive intimacy of Seton's. No salmon parr ever matured as rapidly as the one in "The Last Barrier" (*The Haunters of the Silences*, 1907), and no mallard ever flew so fast as the one in "The Nest of the Mallard" (*The Backwoodsmen*, 1909). Yet if he is guilty of misrepresenting facts he is not of misinterpreting them in the wider orientation of the "laws" of nature.

Although free from Seton's practice of upstage comment and generally less subjective, Roberts can be excessively anthropomorphic. In the name of animal "personality," a fox may "fling dignity to the winds," a moose "look with longing eyes," a rabbit "wave long ears of admiration" at a "comely" mate. Again he may present an animal hero almost allegorically as in *Wisdom of the Wilderness* (1922), when "The Little Homeless One" lays down his life during a "moonlit revel" to save the other rabbits. Normally, however, he lets nature speak dramatically through the interplay of protagonist and incident.

Roberts's stories fall into three groups—the animal biography, the story of action, and the "sketch." The first of these, as Roberts handled it, uses event less to present animal habits than to examine animal "conduct." "The Keeper of the Water Gate" in *The Watchers of the Trails* is typical in its stress on the motives and reactions of its muskrat protagonists. The second kind of story subordinates animal personality and natural history to incident and plot as in "The White-slashed Bull" (*The House in the Water*, 1908), an episode in which a moose escapes death through a hunter's mercy. Men almost always appear in these stories, as participants or as choric observers. The third type, the graphic sketch-like story, isolates and dramatizes a single episode that suggests an elemental force governing the natural world from without, rather than within, or "Fate," as Roberts calls it in "The Iron Edge of Winter" (*The Backwoodsmen*). Here a weasel, about to seize a squirrel, is itself seized and carried off by a hawk. Stories of this kind often read as if Chance were a whimsical god playing jokes on his children of the wild, or having a game in which the rule of "survival of the fittest" no longer holds. The "sketch" Roberts wrote less and less frequently and in his later books not at all.

As an artist Roberts has many merits. He writes a fluent prose. He knows how to create suspense by hinting, withholding information, and working toward a major climax—techniques that "The Haunter of the Pine Gloom" (*The Kindred of the Wild*) admirably demonstrates. He gives individuality to essentially type characters by selecting the fleetest, strongest, and wisest as heroes—the "kings" of the species. Unfortunately this practice tends to turn his protagonists into noble savages, thus detracting from his work as natural history. He knows, also, how to unify his stories, opening and closing them with descriptions as if they were the curtains of a play. Yet the descriptions are not separate from the narrative. They are not simply realistic settings, the curtains of a play, or prose lyrics framing a story. They are his way of disclosing, within the transitory, something of the permanence of the natural world. Or again he begins *in medias res* and ends with a denouement that brings the narrative full circle. Even the longer animal biographies he can keep from sprawling by shaping them around some centre as in "The Last Barrier" (*Haunters of the Silences*). This starts and finishes at a falls that a salmon parr descends on his way to the sea and to which he returns years later.

Whatever the story, it also has a unifying theme: the amorality of nature, the struggle for survival, the cyclical aspect of time. This is as true of the longer as of the shorter stories. "The King of Mamozekel" and "The Lord of the Air" (*The Kindred of the Wild*) both depend greatly on narrative and on the facts of life history for their interest, but neither is unified solely as biography. In the one a moose reveals the power of the instinct for the preservation of species; in the other an eagle becomes the embodiment of nature's freedom of spirit forever reasserting itself in defiance of man's attempts to destroy it.

Roberts's adherence to the concept of the animal hero and of nature as conflict frequently leads to the sensational and spectacular. His stories abound in "desperate encounters" (or duels) of courageous beasts, like epic heroes, battling to the death. At times, however, he resolves plot conflict in a conclusion that has wider and subtler implications.

Just about this time a visitor from the hills had come shambling down to the river's edge—one of the great black bears of the Quahdavic valley. Sitting contemplatively on her haunches, her little, cunning eyes had watched the vain leaps of the salmon. She knew a good deal about salmon and her watching was not mere curiosity. As the efforts of the brave fish grew feebler and feebler she drew down closer and closer to the edge of the water, till it frothed about her feet. When, at last, the salmon came blindly into the eddy and turned upon his side, the bear was but a few feet distant. She crept forward like a cat, crouched,—and a great black paw shot around with a clutching sweep. Gasping and quivering, the salmon was thrown upon the rocks. Then white teeth, savage but merciful, bit through the back of his neck; and unstruggling he was carried to a thicket above the Falls. ("The Last Barriers," *The Haunters of the Silences*, pp. 68–69.)

This has some of the pathos so typical of Seton's endings, but it has more than pathos. It contains Roberts's comment on the grim irony and amorality of life in the world of nature.

As Roberts continued to add more and more animals to his "ark" with *Kings in Exile* (1909), *Neighbours Unknown* (1911), *More Kindred of the Wild* (1911), *The Feet of the Furtive* (1912), *Hoof and Claw* (1913), *Children of the Wild* (1913), *Secret Trails* (1916), *They Who Walk in the Wild* (1924), to list some not already mentioned, he tended, in the cause of entertainment, to resort to more derring-do and far-fetched incident and to reduce his stories to formula. This latter development was almost inevitable since there is a sameness about the situations and themes available to him. His grumpy bears and wary foxes and other animals, despite their personalities, of necessity become types—within a species one creature's habits scarcely differ from another's. Consequently many later stories become monotonous variations in terms of species or situation on his fresh and original early work. Yet at their best, whenever written, they are an impressive fusion of art, fiction, and natural history.

The history of the book-length animal biography after Roberts and Seton concerns the writing of only five men. The versatile and talented Haig-Brown has turned to it twice with *Silver: The Life of an Atlantic Salmon* (1931) and the much longer *Return to the River* (1941), the biography of a Columbia River Chinook. Both are excellent as narratives and natural history, but differ from Seton's and Roberts's biographies, for Haig-Brown writes more obviously as scientist than field-naturalist and stresses biology rather than conjectural animal psychology. His first book, *Silver* (which has a British not a Canadian setting) reads, however, as if he were a kindly angler addressing a child, and occasionally stopping to wag a finger about the conservation practices of the "Good Fisherman." *Return to the River* is concerned with similar questions, but is an adult's book, a fictionalized documentary that takes up the broader issue of the wastage of natural resources and man's inhumanity to nature. (Haig-Brown's *The Living Land* (1961) discusses very fully the use and conservation of the natural resources of British Columbia.)

Another book in this category, Gray McClintock's *Itinerants of the Timberlands* (1934), the life story of two Western Canadian wolves, Radus and Lemus, reverts to type. Anecdotal and sensational, like the stories and essays in McClintock's earlier *The Wolves of Cooking Lake* (1932), it manages to incorporate enough heroics and perils to turn it into an animal adventure story.

Shortly after McClintock's book appeared, Kenneth Conibear (b. 1907) published *Northland Footprints* (1936), a trapper's tale about a tame muskrat and a whiskey Jack that saves the life of its snow-blind "master." Conibear writes imaginatively and affectionately of the wild things, and his observations have the authority that comes from his many years in the North. Frank Conibear, like Kenneth, with whom he wrote a dog story, *Husky* (1940), also turned his experiences as a trapper to account (with the help of J. L. Blundell) in *Water Trio* (1948). A biography of a beaver family, it would seem to reveal Grey Owl's influence in the detailed and kindly manner with which it presents their story. That Conibear sets up a plot by introducing Indian trappers adds little to its interest as narrative, but fortunately detracts nothing from its interest as a study of wildlife.

The latest of the animal biographers is Fred Bodsworth, who in 1955 published the *Last of the Curlews*, a book which assuredly begot his later *The Strange One*, for each celebrates the heroic animal in Seton-like fashion —emotionally and admiringly. The *Last of the Curlews* (there have been sight records since 1955) gives exact scientific data, but combines them with a story of interest and poignancy based on the old motifs of the search and the hero's plight as the last of a vanishing race, a victim of man's greed and insensitivity.

Animal stories like Roberts's and Seton's have not been especially numerous. The Reverend Egerton Young's *My Dogs of the Northland* (1902), Fraser's *Thirteen Men* (1906), Alan Sullivan's *The Passing of Oul-I-But* (1913) and *The Cycle of the North* (1938), and Kerry Wood's *Willowdale* (1956) have included some of the kind. Only a few books have been solely collections of animal stories. William MacMillan's *Northland Stories: Tales of Trapping Life in the Canadian Wilderness* (1922) has as its subjects foxes, moose, otters, and a wolverine, a beast that seems to fascinate nature writers with its "villainy." McKishnie's *Mates of the Tangle* (1924) is misnamed; it might better be entitled *Perils of the Tangle*, since the conventional struggle of beast against beast or man is its central theme. Dickie's *Umingmuk of the Barrens* (1927) eulogizes several dogs, but does include a long biography of a musk-ox, which is largely a story of action. *The Silent Call* (1930), by Evans, contains fifteen stories about wildlife (mainly fish) and Indians on the West Coast. Of these only "The

Spark of Life," a dramatic illustration of man's destructiveness, and "Morsels of Chance," a story of a man's defeat in a grim battle with nature, revolve around anything beyond the usual demonstrations of animal courage, loyalty, and shrewdness. Zella Manning's *Lords of the Wilderness* (1933), an anthology of animal stories, contains several by Canadians. Gillese's *Kirby's Gander* (1957), the latest book of the kind, is largely romantic in outlook. Aside from "A Fox is where you find him," a straight forward biography, it is somewhat contrived, highly subjective, and concerned much with crises.

Nature writing, particularly the animal story, had its hey-dey in the late nineteenth and early twentieth centuries. It has long passed. Perhaps the literary vein has been worked out. Perhaps people tired of learning that animals and men are alike and learned from two world wars that they are too much alike. Perhaps urban people, now removed three or four generations from their country forebears, have lost touch with nature almost completely. Unquestionably the biological sciences have been replaced in public imagination by the physical. What might once have been a nature story is now science fiction. Although man has again turned his face to the stars, he may discover once more, however, that a mouse is "miracle enough to stagger sextillions of infidels."

20. Lampman and Roberts

ROY DANIELLS

IT IS CUSTOMARY, in calling the roll of Confederation poets, to commence with Roberts, as the oldest and as the author of *Orion and Other Poems* (1880) which is a landmark in this country's literary history. The other three members of the principal group were, however, all born within the next year or two and the importance of *Orion* is simply that it demonstrated that poetry could be written and published in Canada. It is possible therefore to begin with Lampman and gain the advantage of encountering at the outset the best corpus of poetry, the most attractive of the four personalities, and the most typical critical problem.

Lampman's brief career—he was born in 1861 at Morpeth, in western Ontario, and died in Ottawa in 1899—is all of a piece and the reverse of episodic. The writing of poetry dominated his life and, like his life, his poetry exhibits a consistent wholeness which makes a chronological arrangement of his poems of little importance. The heart of Lampman's poetic achievement, which in turn is the dominant fact and central achievement of his life, consists of a small group of nature poems, the product of his excursions, at all seasons of the year, into the Ontario woods and fields. His first collection, *Among the Millet*, was published in Ottawa in 1888, the second, *Lyrics of Earth*, in Boston in 1893. A collected *Poems* was issued in 1900, just after his death.

The first thing that will strike anyone coming fresh to Lampman is his loving indebtedness to Wordsworth, Shelley, Arnold, Tennyson and Keats. He writes of Keats, "I have an idea that he has found a sort of faint reincarnation in me." At the beginning of his poetic career the influence of Keats was, indeed, predominant. His poem "April" begins,

> Pale season, watcher in unvexed suspense,
> Still priestess of the patient middle day....

Elsewhere we have re-creations of the poetic world of Arnold. In "Between the Rapids" a scene of bygone affections is revisited—

> Aye there they are, nor have they changed their cheer,
> The fields, the hut, the leafy mountain brows;
> Across the lonely dusk again I hear
> The loitering bells, the lowing of the cows,

> The bleat of many sheep, the stilly rush
> Of the low whispering river, and through all,
> Soft human tongues that break the deepening hush
> With faint-heard song or desultory call. . . .

In an occasional poem such as "Drought" he borrows from Coleridge: "men /Dropped dead beneath the moon," and then

> Into the mocking sky uprist,
> Like phantoms from the burning west
> Dim clouds that brought no rain

and so on until "Down came the rushing rain."

Innumerable passages of this kind attest Lampman's willing dependence on the Romantics and the Victorians for the tools of his trade and many of the materials of his craft. And it is also clear that in a large overriding sense he is consistently Wordsworthian; he finds his consolation, his sense of the divine, his daily sensuous delights, all in the countryside, the world of farm and forest, lake and rock and stream.

It is easy, if one approaches Lampman from the direction of the great nineteenth-century English poets, to write him off as no more than their pale imitator and ineffectual disciple. It is only in a Canadian context that this judgment can be seen for what it is, somewhat less than a half-truth. Lampman has in fact erected, though on narrow foundations, a small poetic edifice securely his own and the excellence of his best work is conditional upon its not attempting anything beyond these narrow limits. "Winter Uplands," written just before his death, illustrates his strength within these self-imposed bounds:

> The frost that stings like fire upon my cheek,
> The loneliness of this forsaken ground,
> The long white drift upon whose powdered peak
> I sit in the great silence as one bound;
> The rippled sheet of snow where the wind blew
> Across the open fields for miles ahead;
> The far-off city towered and roofed in blue
> A tender line upon the western red;
> The stars that singly, then in flocks appear,
> Like jets of silver from the violet dome,
> So wonderful, so many and so near,
> And then the golden moon to light me home—
> The crunching snowshoes and the stinging air,
> And silence, frost and beauty everywhere.

That the bounds were self imposed and to some degree consciously so is apparent from the last two lines of this sonnet which in first draft ran thus:

> Though the heart plays us false and life lies bare
> The truth of Beauty haunts us everywhere.

Philosophic generalization, that stock-in-trade of the Victorians, was never Lampman's forte.

In the small central core of his poems, which alone entitles him to our present consideration, Lampman makes to the Ontario landscape a characteristic response, to which we must apply the word of his own choice—dream. In the early poem "April" he is "Dreaming of Summer and fruit-laden mirth." In "The Frogs" he is "content to dream" with them.

> That change and pain are shadows faint and fleet,
> And dreams are real, and life is only sweet.

The impressions in his well-known poem "Heat" are "in intervals of dreams." In "Among the Timothy" he finds it sweet to lie in the field, "Nor think but only dream." At the conclusion of the Wordsworthian "Winter Hues Recalled" he wakes "As from a dream." In "Song of the Stream-Drops" the waters move on "dreaming and dreaming" of their mother, the sheltering sea. The lesson of "What do Poets want with Gold" is that they should "Ever dream, but never know." In "Athenian Reverie," the dream wish is made more explicit:

> Happy is he,
> Who, as a watcher, stands apart from life
> From all life and his own, and thus from all,
> Each thought, each deed, and each hour's brief event,
> Draws the full beauty, sucks its meaning dry.
> For him this life shall be a tranquil joy.
> He shall be quiet and free. To him shall come
> No gnawing hunger for the coarser touch,
> No mad ambition with its fateful grasp;
> Sorrow itself shall sway him like a dream.

That his dream is a protection from actualities is hinted in "The City" which, characteristically, he finds beautiful at a distance:

> I see with dreaming eyes
> Even as a dream out of a dream, arise
> The bell-tongued city with its glorious towers.

In "Comfort of the Fields" he desires, when stricken with grief and weariness, to wander

> Where the long daylight dreams, unpierced, unstirred,
> And only the rich-throated thrush is heard.

"At the Ferry" concludes with his characteristic stance:

> Beyond the tumult of the mills,
> And all the city's sound and strife,
> Beyond the waste, beyond the hills,
> I look far out and dream of life.

Lampman's ideal natural man, in "The Woodcutter's Hut" endures the long hours of blizzards in his refuge "Without thought or remembrance, hardly awake, and waits for the storm to tire." How closely the idea of this beneficent, salutary dream is associated with Lampman's whole realization of life appears once more in "By the Sea":

> I walk as in a dream 'twixt sea and land—
> The meadows of wise thought, the sea of strife—
> And sounds and happy scents from either hand
> Come with vast gleams that spread and softly shine,
> The joy of life, the energy divine.

The verse echoes Arnold but with none of Arnold's commitment to social struggle.

All of Lampman is summed up and contained in this dream, this moment of trance, of conscious but unspecific self-realization. It is close to the familiar Wordsworthian experience of being "laid asleep in body" to "become a living soul"

> Till with an eye made quiet by the power
> Of harmony and the deep power of joy
> We see into the life of things.

Several concomitants, however, save Lampman from the charge of being Wordsworth's pale imitator. The experience is clearly his own, slowly and often after pain and grief realized, occasion by occasion, in the minutely felt and specifically realized contacts with a local and un-English landscape. Lampman's pervasive, unconscious, and complete honesty, moreover, keeps his poems from the least taint of the facile, of easy rhetoric, of inflation or pretence. In his best poems he says least about the subject of his dreams; they seem to partake of sensations, of an expansive feeling of peace and the resolution of all difficulties, but not to provide him with Shelleyan vision, Wordsworthian philosophy, or Arnoldian didacticism. The conclusion of "Heat"

> In the full furnace of this hour
> My thoughts grow keen and clear

gives not the least clue as to what these thoughts are, though from the imagery of the poem we may be certain that a sense of the goodness of life, the reconciliation of opposites, and the beauty of the earth and seasons pervades them. But it is notable that Lampman refuses to give specific content to his dream or to allow his dreaming to lead him towards philosophic or theological concepts or to make of his dreams any incitement or prelude to action. It follows that as we move outward from this dream, this centre of his poetic experience, we move into spheres which are less and less relevant to his vision. It is nature, and we may say with some confidence only nature, that induces in him the trance of insight into the life of things.

That his brief trances of delight in the experience of natural beauty gave scale and shape to his best poems Lampman himself realizes. In "Ambition" he characterizes his own poetic gift:

> From other lips let stormy numbers flow:
> By others let great epics be compiled;
> For me, the dreamer, 'tis enough to know
> The lyric stress, the fervour sweet and wild:
> I sit me in the windy grass and grow
> As wise as age, as joyous as a child.

In "The Minstrel," another self-characterization, he escapes from the city and its demands upon his song, to the fields and hillsides under a night sky, to sing once more only from the depth of his own spirit.

If we take the normal critical course of inquiring into the influences that shaped Lampman's mind during his formative years, we shall not in fact find anything contrary to what has just been said. He was something of a classical scholar, he lived in a nominally Christian community, he could scarcely avoid the climate of wistfully idealistic and utopian sentiment that pervaded his Victorian world, he could not escape some contact with current Canadian affairs, he assuaged his melancholy and even hypochondriac moments by retreating to his woods and streams and meadows, where his idealism became a dream of perfection.

Well grounded in the classics at school and later in Trinity College, he was enthusiastic about the value of Greek. We find him writing to a friend in 1894, "There never was and never will be another language like the Greek. It is worth while giving two or three years of one's life even to get a moderate knowledge of it." And a few weeks before his death he writes, "I have revived my knowledge of Greek a good deal in the past year or two and read a little every day. I have got so that I can manage a page or two of Homer in a few minutes before breakfast—a good deal easier than Browning." His classicism appears to have made him a careful and sensitive versifier. He writes to a friend, "I send you a little poem written in the strophe that Sappho used to use. I rather like it. Most men who have attempted to write sapphics in English have misused the metre horribly . . . but I flatter myself that these are real sapphics and the proof of it is that the movement is musical." And from his classical reading he derived an ideal of life, in the forms provided by the ancient Greek cities. Like Keats, he finds in Greece an unchanging perfection.

> I remember how of old
> I saw the ruddy race of men,
> Through the glittering world outrolled,
> A gay-smiling multitude,
> All immortal, all divine,
> Treading in a wreathèd line
> By a pathway through a wood.

His long poem "The Land of Pallas" merely amplifies this vision. The story of Sostratus fills him with delight:

> Yet like a gleam out of primitive shadow revealing
> Worlds of old joy and wonder of living and effort
> Named in the book of Herodotus still shall you find him.

It is of interest to see that this delight in the crystallized, unchanging beauty of Hellas, so like Keats's, is all of a piece with his dream of beauty and wonder and that neither the one nor the other is associated with any kind of concrete political or social reform. In spite of many resemblances between Lampman's vocabulary and versification and the techniques of Arnold, Lampman is in temperament far closer to Keats and even to Wordsworth.

Lampman's connection with the Christian tradition is of the most exiguous and awkward kind, and here again we find him in company with many of the English Romantics. His feeble attempts to realize Christian themes in his poems are better evidence, in this context, than any proof that he disliked churchgoing. In his "New Year's Eve" the

> White-haloed groups that sought perpetually
> The figure of one crowned and sacrificed

are totally unconvincing. In "Easter Eve" we have another vision of Christ poetically feeble and psychologically disquieting. The authentic voice of Lampman is heard rather in "A Prayer":

> O Earth, O mighty mother, breathe on us.
> O mother, who wast long before our day,
>   And after us full many an age shalt be,
> Careworn and blind, we wander from thy way:
>   Born of thy strength, yet weak and halt are we;
> Grant us O mother, therefore, us who pray,
>   Some little of thy light and majesty.

As we consider Lampman's relation to contemporary issues and current ideas, we must be prepared to distinguish, all along the line, between Lampman the man and Lampman the poet. The former was interested in reform measures, was said to be a Fabian, and certainly believed in a socialist programme of government. The city and its social inequalities, based on wealth, repelled him. Much of his mildly utopian thinking was identical with the sentiments of *News from Nowhere*. But none of these considerations leads us towards the centre of Lampman's creativity. Like Keats, who influenced him more than any other of the great Romantics and Victorians, his was primarily a life of sensation.

It will be asked, then, why he was not a love poet and the answer illuminates both the man and his situation. His small sonnet sequence "The Growth of Love" was inspired by Maud Playter, whom he married when she was eighteen. The story goes that he pinned together those pages in his manuscript book containing the dozen sonnets of "The Growth of Love," requesting his friends to respect the concealment as they went through the book. It is easy to guess why. The passionate simplicity, purity, and intensity of Lampman's love make of these sonnets a personal rather than a poetic revelation. "With this key" Lampman unlocked his heart, the worse poet he. Few of the great poets who influenced him wrote as well of love as they did of nature. Love as a theme is infinitely complex; some elaborate convention, whether learned as in Dante or popular as in Burns, seems essential to the success of love poetry. Lampman put his emotions directly into simple sonnet form and the results do no more than fill us with sympathy and affection for Lampman the man.

> For like a saint's her yellow hair doth shine
> Most lovely when the soft locks fall amiss,
> And I would call her mouth one perfect bliss
> Of glimmering dimple and pale laughter-line,
> Enough to make a man's heart faint and pine
> To take them all up with one blinding kiss.

One work of Lampman's which deserves special attention is "At the Long Sault: May, 1660," a poem just short of a hundred lines, which was first published in 1943 with an introduction by E. K. Brown. It recounts the historic heroism of Adam Daulac and his band who fought to the death to save their countrymen from massacre by the Iroquois. The best passages, the memorable ones, are the introduction, the conclusion, and the fine simile of the bull-moose fighting a pack of wolves. The opening lines are Lampman at his best:

> Under the day-long sun there is life and mirth
>   In the working earth,
> And the wonderful moon shines bright
>   Through the soft spring night,
> The innocent flowers in the limitless woods are springing
>   Far and away
>   With the sound and the perfume of May,
> And ever up from the south the happy birds are winging,
>   The waters glitter and leap and play
>   While the grey hawk soars.

The moose, fighting for life, is realized briefly and with great force,

> Till, driven, and ever to and fro
> Harried, wounded and weary grown,
> His mighty strength gives way
> And all together they fasten upon him and drag him down.

The poem ends:

> But afar in the ring of the forest,
>   Where the air is so tender with May
> And the waters are wild in the moonlight,
>   They lie in their silence of clay.
>
> The numberless stars out of heaven
>   Look down with a pitiful glance;
> And the lilies asleep in the forest
>   Are closed like the lilies of France.

Repeated readings confirm the impression that this poem, like Wordsworth's "Hart-Leap Well," is an account of violence in a context of the serenity and beneficence of nature and yet Lampman goes on to insist, in his evocation of the magnificent bull-moose, that nature itself is productive of cruelty and violence. The elements of the poem are not fully resolved; it is fittingly, as published in 1943, an addendum to Lampman's major work; it is not an entrance into some region of more complex and mature sensibility than we find in the earlier nature poetry.

It is to this nature poetry that the appreciative reader of Lampman must continually return. His vague Victorian forays into the Viking world ("Ingvi and Alf"), Tennysonian idyll ("The Story of an Affinity"), Old Testament history ("David and Abigail"), or idealized classicism ("The Land of Pallas") are all of some interest as they reveal Lampman's character and temperament but were they the substance of his achievement we should not now be considering him.

The craftsmanship of his nature poetry is of a high order. He was rightly pleased with his "Sapphics," a real test of skill surmounted without apparent effort:

> Brief the span is, counting the years of mortals,
> Strange and sad; it passes, and then the bright earth,
> Careless mother, gleaming with gold and azure,
>   Lovely with blossoms—
> Shining white anemones, mixed with roses,
> Daisies mild-eyed, grasses and honeyed clover—
> You and me, and all of us, met and equal
>   Softly shall cover.

But under the smooth recording of the natural scene, there is frequently an identifiable tension of opposites, a need for resolution. It has been well said that the poem "Heat" provides oppositions between movement and stillness, coolness and warmth, sound and silence, darkness and light. The fundamental pulse in Lampman is between apprehensive weariness on the one hand and the reassurance of renewed strength on the other. It has been noted that he comes to nature from something other and often opposite. He walks, typically, from the city into the "comfort of the fields."

> To roam in idleness and sober mirth,
> Through summer airs and summer lands, and drain
> The comfort of wide fields unto tired eyes.

Without this tension of opposites, it is questionable whether Lampman's work could have had any meaning. It is a fair inference that when most desirous of retiring into rural seclusion to write he was still completely dependent for his best poetic effects upon the dichotomy of his experiences.

In this connection it is worth looking rather closely at "The Woodcutter's Hut," one of his best and most original poems.

> The hut of the lonely woodcutter stands, a few rough beams that show
> A blunted peak and a low black line, from the glittering waste of snow.

The woodcutter, even when most isolated and inarticulate, when stormbound "he lies through the leaguering hours in his bunk / Like a winter-hidden beast," awakens the poet's admiration. He is "The animal man in his warmth and vigour, sound, and hard, and complete." Yet when spring comes, with its sunshine and flowers, its gushing streams and liberation from winter's bondage, the woodcutter is gone. "He is gone where the gathering of valley men another labour yields"; he is in fact one of the habitants gone back to the farm after a winter of woodcutting. And the end of the poem is fruitfully ambiguous; the hut stands buried in triumphant forest vegetation,

> And he who finds it suddenly there, as he wanders far and alone,
> Is touched with a sweet and beautiful sense of something tender and gone,
> The sense of a struggling life in the waste, and the mark of a soul's
>   command,
> The going and coming of vanished feet, the touch of a human hand.

In the woodcutter Lampman palpably recognizes his own alter ego, the man to whom total dreaming commitment in natural surroundings is a supreme good, without an articulate philosophy of life but with a vigorous full realization of life, yet this same man committed to another world of activity, an organized community, to explore which is no part of Lampman's poetic intention, and yet without which the refuge in the woods would have no meaning, would not even be possible.

It is worth noting that, like Wordsworth in the early scenes of *The Prelude*, Lampman has a double experience of natural surroundings. There is the harvest of the quiet eye, the reward of solitary excursions into the Ottawa countryside, and there is active participation in snow-shoeing and canoeing, in which we know (with all the regret of hindsight for the harm it must have done to his damaged heart) Lampman took the greatest delight.

An element of unnecessary controversy has entered into the appreciation of Lampman. A dichotomy has been evoked between the enchained and resentful civil servant and the wanderer among woods and meadows and some confusion has arisen between the young man keenly interested in contemporary ideas and the poet whose best work is virtually innocent of ideas. But that Lampman was in any real sense a divided personality seems very unlikely. If we bring into touch the various sides of his character they take their places as facets of a mind of singular purity and simplicity—if it is any longer possible to use these words in their traditional sense. At the centre of his being there burned a small clear flame.

Toward this centre the reader of Lampman is continually drawn. Thoroughly representative of the liberal tradition of his time and place and one of a group of friends to whom a classical education on a British model was the natural road to a career of teaching and writing, Lampman is nevertheless unique in that, like Cézanne, he has his own little sensation in the face of nature which, without alienating him from his surroundings, lifts him into another sphere. This private sensation is not incompatible with what has been well characterized as picturesque realism, "the fusion of a large, general effect with sharply observed detail," but grows directly out of it. The marked quality and indeed the saving grace of Lampman's sensation when confronted by the face of nature is that it does not issue in ideas. It is, as he fully realized, in the whole *ordonnance* of the poem; it is not stated and elaborated. Some lucky inner check in Lampman saved him, when at his best, from going on into the moralized path beaten by Wordsworth and Arnold. What wakes in his blood at the moment of revelation is "A pleasure secret and austere," communicating itself to the reader by a simple shock of recognition for which the tactical dispositions of the poem have already prepared him. This poetry of a secret sensation shared by the prepared and now perceptive reader is all of Lampman that we shall not willingly let die. And it suffices.

It is impossible, however, to leave Lampman without some expression of the affection every reader of his life and works must feel for him. He is not a tragic figure but his struggles, his poverty, his early death throw into relief his eagerness and gaiety which perpetually contended with his frustrations and spells of melancholy and hypochrondria. As he modestly realized, he is much like Keats. He has moreover the innocence and idealism of the Victorians without the least touch of hypocrisy or sentimentality. His outlook on life was classical rather than Christian. He believed in natural happiness, in the capacity of the natural man for insight and for creative effort.

Of less significance than Lampman as a poet, but of more importance as an influence on Canadian writing, is Charles G. D. Roberts (1860–1943). He superficially resembles Lampman in occupying himself, when at his best, with the Canadian landscape, within a framework of late Romantic convention, heavily influenced by the tradition that runs through English poetry from Wordsworth to Tennyson. Like Lampman, he arrives at his most personal utterance by developing the debate between optimism and melancholy in a context of symbols provided by observed nature. "The Solitary Woodsman," one of his few poems without formal flaw, is in subject and treatment closely parallel to "The Woodcutter's Hut" of Lampman. Where the two men differ is in their power to achieve poetic form organized from within. The most commonplace of Lampman's poems bears the marks of growing from a single impulse while even the best of Roberts's pieces reads as though constructed to fit a theme. It is too facile to regard Lampman as an integrated and Roberts as a dishevelled personality but it is fair to point out that Lampmans' life was centripetal upon his creative work and that Roberts's was a life "without a centre."

It has been pointed out that the friends and critics of Roberts who urged him to write on patriotic and philosophical themes were among the worst enemies of his present reputation and the same may be said for the editors who published the love poems later collected as *New York Nocturnes* (1898). Roberts has been rightly praised as a patriot but his verses in praise of his country make painful and embarrassed reading:

> O strong hearts of the North
> Let flame your loyalty forth,
> And put the craven and base to an open shame,
> Till earth shall know the Child of Nations by her name!

Or, regarding Riel's rebellion,

> Saskatchewan, whose virgin sod
> So late Canadian blood made sweet.

It is unfortunate that Roberts shows little if any development of ideas and techniques which permit the reader to pass over early inadequacies with the assurance of better things to come. The love poems written at the turn of the century are frankly appalling whereas *Orion* in 1880 had brought a letter of encouragement from the pen of Matthew Arnold. Not even in his appreciation of a cosmic spirit in nature does his poetry show any advance; he records the healing power of nature as clearly in the poems written before 1880 as in anything later and with more hope and freshness of spirit, and confidence of comforting mankind:

> Yet would I cheer them, sharing in their ills,
> Weaving them dreams of waves, and skies, and hills;
> Yet would I sing of Peace, and Hope, and Truth,
> Till softly o'er my song should beam the youth,—

> The morning of the world. Ah, yes, there hath
> The goal been planted all along that path;
> And as the swallow were my heart as free
> Might I but hope that path belonged to me.

The realization of this dream was too often to dwindle into vague and ill-expressed commonplaces:

> Little brothers of the clod,
> Soul of fire and seed of sod,
>   We must fare into the silence
> At the knees of God.

The best of Roberts is to be found in his descriptions of Canadian landscape. In these he is capable of recording impressions with the fidelity of a genuine devotion, of evoking the *genius loci* of the Fundy shore, of catching the turn of a Canadian season. In a small handful of such descriptive pieces he achieves memorableness. Among them are a group of sonnets on a Sower, an Old Barn, Salt Flats, Pea-Fields, the Potato Harvest, the Mowing. Here the vague moralizing of his weaker poems is absent, his unsureness of diction is reduced to a minimum, and the conventions of the sonnet form supply some firmness of structure.

> Tons upon tons the brown-green fragrant hay
>   O'erbrims the mows beyond the time-warped eaves,
>   Up to the rafters where the spider weaves,
> Though few flies wander his secluded way.
> Through a high chink one lonely golden ray,
>   Wherein the dust is dancing, slants unstirred.
>   In the dry hush some rustlings light are heard,
> Of winter-hidden mice at furtive play.
>
> Far down, the cattle in their shadowed stalls,
>   Nose-deep in clover fodder's meadowy scent,
>   Forget the snows that whelm their pasture streams,
> The frost that bites the world beyond their walls.
>   Warm housed, they dream of summer, well content
>   In day-long contemplation of their dreams.

It is possible that Roberts, had he regarded poetry as his sole vocation, might have found in the Romantic tradition a form which carried its own built-in disciplines and might thus have circumvented his own unsureness of phrasing, rhythm, and structure. Some support for this suggestion is found within one group of poems that recount Greek myths in Tennysonian form. The best of these is "Marsyas":

> Then to the goat-feet comes the wide-eyed fawn
> Hearkening; the rabbits fringe the glade, and lay
> Their long ears to the sound;
> In the pale boughs the partridge gather round,

And quaint hern from the sea-green river reeds;
The wild ram halts upon a rocky horn
O'erhanging; and, unmindful of his prey,
The leopard steals with narrowed lids to lay
His spotted length along the ground.
The thin airs wash, the thin clouds wander by,
And those hushed listeners move not. All the morn
He pipes, soft-swaying, and with half-shut eye,
In rapt content of utterance,—
                     nor heeds
The young God standing in his branchy place,
The languor on his lips, and in his face,
Divinely inaccessible, the scorn.

Part of the success of this poem may arise from the poet's identification of himself with the subject.

The poems marked by a personal tone and some distinctiveness of utterance are nearly all reminiscences of what could be seen from the bedroom window of his boyhood home, the vista across the marshes of Tantramar and the waters of the Bay of Fundy to the Minudie Hills. *In Divers Tones* (1886), his second collection, contains "Tantramar Revisited" in which is developed a theme and an attitude to which he was often to return but never with such fullness and conviction.

Here where the road that has climbed from the inland valleys and
    woodlands,
Dips from the hill-tops down, straight to the base of the hills,—
Here, from my vantage-ground, I can see the scattering houses,
Stained with time, set warm in orchards, meadows and wheat. . . .
Yonder, toward the left, lie broad the Westmoreland marshes,—
Miles on miles they extend, level, and grassy, and dim,
Clear from the long red sweep of flats to the sky in the distance,
Save for the outlying heights, green-rampired Cumberland Point;
Miles on miles outrolled, and the river-channels divide them,—
Miles on miles of green, barred by the hurtling gusts.

As the description proceeds, some unexplained accession of poetic tact prevents the intrusion of patriotism, philosophy, love, and religion; we have nothing but the evocation of past happiness by a distant scene. It is enough.

Ah, the old-time stir, how once it stung me with rapture,—
Old-time sweetness, the winds freighted with honey and salt!
Yet will I stay my steps and not go down to the marsh-land,—
Muse and recall far off, rather remember than see,—
Lest on too close sight I miss the darling illusion,
Spy at their task even here the hands of chance and change.

Another poem which strengthens the conviction that Roberts would have done well to stay with his early impressions and to cultivate the virtues of provincialism is "The Solitary Woodsman," already mentioned. Like Lampman, Roberts shows an inexplicit recognition of the woodcutter as an alter ego, one who, in close and solitary fellowship with nature, labours actively without philosophizing.

> Green spruce branches for his head,
> Here he makes his simple bed,
>   Couching with the sun, and rising
> When the dawn is frosty red.
>
> All day long he wanders wide
> With the grey moss for his guide
>   And his lonely axe-stroke startles
> The expectant forest-side.
>
> Toward the quiet close of day
> Back to camp he takes his way,
>   And about his sober footsteps
> Unafraid the squirrels play. . . .
>
> And the wind about his eaves
> Through the chilly night-wet grieves,
>   And the earth's dumb patience fills him,
> Fellow to the falling leaves.

It is possible and, indeed, at some point essential to see Roberts and his friends from the stance of the English reviewer, who noted that "Charles G. D. Roberts is still read by schoolboys, for his animal stories," and that "Carman and Lampman have written a few good lyrics." It is quite necessary to see Roberts, in some context, as a restless and unstable wanderer, with a limited capacity for intellectual experience and an emotional life impoverished by wilful separation from his family. It is certainly not possible now to believe that Roberts's prose possesses even the limited aesthetic value of his poetry. The stilted Romanticism of his fiction, its factitious plots, puppet characters, and wooden dialogue have no longer any but an historic interest. His animal stories have had the longest popularity but even they exist in the uncomfortable limbo between deliberate fable and true understanding of animal psychology.

All this, however, would be to ignore the fact that Roberts is nevertheless, to our tradition, "ancestral, important, haunting." His influence on others was widespread and enduring. He early became, and long remained, a symbol. And the achievements which led to this symbolic status are by no means factitious.

All readers of Lampman know the story of his first looking into Roberts's *Orion*, how the recognition that these verses, with their classical background and their Tennysonian manner, "written by a Canadian, by a young man, one of ourselves," "was like a voice from some new paradise of art, calling to us to be up and doing." All the elements of Roberts's influence on Canadian letters are present in this initial and symbolic episode. Early in the bare field, he became the first Canadian man of letters whom his own countrymen and the world at large could recognize. He accepted the editorship of *The Week* in 1880, was elected a fellow of the Royal Society of Canada in 1890 and of the Royal Society of Literature in 1892. In 1893 we find him writing to a friend, "I am sure there are many who would consider that either Carman or Lampman take precedence of me. I am always more than content to be counted the equal of those two. And as for the others,—Campbell and the two Scotts,—they certainly show great possibilities, and any one of them may yet turn out to be the Captain of the whole crowd of us."

It is easy to underestimate *Orion* by basing one's estimate on a wrong premiss. The story begins in a Romantic version of classical landscape:

> Where the slow swirls were swallowed in the tide,
> Some stone-throws from the stream's mouth, there the sward
> Stretched thick and starry from the ridge's foot
> Down to the waves' wet limits, scattering off
> Across the red sand-level stunted tufts
> Of yellow beach-grass, whose brown panicles
> Wore garlands of blown foam. Amidst the slope
> Three sacred laurels drooped their dark-green boughs
> About a high-piled altar.

And as the classic story draws to conclusion,

> Out of their deep green caves the Nereids came
> Again to do him honour; shining limbs
> And shining bosoms, cleaving, waked the main
> All into sapphire ripples, each where crowned
> With yellow tresses streaming. Triton came
> And all his goodly company, with shells
> Pink-whorled and purple, many-formed, and made
> Tumultuous music.

The contemporary reader feels these cadences, this language and sentiment, as Tennysonian and so clearly derivative as to awaken no interest. But to its first readers, especially those in Canada, it was a demonstration that the high style as the Victorians understood it could be achieved by a Canadian. Even from outside there came recognition which to our contemporary uncorrected view seems extravagant. Matthew Arnold, on receipt of *Orion*, wrote a "very kind and helpful letter of three pages" and Oliver Wendell Holmes a long letter "of hearty commendation." Kipling, on receiving a copy of Francis Sherman's *Matins* (1896) from Roberts, wrote that he seemed to see in the giver "a man with a broom sweeping clear the tired literatures, and making way for the fresh, young, sincere work which you Canadian fellows are doing."

Roberts's sense of identity with the whole group of Canadian writers meant that all were heartened by the recognition he received. He was an indisputable Man of Letters. Everything that it lay within his powers to do for literature in Canada, either by intention or by happy accident, he accomplished. The affectionate encouragement he gave to his friends was an extension of the pride and pleasure he took in the literary efforts of his own family. Arthur Stringer recorded in 1904 the general gratitude and esteem: "No man better deserves to be designated as the father of his country's poetry than does Professor Roberts, maintaining, as his poetry does, those traditions of form and phrase-making toward the most perfected expression of man's emotions and aspirations, and yet naturally and harmoniously introducing that newer local note which we now pride ourselves on as distinctively Canadian . . . still again must we call Professor Charles G. D. Roberts *The Father of Canadian Poetry*." Though this and other tributes preserved in the pages of the Pomeroy biography of Roberts are all too reminiscent of Sarah Binks, we may give both Roberts and Stringer credit for complete sincerity. It was possible before 1914 to wave a flag or loudly praise a friend for loyal service to the nation without today's hesitant reservations.

Stringer is right in saying that Roberts combined tradition and innovation. His history of Canada, his excursions into travel guides, his translations of French-Canadian fiction and verse, his regional tales of adventure, his animal stories, all these amounted to a demonstration that Canadian history and landscape and the Canadian sensibility could be projected into literate forms which the English-speaking world was happy to read. The patriotic endeavour was explicit:

> And so I end my random song, returning
> To that which makes perchance its only worth,—
> The patriot warmth within my bosom burning
> Through all my wanderings o'er the curious earth.

Roberts's part in making Confederation a spiritual as well as a political act is not to be passed over. In 1886, he writes, apropos of the literary future of Nova Scotia, "We must forget to ask of a work whether it is Nova Scotian or British Columbian, of Ontario or of New Brunswick, until we have inquired if it be broadly and truly Canadian." He refuses to regard the inhabitants of Upper Canada from the old viewpoint of Howe who thought them "an inland population, frozen up nearly half the year."

Roberts early perceived that the terrain of Canada, as it conditions Canadian life, was the primary subject-matter for Canadian poetry. To extend the vocabulary of the English Romantics to cover the Canadian scene was not easy and many awkwardnesses of style even in his best poems are traceable to this inherent difficulty of adaptation.

Black on the ridge, against that lonely flush,
A cart, and stoop-necked oxen; ranged beside,
Some barrels; and the day-worn harvest-folk,
Here, emptying their baskets, jar the hush
With hollow thunders.

Here the fusion of the two levels of diction is incomplete but the intention is patent.

By being recognized, by being prolific in a variety of forms, and by acquiring a public outside Canada, Roberts demonstrated that Canadian literature was a going concern. By working hard and writing voluminously he was an object lesson to all Canadian writers, too many of whom to this day are authors of one book, or specialists in unrealized potentiality. The bald fact that Roberts made his living as a writer becomes a mark to shoot at. His novel *Barbara Ladd* (1902) sold 80,000 copies in the United States and was published in England by Constable, to whom Meredith recommended it. That no one wishes to read *Barbara Ladd* now is in this context irrelevant.

Less and less, as time goes on, do we recover aesthetic satisfactions or imaginative stimulus from Roberts's poems. But his symbolic stature increases. His true role can now be appreciated and a genuine admiration can be achieved for the spirit in which he conceived and carried it out. He was quite literally Canada's first man of letters and the knighthood he received in 1935 was not an inappropriate honour. He had done something for the concept of the Dominion.

21. Crawford, Carman, and
D. C. Scott

ROY DANIELLS

ISABELLA VALANCY CRAWFORD (hereinafter referred to as Crawford because Miss Crawford will not do, any more than Miss Brontë would do for the author of *Wuthering Heights*) was born in Dublin in 1850 and came with her family to Ontario as a small child. She was nine years older than Roberts and her life was briefer even than Lampman's (she died in Toronto in 1887) but she is part and parcel of the post-Confederation group we are considering. Indeed, the familiar pattern of indebtedness to English Romantics and Victorians, concern with Canadian landscape, knowledge of classical literature, possession by powerful but vague idealism—all this is immediately apparent to any reader. Her major work appeared in Toronto in 1884, *Old Spookses' Pass, Malcolm's Katie, and Other Poems*, and a *Collected Poems* in 1905.

What distinguishes Crawford from the others is, biographically, her consistent ill fortune which only her indomitable spirit saves from the aspect of tragedy, and, poetically, her endowment of inner, creative intensity, which none of the men can match. This peculiar gift is more difficult to identify or illustrate than the corresponding "dream" of Lampman; his uniqueness is concentrated in a few unflawed poems whereas Crawford's vision flashes unexpected, anywhere in her work. If one poem must be cited, it should probably be "Said the Canoe."

As night falls, two hunters lay their birch canoe on a soft bed of pine and cedar and cover it with fur robes:

> "Now she shall lay her polished sides
> As queens do rest, or dainty brides,
> Our slender lady of the tides!"

This slightly overwrought image, in which the simple element of a camp by a lakeside becomes elegant and erotic, sets the key of the ensuing description. The fire, called simply the "camp-soul," is lit, and animates in the most literal sense this dark site in the bush. Light clings to the trunks of surrounding trees,

> Like a shy child that would bedeck
> With its soft clasp a Brave's red neck,
> Yet sees the rough shield on his breast,
> The awful plumes shake on his crest,
> And, fearful, drops his timid face,
> Nor dares complete the sweet embrace.

Once more, the unexpectedness of the image, its intensity beyond the needs of the situation, stir the reader into a realization that "more is meant than meets the ear." How completely the normal Canadian locale is becoming a secret landscape of the sensibilities reveals itself as the description progresses:

> Into the hollow hearts of brakes—
> Yet warm from sides of does and stags
> Passed to the crisp, dark river-flags—
> Sinuous, red as copper-snakes,
> Sharp-headed serpents, made of light,
> Glided and hid themselves in night.

And from this loving interplay of bright and dark there develops a piercing image of death, unique and unforgettable:

> My masters twain the slaughtered deer
> Hung on forked boughs with thongs of leather:
> Bound were his stiff, slim feet together,
> His eyes like dead stars cold and drear.
> The wandering firelight drew near
> And laid its wide palm, red and anxious,
> On the sharp splendour of his branches,
> On the white foam grown hard and sere
>   On flank and shoulder.
> Death—hard as breast of granite boulder—
>   Under his lashes
> Peered thro' his eyes at his life's grey ashes.

The next stage in this extraordinary pastoral is a delicate, light song of love, the pursuit of flowers, stars, and jewels. Then back to death.

> They hung the slaughtered fish like swords
>   On saplings slender; like scimitars,
>   Bright, and ruddied from new-dead wars,
> Blazed in the light the scaly hordes.

Then round this simple Canadian scene, so suddenly disclosed as full of love and light and life, yet replete with images of the hunter and the hunted and the presence of death, night closes in.

> The darkness built its wigwam walls
>   Close round the camp, and at its curtain
>   Pressed shapes, thin, woven and uncertain
> As white locks of tall waterfalls.

It has been worth our while to look at this poem in detail because it succinctly and clearly embodies the elements of Crawford's originality as a poet. The Canadian landscape, the landscape of a pioneer country, is grasped objectively; yet it is at once and completely infused with intensely subjective realizations of love and struggle and death. James Reaney has remarked (in *Our Living Tradition*, III) that "Crawford sees the Canadian landscape as half-human—as potentially under human imaginative control" and that "she was one of the first to translate our still mysterious melancholy dominion into the releasing potentially apocalyptic dominion of poetry."

This capacity for an intense projection into her poems of her feelings about love and struggle and death separates her from the other post-Confederation poets; she is in the line of Emily Brontë rather than Wordsworth or Tennyson. It also differentiates her poems from the general run in her generation, in that they tend to invite two readings—a straightforward and an esoteric—with very different results. *Malcolm's Katie*, her longest and best known piece, is on the face of it a preposterously romantic love story on a Tennysonian model in which a wildly creaking plot finally delivers true love safe and triumphant. To add that there are some nice pictures of the struggles and satisfactions of clearing the land and building homes in the wilderness is not to add much. What makes this poem also "ancestral, important, haunting" is its ability to pull the raw landscape into an interior world of living passion and fulfilment. Katie's lover, Max, achieves this movement of absorption in a superb passage, central to the poem. It follows an objective description of felling and burning trees.

> And Max cared little for the blotted sun,
> And nothing for the startled, outshone stars;
> For love, once set within a lover's breast,
> Has its own sun, its own peculiar sky,
> All one great daffodil, on which do lie
> The sun, the moon, the stars, all seen at once
> And never setting, but all shining straight
> Into the faces of the trinity—
> The one beloved, the lover, and sweet love.

As we should expect, these images are counterpointed by others, of utter insensibility and the threat of death by water.

> O you shall slumber soundly, tho' the white,
> Wild waters pluck the crocus of your hair,
> And scaly spies stare with round, lightless eyes
> At your small face laid on my stony breast!

In contrast to Lampman, who like Wordsworth knew very well how to induce in himself a state of "dream" by wise passiveness in the presence of nature, Crawford achieves her fusion of inner and outer worlds as if by accident. "Old Spookses' Pass" begins as a shapeless tale of cattle-driving by an illiterate cowboy with a turn for moralizing, but before the poem ends we have experienced the authentic shudder of a haunted mountain defile, of a stampede in darkness and the crash of thunder. The landscape imposes its inner presence unmistakably, though the poem seems to have few formal merits. Elsewhere—notably in such pieces as "The Mother's Soul" and "Said the Skylark"—we find standard Victorian diction, versification, and sentiment emitting an unexpected intensity and sincerity of emotion and the occasion is always the same, an escape of the soul into a natural universe filled with love. The child's soul springs into the arms of its dead mother under the kind light of moon and stars. Or to the caged bird comes the cloud from the open sky,

> And murmuring to him said:
> "O Love, I come! O Love, I come to cheer thee!
> Love, to be near thee!"

It has been often remarked that Crawford is unusual among Canadian poets by her strong mythopoeic feeling for nature. Yet the passages where this faculty is most apparent may be read simply as her habitual infusion of external landscape with her passionate apprehension of love, of struggle, of death. Thus the dark Stag of Night is hunted by the Sun:

> His antlers fall; once more he spurns
> The hoarse hounds of the day;
> His blood upon the crisp blue burns,
> Reddens the mounting spray;
> His branches smite the wave—with cries
> The loud winds pause and flag—
> He sinks in space—red glow the skies,
> The brown earth crimsons as he dies,
> The strong and dusky stag.

Comparisons between Crawford and the great Victorians and parallels between her and other post-Confederation poets can be multiplied. She has the same range of subjects as, say, Longfellow, the spectrum that runs from an immediate sensuous knowledge of woods and fields to a scholarly and poetic feeling for Rome and Greece. Her poems bring us medieval lovers, the helot of Sparta, Margaton by the stream, classical shepherds, Vikings of the sagas, Indians of legend or real life, biblical figures, and poor exiles from Erin. Patriotism, faith and hope and charity, the round of the seasons, farewells and welcomes: the standard items of Victorian sensibility are present, down to dialect stories of simple countryfolk.

Ideal love is her dominant theme and best expressed obliquely, as we have seen, through some description of nature. Her overt love poems, like Lampman's, lack proper psychic distance, are too immediate, too revealing.

A golden heart graved with my name alone ...
"A golden prophet of eternal truth,"
I said, and kissed the roses of her palms,
And then the shy, bright roses of her lips;
And all the jealous jewels shone forgot
In necklace and tiara as I clasped
The gold heart and its shamrocks round her neck.
My fair, pure soul! My noble Irish love!

Her true and characteristic inner intensity is better revealed in such a poem
as "The Lily Bed":

His cedar paddle, scented, red,
He thrust down through the lily bed;

Cloaked in a golden pause he lay
Locked in the arms of the placid bay. . . .

All lily-locked, all lily-locked,
His light bark in the blossoms rocked.

Their cool lips round the sharp prow sang,
Their soft clasp to the frail sides sprang. . . .

There are many passages, especially in "Malcolm's Katie," where the
dogged, hopeful spirit of pioneer settlers is expressed and this has some
interest of an historical and sociological kind. But the conquest of our
terrain in which she played her real part was the assimilation of Canadian
landscape into the realm of the imagination, or, conversely, the infusion
of passionate love, love strong enough to overcome death, into the substance
of the simple Canadian scene. This is her triumph, her spiritual victory, her
legacy to our uncertain age.

There are a few poets in every generation—and Isabella Crawford is one
of them—whose personality shines through their achievement. She had a
year less of life than Lampman and her brief history is one of unremitting
courage, dignity, and hopefulness in the face of ever recurring calamity. She
had all the virtues of romanticism—and predominantly a sense of the power
and pre-eminence of the human spirit. From the typical weaknesses and
disabilities of romanticism she seems to have been quite immune. She
deserves to be remembered, and even longer for her life than for her work.

Bliss Carman (1861–1929) was a product of the same social and educational background as his cousin, Charles Roberts. Both fell under the
influence of George Parkin, headmaster of Fredericton's collegiate school, in
a classroom where "the *Aeneid* was often interrupted by the *Idylls of the
King* or *The Blessed Damozel*, and William Morris or Arnold or Mr. Swinburne's latest lyric came to us between the lines of Horace." Like Roberts
Carman hesitated over embarking on an academic career and was finally

unwilling to stay in New Brunswick. Like Roberts he was misdirected by his friends.

After 1886 most of his time was spent in New England, though his restless and indecisive spirit kept him on the move. During his brief career as a student at Harvard, he fell under the influence of Josiah Royce and, less definitely, Francis Child. From Royce's lectures on monism and on Spinoza Carman without doubt derived a large part of the philosophy of life which diffuses itself through his poems. While at Harvard he made the acquaintance of Richard Hovey; the "Vagabondia" which they collaborated in creating remains an essential and extensive part of Carman's poetic landscape. In 1897 he met Mary Perry King, the wife of a New England doctor, and to the Kings he owed a measure of security and stability, which lasted for the rest of his life. Beginning with *Low Tide on Grand Pré* (Toronto, 1893), a series of volumes appeared in the nineties and after the turn of the century in the United States and England, including the five volumes of the *Pipes of Pan* (1902–5).

The significant elements in Carman's poetry are not hard to single out. He is a poet of one mood, an accession of power and insight, in the presence of nature, which fills him with realizations of love and of death. What gives his poems their value, however, is less their ostensible or direct theme than their lyric cry, the cadence of which is the hallmark of his achievement.

> There is something in the autumn that is native to my blood—
> Touch of manner, hint of mood;
> And my heart is like a rhyme,
> With the yellow and the purple and the crimson keeping time.
>
> The scarlet of the maples can choke me like a cry
> Of bugles going by.
> And my lonely spirit thrills
> To see the frosty asters like a smoke upon the hills.
>
> There is something in October sets the gypsy blood astir;
> We must rise and follow her,
> When from every hill of flame
> She calls and calls each vagabond by name.

In this world of brightened colours, of enlarged and simplified symbols, of vague but saturating emotion, a continuous plangent rhythm becomes the principle of unity. Carman's landscapes dissolve as he leaves them. They have nothing of the large objectivity of landscape in Wordworth or Keats. They are the creations of an inner rhythm of the poet, like the scenes that Morris or Swinburne can create. It follows that what matters in Carman's world is not the actuality of love or death but the experience of nature which provides vague but powerful images for lost love or death impending. There is no dialectic, no progression of thought, no resolution or conclusion. There is the simple image of nature which evokes the single, undeviating lyric cry. All the poems of Carman that can be re-read with pleasure are of this kind.

It is paradoxical that Carman's deficiencies were the source of his uniqueness as a poet of the Canadian landscape. He had none of Roberts's practical and prompt character. He shows nothing of the instinct for perfection or the close scrutiny of natural scenes so characteristic of Lampman. Yet his very indiscipline and dishevelment kept him in more senses than one a vagabond, and elicited from him the cheerful songs of morning and the open road or the laments that came with darkening night and thoughts of lost years and lost loves. Vague and imprecise to his unfocusing gaze, nature nevertheless impressed him with her magnified and splendid image, her whispers of immortality, her spectral and haunting presence. "Low Tide on Grand Pré," probably the best known of his poems, is characteristically composed of the *disjecta membra* of romantic inner landscapes, and, although set among the same sea-marshes as delighted Roberts, has none of Roberts's ordered observation and precision of detail.

> So all desire and all regret,
>   And fear and memory, were naught;
> One to remember or forget
>   The keen delight our hands had caught;
> Morrow and yesterday were naught.
>
> The night has fallen and the tide . . .
>   Now and again comes drifting home,
> Across these aching barrens wide,
>   A sigh like driven wind or foam:
>   In grief the flood is bursting home.

In this world of nature's changing face there is sorrow but no tragedy, hope but no urgency, happiness but no resolved fulfilment. Even death is subdued to the beauty of the world:

> With looming willows and gray dusk
>   The open hillward road is pale,
> And the great stars are white and few
>   Above the lonely Ardise trail.
>
> And with no haste nor any fear,
>   We are as children going home
> Along the marshes where the wind
>   Sleeps in the cradle of the foam.

That Carman consciously committed himself to the expression of undirected aspiration and imprecise emotion is clear from his own pages:

> Right were you to follow fancy, give the vaguer instinct room
> In a heaven of clear color, where the spirit might assume
> All her elemental beauty, past the fact of sky or bloom.

> Paint the vision, not the view,—the touch that bids the sense
>   good-bye,
> Lifting spirit at a bound beyond the frontiers of the eye,
> To superb unguessed dominions of the soul's credulity.

The nearest Carman comes to a statement of faith is in such poems as "The Winter Scene," where the splendour of Orion and Sirius reassures him that

> There are no hurts that beauty cannot ease,
> No ills that love cannot at last repair
> In the victorious progress of the soul.

It is only fair to add that such dilute Wordsworthian pantheism was in fashion at the time and that the Emersonian transcendentalism into which he plunged carried him into the same stream of sensibility.

How much Carman owes to the diffused transcendentalism derived from Harvard and his long residence in New England may be seen in his prose works. These are calculated to induce a gentle moral uplift and are filled with overtones of Emerson, Whitman, Lanier. The sweetness of tone, the purity of language, the total lack of urgency, all reveal Carman the man and the writer. At times it is as though we are listening to Ruskin at a distance which reduces each admonition to a whisper. He considers, for instance, the old dichotomy of the active and the contemplative life:

In that great pageant of the seasons which passes by our door year after year, in the myriad changes of the wonderful spectacle of this greening and blanching orb, in all the processes of that apparition we call Nature, do I not see both strife and calm exemplified? . . . It may very well happen that circumstances have placed you in the forefront of the fight, where all your splendid life long you shall have never a minute to call your own, where you shall never once be able to rest or meditate or sun your spirit in a basking hour of leisure. Complain not. . . . It may be, on the other hand, that inactive doubt and timorous incertitude beset me, and that I am becoming stale for lack of use. Never mind, the hour will one day strike, and the lethargic torpor of temperamental incapacity will be broken up, and I shall be remoulded into something more trenchant and available for the forwarding of beneficent designs.

It was Carman's extreme misfortune to find himself in a society where neither poets nor moralists nor purveyors of culture were required to deal with any kind of dialectic or to master any body of knowledge. This relaxed intellectual environment, joined to a haphazard way of life and a congenital indecisiveness, robbed his poetry of substance and vitiated its form. Few of his poems take the reader, either intellectually or emotionally, from one point to another and the reader who tries the small trick of transposing stanzas will find it seldom matters much in what order they come. It is necessary to make these apparently disabling admissions if we are to come to the real nature of Carman's achievement. He was widely read on both sides of the Atlantic and remains among the "ancestral, important, haunting" voices of the elder Canadian world.

He is first of all, in spite of the diffuseness of his imagery, a definably regional poet. He belongs to the geographical continuum of the Canadian Maritime provinces and the New England states, where winter and spring signify emphatic change, where deciduous forests, indented hills, and quick rivers running into arms of the Atlantic combine to provide a familiar set of variations within the compass of a day's walk. This is the background of Vagabondia, the ideal country which is less of an affectation than it appears. Here, let us admit, is Carman's habitat, if not home. Here he lives and moves and has his being.

He provides, and this is the secret of his early popularity, a pattern of response to nature which almost any reader can at once in some degree experience. The vagueness itself is in this context a positive advantage. The canoe trip, the walk along a quiet woodland road, the night spent in some cabin under a great maple: these experiences bring physical health, mental calm, and spiritual insight, without definable proportions or progressions. To step into Carman's world is to move from ordinary self to best self in one easy motion. Simple expansive feelings about love and death come so inevitably out of the forms of nature that questions of subjective and objective never arise.

> What is it to remember?
> How white the moonlight poured into the room,
> That summer long ago!
> How still it was
> In that great solemn midnight of the North
> A century ago!
> And how I wakened trembling
> At soft love-whispers warm against my cheek,
> And laughed it was no dream?
> Then far away
> The troubled, refluent murmur of the sea,
> A sigh within a dream!

But Carman, like other good popular poets, not only provides a form for what everyone is willing to feel; he gives this feeling what seems, if only for a moment, to be its ultimate expression.

> Lord of my heart's elation,
> Spirit of things unseen,
> Be thou my aspiration
> Consuming and serene!
>
> Bear up, bear out, bear onward
> This mortal soul alone,
> To selfhood or oblivion,
> Incredibly thine own,—

> As the foamheads are loosened
> And blown along the sea,
> Or sink and merge forever
> In that which bids them be.

Like Swinburne, Carman is up to a point easy to parody and even given to self-parody, but, again like Swinburne, he rises to an authentic and unmistakably personal note in a few of the best of his poems. In these there is a splendid and genuine largeness of utterance sustained by some simple, gorgeous, and quite adequate image.

> All night long my cabin roof resounded
> With the mighty murmur of the rain;
> All night long I heard the silver cohorts
> Tramping down the valley to the plain.

Or this:

> Come, for the night is cold,
>   The ghostly moonlight fills
> Hollow and rift and fold
>   Of the eerie Ardise hills!
> The windows of my room
>   Are dark with bitter frost,
> The stillness aches with doom
>   Of something loved and lost.

To be shown that an individual and unforced response to nature brings health, peace of mind, and spiritual insight was of real benefit to the Canadian reader of Carman's generation. Not only was it being established that poetry could be written in Canada; it was also being demonstrated that the simple surrounding landscape, if poetically apprehended, could provide "all ye need to know." Such a sufficiency within the visible natural world could only be plausible in a new country where the terrain carried few memories or associations, where no standing stones witnessed to the past, where no gods inhabited the mountains. Here the poet's eye could preserve an innocence and immediacy impossible to any other Canadian generation. It was still feasible to avert one's gaze from the visible evidences of industrialism; the acceleration of technology which has proved to be the distinguishing mark of the twentieth century was not yet evident. Mass media, global involvement, mechanized culture: all these were outside Carman's range. But he perfectly expressed the latent feelings of his contemporaries and satisfied their need for a simple, local, accessible, native ethos. That his popularity has steeply declined does not detract from his significance. He is read in the schools where the pure in heart may still be found, and there are few Canadians who would willingly let die the few score lines of verse in which Carman voices our instinctive and traditional response to the Canadian seasons.

> Now is the time of year
> When all the flutes begin,—
> The redwing bold and clear,
> The rainbird far and thin. . . .
>
> How every voice alive
> By rocky wood and stream
> Is lifted to revive
> The ecstasy, the dream. . . .

The most obvious characteristic of Duncan Campbell Scott (1862–1947) is that neither as man nor as poet is he so immediately apprehensible as the other members of his group. A tendency towards shyness and withdrawal and an innate intellectual austerity combined to inhibit the growth of any personal legend, and the technique of his verse, more astringent and more uncertain than that of his contemporaries, delayed recognition of his achievement. He was a friend of Lampman, who indeed first encouraged him to write, and he was well enough known to be included in Lighthall's *Songs of the Great Dominion* (1889), and yet to this day anyone commenting on Canadian poetry, regardless of how he permutes the names of the four men under discussion, will invariably put the name of Scott last on the list. His first collection, *The Magic House and Other Poems*, was published in 1893, when he was thirty, and Carman's first collection also appeared. Further volumes came out in 1898, 1905, 1906, 1916, 1921, 1935 reflecting a long span of writing, and there were collections in 1926 and 1951.

It is useful to think of Scott against the same general background as Lampman's. Both were civil servants in Ottawa and Scott's long and beautifully appreciative preface to the volume of Lampman's collected poems (1900) reveals how similar their responses were to the natural and intellectual climates in which they lived. It is also useful to remember the large resemblances between Scott and the two New Brunswick poets. All were concerned with Romantic subjects, attitudes, and techniques. Scott's address to "the November pansy" is the epitome of his Romantic aspiration.

> And far above this tragic world of ours
>   There is a world of a diviner fashion;
>   A mystic world, a world of dreams and passion
> That each aspiring thing creates and dowers
>   With its own light;
> Where even the frail spirits of trees and flowers
>   Pause, and reach out, and pass from height to height.
>
> Here will we claim for thee another fief,
>   An upland where a glamour haunts the meadows,
>   Snow peaks arise enrobed in rosy shadows,
> Fairer the under slopes with vine and sheaf
>   And shimmering lea;
> The paradise of a simple old belief,
>   That flourished in the Islands of the Sea.

This world of dreams and passions accounts for the poet's vague personal sadness, his search for an "inappellable" secret, his excursions into fantasy as a means of objectifying dream, and the irresolution of his best and best-known poems of the wilderness.

Scott shares with the others a moralizing tendency associated with an evolutionary view of life and an unfocused Christian outlook. The imprecision of his views is in part the result of having nothing specific to oppose. Emerson, Thoreau, Byron, Shelley, and Arnold were all able in their different ways to identify the enemy, but Scott could feel only the irremediable hardship of the northern wilderness, the unavoidable increase of urban industrialism, and the mysterious sorrow of individual lives. Very occasionally, as in his poem "The Harvest," he has a vision of social revolution but it is contradictory and obscure:

> Then when they see them—
> The miles of the harvest
> White in the sunshine,
> Rushing and stumbling,
> With the mighty and clamorous
> Cry of the people
> Starved from creation,
> Hurl themselves onward,
> Deep in the wheat-fields,
> Weeping like children,
> After ages and ages,
> Back at the breasts
> Of their mother the earth.

Even more tenuous is his residual Christian aspiration:

> Shall we not search the heart of God and find
> That law empearled,
> Until all things that are in matter and mind
> Throb with the secret that began the world?

It is not surprising that neither a transcendental realization of life nor a tragic view of man's fate is possible in the context of this vague idealism, and certainly Scott fails to move towards either of these poles. He stays with the central perception that nature is on the whole good, if not always beneficent, and he holds to the hope that man's future is one of ceaseless evolution towards better things, however repellent some stages of the journey may prove to be.

In the midst of this general resemblance to his fellow poets, Scott nevertheless stands out quite distinctly, not only by the slower growth of critical recognition but by the greater variety in his tone and technique, which, because it produced a less clear image of the poet for the reader, was itself a contributing cause of delayed recognition. His reading of late Victorians induced in him a current of fantasy which remained intermittent and unsatisfying to the end. Even the often quoted "Piper of Arll" is lacking the compulsion of true magic and such poems as "The Music House" and "In the House of Dreams" reveal only the fascination exercised upon a Canadian mind by the last enchantments of the age of Tennyson. If this predilection of Scott's for "mementoes of destroyed desire" had resulted only in a succession of weak poems, it would be of little account. There was another and more serious effect, however. His diction, phrasing, and cadence remained uncertain and unstable to the end. In a poem of close observation entitled "Leaves," we pass from the firmness of "berries in dense clusters of dark coral / Which the pine grosbeaks share" to the inanity of, "while we muse, there falls a fairy jar / That subtly tells us where we really are."

Unlike Carman and Lampman, Scott had little natural gift for melody; he needed exemplars and models which could have taught him to "build the lofty rhyme" and these he never found. The result is that a number of his longer poems reveal in the clearest way a gap between personal sincerity and poetic sincerity. In this category are memorial poems to Edmund Morris and William McLennan, "The Dame Regnant," "Spring on Mattagami," and a long set of variations on a passage from Henry Vaughan. Of these it is perhaps "Spring on Mattagami" that reveals most clearly the problem of relating a vaguely apprehended European Romanticism to a deeply felt experience of the Canadian landscape. This poem begins in the northern wilderness:

> Through the lake furrow between the gloom and bright'ning
> Firm runs our long canoe with a whistling rush,
> While Potàn the wise and the cunning Silver Lightning
> Break with their slender blades the long clear hush.

Night falls on the camp in the forest and the poet dreams of Venice and the ideal woman he loved and lost there.

> Once when the tide came straining from the Lido,
> In a sea of flame our gondola flickered like a sword,
> Venice lay abroad builded like beauty's credo,
> Smouldering like a gorget on the breast of the Lord.

Were this pale, proud woman with him in the pure, elemental world of the northern forest, she would be his, "for ever and for ever." But, "vain is the dream" and the reason is not hard to discover: nothing will bring these two worlds together either in real life or in any realm of the imagination to which Scott has access. His final stanza moves towards an attempted resolution in the ultimate depths of nature but a resolution without context of any kind.

> Venus sinks first lost in ruby splendour,
> Stars like wood-daffodils grow golden in the night,
> Far, far above, in a space entranced and tender,
> Floats the growing moon pale with virgin light.

> Vaster than the world or life or death my trust is
> Based in the unseen and towering far above;
> Hold me, O Law, that deeper lies than Justice,
> Guide me, O Light, that stronger burns than Love.

It seems probable that Scott never resolved or passed beyond these problems of style and of subject-matter. But he had a capacity for edging his way out of them, from time to time, into areas controlled by a simpler form of sensibility. To this ability of his we owe the small group of poems on which his reputation ultimately rests. The best of these is probably "Night-Hymns on Lake Nipigon."

We should remind ourselves, before considering this poem, how deeply Scott was committed by profession and by temperament to the Canadian northern wilderness. He was head of the Department of Indian Affairs when he retired in 1932, after more than fifty years of service in the Department. His concern with Indians as wards of the Canadian government was sincere and deep; within the somewhat narrow limits set by official policy he laboured unceasingly for them. All the poems for which he is likely to be remembered are concerned with the northern wilderness, Canada's Indian territory.

The poem opens in an atmosphere of impending gloom and tempest:

> Here in the midnight, where the dark mainland and island
> Shadows mingle in shadow deeper, profounder,
> Sing we the hymns of the churches, while the dead water
>   Whispers before us.
>
> Thunder is travelling slow on the path of the lightning;
> One after one the stars and the beaming planets
> Look serene in the lake from the edge of the storm-cloud,
>   Then have they vanished.
>
> While our canoe, that floats dumb in the bursting thunder,
> Gathers her voice in the quiet and thrills and whispers,
> Presses her prow in the star-gleam, and all her ripple
>   Lapses in blackness.

Then, prepared for by the classical cadence of these unrhymed stanzas, the Christian theme is introduced, for once perfectly harmonized to the wild Canadian landscape through the irony and pathos of the Adeste Fideles chanted by those who have no future:

> Sing we the sacred ancient hymns of the churches,
> Chanted first in old-world nooks of the desert,
> While in the wild, pellucid Nipigon reaches
>   Hunted the savage.
>
> Now have the ages met in the Northern midnight,
> And on the lonely, loon-haunted Nipigon reaches
> Rises the hymn of triumph and courage and comfort,
>   Adeste Fideles.

Tones that were fashioned when the faith brooded in darkness,
Joined with sonorous vowels in the noble Latin,
Now are married with the long-drawn Ojibwa,
    Uncouth and mournful.

Nowhere do we see more clearly the dominant role which wild nature plays in Scott's imagination and what might be called its power of absorption. The irony of his Indians, whose way of life is doomed, being nevertheless in some sense joyful and triumphant—this irony is not expanded. Nor is the resolution of conflicting emotions ever made explicit. Instead we have the storm itself, by its own return to peace and calm, providing a conclusion. This envelopment of the subject by the surrounding scene is a recurring and deeply significant feature of Scott's best works. Nowhere do we see it more beautifully handled than in this poem.

Soft with the silver drip of the regular paddles
Falling rhythm, timed with the liquid, plangent
Sounds from the blades where the whirlpools break and are carried
    Down into darkness;

Each long cadence, flying like a dove from her shelter
Deep in the shadow, wheels for a throbbing moment,
Poises in utterance, returning in circles of silver
    To nest in the silence.

All wild nature stirs with the infinite, tender
Plaint of a bygone age whose soul is eternal,
Bound in the lonely phrases that thrill and falter
    Back into quiet.

Back they falter as the deep storm overtakes them,
Whelms them in splendid hollows of booming thunder,
Wraps them in rain, that, sweeping, breaks and onrushes
    Ringing like cymbals.

In most of Scott's wilderness pieces violence of emotion matches the rigour of the land itself. Besides "Night-Hymns" the principal poems in this group are "On the Way to the Mission," "The Forsaken," "The Half-Breed Girl," and "Powassan's Drum." Two other poems, "At the Cedars" and "Night Burial in the Forest," show how easily poems dealing with trappers or lumberjacks associate with the specifically Indian or Métis pieces. It should be added that these themes and settings reappear in the best of Scott's short stories.

It is easy to regard these poems as studies of life in the wilds or manifestations of their author's deep sympathy with the lot of the northern Indians. This is to miss their ultimate meaning, which is the resolution of violence either into the calm of nature or into nature's own impersonal fury of stormy wind and rushing water. If the half-breed girl seems an exception, it is because the adulteration of her true heritage of blood has made her unable to hear when "A voice calls from the rapids, / Deep, careless and free."

We must concede that only nature, and preferably nature in her most primitive and untamed aspect, is capable of releasing Scott's powers as a poet, by providing him with some counterpart or correlative to his own emotions. As we have shown, this correlation is not argued out nor is the transition from human terror or violence to the peace or power of nature logically achieved. Whereas Lampman takes us easily from urban frustration to rural release, Scott transports us to his wild northland, without centre or circumference, by the compulsion of an inner necessity. Unlike those English Romantics who moved into the wilder hills along avenues of pastoral tradition or cheerful pantheism, Scott has trouble in interpenetrating nature with human life. At one moment he is the educated, non-participating observer of a scene of violence or distress; the next instant he has been carried into a commitment to an absolute in nature. Even in the occasional poem such as "The Height of Land" where he appears to employ some apparatus of argument, the conclusion is a movement into the mystery of nature and of life. We feel

> The long light flow, the long wind pause, the deep
> Influx of spirit, of which no man may tell
> The Secret. . . .

This perception, deep and vague, corresponds so well to the permanent needs and possibilities of the Canadian mind that Scott is everywhere felt to belong among the little group of ancestral voices, indispensable to our tradition, haunting to the imagination. In this context the fact that his patriotic poems appear stilted, his love poems conventional, and his odes to Debussy and Keats formless is totally unimportant. And the careful reader who moves among even his least inspired pages will find the occasional line or stanza open like a window upon the natural world of Scott's Ontario. He will see "The wan grey under light of the willow leaves" or watch where "Pallid saffron glows the broken stubble."

For this revelation of Canada's wildness and beauty, of peacefulness or rushing fury in nature as counterparts to our own feelings, Scott will deserve the gratitude of succeeding generations of readers, however urbanized or mechanized their lives may become.

22. Minor Poets
1880-1920

ROY DANIELLS

AMONG MINOR POETS of the period 1880–1920 a half-dozen call for individual attention. William Henry Drummond (1854–1907) was born in Ireland and came to Canada as a small boy. At the age of thirty he achieved a medical degree and, after several years as a country doctor, established a practice in Montreal. Cheerful and kindly, a devotee of winter sports, a good after-dinner speaker, he was everywhere popular. His poems of *habitant* life, the first volume of which in 1897 contained a sympathetic introduction by Louis Fréchette, and which appeared also in four other volumes between 1898 and 1907, were widely read and have never lost their appeal. The picture of *habitant* life is superficial, comedy and pathos are precariously related, the presentation of "un pauvre illettré" (in Fréchette's phrase) as a national type is itself hazardous. But Drummond's transparent goodwill and the sincerity of his regard for his characters serve to overcome his limitations. Behind the clown's mask and the broken English interlarded with French we cannot fail to see "un personnage bon, doux, aimable, honnête, intelligent et droit, l'esprit en éveil, le cœur plein d'une poésie native stimulant son patriotisme, jetant un rayon lumineux dans son modeste intérieur, berçant ses heures rêveuses de souvenirs lointains et mélancoliques." So few Canadian poets induce their characters and readers to join in cheerful and kindly laughter that Drummond has the advantage of being almost unique. Unique also is the illusion he gives of an easy and amiable interchange between the two cultures, French- and English-speaking. The complexities of the actual situation have proved less tractable.

The life of Wilfred Campbell (1861?–1918) conforms fairly well to the standard biographical pattern for Canadian poets of his generation. His father, a clergyman, saw that he was given a classical education. He took holy orders but school teaching and preaching were succeeded by a literary career sustained by grudging appointments in the civil service. He lived for five years in the United States, was influenced by transcendentalism, made repeated visits to Britain, became an Imperialist. Possessing three English great-grandfathers, he regarded himself as a Scottish clansman; he was important as an index to Canadian thought and taste; he will be remembered for half-a-dozen poems, all written early and all concerned with the Canadian landscape. There were volumes published in 1889, 1893, 1899, collections in 1905 and 1923, war poems during the First World War.

His theory of composition was of the simplest. "Poetry is first and last a high emotion"; "the highest class of poetry . . . is that dealing with the eternal tragedy of life in the universe." The reader of poetry "needs no subtle insight into the intricacies of language and the laws of prosody." Campbell read and admired many poets—Homer and Virgil; Shakespeare, Gray, Scott, Byron, Coleridge, Tennyson, Thomas Campbell, Hood, Swinburne; among Americans, Emerson, Poe, Longfellow, Bryant, Whittier. He was atypical in not being attracted to Wordsworth and Arnold. His relations with other Canadian poets were exiguous. He collaborated with Scott and Lampman in the famous "Mermaid Inn" newspaper column but his violent independence of spirit made him a difficult associate.

Campbell's feeling for poetic style was never reliable. There is something wilful about his deliberate infelicity of phrase, insensitive rhythm, obliviousness to requirements of structure and delight in clichés. He attempted a defence of his practice: "The uneven poem may be as necessary to the line or stanza of beauty therein as is the wood or heaven to the flower or star." Or, more emphatically,

> 'Tis the dream, and not the deed
> That doth, eternal, endure;
> The spirit, and not the form,
> That makes earth's literature.

His variant of "true British idealism" enabled him to combine a devotion to tradition with an Emersonian self-reliance, a consciously Scottish independence, and Canadian forthrightness of expression. How well he caught public sentiment at the turn of the century may be judged from the five hundred copies of his *Collected Poems* ordered by Andrew Carnegie for the Carnegie libraries, and from the honorary degree he received in 1906 at Aberdeen University, at which time he was presented to Their Majesties. Regarding himself as a citizen of "vaster Britain," he endeavoured to be a poet of the people in the service of the highest national ideals. In the years preceding his death on January 1, 1918, he threw himself energetically into the Canadian war effort.

It is not for his "Sagas of Vaster Britain" or for his plays in Romantic Shakespearean manner that Campbell will be remembered. Rather for "An

August Reverie," where the common ground that he shared with Lampman is evident, or for "How One Winter Came in the Lake Region":

> That night I felt the winter in my veins,
>   A joyous tremor of the icy glow;
> And woke to hear the north's wild vibrant strains,
> While far and wide, by withered woods and plains,
>   Fast fell the driving snow.

The Bruce Peninsula, lying between Lake Huron and the Georgian Bay, had in the event an intimate claim on Wilfred Campbell that no vaster region, even among regions of the mind, could match.

Robert Service (1874–1958) was born in England and came to Canada at the age of twenty. His wanderings on the West Coast took him up to the Yukon where he worked for eight years in Whitehorse and Dawson, as an employee of the Bank of Commerce. Though the peak of the gold rush was past, the independent miner was still predominant and Service found ready to hand the materials for such pieces as "The Law of the Yukon," "The Shooting of Dan McGrew," and "The Cremation of Sam McGee." Service's ballads, full of Kipling's earlier devices and thick with melodramatic pathos and humour, were immediately and enormously successful. From 1907 with *Songs of a Sourdough* volumes continued. Poems such as those mentioned gave the illusion of realism, they were exotic in their locale, and their driving rhythms and clanging rhymes invited public recitation. These verses, for which he himself claimed little in the way of poetic merit, are nevertheless an ineradicable part of Canadian tradition and in their stereotype they keep the image of the frozen north, the trail of '98, the half-mythical mining towns. Their hallmark is an enormous expansiveness which still appeals because it has a certain real counterpart in Canadian life of the upper latitudes:

> The strong life that never knows harness;
> The wilds where the caribou call;
> The freshness, the freedom, the farness—
> O God! how I'm stuck on it all.

No case can be made for Service as a poet, yet no history of Canadian letters could fail to find him a place. Like the unknown miner in the ballad of Dan McGrew, he achieves effects outside the ordinary canons of performance:

> The rag-time kid was having a drink; there was no one else on the stool,
> So the stranger stumbles across the room, and flops down there like a fool
> In a buckskin shirt that was glazed with dirt he sat, and I saw him sway;
> Then he clutched the keys with his talon hands—my God! but that man
>   could play.

Marjorie Pickthall (1883–1922) came from England to Toronto as a child. She lived in England again from 1913 to 1920, engaging in the war effort, and returned to the far West of Canada, to die in Vancouver. Her first volume was published in 1913, with others in 1915, 1916, 1922 and 1925 and a *Complete Poems* in 1925. She was the antithesis of Campbell and Service in that she worked within narrow limits with great technical proficiency and a very delicate sensibility. While some of her poems deal with Canadian subjects, they are Pre-Raphaelite in tone and overcast with Celtic twilight. Every subject becomes small and delicate; every mood is suffused with love and weariness in the presence of beauty. Père Lalemant in the remote wilderness dreams of the missions founded by his order,

> There where we built St. Ignace for our needs,
> Shaped the rough roof tree, turned the first sweet sod,
> St. Ignace and St. Louis, little beads
> On the rosary of God.

The literary historian, moving from the poets born twenty years earlier to consider Marjorie Pickthall, will emphasize, with regret, the loss of momentum, weakening of grasp, reduction of resonance. She is at too many removes from the original sources of strength. If we think of her, however, as a disciple of Christina Rossetti, it is possible, as in the poem "Resurgam," to find a true poignancy behind her controlled phrasing:

> I shall say, Lord, "We will laugh again to-morrow,
> Now we'll be still a little, friend with friend.
> Death was the gate and the long way was sorrow.
> Love is the end."

The reputation of Pauline Johnson (1862–1913) is at once surprising and significant. Her collected poems, *Flint and Feather* (1912), have been in demand for fifty years. "The Song My Paddle Sings" every schoolchild knows. She was the daughter of an Indian chief and born on the Six Nations Indian Reserve; her mother was an Englishwoman. Her first public reading in Toronto in 1892 was followed, over a period of sixteen years, by hundreds of recitals of her poems in Canada, England, and the United States. She was consciously Indian in her outlook. "My aim, my joy, my pride is to sing the glories of my own people." Her concern with Indian history and legend extended to the ultimate West and a memorial in Stanley Park marks her grave. Such biographical and symbolic elements make up the substance of her reputation. It is somehow fitting that part of her small estate was used towards the purchase of a machine gun which was named after her and "did great service" on the Western front.

What value her poems will have when the memory of her vigorous personality has faded it is difficult to say. In "The Corn Husker" and one or two other descriptive lyrics there appears the pathos of Indian wrongs or the intimacy between Indian life and western landscape. But it is not by such residual pieces that her popularity has over half a century been maintained. It is rather that Pauline Johnson is still what she was at the very beginning, a symbol which satisfies a felt need. Like Service and Campbell, she associates a broadly Romantic view of life with the elements of the vast natural landscape. This need to realize topography in terms of life is, of course, the fundamental fact of Canadian experience.

There is more, however, than Canadian sensibility. Theodore Watts-Dunton, reviewing Lighthall's *Songs of the Great Dominion* in 1889 for the London *Athenaeum,* quoted Pauline Johnson's lyric "In the Shadows," which he regarded as "a new note—the note of the Red Man's Canada." The poem haunted him. He was delighted to find that its author belonged to the Mohawks of Brantford, "that splendid race to whose unswerving loyalty during two centuries not only Canada, but the entire British Empire owes a debt that can never be repaid." Neither "In the Shadows" nor "At the Ferry," her only other contribution to Lighthall's volume, will strike the modern reader as more than pleasant renderings of standard Romantic landscape,

> When the river mists are rising,
> All the foliage baptizing
>   With their spray;
> There the sun gleams far and faintly,
> With a shadow soft and saintly
>   In its ray.

Pauline Johnson's reputation would appear to be securely based, not on her poetry as such but on the need, felt in England at the turn of the century, for fresh contact with primitive and unspoiled life, and on the continuing secret desire of all Canadians to reach back into an innocent and heroic world of wild woods and waters before the white man came and the guilt of conquests, whether French or English, was incurred.

Francis Sherman (1871–1926) brought out four books of verse at the turn of the century and aptly illustrates the plight of the Canadian poet at that time. Like Marjorie Pickthall, he was induced by the taste of his generation to follow masters and models too far removed from the primal source of Romanticism, and he was at the same time too early for post-war developments in poetry to be of any use. His feeling for landscape and his sense of personal tragedy in life are embodied in the verse conventions of William Morris; the metrical facility is there but not Morris's power to suffuse a landscape, and all these poems of love and death in a context of natural beauty lead simply to the regret that so admirable a man should have been so badly supplied with the tools of the poetic craft. On the rare occasions that he fuses his excellent sense of verse rhythm with the New Brunswick landscape and his own inner emotional struggle, we get a sense of what he might have become had he lived in another poetic environment:

> And yet, should I go down beside the swollen river
> Where the vagrant timber hurries to the wide untrammelled sea,
> With the mind and the will to cross the new-born waters
> And to let the yellow hillside share its peace with me,
>
> —I know, then, that surely would come the old spring-fever
> And touch my sluggish blood with its old eternal fire;
> Till for me, too, the love of peace were over and forgotten,
> And the freedom of the logs had become my soul's desire.

Other minor poets between 1880 and 1920 may be usefully considered as a chorus to the tragi-comedy of Canadian cultural decline, a chorus which "did nothing in particular and did it very well." It is convenient to think of two roughly equal periods: 1871–1896, 1896–1921. During the first of these a community of aims among the poets is easy to discover. They work within the conventions of the English poetic tradition; if they borrow ideas or devices from Emerson or Longfellow it is because these do not deflect them from the path of discipleship to the great Romantics and Victorians. The high colonialism of the Golden Age does not call for any revolt from tradition or for obtrusive originality. A. W. Eaton (1849–1937) in one of his many volumes, apostrophizes L'Isle Ste. Croix,

> Sing on, wild sea, your sad refrain
> For all the gallant sons of France,
> Whose songs and sufferings enhance
> The romance of the western main.
>
> Sing requiem to these tangled woods,
> With ruined forts and hidden graves;
> Your mournful music history craves
> For many of her noblest moods.

If this reminds the reader of *In Memoriam*, we may be certain it was intended to.

It follows from the self-consciousness of high colonial culture that we should expect certain models to be held in general high regard. And such is the case. The *Canadian Monthly*, in three articles on Matthew Arnold, numerous reviews and several discussions of poetry as an art, rehearses the desiderata of good poetry. LeSueur, for example, praises Arnold as a worthy son of Thomas Arnold, having the same honesty, open-heartedness, amiability, firmness, and sagacity, and, in addition, a delicate sensibility and intellectual alertness all his own. "Kensington Gardens" shows that, without pretentions to Wordsworth's mystical insight, Arnold can faithfully render the beauties of nature in everyday language, adding an "earnestness of aspiration which seems to give strength to the will." He has a breadth and calmness of manner which distinguishes the great minds of Greek antiquity; he speaks in "noble accents"; "his influence as a writer tends constantly to the refining of our taste and the ennobling of our moral sense."

In one form or another, all the critics agree with LeSueur. Some make the moral function of ideal poetry more specifically Christian—there is a sharp rejection (1878) of Arnold's scepticism. Some lay more stress on the decorum of verse: "a graceful command of expression and of literary form is spreading among a wide circle" or, more naively,

> Only the same old thoughts
> Clothed with a sweeter sound:
> And lo! a poet's brow
> With laurel leaves is crowned.

With such criteria at hand, there is appreciative reading of the American poets. Longfellow is praised for "his clearness of thought and expression," for "earnest moral purpose," for the humanity which makes him popular.

If to the above considerations we add the predominance, already discussed, of the Canadian terrain as a subject for Canadian poetry the consistency of performance among the minor poets will cause no surprise. What is surprising, and agreeably so, is the frequency with which, in this chorus to the historical drama of high colonialism, the slight poetic mask fails to conceal an honest and charming personality behind it. The inextinguishable "Fidelis" combines a real feeling for the Canadian scene and its seasons with idealist aspiration and Christian hope in dozens of poems for the periodicals. Helena Coleman (1860–1953) contributed many poems of precise form and clear sentiment. George Frederick Cameron (1854–1885) embodied his enthusiasms for political freedom in verses with subjects ranging from Cuba to Ireland and Russia. Mrs. Sarah Anne Curzon (1833–1898) came to Canada in 1862. She had contributed in England to *The Leisure Hour*. She became a journalist and identified herself with the cause of women's suffrage. In 1887 she published *Laura Secord, the Heroine of 1812: A Drama, and Other Poems*. Sir James Edgar (1841–1899), Speaker of the House of Commons, is remembered for "The Canadian Song Sparrow." Mrs. J. F. Harrison (1859–1935), better known as "Seranus," contributed to periodicals, edited an anthology of Canadian poetry in 1887, and published collections of her own, of which the best known is *Pine, Rose and Fleur-de-lis* (1891). Nicholas Flood Davin (1843–1901), came to Canada in 1872 and achieved a career as a lawyer, journalist, and politician. His Irish eloquence flowers in "Eos—an Epic of the Dawn" where Canada is seen to possess "large promise of the mightier day." Edward Hartley Dewart (1828–1903) is remembered not only for his own poems but also as editor of *Selections from Canadian Poets* (1864). His introductory remarks are sometimes applicable to the whole history of Canadian poetry: "Many writers of undoubted genius have been deficient in that thorough literary culture essential to high artistic excellence. But in many instances this want of finish may be traced to want of application, resulting from a low estimate of poetry as an art." Lieutenant-Colonel John Hunter-Duvar (1830–1899) belongs to an older tradition than other post-Confederation poets. Two verse dramas were followed by *Annals of the Court of Oberon* (1895); here romantic fancy and exact observation are embodied in crisp, confident stanzas. John E. Logan (1852–1915) wrote some vigorous descriptions of the Northwest under the pseudonym "Barry Dane" and was sufficiently popular to get liberal representation in *Songs of the Great Dominion*. John McCrae (1872–1918), a medical officer with Canadian forces in the First World War, wrote the best known of all Canadian poems, "In Flanders Fields." It is a restrained, formal, flawless expression of Canadian feeling in 1915. Thomas O'Hagan (1855–1939) is the perfect exemplar of minor poetry of the Golden Age. *In Dreamland and Other Poems* was reviewed (1893) as a "charming volume of poems, each one a tacit protest against worldliness." Theodore Harding Rand (1835–1900) edited *A Treasury of Canadian Verse* (1900); as a poet he is chiefly memorable for his association with the New Brunswick scene; the first edition of *At Minas Basin* appeared in 1897. John Reade (1837–1919) is mainly remembered as a journalist but *The Prophecy of Merlin and Other Poems* (1870) brought him a considerable reputation, Lighthall regarding him as "one of the chief figures in Canadian literature, and probably the sweetest poet," "the *doyen* of English poetic literature in the Province of Quebec." Theodore Goodridge Roberts (1877–1953), a younger brother of Charles G. D. Roberts, shows considerable formal skill in such a poem as "The Blue Heron," where exact description of the details of a natural scene fixes its mood. His themes are contained within a romantic view of life and he records with fidelity the visual effect of exotic places. Carroll Ryan (1839–1910), who is best thought of as a journalist, a Christian Zionist, and a crusader against injustice, published several volumes of poetry, which are marginal to his active public life. Marginal also to a devoted life are the poems of Frederick George Scott (1861–1944). They reflect his love of the Laurentian landscape and the faith and courage which won him wide regard during his service as an army chaplain in the First World War. John Talon-Lesperance (1838–1891) writes with conviction of love and loss, of Canada and its changing seasons; he was "known for his strongly individual style, his learning and his kindliness, all over the

Dominion." Agnes Ethelwyn Wetherald (1857–1940) was a prolific writer whose feeling for Nature is thoroughly representative of the age of Lampman:

> When spring unbound comes o'er us like a flood
>   My spirit slips its bars,
> And thrills to see the trees break into bud
>   As skies break into stars. . . .
>
> And feels its sordid work, its empty plan,
>   Its failures and its stains
> Dissolved in blossom dew, and washed away
>   In delicate spring rains.

By 1920 the chorus of minor Canadian poets was seriously diminished and the survivors of the group under discussion, together with Roberts, Carman, and Scott, were of an average age of well over fifty. In a wider and looser Canadian community new lines of thought, sceptical, divergent, and centrifugal were now appearing; the centralizing impulse of Confederation had spent its force.

23. Philosophical Literature

to 1910

JOHN A. IRVING, ADAPTED BY A. H. JOHNSON*

THE LITERATURE OF PHILOSOPHY frequently has been produced by men whose interests, training, and professional appointments were not confined to philosophy. In some cases, the amount of their philosophical writing was not great. However, these men helped to establish an environment in which later generations of professional philosophers could flourish. This was very evident in the earliest period of Canadian philosophical literature. A prime example is provided by Thomas McCulloch who came from the old Scotland to the new and exerted a profound influence on the intellectual and social life of Nova Scotia.

An understanding of McCulloch's achievement requires some knowledge of his career as a religious and educational leader.† He was born in 1776 at Fereneze in the parish of Neilston, Renfrewshire, Scotland. Owing to his extreme reticence, nothing is known of his early life and education in his native parish school. At the University of Glasgow, where he studied both Arts and Medicine, he was such an excellent student of Oriental languages that, at the age of twenty, he was conducting a private tutorial class in Hebrew. Although he seems to have completed the course requirements, he never proceeded to the degree of Doctor of Medicine.

*Professor Irving was unfortunately seriously ill while this book was in progress and Professor Johnson kindly undertook to prepare a revision of writing previously published by Professor Irving on this subject. In this chapter he has used material in *The Stepsure Letters* (edited by Malcolm Ross, the New Canadian Library, McClelland and Stewart, Toronto 1961) under the heading of "The Achievement of Thomas McCulloch" by John A. Irving; and other material previously published by Professor Irving in the *Canadian Historical Review*, XXXI (Sept., 1950), 252–87; *University of Toronto Quarterly*, XX (Jan., 1951), 107–123; *Philosophy and Phenomenological Research*, XII (Dec., 1951), 224–45; *Philosophy in Canada: A Symposium* (Toronto: University of Toronto Press, 1952); and *The Culture of Contemporary Canada*, edited by Julian Park (Ithaca, N.Y.: Cornell University Press, 1957), 243–73.

†The subsequent discussion of McCulloch is a revision of "The Achievement of Thomas McCulloch" by John A. Irving in *The Stepsure Letters* (New Canadian Library, Toronto: McClelland and Stewart). A.H.J.

In 1799, after the usual period of study at the Secession Divinity Hall at Whitburn, McCulloch was licensed to preach by the Presbytery of Kilmarnock. He was ordained in the Secession Church at Stewarton. Following a successful ministry of four years there, he volunteered for colonial missionary service and was designated by the General Associate Synod to Prince Edward Island. On arriving in Nova Scotia, late in 1803, he was persuaded to take a temporary appointment as minister at Pictou until the spring, a decision which was to keep him there for nearly thirty-five years.

In a short time McCulloch's learning, medical knowledge, and powerful preaching made him one of the best known personalities of his time in Nova Scotia. Despite success and fame he was unhappy, for he had become profoundly concerned with the religious exclusiveness of the two existing institutions of higher education: King's College and Academy at Windsor and the Halifax Grammar School. Finally, in 1816, his dream of a different type of college was realized by the foundation of Pictou Academy. During the next twenty-two years McCulloch's heroic work as principal and teacher raised this institution to the unique place it occupies in the educational history of Nova Scotia.

McCulloch taught logic, moral philosophy, science, Hebrew, and theology. If not quite the first, he was certainly the second teacher of modern philosophy to appear in what is now English Canada. From the beginning he tried to develop a library, to obtain laboratory apparatus, and to build up museum collections. The quality of teaching at Pictou Academy under his *régime* was recognized very early by the University of Glasgow, which conferred the degree of M.A., after the usual examinations, on three of its first graduates. Although McCulloch was perennially thwarted by vested religious interests in his efforts to secure degree-granting powers in Arts for Pictou Academy, he did realize a second great educational ambition—the training of a native ministry.

Towards the end of his life, in a totally unexpected manner, McCulloch finally achieved his ambition of presiding over a degree-granting institution. In 1838 he was appointed the first principal of Dalhousie College, twenty years after its foundation by the Earl whose name it bears. Here as professor of philosophy and political economy, he imbued the students of a pioneer community with a lasting respect for the scholarly and scientific heritage of Western civilization. He worked tirelessly, as at Pictou, to develop a library, to acquire scientific apparatus, and to build up museum collections as aids to the study of the humanities and the natural sciences. When he died in 1843, Nova Scotia had lost its ablest and most persistent champion of liberal education.

McCulloch's educational ideals had been powerfully expressed a quarter of a century before his death in a remarkable address, *The Nature and*

Uses of a Liberal Education Illustrated, delivered at the opening of Pictou Academy in 1818, and published at Halifax in 1819. As a philosopher, he begins with a discussion of human nature and society. An adequate idea of man, he argues, must consider what is innate or natural in the human constitution and what is due to its physical and social environment. Without becoming involved in current controversies, he notes that the mind of man seems to possess an infinite capacity to respond to the challenge of its environment.

It is this flexibility of the mind that underlies McCulloch's optimistic philosophy of education. After a digression into genetic psychology and a discussion of the educational methods of primitive and modern societies, he insists that the ideal of a practical education limited to the three R's must be replaced by the ideal of a liberal education. A liberal education, he declares, strives for "the improvement of man in intelligence and moral principle, as the basis of his subsequent duty and happiness." The fulfilment of this ideal requires that man must be considered "as he exists in society, having property, social relations, and an interest in the general prosperity." Further, society itself must be envisaged "merely as a link in the chain of existence, and equally connected with the past and future ages." A liberal education is therefore essential not only for the members of such learned professions as law, medicine, and theology, but for everybody engaged in the world's work. Each individual, no matter what his occupation may be, must live in organized society and therefore needs to understand the principles of his art or trade and the spirit of his culture. While making it clear that he had no quarrel with the conventional classical curriculum of his time, McCulloch boldly advocated the claims of philosophy, mathematics, and the natural sciences as subjects that would best enable the student to understand nature, man, and society.

McCulloch's strong concern for the Protestant approach to religion led him to write three major volumes in the field of theology. One of these, *Calvinism* (published posthumously in 1849) provides further evidence of his philosophical insight and skill.

II

During the period from 1880 to 1910 the religious and educational life of the Maritimes derived great enrichment from the university careers of a number of clergymen (and a few non-clergymen) who like McCulloch manifest obvious philosophical interests and abilities. Because Thomas McCulloch (in this survey) serves as an outstanding example of this type of person, only very brief reference will be made to the individual members of this group. At Dalhousie, instruction in logic, ethics, and political economy was provided by one of McCulloch's most impressive students, the Reverend James Ross who was the second president of the College (1863–85). James

De Mille, Professor of History and Rhetoric (1865–80), also lectured in logic in those years. In 1884, Dalhousie's great benefactor, George Munro, established a chair of Metaphysics and assigned to it Dr. Jacob Gould Schurman.

Acadia University appointed in 1838 the Reverend Edmund A. Crawley to a professorship of logic, mental philosophy, rhetoric, and mathematics. He also served briefly as president (1853–55). From 1851 to 1869, the Reverend John A. Cramp was Professor of Mental and Moral Philosophy and Theology. He was succeeded by the Reverend A. Wayne Sawyer (1869–96) who also served as President (1869–88). During part of this period, from 1882 to 1905, the Reverend E. Miles Keirstead was Professor of English Literature and Logic.

Three presidents of Mount Allison (all clergymen) taught philosophy in the early days of this institution: Humphrey Pickard, James Inch, and David Allison. Their work in moral philosophy was continued by two other clergymen, Charles Stewart and William Watson.

At the University of New Brunswick,* Dr. Charles Harrison of Trinity College, Dublin, had been for fifteen years Professor of English and Philosophy when, in 1885, he was appointed President and Professor of Mathematics. He remained in this capacity until 1906. John Davidson (M.A., Edinburgh), Professor of Philosophy and Political Science from 1892 to 1902, was the author of numerous volumes in the field of economics. In his courses in philosophy, he stressed the great Greeks, Spinoza, Kant, Mill, and Green. His most impressive student was W. C. Keirstead who taught at the University of New Brunswick from 1906 until 1945. (Chronologically Keirstead belongs in a later period, but for the purposes of this survey it is more appropriate to refer to him at this point.) He was an ardent admirer of John Dewey. Following the example of Davidson and after similar influences at Chicago, Keirstead found it impossible to restrict his energies to the narrow scope of traditional academic philosophy. Lecturing on economics, political science, education, and psychology as well as philosophy, he influenced his students in an unusually profound fashion.

The official histories of the Maritime universities mentioned indicate that these men did not publish books or monographs in the field of philosophy, but rather built up a tradition of philosophical inquiry through their teaching. The situation was otherwise in the case of clerical and non-clerical professors of philosophy in central Canada. They did publish books and monographs which made contributions to Canadian philosophical literature.

---

*The University of New Brunswick, established in 1859, is the lineal descendant of the College of New Brunswick (1785–1829) which was replaced by King's College (1829–1859). In his address to the graduating class of the College in 1828, the Reverend Dr. James Somerville referred to their instruction in logic and moral science. It is also recorded that Principal Edwin Jacob of King's College was a lecturer in logic and the Reverend George McCawley, a member of the staff from 1829 to 1836 (he was a graduate of King's College, Windsor, Nova Scotia), taught metaphysics.

III

In the last half of the nineteenth century, there were professorships in philosophy at the University of Toronto, Queen's, and McGill. The outstanding authors in philosophy were John Watson of Queen's and John Clark Murray of McGill. Others produced books and monographs, but no one equalled these two men in the quality and quantity of philosophical publication. James Beaven and George Paxton Young of Toronto were dedicated teachers, who participated actively in the life of their universities and communities. They wrote in other fields. But although they did not engage in extensive philosophical publication, they, like Thomas McCulloch in earlier days, helped to establish the intellectual and social climate in which men of later generations were stimulated to produce the considerable flowering of philosophical literature which took place in Canadian universities in the twentieth century. Their contributions must, of course, be kept in proper perspective. In all these activities, as in the production of the literature of philosophy, Watson and Murray were also the dominant figures.*

The distinction of being the first academic philosopher in central Canada belongs to James Beaven. He was born in 1801 in Wiltshire and educated at St. Edmund's Hall, Oxford, where he obtained his B.A. in 1824 and his M.A. in 1827. On going down from Oxford, where he had devoted himself mainly to classics and theology, he took holy orders and spent fifteen years in clerical and educational activities. In 1841 he published, in London, *An Account of the Life and Writings of St. Irenaeus*, for which Oxford awarded him the degree of Doctor of Divinity. His book evidently attracted some attention, for the year following its publication saw his appointment as Professor of Divinity in King's College, Toronto. In 1850 he became Professor of Metaphysics and Ethics in the newly reconstituted University of Toronto, a chair he held until his resignation in 1871, when he accepted the position of rector of the Church of England at Whitby, where he died in 1875. In addition to his book on St. Irenaeus, Beaven published through Rivingtons of London two other scholarly works, *Elements of Natural Theology*, in 1850, and an edition of Cicero's *De Finibus* in 1853.

When Beaven, at long last, resigned his professorship in 1871, the appointment of his successor immediately aroused enthusiastic and universal approval. George Paxton Young had already lived in Ontario for twenty-four years, and his extraordinary abilities and scholarship had won him a great influence in religious and educational circles. Born in 1818, in the manse at Berwick-

*The subsequent discussion of Canadian philosophical literature is a revision of John A. Irving's "The Development of Philosophy in Central Canada from 1850 to 1900," *Canadian Historical Review*, vol. XXXI, no. 3 (Sept., 1950), 252–287. An epilogue has been added. A.H.J.

on-Tweed, Young was educated at both the high school and the University of Edinburgh. During his university course he was a distinguished student in his favourite subjects of mathematics and philosophy. On taking the degree of M.A., he taught mathematics at Dollar Academy for a number of years. Then came the great disruption of the Church of Scotland, and Young was so attracted by Chalmers's liberal cause that he entered the Free Church Theological Hall, was subsequently ordained, and given a call to the Martyrs' Church, Paisley. But after a few months he emigrated to Canada. Three years later, in 1850, he became minister of Knox Church in the rising city of Hamilton. In 1853, he was appointed Professor of Mental and Moral Philosophy at Knox's College (as it was then called), where, during the next eleven years, he exhibited his great versatility by filling various chairs in succession: it is said that he lectured in almost every department of the College.

Young's contemporaries were astonished by his phenomenal range of scholarship; they believed that he could have taught Oriental languages, classics, or mathematics as effectively as he taught theology and philosophy. Certainly his contributions to mathematics suggest that he may have missed his calling. He published no less than ten important mathematical papers, six of them in the *American Journal of Mathematics*, mainly in the theory of quintic equations. His colleague in Natural Philosophy, J. B. Cherriman, considered that Young was the most remarkable mathematician of that generation. That his mathematical researches were not entirely unrelated to his philosophy is evident from a paper entitled "Boole's Mathematical Theory of the Laws of Thought" which appeared in the *Canadian Journal* of 1865.

Young published little in philosophy (in the narrowest sense of the term) except several monographs. One entitled *Freedom and Necessity* appeared at the urgent request of the students of Knox College to whom he had delivered a lecture on this topic in the spring of 1870. Henry Calderwood in the *Knox College Monthly* of 1889 characterized this lecture, in which the theories of Edwards, Locke, and J. S. Mill are discussed and the "Liberty of Indifference" attacked, as "a fine example of clear definition, critical acumen, and true appreciation of the difficulties besetting the problem." During his student days at Edinburgh Young had come under the powerful influence of Sir William Hamilton and the philosophy of Common Sense. In an elaborate essay on *The Philosophical Principles of Natural Religion*, which was published in 1862, he explicitly rejected, "root and branch," the doctrines of this school. He then transferred his allegiance to Idealism as expounded by John Watson and T. H. Green.

IV

Queen's University was established in 1841, but it was not until the appointment of James George to a chair of Logic and of Mental and Moral

Philosophy in 1853 that philosophy was specifically recognized as distinct from theology. Queen's first philosopher was not a newcomer: in 1846 he had been appointed Professor of Systematic Theology. After a colourful, if somewhat controversial, nine years in philosophy he returned to a pastoral charge at Stratford, Ontario, where he died in 1870. At least seven of his monographs have survived, including two addresses delivered in his capacity as vice-chancellor (1853–57) at the opening of the fourteenth and fifteenth sessions of Queen's; an address to the Senate and students of Queen's on the occasion of the first conferring of the degree of M.D.; and two public lectures entitled *The Poetic Element in the Scottish Mind*, and *What is Civilization?* His style was characterized by a luxuriant imagination and a certain splendour of illustration which invested the most familiar subject with charm and freshness.

In his address to the first medical graduates of Queen's he naturally warned the new doctors to be on their guard against the materialism of the eighteenth century, which he characterized as "a mass of gratuitous assumptions, supported by such childish and superficial arguments, as to make all men of sense and learning thoroughly ashamed of it." At the same time, he had come to realize, as a result of his pastoral experience, that the connection between mind and body is so subtle and so constant that the role of mental factors in many bodily diseases cannot be denied. The physician who would attain "solid distinction" in the art of healing must, therefore, go through a severe course of training in mental philosophy.

The range of George's sympathies is perhaps best illustrated in his monograph, *What is Civilization?* Civilization, the philosopher affirmed, does not consist in the accumulation of wealth among a people, or in the achievement of splendour, elegance, and excellence in the arts, or in the attainment of polished manners, or even in the creation of literature of a sort. Civilization consists essentially "in the conscience and intellect of a people thoroughly cultivated, and the intellect in all cases acting under the direction of an enlightened conscience." In George's opinion four factors were responsible for the current decay of civilization: insubordination to law and government; dishonest dealings in the ordinary transactions of life; the growing practice on this continent of assassination; and the prevalence of atheism. These dissolving factors were more than counter-balanced, however, by the operation of constructive forces: the triumphs of physical science; the development of worldwide communications; and the extension of Christianity.

v

Born in Glasgow in 1847, John Watson received his early education at the Free Church School, Kilmarnock. He then spent six years at the University of Glasgow where he distinguished himself in philosophy, classics, and English, and from which he received the degree of M.A. in 1872. A few months after graduation he was appointed, on Edward Caird's recommendation, to the chair of Logic, Metaphysics, and Ethics at Queen's. Here he taught philosophy with great learning, rare wisdom, and high authority for the next fifty-two years, and from 1901 to 1924 was Vice-Principal of the University. He survived retirement for fifteen years, dying in 1939 within a month of his ninety-second birthday after having lived in Kingston for sixty-seven years. He was the first, and, up to the present, the only Canadian to receive the high honour of an invitation to give the Gifford Lectures. One of the great teachers of philosophy in Canada during the last hundred years, Watson was the first philosopher in this country to achieve an international reputation through his writings. British and American historians of philosophy always list him as one of the leading representatives of the idealistic movement in the Anglo-Saxon world.

It is difficult to understand Watson's philosophy and influence without some appreciation of the role of Edward Caird in his intellectual development. As a student, and later as a fellow, at Oxford, in the early 1860's, Caird was associated with his tutor, Benjamin Jowett, and his friend, Thomas Hill Green, in the early development of that great philosophical movement known as British Idealism. Green assumed the role of critical analyst of systems opposed to Hegel's, while Caird expounded and examined the critical philosophy of Kant with the object of showing that this philosophy, if interpreted rationally and consistently, led to the absolute idealism of Hegel.

As the new idealism developed, it gradually became apparent that a more rational and more liberal interpretation of Christianity than had hitherto existed was possible. Confronted with the advance of science, the theory of evolution, the new biblical criticism, and an aggressive enlightenment, Edward Caird and his elder brother John Caird, who became Professor of Divinity at Glasgow in 1862, sought to show that absolute idealism preserved the essence of traditional religion while giving to it a more rational and enlightened form.

In 1866, when the young Watson entered the University of Glasgow with the intention of studying for the ministry, Edward Caird had just been appointed Professor of Moral Philosophy. Caird's inaugural lecture made a profound impression upon the new student. Over forty years later Watson remembered the "curious way" in which Caird had linked Socrates and Christianity, Aristotle and St. Paul. He had been accustomed to regard Christianity in a strict Calvinistic fashion, but he now received from Caird a new insight into the kinship of Greek philosophy and the Christian religion. Later, as a student of Caird's for three years, he saw exhibited the process by which Greek philosophy gave rise to the categories by means of which Christian experience was gradually developed into a theology that enabled it to conquer the world.

Watson, aged 25, had barely arrived at Queen's when, on October 16, 1872, he charted his future course in an inaugural lecture, published a year later as a monograph, *The Relation of Philosophy to Science*. It was by any standard a remarkable performance for a man of his years. In it, Watson surveyed incisively and maturely the spheres and limits of philosophy, science, and religion. The presuppositions and weaknesses of T. H. Huxley's scientific materialism, Herbert Spencer's evolutionary naturalism, and J. S. Mill's empiricism were pointed out; and the claims of religion were vindicated by an appeal to the Kantian critical philosophy, to which were added the overtones of Caird's idealism. Watson concluded:

Philosophy elevates itself above all mere opinions, above all untested assumptions, above all caprice and impulse—in short, above all that is peculiar to this or that individual—and lives and moves in the realm of necessary truth. . . . All men, consciously or unconsciously, participate in universal truth, and thus there is a universal consciousness, given *through* the consciousness of the individual, but in no way *dependent* upon it. In thus revealing necessary truth, Philosophy at the same time reveals Him who is Truth itself . . . the assurance which Religion gives to the individual man of the existence of a Supreme Being whom he must reverence and love, Philosophy endorses and supports. The fundamental notions with which it is the office of Logic to deal may not inappropriately be termed the plan of the universe as it existed in the Divine mind before the creation of the world; the long but sure path, by which Metaphysic ascends from the inorganic world to the world of living beings, and thence to the realm first of individual consciousness, and next of universal thought, at last terminates and loses itself in the all-embracing glory of God; and the highest lesson that Ethics has to teach is that only by unity with the divine nature, only by the elevation of his individual will to the high standard of duty, can man enter into the glorious liberty wherewith the truth makes free.

Such was the conception of philosophy that was destined to remain dominant in Canada for the next half-century.

Perhaps the most astonishing aspect of Watson's career is the sheer volume of his publications, amounting to fifteen large books, over sixty major articles, and uncounted book reviews. He contributed to both technical and popular journals in Britain, Germany, the United States, and Canada; and there was scarcely a current philosophical controversy in which he did not engage. Shortly after coming to Canada he identified himself with the St. Louis Hegelians (a remarkable group of enthusiasts for classical German philosophy which had been organized by H. C. Brokmeyer and W. T. Harris), and contributed various articles to their *Journal of Speculative Philosophy*. When the *Philosophical Review* was established in 1892, Watson was the honoured author of its second article on "The Critical Philosophy and Idealism." Such semi-popular magazines as *Canadian Monthly, Rose-Belford's Canadian Monthly, New World*, and the *Queen's Quarterly* (of which he was one of the mainstays for over thirty years) carried numerous articles from his pen. He was constantly on the war-path against Tyndall, Nietzsche, Spencer, and the American pragmatists; but he was also constantly building up constructive approaches to Kant, Hegel, and his contemporaries in the idealistic movement.

Philo and the New Testament, Gnostic theology, Dante and medieval thought, Leibniz and Protestantism, Lessing and art criticism, the poetry of Browning—all were grist for his mill, and the mill was continually turning out a product of the highest quality.

Watson's books fall into four main groups, according as they are concerned with (1) classical German philosophy, (2) hedonism, positivism, and empiricism, (3) the philosophy of religion, or (4) political philosophy. While it is not within the scope of the present survey to present a technical analysis and evaluation of these varied contributions, nevertheless certain brief comments may enable the reader to appreciate the nature of their author's international reputation. On German philosophy, Watson wrote such authoritative books as *Kant and His English Critics* (1881), *The Philosophy of Kant Explained* (1908), and *Schelling's Transcendental Idealism* (1882). German scholars regarded him as one of the foremost authorities on Kant in the nineteenth century, and Hans Vaihinger invited him to contribute articles to *Kantstudien*, a highly technical journal. In addition to these expository and critical works, he edited and translated *Selections from Kant*, a book which was revised and reprinted eleven times between 1882 and 1934. This project grew out of a deep-seated belief that if students of philosophy were to pass from a lower to a higher plane of thought they must read the classical texts for themselves. He would set his own class of more advanced students at work upon extracts from the philosophy of Kant, watch them as they struggled with its perplexities, and give helpful instruction only when it was needed. This method was adopted at Harvard and spread thence to many other leading American universities. It is no exaggeration to say that Watson did more to promote the study of Kant on this continent than any other North American philosopher.

In 1891 Watson performed a similar service for the empirical school with the publication of *The Philosophy of John Stuart Mill*, a book of extracts. This was followed in 1895 by *Comte, Mill, and Spencer*, ostensibly a critical exposition of nineteenth-century positivism, empiricism, and evolutionism, but actually a constructive introduction to philosophy in general. In 1898 an elaborate addendum, *Notes, Historical and Critical, to Comte, Mill and Spencer*, appeared, and later that year the two volumes were fused and published under a new title, *Outline of Philosophy*. During the next twenty-five years this book ran through half a dozen editions, and formed the basis of the introductory course in philosophy in many American and Canadian universities. Its wide acceptability in that period was guaranteed, of course, by Watson's statement of his position in the preface: "The philosophical creed which commends itself to my mind is what in the text I have called Speculative Idealism, by which I mean the doctrine that we are capable of knowing Reality as it actually is, and that Reality when so known is absolutely rational." The criticism of the empirical tradition in philosophy was supplemented in 1895 with *Hedonistic Theories from Aristippus to Spencer*, an uncompromising demonstration of the view that no hedonistic theory can plausibly explain morality without assuming ideas inconsistent with its asserted principle.

In the popular consciousness Watson is usually associated with the provision of more adequate philosophical foundations for Christian theology. The popular view is, on the whole, correct, but it should be emphasized that he preferred to regard Christianity as an ideal of conduct rather than a historical theology. This approach was developed in a series of lectures given before the Philosophical Union of the University of California and published in 1897 as *Christianity and Idealism*. Here Watson argued that Christianity and idealism, when each is understood, lend each other mutual support. Each proved the other true; each is seen to be but a different expression of the same indivisibly threefold fact—God, freedom, and immortality. Idealism is the principle of morality and the principle of advancing history. Christianity is the germ of which idealism is the full issue. This conception of the relationship between idealism and Christianity was developed further in 1907 in *The Philosophical Basis of Religion*, a series of essays in the reconstruction and history of religious belief which had been delivered before the Brooklyn Institute of Arts and Sciences. Watson's mature philosophy of religion found expression, of course, in the Gifford Lectures which he delivered in the Union of Glasgow during the years 1910 to 1912, and which were published in two massive volumes as *The Interpretation of Religious Experience* (1912). This work, the crowning achievement of his philosophical career, concludes with a passionate plea for a faith which has a rational basis—in idealism:

... the religious interests of man can be preserved only by a theology which affirms that all forms of being are manifestations of a single spiritual principle in identification with which the true life of man consists. Living in this faith the future of the race is assured. Religion is the spirit which must more and more subdue all things to itself, informing science and art, and realizing itself in the higher organization of the family, the civic community, the state, and ultimately the world, and gradually filling the mind and heart of every individual with the love of God and the enthusiasm of humanity.

The First World War drove Watson to a deeper consideration of the problems of political philosophy which he, unlike most of the British idealists, had hitherto largely neglected. Two articles in the *Queen's Quarterly* on "German Philosophy and Politics" (1915) and "German Philosophy and the War" (1916) heralded the publication in 1919 of his last book, *The State in Peace and War*. Notable for its detachment, this book contains a survey of the evolution of political ideas from the origin of the city-state to the rise of the modern nation-state, an analysis of the latter in terms of its great associations and institutions, and a lengthy discussion of international relations in peace and war. At the age of seventy-two the sage of Kingston prophesied that the treatment of the defeated Central Powers, as well as the structure of the League of

Nations, would lead to a renewed war. He died seven months before this dire prediction was realized. Even a brief sketch of his writings must indicate that if any Canadian philosopher of the nineteenth century is remembered in future ages it will surely be John Watson.

VI

John Clark Murray was the son of David Murray, Provost of Paisley, Scotland, and his wife, Elizabeth Clark. Born in 1836, he was educated at the Paisley Grammar School and at the universities of Glasgow and Edinburgh, obtaining the degree of M.A. from the latter. From Edinburgh he went to Heidelberg and thence to Göttingen. During Murray's student days in Scotland the reigning philosopher was Sir William Hamilton; and it was to the Scottish Common Sense school of Thomas Reid, Dugald Stewart, and Hamilton that he ultimately belonged. But his studies on the Continent convinced him that the work of this school had to be supplemented by ancient, as well as by modern French and German, philosophy. A student should be presented with the points of view of representative classical systems.

At the age of twenty-six he was already so thoroughly trained and so well known that he was called to the chair of Mental and Moral Philosophy at Queen's University where he remained for ten years, serving as secretary to the Senate during part of this period. Murray then accepted the chair of Mental and Moral Philosophy at McGill, and his life was identified with this university for the next forty-five years.*

While teaching at McGill, Murray became more and more interested in the moral and ethical values of the great speculative systems of the past. Such an emphasis led certain of his students during the last decade of the nineteenth century to suppose that he must be a member of the idealistic school. They were perhaps influenced in this direction by his conception of philosophy as "the key which would unlock the secret of life's divine significance." He overrated Berkeley; and his distaste for empiricism, coupled with the influence of nineteenth-century Hegelian historians of philosophy, caused him to underestimate Locke and Hume. It is difficult to classify Murray in terms of the conventional schools. He had been trained in theology; and it would seem that he never achieved an entirely satisfactory synthesis of Calvinism, Scottish common sense, and German idealism. His final philosophical position is

---

*McGill University was the earliest of the central Canadian foundations, but philosophy seems not to have been recognized as a subject distinct from theology until 1853. In that year William Turnbull Leach (M.A. Edinburgh 1827, ordained by the Church of Scotland 1931 and later as an Anglican priest) was tranferred from the chair of Classical Literature, which he had accepted on the advice and request of Bishop Mountain in 1846, to a professorship of Logic, Rhetoric, and Moral Philosophy. From 1846 he served as Vice-Principal of the University, and from 1853 as Dean of the Faculty of Arts. In 1881 he resigned the Molson chair of English Literature (which he had held since 1858), but retained the administrative positions until his death in 1886.

perhaps best described as eclectic idealism. But Sir William Hamilton was never far beneath the surface.

For a philosopher Murray's scientific knowledge was exceptional. His Scottish training had included a thorough grounding in physics, which had been supplemented by further scientific study in Germany. Throughout his life, he kept up with the latest developments in physics and physiology, and this knowledge gave to his teaching of psychology and metaphysics a refreshing concreteness that was lacking in his philosophical contemporaries in central Canada. At Göttingen and Heidelberg he was also strongly influenced by the new biblical criticism, an influence which confirmed the insight, derived from Spinoza and Kant, that all religious values must be freely examined. Extensive work in psychology enabled him to appreciate also the significance of anthropology and comparative mythology for the study of religious origins.

Although he toiled single-handed in his teaching activities at Queen's and McGill for over forty years, Murray published nine books, some forty articles, a large number of reviews, and occasional verse. Of his nine books, one is concerned with Sir William Hamilton; two deal with ethics, two with psychology, and four with literary themes. His *Outline of Sir William Hamilton's Philosophy*, published at Boston in 1870, is the first technical philosophical book written in Canada. It had been preceded by a series of four articles on Hamilton in the *Canadian Journal* during the years 1866 and 1867. The *Outline* itself was introduced and highly recommended by James McCosh, President of Princeton and leading exponent of the Scottish philosophy in the United States. McCosh and Murray both believed that Hamilton was the great metaphysician of his age and that his writings would be studied by all thinking people in future centuries. It was imperative, therefore, that Hamilton's philosophy should be presented in systematic form, and this was the task Murray had set himself. In view of the diffuse, often chaotic, character of Hamilton's writings it is surprising that Murray should have succeeded in presenting such a tightly articulated, and altogether fair, exposition of his system. In 1870 he was still too much under the influence of Hamilton to venture any criticism of the latter's doctrines, but this defect only enhanced the value and influence of the *Outline* in circles where the Scottish philosophy was still generally accepted, and more especially in the United States.

In his *Introduction to Ethics* (1891), Murray's style is seen at its best, clear, vigorous, thought-compelling, on occasion even passionate. At the time of its publication this book was noteworthy in that it was not confined to the exposition of ethical concepts in their abstract generality but considered also the concrete application of moral concepts to the principal spheres of human duty. Its method throughout was strongly influenced by the new historical or evolutionary approach; and the conditions under which the principal moral ideals of humanity had been developed were given extended treatment. "The requirements of the moral ideal in any age," wrote Murray, "can be definitely comprehended only when we come to know how it has been formed, just as the precise meaning of a word is often to be reached only by tracing its history; and even if the obligations of the moral life demand an elevation or modification of the existing ideal, the proposed moral advance can itself be understood only when it is viewed as a continuation of the process through which that ideal was attained." The *Introduction* was translated into several languages, including Russian. Several years after his retirement, Murray published *A Handbook of Christian Ethics* (1908) in which the principles developed in his earlier ethical studies were applied to an exposition and philosophical interpretation of Christian ethical ideals. Like Young and Watson, Murray was unalterably opposed to hedonism and utilitarianism, yet he always succeeded in presenting theories with which he differed clearly and honestly.

It was taken for granted until long after Murray's retirement that psychology was a branch of philosophy, and he gave regular lectures in this field during his entire period at McGill. These lectures formed the basis of *A Handbook of Psychology* (1885) and *An Introduction to Psychology* (1904). Both texts were widely used in the United States, the former running through at least five editions in fifteen years. They were eventually displaced, of course, by the writings of William James and his disciples who emphasized a much more physiological and experimental, and a less exclusively analytical, approach to psychology. It is not surprising that Murray's treatment of psychology was not yet freed from epistemological and metaphysical intrusions. But it is remarkable that he should have been so receptive to the scientific material that had become available as an aftermath of the Darwinian biology. His psychology is an interesting blend of Sir William Hamilton and Wilhelm Wundt, the "founder" of experimental psychology. In the later volume the German influence became predominant, and the science of psychology was defined in terms of the conceptual framework laid down by Wundt. Much more extensive use was also made of anthropological material. But to the end the persistent influence of the Scottish School prevented Murray from reaping the fullest harvest of his remarkable alertness to late nineteenth-century movements of thought in science and philosophy.

VII

It is evident that the philosophical literature of nineteenth-century Canada was almost exclusively characterized by a positive religious orientation and devotion to Scottish Common Sense philosophy or some variety of Idealism. Murray was a partial exception. In his case there was a serious interest in natural science and a tendency to break away from the major philosophical emphases and heroes of his contemporaries. To this extent he was a "transition man" who pointed unmistakably towards the more heterogeneous world of twentieth century Canadian philosophical literature.

24. Scientific Writings

A. VIBERT DOUGLAS

THE SUBJECT-MATTER of his choice is not the determining factor as to whether a scholar's writing will or will not have literary merit, perhaps even literary excellence. The useful classification of knowledge into divisions and subdivisions has been done by erecting arbitrary walls where no intrinsic boundaries exist. All branches of knowledge interpenetrate one another, hence to affirm the oneness of all knowledge is no meaningless assertion. It was therefore essential to include a chapter on the literature of science in the present volume. To have done otherwise would have been to neglect a rich field of Canadian scholarship, a field which for more than a century can claim among its expositors men who have handled the English language with distinction and discrimination.

"We approach Nature in the same spirit as we are bidden to approach the Kingdom of Heaven, that is, as little children, and patiently strive by observation and experiment to find out what she is" . . . "the scientific idea of truth is a principle which brings order and harmony into phenomena . . . not arrived at by any mechanical stringing together of facts but by a flash of insight which may be compared to inspiration": so wrote Professor E. W. McBride in the *McGill University Magazine* in 1908 in an essay "The Criterion of Truth." The words "not arrived at by any mechanical stringing together of facts" deserve to be repeated with emphasis since many scholars trained too exclusively in the classical, literary, and social studies fall into the grievous error of imagining that science is in fact no more than just that. "The dramatic fancy which creates myths," wrote Dean W. R. Inge with an all too rare insight, "is the raw material of both poetry and science."

Unavoidable curtailment of space allotted to this chapter necessitated drastic and arbitrary limitation of the scope and depth of the survey and of the interpretation of the phrase "literature of science." The survey is restricted to books and articles of literary merit which are designed to expound and interpret science to the general reader. This rules out all technical papers and reports, and the many catalogues of fish, birds, animals, plants, and rocks, no matter how important these have been in the history of scientific achievement. Hence the names of most of Canada's outstanding scientists do not appear in the pages that follow.

References will be found to astronomy and physics, chemistry and geology, the biological, medical, and applied sciences; but no attempt has been made to cover agricultural science (with the exception of reference to one famous book) or anything pertaining to the Arctic regions. Where there are hundreds of books and essays to be considered, the selection of a few is obviously a very personal choice. In the bibliographies from 1751 to 1867 alone, some 108 authors are listed. After this date, the volume of scientific writing increases, and with striking acceleration in this century. The attempt is here made to select some typical and some of the most outstanding contributions made by native Canadians and by residents of Canada, whether their stay in this country was of long or short duration.

I

Prior to 1800 very little if any literature of science seems to have appeared in Canada. One finds references to almanacs and to practical instructions relating to husbandry, health, the practice of dentistry, and so forth. As R. O. Earl has pointed out in *The Culture of Contemporary Canada* (1957) "the early days of pioneer settlement were not appropriate for the development of scientists nor were scientists likely to come to a country in this stage."

But by the nineteenth century many well-educated professional men were coming out as officers in the army, as surveyors, teachers, medical men, or ministers of religion. In the old Scottish universities, particularly, many of them had acquired considerable knowledge of geology and natural history and they were keenly observant of nature. Scholarly articles and a few books on scientific topics began to be written in Canada.

In Nova Scotia, as early as 1818, the "Letters of Agricola" appeared weekly in the *Acadian Recorder*. Their author, John Young (1773–1837), not only stimulated farmers of the Maritimes to improve their methods and to form groups for the discussion of general and local problems, but he gave them food for thought in a variety of ways. Good examples are Letters 6 and 7 on climate, and Letters 27–32 on manures. In this latter category he included lime. The discursive nature of his writing is illustrated by his digression to recall a visit to the last resting place of Burns where an old gardener talked with him about the poet and then remarked upon the greatly increased fertility of Ayrshire since the poet's day, ascribing this to the application of lime to the fields. Young then advocated this treatment and described the various types of occurrence of lime in Nova Scotia and how best to prepare it for spreading. So highly were these letters regarded and so great was their influence that they were published as a book under the same title in Halifax in 1822.

In 1847 Abraham Gesner, M.D. (1797–1864), who became a surveyor in New Brunswick, geologist, investigator of fisheries, pioneer in extracting kerosene and oils from bituminous substances, published in London *New Brunswick; with Notes for Emigrants*, a book which contains chapters on natural history, climate, soils, and wild life.

One manifestation of growing intellectual activity was the formation by groups of inquiring spirits in Montreal, Quebec, and the Maritimes of natural history societies or literary and scientific societies. The Montreal Natural History Society was founded in 1827, shortly after the Literary and Historical Society of Quebec; a museum was established and the papers read at its meetings were published subsequently in the *Canadian Naturalist*. This magazine undoubtedly helped to form the intellectual atmosphere of those early years.

In Upper Canada a similar function was performed by the *Canadian Journal*, organ of the Royal Canadian Institute which was established in Toronto in 1849. Through its public lectures, its *Journal* (1852–78), and its subsequent *Proceedings* and *Transactions*, the Institute has richly contributed to the intellectual growth of this country. In its Centennial Volume (1949) are found ten essays on "One Hundred Years of Science in Canada."

The Nova Scotia Literary and Scientific Society was established in January 1859 "for the reading and discussion of original communications . . . in Literature, Science, Political Economy, Commerce, Statistics and the Arts . . . to foster a spirit of enquiry and enterprise and generally promote the advancement of science, learning and the useful arts." Many of the papers are of high quality, couched in the dignified, often somewhat ponderous style of the period. In one of the first papers read before the Society, on the "Fossiliferous Rocks of Arisaig," the Rev. David Honeyman wrote: "we see nature, by chemical constituents of these rocks, often times embalming their entombed inhabitants as no Egyptian physician could embalm, not to present, after a few thousand years, a dry and withered mummy, but, after years whose numbers we cannot imagine, to present them almost, if not altogether, as lovely as when they were first entombed."

This somewhat too all-embracive society was modified in 1863 when the Institute of Natural Science was founded and began publication in its *Transactions* of the papers read at its meetings. The seventh paper for that year was by R. G. Haliburton, F.S.A. (1831–1901) (son of Judge Haliburton, satirist), on "The Festival of the Dead," afterwards published in Halifax as the first part of his book *New Materials for the History of Man* (1863). In this he showed that ancient and more recent inhabitants of four continents regulated their Festival of the Dead and their date of the beginning of the new year from the heliacal rising or the midnight culmination of the Pleiades. Haliburton communicated these ideas to Professor Piazzi Smith, and they led the latter to base one of his dates for the construction of the Great Pyramid on the present altitude of the Pleiades at culmination relative to the inclination of a passage to the south face, up which, because of the procession of the equinoxes, the Pleiades could have been seen in 2170 B.C.

In the previous year, 1862, the Principal of Queen's University, Rev. Dr. William Leitch (1814–1864), published in London a little book which gave a good account of the astronomical knowledge of the day with reproductions of the Earl of Rosse's drawings of galactic, elliptical, and spiral nebulae. The tone of the book is set by its title, *God's Glory in the Heavens*. Published also in New York, it ran to a third edition in 1866.

H. Beaumont Small (1832–1919) was the author of *The Animals of North America* (Montreal, 1864), illustrated with many attractive woodcuts and written to meet "a growing desire for further acquaintance with . . . the pleasing study of Natural History . . . felt among a large and increasing class of intelligent readers." Of this little book the Montreal *Gazette* wrote "we can almost imagine 'old Isaak' recommending it to his pupil Venator," and the *Athenaeum* praised it as "well worth perusal, written in a style seldom met with in a concise handbook."

II

A striking feature in our development is the early interest in Canada in the repercussions of advancing scientific knowledge upon religious beliefs. One evidence of this is a work by Henry Taylor (fl. 1819–1860) which seems to have had considerable influence in Great Britain. Published by Coates in Toronto in 1836, it bears the title *An Attempt to Form a System of the Creation of our Globe, of the Planets, and the Sun of our System*. It is founded on the first chapter of Genesis, on the geology of the earth, and "on the modern discoveries in that science and the known operations of the laws of Nature, as evinced by the discoveries of Lavoisier and others in pneumatic chemistry." The author set out "to reconcile the present Geological appearances of our Earth with the Mosaic account of creation" by taking literally "the waters" of the second, sixth, and seventh verses of Genesis and explaining them in the light of "the wonderful discoveries in pneumatic chemistry, of the gaseous bodies and . . . the component principles of water." Out of this "Universal ocean" sun, moon, planets are born, the "days of creation" being successive cycles of time. His manuscript, composed between 1819 and 1825, was shown to Archdeacon Mountain, and to the Bishop of Quebec, who encouraged him to take it to England where he gave a copy to the Lord Bishop of London, to a theologian named Fairholme, and in 1833 to the Royal Institution in London. When he learned in 1836 that Professor Buckland and the theologians Pusey, Chalmers, and Gleig were advocating these very ideas, he hastened to publish his work, fully believing that he was the originator of the ideas. It went through nine editions between 1836 and 1854.

The same serious motive led Thomas Trotter (1853–1918), minister of the Presbyterian Church of Antigonish, to publish in 1845 in Pictou his *Treatise on Geology*, "in which the discoveries of that science are reconciled with the Scriptures, and ancient revolutions of the earth are shown to be of benefit to man." This book was written in the belief that "a comprehensive, connected and scientific view of these events would render an important service to Religion by silencing many of the cavils of the infidel, and solving some of the greatest difficulties which perplex the mind of the inquisitive Christian."

"It is utterly unworthy of the cause of our holy religion, which professes to rest on truth . . . to shrink from confronting any of the established truths of science," wrote Rev. Moses Harvey of St. John's, Newfoundland (1820–1901), and with eloquence and many poetic references he reviewed current advances in geology and astronomy in *The Harmony of Science and Revelation* (Halifax and St. John's, 1856). In this book he upheld the speculative musings of Sir David Brewster on the plurality of inhabited planets in the universe. A different treatment of this theme was T. W. Goldie's *Mosaic Account of Creation of the World and the Noachian Deluge Geologically Explained*, which ran to two editions in Quebec in 1856.

Thoughtful and scholarly men in Canada viewed with the same deep interest and grave concern the great wave of new biological knowledge and speculation which swirled around the words Evolution and Natural Selection throughout the latter half of the nineteenth century and far into the twentieth. The names of Lyell, Darwin, Lamarck, Spencer, Huxley, Haeckel, produced feelings of hopeful exhilaration or of dismay according to the reader's knowledge and temperament. The concern was of two kinds: unreasoned opposition to the new knowledge on the assumption that it was undermining spiritual faith; and honest acceptance leading to earnest and often ingenious efforts to reconcile new scientific knowledge with biblical cosmology. In 1859, the same year in which *The Origin of Species* appeared in London, Dr. James Bovell, M.D. (1817–1880), published in Toronto *Outlines of Natural Theology* of which Professor Chapman wrote in the *Canadian Journal*, "It deserves the attention of all interested in the progress of Canadian Literature." In this book the author, who believed "that a Being exists, who through his works reveals himself, as an author in his volume," proceeded to outline the current state of knowledge in geology, zoology, physiology, quoting numerous authorities such as Lyell, Humboldt, Darwin, Murchison, Huxley, Solly, and Agassiz, stating unequivocally where he agreed or differed with their metaphysical or theological deductions. The influence of

Dr. Bovell on the thinking and activities of the youthful William Osler (afterwards Sir William Osler, M.D.) was a potent one and continued to be a factor throughout Osler's life.

In the opposite camp was a Nova Scotian author, Hon. John G. Marshall (1786–1880), whose letters published in 1863 in the *Christian World* (London) opposed Sir Charles Lyell's views as to the age of the earth, transmutation of species, and gradual development in the natural world. Also among the reactionaries was a schoolmaster, Ezekiel S. Wiggins (1839–1910), whose book published in Montreal in 1864 carried the title and explanation, *The Architecture of the Heavens,* "containing a new theory of the Universe, the extent of the Deluge, the testimony of the Bible and Geology in opposition to the views of Dr. Colenso." Dr. Colenso, it will be recalled, was an Anglican ecclesiastic and mathematician, a pioneer in the Higher Criticism, who became Bishop of Natal but was excommunicated for his liberal views by the Bishop of Capetown.

The proponents of a reconciliation of science and religion had an eloquent champion in that distinguished and prolific Canadian scholar, Sir John William Dawson (1820–1899). Only five of his books will be mentioned here. His classic *Acadian Geology* (Edinburgh and London, 1855), of whose "high scientific merit, very considerable literary merit" Hugh Miller wrote in the *Edinburgh Witness,* is far from being in the category of an ordinary textbook, *vide* his beautiful and dramatic description of the incoming tide in the Cobequid and Chignecto bays and his pages on the history of the name Acadia. Dawson's *Archaia; or, Studies of the Cosmogony and Natural History of the Hebrew Scriptures* (Montreal and London, 1860), was so widely read and valued that he revised it in 1877 and it reappeared under the title *The Origin of the World according to Revelation and Science.* His prestige both in Canada and in Great Britain is further indicated by the reception accorded to two later books. *The Chain of Life in Geological Time* was published in London in 1880, with a second edition in 1885, and a third in 1888. From this little book is taken a passage in the final chapter:

What general conclusions can we reach as to this long and strange history of the progress of life on our planet? Perhaps the most comprehensive of these is that the links in the chain of life or rather its many chains are not scattered and disunited things but members of a great and complex plan. . . . It must also appear that the original plan of nature both in the animal and vegetable worlds, was too vast to be realized at one time on a globe as limited as ours, but had to be distributed in time as well as in space . . . successive aeons in which, one after the other, the work of creation could rise to successive stages of perfection and completeness till it culminated in man.

Dawson's *Modern Ideas of Evolution as related to Revelation and Science* (London, 1890) provided, amongst other topics, a critical examination of the views of Haeckel and Huxley. A tenth impression appeared in 1910.

III

During the latter half of the last century, the scientific magazines like the *Canadian Naturalist*, the *Canadian Journal*, the *Anglo-American Magazine* were providing well-written articles on a wide range of scientific topics: T. Sterry Hunt on chemistry, mineralogy, and geology; John Matthew Jones, F.L.S., on ocean drifts and currents; Sir William Dawson's presidential address, 1864, to the Natural History Society, in light whimsical vein, and his tribute to Sir William Logan's *Report of the Geological Survey*; Sir Sandford Fleming's tribute to Logan, 1856; Rev. A. De Sola's address in 1868 when he said, "Possibly Robinson Crusoe himself was not so much astonished at the footprints on the sands of his desolate island as the naturalist who first saw the footmark of birds on a slab of sandstone which was turned up by the plow . . . in 1802 at South Hadley in the valley of the Connecticut River"; papers on the great Niagara suspension bridge (1853), on the wave principle in marine architecture (1852), on dew (1853), on the Victoria Bridge (1855); John Langton, Auditor-General and Vice-Chancellor of the University of Toronto, on the age of timber trees (1862) and ethnological investigations (1866).

The *British American Journal* (Montreal, 1845, with a new series beginning in 1860) contained articles and reviews on medical subjects both general and specific. The report on "Quackery, Imposition and Deception" by Dr. William Marsden (1860) reads like a chapter from a modern detective tale.

The growth of productive scholarship in Canada was greatly stimulated by the increase in the number of universities across the country in the latter part of the nineteenth century. These, with their faculties of letters, social, and scientific studies, attracted and encouraged able, ambitious scholars. To provide new outlets for the publication of their ideas, the *Queen's Quarterly* [*Q*] was founded in 1893, *McGill University Magazine* [*M*] in 1901 and *Dalhousie Review* [*Dal*] and *University of Toronto Quarterly* [*T*] twenty years later, as well as the *Canadian Forum* [*F*]. True, high-quality journals like the *Atlantic Monthly* [*A*] (1857) from the United States and the *Hibbert Journal* [*H*] (1902) and *Discovery* [*Disc*] (1920) from Great Britain had found some devoted readers among thoughtful Canadians, but very few Canadian scientists had published in their pages. Canadian periodicals were therefore very necessary and in them much excellent writing is to be found including expositions of scientific ideas and achievements designed for the enlightenment of general readers, articles on the overlapping fields of science, philosophy, and religion, and a large number of able reviews of scientific books. That even the *Canadian Forum* should carry so many such reviews is convincing evidence of the widespread interest in science during the last forty years.

The following names recur time and again in one or in several of these periodicals; by the initials following each name, identification of the periodicals to which each contributed may be made: Frank Allen (*T*), W. C. Baker (*Q*), S. Basterfield (*T,F*), N. J. Berrill (*A*), G. S. Brett (*T,F*), N. R. Carmichael (*Q*), A. L. Clark (*Q*), C. K. Clarke (*Q*), A. P. Coleman (*T,F*), A. V. Douglas (*Q,T,H,A,Disc*), N. F. Dupuis (*Q*), R. O. Earl (*Q*), Sandford Fleming (*Q*), W. L. Goodwin (*Q*), D. Fraser Harris (*Dal,H*), A. P. Knight (*Q*), A. Macphail (*M,Q*), W. T. McClement (*Q*), E. W. McBride (*M,H*), J. Markowitz (*F*), R. E. K. Pemberton (*F*), J. K. Robertson (*Q*).

With the increasing emphasis on scientific research since the close of the First World War, university research laboratories and federal, provincial, and industrial laboratories have proliferated, one result being an ever increasing flow of published papers, reports, and surveys. While one does not turn to such sources primarily for the delight of finding literary quality, such writing is not absent. It is important to note that the Society of Technical Writers and Publishers is actively promoting higher standards for their work. Many of these writers realize that scientific accuracy, clarity, and succinctness are not incompatible with a good style of expression and a discriminating choice of words.

Some seventy-five Canadian scientific journals and publications are listed in *The Culture of Contemporary Canada* (pp. 327–66). Mention will only be made here of the annual *Proceedings and Transactions* of the Royal Society of Canada, and attention is drawn to some of the presidential addresses delivered to the Society or to one of the science sections. It may appear invidious to single out a few from so many, nevertheless mention may be made of "The Progress of Biology," R. Ramsay Wright, 1911; "The National Domain in Canada and its Proper Conservation," Frank D. Adams, 1914; "The 'Miraculous' Micro-organism," F. C. Harrison, 1924 (Section V); "Time and Life," W. A. Parks, 1926; "Continuity and Discontinuity," J. K. Robertson, 1945; "Mutations," W. P. Thompson, 1948; "Microbes and Men," G. B. Reid, 1953; "Micheli and the Discovery of Fungi," A. H. Reginald Buller, 1915 (Section V), and by the same author as President of the Society in 1928, "The Plants of Canada Past and Present," from which address three passages follow: "Among the great generalizations of science not one seems more secure than that of organic evolution." . . . "What are the first traces of plant life within the boundaries of this broad Dominion? For an answer to this question we must go with the palaeontologist to the oldest rocks of our country and with hammer and chisel extract from them their fossil remains. 'In the never-idle workshop of nature,' as Matthew Arnold has called it, many strange plants have been woven on the looms of time and have left the traceries of their stems and leaves and the beautiful hexagonal pattern of their internal tissues in the sedimentary rocks, but the first products of the loom were doubtless too delicate and too frail for proper preservation." . . . "It is possible that *Eozoon* [J. W. Dawson's discovery in the Precambrian] is one of the rocks that owe their origin to the activity of Blue-green Algae."

IV

When we come to consider the books written at the close of the last century and during six decades of this century, we note the wide range of subject-matter, the almost complete absence of sermonizing, the rarity of adventure into metaphysical regions, the rich sense of history, and an evident pride in solid scientific achievement by men, many of whom have been inspiring teachers and citizens as well as able researchers.

In the broad field of natural science the books of Ernest Thompson Seton have been very widely read by three generations. Seton's keen observation of wild life in Ontario and Manitoba between the ages of four and twenty-four provided the material for his life stories of foxes, rabbits, wolves, grouse, prairie chicken, etc., published in the *Canadian Journal*, *St. Nicholas*, *Scribner's* and other magazines. Later sojourns in New York, London, Paris, and eventually New Mexico, added their quota. His books began with *Wild Animals I Have Known* (1898), and include in rapid succession *Lives of the Hunted*, *Biography of a Grizzly*, *Animal Heroes*, *The Trail of the Sandhill Stag*, *Monarch: The Big Bear of Tallac*. Later came his *Life-Histories of Northern Animals* in two volumes, *Lives of Game Animals* in four volumes, and at the age of 80 in 1940 the charming autobiography *Trail of an Artist-Naturalist*. These works are discussed more fully in chapter 19 on nature writers.

A Canadian-born naturalist whose life was lived chiefly in England and Europe was Grant Allen (1848–1899). Some ten books became well known in the last two decades of the century. *The Story of Plants* (1895) was reprinted in London in 1927. His observations and conclusions as a field botanist won praise from Darwin and Spencer, while T. H. Huxley complimented him on his ability to achieve in his writings "precision with popularity." He termed himself "a scientific middle-man," but he was much more.

A friend of Seton's, William Perkins Bull (1870–1948), wrote the beautifully produced books *From Humming Bird to Eagle* (1936) and *From Amphibians to Reptiles* (1937), and *From Medicine Man to Medical Man* (1934) in which he traced "the efforts of men of science through the past century and a half, not only to increase the pleasure of living, but also to lengthen the span of human life." Sir W. Arbuthnot Lane considered the latter "an important contribution to the literature of public health, particularly for the closely defined area of one Canadian County [Peel Co.]."

From the prolific pen of a contemporary zoologist, N. J. Berrill, have come a series of books for the lay reader: *The Living Tide* (1951), *Journey into Wonder* (1952), *Sex and the Nature of Things* (1954), *The Origin of Vertebrates* (1956), *You and the Universe* (1958), *Man's Emerging Mind* (1961).

To A. G. Huntsman we owe *Life and the Universe* (1959), a veteran biologist's examination of thought, science, will, faith, and purpose. A question of perennial importance is ably discussed by Robert McRae, philosopher, in *The Problem of the Unity of the Sciences* (1961).

Textbooks are not often remarkable for their literary value, but in the eyes of his contemporaries those of Dr. William Clauser Boyd are in this category: *Surgical Pathology* (1925), with a sixth edition in 1947 and a *Text-Book of Pathology* (1933) with a sixth edition in 1953; *An Introduction to Medical Science* (1937); *Fundamentals of Immunology* (1943) with a third edition in 1956; *Pathology for the Physician* (1958).

The history of science has claimed the interest of not a few Canadian scientists, among whom are F. D. Adams, whose erudite *Birth and Development of the Geological Sciences* (1938) is a classic; Sir William Osler in his learned and wholly delightful *Evolution of Modern Medicine* (1921) and *Incunabula Medica, 1467–1480* (1922); Walter Libby, *A History of Medicine in its Salient Features* (1921); Maude E. Abbott, *History of Medicine in the Province of Quebec* (1931); J. J. Heagerty, *Four Centuries of Medical History in Canada and Newfoundland* (1928) and *The Romance of Medicine in Canada* (1940); Frank Allen, *The Universe, from Crystal Spheres to Relativity* (1931); Lloyd G. Stevenson, *The Meaning of Poison* (1959); C. J. S. Warrington and R. V. V. Nicholls, *A History of Chemistry in Canada* (1949), which opens thus: "A thread of metal runs through the whole fabric of Canadian history. The period spans the epoch between the last years of alchemy and the beginning of the atomic era."

Some biographies of men of science are enriched by informative accounts of scientific work and discoveries: *Loring Woart Bailey* by Joseph Whitman Bailey (1925) containing many quotations from L. W. Bailey's notes, letters and his *Reminiscences*; *Thomas Sterry Hunt* by F. D. Adams (1933); *The Life of Sir Thomas Roddick* (1938) and *Maude Abbott: A Memoir* (1941) by H. E. MacDermot; *Sir Frederick Banting* by Lloyd Stevenson (1946); *Arthur Stanley Eddington* by A. Vibert Douglas (1956); *Sir William Osler*, a memorial volume of 119 articles edited by Maude E. Abbott (1920) whose expressed aim was to supply "the unsmelted ore from which the future historian may extract that firsthand evidence which may enable him rightly to estimate the service which William Osler rendered to his day and generation . . ."; *Young Endeavour* (1958) by William C. Gibson, summarizing the "contributions to science by medical students of the Past Four Centuries";

Medicine in the Making (1960) by Gordon Murray and *Amid Masters of Twentieth Century Medicine* (1958) by Leonard G. Rowntree, both containing vivid descriptions of the fight against disease and of the developments in surgical practice made by these masters and their medical contemporaries. *The Chord of Steel* by Thomas B. Costain (1960) portrays the early years of Alexander Graham Bell and his discoveries culminating in the telephone. Leopold Infeld, for many years a professor in Toronto, wrote an inspiring biography, *Albert Einstein: His Work and its Influence on our World* (1950), and an autobiography, *Quest* (1941), recounting not only his life in Europe and America but his intellectual quest in the realm of mathematical physics wherein we read: "The transition from particle physics to field physics is undoubtedly one of the greatest, and as Einstein believes, *the* greatest step accomplished in the history of human thought. Great courage and imagination were needed to shift the responsibility for physical phenomena from particles into the previously empty space and to formulate mathematical equations describing the changes in space and time." Thanks to the Engineering Institute of Canada some important books have been produced. One entitled *Daylight through the Mountain: The Letters and Labours of Civil Engineers Walter and Francis Shanly* (1957) is edited by Frank Norman Walker. Another is the life of one of the founders of the Institute, *Sir Casimir Stanislaus Gzowski* (1959) by Ludwik Rabcewicz-Zubkowski and William Edward Greening.

In the field of applied science R. F. Legget's *The Rideau Waterway* (1955) recounts a great achievement of historic significance to Canada, and his *Geology and Engineering* (1939) is a stimulating book. So too is *Modern Railroad Structures* (1949) by C. P. Disney and R. F. Legget. D. M. Le-Bourdais in his *Sudbury Basin: The Story of Nickel* (1953) and G. B. Langford in *Out of the Earth: The Mineral Industry in Canada* (1954) have produced books of extreme interest about mineral deposits in Canada and the problems and achievements of mining engineers.

The year 1960 saw the publication of three books on evolution, *Evolution: Its Science and Doctrine*, edited by T. W. M. Cameron, *Darwin in Retrospect*, edited by H. H. J. Nesbitt, and *The Ascent of Life* by T. A. Goudge, indicating the widened scientific, philosophical, and social significance of the theory a century after Darwin's *Origin of the Species*. Goudge has contributed essays in this field to various journals including *Mind* (1954) and *British Journal for the Philosophy of Science* (1955, 1958–59).

Special mention should be made of J. Tuzo Wilson's *I.G.Y., the Year of the New Moons* (1961) where chapters on his journeys and observations from Arctic to Antarctic and to every continent are interspersed with clear informative chapters on the discoveries and new problems confronting science as a result of researches in which men of 67 nations cooperated.

Bare mention of many books of high quality could run to an undue length for this limited chapter; hence only a few more are selected for inclusion. *Nerves and Personal Power* (1922) by Dougall MacDougall King (brother of W. L. Mackenzie King), is an eloquent book by a physician who knew his days were few; *On Understanding Physics* (1938) by W. H. Watson, one of the few philosophical books written by a physicist in Canada; *Our Mobile Earth* (1926) by Reginald A. Daly; *Ice Ages, Recent and Ancient* (1926) and *The Last Million Years* (1941) by Arthur P. Coleman; *Our Wonderful Universe* (1928) by C. A. Chant; *The Stress of Life* (1956) by Hans Selye; *Memory, Learning and Language: The Physical Basis of Mind* (1960) edited by William Feindel with contributions by A. Hoffer, J. W. T. Spinks, Arthur Porter, and Wilder Penfield, O.M., and his own chapter on "The Brain considered as a Thinking Machine," containing the following paragraph:

Each of us has in his possession the most remarkable of galaxies—twelve billion nerve cells with their myriads of subconstellations in the compact universe of the brain. It is this inner space of the mind which surely, of all our natural resources, offers the most exciting potentialities. Consideration makes us realize that we are far from exploiting this thinking machine as efficiently as we might in the broad field of creative learning. To paraphrase Cassius, "The fault, dear Brutus, lies not in our brains, but in ourselves, that we are underlings."

The concluding word must be an exhortation to scientists to take time to interpret science to non-scientists, to bridge the chasm which too often exists between the disciplines. Men with a flair for literary expression, whose interests embrace the exposition of scientific ideas and achievements, are needed in our country. When their "apples" of pure scientific "gold" are given to a hungry reading public in "baskets" of literary "silver" these writers are making an important contribution to the literary history of Canada.

25. Literature of Protest

F. W. WATT

IT HAS LONG BEEN RECOGNIZED that the creation of the Dominion of Canada in 1867 was primarily a conservative act—conservative in the sense of attempting to preserve in the new political entity the character, traditions, and advantages of its colonial components, and to avoid a revolutionary rupture with the circumstances of the past. But from the very beginning Canadians found their energies drawn into a difficult and paradoxical endeavour. They had to devise unique political and economic strategies (and the vocabulary and imagery in which to shape them) in order to project the past into the future along a path never travelled before. This chapter does not concern itself, however, with the conservative tradition which is mainly responsible for the building of the nation of Canada as it is today, but rather with the spirit of protest and dissent which, sometimes deliberately, resisted the main current, and which as a consequence of the necessities of nation-building was almost, but never entirely, stifled.

In the half-century following Confederation most Canadians came to share the social ideals of the nation-builders: religious, political, and racial harmony; rapid commercial and industrial growth; high immigration; continental expansion from sea to sea. Their desire for unanimity produced a national temper or ethos which offered no adequate outlet (except emigration) for those who had criticisms, reservations, or competing ideals. In Victorian Canadian society controversial issues were habitually played down, and conciliation became the national virtue. The major political divisions ceased to reflect any fundamental differences in principles. In the lower orders of society, however, a movement impelled by other motives and opposed or indifferent to the ideals of the conservative tradition appeared and continued to grow during the first fifty years of Confederation, though not until the 1920's did it emerge as a factor of major importance for all levels of society.

The conservative tradition found its first practical form and its symbol in the National Policy of 1879, a programme of economic nationalism. By its chief strategy, the raising of tariff barriers against imported manufactured goods, the N.P. stimulated home industries, linked commercial and manu-facturing interests with national existence and material progress, and com-mitted the country to industrial urban expansion as rapidly as world economic conditions would allow. In 1867 the grimmer realities of industrial urbanism, which had long ago loomed large in the lives and minds of Englishmen, and which were rapidly appearing in the United States, had as yet little meaning in the Canadian economic environment, but this situation was soon to change. Growing hints of the future were there for those who had eyes to see them, and radical ideas and protest movements active in Europe and the United States were beginning to receive some attention in the Canadian press by the 1870's. Radicalism such as that which inspired the notorious International Workingmen's Association and Karl Marx, the founder of modern communism, at first seemed not so much repulsive as utterly meaning-less and unrelated to the Canadian situation, as early allusions (for instance in the *Canadian Monthly and National Review*) indicate. By the 1880's and early 1890's journalists and men of letters were showing more familiarity with and understanding of Marxian and other serious ideological critiques of capitalist free enterprise and its weaknesses. Governmental concern was growing too. In 1889, ten years after the adoption of the Tory National Policy, the *Report of the Royal Commission on the Relations of Labor and Capital* was submitted, which gave credit to the N.P. for the rapid industrialization of Canada during the previous decade, but which officially recognized the existence of industrial evils—sweated labour, children and women working long hours, unsanitary factory conditions and slum dwellings —and which advocated Parliament's "paternal care" as a necessity for labour as well as for capital. The industrial revolution and all its consequences had reached Canada. By 1894 a social observer in the highly respectable *Canadian Magazine* was able to advance a criticism of the contemporary social order in the manner of the middle-class American "progressives." The essay "Canadian Democracy and Socialism" by John A. Cooper points out the existence of varieties of socialism, from its mildest, comprising such generally accepted social features as the public school system, to more extreme forms, that of Karl Marx, whose *Das Kapital* "has now great influence in the United States and Canada," and that of the extremist Bakunin:

His Second International has caused no end of trouble to the governments of Europe, and there is little doubt that it has many members in the United States and a few in Canada. Its aim is destruction, and its means are the knife and the bomb. Such is the extreme socialism that may some day in the near future force itself into Canada. Among the laborers of this country who have felt the bitter stings of poverty, it smoulders.

"Great soulless corporations" and the unequal distribution of wealth were a good deal to blame; if moderate reforms were adopted now, "extreme socialism would cease to be a menace and anarchism cease to be a nightmare."

But attacks on corporations and trusts, on bigness in business, were rare. More often Canadians, partly because they were accustomed to the large-scale development of resources by government-supported operations, were ready to accept the presence of large and semi-monopolistic enterprises as natural and desirable—an "inevitable stage in the evolution of society," as another witness to these developments expressed it in 1898 (E. R. Peacock in the *Queen's Quarterly*, VI). Threats of monopolistic domination and other abuses, the growth of trade unionism and labour unrest, the increase in complexity and interdependency in industrial urban conditions, the rise of unemployment and slumdom, were features in the "collectivism" of the late nineteenth century which largely came about or were prepared for in the short space of a quarter of a century. Something of a "great social revolution" (see Henry Stephens, *Canadian Monthly*, I, 1872) was indeed taking place, and elsewhere in the world its issues formed the substance of public controversy and political battles. In nineteenth-century Canada the conservative temper and the exigencies of nation-building remained so dominant that it never became a central preoccupation, the issues involved were rarely seriously brought into the arena of public debate and were never sharply drawn, despite the efforts of a militant minority.

As one would expect, the men of letters of Victorian Canada were on the whole no more preoccupied with radical ideologies and the social evils which gave them encouragement than were the politicians and the social and economic theorists. The eminent Torontonian and sometime Oxford Professor of History, Goldwin Smith, was a distinguished exception. He took an intelligent interest in aspects of the "social revolution" at an early stage when Canadians of his class seemed scarcely aware of its significance. In the early 1870's he was drawing attention to the growing power of the working classes whose rallying cry "Union is Strength" was beginning to be taken up by the small Canadian labour force. In the 1880's he frequently pointed out the internationalist implications of the growth of unionism, particularly the rise of the Knights of Labor just then entering Ontario: the movement was towards a "denationalized" working class. Also in the 1880's Smith was among those few Canadians concerned over symptoms of the encroachments of the darker side of industrial urbanism in North America, tramps and paupers and the like: "We admit it with reluctance, but we are everywhere looking forward to the necessity of a public provision for the poor." Though an ardent individualist, Smith was typically prepared to give the devil his due, and so we find him studying extreme varieties of late nineteenth century social panaceas largely shunned by respectable Canadian writers. In 1872 he offered a lengthy and careful review of J. H. Noyes's classic *History of American Socialism*; in the 1880's he repeatedly drew attention to the implications of Henry George's land nationalization schemes; in 1893 he subjected Edward Bellamy's social utopia *Looking Backward* to a detailed analysis. Opposed to state control in any form and holding to his conception of "natural" economic laws, Smith could throw down a challenge to Single Taxer, Socialist, or any other advocate of governmental control alike: "let him ask himself whether his government, or his group of governments, is likely to do better than *nature*" (my italics).

In short, Goldwin Smith was curiously both radical and reactionary. A "liberal of the old school," he felt compelled to examine freely and without prejudice any institution, belief, or theory, but he was passionately committed at the same time to his primary assumption: the right, duty, and ability of each individual to fend for himself. The modern world was producing certain changing conditions which were making it increasingly difficult for the unorganized and independent individual to exist, in actuality or in social theory. Having formed leading ideas of liberalism in the England of the 1840's and 1850's, which he determinedly expounded in North America in the 1880's and 1890's, Goldwin Smith was a man between two worlds, at home in neither.

Another well-known controversialist, though not of Smith's international stature, W. D. LeSueur, was theoretically much more unorthodox and radical in his views. He was, in fact, that almost unique phenomenon of nineteenth-century Canada, a disciple of Auguste Comte. LeSueur fully and explicitly endorsed the "positivist ideal" with its religious scepticism and its faith in science, reason, and progress. "Scepticism," he brashly argued in the 1870's, "occupies somewhat the same position at present that Christianity held before its official recognition as the religion of the Roman Empire." The potential achievements of emancipated reason are great: "faith in reason and faith in progress are sentiments so closely allied they are seldom seen apart. . . . If . . . there are no assignable limits to the conquests of the human mind, there can be none to the progress of society." The religion of the future should take the form of "an earnest study of the laws of life and of morality, personal and social" and its end will be to "transfigure society." These heretical doctrines, so antithetical to the accepted pieties of Canadian Victorians, and revealing that unholy fusion of secularism, science, and social discontent which conservatism thoroughly feared and condemned, remained at the level of the most abstract theory, and LeSueur though criticized was never obliged to forfeit his seat among the respectable.

LeSueur's disinterestedness was the kind Matthew Arnold preached—aloofness from action and immediate practice; and Canadian social and literary critics alike tended to accept this doctrine. A too-active social conscience was looked upon as unhealthy and out of place in the Canadian scene. Writers were praised for their idealism, their respect for the conventional virtues, and their sense of decorum, and by and large they were careful to merit such praise. The case of Agnes Maule Machar's social criticism is instructive. The hero of her *Roland Graeme, Knight: A Novel of Our Times* (1892) reads Henry George along with the Higher Criticism, becomes in effect a Christian socialist, edits a radical newspaper, and throws in his lot with the working class under the inspiration of a "vision of a fair Utopia which might become the noble aim of a modern crusade." His kind of vague socialist idealism, secular in theology but Christian in ethics, was finding its outlet in the rapid spread of the Knights of Labor movement in Canada in the 1880's and 1890's. Miss Machar's novel, however, is set in the United States. And though protesting the selfishness and ignorance of the wealthier classes of society and exhibiting in a relatively favourable light radical and unconventional ideas, it is still basically in the genteel tradition. For all the weight it gives political and economic issues and for all its sympathy for the lower classes, it is essentially a romantic story of high society, and it preaches not social or political revolution but *noblesse oblige*.

Two poetasters, John Henry Brown (b. 1859) and Walter Ratcliffe (b. 1860), flouted decorum to give less inhibited support to the cause of social revolution. Brown's *Poems: Lyrical and Dramatic* (1892) presents the flamboyant person of an atheistical and free-thinking rebel. Politically he proclaims his faith in democracy, is repulsed by the squalor of modern industrial civilization, and propagandizes for a planned society (of the Comtean sort) where scientists replace priests and freedom and social justice prevail. To the poet who looks at the contemporary scene, Brown observes, "Life is barren and grey, Life is gross and vulgar and dull." Two responses are possible; the first, escapism, romantic nostalgia, or "looking backward," Brown emphatically rejects. The other response, which the poet elects in what amounts to a conversion, brings him to the position of the proletariat, and as poet, to a proletarian aesthetic: "I looked on the world and accepted it. . . . Henceforth, I said, the function of the poet is changed. . . ." The poet vows to "accept no good that is not the right of every man."

Walter Ratcliffe's less melodramatic *Morning Songs in the Night: Poems* (1897)—the title alludes to the poet's blindness—contains verse which is more sombre, direct, and earnest. The poet's protests against the vices of capitalistic oppression and social inequalities are strong, however, and, as W. D. Lighthall points out in the Preface, "socialistic." Poems like "Looking Backward" and "The Land Monopolist" indicate by their content as well as their titles the influence of Bellamy and Henry George on Ratcliffe's thinking; and his verse is motivated by the same fervour of sympathy and indignation exhibited by these reformers. "To Canada," a variation on the well-established Confederation ode, explicitly takes issue with the traditional ideals of the nation-builders:

> . . . Love thee? Ay, love thee and mourn
> That the crown of thy glory is dross.
> Tinsel and bunting and smoke
> Are not of greatness the pledge.

Among those late Victorian poets whose work retains most literary value, Archibald Lampman and D. C. Scott were almost alone in demonstrating social and ideological concerns of an unorthodox nature. Both reputedly took part in Fabian discussion groups in Ottawa; both wrote poems of revolutionary or utopian inspiration. The title of Scott's second book of verse, *Labor and the Angel* (1896), is a sign of his temper and interest at this period: his sympathy with the underprivileged and dismay and indignation at social squalor and injustice were evidently strong; but after 1900 Scott turned away almost entirely in his verse from social preoccupations. Lampman is a more complex case, for throughout his briefer poetic career he vacillated between the claims of a mild, retiring, sensitive nature-loving temperament and a socially oriented, ambitious, puritanical will—between the idealized rural landscape and the mechanized and vulgarized city, between romantic reverie and social protest. "The City of the End of Things" is a nightmare projection of contemporary industrial civilization; "The Land of Pallas" offers the alternative vision: a utopian society based on idealistic communism. In between nightmare and dream are such direct daylight attacks on the perversions of modern commercial society as "To a Millionaire" and "Epitaph on a Rich Man." Because he is known by his best work, his meditative nature poetry, Lampman has been condemned for turning his back on the contemporary scene, a curious fate for the poet probably most inclined of any of the Group of the Sixties to social analysis, commentary, and protest.

As we have seen, most of the cultivated writers in the years following Confederation accepted and did not seriously explore the social implications of the National Policy and the nation-building programme. In the same period, however, a radical critique of it began to emerge, paradoxically, from that group whose strength and size seemed especially to depend on its success: the working class. The working class had appeared for the first time as a significant national force in the Nine Hour Movement in 1872, finding its voice in the weekly newspaper, the *Ontario Workman*. From then on a proletarian spirit can be seen evolving in the small radical labour press which struggled to support the interests of that class. First there was a simple desire for higher wages and shorter hours (the Nine Hour Movement); then there was the phase of growing class consciousness and eclectic interest in such social theories as those of Henry George, the Knights of Labor, and Edward Bellamy; and later came more dogmatic and exclusive ideologies based on communist and socialist principles. The proletarian spirit from the 1870's to the 1890's manifested itself in disillusion with and radical criticism of the programme of nation-building, and in an inclination to associate the patriotic forces which supported the National Policy with the motives and methods of capitalist exploitation. "Patriotism indeed!" cried the editor of the *Palladium of Labor* (Hamilton) in 1883:

It is all very well for the millionaire, for the Government pensioner, for the oil-tongued politician, and the full-paunched bourgeois to be patriotic. They have reason to—the country has filled their pockets. Its laws are made in their interests. Its institutions permit them to plunder the poor with impunity. Let them throw off their hats and cheer for the Queen or Canadian independence as they prefer; but as for the mass of humanity, they have little to care the toss of a copper what form the Government assumes, or whether we are ruled from Ottawa, Downing Street, or Washington. (Dec. 1, 1883)

Simultaneously there was a growing realization, manifested in savage criticism of the "literary hacks" of "bourgeois" culture (among them "Goldwin Smith, that notorious corrupter of public opinion" *Labor Union*, Sept. 1, 1883), that culture was no mere veneer to grace the lives of the upper classes, but a potent force active in moulding and preserving the social structure. A writer in the *Palladium of Labor* had this realization in mind when he expressed the hope that "the literature of the future will be the powerful ally of Democracy and Labor Reform, instead of the prop and buttress of every form of legalized wrong and injustice" (Aug. 29, 1885). And the editor of the *Labor Union* saw the labour press as a propaganda agent for the insurgent working class: "They should be led to see that the ultimate object in view is not merely to tinker and patch a rotten and corrupt social system, but to replace it by a better and juster one" (March 3, 1883).

The enemies against which the labour press particularly fought were the class interests implied in the National Policy's protective tariff ("Protection for Labor as well as for Capital" was the worker's cry); snobbery; that callous indifference to the underprivileged which was masked by the doctrine of *laissez-faire* individualism; and the harnessing of evolutionary science and capitalistic social philosophy in what has since been called Social Darwinism: the theory that beneficent effects result from competition and the survival of the fittest in human society. The editor of the *Labor Union* did his best to demolish this last pernicious theory: "To accept the doctrines of the survival of the fittest as applied to present industrial conditions is simply to put a premium upon greed, cunning, injustice and dishonesty—and to stamp the virtues and graces which alone make life endurable as so many hinderances to advancement." Against the tenacious doctrines of *laissez-faire*, the labour press opposed evidence of growing "collectivism" in society and the idealistic communal theories of the Knights of Labor and Henry George. Against the indifference of the haves to the have-nots, they opposed the Christian socialist vision: "a religious society recognizing the Fatherhood of God and the Brotherhood of Man, and insisting justice to the Toiler be the outcome" *Labor Union*, Oct. 27, 1883). The radicals of the eighties recognized fully how remote they were from any of the political platforms of the day, but their strength lay in their faith that "the 'Utopian visions' of today are the established facts of tomorrow" (*Palladium of Labor*, April 25, 1885).

The *Labor Advocate* of the 1890's was the vehicle for a less utopian idealism. Its readers were brought in touch with radical movements elsewhere in the world by weekly "Socialist Notes," along with accounts of Edward Bellamy's "Nationalism" propounded in *Looking Backward* (1888) and in other works, of the limitations of Henry George's theories, and of the ideas of the newly emerging Fabian society. T. Phillips Thompson (1843–1933), editor and most eloquent polemicist of the *Labor Advocate*, propagandized for a radical solution to economic evils: "no permanent or satisfying solution is possible which does not change the underlying conditions of industrial servitude, by an entire reorganization of the system of distribution." Elsewhere, in his book *The Politics of Labor* (1887), Thompson had already launched a vigorous attack on the exploiting capitalist class and in particular on the attitudes embodied in the culture and traditions which support it—"the bitter hostility of the supercilious and cynical 'culture' which apes European models and cultivates undemocratic habits of thought, from the ranks of which capitalism recruits its host of literary hirelings and professional henchmen" (p. 143). His main target, however, was the doctrine of Social Darwinism and all it entailed, and Thompson subjected the conclusions of Herbert Spencer, leading spokesman of those who applied evolutionary determinism to man's social life, to a destructive analysis, using Spencer's own ideas to arrive at opposite conclusions. With the uninhibited and vehement protests of such writers as Thompson, it is obvious that the developments of a quarter of a century since the *Ontario Workman* of 1875 had carried proletarian ideology a long way.

During these early stages of Canadian radicalism, the potential power of literature was gradually realized. Seeds of the understanding were already present in the *Ontario Workman*. For despite the editorial view that creative writing was mere entertainment and diversion from the troubles of daily life ("In these columns we will be invited now and then to turn aside from the turmoil and strife of the world, and find peaceful enjoyment"), the newspaper published a good deal of didactic and hortatory doggerel in favour of the workingman's cause, and, beginning on June 27, 1872, one lengthy and notable piece of fiction, the serialized economic novel, *The Other Side*, by a trade unionist and leader in the Canadian Nine Hour Movement, M. A. Foran. A melodramatic tale of factory life, trade unionism, and the eventual triumph of the labour movement over the tyrannical oppression of the capitalist class, it is noteworthy as an early fictional critique of industrial urban society, its class divisions and its economic basis, though it never escapes the limitations of the "bourgeois" novel and its aesthetic qualities are modest to say the least. In the 1880's the pages of the *Labor Union* and the *Palladium of Labor* are adorned with a variety of revolutionary verse, from imported traditional gleanings like Shelley's "Men of Labour" and the Chartist poems of Vincent, Jones, and Massey, to contemporary and local pieces, many written especially for these labour journals: utopian idealism, chiliastic vision, indignation at social injustice, exhortations of general and specific kinds, most of them betraying their semi-literate origins all too clearly. The *Labor Advocate* in the 1890's cast a wider net for English and American literature, and included Chartist verse, selected poems by sympathetic writers like Whitman and William Morris, an economic novel by Ignatius Donnelly printed serially, excerpts from Edward Bellamy. Its editor, Phillips Thompson, was himself a poet of sorts: "The Political Economist and the Tramp" is a facetious exposure of the Social Darwinist fallacy; "Always with You" is a bitter attack on the church's support of the economic *status quo* ("the poor shall always be with you"); and *The Labor Reform Songster* (1892) is a collection of Knights of Labor chants and battle hymns. Worthy of notice too is the *Palladium* series "Our Social Club," in which the anonymous author sets out to provide a Spectator Club for Canadian workers, to entertain his readers with fictional meetings involving a range of typical workers, while at the same time exploring and propagating radical social and political doctrines.

Both in theory and in practice proletarian literature grew in complexity through the 1870's, 1880's, and 1890's. In quality it rarely rose above the level of the crude, naive, sentimental, or melodramatic. But its existence is worth recording because it remained alive to a range of ideals and social experiences largely ignored by the respectable Canadian tradition of the period, and awareness of it places that main tradition in a truer perspective.

II

The causes and nature of Canada's spectacular "boom" beginning about 1896 and lasting with varying intensity for two decades are now generally understood. International and domestic circumstances combined to send a wave of immigration breaking over the empty western prairies, and eastern industries strained and expanded to meet the new demands. It was a time of immense enthusiasm and optimism, succeeding the discouragements of the post-Confederation era. "As the 19th century was that of the United States,"

Wilfrid Laurier proclaimed, "so I think the 20th century shall be filled by Canada." Big business enthusiasts, noting happily the rise of great trusts and corporate enterprises, praised the workings of social evolution in which this process appeared to be a late stage. "If we except a certain class of American politician," wrote a contributor to the *Canadian Magazine* in 1900 (XIV, 243 ff.), "we shall be able to find few persons who are unwilling to believe that trusts are a natural growth, and are the result of a process of evolution." The expansive spirit of the times was caught by poets and novelists like Service, Stead, MacInnes, and Stringer, who were undismayed by the moral and social upheavals of rapid material and population growth. "Sweet is the breath of the prairie," Stead chanted, "where peace and prosperity reign, / And joyous the song of the city, where all is expansion and gain."

Not everyone was so enthusiastic, however. At another extreme the agrarian evangelist Peter McArthur bitterly attacked big business in all its aspects, condemned the growth of mechanistic urban society, and sang the praises of the fast disappearing rural Eden where individualism flourished and farming was a way of life, not a commercial enterprise. A less utopian writer, Stephen Leacock, stood as firmly as McArthur for the cause of individualism and the quietness and simplicity of life being devoured and destroyed by rampant commercial and industrial expansion. The crudeness and stupidities of the new plutocracy are pilloried unmercifully in *Arcadian Adventures with the Idle Rich* (1914), and in *Sunshine Sketches of a Little Town* the virtues of Mariposa are opposed, albeit with whimsy and satire as well as nostalgia, to the corruptions of the big city which it so foolishly tries to imitate. Still others, like the poetess Marjorie Pickthall, shut out the turmoil and noise of contemporary reality altogether to create a fairer dream-world, or like D. C. Scott in "Ode for the Keats Centenary" lamented the flight of "Beauty" from the modern world, "that grew too loud and wounding."

The working classes reached out for their share in the new material prosperity. Trade unions rapidly increased in size and numbers. Internecine battles and ideological disagreements were numerous, but for the most part Canadian unions travelled the path of "business unionism" rather than of political action, that is, the American rather than the British path. But radical workers' parties also sprang up in the era of the boom, and new radical newspapers appeared to give them voice across the country. Though now largely forgotten, sects and schisms in confusing numbers propagandized vigorously in their journals and in public meetings, spreading, for the most part on still barren soil, the doctrines of socialism and communism. In general, despite the extreme dissidence of these dissenters among themselves, it can be said that they looked upon their beliefs as "hard" socialism rather than "soft"— that is, they aimed to be practical in their political and industrial warfare, not utopian dreamers as they saw their predecessors. Second, they were for the most part infected by the evolutionary optimism of "Canada's century," so that they believed in an inevitable movement towards socialism, however unsympathetic the immediate climate—in other words they were proletarian Social Darwinists. "Today," J. Connell argued in "Socialism and the Survival of the Fittest" in the *Western Clarion* in April 1913, "capitalist individualism seems firmly rooted and strongly knit, but the laws of nature are fighting on our side. . . . The time is coming when the waves of the evolutionary tide will break and roar far, very far above it."

The "scientific" or "hard" socialist was interested in the works of Marx, Engels, Sidney Webb, the Fabian Shaw, but was less sympathetic to imaginative literature than his more utopian predecessors. "The Scientific Socialist," wrote one of the Canadian radicals in *The Lance* (Oct. 9, 1909), "unlike his utopian brothers, is not an artist." And the editor of the *Western Clarion* grumbled, "we have no particular desire to pick any quarrel with working-class poets, but we think that straight plain prose is about the best form in which our views can be presented to the proletaire" (Feb. 14, 1914). Nevertheless, in the area of the shorter lyric a large number of proletarian poetasters were active, including at least two whose main work for the radical cause was as party organizers and lecturers: Alfred Budden and Wilfred Gribble. The career of the latter apparently ended in 1916 when he was arrested on charges of sedition while speaking for socialism in the streets of Saint John, New Brunswick.

It will be recognized that political radicalism in Canada has a history going back well before the Russian Revolution, which in 1917 inevitably established itself as the centre of attraction or repulsion for all revolutionary theory and practice in modern times. Between Confederation and the First World War the processes of nation-building were occupying the energies and idealism of the majority of Canadians largely to the exclusion of questions of equality, social justice, and welfare, and only in the small radical press do we find vigorous and uninhibited criticism of the social, political, and economic patterns being laid down. By the end of World War I, however, most of the goals of the National Policy were within reach or attained—the East-West communications had been developed, the West was populated through soaring immigration, home industries had flourished to make Canada, by 1920, a predominantly urban country. Radical criticism of its nature could now be entertained without endangering national existence, and for the first time a critique emerged not merely from the dissident minority among the working classes, but from the respectable middle class intellectuals who had earlier remained aloof.

The optimistic and jingoistic spirit of "Canada's century" which characterized the early 1900's and the World War I period continued into the 1920's. But though the commercial nationalism of the Canadian Manufacturers Association (Buy Canadian Goods) and of the Canadian Authors Association (Buy Canadian Books) was typical, there was also a new and more demanding patriotism, where concern with country was coupled with an earnest desire to see and remedy shortcomings. It is this kind of patriotism which provided the adjective for the titles of such new intellectual journals as the *Canadian Forum* (1920–   ) and the *Canadian Mercury* (1928–29). The older attitudes found their home in journals like *Willison's Monthly*, also born in the 1920's, which was devoted to the "upbuilding of Canada" through such traditional means as higher tariff protection, buying Canadian goods, and lower taxes on capital. This journal deplored the rise of aggressive democracy, Bolshevism, and the "Jazz psychology" of modern writing. "Repose, conservatism, and stability" are what the world desires, wrote the editor in 1925; and the journal found these ideals in contemplation of the real or imagined nineteenth-century past and in the literary and social amenities of the genteel tradition.

The vital spirit of the 1920's, however, was not retrospective and nostalgic but critical. *The Rebel*, the University of Toronto magazine appearing in 1917, had as its purpose "an honest criticism of things as they are" (I, Feb.). It matured into the *Canadian Forum*, of which the chief aim was "to secure a freer and more informed discussion of public questions" (Oct., 1920). The social philosophy of the *Canadian Forum*'s editorial board was acknowledged to be "progressive," and in general the journal became a focus for those who welcomed or were sympathetic towards the new in art, social attitudes, and politics. In each area it published sufficient articles of a vigorous, witty, caustic, or iconoclastic order to justify the belief that there was indeed in progress a "revolt of the 1920's." By the late 1920's a new journal, the *Canadian Mercury*, announced an even more emancipated critical spirit. Its chief objects of attack were the inhibitions and narrowness of "respectable" Canadian social life and of the Maple Leaf School of writers; its aim was "the emancipation of Canadian literature from the state of amiable mediocrity and insipidity in which it now languishes" (Dec., 1928).

The post-World War I mood of disillusion was an international phenomenon; but local reasons for the growth of a critical spirit among Canadian intellectuals in the 1920's are not far to seek. The Royal Commission on Industrial Relations which published its report on Canada's miniature Russian Revolution, the Winnipeg Strike of 1919 (see the *Canadian Annual Review*) listed at length social evils which were only added to in the 1920's and 1930's, and which were sure signs not only of the impact of the war, but that all the problems of a contemporary industrial urban civilization had arrived in Canada as part of her nationhood. The 1920's were indeed a decade of ferment. The failure of the Winnipeg Strike split the radicals into revolutionary and evolutionary camps, the former eventually leading into Tim

Buck's communism, the latter into Woodsworth's socialism, the Cooperative Commonwealth Federation, and the League for Social Reconstruction of the 1930's. Out of the same ferment the western farmers made their powerful but short-lived protest against eastern big-business ascendancy with the Progressive party. Though in the 1920's the intellectuals continued to remain aloof from political commitments of a radical kind, it is not surprising to find a writer advertising in an article in the *Canadian Mercury* in March of 1928, "Wanted—a Gospel," and lamenting that everywhere Canadians "are searching and wavering, losing one ideal after another, waiting vainly for the stimulus which would be provided by initiation into some combination of writers, poets, and all people with the vision of a socially progressive Canada." A gospel was indeed soon to be found (though, incidentally, not to that same writer's liking) when the calamity of the Great Depression abruptly descended on the land. The aesthetic and moral revolt of certain intellectuals of the 1920's became, in the dark years of the 1930's, aggressively political. The critical tools of Marxism were discovered and seized upon as answering a great need, and economic and political theories once only of interest to a small minority of the lower orders of society became palatable and even desirable to large numbers in every walk of life. The first socially committed organization of radical intellectuals, the League for Social Reconstruction, set to work to articulate a radical social philosophy to meet the challenges of the Depression, and it had an important contribution to make to that fusing of proletarian, agrarian, and old-time socialist rebels in the C.C.F. party in 1933. In the 1930's what had been an insignificant proletarian minority swelled in numbers and power and became, for the first time, of major literary and cultural significance.

The *Canadian Forum* reported the activities of the new left wing with sympathy, and indeed for a short period fell under the sway of the L.S.R., but generally it lived up to its name and provided a forum in which critical discussion could take place. From the pens of left-of-centre intellectuals, especially from that witty, vital, and provocative professor of history, F. H. Underhill, came a critical commentary on Canadian society and politics which had vigour and acuteness rarely achieved before. But angrier and more aggressive periodicals emerged in the 1930's to satisfy the needs of extremists. For two years (1932–34) *Masses* acted as a spokesman for the revolutionary proletariat, preaching Marxist doctrine with considerable violence and lashing its enemies to the right without restraint. *New Frontier* (begun in 1936) was more temperate and literate, but equally distinguishable from the *Canadian Forum*, as its attack on that journal's middle-left affiliation made clear enough: "the depression-born Canadian social democratic party with its professorial brain-trusters is a rather genteel sprig clipped from the suburban hedge of British Fabianism" (April, 1936). Unlike the *Canadian Forum*,

New Frontier purported to be fully engaged in the contemporary political scene. Typically, in December 1936, it published a special issue on Spain, which included the replies of a number of well-known Canadians to the problem, "Where I stand on Spain." The answers, which ranged from W. A. Deacon's "we should cut clear of the Empire and the whole continent of Europe" to E. J. Pratt's "My sympathies in the Spanish situation are wholly with the Popular Front," give a lively indication of the extent to which Canadian society was divided by the international and ideological debate between left- and right-wing ideas and attitudes.

The collapse of the Spanish Loyalists, the triumph of European fascism, and the non-aggression pact between Soviet Russia and Germany in 1939 were blows felt alike by moderate and extreme social revolutionaries in Canada. But soon the *deus ex machina* of global war appeared to close the dying action of this era, and to unravel in its own effective way those tangled social problems of the country which the dialectic of ideas had left unsolved. A remarkable change had taken place, however, in the temper of Canadian thought from the years following Confederation to the years of the Great Depression. In those earlier days any serious social concerns of the intellectual were likely to be associated with or conditioned by nationalism in one of its possible forms. Differences in social ideals were slight, or if they were not, the pressures were all towards making them appear decorously so. Conciliation and compromise were the key notes of public discussion, and basic principles tended to be assumed rather than considered. But in the 1920's and 1930's a range and violence of opinion not imagined before appeared to be possible and indeed to be demanded. Conflicting theories of art and social life were thrust forward with urgency and vehemence, while both domestic and international social realities became inescapable.

Already in the twenties there had been a critical reaction against the poetry of romantic sensibility in favour of the literature of ideas, social realism, and even naturalism. When in the 1930's the break with the nineteenth century tradition was intensified, debate raged as to the nature and validity of Marxist theories of art. Interpretations of proletarian aesthetics were numerous and subtle enough to constitute a new scholasticism, but it is true that many of the better Canadian writers of the time were in agreement at least to the extent of endorsing the literature of social conscience. Few revolutionaries or fellow travellers went so far as Earle Birney who argued in the *Canadian Forum* that art must temporarily cease until revolutionary action had built a new society where true creativity was possible, but just as few writers remained at the opposite pole with Robert Finch, whose verse exhibited a controlled aestheticism and formalism justifying his manifesto: "Beauty my fond fine care." By the middle thirties Canadian literary theory had swung away from "escapist" or "pure" subjective art towards a conception of art as propagandizing for or at least symptomatic of social revolution. The Victorian Canadian assumption that art was the product and ornament of a social and cultural élite had found its antithesis in the belief that the only vital art was derived from the insurgent lower orders of society. Upper- and middle-class culture had met its opposite, proletarian culture.

From the mid-twenties the gulf between proletarian ideals and aspirations and the sympathy of men and women of culture and talent can be seen closing. By the latter part of the decade poems and stories began to appear in the journals of the intellectuals which reflect an increased concern for the condition of the lower orders of society, farmers and labourers and their way of life. The new "angry" note ("sharp shame and dim anger, / Anger at civilization," as B. H. Chambers in "Nocturne" put it in the *Canadian Forum*, XII, 1931–32), is sounded frequently in the *Forum* and consistently in the *Canadian Mercury*, both in poetry and in the stories, where the marks of psychological and sociological realism and a willingness to see things as they are, however unpleasant, appear as never before. With Vernal House's "Eternity goes down the sewer" (*Masses*, I, 1932) and Leo Kennedy's "Life's like a garbage can" (*Canadian Mercury*, June 1928) the alleged complacencies of the Victorian era received their quietus.

As the events of the 1930's proceeded to channel this critical reaction along ideological lines, the impact on both poetry and prose was marked. There appeared numerous examples of "reportage," a new prose form defined in the popular American anthology, *Proletarian Literature* (1935) in this way:

> Reportage is three-dimensional reporting. The writer not only condenses reality; he must get his readers to see and feel the facts. The best writers of reportage do their editorializing via their artistry. . . . Reportage . . . requires delineation of character, of locale, of atmosphere. (P. 211.)

Dorothy Livesay was one of the best practitioners of this genre, as her intense sketch "Corbin—A Company Town Fights for its Life" in *New Frontier* (April 1936) illustrates, but it was a much used form. It required a certain discipline: a balance between editorializing and artistry, an eye for vivid and telling detail, powers of concentration. Its significance was not so much in itself, however, as in the movement which it symptomized and encouraged: the movement towards contemporaneity and realism in fiction. The result was the early domination of fiction, for the first time in Canadian literary history, by contemporary themes. The Depression short story, dealing with unemployment, its causes and consequences, flourished in the early thirties, to such an extent that readers of the *Canadian Forum*, *Masses*, and *New Frontier* became sated and bored. Most writers of the day tried their hand at the form, among them F. P. Grove, A. M. Klein, Morley Callaghan, M. Q. Innis, L. B. Creighton. Grove and Callaghan showed even more vividly in their novels the impact of the Depression and its ideological debates.

Grove's *Master of the Mill*, with its symbolic exploration of the chief contemporary "isms," is in certain respects the most penetrating ideological
analysis to come out of the writing of the thirties. Callaghan, from the shabby
urban naturalism of *Strange Fugitive* (1928) to the troubled dialectics of
They Shall Inherit the Earth (1935), took his settings, actions, and themes
from the contemporary Canadian scene. Grove and Callaghan both strove for
artistic detachment in their works, but the result is a searing protest against
the rottenness of the social and political structure of the day. Fictional
exploitation of this period is likely to continue as its significance becomes
easier to hold in perspective. The direct and savagely indignant protests of
Irene Baird's *Waste Heritage* (1939) have no doubt permanently given way
to the subtler and more profound probings and ironies of works like Gabrielle
Roy's *The Tin Flute* and Hugh MacLennan's *Watch That Ends the Night*,
but recent novelists (Ethel Wilson, John Marlyn, Earle Birney, Roger
Lemelin) have drawn attention to rather than exhausted the richness of the
material.

The leftward swing of the 1930's produced no more permanently valuable
poetry than prose, but here the impact is easier to trace, and in many respects
is more striking, for the Depression era was like an intense magnetic field that
deflected the courses of all the poets who went through it. (That poet
laureate of communism, J. S. Wallace, had already set his course long before
the Great Depression.) A few like Dorothy Livesay, Leo Kennedy, and
Abraham Klein underwent a sudden and dramatic veering. Dorothy Livesay,
seeking to "see with the sun's bright honesty," accepted almost overnight the
Marxian answer to the current social chaos, and dedicated her art to the
revolutionary cause. Like her, Kennedy and Klein turned their backs on "pure
poetry" to write hortatory chants and indignant diatribes for the insurgent
proletariat. These two, along with F. R. Scott, whose socialism and social
satire pre-date the Depression era, justify the symbolical title of the mid-
thirties anthology, *New Provinces*, in which they appeared, in company with
Finch, A. J. M. Smith, and E. J. Pratt. Even the last two of these more conservative poets showed clearly in their verse the pressure of the Depression
ethos. Social injustice and disorder; poverty and suffering among the underprivileged; greed and complacency in high places; the concepts and theories
of reform and revolution: these had become the dominant subject-matter of
Canadian literature.

In the early 1920's A. J. M. Smith and others were deploring the Canadian writer's inhibitions, his lack of freedom in the choice and treatment of
subjects, and the reluctance of Canadian readers, critics, and authors alike to
accept the elements of realism and satire in literature. But in the 1930's the
realistic mode, the cynical pose, and the weapons of satire were exploited to
their fullest. For many the immediate result was a new ideological enslave-

ment. Much of the literature of the Hungry Thirties has little purely aesthetic value and therefore it has understandably been forgotten by its original readers, perhaps even by its writers. But to ignore it is to ignore work which, for some of the chief writers of the present day, "has significance for the authors in the evolution of their own understanding"—to adopt a phrase from the introduction to *New Provinces*. After the 1930's a wide range and freedom were seen to have been won. The old debate about the degree to which a writer should be personally involved in society and committed to an ideology was not over, yet demands upon the artist to be socially committed were not likely to be so naive again nor attacks on "aestheticism" so crude. Taboos with respect to subjects and themes and modes still remained, but the potential range of art in matter and in manner was immeasurably increased. The "new provinces" of radicalism brought disillusion, but their exploration was a cathartic experience for Canadian writers. The conservative culture of nation-building met in full dialectical play the art and politics of protest and rebellion, and each was transformed by the collision. "A culture is not a flow, nor even a confluence," Lionel Trilling has argued in *The Liberal Imagination*; "the form of its existence is struggle, or at least debate—it is nothing if not a dialectic." If this is true, the late emergence of a vigorous literature of protest heralded the emancipation and the maturity of Canadian culture.

BIBLIOGRAPHY AND NOTES

INDEX

Bibliography and Notes

SPECIAL BIBLIOGRAPHIES, BY CHAPTERS

EDITORS' NOTE: As a general rule, footnotes to the chapters were avoided in favour of inclusion in the text of all relevant material and an indication of the sources of most references and quotations. For some chapters, therefore, no additional notes are supplied. For others, the reader will find in this section the contributors' lists of the most useful printed sources which they have consulted, together with their suggestions for further reading.

The appropriate items in Watters' *Check List* and in our "General Bibliography" should be consulted for each chapter of this *Literary History*; abbreviations in the notes (e.g. Staton and Tremaine) refer to such items.

CHAPTER 1. THE VOYAGERS

Many books have been written about the voyages to the New World in the sixteenth and seventeenth centuries, and only a few of them can be mentioned here.

Of the numerous bibliographies of early Americana, two that I have found especially useful are: E. G. Cox's *A Reference Guide to the Literature of Travel*, vol. II, *The New World* (Seattle: University of Washington Press, 1938), and Joseph Sabin's *A Dictionary of Books relating to America from its Discovery to the Present Time* (29 vols.; Amsterdam: N. Israel, 1961–62). An excellent guide to manuscript material is *A Guide to Manuscripts Relating to America in Great Britain and Ireland*, edited by B. R. Crick and Miriam Alman (London: British Association for American Studies, 1961). Watters' *Check List* is of little use for sixteenth- and seventeenth-century source material because only one item in it, Robert Hayman's *Quodlibets* . . . (London, 1628), is dated earlier than the year 1700.

The most valuable collections of voyage literature are, of course, those of Hakluyt and Purchas, both of which have been printed in twentieth-century editions. Richard Hakluyt's *The Principal Navigations, Voyages, Traffiques & Discoveries of the English Nation* was published by Maclehose (12 vols.; Glasgow, 1903–5) and by Dent (London, 1927–28). There is also a cheap Everyman edition. Samuel Purchas's *Hakluytus Posthumous or Purchas His Pilgrimes* was published by Maclehose (20 vols.; Glasgow, 1905–7). The publications of the Hakluyt Society (London, 1849–   ) provide further accounts of the voyages, some of them not in Hakluyt or Purchas. An unpublished doctoral dissertation by William Beckler White, "The Narrative Technique of Elizabethan Voyage and Travel Literature from 1550 to 1603" (Lehigh University, 1955) is useful in its assessment of the literary merits of voyage literature in the second half of the sixteenth century.

Boies Penrose's *Travel and Discovery in the Renaissance, 1420–1620* gives a good survey of two hundred years of travel in different parts of the world, but it is annoying for the serious student to find that Penrose does not give the sources for so much of his information. Of more relevance to students of Canadian history and literature is the sometimes inaccurate and biased, but nevertheless valuable, *A History of Newfoundland* (London: Eyre and Spottiswoode, 1896) by D. W. Prowse, and *A Historical Geography of the British Colonies*, vol. V, Part IV, *Newfoundland* (Oxford: Clarendon Press, 1931), by J. D. Rogers. G. P. Insh's *Scottish Colonial Schemes, 1620–1686* (Glasgow: Maclehose, Jackson & Co., 1922) deals with Scottish settlements in Nova Scotia and in other parts of the New World. Two books by R. R. Cawley, *The Voyagers and Elizabethan Drama* (Boston: Modern Language Association of America, 1938), and *Unpathed Waters: Studies of the Influence of the Voyagers on Elizabethan Literature* (Princeton: Princeton University Press, 1940), deal with the impact of the voyagers on the literature of sixteenth- and seventeenth-century England, and contain useful bibliographies.

NOTES

1 (p. 3). *The First Three English Books on America*, ed. Edward Arber (Birmingham, 1885), 71.

2 (p. 3). *The Plays and Poems of Robert Greene*, ed. J. Churton Collins (Oxford, 1905), I, 224. Edmund Waller, *The Poems*, ed. G. Thorn Drury (London, n.d. [1893]), I, 67.

3 (p. 5). It is unlikely, I think, that more than three or four hundred copies of such large and expensive volumes as *The Principal Navigations* were printed. We know very little about the numbers of individual editions of books printed during the Elizabethan period, but "of John Dee's *General and Rare Memorials pertaining to the Art of Navigation*, 1577, as we know from a statement in the dedication, only 100 copies were printed." See R. B. McKerrow, *An Introduction to Bibliography* (Oxford, 1951), 131–32.

4 (p. 5). J. Holland Rose, *The Cambridge History of the British Empire* (Cambridge, 1929–   ), I, 96; R. B. Nye and J. E. Morpurgo, *A History of the United States* (Penguin Books, 1955), I, 20.

5 (p. 5). For a brief discussion of the map and globe, see George Bruner Parks, *Richard Hakluyt and the English Voyages* (New York, 1928), 186.

6 (p. 5). The broadside ballads were an ephemeral form of "literature" and the majority of them have probably been lost. It is, also, sometimes difficult to decide whether a ballad is *primarily* or *incidentally* about the New World. By my calculations, however, there were 32 ballads about the Northern Rebellion and 25 about the New World. Hyder E. Rollins, *An Analytical Index to the Ballad Entries (1557–1709) in the Registers of the Company of London* (University of North Carolina Press, 1924), lists 24 ballads on the New World and 27 on the Northern Rebellion. V. de Sola Pinto and A. E. Rodway, *The Common Muse* (London, 1957), write: "no less than a hundred ballads were licensed at Stationers' Hall for publication in 1569–70 alone, and about three-quarters of them dealt with the Northern Rebellion" (p. 17).

7 (p. 6). Rastell's *New Interlude* was edited by W. C. Hazlitt in Dodsley's *Old English Plays* (4th ed.; London, 1874–76), vol. I, and often reprinted.

8 (p. 7). William Beckler White, "The Narrative Technique of Elizabethan Voyage and Travel Literature from 1550 to 1603" (unpub. doct. diss., Lehigh University 1955), finds that 54 out of 176 accounts (some not in Hakluyt) have "significant literary merit."

9 (p. 8). *Ibid.*, 579, 587.

10 (p. 9). Howard Mumford Jones, "The Image of the New World," in *Elizabethan Studies and Other Essays in Honor of George R. Reynolds* (Boulder, Colorado, 1945), 68.

11 (p. 9). *Roxburghe Ballads*, ed. J. W. Ebsworth (London, 1877), VI, 377. Another, and slightly different, version is preserved in Ashmolean MS. 36 in the Bodleian Library. De Sola Pinto and Rodway reprint the MS. version in *The Common Muse*, 39–40.

12 (p. 9). Ashmolean MS. 208; reprinted in *Ballads from Manuscripts*, ed. W. B. Morfill (London, 1873), 282–83. Another poem, "A Commendation of Martin Frobisher," in the same MS., and reprinted in the same volume (pp. 284–85), seems to be of later date.

13 (p. 10). References to Zuniga, Rich, and Price may be found in Alexander Brown, *The Genesis of the United States* (London, 1890), I, 147, 312–16, respectively.

14 (p. 11). Marc Lescarbot, *The History of New France* (3 vols.), English translation by W. L. Grant, introduced by H. P. Biggar (Toronto: Champlain Society, 1907–14). Part of Lescarbot's work was translated into English by P. Erondelle (London, 1609), under the title of *Nova Francia*.

15 (p. 11). *The Works of Samuel de Champlain* (6 vols.), ed. H. P. Biggar *et al.* (Toronto: Champlain Soc., 1922–36).

16 (p. 11). *Travels and Explorations of the Jesuit Missionaries in New France* (73 vols.), ed. R. G. Thwaites (Cleveland, 1896–1901).

17 (p. 11). Mason Wade, *The French Canadians: 1760–1945* (London, 1955), 25.

18 (p. 11). Donald Creighton, *Dominion of the North* (Toronto, 1957), 128.

19 (p. 12). Helmut Kallmann, *A History of Music in Canada, 1534–1914* (University of Toronto Press, 1960), 25.

20 (p. 12). *The Voyages and Colonising Enterprises of Sir Humphrey Gilbert*, ed. D. B. Quinn (London: Hakluyt Soc., 1940), 440.

21 Guy's letter may be read in *Purchas His Pilgrimes*, published originally in 1625 (in the edition of 1905–7, xix, 410–16).

22 (p. 14). For a brief discussion of the problem as to who wrote the first verse in English in North America, see Richard Beale Davis, *George Sandys: Poet Adventurer* (London, 1955), 225–26. Sandys' *Ovid* was, of course, a translation. Davis considers Vaughan as a candidate, but Mark Eccles, "A Biographical Dictionary of Elizabethan Authors," *H.L.Q.*, V, 286, writes that he "can find no evidence that Vaughan crossed the Atlantic at all."

23 (p. 15). George Pratt Insh, *Scottish Colonial Schemes, 1620–1686* (Glasgow, 1922), p. 43.

24 (p. 16). J. L. Lowes, *The Road to Xanadu* (London, 1930), 337, 133.

25 (p. 17). Bacon and Drummond are quoted by R. R. Cawley, *The Voyagers and Elizabethan Drama* (Boston, 1938), 310n, 352n.

26 (p. 17). "Englands Honour Revived. By the valiant exploytes of Captain *Kirke*, and his adherents, who with three Ships, *viz.* the *Abigaile* Admirall, the *Charitie* vice Admirall, and the *Elizabeth* the reare Admirall: did many admirable exploytes: as is exactly showne in the iusuing [*sic*] story." This broadside ballad was written by "M[athew] P[arker]" and "Printed for M. Trundle, Widdow" in 1628. It was edited by J. Stevens Cox and reprinted by the Toucan Press, Beaminster, Dorset, England, in 1964. "Here, celebrated in a hundred and thirty two lines of jovial pedestrian verse, is a tribute to the first expedition to Canada of David Kirke and his two brothers who in 1628–29 drove out the French and took possession of the shores of the St. Lawrence and the fortress of Quebec for the English Crown."

27 (p. 17). Gilbert Chinard, *L'Amérique et le rêve exotique* (Paris, 1934), 169.

28 (p. 18). For a full account of the visit of the Indian kings see Richmond P. Bond, *Queen Anne's American Kings* (Oxford, 1952).

CHAPTER 2. EXPLORERS BY LAND (TO 1867)

There is almost no literary criticism published on the writings of Canadian explorers. Ray Palmer Baker's *History of Canadian Literature to the Confederation* (1920) contains a brief and sketchy chapter on the subject, as does Thomas Guthrie Marquis's *English-Canadian Literature* (1913), a reprint from *Canada and Its Provinces*. Historical works sometimes give hints in passing about the literary quality of their sources, or show some literary appreciation in their choice of quotations. Such works include Arthur S. Morton's *History of the Canadian West* (1939 and to be reissued), E. E. Rich's *History of the Hudson's Bay Company* (1958–59), John Bartlet Brebner's *The Explorers of North America* (1933), Jeanette Mirsky's *To the Arctic!* (1948) and Leslie H. Neatby's *In Quest of the North West Passage* (1958). Also, editors of particular texts sometimes show appreciation of their character as literature, for instance, Richard Glover in his edition of Hearne's *Journey to the Northern Ocean* (1958). Similarly, some biographical studies such as Grace Lee Nute's *Caesars of the Wilderness* (1943) yield hints.

Among bibliographies Marie Tremaine's *A Bibliography of Canadian Imprints* (1952) and *Arctic Bibliography* (1953–   ) are very useful, as are also Lorne Pierce's *An Outline of Canadian Literature* (1927) and Watters' *Check List*. However, none of these can be considered as giving a complete list of either primary or secondary works about Canadian exploration. Several studies, such as some mentioned in the first paragraph, or Catherine M. White's *David Thompson's Journals Relating to Montana* (1950) contain useful special or background bibliographies.

In many ways the literature of Canadian exploration is more extensive than the chapters concerned indicate. Many journals and narratives written before 1860 are not referred to, although perhaps they deserve mention. Such omissions may be due to ignorance or oversight, but in many cases I feel that the material is of slight literary interest. Examples are the journals of Philip Turnor and the letters of John Henry Lefroy, although they have some importance in history and geographical science. In discussing early naturalists, Philip Akrigg's article "The Naturalists Discover British Columbia" (*B.C. Historical News*, November 1972) was most helpful. In an introduction to a reprint (1973) of Margaret McNaughton's *Overland to Cariboo*, I discuss the literature of the Cariboo gold rush and the Overlanders.

CHAPTER 3. EXPLORERS BY SEA: THE WEST COAST

In general, the note on chapter 2 applies to the ocean explorers of the West Coast. The best discussion of primary documents is F. W. Howay's 1924 address to the Royal Society of Canada, "The Early Literature of the North-West Coast," printed in the *Proceedings and Transactions of the Royal Society of Canada*, 3rd series, XVIII (1924), Section II, pp. 1–31. Although primarily an historian, Howay is alert to literary quality. Howay's other essays and introductions to editions of various works are also valuable. The most useful history is E. O. S. Scholefield's volume I of Howay and Scholefield's *British Columbia* (1914). It includes a helpful bibliography. Dorothy O. Johansen's *Empire of the Columbia* (1957) is good for background, as is Marius Barbeau's *Pathfinders in the North Pacific* (1958). Some editions of texts have valuable introductions, for example Gordon Grant's edition of *The Life and Adventures of John Nicol, Mariner* (1936).

Some readers may wish to follow up some of the topics touched on during this chapter. The question of apocryphal voyages is well treated by Henry Raup Wagner in his *Apocryphal Voyages to the Northwest Coast of America* (1931) and his *Cartography of the Northwest Coast of America* (1937). Possible early Chinese voyages to America are discussed at length but not very satisfactorily in

Edward P. Vining's *An Inglorious Columbus* (1885). W. Kaye Lamb has assembled the facts and documents about Mrs. Barkley's Diary in the *British Columbia Historical Quarterly* for January 1942. The University of British Columbia Library has photostats and microfilms of the unpublished diaries of Captain Vancouver's crews. It also has a typescript translation by William L. Schurz of a copy of Estevan's journal.

Steller's narrative (mentioned on page 42) may be read in English in the second volume of *Bering's Voyages* (1925), edited for the American Geographical Society by F. A. Golder.

CHAPTERS 8 AND 9. LITERARY ACTIVITY IN THE
CANADAS, 1812–1841 AND 1841–1880

The most useful general lists are Henry J. Morgan's *Bibliotheca Canadensis* (Ottawa, 1867); Philéas Gagnon's *Essai de bibliographie canadienne* (Vol. I, Québec, 1895); Vol. II, Montréal, 1913); Staton and Tremaine with Boyle's Supplement; Watters' *Checklist*. William Kingsford's *The Early Bibliography of the Province of Ontario* (Toronto, 1892) is interesting, but unreliable. Early writing in the Canadas (now Quebec and Ontario) was largely neglected by literary historians. Three good surveys should be mentioned: John Reade's "English Literature and Journalism in Quebec," in J. Castell Hopkins, ed., *Canada, an Encyclopedia of the Country* (Toronto, 1899, V, 147–65), and Lawrence M. Lande's *Old Lamps Aglow: An Appreciation of Early Canadian Poetry* (Montreal, 1957). Ray Palmer Baker's *A History of English-Canadian Literature to the Confederation* (Cambridge, Mass., 1920) was devoted primarily to the Maritime Provinces.

Research for these chapters brought out much detailed information about various authors which could not be included in the text. For details the reader may consult articles in *Ontario History* (the publication of the Ontario Historical Society) on Galt, Richardson, and Holmes (XLV, 1953, 155–63), on Major Richardson (XLVIII, 1956, 101–7), and on Galt (XLIX, 1957, 187–94). There are articles on Adam Kidd in *Queen's Quarterly* (LXV, 1958, 495–506); on Levi Adams in *Dalhousie Review* (XL, 1960, 34–42); and on S. H. Wilcocke in *Journal of Canadian Fiction* (II, no. 3, 1973), 13–21. Introductions to the New Canadian Library editions of Frances Brooke's *Emily Montague*, John Richardson's *Wacousta* and *"Tiger" Dunlop's Upper Canada*, Susanna Moodie's *Roughing It in the Bush*, and Rosanna Leprohon's *Antoinette de Mirecourt* are easily obtainable. See also the introduction and notes to *The Poems of Adam Hood Burwell* ("University of Western Ontario History Nuggets, no. 30"), and *William "Tiger" Dunlop, Blackwoodian Backwoodsman* (Toronto, 1958).

The author is indebted to the work of some postgraduate students of the University of Western Ontario and their M.A. theses: Carl Ballstadt's "The Quest for Canadian Identity in Pre-Confederation English-Canadian Literary Criticism"; Marilyn I. Davis's "*Belinda* and the Sentimental Seduction Tradition" (1963); Kathleen O'Donnell's "Thomas D'Arcy McGee's Irish and Canadian Ballads" (1956); Mary (Markham) Brown's *Index to the Literary Garland (Montreal 1838–1851)*, which was published by the Bibliographical Society of Canada in 1962. Charles R. Steele's Ph.D. thesis, "Canadian Poetry in English: The Beginnings" (1974), presents analyses and conclusions regarding poetry in the Canadas up to 1851.

Canadian Literature (U.B.C.) and the *Journal of Canadian Fiction* (Montreal, 1972–   ) contain many articles on early Canadian literature.

Studies of the life and works of Major John Richardson are increasing and are establishing the reputation of the first novelist of Upper Canada. See A. C. Casselman's edition of *War of 1812* (1902); Ray Palmer Baker's *History* (1920), 125–39; W. R. Riddell's bio-bibliographical survey [1923]; Desmond Pacey's "A Colonial Romantic" in *Canadian Literature* (U.B.C.) 2 and 3 (1959–1960); Carl Ballstadt's selection of reviews and criticism (Lande Foundation, 1972); William F. E. Morley's *A Bibliographical Study* (Bibliographical Society of Canada, 1973); *Westbrooke the Outlaw* (Grant Woolmer Books, 1973); "Frascati's; Or, Scenes in Paris" in the *Journal of Canadian Fiction* II, no. 3 (1973); and the continuing discoveries by David R. Beasley.

The reputation of David Willson of Sharon, a religious poet of the early nineteenth century, has been enhanced by Professor James Reaney in his lectures, but not yet in a published article or book.

CHAPTER 11. LITERARY PUBLISHING

For the early press in Canada, the standard works are Aegidius Fauteux, *The Introduction of Printing into Canada* (Montreal: Rolland Paper Co., 1930); Marie Tremaine, *Bibliography of Canadian Imprints, 1751–1800* (Toronto: University of Toronto Press, 1952); John Hare et L.-P. Wallot, *Les Imprimés dans le Bas Canada, 1801–1840* (Montreal: Les Presses de l'Université de Montréal, 1967) I, 1801–1810; Frances M. Staton and Marie Tremaine, *A Bibliography of Canadiana . . .* (Toronto: The Public Library, 1934); *The Lawrence Lande Collection of Canadiana in the Redpath Library of McGill University: A Bibliography Collected, Arranged, and Annotated by Lawrence Lande* (Montreal: McGill University Press, 1965). See also the following by H. Pearson Gundy: *Early Printers and Printing in the Canadas*, 2nd ed. 1964, and *Book Publishing and Publishers in Canada before 1900*, 1965, both published in Toronto by the Bibliographical Society of Canada; *The Spread of Printing: Canada* (Amsterdam: Van Gendt & Co., 1972); "The Development of Trade Book Publishing in Canada" in Ontario Royal Commission on Book Publishing. *Background Papers* (Toronto: Queen's Printer and Publisher, 1972).

A few Canadian publishing and printing firms have issued house histories, e.g. Lorne Pierce, *The Chronicle of a Century, 1829–1929* (Toronto: Ryerson, 1929) and *The House of Ryerson* (Toronto: Ryerson, 1954); *A Canadian Publishing House* [The Macmillan Company of Canada Limited] (Toronto: Macmillan, 1923); *Warwick Bros. & Rutter Limited: The Story of a Business, 1848–1923* (Toronto: Warwick, 1923); George L. Parker, "History of a Canadian Publishing House: A Study of the Relation between Publishing and the Profession of Writing, 1890–1940," unpublished Ph.D. thesis, University of Toronto, 1969; Gordon Roper, "Mark Twain and his Canadian Publishers: A Second Look," *Papers of the Bibliographical Society of Canada*, V (1966), 30–89; Eleanor Harman, (ed.) *The University as Publisher* (Toronto: University of Toronto Press, 1961).

Two early trade journals are also useful, *Canada Bookseller*, 1872, and *Books and Notions*, 1884–85, both published in Toronto.

The best survey of the newspaper press is W. H. Kesterton, *A History of Journal-*

ism in Canada, Carleton Library No. 36 (Toronto: McClelland & Stewart, 1967). There are also valuable notes in *Canadian Newspapers on Microfilm: Catalogue* (loose-leaf, multilithed) issued by the Canadian Library Association (Ottawa, 1959, and continuing); also J. Russell Harper, *Historical Directory of New Brunswick Newspapers and Periodicals* (Fredericton: University of New Brunswick, 1961), and Edith Firth, *Early Toronto Newspapers, 1793–1867* (Toronto Public Library, 1961). The best study of the periodical press in Canada to 1900 is R. L. McDougall, "A Study of Canadian Periodical Literature of the Nineteenth Century," unpublished Ph.D. thesis, University of Toronto.

The history of book publishing in Canada is a virgin field for research. The late Dr. Lorne Pierce was unable to complete the collaborative work on which he was engaged at the time of his death. The present writer has prepared for publication by the Bibliographical Society of Canada a book entitled *Book Publishing and Publishers in Canada before 1900*. A few Canadian publishing and printing firms have issued house histories, e.g. Lorne Pierce, *The Chronicle of a Century, 1829–1929* (Toronto: Ryerson, 1929) and *The House of Ryerson* (Toronto, Ryerson, 1954); *A Canadian Publishing House* [The Macmillan Company of Canada Limited] (Toronto: Macmillan, 1923); *Warwick Bros. & Rutter Limited: The Story of the Business, 1848–1923* (Toronto: Warwick, 1923); Eleanor Harman (editor), *The University as Publisher* (Toronto: University of Toronto Press, 1961).

George H. Doran, *Chronicles of Barabbas, 1884–1934* (New York: Reinhart, 1952), in the opening chapter, deals with publishing in Toronto at the turn of the century. For the earlier period the only first-hand account is Samuel Thompson's *Reminiscences of a Canadian Pioneer for the last Fifty Years: An Autobiography* (Toronto: Hunter, Rose, 1884). Two trade journals are useful, *Canada Bookseller*, 1872, and *Books and Notions*, 1884–85.

For the early press in Canada the standard works are Aegidius Fauteux, *The Introduction of Printing into Canada* (Montreal: Rolland Paper Co., 1930), and Marie Tremaine, *Bibliography of Canadian Imprints, 1751–1800*. See also Miss Tremaine's article "A Half-Century of Canadian Life and Print" in *Essays Honoring Lawrence C. Wroth* (Portland, Me., 1951), and *The Canadian Book of Printing* (Toronto: Toronto Public Library, 1940). A monograph by the present writer, *Early Printers and Printing in the Canadas*, was published by the Bibliographical Society of Canada (Toronto, 1957).

For the newspaper press there are valuable notes in *Canadian Newspapers on Microfilm: Catalogue* (loose-leaf, mimeographed) issued by the Canadian Library Association (Ottawa, 1959, and continuing); also J. Russell Harper, *Historical Directory of New Brunswick Newspapers and Periodicals* (Fredericton: University of New Brunswick, 1961), and Edith Firth, *Early Toronto Newspapers, 1793–1867* (Toronto Public Library, 1961). The best study of the periodical press in Canada is R. L. McDougall, "A Study of Canadian Periodical Literature of the Nineteenth Century," unpublished Ph.D. thesis, University of Toronto.

CHAPTER 12. CONFEDERATION TO THE FIRST WORLD WAR

See Alfred G. Bailey, "Creative Moments in the Culture of the Maritime Provinces," *Dalhousie Review*, XXIX, 231–44; Claude T. Bissell (ed.), *Our Living*

Tradition (University of Toronto Press, 1957); S. D. Clark, *The Social Development of Canada* (University of Toronto Press, 1942); Donald G. Creighton, *Dominion of the North* (Boston: Houghton Mifflin Co., 1944); William Douw Lighthall (ed.), *Songs of the Great Dominion* (London: Walter Scott, 1889) and (Wilfred Chateauclair, pseud.), *The Young Seigneur* (Montreal: Wm. Drysdale and Co., 1888); Robert L. McDougall, "A Study of Canadian Periodical Literature of the Nineteenth Century," unpublished Ph.D. thesis, University of Toronto; Robert L. McDougall (ed.), *Our Living Tradition*, Second and Third, and Fourth Series (University of Toronto Press, 1959 and 1962); W. L. Morton, *The Kingdom of Canada* (Toronto: McClelland and Stewart, 1963); Desmond Pacey, *Creative Writing in Canada* (new edition; Toronto: Ryerson Press, 1961); Elisabeth Wallace, *Goldwin Smith: Victorian Liberal* (University of Toronto Press, 1957); Frank W. Watt, "Radicalism in English-Canadian Literature since Confederation," unpublished Ph.D. thesis, University of Toronto, 1957.

CHAPTER 13. HISTORICAL WRITING IN CANADA TO 1920

In addition to an examination of the books discussed, the private papers of the more important historians were consulted when available. The following list contains the more useful collections. The code number of the Union List of Manuscripts in Canadian Repositories is included in cases where it has been determined. *Thomas Beamish Akins Papers*, Public Archives of Nova Scotia, Halifax, (1–26); the *George Bryce Papers*, Public Archives of Manitoba, Winnipeg, (9–32); *William Wilfred Campbell Papers*, Douglas Library Archives, Queen's University, Kingston; *William Canniff Papers*, Ontario Archives, Toronto, (8–70); *James Henry Coyne Papers*, Lawson Memorial Library, University of Western Ontario, London; *Arthur Doughty Papers*, Public Archives of Canada (hereafter referred to as P.A.C.), Ottawa; *George Taylor Denison Papers*, P.A.C. (7–1111); *John Skirving Ewart Papers*, Public Archives of Manitoba (9–97); *George Monro Grant Papers, William Lawson Grant Papers*, P.A.C.; *John Castell Hopkins Papers*, P.A.C. (7–758); *Joseph Howe Papers*, P.A.C.; *George Johnson Papers*, P.A.C.; *Stephen Leacock Papers*, Stephen Leacock Memorial Home, Orillia, Ontario (95–1); *William Dawson Le Sueur Papers*, P.A.C.; *Lizars Papers*, Lawson Memorial Library, University of Western Ontario; *Charles Mair Papers*, Douglas Library Archives, Queen's University (75–28); *James Mavor Papers*, University of Toronto Library (16–356); *Henry James Morgan Papers*, P.A.C.; *W. B. Munro Papers*, Huntington Library, San Marino California; *Duncan Campbell Scott Papers*, University of Toronto Library (16–19); *Adam Shortt Papers*, Douglas Library Archives, Queen's University (75–37); *Goldwin Smith Papers*, Mann Library, Cornell University, Ithaca, New York. Some of the Cornell collection is on microfilm in the P.A.C. (7–1639) and copies of the Smith letters in the New York Public Library are on microfilm in the University of Toronto Library (16–256); *Sir Byron Edmund Walker Papers*, University of Toronto Library (16–391); *Sir Daniel Wilson Papers*, Ontario Archives (8–342); *Sir Daniel Wilson Typescripts*, University of Toronto Library (16–283); *G. M. Wrong Papers*, University of Toronto Library. An intensely interesting collection not used in this survey is the *E. B. O'Callaghan Papers*, P.A.C. Irish born, O'Callaghan (1797–1880) was implicated in the rebellion of 1837 in Lower Canada. He became the historian and archivist of New York State and compiled *The Documentary History of the State of New York* . . . (4 vols., 1849–51) and the first 11 volumes of *Documents Relative to the Colonial History of the State of New York* . . . , which appeared between 1853 and 1861. He also wrote a *History of New Netherlands; or, New York under the Dutch* (2 vols., 1846–48).

The ruminations of the presidents of the Canadian Historical Association printed in the annual *Report* (1922–   ) contain many useful suggestions, summaries, and criticisms. For the period under discussion the most useful interpretive article is J. K. McConica, "Kingsford and Whiggery in Canadian History," *Canadian Historical Review*, XL (1959), 108–20. Also very helpful was V. L. O. Chittick, *Thomas Chandler Haliburton ('Sam Slick'): A Study in Provincial Toryism* (New York: Columbia University Press, 1924). On Parkman, particularly useful were William J. Eccles, "The History of New France According to Francis Parkman," *William and Mary Quarterly*, 3rd series, XVIII (1961), 163–75, and G. M. Wrong, "Francis Parkman," *Canadian Historical Review*, IV (1923), 289–303. On Goldwin Smith, see Elisabeth Wallace, *Goldwin Smith: Victorian Liberal* (Toronto: University of Toronto Press, 1957) and, by the same author, "Goldwin Smith on History," *Journal of Modern History*, XXVI (1954), 220–32. On the professional study of history, see Chester Martin, "Fifty Years of Canadian History," *Royal Society of Canada: Fifty Years Retrospect: Anniversary Volume 1882–1932* (n.d., n.p.), 63–69 and "Professor G. M. Wrong and History in Canada," *Essays in Canadian History presented to George MacKinnon Wrong for his Eightieth Birthday* (Toronto: Macmillan, 1939), 1–23. On the development of archives in Canada, see Duncan McArthur, "The Canadian Archives and the Writing of Canadian History," *Canadian Historical Association, Report*, 1935, 5–17. On the teaching of history in Canadian universities, see Richard A. Preston, "Breakers Ahead and a Glance Behind," Presidential Address read before the Canadian Historical Association, June, 1962, printed in the *Canadian Historical Association, Report*, 1962, 1–16. As an example of the development of local history, see Hugh A. Stevenson, "James H. Coyne: An Early Contributor to Canadian Historical Scholarship," *Ontario History*, LIV (1962), 25–42.

CHAPTERS 15, 16, 17. FICTION (1880–1920)

The most comprehensive bibliography of Canadian fiction from 1880 to 1920 is embedded in R. E. Watters' *Checklist*, pp. 233–423 and 995–1001 (2nd edition, 1972). The first comprehensive bibliography was by Lewis Emerson Horning and Lawrence J. Burpee, *A Bibliography of Canadian Fiction* (English) (Toronto, 1904).

Large or special collections of Canadian fiction are in the Library of Parliament, Ottawa, the Toronto Public Library, and the libraries of the following institutions: Dalhousie University, Halifax; Massey College, University of Toronto; McGill University, Montreal; Queen's University, Kingston; University of British Columbia, Vancouver; University of New Brunswick, Fredericton; University of Toronto; Victoria University, Toronto; the University of Western Ontario, London; the British Museum; the Library of Congress, Washington; and the University of Texas, Austin, Texas.

Biographical information on some or many of the writers mentioned in these chapters will be found in O. F. Adams, *A Dictionary of American Authors* (5th edition; Boston, 1904); W. J. Burke and Will D. Howe, *American Authors and Books* (New York, 1943); *Encyclopedia Canadiana* (Ottawa, 1957); S. J. Kunitz and H. Haycroft, *American Authors, 1600–1900* (New York, 1928); R. J. Long, *Nova Scotia Authors and their Work* (East Orange, N.J., 1918); W. G. Mac-Farlane, *New Brunswick Bibliography* (Saint John, 1895); A. N. Marquis, *Who's Who in America*, vol. I (Chicago, 1900); *Who's Who among North American Authors*, vol. I (Los Angeles, 1921); Rev. W. E. McIntyre, *Baptist Authors* (Montreal and Toronto, 1914); H. J. Morgan, *The Canadian Men and Women of the Time* (Toronto, 1898; revised, 1912); Sir C. G. D. Roberts and A. L. Tunnell, *A Standard Dictionary of Canadian Who Was Who* (Toronto, 1934–1938); W. S. Wallace, *The Dictionary of Canadian Biography* (Toronto, 1945); W. S. Wallace, *A Dictionary of North American Authors, deceased before 1950* (Toronto, 1951); W. S. Wallace, *The Encyclopedia of Canada* (Toronto, 1935); W. Stewart Wallace, *The Macmillan Dictionary of Canadian Biography* (Toronto, 1963).

Information on the literary and social milieu is to be found in articles on fiction and book reviews in Canadian magazines and newspapers, especially in Goldwin Smith's *The Week* and in the *Canadian Magazine*. Reviews also are to be found in British and American periodicals. See also the autobiographies by Charles Gordon (Ralph Connor), Nellie McClung, Frederick Niven, Roger Pocock, Robert Service, Ernest Thompson Seton, and Henry Beckles Willson (Watters, pp. 333–429), and the volumes of Hector Charlesworth (Watters, p. 446). For more information on the Anglo–North American literary currents, see James D. Hart, *The Popular Book: A History of America's Literary Taste* (New York, 1950); Frank Luther Mott, *Golden Multitudes: The Story of Best Sellers in the United States* (New York, 1950), and Richard Altick, *The English Common Reader* (Chicago, 1957).

Descriptive and critical studies of Canadian fiction are contained in the histories of Canadian literature by Logan and French, Archibald MacMechan, Archibald MacMurchy, T. G. Marquis, Lorne Pierce, V. B. Rhodenizer, Lionel Stevenson, and O. J. Stevenson (see Watters, pp. 642–73). Special studies have been made by Edward McCourt, *The West in Canadian Fiction* (Toronto, 1949), and Frank William Watt, "Radicalism in English-Canadian Literature," unpublished doctoral dissertation, University of Toronto, 1957.

For studies of individual writers, see bibliographies in C. F. Klinck and R. E. Watters, *Canadian Anthology* (Toronto, 1955; revised 3rd edition, 1974). For a bibliography of Stephen Leacock, see Ralph L. Curry, *Stephen Leacock* (Philadelphia, 1956). See also C. F. Klinck's annual mimeographed listing of M.A. and Ph.D. theses on Canadian writers.

CHAPTER 20. LAMPMAN AND ROBERTS

See Claude Bissell, "Literary Taste in Central Canada during the late Nineteenth Century," *Canadian Historical Review*, XXXI (September 1950), 237–51; A. S. Bourinot (editor), *Some Letters of Duncan Campbell Scott, Archibald Lampman and Others* (Rockcliffe, Ottawa: the editor, 1959); E. K. Brown, *On Canadian Poetry* (Toronto: Ryerson, 1943); James Cappon, *Charles G. D. Roberts* (Toronto: Ryerson, n.d.); Archibald Lampman, *Poems* (fourth edition; Toronto: Morang and Co., 1915); John P. Matthews, *Tradition in Exile* (University of Toronto Press,

1962); James Reaney, "The Canadian Poet's Predicament," *University of Toronto Quarterly*, XXXVI, 284–95; Charles G. D. Roberts, *Poems* (Boston: L. C. Page & Co., 1907); Lloyd Roberts, *The Book of Roberts* (Toronto, Ryerson, 1923); E. M. Pomeroy, *Sir Charles G. D. Roberts: A Biography* (Toronto, Ryerson, 1943); Frank W. Watt, "The Masks of Archibald Lampman," *University of Toronto Quarterly*, XXVII, 169–84.

CHAPTER 21. CRAWFORD, CARMAN, AND D. C. SCOTT

See E. K. Brown, *On Canadian Poetry* (Toronto, Ryerson, 1943); James Cappon, *Bliss Carman* (Toronto, Ryerson, 1930); Isabella Valancy Crawford, *Collected Poems* (Toronto, Wm. Briggs, 1905); Katherine Hale, *Isabella Valancy Crawford* (Toronto, Ryerson, 1923); Muriel Miller, *Bliss Carman: A Portrait* (Toronto, Ryerson, 1935).

CHAPTER 22. MINOR POETS (1880–1920)

See Mrs. W. Garland Foster, *The Mohawk Princess* (Vancouver: Lion's Gate Pub. Co., 1931); Carl F. Klinck, *Wilfred Campbell: A Study in Late Provincial Victorianism* (Toronto: Ryerson, 1942); Desmond Pacey, *Creative Writing in Canada* (2nd edition; Toronto: Ryerson, 1961); R. E. Rashley, *Poetry in Canada: The First Three Steps* (Toronto: Ryerson, 1958); A. J. M. Smith (editor), *The Book of Canadian Poetry* (3rd edition; Toronto, W. J. Gage, 1957); A. J. M. Smith (editor), *The Oxford Book of Canadian Verse* (Toronto, Oxford University Press, 1960).

CHAPTER 23. PHILOSOPHICAL LITERATURE (TO 1910)

For pages 435–36, in text above, see a bibliography of Young's mathematical papers in [W. J. Alexander], *The University of Toronto and Its Colleges, 1827–1906*, pp. 253–54. A recent discovery of C. B. Sissons suggests that President S. S. Nelles must have offered Young the chair of Mathematics in Victoria University towards the end of the latter's service with the Department of Education. In Nelles's unpublished diary, under date January 8, 1868, the following entry appears: "Called on Prof. Young. Find he has fully decided not to come as Prof. of Mathematics." For pages 437–42, see a bibliography of Watson's writing between 1872 and 1922 in *Philosophical Essays, Presented to John Watson* (Kingston, Ontario, 1922), pp. 343–46. For pages 442–44, see a bibliography of Murray's writings from 1867 to 1894 in *Proceedings of the Royal Society of Canada*, XII (1894), 61–62.

CHAPTER 25. LITERATURE OF PROTEST

Page 458, above, line 15: *Canadian Monthly and National Review*, I (1872), 93–94. Pp. 459–60: articles by Goldwin Smith in *The Week*, III (1885–86), 75; *Canadian Monthly and National Review*, I (1872), 425 and II (1872), 524; also *CMNR*, VI (1874), 425 ff; *Questions of the Day*, 11 and 50 ff. Pp. 460–61: articles by LeSueur in *The Nation* (Dec. 31, 1874), p. 474; *CMNR*, VII (1875),

322–25; "Mr. Malloch on Optimism," *Popular Science Monthly*, XXXV (1889), 541. P. 461, line 2: for example *CMNR*, VI (1874), 386–88; *The Week*, IX (1892–93), 800–2. P. 462, line 33: see F. W. Watt, "Sir John Macdonald, the Workingman, and Proletarian Ideas in Victorian Canada," *Canadian Historical Review*, XL, no. 1 (March 1959), 1–26, for a more detailed treatment of this subject. P. 467, line 29: see *Western Clarion*, March, 1916. P. 468, line 26: see Elisabeth Wallace, "The Origin of the Social Welfare State in Canada," *Canadian Journal of Economics and Political Science*, XVI (1950), 383–93. P. 468, line 26: this phrase occurs in A. G. Bailey's "Creative Moments in the Culture of the Maritime Provinces," *Dalhousie Review*, XXIX (1949), 231–44. P. 470, line 36: "Proletarian Literature: Theory and Practice," *Canadian Forum*, XVII (1937–38), 58–60.

Index

MacGeorge, Robert Jackson ("Solomon of Streetsville") 165
McGill University Magazine. See, University Magazine.
McGillen, Pete 388–9
McGillivray, Duncan 32–3
MacGregor, Rev. James 88, 95
MacGregor, John 155, 226
MacGregor, Mrs. Mary Esther. *See* "Keith, Marian."
Machar, Agnes Maule ("Fidelis") 176, 209, **210–11**, 214, 253, 275, 277, 304, 316, 320, 444, **477**
Machel, P. 378
McIlwraith, Jean Newton 242, 276, 277, 301
"MacInnes, Tom" (Thomas McInnes) 482
MacKay, Isabel Ecclestone 308
Mackay, J. 100–1
Mackenzie, Alexander (explorer) 26, **29–30**, 37, 79, 242, 255
Mackenzie, Alexander (prime minister) 243
Mackenzie, Compton 326
Mackenzie, Roderick 29
Mackenzie, W. Roy 186
Mackenzie, William Lyon 80, 153, **154**, 155, 158, 160, 184, 239, 240, 242, 243–4, 309
Mackenzie, Selkirk, Simpson (G. Bryce) 242, 255
McKibbin, Archibald 307
Mackie, John 312
McKillican, Janet 321
Mackinlay, A. & W. (publisher) 193
McKinnon, William Charles 130
McKishnie, Archibald 276, 277, 307, 309, 321, 351, 395, 396, 403
McKowan, Evah 315, 325
McLachlan, Alexander 150, **165–6**, 168, 220
McLachlan, Mrs. 160
McLean, John (1797?–1890)

39
Maclean, John (1851–1928) (novelist) 312
Maclean's (magazine) 283, 285
Maclear, Thomas (publisher) **196**, 197, 254
MacLennan, Hugh 488
McLennan, William 183, 276, 277, 301, **302**, 321–2, 434
McLeod, A.J. 302
MacLeod, Margaret Arnett 182
McLeod, Robert 385
McLoughlin, John 38–9, 40, 44
MacMechan, Archibald 355–6
McMicking, Thomas, 42, 43
Macmillan, Cyrus, 179, 394
McMillan, J. & A. (N.B. publisher) 192
McMillan, John 192
MacMillan, William 403
Macmillan's Magazine (Eng.) 279
McMullen, John Mercier 229–30, 248
McNaughton, Archibald 43
Macnaughton, John 243
McNaughton, Margaret 43
McNeill, A.D. 122
MacNutt, W.S. 75
Macphail, Sir Andrew 301, 356, **357–8**, 360, 468
McPherson, John 132–3
MacQueen, Thomas 166
McRae, Robert 470
Mac's of '37, The (1910) 309
Mactaggart, John 155, 181
Madden, Mary Anne. *See* Sadlier, Mrs. Mary Anne.
Madison, Grant 392, 395
Madison, James 262
Madonna of a Day, The (1895) 314, 334
Magic Fiddler, The, and Other Legends of French Canada (1968) 180
Magic House, The, and Other Poems (1893) 432
Magic Lantern, The (Montreal journal) 163

Maginn, William 146, 148
Magnalia Christi Americana (1702) 12
Magpie's Nest, The (1917) 313
Magrath, Thomas William 155, 387
Magrath family 267
Maid of Many Moods, A (1902) 321
Mail (Niagara) 172
Mail (Toronto) 240, 254
Main Street (1920) 306
Main Travelled Roads (Garland) 296
Mainer, Henry 307
Mainly about Wolves (1937) 398
Mair, Charles 80, 168, 172, **173–4**, 201, 271, 311
Maitland, Sir Peregrine 153, 234
Major, The (1917) 325, 337
Major, Charles 295
"Makers of Canada" (series) 237, **241–6**, 248, 250, 255, 258
Making Good in Canada (F.A. Talbot, 1912) 378
Making of a Man, The (1918) 310
Making a Start in Canada (Church, 1889) 364
Malaeska; or, The Indian Wife of the White Hunter (Stephen) 292
"Malcolm" (Coll MacLean Sinclair) 309
Malcolm's Katie. See, Old Spookses' Pass ...
"M.A.M.". *See* Sadlier, Mrs. Mary Anne.
Man from Glengarry, The (1901) 284, 306, 308, 336, **337**
Man in the Open (1912) 314
Manby, Thomas 62
Manitoba: Its Infancy, Growth, and Present Condition (1882) 232–3
Manitoba Chore Boy, A: The Experience of a Young Emigrant ... (1912) 311